W9-DEE-382

THE ECONOMY OF
THE CHINESE MAINLAND

The Economy of the Chinese Mainland: National Income and Economic Development, 1933-1959

TA-CHUNG LIU • KUNG-CHIA YEH
CORNELL UNIVERSITY • THE *RAND* CORPORATION

PRINCETON, NEW JERSEY
PRINCETON UNIVERSITY PRESS
1965

Published, 1965, by Princeton University Press

L. C. Card No. 64–12223

Printed in the United States of America
by The Colonial Press Inc.
Clinton, Massachusetts

PREFACE

This book presents a quantitative study of the economic development of the Chinese Mainland during 1952–59 and a comparison of changes over this period with the condition of the pre-Communist and prewar Chinese Mainland economy in the 1930s.

The method is that of national income accounting: detailed estimates of Domestic Product by Industrial Origin, and Domestic Expenditures by End Use are derived for the years 1933 and 1952 through 1957. Very tentative estimates are offered for 1958–59. Selection of the years covered by the estimates and the detail of analysis were determined by conditions in China and the availability and quality of statistical data. 1933 was chosen as a reasonably normal prewar year offering relatively good data coverage for both China proper and Japanese-occupied Manchuria.

The year 1952 was selected as the starting point of the postwar series, to eliminate not only the disturbed (and statistically obscure) period of the Sino-Japanese war (1937–45) and the immediate postwar period (1946–48), but also the first three years of the Communist regime (1949–51), when the economy was dislocated and the statistical coverage was meager and even less reliable than for the later years. The most detailed and intensive estimates are those for 1952 and the First Five Year Plan period 1953–57, when the supply of data expanded to a point where we could apply a variety of methods to appraise the accuracy of the data and use them to estimate the domestic product.

The difficulties in collecting, evaluating, and analyzing the statistical and other data necessary for this research were recognized at the outset. The Chinese Communists themselves admit that their economic data are unsatisfactory in many respects even for the period before the so-called Great Leap Forward in 1958; and the quality of their statistics deteriorated greatly afterward. In view of the weakness in the basic data, it might appear questionable whether an elaborate estimate of national income is justified. On the other hand, an attempt to estimate national product by industrial origin and national expenditure by end use is in fact the most systematic and comprehensive method of checking the plausibility and consistency of the Communist data. Any impression of the working of the economy of the Chinese Mainland obtained by rougher studies without going through the process of estimating national product and expenditure and their components would be even less reliable.

In dealing with the difficult problem of evaluating and interpreting Chinese Communist data, the authors adopted the following procedure: The Communist estimates of national income are given and fully documented, and are labeled "Communist estimates"; those so labeled are not adjusted or corrected by us in any way. Using the basic Communist economic statistics, especially those on output, prices, and employment, we have derived a set of national income estimates, adjusted to conform to standard Western concepts of national income accounting. This set of estimates, labeled "adjusted estimates," is, however, uncorrected for accuracy in the basic data. Wherever the reliability and plausibility of the basic data are in doubt, and if a reasonable method of correcting the biases can be formulated, corrections are made and fully explained. The results so obtained are called the "authors' estimates." Unless specified as adjusted or Communist estimates, the estimates referred to in the text are the "authors' estimates." This way of presenting the data and the findings makes it possible for the reader to understand the sources and magnitudes of the differences between the Communist and the authors' estimates, in total and by sector. Although we feel we have corrected the most important defects in the Communist data for 1952–57, occasionally we have not been able to formulate reasonable methods to correct doubtful data. Rather than risk making hasty judgments on unsure criteria, we have not made corrections in such cases.

The core of the study, then, is the annual series of estimates for 1952–57, the accounts for 1933, and the resulting comparisons, both over the 1952–57 period and between that period and the 1933 economy. The intertemporal comparisons are based on use of three alternative sets of price weights for most estimates: 1933, 1952, and 1957 prices. This procedure makes it possible to bring out and study the effects on the growth and structure of national product of the transition from the price structure of the free-market economy of 1933 to that of a centrally planned, industrialization-oriented "Soviet-type" economy.

Chapter I provides a brief historical background for the quantitative study presented in this book. The data, methods, and estimates of domestic product by industrial origin, and of domestic expenditure by end use, are summarized in Chapter II. This chapter orients the reader to the detailed explanation given in Chapter IV (estimates of domestic product) and Chapter V (estimates of domestic expenditure) and the supporting appendixes. For the general reader, Chapter II alone contains sufficient background for the analysis presented in Chapter III, which covers a wide range of subjects including the cost and the result of the Communist drive for industrialization; the speed of development and the changes in the structure of production; distribution of labor force and employment; and measurement of inflationary pressure in the economy during the postwar years. Chapters IV and V and the appendixes are intended for specialists on China and for those concerned with problems of national income accounting for underdeveloped countries.

T. C. Liu is responsible for formulating the approaches and making the major assumptions underlying the estimates. The sections on investment and capital formation in Chapter V, however, are entirely the work of K. C. Yeh. The idea of pooling the major sources of data on prewar agriculture (mainly the contributions of John Lossing Buck and the National Agricultural Research Bureau of the National Government), and of evaluating postwar food consumption through calorie intakes and rationing regulations, was developed by Liu as an advance on his earlier study, *China's National Income, 1931–1936* (The Brookings Institution, 1946). Chong Twanmo assisted Liu in carrying out the computations on agriculture. The first three chapters were written by Liu; and the sections on agriculture and total population in Chapter IV, and Appendixes A-E, were prepared by him with the assistance of Twanmo. Yeh made the computations for the nonagricultural sectors and drafted the rest of the manuscript under the direction of Liu.

This study was undertaken by The RAND Corporation for the United States Air Force as a part of the Project RAND research program. Instrumental in initiating this work at RAND were Joseph A. Kershaw (now Provost of Williams College) and Charles J. Hitch (now Assistant Secretary of Defense, Comptroller). A constant source of inspiration and guidance has been Simon Kuznets of Harvard University, who, at the invitation of the National Government in China in 1946 (in addition to supervising a number of other investigations), undertook a critical examination of the studies of prewar national income by P. S. Ou and T. C. Liu. Kuznets read the manuscript of the present study at various stages and offered many valuable suggestions.

Special thanks are due a number of colleagues associated directly with the research: Chong Twanmo, now with the United States Information Agency, whose expert knowledge of Chinese agriculture was invaluable in completing the estimates for this sector of the economy; Mrs. Amy Wu, now with the United States Department of Health, Education, and Welfare, who assisted the project in general and the preparation of the manuscript in particular; Kenneth Chiang, now of Wilkes College, Wilkes-Barre, Pennsylvania, who participated in the research in its earliest stage; Ronald Hsia, of the University of Hong Kong, who helped in the collection of part of the price data; and Hang-sheng Cheng, now of Iowa State University, who checked some of the computations on agriculture.

The book has benefited greatly from the comments and suggestions of the authors' colleagues at RAND. In addition to Joseph A. Kershaw, Paul G. Clark (RAND consultant and Professor of Economics at Williams College), Edmund Dews, Oleg Hoeffding, and Richard Moorsteen reviewed the whole of an earlier draft, and Harold J. Barnett (RAND consultant), Hans Heymann, Jr., and Frederick T. Moore read various sections and gave thoughtful criticism.

The deficiencies and defects that may remain would in all likelihood have been overcome if it had been possible for the authors to accept all the suggestions made by their colleagues and the other scholars mentioned above. For any shortcomings, the authors alone must be held responsible.

TA-CHUNG LIU
Cornell University
KUNG-CHIA YEH
The RAND Corporation

CONTENTS

LIST OF FIGURES

LIST OF TABLES

Table *Page*

NOTES ON CHINESE UNITS

1. In this study, the statistics are given in terms of the Chinese standard system of weights and measures. Their conversion ratios to other systems are given below:

1 *mow* (*shih mow*)

= 0.1647 acre
= 0.0666 hectare

1 *picul* (*tan* or *shih tan*)

= 100 catties (*chin*)
= 0.05 metric ton
= 50 kilograms (Kg)
= 110.25 pounds

2. A *hsien* is an administrative unit under a province, corresponding to a county.
3. The estimates in value terms are given in the following Chinese monetary units: the 1933 yuan, the 1952 yuan, and the 1957 yuan. The official rates of exchange are, respectively:

1 U.S. $ = 3.839 yuan in 1933
1 U.S. $ = 2.343 yuan in 1952
1 U.S. $ = 2.617 yuan in 1957

* * * * * * * * * * *

In many of the tables in this volume sub-items do not sum up to the totals due to rounding. These minor discrepancies are not annotated individually in the tables.

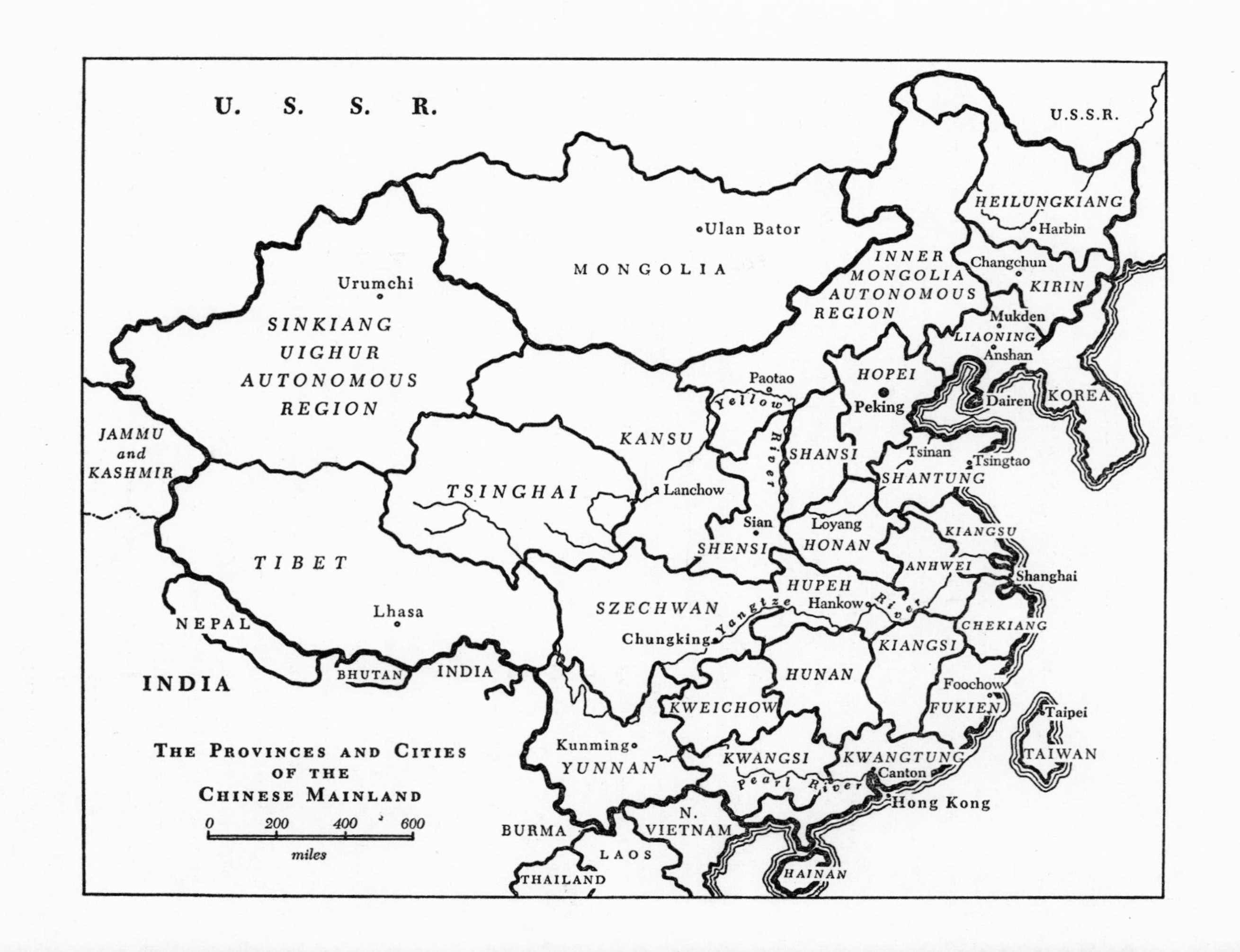

THE PROVINCES AND CITIES OF THE CHINESE MAINLAND

CHAPTER I

INTRODUCTION

DURING the past three decades, changes in political, social, and economic institutions and conditions on the Chinese Mainland have been so intensive, extensive, and violent as to be without precedent in history. Regardless of the direction of future events, this period will remain a significant chapter in the history of mankind.

This work is a modest attempt at a quantitative study of the economy on the Chinese Mainland with regard to its development during the postwar years and in comparison with the prewar economy. The scope of the study is purposely limited, and changes in political and social fields will not be discussed. Changes in economic institutions will be sketched only as necessary to make the quantitative analysis intelligible. Our purpose is to derive estimates of national production, expenditure, and employment, and their important components by various classifications for the prewar and the postwar periods, and to draw such tentative inferences about the pattern of Communist economic development as appear warranted from these estimates. An evaluation of the nature and quality of Communist economic data is an important part of this study.

TIME AND GEOGRAPHICAL COVERAGE

Even within this narrow scope, the present attempt is incomplete with respect to the years covered. For the prewar period it has been possible to make estimates for only the year 1933, as that is the one year for which there are detailed industrial statistics for areas outside Manchuria. There are evidences that development in light manufacturing was fairly rapid in China during the early and middle 1930s. Three trunk railroads were completed during this period.[1] Some development of heavy industry had taken place in Manchuria even before the Japanese occupation in 1931, and a substantial industrial base was developed by the Japanese. A comparison of the pattern of growth during prewar years with the recent Communist development would have been illuminating; however, the priority

[1] The Chekiang-Kiangsi Railway (220 miles), the middle portion of the Canton-Hankow Railway (283 miles), and the western portion of the Lunghai Railway (108 miles).

given to the more recent years in this study has made it impossible to bridge the gaps in industrial statistics for prewar years other than 1933.

The single year estimate for 1933 is significant in that it furnishes a base against which one can measure the standard of living prevailing in recent years. A comparison of the 1933 market prices with the controlled prices in the Communist economy is also useful for many purposes.

Statistics are so scarce and unreliable for the period of the Sino-Japanese War (1937–45) and for the three years of internal warfare (1946–48) that any estimate of national product for these years would have low reliability. The Communist data for the first three years of the regime (1949–51) are also of doubtful quality, and any estimate made on the basis of these figures, when taken with the estimates for the later years, would present a misleading picture of the trend of development over the whole period 1949–57.[2] In the absence of a satisfactory independent estimate for the years 1949–51, it seemed preferable to omit these years from the study.

By 1952, the year immediately before the planning period (the First Five Year Plan began in 1953), the economy had been rehabilitated from the ravages of war. The land redistribution program had been completed and the socialization of private industry and business was well on the way. Between 1952 and 1957, the economy became fully collectivized, and Communist statistics were more abundant and less unreliable than before.[3] Estimates for the years 1952–57 have been made, therefore, to throw some light on the performance of the Communist economy during the First Five Year Plan.

With the year 1958 came the "Great Leap Forward," but the quality of economic data took a sharp turn for the worse. For that year, the Chinese Communists made some grossly exaggerated claims of advances in agricultural and industrial production which they later felt compelled to revise substantially downward. The radical changes in economic and social institutions which took place with the "Leap" have made it even more difficult than before to evaluate the degree of reliability of these data, even though there

[2] See Figure 1 in Chapter II and the discussion regarding pre-1956 data which follows Figure 2.

[3] See Chapter II on source data and the method of estimate.

could be no doubt that the errors were very great. The estimates for 1952–57 have been helpful in determining the plausibility of the 1958–59 data, and we have made some very tentative conjectures as to the magnitude of the national product for 1958 and 1959.

The geographical coverage of the estimate for the prewar year 1933 includes the entire Chinese Mainland, which consisted of the Republic of China, including Manchuria and Outer Mongolia. The existence of the puppet "Manchoukuo" in that year, depriving China of its main industrial base, was a severe handicap to the development of the economy in the rest of the country, but the productive activities in Manchuria must be included in our estimates. For the postwar years, income originating in Outer Mongolia has not been included for the simple reason that we have no access to the data. Any incomparability of the prewar and postwar estimates on this account is negligible; Mongolian production, as it is now, would not show itself in any reasonably rounded estimate of the income of the Chinese Mainland.

HISTORICAL AND INSTITUTIONAL SETTING

No attempt will be made here to provide a detailed description of the historical and institutional background for the periods studied in this volume. We shall present only a general picture of the economy as it existed around 1933, and then sketch briefly the most important changes in the Chinese Communist economy since 1949.

The Pre-Communist Era

International and domestic conditions during the early and middle 1930s were anything but conducive to orderly economic development. After the founding of the National Government in Nanking in 1928, there were at least four major internal revolts by remaining warlords, but they were quickly suppressed. The military campaigns against the Communist forces in 1930 and 1931 were less conclusive. Then in September 1931, Japan invaded Manchuria. Even after the Japanese occupation of Manchuria, China had no breathing spell to enable it to lay the foundation for long-range economic development. Under pressure from the Japanese, a degree of local autonomy had to be granted to a North China Administration. The cutting off of Manchuria and North China deprived China of an important part of what little industrial base it had at that time. A local war with Japan then broke out in Shanghai in 1932. The Province of Jehol was also invaded and occupied. The full-scale Japanese invasion, however, did not come until 1937.

In addition to the military actions, China suffered a major depression in the industrial and trading sectors of its economy during 1934. China had been on the silver standard, and in 1934 United States legislation provided for the purchase of silver at a price far above the previous market price. This caused an outflow of silver from China and a severe contraction of business activities in the cities. The currency reform of 1935 took China off the antiquated silver standard and successfully arrested the downswing in business activities.

Actual fighting and impending full-scale war with Japan further hindered economic development. Yet the very backwardness of the Chinese economy was, ironically, the strength of the country. Neither the military actions in the early thirties (which were relatively limited compared with what was to come after 1937) nor the business depression in the leading cities in 1934 had too much effect on the countryside. Chinese farms were primarily family businesses which did not depend much upon outside supply for either production or consumption. Their produce was sold mostly in nearby localities. What happened in the outside world was more often than not immaterial to, and indeed sometimes unnoticed by, the peasants, except those located along the few railroads. More than the normal quota of floods occurred in the early and middle thirties, especially in 1931 and 1935, but conditions on the farms were otherwise not worse than in other years.

The usual lot of a Chinese peasant family was not an enviable one, but circumstances varied greatly from region to region. The peasants in the rice-tea region in Central and South China probably had the highest standard of living in rural China. Northward through the Yangtze rice-wheat area and the winter wheat-kaoliang area there was increasing poverty among the farmers. The rice region in the southwest (including Szechwan) had fertile soil, but the social structure was backward and the ratio of tenant peasants to owner-farmers was the highest in the country.

The best data on the landlord-tenant situation in China as a whole are given in John L. Buck's study of land utilization. According to Buck, in the early 1930s a little over one-half of the farmers were owners, less than one-third were part owners, and 17 per cent were tenants. Somewhat less than three-fourths of the privately owned farm land was owned by the farmers themselves, and only a little over one-fourth was rented.[4] The labor force per farm, including both family (men, women, and children) and hired labor, amounted to two man-labor units (the equivalent of the work of two adult males); of this, 1.7 was family labor and 0.3 was hired labor.[5] In addition to land rent, many tenant peasants were in debt (more often than not to their landlords), and the interest rates were high. Needless to say, those farmers who owned land had taxes to pay. Relative to their incomes, the financial burden on the peasants was high. But the more basic cause of their poverty was the classical one of an extremely low ratio of land to man. According to Buck, the amount of crop area per person was about 0.43 acres.[6] Droughts, plant diseases, and the lack of fertilizers and effective control of floods were also important contributory causes.

In summary, we believe it is fairly accurate to say that, granted substantial differences in the various regions, the toil and labor of the peasants left them with enough staple food grains (but not much of any other food) to sustain their energy. They had just sufficient resources to maintain low-grade housing, barely adequate clothing and other subsistence requirements and to keep their simple productive facilities and implements repaired and replaced. But they had nothing left over either as provision for a rainy day or as capital for expansion or self-improvement. This bare subsistence was compensated for to some extent by the fairly quiet and stable family life in the villages.

The peasants were the backbone of society, honest and resourceful. But they were still using the same implements and the same techniques that their forefathers had been using for generations to produce the same kinds of crops. There was little cooperation among the peasants either in production or in marketing. To be sure, when disaster fell, neighbors helped each other; but the tiny plots were separated by ridges, and the boundary lines were strictly observed. There was no pooling of land and resources to reap the benefits of a division of labor. Joint selling negotiations with grain merchants, and bulk buying of their very modest production and consumption requirements from the towns and cities, were largely unknown.

[4] Buck, *Land Utilization*, Vol. I, pp. 9, 192–199.
[5] *Ibid.*, p. 292.
[6] *Ibid.*, p. 279.

Along with agriculture there was a handicraft industry, which included on the one hand such artistic perfection as the silk in Hangchow, embroideries in Hunan, chinaware in Kiangsi and carpets in Tientsin, and on the other hand such crude wares as handwoven cloth and hand-milled flour and rice. Most of the handworkers lived in villages and rural towns, but quite a few established themselves in urban areas of good size and in leading cities. The handicraft establishments were mostly family affairs, frequently carried on in peasant households. Apprentices were taken into the family, and, sustained by their masters, they worked without wages until they had learned their trade. The importance of the handicraft industry in the economy can be seen if we realize that the daily life of most Chinese people, except for a small portion of those in the large cities, would have been affected very little if no modern factories had existed at all in China.

Handicraftsmen had existed in China since time unknown, although their skill in different trades rose and fell through the centuries. Mechanical motive power did not make its appearance in China on any significant scale until about the beginning of the twentieth century. At that time half-hearted attempts were made, under the leadership of a few relatively enlightened Mandarin officials, to build some factories on the European pattern. Very few of these industrial enterprises engaged in the production of producers' goods. Most of them specialized in mass-demand items—cotton textile products, manufactured food, cigarettes, and matches—that could be produced by machine in greater volume and more cheaply than in the handicraft establishments. Foreign-owned manufacturing plants, practically all located in the concessions in a few coastal cities, employed many workers, although the ratio of factory workers to handworkers was on the decline from 1931 to the Sino-Japanese War in 1937.

Growth of modern manufacturing was slow before 1930, not only because of political instability and lack of effective demand in the stagnant economy, but also because, by treaty limitations, tariffs on foreign goods were low. The protection of infant industries by high custom duties, which was practiced by many industrial nations, did not exist in China. The National Government gained control of tariffs and customs administration from most countries in December 1928 and from Japan in 1930. Development of certain light industries received immediate stimulus. Substantial expansion of light industry took place during the early and middle 1930s, although a quantitative estimate is difficult to obtain.[7]

In the meantime, substantial industrial development was taking place in Japanese-occupied Manchuria. The emphasis there was on heavy industries for military purposes. Endowed with rich iron and coal deposits and lumber supplies, and with sturdy, hardworking inhabitants (many of whom had migrated from other provinces), Manchuria was then, as now, the obvious base in the initial stage of any program of industrialization. Therefore the loss of Manchuria to Japan in 1931 was a crippling blow to the economy.

Perhaps the most backward aspect of the prewar economy was the use of human power in all forms of transportation. From the movement of people in the cities to the shipment of goods over fairly long distances, human and animal power and primitive vehicles were of overwhelming importance. In the trading sector, too, peddlers with their wares in hand-pushed carts or in baskets fastened to long poles across their shoulders were an essential element in the economy, more important than the stores and shops with fixed locations of business.

It was in this underdeveloped state that the Chinese economy withstood the brunt of Japanese invasion. During a period of four years—1937 to 1941—China fought the much more modern and powerful Japanese war machine alone, mainly by trading space for time. The National Government retreated to the southwestern hinterland in 1938 and remained there until 1945. During the second half of the Sino-Japanese War, hyperinflation further weakened the Chinese economy already worn out by the war.

Industry and commerce did not revive immediately after the Second World War, for internal fighting was soon resumed on a large scale. Military and political developments during the years 1946–48 need not concern us here. The National Government was evacuated to Taiwan early in 1949, and toward the end of that year the Communists gained control of the mainland.

[7] In an earlier study, an index of industrial production for China, excluding Manchuria and foreign enterprises, was constructed mainly on the basis of employment data. Industrial production increased roughly by 50 per cent, from 87 per cent in 1931 to 125 per cent in 1936, with 1933 as 100 (Liu, *Income*, pp. 44–48). Although a substantial part of this increase in fact represented expansion in output, it was later felt that an unknown portion of the increase reflected improvement in statistical coverage. Since it has not been possible to determine the relative magnitude of these two parts, an estimation of the national product of prewar years other than 1933 was not attempted in this study.

The Postwar Years, 1949–57

The "People's Political Consultative Conference," held in Peiping in October 1949, can be considered as the commencement of the Communist regime on the Chinese Mainland. The initial effort of the regime to rehabilitate the economy was fairly successful for three main reasons. First, by the end of 1949, large-scale military operations had practically ended. For the first time in 12 years there was no fighting in the country. This alone was a boon to the whole country for it made possible the resumption of normal economic activities. Second, the successful Communist price stabilization program in 1950 curtailed the inflation which had run uninterrupted from the last years of the Sino-Japanese War, and greatly assisted in rehabilitating the economy. Victory bonds were issued and, quite understandably, private businesses and individuals had to come forward to subscribe to them. Vigorous efforts were made to increase government revenue (for example, to impose taxes in real terms so that tax revenue would increase with the price level). Except for a small surtax on agriculture, taxes were now collected entirely by the central government, and stringent controls were reestablished over the receipts and expenditure of all government organs and state enterprises. These measures were undoubtedly effective in controlling and reducing inflationary pressure. Probably most important to the price stabilization program, however, was the regime's success in ending the flight from cash into commodities. Such transactions were limited, and people did not engage in them because they were afraid of the newly established revolutionary regime. Third, and very important, the mildness of the 1949 "Common Program," to be carried out by Communists and non-Communists alike, succeeded in relieving the urban population's feelings of anxiety and uncertainty toward the Communist regime. Indeed, except for the harsh treatment given the landlords and the so-called rich farmers, the first two or three years of the Communist regime can be considered the "honeymoon" period.

The honeymoon proved to be short lived. A period of intensive liquidation of certain elements of society was followed by gradually tightened regulation and control of every aspect of life during 1952–56. Then in 1956–57 came the strange "Let Hundred Flowers Bloom" campaign and its frightful aftermath. Finally, in 1958, the Chinese Communists, going beyond Russian-style communism, established the communes and instituted a number of drastic measures in the so-called Great Leap Forward.

THE "HONEYMOON" PERIOD, 1949–51

Whereas the "Common Program" proclaimed by the Communists in 1949 was relatively mild in its effects on certain sectors of the urban population, it nevertheless provided for the immediate redistribution of land and the confiscation of the properties of "anti-revolutionaries" and other elements deemed undesirable. The economy was to be controlled according to a central plan and the production of producers' goods would take precedence over the supply of consumers' goods. Private enterprise was supposed to be allowed to exist side by side with state and joint enterprises for a long time, and the Communists went so far as to permit "national capitalists" to play an important role in the "Common Program." When the price stabilization measures became effective and the halt in the rise of the price level brought about a recession in private industry, the Communist regime even came forward with contracts and other kinds of help for private enterprise. To be sure, government contracts were one of the effective means through which private enterprise was gradually being supervised and regulated. Other forms of indirect control included channeling through the government both the supply of raw materials to private enterprises and the distribution of their products. Moreover, in December 1950, "Provisional Regulations Concerning Private Enterprises" were put into effect to govern the scope of operations, production, profit distribution, and labor relations of private business. Nevertheless, there was no outright hostility toward private businessmen who "cooperated" with the regime.

In the meantime, however, a centrally planned economy was first practiced in Manchuria and gradually put into effect in the rest of the mainland. The pattern on which the planned economy was to operate was theoretically as follows. A general outline of the annual plan was determined in the State Council. The various ministries and their subordinate organs would then put the plan in more concrete terms in the form of output targets for specific commodities. These output quotas would be assigned to the enterprises which would in turn prepare detailed plans for meeting the quotas. The detailed plans, covering all aspects of the operation, including raw materials, labor, power, financing, marketing, and transportation, would then be submitted back through the same channels for approval. After these plans were coordinated and modified at the top, they would be returned to the enterprises for execution.

State trading corporations were organized to engage in buying and selling operations so that for consumers in urban areas the government became the major supplier of the following essential commodities: food crops, cotton and textiles, "miscellaneous daily necessities," salt, coal, construction materials, and "miscellaneous local products." In addition, all foreign-trade products were handled by government companies. Salt had always been a government monopoly in China and government marketing of food grains, cotton textiles, and coal had begun during the war, but this was the first time in the history of China that the government actually engaged in the marketing of "miscellaneous daily necessities" and "miscellaneous local products" which included practically all the items entering the consumption basket of people living in urban areas.

In sharp contrast to the moderate policies pursued in the urban areas, the land redistribution was carried out with full force and violence. An unknown number of people were liquidated through mob trials and mass executions. After the redistribution of land, farms were even smaller in size. From an economic point of view, division of labor became more difficult than ever. Discussion of more efficient land utilization frequently turned up in the various publications and undoubtedly paved the way for the collectivization movement soon to come.

Agricultural taxes were collected in kind, and compulsory sales of agricultural products to the government were soon effected. From the very beginning, compulsory sales to the government were transacted at prices determined by the government. Relative to the prices of nonagricultural products, these prices were lower than before the war. Even though some upward adjustments were reported from time to time, the terms of trade between agricultural and nonagricultural sectors were more unfavorable to the peasants at the end of 1957 than in the prewar period.

THE PERIOD OF GRADUALLY TIGHTENED CONTROL, 1952–56

With the completion of the rehabilitation of the economy, the honeymoon was over. The regime had gained some experience in large-scale planning in Manchuria and in the operation of industrial and trading enterprises throughout the mainland. The Communists were now ready to push forward the socialization of the urban economy. Two groups of urban population, heretofore treated rather mildly and courteously, were put under firm discipline in 1951: the rank and file government workers and the owners of private enterprises. A "three-anti-movement" was initiated to single out and punish some of the untrusted civil servants. It was alleged that (1) dishonesty, (2) waste, and (3) inefficiency among government workers and employees of public enterprises were hampering the Korean War effort.

Early in 1952, a "five-anti-movement" evolved which, in effect, amounted to a large-scale nationalization of private business and the liquidation of undesired businessmen. The movement was directed against (1) bribery of public officials, (2) tax evasion, (3) theft of public assets, (4) fraud in fulfilling government contracts, and (5) theft of government information. Continued operation of private enterprise was made so difficult that many businessmen felt relieved to have the government take over. Even independent handicraftsmen found it difficult to secure supplies of raw materials and quickly learned that their difficulties could be greatly eased if they joined cooperatives. The socialization of private industry and business had now begun in earnest.

Although the First Five Year Plan was not announced until 1955, the year 1953 was considered to be the beginning of the five-year period. Several important changes in economic policies did, in fact, start in 1953, among them a new policy toward the peasants. The peasants were urged to render "mutual aid" during busy seasons as early as in 1951, and "mutual aid" teams were formally organized in the spring of 1953. These measures were rather beneficial to the peasants who, in large measure, had the ownership and use of the land.

By the end of 1953, however, the decision had been made to organize agricultural producers' cooperatives. The ownership of land, livestock, and implements remained in the hands of the peasants, though these properties were to be used jointly by members of the cooperatives. From the end of 1953 to July 1955, 630,000 cooperatives were organized, with a total membership of 17 million farm households. This was only a small percentage of the agricultural population. In July 1955 Mao Tse-tung severely criticized Communist Party members for the lack of progress in the cooperative movement. In November 1955 the decision was made to organize first preliminary and then advanced cooperatives. In the preliminary type, the ownership of the land was transferred from the members to the cooperatives; the share a member was entitled to have in the total income of the cooperative was partly determined by the land he had contributed. In addition, the peasants were allowed to own minor livestock and implements and to have a small private plot for growing vegetables and poultry for their own use.

In June 1956 the advanced cooperative was introduced. The feature that distinguished this type from its predecessor was that the amount of land a peasant had contributed to the cooperative no longer determined his share in the cooperative's income. By the end of 1956, about 88 per cent of the peasants were organized into advanced cooperatives; approximately 8 per cent remained in the preliminary type.

Along with the collectivization of the farmers came comprehensive control and rationing of food. Starting in November 1953, a program of "planned purchase and supply" of food crops was put into effect. On the supply side, the peasants were forced to sell a certain amount of their harvest to the government, although they were still permitted to engage in small food transactions in the countryside. In the meantime, the government became the sole supplier of food to urban areas, either directly, or indirectly through food merchants. No city dwellers, food stores, or manufacturers of food products were allowed to buy food supplies directly from the peasants.

The control was further tightened in 1955. A new system of the so-called unified purchase and supply of food grains was introduced throughout the country. In the rural areas the so-called three-fix policy was put into effect—fixing the normal yields, the amount of compulsory sales, and (in the case of food-deficient farming areas) the amount of food purchased from the government. This policy was designed to wipe out whatever free market was left in rural areas. In the meantime, the urban population was subject to strict food rationing according to age and occupation. The control of the supply and distribution of food was now comprehensive and complete. Small free markets for miscellaneous food items appeared briefly in 1957, but since then neither the peasants nor the consumers have had the freedom to sell or buy food except in accordance with strict government regulations. According to reports, however, clandestine dealings are frequent.

During this period, the socialization of private industry and business continued at a rapid pace. One regulation after another was introduced to organize the small business units into cooperatives in which the individual members gradually lost identity, and to transform the larger business concerns into joint or state enterprises. The Communist data on the share of private enterprise in industry and trade are shown in Table 1.

Table 1

PRIVATE ENTERPRISE'S SHARE IN INDUSTRY AND TRADE
(per cent)

	1952	1953	1954	1955	1956	1957	1958
Value of industrial production (excluding handicraft cooperatives and individual handicraftsmen)	39.0	36.8	24.9	16.2	0.1	—	—
Value of wholesale trade	36.3	30.3	10.2	4.4	—	—	—
Value of retail trade	57.8	50.3	26.4	17.5	3.0	3.0	—

NOTE: — Indicates a negligible amount.
SOURCES: Based on Communist data: *1955 Statistical Abstract*, pp. 40–41, 46; *1956 Statistical Abstract*, pp. 29, 57; and *FFYP Communique*, p. 48.

THE "HUNDRED FLOWER BLOOMING" PERIOD AND ITS AFTERMATH

In May 1956 Mao Tse-tung made the dramatic proposal, "Let hundred schools of thought contend and let hundred flowers bloom," meaning that he would welcome free comments and criticisms and would tolerate differences of opinion. The call was first directed toward literary and academic circles. Initially, there was no response. By the spring of 1957 the Communists made a massive effort to invite and encourage many leading personalities in all walks of life (particularly Western-trained intellectuals who had cooperated with them since 1949, such as well-known writers, leaders in higher education, cabinet ministers, and others who occupied responsible positions in the regime) to voice any criticism they might have of the regime and the new society. The slogan went as follows: "Say everything you know; withhold nothing in what you say; those who speak need fear no vengeance; those who listen will know how to discipline themselves; those who have erred will rectify; those who have not erred will try to do better." The flood of severe criticisms, complaints, and accusations that followed were published in the Communist newspapers. Those who spoke included many outstanding Communists. The criticisms had to do with all aspects of the new society, including the regulation and management of the economy. There are reasons to believe that the intensity and the scope of the criticisms went far beyond original expectations.

The reversal of the policy inviting free criticisms soon came in the latter part of 1957, as dramatically as had its advent. Those who held critical views of the regime were first humiliated in public meetings and then removed from positions of influence and responsibility. The number of people involved was not large, but the effect on the non-Communist educated class was total and devastating. The old intelligentsia, including both the classical and Western-trained scholars, long held in great esteem in Chinese society, were now discredited on the surface if not in the minds of the people.

The "Hundred Flower Blooming" episode and its aftermath are exceedingly important, but the analysis of its motives, implications, and consequences is beyond the scope of this work. Two observations should be made here, however. First, it is reasonable to believe that the severe punishment of critics of the economy effectively induced people (including Communist Party members themselves) to echo the statements of the Communist high command. This belief is supported by the quite unprecedented exaggerations in the economic statistics for 1958. Second, the revelation that an important sector of the community was dissatisfied with the Communist regime was probably a contributory cause of the radical measures of control introduced with the advent of the communes in 1958. These developments will be described in Chapter III.

CHAPTER II

DOMESTIC PRODUCT AND EXPENDITURE: A SUMMARY OF DATA, METHODS, AND FINDINGS

STATISTICS on the Chinese economy are scarce compared with those of more industrially advanced nations, but because of the sheer size of the economy, we have been able to use thousands of items of data in this study. We have had to make many assumptions to close the gaps in the available information. Although the estimating method is conceptually straightforward and simple, at times it becomes extremely roundabout and complex. The sources, data, concepts, methods, and estimates obtained are discussed in detail in Chapters IV and V and in their supporting appendixes. The more important aspects of the estimates are summarized in this chapter to serve as a guide to the detailed discussion and to provide background for the analysis presented in the next chapter.

A knowledge of the scope and reliability of the data is needed to understand the nature of the estimates obtained and to guard against attributing to the estimates a degree of precision that they do not possess. Moreover, the estimating method is determined by the available data. Communist statistics have been adjusted in accordance with our judgment of their reliability; the estimates obtained are, in turn, governed by the adjustments. It is convenient, therefore, to discuss the nature of the sources and the method of estimate together.

The first section presents a discussion of the general framework of the estimates. Specific discussions of the estimates for 1933 and for the period 1952–57 follow in the second and third sections. In most cases, neither the description of the data nor the explanation of the method of estimate requires the actual presentation of statistics. So far as possible, the discussion in these three sections is presented in general terms, the exceptions being the description and adjustment of the Communist data on agricultural output and industrial production. Certain prewar data that are relevant to the evaluation of these Communist statistics are also presented, and because of the special importance of the adjustments, a rather detailed discussion is given of the reasons and assumptions underlying the changes we have made. The main estimates are then summarized in Tables 8–11.

The Communist data for 1958 and 1959 are even less reliable than those for 1952–57. As will be explained in Chapter III and Appendix K, only a conjectural estimate has been made for these two years. The results are also presented in Table 8.

CONCEPT AND APPROACH

Although "national income" (the generic term for a whole family of related concepts) is used in the title of this study, the main body of the estimate is concerned with domestic product at market prices. The domestic product is estimated both gross and net of consumption of fixed capital, although the estimate of capital consumption is based on more or less arbitrary assumptions. The concept of domestic product can be explained conveniently by relating it to the more familiar one of national product. National product at market prices is the total market value of production (excluding the value of intermediate products used in the process of production) attributable to the factor services supplied by the residents of a country. Domestic product is obtained from national product by excluding factor income received from abroad and adding factor income remitted abroad. Factor income received from abroad is payment for services supplied by the residents of a country and is therefore included in the national product, but it is not a part of domestic production. On the other hand, factor income remitted abroad is payment for services supplied by nonresidents and is therefore omitted from national product; but it constitutes a part of the domestic output. Information on net factor incomes from abroad, especially for the postwar years, is much scarcer and less reliable than our basic data on domestic production. Only domestic product, therefore, has been estimated. Net factor income from abroad was probably very small compared with domestic product for all the years included in this study. For 1933, net factor income received from abroad was roughly 200 million yuan, less than 1 per cent of the domestic product for that year.[1] There is every reason to believe that the magnitude of this item relative to domestic product has been even smaller during the postwar years. No attempt will be made to express the estimate obtained in terms of factor cost, as that would require a

[1] Liu, *Income*, p. 69.

thorough inquiry into the nature of various taxes and government subsidies and is beyond the scope of this study.

Domestic Product by Industrial Origin: The Heart of Our Estimate

Domestic product can be estimated in three different ways: by summing up the contributions of the different industrial sectors to the total product (the value added or income originating approach); by aggregating distributive shares paid or accrued, such as wages, salaries, interest, rental income, dividends, business savings, and indirect taxes less government subsidies (the income payment or distributive shares approach); or by measuring the value of the final product going into personal consumption, government consumption, and domestic and foreign investment (the end use or final product approach). For the first approach, either data on the value of output and nonprimary input (raw materials used, power consumed, and so on) must be available so that the value added by a given industry can be derived, or the payments to primary inputs must be known so that the income originating in a given industry can be computed. The basic data used in estimating domestic product by the second approach are usually aggregate data on income payments without regard to industrial origin, such as the total salary and wage payments derived from income tax and social security records. To use the third approach, data on family budgets or on retail sales must be available so that personal consumption can be estimated. In addition, data on business investment outlays and government budgets are needed.

It would be ideal if estimates could be made in all three ways, using independent sets of data, but this is seldom possible. In studying the economy of an underdeveloped country, one is grateful to find enough data for a single approach. For China, the data are such that an estimate obtained on the value added approach, using production and employment statistics, is the least unreliable for both the prewar and postwar periods. The least incomplete of the Chinese economic statistics are the production data. Not only are data on the values or physical outputs of important agricultural and manufactured products relatively more abundant, but most of them are also more reliable; or at least their reliability can be more easily judged. Data on commodity prices are also available to some extent.

Information on nonprimary inputs for production purposes is less complete, but estimates for the missing parts can usually be made.

As in other countries, agriculture, manufacturing, mining, utilities, transportation, trade, government administration, finance, personal services, and rental income are all important enough to be treated as separate sectors of the economy. A "work brigades" sector must be added for the postwar period, when an increasing number of people, mostly peasants, were organized to do heavy earth work (without pay) on irrigation, conservation, highway, and railway projects.

The factor that distinguishes the Chinese economy from the more industrially advanced economies is that in manufacturing, transportation and communications, and trade, the modern enterprises can be separated from the traditional. The techniques of production and business organization of the handicraftsmen, and their role in the economy, bore no resemblance to the techniques and organization of the factories, even though their products, in many ways, could be substituted for each other. Similarly, the old-fashioned carriers must be separately reported from the modern transportation and communication services, and the peddlers separately reported from the trading stores. This differentiation between modern and traditional should not be interpreted too literally. Some of the trading stores and shops were quite ancient in their origin and organization, but available data do not permit us to separate them from the other trading enterprises. Some of the mining and construction enterprises were still using antiquated equipment and techniques, but they must remain classified with their more modern counterparts until we have information to separate them. We shall therefore use the term "modern" in a relative sense throughout.

The quality and completeness of the production statistics, of course, are not the same for the different sectors of the economy. Data are generally more adequate and reliable for the modern sectors. The 1933 employment data in certain sectors can be used to supplement the production statistics. A crude estimate of the occupational distribution of the population had to be used to estimate the value added in most of the traditional sectors. For the postwar period, different but equally crude methods had to be used to estimate the incomes originating in sectors for which specific data do not exist.

Estimate of Domestic Expenditure and Employment: The Secondary Results

Data on family budgets and information on capital expenditures of business enterprises, which are necessary for a direct calculation of domestic expenditure, are extremely fragmentary and unreliable. For 1933, they exist for only small samples.[2] For the postwar years, statistics on family budgets are not only limited to small samples but also appear to be of doubtful reliability. They are discussed later in this chapter.

Data on retail sales would be helpful in estimating personal consumption, but they are totally lacking for the prewar years. For the postwar years, the Communists have published a series of retail sales data which even they admit are of poor quality. The Communist Director of the State Statistical Bureau has said that the statistics on trade are poorer than the statistics on industry.[3] The low degree of reliability of the latter will be shown later in this chapter.

Although a direct estimate of domestic expenditure would be even less reliable than the product estimate, it is still possible to derive the major components of domestic expenditure from the product estimate, mainly by the commodity flow method. An estimate for the food and clothing components of personal consumption and for investment expenditure has been so obtained. Since our expenditure estimate is not independent of the product estimate, it cannot serve as an accuracy check, but it does serve many analytical purposes.[4]

Another important by-product of the estimate of domestic product by industrial origin is the estimate of employment in the different sectors of the economy. For 1933, the product and employment estimates are really interdependent, the value added in certain sections being derived from estimates of employment and occupational distribution, and the employment estimates in certain sectors from output figures and rough estimates of value added per worker. For

[2] Buck, *Farm Economy,* pp. 382–421; T'ao Lu-kung, *Livelihood in Peking: An Analysis of the Budgets of Sixty Families,* Peiping, Social Science Research Department, China Foundation, 1928; Lee Ching-han, *Peiping chiao-wai chih hsiang-t'sun chia-ting* (Rural Families in Suburban Peiping), Peiping, Social Science Research Department, China Foundation, 1929.

[3] Hsieh Mu-ch'iao, "Summary Report to the Fourth National Statistical Work Conference," *HHYP,* No. 6, June 1955, p. 148.

[4] See Chapter III on the investment drive and the "real cost" of the investment program.

the postwar years, however, employment estimates for the modern sectors are either compiled from Communist employment data or obtained from sources independent of the output figures. This makes it possible to analyze (in Chapter III) the trend relationships between output and employment in these sectors during the postwar years. The postwar employment estimate is based on data so fragmentary that the derivation, which is explained in Chapter IV, has not been summarized in this chapter.

Three Bases of Valuation: The 1933, 1952, and 1957 Price Weights

The total value of national product and its rate of growth depend not only upon the physical volumes of the component items, but also upon the unit prices used in combining these components in the product total. This is the familiar "index number problem" encountered in many areas in economic analysis. In studying patterns of economic development, it is clearly desirable to weight the constituent parts of the national product by appropriate alternative sets of price weights if relative prices have changed significantly through time.

In our estimation of domestic product by industrial origin, three different price weights were used. The 1933 and 1952 price weights were constructed on the basis of data on actual market prices. The 1957 weights were obtained by converting the 1952 weights on the basis of a few aggregate price indexes published by the Communists. (All the price indexes are given in Appendix I. In the discussion in this section, the sources of the data on prices will not be given separately.)

Data on market prices of most agricultural and industrial goods received by producers are readily enough available for us to estimate the value of production at the source of origin. Estimates of value added by trade, transportation, and other sectors are gross of all taxes and net of government subsidies. The estimates obtained, therefore, are in accordance with the concept of domestic product and expenditure at market prices. As is customary, consumption of agricultural products on farms is included in the domestic product at producers' prices without the addition of transportation and trade margins.

In 1933, indirect taxes and government subsidies were very small in relation to the total product. The estimated gross domestic product was about 30 billion yuan (see Table 8), but total government revenue amounted to less than a billion yuan, a significant portion of which was derived from the land tax. Indirect taxes probably amounted to less than 2 per cent of the domestic product. The amount of government subsidies is unknown, but is felt to have been negligible. Except in Manchuria, arbitrary allocation of resources by public authorities was, for all practical purposes, absent. Hence the 1933 market prices approximate the factor cost valuation of the products and services produced by the economy, and serve as a basis of comparison with the postwar pricing systems under Communist control and planning. The product and expenditure estimates for 1952–57, therefore, have also been computed on the 1933 price weights. In our use of the 1933 price structure as a basis of comparison we do not intend to imply that the 1933 price weights reflect an efficient and desirable system for the allocation of resources. Although monopolistic controls were generally absent, the economy consisted on the one hand of more or less isolated rural districts where division of labor and modern industries were underdeveloped, and on the other hand of a few industrial cities along the sea coast and under Japanese occupation in Manchuria. It is true, however, that the mechanism of supply and demand in a free economy was operating in 1933 to a much greater extent than in later years and that the price structure then in existence sharply differs in many ways from that in the postwar years.

The 1952 price structure has been used to compute product and expenditure estimates for 1933 and all the postwar years for a number of reasons. First, nearly all of the important Communist economic series published prior to 1958 (such as the value of agricultural and industrial production and the volume of retail and wholesale trade) are expressed in constant 1952 prices. Since Communist statistics are necessarily the basic data for our estimate, the 1952 price weights are used in our calculation. Second, a good deal of information is available on actual market prices in that year, even though there is less than for 1933. Third, since the Communist estimate of national income is given in constant 1952 prices, we can make a comparison and reconciliation between their estimates and ours by computing our estimates with the same price weights.[5]

By 1952 the Communist regime was in control of most of the modern sectors of the economy. Although farms were not yet col-

[5] See Chapters IV and V on comparison of estimates.

lectivized and there could not have been really effective control of farm consumption in kind, nor of small trading transactions in the villages, the Communists largely controlled trade among the villages and between rural and urban areas. The regime was the largest buyer and seller of agricultural products through compulsory sales to the government, monopolistic control of the wholesale market, and, to a lesser extent, through control of retail trade in farm output. The Communist government was, therefore, in a position to have an effective influence on a large portion of the agricultural market prices. It had been an important Communist policy to depress agricultural prices relative to other prices in order to increase profits of the government enterprises that used these products as raw materials. This policy also helped the Communist regime to curtail the peasants' demands for consumers' goods and, hence, to reduce inflationary pressure. All prices were higher in 1952 than in 1933, but prices of producers' goods had increased at a higher percentage rate during this period than had prices of consumers' goods. This was partly because of the high initial development costs required for the many new producers' goods. But it was also partly because a considerable portion of consumers' goods were still produced by private enterprises, which, during the five-anti-movement in 1952, suffered a loss in profits.

Using index numbers of 1933 prices = 100, the following prices for 1952 show the differences between the price structures for the two years: Agricultural products, 183; handicraft products, 218; factory-produced producers' goods, 488; factory-produced consumers' goods, 332; net value added by trading stores, 350; personal consumption, 200; government consumption, 225; and investment expenditure, 500. As will be shown in Chapter III, the higher prices of manufactured goods in 1952, relative to the prices of agricultural products, have great effects on the measurement of changes in the industrial structure of the economy, on the pattern of allocation of resources for end use, and on the rates of growth of domestic product and expenditure.

The Communists had succeeded in keeping agricultural prices consistently lower than other prices, but they found it necessary to make occasional adjustments in both the prices of individual products and agricultural output as a whole. It is possible that there were some increases in the prices received by peasants from 1952 to 1957. As implied in certain Communist data, the level of the prices received by farmers in 1957 was 106, with 1952 = 100.[6] On the other hand, as industrialization developed, the prices of many manufactured products declined. Information on the actual degree of the decline is scarce. The Communists reported that the price level of investment goods in 1957 was 89.9, with 1952 = 100. Since investment goods include new products that require high initial costs of development, their price decline should have been more substantial than that of other manufactured products. According to the Communists, however, the price level of industrial output as a whole in 1957 was 89.4 (1952 = 100), almost the same as the price index of investment goods. If this information is reliable, the equally great decline in the price level of consumers' goods from 1952 to 1957 must have taken place because of the greater volume of production in 1957 of such products as cotton textiles.

It is doubtful that the price level for industrial output as a whole actually could have declined as much as that for investment goods. In the absence of more accurate information, we have to postpone judgment as to the reliability of these price data. We have deflated the various components of our product and expenditure estimates for all the years (1933 and 1952–57) and have expressed them in 1957 prices mainly on the basis of this limited and uncertain information on the price structure in 1957, and also, among other data, on the cost-of-living index and the wholesale price indexes. It must be emphasized that the estimates given in constant 1957 prices are very crude and highly tentative. The estimate of the value added *in a given industrial sector* in all the years 1933 and 1952–57 in constant 1957 prices was obtained by deflating the estimate in constant 1952 prices by one and the same index. Therefore, the estimated rate of growth of the given sector is the same in the prices of both years. When all the sectors are taken into consideration, however, the industrial structure of the economy and the pattern of allocation of resources (as they are reflected in the estimates of domestic product and expenditure in constant 1957 prices) are different from those implied in the estimates in constant 1952 prices.[7]

[6] In *Great Ten Years,* p. 14, the gross value of agricultural production in 1957 was given at 60.35 billion yuan in 1952 prices but at 53.70 billion yuan in 1957 prices. The implied price index for 1957 would be 89, with 1952 = 100. Such a calculation cannot be correct, because the product coverages of these two figures are different. When the coverage is adjusted to the same figure, the implied index for 1957 is 106, with 1952 = 100. See also Appendix I.

[7] See Chapter III on the real cost of the investment program and the development and changes in the production structure.

SOURCE DATA AND METHOD OF ESTIMATE: 1933

Prior to the founding of the National Government in 1928, the central government was so weak and ineffectual that national-scale, systematic efforts were never made to collect economic statistics of any degree of reliability. Even the population censuses published in 1912 by the government during the first year of the republic were actually taken during the last years of the Ch'ing dynasty. The data available were so fragmentary and unreliable that the National Government had to start the compilation of statistics from scratch. Major efforts were made to collect comprehensive statistics in both agriculture and industry, and a population census was compiled in 1928. However, only 16 of the 23 provinces actually submitted reports.[8] These statistics were supplemented by two other important sources of data. From 1929 to 1933, John L. Buck organized what was undoubtedly the best sample study of Chinese agriculture. In addition, the Japanese made available a set of industrial statistics for Manchuria. The four sets of industrial and agricultural statistics, together with the population data, constitute the major sources for our value added estimate of prewar domestic product. The data and method we have used separate the industrial sectors into two groups: a "hard" category, consisting on the whole of the more accurate estimates, and a "soft" category of less reliable estimates. Our expenditure estimate is derived from the product estimate essentially by the commodity flow method, and is described below.

The "Hard" Components of the Product Estimate, 1933

AGRICULTURE

Before the Communists took control of the mainland, an annual report of crop production, initially developed by C. C. Chang from 1929 to 1931, was released by the National Agricultural Research Bureau of the National Government. These annual surveys covered all the provinces of China (except Manchuria after 1931). The current yields of all important crops, both food grains and raw materials for industry, were reported by field observers to the Bureau where the total output was computed. This crop-reporting system had a number of important weaknesses. First, the annual output of a crop was estimated by multiplying the yield per mow by the

[8] Ministry of Interior, National Government, *Min-kuo shi-chi-nien ko sheng-shih hu-kuo tiao-cha t'ung-chi* (Population Statistics by Province, 1928), Nanking, 1933, preface and p. 35.

number of mows in cultivation. The data on cultivated acreage were largely taken from the land tax records and were gross underestimates. Second, the field observers were selected local residents (such as postal employees and school teachers) who voluntarily participated without pay. Most of them were intelligent and reliable, but they were not trained in agricultural census taking.

Fortunately, the Bureau's estimate is supplemented by Buck's independent survey which was carried out in various localities under the supervision of the faculty and students of the College of Agriculture of the University of Nanking. The statistical procedure and methods used were as careful as the circumstances and financial resources permitted. The size of Buck's sample, however, was not as large as might be desired, and the areas covered were the more accessible regions which probably had high ratios of cultivated land to total area.

The greatest differences between the Bureau's and Buck's data occur in the total cultivated acreages and in rice production. We have attempted to supplement these two sets of data by other sources of information so that the known downward bias in the Bureau's figures and the apparent upward bias in Buck's data on cultivated acreages are corrected. An estimate of rice production by province was obtained by an exhaustive study of all available information. Our estimate of the production of other crops combines the Bureau's and Buck's data since they have no apparent biases. In this manner, a larger number of independently collected observations are incorporated into the basic data.

Our estimate of total food crop production is given below, together with the Bureau's figure and the estimate derived from Buck's data:

	Million piculs
Our estimate (from Table 2)	3,456
Estimate derived from Buck's data[9]	3,746
The Bureau's estimate[10]	2,507

Our estimate is substantially higher than the Bureau's, but is about 10 per cent lower than the figure derived from Buck's data. No claim is made for accuracy within a small margin of error; in obtaining our

[9] Sum of output in China proper given in *Food Crops*, p. 10; output in Sinkiang and Manchuria given in Appendix A, Table A-9.

[10] *Agricultural Estimates*.

estimate, we have often arbitrarily averaged the various reputable sources. We believe that no valuable information has been overlooked.

There is, in fact, no way to estimate the probable margin of error by any rigorous statistical method. The plausibility of our estimate of food crop production can be examined only by checking the implied per capita consumption figures with the results of certain food consumption surveys. Needless to say, even such a check cannot be expected to result in any definite conclusion about the reliability of our estimate of food crop production. All three sets of figures (food crop production, per capita consumption, and food crop consumption) are subject to unknown margins of error. Nevertheless, these three sets of data were obtained independently. More confidence could be placed in them if they were found to be consistent with one another. As will be seen, the data are only roughly consistent, and the error involved can be interpreted in a number of ways. Moreover, even if they were entirely consistent, this check would remain inconclusive. Production and population might have been overestimated by the same proportion, for example.

As the check is of considerable interest, it is presented here in detail. In Table 2, the total amount of calories supplied by the different food crops is estimated at about 350,000 billion calories per year in 1933. The total population of the Chinese Mainland around 1933 is estimated later in this chapter at roughly 500 million.[11] The intake from all food crops is therefore about 1,940 calories per capita per day.

The information on calorie intake given in several food consumption surveys is summarized in Table 3. According to Buck's study on the rural areas, calories from food crops accounted for 91 per cent of the total calorie intake from all sources, and amounted to about 2,300 calories per day. The estimate of food crop production derived from Buck's data was 10 per cent higher than our estimate. Although Buck's food consumption survey was carried out independently of the output survey, the samples of the two surveys came from essentially the same regions which are more accessible and, we believe, better off than many other localities in China. If we also make a downward adjustment in Buck's estimate of per capita calorie intake from food crops by 10 per cent (that is, the

[11] See Chapter IV.

Table 2

ESTIMATED SUPPLY OF CALORIES FROM FOOD CROPS, 1933

Crop	Total output: Our estimate (million piculs) (1)	Output for food consumption (per cent) (2)	Output for food consumption (million piculs) (3)	Extraction rate (per cent) (4)	Processed products for food consumption (million piculs) (5)	Calories per picul (thou-sands) (6)	Total calories supplied (billions) (7)
Nonglutinous rice	1,600	90	1,440	70	1,008	177	178,416
Wheat	534	73	390	80	312	173	53,976
Millet	255	75	191	80	153	181	27,693
Kaoliang	251	39	98	88	86	181	15,566
Corn	186	66	123	100	123	187	23,001
Barley	152	36	55	80	44	164	7,216
Glutinous rice	82	81	66	70	46	173	7,958
Peas	65	57	37	100	37	167	6,179
Broad beans	60	68	41	100	41	157	6,437
Proso millet	38	84	32	88	28	178	4,984
Oats	13	64	8	80	6	179	1,074
Buckwheat	19	74	14	78	11	173	1,903
Black beans	20	30	6	100	6	161	966
Mung beans	27	68	18	100	18	166	2,988
Sweet potatoes	132	66	87	100	87	142	12,354
Irish potatoes	21	66	14	100	14	190	2,660
Total	3,456	76	2,620	77	2,020	—	353,371

Calories per capita per day, 1,936

NOTES: — Does not apply.

Column (1). Output of rice is taken from Table 31, and those of other crops from Appendix A, Table A-9. Potatoes are given here at their grain-equivalent weight (one-fourth of their natural weight).

Column (2). Percentage for rice is our estimate, an average of Buck's 95 per cent, the Bureau's 82 per cent, and T. H. Shen's 93 per cent (Buck, *Land Utilization*, Vol. III, p. 238; W. Y. Swen, "A Study of the Consumption of Staple Food Products in China," *Crop Reports*, Vol. 2, No. 8, 1934, pp. 63–65; and T. H. Shen, *Agricultural Resources*, p. 201). Percentages for other crops are based on *Crop Reports*, Vol. 5, No. 6, quoted in Pei Yu-lin, "National Income, Consumption and Investment of China," *Shi-yeh jin-yung* (Journal of Finance and Industry), Shanghai, Vol. I, No. 1 (May 1948), p. 70, and *Land Utilization*, Vol. III, pp. 237–238.

Column (3). Column (1) times column (2).

Column (4). Rice is given at 70 per cent in the following three sources: Kung Chi-chih, *Nung-yeh shih-yung shou-t'se* (Practical Agricultural Handbook), Chung-kuo wen-hua shih-yeh-she, Shanghai, 1951, p. 120; Chiao Chi-ming and Chiang Chieh, *Chung-kuo jen-k'ou yu shih-liang wen-ti* (China's Population and Food Problem), Shanghai, Chung-hua Book Company, 1939, p. 39; and Food and Agricultural Organization (of the U.N.), *Report of the Second Session of the International Rice Commission*, Bangkok, 1950, p. 40. Percentages for other crops are based on Food and Agricultural Organization, *Food Balance Sheets*, Washington, D.C., 1949, p. 239.

Column (5). Column (3) times column (4).

Column (6). Taken from Buck, *Land Utilization*, Vol. III, p. 67. The figures given for potatoes are in grain-equivalent weight.

Column (7). Column (5) times column (6).

percentage difference between Buck's and our estimate of food crop production), the amount would be 2,070 calories per day, about 7 per cent higher than our estimate of 1,940 calories per day. For an estimate of this kind, a 7 per cent difference cannot be considered large, though we are inclined to believe that our lower estimate is nearer the actual level. The prewar (1934–38 average) calorie intake per capita per day for Japan was only 2,180, which includes intakes from all sources, not food crops alone. On the basis of our estimate of 1,940 calories from food crops, and assuming that food crops accounted for 91 per cent of the total calorie intake (see Table 3), our estimate of the total calorie intake would amount to 2,130 per capita per day, about the same as that of prewar Japan.

The scattered data on urban communities do not present a consistent picture. Thus, the calorie intake of young male college students in Liaoning, which is located in an extremely cold region, is reported to be 2,456 calories per day, a level lower than the average 2,532 calories for adults and children taken by middle-class families in Shanghai in the summer. The working class in Changsha in South-Central China, where the climate is mild, took 3,008 calories per day, about 400 calories more than the 2,595 calories taken by the low-income class in Peiping in the north.

Among these scattered data for the urban areas, the lower figures are more credible than the higher. If we adjust Buck's estimate of *total* calorie intake downward by 10 per cent, the per capita figure for the rural areas would be only about 2,280 calories per day. It is extremely unlikely that the total per capita calorie intake would be lower in rural areas than in urban areas, even though the proportion supplied by food crops in rural areas would be higher than in the cities. In general, people in the country work harder than people in the city. If factory hands in Shanghai had only about 2,500 to 2,660 calories per day, and the urban middle class in Shantung had only 2,500 calories, then the average for all classes of people and for all age groups should be well under 2,400 calories in the urban areas. The percentage of calories supplied by food crops in urban areas would be substantially lower than the 91 per cent reported by Buck for rural areas. If we assume it to be 80 per cent of the total, calories supplied by food crops in the urban areas would be under 2,000 per day, which is not inconsistent with our estimated 1,940 calories per day for the nation as a whole.

Our estimate of calorie intake, based on food crop production and a population of 500 million people, comes quite close to the more plausible figures reported in food consumption surveys. For estimates of this nature, the three sets of figures can be considered roughly consistent with one another. It must be pointed out, however, that if we assume the amount of per capita calorie intake derived from food crops at the higher level of 2,080 calories per day (Buck's figure as adjusted) and our estimate of food crop produc-

Table 3

CALORIE INTAKE PER CAPITA PER DAY IN PREWAR YEARS
(taken from food consumption surveys)

Buck's data		
Calorie intake per man-labor unit		3,295[a]
Calorie intake per capita		2,537[b]
Percentage distribution of food energy by source:		
(Calories supplied by different products)		
Source	*Per cent*[c]	*Calories (computed)*
Food crops:	91.0	2,309
Grains	(83.1)	
Legumes	(4.0)	
Potatoes	(3.9)[d]	
Soybeans	2.7	68
Vegetable oils	2.0	51
Animal products	2.3	58
Fruits	0.2	5
Vegetables	1.3	33
Sugar	0.5	13
Total	100.0	2,537
Data on urban communities		*Calories per capita per day*
Data submitted by the National Government to the Conference of the Food and Agriculture Organization of the United Nations[e]		
Peiping, university communities		3,044
Peiping, middle schools		2,746
Peiping, middle-class families (summer)		2,471
Liaoning, college communities		2,456
Liaoning, middle schools		2,460
Shanghai, middle-class families (summer)		2,532
Shanghai, factories		2,490–2,660
Nanking, students of army medical college		2,932
Chang Chun-tsun[f]		
Peiping, middle-income class		2,977
Peiping, low-income class		2,595
Shantung, urban middle-income class		2,491
Shanghai, middle-income class		2,544
Nanking, average		2,801
Changsha, labor class		3,008
Wu Hsiang[g]		
Peiping, urban middle-income class		2,901
Nanking, urban middle- and low-income classes		2,829

NOTES: [a] Buck, *Land Utilization*, Vol. I, p. 407.

[b] Based on Buck's ratio of man-labor unit to single person of 0.77. *Ibid.*, Vol. III, p. 66. 3,295 × 0.77 = 2,537.

[c] *Ibid.*, Vol. I, pp. 407–413. Items are arranged according to our classification. Potatoes were included in Buck's table with vegetables, and soybeans with legumes.

[d] Figures in parentheses add to the figure immediately above.

[e] National Government, *Annual Progress and Program Report on Food and Agriculture for China*, August 1947, p. 57.

[f] Chang Chun-tsun in *Min-tsu chien-kang yu ying-yang huan-ching* (Nutritional Environment and the Health of the Nation), Chungking, 1945, pp. 7–9.

[g] Results of prewar studies by professors of the medical schools in Nanking and Peiping, cited by Wu Hsiang in *Ying-yang* (Nutrition), Chengtu, 1944, p. 186.

tion is correct, then the implied population figure would be only about 465 million in 1933.[12] This figure is nearer to the commonly held notion of 450 million and the official figure of 479 million published by the National Government before the war than our estimate of 500 million.[13] However, we believe the lower estimate of 1,940 calories per day is nearer the true amount, and, therefore, that the population estimate of 500 million is more nearly correct than the other estimates. The derivation of our population estimate will be discussed in connection with the "soft" components of the product estimate in this chapter and in Chapter IV.

Estimates of the quantities and prices of animal, forest, fishing, and miscellaneous agricultural products can be obtained, although the basic data are less reliable than those on plant crops. Gross and net value added by agriculture are then found on the basis of scattered information on nonprimary input and arbitrary assumptions on depreciation.

FACTORIES

In 1933, a comprehensive industrial census of Chinese-owned factories, covering all manufacturing plants using mechanical power, was planned and carried out by D. K. Lieu for the National Resources Commission of the National Government. It was the only survey of its kind before the war. Detailed data on the gross value of output, raw materials and power consumed, the number of people employed, and much other information on factories are included in the report. The Commission's survey had a number of defects, some of which can be removed. Unfortunately, the survey was carried out only for the one year 1933. This is the decisive reason for limiting our estimate to that year.

A number of studies of foreign-owned factories in China outside of Manchuria were available for the prewar years, although none is comparable to the Commission's survey. In addition, two studies, made by the Japanese South Manchurian Railway and the puppet Manchoukuo Government, provide us with about the same information on factories in Manchuria as the survey made by the National Resources Commission for China proper. From these data and arbi-

[12] Total calories supplied by food crops estimated at 353,371 billion (see Table 2); 353,371/(2080)(365) = 465 million.

[13] China Handbook Editorial Board, *China Handbook, 1951*, Taipeh, Taiwan, China Publishing Company, 1951, p. 26.

trary assumptions about depreciation, the gross and net value added by factories are estimated for the whole Chinese Mainland.

OTHER "HARD" SECTORS

Data on output, input, and prices are available in sufficient quantity to estimate the value added by mining, utilities, and modern transportation and communications. The basic data on transportation and communications are more reliable than the rest. About 60 per cent of the value added by handicraftsmen can be estimated by data on output, input, and prices, and the estimate obtained is probably on the same level of reliability as our agricultural estimate. This can be considered the "hard" portion of handicrafts; the rest will be explained below.

Value added by construction is estimated as the amount of primary inputs required for work with the construction materials produced, adjusted for import balance; its accuracy is probably of the same order as the estimate of construction materials themselves.[14] In China, especially in the rural areas and in small cities, an overwhelming proportion of major repairs of buildings and workshops, and even a small proportion of new construction, were carried out by owners or occupants with salvaged materials or with straw, clay, and dirt. These have not been included in our estimate of construction materials. To that extent, the value added by the construction sector may have been underestimated.

Value added by government administration and by finance are all estimated on data specific to these factors. They are included in the "hard" group.

The "Soft" Components of the Product Estimates and Data on Population and Occupational Distribution, 1933

In industrially underdeveloped countries where economic statistics are usually deficient, it is certain that an estimate of national product based upon available data on output, input, and employment in specific sectors will fall short of the actual magnitude. For the traditional sectors, specific data are unlikely to exist, since the statistical agencies of the government usually pay little or no attention to them. Accurate information would be difficult to find even if attempts were made to collect it because the individuals serving

[14] Data on construction materials produced can be found in our estimate of agricultural, manufacturing, and mining output in the appropriate appendixes.

in these sectors are usually uneducated and do not keep records. They also tend to be uncommunicative.

There are insufficient data on handicrafts, old-fashioned transportation, and peddlers. For the first, specific data are available on a large portion of the raw materials used in handicrafts, and this portion is included among the "hard" sectors. How much of the total income originating in handicrafts has been so accounted for cannot be determined on the basis of the statistics specific to that sector alone and must be estimated by some other method. For old-fashioned transportation and peddlers, there is almost no information.

A rough estimate of the income originating in these sectors is obtained in this study first by estimating the total population and its occupational distribution. The total number of people employed in manufacturing, whether in factories or in handicrafts, is a part of the estimate of occupational distribution. If the number of workers already accounted for in factories is deducted from the total number of workers engaged in manufacturing activities as a whole, a rough estimate of the total number of handicraftsmen is obtained. The number of workers engaged in old-fashioned transportation can be similarly found by deducting the number working in modern transportation from the total number employed in transportation. In the trading sector, our estimates of both peddlers and trading stores with fixed locations depend partly on the population data.

The estimate of the "soft" components is admittedly very rough and less reliable than that of the "hard" components. However, the inclusion of even such a rough estimate will in all likelihood result in a more accurate determination of the total product than would their exclusion.

TOTAL POPULATION

Ever since W. F. Willcox, the renowned demographer, challenged the validity of Chinese population statistics, they have consistently, and deservedly, had a very low reputation.[15] The Chinese Communist census of 1953, suddenly claiming the Chinese population to be 580 million (about 130 million higher than the commonly held belief) was a great surprise and was suspected of falsification. Although the quality of the census data is indeed very poor, by using the prewar sample studies discussed below, we estimate the Chi-

[15] W. F. Willcox, "The Population of China and Its Modern Increase," *Studies in American Demography*, Ithaca, N.Y., Cornell University Press, 1940.

nese population in the early 1930s to have been roughly 500 million. It cannot be claimed that this estimate is accurate within a narrow margin of error, but there is no reason to believe that it is much less accurate than other Chinese economic statistics, prewar or postwar.

Our conclusion as to the size of the Chinese population was obtained from the following considerations. First, after a painstaking examination of the Chinese official census data, Willcox made an estimate of his own for 1912. However, he was unable to correct for the two fundamental defects in the Chinese population data of which he was fully aware, namely the underreporting of infants and very young children, and the unreasonably high male to female ratio. Since Willcox published his studies, certain sample studies of the Chinese population have been made that are of higher quality than those previously available. On the basis of these sample studies, we have adjusted Willcox's estimate for these defects. Moreover, a rate of growth under unfavorable conditions (rather high mortality rates) can be computed from the samples at 0.78 per cent per year. This low rate of growth has been used to project Willcox's figure to the early 1930s. The result obtained is roughly 500 million.

Second, in 1935, S. T. Wang, a noted Chinese demographer, made a thoroughgoing examination of the existing population figures by province and made many useful adjustments. His data are probably the best selection of the official figures available. He did not, however, make corrections for the two defects in the data mentioned above. When his data are adjusted for these defects, the result is also about 500 million. Third, Wang's adjusted population figures by province are applied to our estimate of the production and per capita consumption of rice by province. The resulting picture of rice surplus or deficiency for the leading rice producing and consuming provinces is roughly in accord with our general impression.

Our estimate of the total population is therefore higher than the commonly believed 450 million and the official figure of 479 million published by the National Government.[16] The absolute differences among these figures are very great indeed; the percentages are neither unexpected for an estimate of this nature, nor alarmingly large. It would be idle to argue that our estimate is definitely more accurate than the other figures. On the other hand, as has been discussed in connection with our estimate of food crop production, the per capita calorie-intake figure obtained with our population esti-

[16] China Handbook Editorial Board, *op. cit.*

mate seems reasonable. Moreover, if we accept the adjusted Willcox estimate for 1912, then the figures for 1933 of 450, 475, and 500 million imply rates of growth of the Chinese population from 1912 to 1933 at about 0.2, 0.5, and 0.7 per cent per year. Of these rates, the highest is still substantially below 1 per cent per year, and appears to be the most plausible. Finally, while we shall not use the Communist population figure of 583 million for 1953 to support our population estimate of 500 million for 1933, it should be pointed out that if the Willcox estimate of 430 million for 1912 and the Communist estimate of 580 million for 1953 are both accepted, then a 1933 figure of less than 500 million would mean a rate of growth of population for the period 1912 to 1933 lower than that for 1933 to 1953. The implied rate of growth from 1912 to 1933 and that from 1933 to 1953 would be about 0.7 per cent per year if we accept 430, 500, and 580 million as the estimates for 1912, 1933, and 1953. The 20 years from 1933 to 1953 were more disturbed by war than were the two previous decades. Hence, it would be unreasonable to take a figure for 1933 lower than 500 million. By the same argument, however, it may be said that if one accepts the Willcox estimate for 1912 and the commonly held impression of 450 million for 1933, then the Communist figure for 1953 would be too high. Actually, the effects of war on both the birth and the death rates in China are far less important than the influences of sanitary conditions and natural calamities. These basic factors were probably quite similar in both the 1912–33 period and the 1933–53 period.

OCCUPATIONAL DISTRIBUTION AND THE "SOFT" COMPONENTS

Our estimate of occupational distribution is definitely less reliable than most of the other statistics we have used. The proportion of the total population having agriculture as its main occupation was given by both Buck and C. C. Chang at about 73 per cent, and this is probably a fairly accurate figure.[17] Data on the nonagricultural occupations, however, are available for only two provinces and one county. Fortunately, one of the two provinces and the county were industrially rather advanced and the other province was very backward, so that the situation in the other provinces can be approximated by various weighted combinations of the three sets of data.

[17] The agricultural population, which we define as people having agriculture as their main occupation, is considerably smaller than the rural population as defined by the Communists. See the discussion on distribution of population in Chapter IV.

There is no way to check the accuracy of the result, but this estimate appears to be consistent with the occupational distribution in 12 leading cities on the one hand and the agricultural subsidiary occupations on the other.

The nonagricultural occupations are classified into four groups: industry, trade, transportation, and all other (nonagricultural) sectors. The industrial category includes handicrafts, factories, utilities, mining, and construction. Since people employed in the last four subcategories have already been estimated, the number of handicraft workers can be obtained as a residual. Employment in old-fashioned transportation is estimated by deducting the number employed in modern transportation from the total number employed in transportation. After the number of people engaged in handicrafts and old-fashioned transportation are roughly estimated from the data on occupational distribution, their total value added can be obtained since the value added per worker in these industries is either known approximately or can be roughly assumed.

The estimate of the trading sector has to be obtained in a special way. Some sample studies of the ratio of stores to population and of the number of workers employed per store are available. Given the total population figure, income originating in trading stores can be estimated on the basis of these ratios and certain information on profits and workers' wages. Value added by peddlers can then be estimated on the basis of occupational distribution data by deducting the number of workers in stores from total employment in trade. The result obtained for the trading stores is probably more reliable than that for the peddlers. The figures given for rent are very crude estimates obtained from population data and other fragmentary information.

The Expenditure Estimate, 1933

It is a simple step to estimate the total magnitude of net domestic expenditure since it is equal to net domestic product plus the import balance of international trade. The problem is to obtain an estimate of the three major components of domestic expenditure: personal consumption, government consumption, and investment. Government consumption can be computed rather easily from government budgetary data but the other two components are more difficult to estimate.

The value added by the different sectors of the economy can be used to compute investment and the food and clothing components of personal consumption by the commodity flow method. This method is conceptually simple, even though many bold assumptions have to be made in applying it to the Chinese data. In food consumption, for example, the value of food output at producers' prices and services rendered by manufacturing, transportation, and trade in connection with food products are successively added to obtain the value of food consumption to consumers. The procedure is similar in the case of clothing consumption and investment, except that the starting point in clothing consumption is the output of textile fiber materials and in investment, capital goods produced. In all three cases, domestic output is adjusted by import balance.

Food and clothing accounted for by far the major share of personal consumption; the rest consisted of fuel and lighting, and housing, which can be directly estimated, and a miscellaneous category on which information is completely lacking. However, since both total domestic expenditure and all the other components of the total are now known, miscellaneous personal consumption can be obtained as a residual. Residual estimates are risky because they embody the errors of the estimates of all other components. There is the possibility that these errors might not be cumulative, but could cancel one another out to some extent. We have accepted this residual as the estimate of miscellaneous personal consumption because in our opinion its proportion to total consumption, 14 per cent, appears reasonable. It is unlikely that the Chinese people could have spent more than 14 per cent of their total consumption on items other than food, clothing, housing, fuel, and lighting. If the estimate is biased, it errs in the upward direction.

Since our estimate of domestic expenditure is obtained from domestic product, the accuracy of the total figure can differ from that of the product only by the margin of error of the estimated import balance of international trade. The import balance is very small compared with the total expenditure; whatever the margin of error, there would be little effect on the accuracy of the total. However, the estimates of the different components of domestic expenditure are definitely less reliable than the sector estimates of domestic product, because arbitrary assumptions had to be made to allocate the transportation and trade margins to the various consumption components and to investment.

SOURCE DATA AND METHOD OF ESTIMATE: 1952–57

Prewar statistics are admittedly scarce and inaccurate; the poor quality of these data was the result of unsystematic collection efforts and insufficient training and experience of personnel. With the exception of the downward bias of the Bureau's food production statistics which we believe we have corrected, there are no grounds for suspecting institutional bias in any particular direction. For the postwar period, the reliability of the Communist data is a more controversial and difficult question, and much of our study is concerned with this problem. The nature of Communist statistics will be discussed briefly and in general terms in the next section. Detailed discussion of specific Communist data, especially those on agricultural and industrial outputs, will be presented in connection with the description of the methods by which our estimates are derived.

A Preliminary Discussion of Communist Statistics

It has sometimes been said that the Communists keep two sets of books, one for internal use and another for propaganda purposes. Whatever the true situation is, it is idle to argue in general terms for Communist statistics as a whole. There are, in all likelihood, different degrees of reliability for different categories of data. The very indications of implausibility and unreliability with respect to certain data might provide a clue for making a more accurate estimate. The important problem is to determine the extent of bias. On the other hand, if indications of unreliability are not present, even a definite knowledge of two sets of books would not help us to estimate the degree of falsification.

The Communist economy is almost totally planned; every plan, decision, and move require (and are presumably guided by) concrete statistics and information. But this should not lead one to believe that the Communist data are largely reliable. The necessity for reliable data in running a Communist economy does not in itself guarantee the availability of such data. There are certain basic physical and human elements that must have worked against the Communists in their attempt to gather reliable economic information. To use Chinese Communist data, it is necessary to examine their plausibility and accuracy in every respect and to use all the evidence, direct and indirect, without preconceived notions about their reliability.

It is hardly necessary to point out that the Chinese Mainland covers a very large area. In this territory, the means of communication were inadequate, to put it mildly. Moreover, there was an exceedingly large number of economic units in the traditional sectors. Countless small farms, handicraftsmen, peddlers, and village stores were scattered all around the country, some in regions with very limited access to and from the outside. It is true that even before the advent of the communes many of these small economic units had been organized into cooperatives of one kind or another; but it is equally true that before 1958, the traditional sectors had not been organized on a military pattern. A mere 12 million Communist Party members (the approximate number in 1957), scattered among a population probably more than 50 times as numerous and over an area of roughly 3.5 million square miles, would not have been in a position to keep track of the productive pursuits of all the people on the mainland in minute detail prior to 1958. However, even before 1958 the people generally were not in a position to oppose or even to evade major Communist policies. For example, compulsory sales of food by the peasants to the regime had to be made more or less to the satisfaction of the Communists. When the peasants were told not to sell their food directly to the urban areas, most of them probably stopped doing so. Of course, it would have been extremely difficult for the government in Peiping to know the exact amount of agricultural production in all the provinces and counties. The situation was undoubtedly similar in the control of the handicraftsmen and small traders.

For most individuals, there were strong incentives not to let the Communists know the true situation. Practically all the Communist regulations and controls were designed to promote the interest of the government at the expense of the individual. The pressure that the regime has exerted on party workers to fulfill productive targets and quotas in various fields worked against them in their effort to collect reliable data. The success or failure of party workers in fulfilling these quotas and targets would literally decide their futures, and many of them undoubtedly manipulated the reported data in their favor.

The need to guard against the uncritical use of Communist statistics is further confirmed by the developments since 1949. During the period of internal warfare after the defeat of Japan, the regions under the control of the National Government were divided into pockets connected by precariously held lines of communication. The managers of government enterprises in various regions had to keep their businesses in operation in a makeshift manner and largely on their own initiative. Much depended upon whether raw materials could be obtained and finished products could be shipped out. Factories and plants could not have been well maintained and whatever records and statistics were kept were of doubtful quality.

The Communists took over these enterprises during 1949 and 1950 and added to the confusion. They therefore did not have data with any degree of reliability for those years. Since that time, they have made determined efforts to collect and improve upon their statistics. Surveys of government and joint enterprises were conducted as early as 1950, and statistics on the value of agricultural production, industrial production, and wholesale and retail trade were published as early as 1949 and 1950, but data published during these early years are of particularly questionable reliability. This conclusion is based upon the consideration that comprehensive surveys of the different sectors of the economy were carried out much later. The statistics published before these surveys were probably rather crude estimates. Moreover, the State Statistical Bureau was not established until 1952.

The Director of the State Statistical Bureau reported in November 1957 that in addition to the well-known population census taken in 1953,

> ". . . in 1953, we gradually established and improved upon our statistical collection work concerning private industry and trade, handicrafts and agricultural production. In 1954, we organized a comprehensive survey of private industry and handicrafts. In 1955, we conducted a comprehensive survey of private trade and began to investigate the receipts and expenditure of the agricultural production cooperatives. In 1955 and 1956, we started to survey family budgets of farmers and workers and began to estimate national income." [18]

[18] Hsieh Mu-ch'iao, "Our Experience in Statistical Work During the First Five Year Plan Period and Our Future Tasks," *TCKT,* No. 21, November 1957, p. 2.

In other words, Communist data on handicrafts and private industry before 1954, and data on private trade before 1955, were not obtained through comprehensive surveys.

One might hurriedly conclude that as a consequence of the Communists' efforts to improve their statistical reporting systems, their data for the later years, say 1955–57, are better than those for 1952–54. This conclusion is unwarranted for it is precisely during these later years that the First Five Year Plan was formally put into effect and that there were increased pressures on the managers of enterprises and local party members to fulfill or overfulfill the assigned quotas. The inflation of statistical reports probably increased as the drive to reach one target after another was intensified, and this tended to cancel out the effects of the improvements in the statistical reporting system. The unprecedented inflation of data on agricultural production in 1958 can be considered the climax of the "effort" and "response" made by local party workers and managers to satisfy the desire of the central authorities for an accelerated increase in production. The improvements in the data collecting system were completely negated. Moreover, it should be pointed out that most of the data published for the years 1952–54 were revised after the comprehensive surveys were completed. Precisely because they were *ex post* estimates, they should be free from the kind of inflating pressure that was exerted on the data for the later years. It is therefore entirely possible that the data for 1952–54 are more reliable in certain fields than the later data. There is no possibility, however, that the data for the years 1949–52 are better than the post-1952 data, as there was really no basis on which the Communists could have improved these figures in later years.

Apparently no uniform description can be offered for the accuracy of the different categories of Communist data or for the reliability of the data for any period as a whole. Each category for each year must be examined on the basis of the objective evidence. We might mention in this connection that we have found the Communist data on agricultural production for 1956–57 to be more plausible and reliable than those for earlier years. The opposite is true for their data on industrial production. These conclusions are not based on our judgment of the relative importance of such factors as the Communist effort to improve their statistical collecting system and the tendency to inflate statistical reports under pressure to meet production targets; rather, they are reached on the basis of indications and evidences that can be more objectively evaluated, as will be discussed in the following section.

The "Hard" Components of the Product Estimate, 1952–57

AGRICULTURE

Communist data on the total output and per capita consumption of food crops for the postwar years are presented in Figure 1, together with the following three estimates for the year 1933: (1) that of the National Agricultural Research Bureau, (2) that obtained from Buck's data, and (3) our own estimate. The estimates for the years 1946 and 1947, published by the Bureau before the National Government moved to Taiwan, are also given, together with our own estimates for the postwar years.

Food crops are compared both by natural weights and with potatoes included at one-fourth of their natural weight (used as the grain-equivalent weight). The Communists have consistently counted potatoes by grain-equivalent weight, and there is a great deal to be said for this practice. One pound of potatoes generates only about one-fifth as many calories as one pound of rice or wheat flour.[19] (The per-mow yields of potatoes are, in terms of weight, roughly three times that of rice and more than seven times that of wheat.[20]) Potatoes accounted for about one-seventh of the total production of food crops by natural weight in 1933, but their proportion in the total increased to about one-third during the postwar years. This is unprecedentedly high for China where rice and wheat are vastly preferred. To express potatoes in their natural weight would exaggerate both the energy-generating capacity of food crop production and the productivity of agriculture in postwar years.

Figure 1 is almost sufficient in itself to tell that the Communist data on food crops for the earlier years of their regime are unreliable. The pre-1956 Communist figures are gross underestimates of the actual output. It is probable that the data for 1949 and 1950 were collected more or less by continuing the old crop-reporting system of the Bureau. Not only was there a degree of continuity in these figures with the Bureau's 1946 and 1947 data, but there simply had not yet been time for the Communists to develop their own system of reporting. The downward bias in the figures published by

[19] Buck, *Land Utilization,* Vol. III, p. 67.
[20] Appendix A, Tables A-3 and A-9.

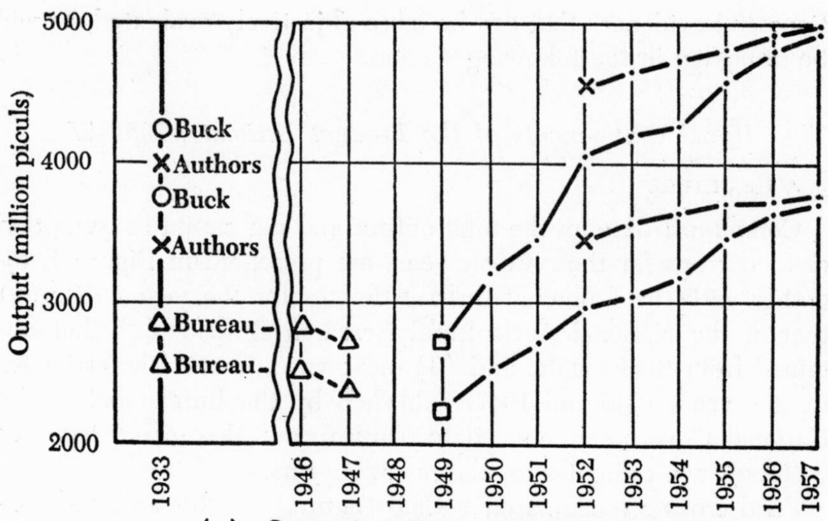

(a)—Output in millions of piculs with potatoes at natural and grain-equivalent weights

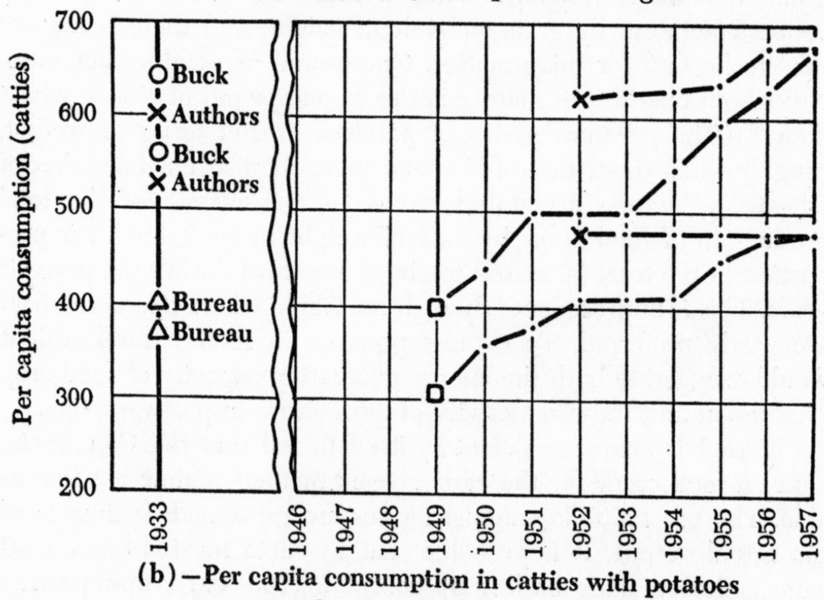

(b)—Per capita consumption in catties with potatoes at natural and grain-equivalent weights

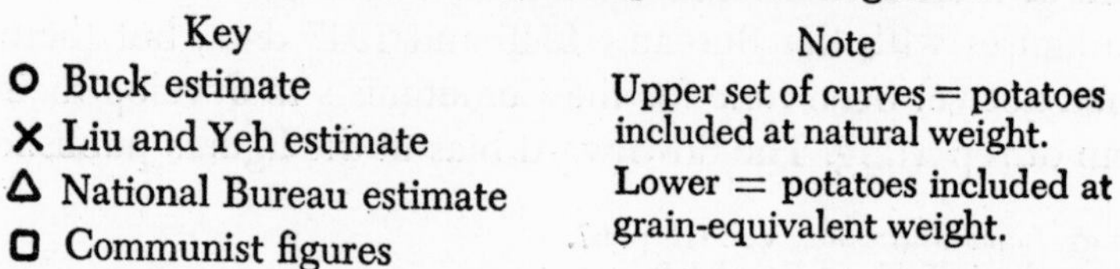

Figure 1. Total output and per capita consumption of food crops, 1933 and 1952–57

the Bureau has been explained earlier in this chapter. The Communist data for 1949–51 are therefore also underestimates. Even their 1952–55 figures are still unreasonably low. It is clear from Figure 1(b) that per capita consumption (especially with potatoes at grain-equivalent weight) during these years was so much below both Buck's and our estimates of the prewar level that even the Chinese people, long accustomed to hardships, could not very well have survived as a nation on this starvation diet for such a long time.

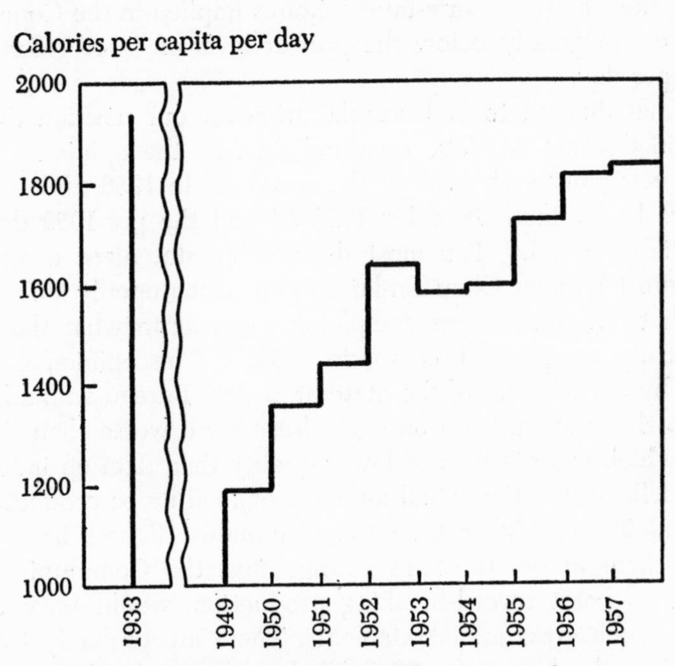

Figure 2. Per capita calorie intake from food crops

Figure 2 shows the 1933 estimate for daily per capita calorie intake derived from food crops, together with the corresponding estimates from Communist data on postwar production. Clearly, the Communist crop production data for all the years 1949–55 are grossly underestimated. Our estimate of the 1933 calorie intake derived from food crops is only about 1,940 calories per capita per day.[21] Calorie intake from other sources was very small; for the country as a whole it is in all probability not much more than 10 per cent

[21] See Table 2.

of that taken from food crops.[22] The Chinese diet in 1933 not only lacked protective elements, it was far from abundant as a source of energy. There was little room for reduction from the prewar level without the risk of national starvation. Yet, if the Communist data on food production for 1949–55 had been even roughly correct, the Chinese people would have endured a diet far below the starvation level for seven years. There were many reports about the shortage of food on the mainland, but prior to 1960 there was no evidence of starvation *on a national scale.* Even with the 1949–51 data discarded, the 1952–55 calorie-intake figures implied in the Communist data are still greatly below the prewar level of 1,940 calories per capita per day.

It is not difficult to find corroboration for our position that the pre-1956 Communist data are unreliable. In the opinion of some Indian economists who visited the mainland in 1956, the 1955 figures are better than those for 1952–54 and the pre-1952 data are not reliable at all.[23] The most devastating statement came from Communist Premier Chou En-lai himself. Chou openly admitted in 1956 that "we are not yet completely clear as to what the actual amount of food production was in 1954." [24] This opinion was supported by the Director of the State Statistical Bureau who admitted in 1955 that the statistics on agriculture were worse than data on trade, which were in turn of lower quality than data on industry.[25]

We believe that the actual amounts of food crops produced during 1949–55 are higher than the Communist figures have represented them to be. It seems strange that the Communists, ever anxious to boast record-breaking production, would have chosen to make such gross understatements. There are probably two reasons. First, the figures for 1949–55 show a steeply rising trend to which the Communists have called attention as a proof of their achievement. In so doing, they have, of course, overlooked the shockingly low calorie-intake figures for the years prior to 1956. Second, it must be borne in mind that the crop-reporting system of the National Bureau was the only reporting mechanism in existence.

[22] See Table 3.

[23] Government of India, *Report of the Indian Delegation to China on Agricultural Planning and Techniques,* New Delhi, 1956, pp. 81, 86.

[24] Chou En-lai, "Report on the Proposal of the Second Five Year Plan," *HHPYK,* No. 20, October 1956, p. 37.

[25] Hsieh Mu-ch'iao, "Summary Report to the Fourth National Statistical Work Conference," *HHYP,* No. 6, June 1955, p. 148.

The Communists could be expected to have made use of it in the earlier years of their regime without any great doubts of the validity of the reports. Buck's studies were familiar only to academic circles in China even in prewar years, and since they were research done by American- and Western-trained Chinese scholars under the leadership of an American economist, they were not given the attention they deserved during the early postwar years.[26]

It is difficult to say how accurate are the Communist 1956 and 1957 data on food crop production. The Communists themselves were criticizing their crop-reporting system at that time. However, for these years there is no longer any convincing evidence of significantly underestimated or overestimated outputs. This tentative conclusion is based on the mainland rationing standards and the subsistence requirements of the Chinese people.

It is unlikely that the 1956 and 1957 figures are clear-cut underestimates of the actual output, because the per capita consumption figures implied in the data for these years[27] are as much as 14 per cent higher than the estimated average ration allowed by the Communist regime.[28] It is reasonable to assume that the Communists, knowing that rationing and control regulations could not be completely enforced, would fix the ration at a lower level than the actual amount of consumption. But the Communist rationing and control systems were probably effective enough for actual consumption not to have been more than 10 to 15 per cent higher than the ration amounts allowed. This point is sufficiently important to justify a detailed computation. The essential data on the Communist rationing regulations by occupations and age groups are given in Table 4. In Table 5, the ration amounts given in Table 4 are weighted by the Communist data on age distribution and by our estimate of the occupational distribution of the population. Table 6 then weights the Table 4 amounts by the Communist data on age and occupational distribution. In both cases, the national average

[26] More recently, Buck's studies have been the subject of criticisms by the Communists. *CCYC*, No. 5, October 1958, p. 9.

[27] The per capita consumption figures implied in the output data are very similar for these years—481 catties per year for 1956 and 486 catties per year for 1957.

[28] Although the strict control of food distribution in rural areas was enforced through a system separate from that in urban areas (both were put into effect on August 25, 1955), it is probable that the official amounts allowed by the rationing regulations and the actual per capita consumption were very much the same. We refer to the consumption of food crops only. The per capita consumption of all kinds of food, including meats and vegetables, *by middle- and higher-income classes in the cities* would be higher than in the rural areas.

Table 4

COMMUNIST FOOD RATIONING SCHEDULE, 1955–57
(in catties of processed food crops per person)

Occupation and age group	In areas where rice is the staple food[a] (per month)	(per year)	In areas where miscellaneous food crops and wheat flour are the staple foods[a] (per month)	(per year)	National average[b] (per year)
Workers doing exceptionally heavy physical labor	50	600	55	660	634
Workers doing heavy physical labor	40	480	44	528	508, 516[c]
Workers doing light physical labor	32	384	35	420	405
Workers in government agencies, civil groups, personnel of public and private enterprises, shop assistants, and others doing nonphysical labor	28	336	31	372	357
University and middle-school students	32	384	35	420	405
General residents and children	25	300	27.5	330	317
Children between 6 and 10 years	20	240	22	264	254
Children between 3 and 6 years	13	156	14	168	163
Children under 3	7	84	8	96	90

NOTES: [a] Based on Communist State Council, "Provisional Measures for Fixed Supply of Food Crops," proclaimed on August 25, 1955. *HHYP*, No. 9, September, 1955, pp. 163–164.

[b] Weighted average of the two area figures, the weights being the percentage shares of rice (44 per cent), and miscellaneous food crops and wheat (56 per cent), in the total food crop production. Potatoes are included as miscellaneous food crops at their grain-equivalent weight. Actual computation for this column is based on unrounded figures of the percentages of rice, miscellaneous food crops, and wheat.

[c] Arithmetic average of the three component figures.

per capita ration comes to about 420 catties of unprocessed grains—about 14 per cent lower than the 486 catties estimated from the 1957 Communist production figures.

In computing the ration in Tables 5 and 6, we have included the rural population in the calculations. It may be argued that control was more difficult to enforce on the farms where food crops are produced, and that as a result, per capita consumption in rural areas was higher than the average ration allowed in urban areas by more than, say, 15 per cent. If this were true, the 1957 Communist output

Table 5

RATIONS OF FOOD CROPS, 1955–57, WEIGHTED BY COMMUNIST DATA ON AGE DISTRIBUTION AND BY AUTHORS' ESTIMATE OF OCCUPATIONAL DISTRIBUTION

Age group (1)	Per cent in total (2)	Ration per capita per year (catties) (3)	1955 Population (million) (4)	1955 Food (million piculs) (5)	1956 Population (million) (6)	1956 Food (million piculs) (7)	1957 Population (million) (8)	1957 Food (million piculs) (9)
0–2	9.5	90	58	52	59	53	61	55
3–5	8.1	163	49	80	50	82	52	85
6–9	8.1	254	49	124	50	127	52	132
10–11	4.1	317	25	79	25	80	26	82
12–64	65.8		400		409		419	
Nonagricultural, total			159		160		168	
Students		405	5	20	6	24	7	28
Physical laborers		516	45	232	47	242	48	248
Office workers		357	12	42	13	46	13	46
Military personnel		516	3	15	3	15	3	15
Housewives, idle and unemployed		357	94	336	91	325	97	346
Agricultural, total			241		249		251	
Physical laborers		516	182	939	185	955	186	960
Others		357	59	211	64	228	65	232
65 and over	4.4	317	27	85	27	85	28	89
Total population			608		621		637	
Total ration of food crops:								
Processed				2,215		2,262		2,318
Unprocessed				2,576		2,630		2,695
National average food ration of unprocessed food crops (catties) per person per year			424		424		423	

NOTES: *Columns (1) and (2).* The percentage figures of the different age groups are extrapolated from the figures given in Table 52 to correspond to the age groups given in the rationing schedule. These percentages, originally referring to 1953, are used for 1955–57 without modification. The resultant errors should not be very large. (Percentage figures are not given for students, nonagricultural workers, and agricultural workers in age group 12–64, for they vary from year to year.)

Column (3). Figures taken from appropriate groups in Table 4.

Columns (4), (6), and (8). Estimates of the total number of persons in each of the six age groups are obtained by applying the percentage figures given in column (2) to the total population given at the bottom of this table. For nonagricultural population of age group 12–64 and nonagricultural students in the same age group, see Table 24. The category of "physical laborers" includes labor in industry, transportation and communications, construction, peddlers, restaurant and service workers, and work brigades. For the number of workers employed in these industries, see Tables 57, 59–61, and 63. The category of "office workers" includes shop attendants, finance workers, and government nonmilitary workers. For the numbers of workers employed in these sectors, see Tables 61–63. Estimates of the total military personnel are given in Table 62. The number of idle and unemployed housewives is derived by deducting the sum of students, physical laborers, office workers, and military personnel from total nonagricultural population of age group 12–64. Estimates of the total agricultural population of this group are obtained by subtracting nonagricultural population of age group 12–64 from the total population of the same age group. The number of agricultural workers in the category of physical laborers is derived as follows: The numbers of agricultural workers of age group 7–64 were estimated at 211, 215, and 216 million in 1955–57 (see Table 11). The numbers of agricultural workers of age group 12–64 are derived by multiplying the number of those in age group 7–64 by a factor equal to the ratio of the total population of age 12–64 to that of age 7–64. This ratio is computed at 86 per cent on the basis of the data on age distribution given in column (2) of this table. Estimates of agricultural population of age group 12–64 in the "other" group are obtained as residuals by deducting the estimates for physical labor from total agricultural population of age group 12–64.

Columns (5), (7), and (9). Food requirements are obtained by multiplying the population figures given in the immediately preceding columns by the corresponding ration per capita given in column (3).

The four lines at the bottom of the table. Total population figures are taken from Table 32. The conversion ratio between unprocessed grains and processed grain is 100:86. Chen Yun, "Questions Concerning the Unified Purchase and Unified Supply of Food Crops," *HHYP*, No. 8, 1955, p. 51.

Table 6

RATIONS OF FOOD CROPS, 1955–57, WEIGHTED BY COMMUNIST DATA ON AGE AND OCCUPATIONAL DISTRIBUTION

Age group (1)	Per cent in total (2)	Ration per capita per year (catties) (3)	1955 Population (million) (4)	1955 Food (million piculs) (5)	1956 Population (million) (6)	1956 Food (million piculs) (7)	1957 Population (million) (8)	1957 Food (million piculs) (9)
0–2	9.5	90	58	52	59	53	61	55
3–5	8.1	163	49	80	50	82	52	85
6–9	8.1	254	49	124	50	127	52	132
10–11	4.1	317	25	79	26	80	26	82
12–64	65.8		400		409		419	
Nonagricultural, total			168		163		148	
Students		405	5	20	6	24	7	28
Physical laborers		516	44	225	44	225	48	248
Office workers		357	12	42	13	46	13	46
Military personnel		516	3	15	3	15	3	15
Housewives, idle and unemployed		357	104	371	97	346	77	275
Agricultural, total			232		246		271	
Physical laborers		516	174	898	183	944	196	1,011
Others		357	58	207	63	225	75	268
65 and over	4.4	317	27	85	28	89	28	89
Total population			608		621		637	
Total ration of food crops:								
Processed				2,198		2,256		2,334
Unprocessed				2,556		2,623		2,714
National average food ration of unprocessed food crops (catties) per person per year			420		422		426	

NOTES: *Columns (1) and (2)*. The percentage figures of the different age groups are extrapolated from the figures given in Table 52 to correspond to the age groups given in the rationing schedule. These percentages, originally referring to 1953, are used for 1955–57 without modification. The resultant errors should not be very large. (Percentage figures are not given for students, nonagricultural workers, and agricultural workers in age group 12–64, for they vary from year to year.)

Column (3). Figures taken from appropriate groups in Table 4.

Columns (4), (6), and (8). With the exception of the estimates for two categories of nonagricultural population of age group 12–64 (physical laborers and idle and unemployed housewives), all the estimates are derived in the same manner or taken from the same sources as those for Table 5. Estimates of nonagricultural physical laborers are the sum of estimates for factories, mining and utilities, handicrafts, transportation and communications, construction, peddlers, restaurant and service workers, and work brigades given in Chapter IV. The numbers of idle and unemployed housewives are obtained by deducting the sum of the numbers of physical laborers, office workers, and military personnel from total nonagricultural population of age group 12–64.

Columns (5), (7), and (9). Food requirements are obtained by multiplying the population figures given in the immediately preceding columns by the corresponding ration per capita given in column (3).

The four lines at the bottom of the table. Total population figures are taken from Table 32. The conversion ratio between unprocessed grains and processed grain is 100:86. Chen Yun, "Questions Concerning the Unified Purchase and Unified Supply of Food Crops," *HHYP*, No. 8, 1955, p. 51.

figure would underestimate the actual output. In fact, there have been reports that in 1955 and as late as in 1956, the cooperatives were underreporting crop production.[29] However, it is probable

[29] These reports came out while the 1957 statistics were being collected. In May 1957 the principal Communist statistical journal stated that because of the change to the cooperative form of organization and the concurrent reassignment of the statistical staff, only the output of the cooperatives had been reported, and production on members' private plots and the output of individual peasants were omitted from

that attempts made by the cooperatives to underreport have been compensated for by an equally strong urge on the part of some Communist officials to overstate the achievement in production. Per capita consumption of food crops could not have been significantly higher in the country areas than in the cities, for, in spite of the low rations allowed in the urban areas, country people still tried hard to get into the cities in 1957. In a subsistence economy, food is usually the main motivation for population movements. The harsh controls over daily life in the country, which came with the advent of the communes, had not yet been imposed, but the Communist systems of taxation in kind and of compulsory purchases of agricultural products were probably effective.[30]

---

the report. In addition, it was pointed out that numerous cooperatives had underreported their production and that there was repeated underreporting through the statistical network. A first secretary of a county party organization stated that "we must overcome the selfish tendency of underreporting acreages and production" (*TCKT*, No. 10, May 1957, p. 22; No. 17, September 1957, p. 27; No. 4, February 1958, p. 4; No. 11, June 1958, p. 9). The Director of the State Statistical Bureau was very candid. He said that the collection of data on agricultural production was still a weak link of their statistics and that, as the statistical collection mechanism at the hsien level had not yet been really established, the reliability of the data on agricultural production could not be guaranteed (Hsieh Mu-ch'iao, "We Must Strive To Improve Agricultural Statistical Work," *TCKT*, No. 22, November 1957, p. 9).

[30] It is possible that consumption of food crops, in spite of the greater difficulty in the enforcement of any food consumption regulations, might have been even lower in the rural areas than in the urban areas. As we have mentioned, per capita consumption of meat, vegetables, and food other than staple crops is likely to be higher for middle- and high-income classes in the cities than for the peasants in the rural areas. This could certainly not have been a factor inducing the peasants to come into the cities, because they could not afford expensive food items in the cities any more than they could in the rural areas. In the consumption of food crops, it is unlikely that there was any great difference between the low-income laboring class in the cities and the peasants in the rural areas. The peasants unquestionably worked as hard as the hardest working group in the cities, and less than 486 catties per year of food would not have sustained either group.

The Communists themselves provided conflicting data. In one source, per capita consumption of food crops in the cities was given at about 560 catties per year for all the years from 1953 to 1957. The per capita amount in the rural areas is given at 518 catties for 1956–57, about 8 per cent lower than the corresponding amount given for the urban population (SSB, "The Basic Situation of Planned Purchase and Planned Supply of Food Grains in China," *TCKT*, No. 19, October 1957, p. 28). The still lower amounts given for the earlier years for the rural population simply reflect their lower production figures, and should be taken less seriously. The total amount of food crop consumption given in this source, on the basis of the percentage of production used for food given in the same source, does not agree with the total amount of food crops produced. In another source, the per capita use of food crops in the rural areas is reported to be as high as 650 catties for 1956 and 610 catties for 1955 (Chu Han, "The Basic Condition of China's Food Grain Supply in the Current Year," *TKP*, Peiping, October 8, 1956, p. 2). Of the 610 catties for 1955, 540 catties were used for food. If so, the amount used for food in 1956 in rural areas, estimated proportionally, would be higher than the 560 catties reported in the first source.

On this rather circumstantial evidence, we tentatively conclude that the Communist food crop production data for 1956 and 1957 probably do not significantly underestimate the actual production.

We believe that the Communist 1956 and 1957 figures do not overestimate the actual output. It is true that the data for these years show substantial increases over the figures for earlier years. In fact, as shown in Figure 1(b), the Communist figures for per capita food consumption in 1956 and 1957, with potatoes included at their natural weight, are about 6 to 8 per cent higher than our estimate for 1933. However, with potatoes included at their grain-equivalent weight, the Communist figures for per capita food crop production in 1956 and 1957 are about 6 to 8 per cent *lower* than our 1933 estimate. Indeed, as shown in Figure 2, the daily per capita calorie intake derived from food crops, as implied in the Communist data, are 1,816 for 1956 and 1,833 for 1957, or 5 to 6 per cent lower than our prewar estimate of 1,940. This per capita consumption is not much above the starvation level, but since there is no evidence of nationwide starvation or impairment of health in 1956–57, it is unlikely that the figures are overestimates.

Unless convincing reasons are found for doubting the 1956 and 1957 Communist figures for food crop production, we shall tentatively accept them, but we reject Communist data on 1952–55 output as being definitely too low. It is an exceedingly difficult task to estimate the amount of production in these years; at the very best, we can give no more than an educated guess. There is no reason to assume that per capita consumption of food crops had been increasing during 1952–57. In fact, the control of food consumption had been gradually tightened throughout the period, and this would have been unlikely had there been increases in per capita supply of food crops, a point elaborated on later in this chapter. On the other hand, there is no evidence that per capita consumption was reduced during this period; it seems reasonable to assume that it was more or less constant throughout 1952–57.

The assumption enables us to estimate the production of food crops for all the years 1952–57. Crops were increasingly used for food, and the data are available on the annual percentage used for food in total food crop production, including quantities exported. If we assume that the importation of food crops had been negligible and that there had been no change in the amount in storage, the output can be easily computed for 1952–57 on the basis of the population data. The result of this "backward projection" from 1957 to the 1952–56 period is presented in Figure 1. The increase in total production therefore reflects the growth of population, modified only by the increasing percentages of crops used for food.

A number of criticisms can be raised against this estimate. First, it might be questioned whether the rehabilitation of agricultural production would have been so complete by 1952 that the total production could be as high as in 1933. (See Figure 1.) The level of production after the war could have recovered quickly to that of 1933 because the technique of cultivation used in China was simple and the implements primitive; almost no chemical fertilizers were used. As soon as hostilities with Japan ended and internal warfare stopped, cultivation could have been immediately resumed, and normal production could have recovered within one year, certainly within two or three years. Before the collectivization drive in 1955–56, party workers interfered in agriculture less than in later years. It is likely that peasants worked with greater enthusiasm than they did later. There is every reason to believe that by 1952 at the latest, output was in the neighborhood of the prewar level.

Second, it might be thought that increased use of fertilizers, insecticides, and mechanized implements, and the completion of many irrigation and flood control projects, which were claimed by the Communists from 1952–57, have not been sufficiently reflected in our estimates. However, as shown in Figure 1, with potatoes included at their grain-equivalent weight, total production increased from 3,510 million piculs in 1952 to 3,700 million in 1957, an increase of 5 per cent, and with potatoes included at their natural weight, from 4,620 to 5,000 million piculs, an increase of 8 per cent. If it is borne in mind that formerly uncultivated and inferior land had to be brought under cultivation and that the increased use of fertilizers and mechanical implements was extremely small relative to the total cultivated land area, one realizes how difficult this increase must have been to achieve. It probably was attained only because the peasants had to work harder each year to avoid hunger.

Third, it might be argued that the introduction of rationing in 1953 and the tightening of controls in 1955 were not the result of an inadequate food supply. The controls, the argument goes, were necessary to prevent an increase in the consumption of food crops from an already adequate level in response to higher income. This argument is not valid because, with potatoes included at their grain-equivalent weight, the ration allowed was about 20 per cent below the prewar level. Only if the per capita ration allowed were higher than, or nearer to, the prewar consumption level could one say that rationing was imposed to prevent increasing consumption of basic foods in response to higher real income. The fact seems to be that there has been barely enough food to maintain the people, and close supervision of its distribution was necessary. Moreover, the demand for basic food crops is quite income inelastic. It is reasonable to believe that if and when the prewar level of per capita consumption of food crops is restored, increase in real income would lead only to greater demands for meat, fats, eggs, vegetables, and fruits, and not to noticeably greater demands for food crops. In fact, if the prewar consumption is restored, the demand for food crops might actually *decrease* with an increase in real income. The share of food crops in the Chinese diet was, and must still be, exceedingly high by any standard.[31]

Fourth, it might be felt that our estimate is unsatisfactory in that it does not reflect the varying degrees of severity of the natural calamities that occurred in the years covered. This criticism is valid. Although it is certainly not an acceptable reply to the criticism, the Communist data also do not quite reflect these effects. The Communist data on crop production are given below, together with their description of harvest conditions in the years covered.

	1952	1953	1954	1955	1956	1957
Crop production (million piculs)	3,088	3,138	3,209	3,496	3,650	3,700
Harvest conditions	Good	Average	Bad	Good	Bad	Average

These figures indicate that "bad" years 1954 and 1956 were substantially better than "average" year 1953; and "bad" year 1956 was even better than "good" year 1955.

The Communist data are used without adjustment for the rest of the agricultural sector, except for hog production. Communist figures on the number of hogs throughout the years 1953–56 do not appear to be unreasonable. Hogs increased by 6.3 per cent in 1953 and 14 per cent in 1956, and decreased 4.2 per cent during 1954 and 9.3 per cent during 1955.[32] However, the number of hogs is

[31] According to Buck, 91 per cent. See also Table 3.

[32] See Appendix C, Table C-2. The 14 per cent increase during 1956 might not be unreasonably large in view of the 9.3 per cent reduction in 1955.

reported to have increased suddenly by as much as 47 per cent during 1957. It is true that in February 1957, realizing that the peasants lacked incentive to raise hogs, the Communists issued an order increasing official purchase prices of hogs. Nevertheless, it is unlikely that the hog production could have increased in the same year by such a large amount. Not only is there no evidence of any increase in food crops used as animal feeds, but there is in fact some reason to believe that the amount of food crops so used declined from 1956 to 1957. The total output of food crops was reported to be about the same in 1957 as in 1956, but the proportion used for human consumption was higher in 1957. (See Table 32.) The feed consumed by hogs always accounts for the major portion of all animal feeds. Moreover, if the number of hogs had increased by about 50 per cent during 1957, one would expect to see impressive increases in the consumption of pork toward the end of 1957 and during the following years, but there have been no announcements of such increases. Furthermore, following the announced increase in the supply of hogs in 1957, there were reports of reduced exports of pork and reduction in the stocks of pork held by government trading enterprises.[33] Since the reported increase in hog production was presumably the result of the increase in government purchase prices of hogs, it would be unreasonable to assume that the peasants were holding large stocks without selling them. They would not have had the feed to do so even if they had wanted to. One is forced to conclude that like the spectacular increases reported after the Big Leap Forward in 1958, the 50 per cent increase reported in the hog population during the single year 1957 was mainly a local "statistical response" to the pressure from Peiping.

Since there is no evidence of increases in exports and consumption of pork in the years following 1957, it seems reasonable to assume a percentage increase in the number of hogs equal to the rate of increase of human population during 1957. An estimate of the hog population at the end of 1957 can then be easily calculated. The decrease in consumption of animal feeds would seem to bear out that this is not an underestimate. Moreover, the rate of increase of hog population assumed for 1957—2.6 per cent—is higher than the average annual rate of increase—1.7 per cent—during 1953–56.

[33] SSB, "A General Survey of Supply of Goods in the Domestic Market in 1957," *TCYC*, No. 4, April 1958, p. 24.

FACTORIES

Two kinds of Communist statistics are available for 1952–57 which, together with our prewar data and certain other information on cost deductions, have enabled us to estimate the value added by factories during the postwar years. First, for 12 kinds of producers' goods (pig iron, steel, rolled steel, machinery, cement, sheet glass, construction materials, coke, chemicals, paper, gunny sacks, and auto tires), and 14 kinds of consumers' goods (cotton yarn, cotton cloth, silk, silk piece goods, woolen textiles, "grass cloth," clothing and knitted goods, sugar, milled rice, wheat flour, edible vegetable oils, cigarettes, matches, and rubber footwear), the gross value of output is either directly given by the Communists or can be estimated from their quantity and price data. Certain data on cost deductions, mostly for factories in Manchuria (in 1939) and North China (in 1943), can then be used to estimate the value added by factories producing these 26 kinds of goods, which will be called the "identified" portion of the output.

Second, the global value of all factory-made producers' goods can be derived from the Communist data on the "gross value of industrial production." This global value is, of course, higher than the sum of the values of the identified producers' goods, which account for about 73 per cent of the global total in 1952. Similarly, a global value of all consumers' goods can be derived from Communist data. It is also higher in value than the identified consumers' goods, which account for about 74 per cent of the global total in 1952.

Our problem now is to estimate the value added by the unidentified portion of the producers' and consumers' goods produced by factories. This is a difficult problem; fortunately, our 1933 estimate suggests a solution. In our 1933 estimate of producers' goods we have a global figure for all the producers' goods produced by factories in that year, as well as specific information for the 12 kinds of producers' goods identified in the Communist data for the postwar years. In addition, we know the nature and cost deductions of the various producers' goods other than those 12 kinds. It is reasonable to assume that the unidentified goods in the postwar Communist data are not greatly different from those in the corresponding group in 1933. Although there had been considerable industrial development during the postwar years, this assumption is reasonable because the 12 identified kinds of producers' goods would include most of the newly developed products, and they accounted for as much as 73 per cent of the total value of production of producers' goods in 1952. If we apply the prewar percentages of cost deductions of this group of goods to the postwar unidentified portion, the value added is obtained for the latter. The same procedure is followed to estimate the value added by the unidentified consumers' goods for the postwar years. It should be pointed out that the percentage cost deductions we have worked out for the producers' and consumers' goods are very close to some of the Communist figures.[34]

The Communist data on the gross value of industrial production and on the value of output of certain important kinds of producers' and consumers' goods have been used to estimate the value added by the factories from 1952–57. A large number of the factories, especially in the producers' goods industry, consisted of state enterprises. The Communists paid the greatest attention to this sector, and it was the central point of their planning system. Therefore, their statistics on factories should be better than their other economic data. Nevertheless, it is a mistake to believe that these data are reliable within a narrow margin of error. Communist annual figures on the gross value of industrial production are misleading for a number of technical reasons, and the Communists themselves have revealed a lack of confidence in their data on factories.

Among the technical factors are the degree of double counting in the valuation of industrial production because of changes in industrial organization, and the "new product effect." In computing the gross value of industrial production, the Communists followed the practice of subtracting from the total global figure the value of intra-enterprise use of raw materials and intermediate products (used for further production in the same enterprise that produced them), but counting purchases for interenterprise production twice. Decentralization of a big enterprise into a number of smaller ones would exaggerate the increase in the value of industrial production reported after the decentralization had taken place. A merger of small units into larger ones would have the opposite effect. It cannot be ascertained which of these two influences was stronger during 1952–57, but the net effect was perhaps not too great. It has been reported that even the quota or the production target that an enterprise had to meet during a period of time was determined in the same way as its contribution to industrial production (that is,

[34] See the discussion on comparison of our estimates and the Communist estimates in Appendix F.

the value of production was net of intra-enterprise production but gross of interenterprise purchases).[35] As a result, there would have been a tendency *not* to economize on interenterprise purchases, and the value of production would be inflated all around.

The second technical factor, the "new product effect," is the result of valuing newly produced manufactured goods at high initial costs. This is one aspect of the "Gerschenkron effect," that is, relative outputs and relative prices are negatively correlated through time. In compiling their data on the value of industrial production, the Communists originally used 1952 prices as weights for the different products in the total value. As new products were developed, they entered into the value of industrial production at their initial cost of production. For products developed later than 1952, a price deflator was used to convert their prices to the 1952 level. This process of deflation, however, would not affect the excess that resulted from high initial development costs and small scale of production. As the volume of production increased, the unit cost usually declined. However, the price weights remained at the original, higher level. During the process of industrial development, this new product effect could be a source of serious upward bias in the reported value of industrial production because it would be present not only in complicated goods that required high costs of development, but also in common consumers' goods that first came into production in very limited quantities. The Communists were aware of this source of bias. They announced that in the future the 1957 price weights would be used in computing economic data.[36] The 1957 value of industrial production is about 10 per cent lower in 1957 prices than in 1952 prices. This information, together with some other data, has enabled us to express our product and expenditure estimates for all the years in terms of 1957 prices. Although the 1957 price weights have somewhat corrected the exaggeration of the importance of the contribution of the industrial sector to the total product as computed in the 1952 price weights, they have not corrected the new product effect on the rate of growth of industrial production itself from 1952 to 1957.

In addition to these factors, data on industrial output may also be unreliable for other reasons. It has been admitted that errors

[35] Fang Fa, "Tabulation Forms for Industrial Production Planning," *CHCC*, No. 1, January 1957, p. 28.

[36] Tien Chi, "Several Problems in the Revision of Constant 1952 Industrial Prices," *TCKT*, No. 1, January 1957, p. 16.

occurred in industrial statistics because of insufficient training and lack of experience of statistical and accounting personnel and, in some instances, deliberately false reporting.[37] It has also been said that many enterprises have exaggerated their figures in order to meet, or to exceed, targets or quotas.[38] Moreover, substandard output was included in the total value reported, and no adjustment was made in the final figures after the low-quality products were rejected.[39] All these factors contributed to the unreliability of the data, mostly resulting in upward bias in the figures on individual items. The very nature of these errors would cause the extent of the bias to be unknown even to the Communists themselves. It is not even possible to say that the reliability of the data necessarily improved from 1952 to 1957, quite apart from such considerations as the new product effect, which has presumably been increasing in intensity throughout the period.

It has often been thought that such errors could be detected by checking the internal consistency of these data on simple input-output relationships, but this kind of investigation usually failed to reveal any inconsistency.[40] The data on which such checks can be

[37] Chia Chi-yun, "Statistical Work in 1954 and Suggestions for 1955," *HHYP*, No. 4, April 1955, pp. 149–154.

[38] *People's Daily*, September 12, 1953.

[39] *TCKT*, No. 11, June 1958, p. 17.

[40] We performed a large number of such checks: (1) Output, production capacity, and utilization of the iron and steel industry. The productive capacities of the pig iron and steel industry in 1952 were 2.10 million and 2.17 million tons. (See Yang Chien-pai, "A Comparative Analysis of China's and Soviet Russia's First Five Year Plan," *HHYP*, No. 9, September 1955, p. 194.) The rates of utilization of capacity were given at 84.4 for pig iron and 58.6 for steel (SSB, *Socialist Industrialization*, p. 58). Whether the rates of utilization were calculated on the basis of rated capacity or maximum operating capacity of the equipment, which might not be the same, is not known, but any differences would not be serious enough to affect our rough comparison. From this information it is possible to derive the output of pig iron at 1.77 million tons and steel at 1.27 million tons. These figures compare fairly well to the official data of 1.90 million tons and 1.35 million tons. (2) The input-output relationships in the cigarette industry. The State Statistical Bureau estimated that the average quantity of cured tobacco used in the production of one case of 50,000 cigarettes in 1952 was 60.7 kg. (SSB, *Technological Level*, p. 31). Output of cigarettes in 1952 was 2.65 million cases (Appendix F, Table F-8) which would require 161,000 tons of cured tobacco. If the total output of cured tobacco was 222,000 tons in 1952 (*1955 Statistical Abstract*, p. 43), the above figures seem quite plausible, since annual exports of cured tobacco average 40 to 50 thousand tons (*People's Daily*, March 24, 1958, p. 2). (3) Employment in the machinery industry. Based on 1952 yuan, the net value of fixed assets in the machinery industry in 1952 was given at 1.01 billion yuan, or 7.1 per cent of that for industry as a whole, which was 14.32 billion yuan (SSB, "A General Survey of National Industrial Capital," *TCKT*, No. 1, January 1957, p. 32). Fixed assets per worker in the machinery industry were given in another source at 4,570 yuan (SSB, *Technological Level*, p. 30). From these

made are often concerned with small segments of the industry, and an infinite number of checks would have to be made before one could reach any conclusion as to the nature and the extent of the biases in such an important aggregate statistical series as the gross value of industrial production. Such sources of inaccuracy as the inclusion in the value of output of substandard and rejected products cannot be detected by this method.

In order to test the validity, or rather the plausibility, of the industrial statistics, one has to go beyond the input-output relationships for small segments of industries and examine the relationships among categories of data. One way to test the plausibility of the data on industrial production is to examine the size of the unidentified portion in relation to the total gross value of industrial production. The relevant data are presented in Figure 3. In the postwar years unidentified producers' goods remained fairly constant at 27 to 32 per cent of the total, compared with 56 per cent in 1933. It is probable that the trend in the Communist statistics to increase the value of production of producers' goods contains an element of the new product effect and other upward biases discussed above, but the fact that the postwar unidentified share is smaller than the prewar gives no clue as to whether this share is padded. However, as shown in Figure 3, unidentified consumers' goods accounted for 26 per cent of the total gross value of consumers' goods produced in 1952 compared with 20 per cent in 1933; this figure increased steadily to 42 per cent in 1957. If the unidentified portion accounted for more and more of the total, it was increasing at a faster rate than the identified portion. In fact, from 1952 to 1957, the unidentified portion is reported to have increased by 200 per cent, whereas the identified portion increased by only 45 per cent.[41]

As was shown at the beginning of this section, the identified portion includes all the major items of manufactured daily necessi-

---

figures, the number of workers in this industry can be estimated at 0.21 million. Total employment in this industry in 1952 is reported to be 0.32 million, including office employees and nonproductive workers (Ching Lin, *Ti-yi-ke wu-nien-chi-hua chung ti chi-che chi-tso-yeh* [The Machinery Manufacturing Industry in the First Five Year Plan Period], Peiping, Chung-huo chuan-kuo k'o-hsueh pu-chi hse-hui, 1955, p. 18). The proportion of productive workers in the total is not known. For our purposes, it can be assumed to be roughly 69 per cent, the same as that for the iron and steel industry (Yin Hsin, "Emphasizing the Economy of Labor Is an Effective Means of Increasing Accumulation of the Enterprise," *Lao-tung* [Labor], Peiping, No. 6, March 1955, p. 9). On this assumption, the number of productive workers should be 0.22 million, which checks well with the above estimates.

[41] See Table 41

ties consumed by the Chinese people. With rationing of food and clothing strictly enforced, the reported rate of increase of unidentified consumers' goods would require a great deal of supporting evidence. No such evidence can be found. From 1952 to 1956 the Communists published some aggregate data on daily consumption

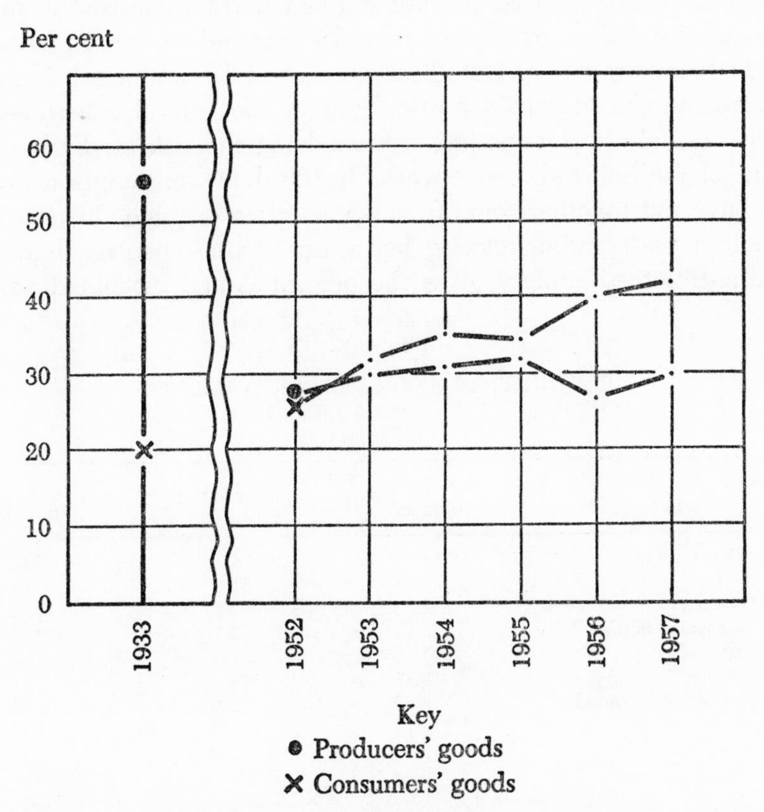

Figure 3. Percentage of unidentified items in total value of output, producers' goods and consumers' goods

items including china and earthenware; consumers' metal products; leather and fur products; glass products; furniture; soaps and cosmetic products; cultural, educational, and "technical" products; and an unnamed "others" category which varied in size from one-fifth to one-third of the total. The gross value of output of this aggregate group of consumers' goods increased 44 per cent from 3.7 billion yuan in 1952 to 5.3 billion yuan in 1956.[42] This is about equal

[42] Chao Yi-wen, *Hsin-chung-kuo ti kung-yeh* (New China's Industry), Peiping, T'ung-chi chu-pan-she, 1957, p. 59.

to the rate of increase of the identified portion of the total value of consumers' goods but is a great deal less than the 200 per cent increase reported for the unidentified portion from 1952 to 1956. This information fails to support the claim made for the rate of increase of the global total of the output of consumers' goods.

It can be argued that the unidentified portion consists of goods that are not daily consumption requirements and were not produced at all before the war. But these goods can be nothing but those covered in the identified portion and in the several categories of daily consumption items just discussed. At the risk of duplicating some of the items already covered in the daily consumption items, we have put together some fragmentary data on such "luxuries" as fountain pens, radios, clocks, hot water bottles, pencils, bicycles, and antibiotics. Table 7 gives the quantities and estimated values

Table 7

PRODUCTION AND ESTIMATED VALUES OF SELECTED CONSUMERS' GOODS, 1957
(1952 yuan)

Item	Quantity (million)	Estimated unit price	Total value (million)
1. Fountain pens	51	2	102
2. Radios	0.38	50	19
3. Clocks	1.78	3	5
4. Hot water bottles	22	5	110
5. Pencils	500	0.1	50
6. Bicycles	0.81	100	81
7. Antibiotics (grams)	18.30	1.0	18
8. Books	1,278	0.5	639
9. Magazines	315	0.2	63
			1,087

SOURCES: Items 1, 4, and 5: *TKP*, Peiping, April 12, 1958, p. 1.
Items 2 and 3: *TKP*, Peiping, March 20, 1958, p. 1.
Items 6, 7, 8, and 9: *Great Ten Years*, pp. 86, 88, 183.

of production of these items in 1957. The total value of these goods (in 1952 yuan) cannot exceed about 1.1 billion, but there was a total value of 9.6 billion yuan worth of unidentified consumers' goods (again in 1952 yuan).[43] However fast the rate of increase of the "luxury" items may have been, their increased production could

[43] See Table 41.

not possibly explain a 200 per cent increase from 1952 to 1957 of the unidentified portion of the gross value of consumers' goods to a total of 9.6 billion (1952) yuan.

There is only one possible (but very weak) defense for the Communist data: the increases in the unidentified portion of consumers' goods production were for exports. But even exports of consumers' goods would have been included either in the identified portions, in the daily consumption items, or in the "luxury" items listed in Table 7.

The 200 per cent increase in the unidentified portion of consumers' goods from 1952 to 1957 is therefore inexplicable. Actually, even an increase of 45 per cent in the identified portion of consumers' goods from 1952 to 1957 is probably too high in view of the fact that resources are increasingly channeled to investment and government consumption. The nature of the identified consumers' goods is largely known, and we have no reasonable basis on which to make an adjustment in the data; but there can be no doubt that the rapid rate of increase reported for the unidentified portion is exaggerated. To use the data on the value of production of consumers' goods without adjustment would result in an overestimate of the rate of growth of the national product. We have recomputed the total annual value of consumers' goods production from 1953 to 1957 by assuming that the unidentified portion increased at a rate equal to that of the identified portion. If that assumption is wrong, it overstates the increase in unidentified goods, and our estimate errs in the upward direction.

OTHER "HARD" SECTORS

As with the 1933 estimate, specific data are available for estimating the value added by mining, utilities, and modern transportation and communications. These are probably more reliable than most of the other Communist economic statistics. On the other hand, output, input, and price data are available for a much smaller portion of handicrafts in 1952–57 than in 1933. The rest of the income originating in handicrafts was estimated as explained later in this chapter.

Data on the value added by the construction and trading sectors are used without adjustment. Statistics on construction, a most important item in the Plan, should be as reliable as any of the other data. Although the total value of wholesale and retail trade, as reported by the Communists, is among the least reliable of their statistics, the value added, consisting mainly of taxes and profits of state enterprises, should be more accurately known to them.

Income originating in government administration and finance in 1952 is estimated from the employment data in those sectors. The estimate of government net product for the other years is obtained by extrapolating from the 1952 figure on the basis of an index of certain expenditures in the government budget. Value added by the finance sector in the other years is estimated by extrapolating from the 1952 figure on an index that represents the sum of values added in a few important sectors.

The "Soft" Components of the Product Estimate, 1952–57

The small portion of the handicraft net product that can be identified in terms of specific commodities has already been estimated. It must fall far short of the total handicraft output. The 1952–57 output is estimated by extrapolating from the 1933 figure on the basis of an index that represents the sum of the gross value of agricultural and mining output for 1933 and 1952–57. It is assumed that total handicraft output varied in proportion to the output of the two sectors that supplied its raw materials.[44] This procedure can be criticized on the ground that there must have been some substitution of factory output for handicraft output between 1933 and the postwar years. Hence, an estimate of handicraft output obtained on the assumption of a constant ratio of handicraft output to agricultural and mining production would be an overestimate. This criticism is probably valid. However, the margin of overestimation cannot be very great, because the estimated output in 1952 is virtually the same as in 1933 and the increases during 1952–57 are quite modest.

Although the total value added by trade is considered to be a "hard" component, its classification into trading stores and restaurants on the one hand, and peddlers on the other, is based on rather fragmentary employment data. Value added by old-fashioned transportation is also estimated on some fragmentary employment data, first for 1957 and then by extrapolating from 1957 to the other years on the basis of the volume of goods transported, adjusted for the expansion of modern means of transportation. The estimates of

[44] For the estimate, see line 3 of Table 8. The estimated "others" portion, given in line 3.b., is the difference between the total and the identified portion.

personal services, rent, and work brigades are the "softest" components of our product estimate.

The Expenditure Estimate, 1952–57

Our estimate of the total domestic expenditure is derived simply by adding the import balance of international trade to the estimate that we obtained for domestic product. A direct estimate of domestic expenditures on the basis of Communist data has not been attempted. Communist data on family budgets are among the least reliable data that they have published. For instance, the Communists have claimed per capita consumption of rural population in 1956 to have been 37 per cent and that of urban population 54 per cent above the 1936 levels.[45] If these reports were reliable, overall per capita consumption would have increased by about 40 per cent. Such an increase, together with a 20 per cent increase in population and a sixfold increase in investment, would imply that the national income doubled from 1936 to 1956. Even the Communists themselves have not made this claim.

Total domestic expenditure can be broken down into a few major categories. The food and clothing components of personal consumption expenditures are derived from the product estimate by the commodity flow method in the same way that the 1933 estimates were obtained. The fuel and lighting component is assumed to be the same on a per capita basis as in 1933. If our estimate of this item errs, it is probably in the upward direction. The rent component has already been estimated in our product account.

Government consumption can be estimated in a relatively easy way from Communist data on government purchases of goods and services and from our estimate of wage and salary payments to government employees and servicemen. No attempt is made to estimate investment expenditure by the commodity flow method. Instead, Communist figures on investment are tentatively used in our estimate with some minor adjustment. A rough estimate of the investment made by work brigades and the service rendered by passenger traffic and finance in connection with investment are added to the Communist figures; and ancillary expenses, which are included by the Communists in investment expenditure, are ex-

[45] *People's Daily*, February 24, 1957, p. 2; and SSB, "A Preliminary Study of the Production and Distribution of China's National Income," *TCYC*, No. 1, January 1958, p. 13

Table 8

DOMESTIC PRODUCT BY INDUSTRIAL ORIGIN, 1933 AND 1952–57, IN CONSTANT 1933 AND 1952 PRICES

	1933	1952	1953	1954	1955	1956	1957	1933	1952	1953	1954	1955	1956	1957	1958	1959
	(billions of 1933 yuan)							(billions of 1952 yuan)							Conjectural (billions of 1952 yuan)	
Net value added in:																
1. Agriculture	18.76	18.39	18.73	19.16	19.39	19.77	19.85	33.86	34.19	34.82	35.50	35.84	36.97	37.16	40	42
2. Factories	0.64	1.09	1.39	1.60	1.70	2.35	2.57	3.33	6.45	8.28	9.58	10.36	14.51	15.99	19	25
a. Producers' goods	0.16	0.46	0.65	0.77	0.92	1.39	1.63	0.84	3.15	4.37	5.25	6.25	9.44	11.07	14	19
b. Consumers' goods	0.47	0.63	0.75	0.82	0.78	0.97	0.94	2.48	3.30	3.92	4.33	4.12	5.07	4.92	5	6
3. Handicrafts	2.04	2.14	2.19	2.26	2.33	2.39	2.44	4.41	4.72	4.81	4.98	5.12	5.25	5.38	6	6
a. Identified portion	1.24	0.66	0.75	0.72	0.74	0.84	0.86	2.67	1.45	1.65	1.58	1.62	1.86	1.90	—	—
b. Others	0.80	1.48	1.44	1.54	1.59	1.55	1.58	1.74	3.26	3.16	3.40	3.50	3.39	3.48	—	—
4. Mining	0.21	0.63	0.62	0.78	0.99	1.02	1.31	0.50	1.47	1.46	1.82	2.32	2.38	3.07	4	5
5. Utilities	0.13	0.31	0.38	0.44	0.48	0.60	0.72	0.14	0.31	0.37	0.43	0.48	0.59	0.71	1	1
6. Construction	0.34	0.60	0.75	0.88	0.96	1.64	1.52	1.03	1.83	2.28	2.68	2.93	4.97	4.62	6	8
7. Modern transportation and communications	0.43	0.83	1.00	1.14	1.22	1.38	1.50	1.09	2.10	2.55	2.90	3.10	3.52	3.82	4	5
8. Old-fashioned transportation	1.20	1.20	1.11	1.07	1.06	1.13	1.10	2.61	2.65	2.45	2.35	2.34	2.48	2.43	3	3
9. Trade	2.71	2.88	2.97	2.99	3.00	3.16	3.23	8.19	9.66	9.97	10.27	10.49	11.15	11.45	12	14
a. Trading stores and restaurants	1.75	1.97	2.02	2.20	2.30	2.50	2.57	6.12	7.66	7.87	8.54	8.95	9.71	10.01	—	—
b. Peddlers	0.96	0.91	0.95	0.79	0.70	0.66	0.66	2.07	2.00	2.10	1.73	1.54	1.44	1.44	—	—
10. Government administration	0.82	1.84	2.11	2.26	2.33	2.76	2.92	1.43	3.27	3.70	3.95	4.07	4.76	5.03	5	6
11. Finance	0.21	0.80	0.85	0.90	0.93	1.04	1.08	0.35	1.31	1.39	1.47	1.52	1.70	1.77	2	2
12. Personal services	0.34	0.34	0.34	0.34	0.33	0.31	0.31	0.55	0.55	0.55	0.54	0.54	0.51	0.51	1	1
13. Residential rents	1.03	1.17	1.19	1.22	1.25	1.28	1.31	2.00	2.28	2.32	2.37	2.44	2.48	2.55	3	3
14. Work brigades		0.28	0.17	0.20	0.34	0.37	0.39		0.62	0.38	0.44	0.75	0.81	0.85	3	3
Net domestic product	28.86	32.50	33.80	35.24	36.31	39.20	40.25	59.49	71.41	75.33	79.28	82.30	92.08	95.34	108	125
Depreciation	1.02	1.33	1.47	1.59	1.65	1.94	2.04	2.19	3.26	3.66	4.03	4.27	5.20	5.48	6	8
Gross domestic product	29.88	33.83	35.25	36.83	37.96	41.14	42.29	61.68	74.67	78.99	83.31	86.57	97.28	100.82	114	133

NOTE: — Not available.

SOURCES: *Constant 1933 Prices:* Chapter IV, Tables 36, 37, 44, 47, 48, 49, and the discussions following these tables.
Constant 1952 Prices: Tables 36, 37, 44, 48–50, and for the conjectural estimate for 1958–59, Appendix K.

cluded from our estimate. The Communist figures on investment will be analyzed in Chapter III. The estimate of domestic expenditure is now complete except for a miscellaneous category of personal consumption to be derived as a residual when all other categories of personal consumption and investment are deducted from the total domestic expenditure.

The Communist definition of basic construction, from which the present estimate of investment is derived, can be given a different interpretation from that used in the text. In addition, other statistical data are available for estimating working capital investment. These alternatives are discussed in Appendix L.

SUMMARY OF ESTIMATES

The results of our estimates are presented in Tables 8 through 11. Although many assumptions have been introduced and numerous adjustments have been made in the available data, the concepts underlying the different categories and items given in these tables are the same as those used in accepted Western practice. Reconciliations with estimates computed without adjustment from Communist data and with the Communist definitions and concept of national income are presented in Chapters IV and V.

The estimate for domestic product by industrial origin is given in Table 8 in constant 1933 and 1952 prices, and in Table 9 in 1957

Table 9

DOMESTIC PRODUCT BY INDUSTRIAL ORIGIN, 1933 AND 1952–57, IN CONSTANT 1957 PRICES
(billions of 1957 yuan)

	1933	1952	1953	1954	1955	1956	1957
1. Agriculture	35.99	36.35	37.01	37.74	38.10	39.30	39.50
2. Manufacturing, mining, and utilities	7.53	11.63	13.40	15.10	16.43	20.41	22.58
3. Others	20.97	27.94	28.99	30.56	31.98	36.97	38.03
4. Net domestic product	64.49	75.91	79.40	83.40	86.50	96.68	100.11
5. Depreciation	1.98	2.95	3.31	3.64	3.86	4.70	4.95
6. Gross domestic product	66.47	78.86	82.71	87.04	90.36	101.38	105.06

Source: Appendix I.

prices. The estimate in Table 9 is more aggregated because of the much more limited price information available for 1957. The con-

Table 10

DOMESTIC EXPENDITURE BY END USE, 1933 AND 1952–57, IN CONSTANT 1933, 1952, AND 1957 PRICES

	1933	1952	1953	1954	1955	1956	1957	1933	1952	1953	1954	1955	1956	1957	1933	1952	1953	1954	1955	1956	1957
	(billions of 1933 yuan)							(billions of 1952 yuan)							(billions of 1957 yuan)[a]						
1. Personal consumption	28.02	27.56	27.15	28.41	29.26	30.93	31.53	56.53	54.60	51.84	54.96	56.99	62.60	64.49	61.73	59.62	56.61	60.02	62.23	68.36	70.42
a. Food	18.13	17.36	17.72	19.10	18.97	19.48	20.19	33.19	33.08	33.59	36.44	36.35	36.64	38.39							
b. Clothing	2.17	2.38	2.69	2.55	2.40	3.27	3.09	7.56	7.89	8.79	8.43	7.82	10.40	9.62							
c. Fuel and light	2.16	2.46	2.51	2.57	2.63	2.68	2.75	4.49	5.11	5.22	5.35	5.46	5.58	5.72							
d. Housing	1.37	1.56	1.59	1.62	1.67	1.70	1.75	2.66	3.04	3.10	3.16	3.25	3.31	3.40							
e. Miscellaneous	4.19	3.80	2.64	2.57	3.59	3.80	3.75	8.63	5.48	1.14	1.58	4.11	6.67	7.36							
2. Communal services	0.14	0.80	0.97	1.00	0.97	1.36	1.40	0.32	1.94	2.45	2.46	2.32	3.26	3.29	0.34	2.11	2.67	2.68	2.53	3.55	3.58
3. Government consumption	1.06	2.35	2.87	2.59	2.79	2.66	2.92	2.36	5.34	6.64	5.49	6.11	5.23	5.92	2.57	5.81	7.23	5.97	6.65	5.69	6.45
4. Net domestic investment	0.51	2.25	3.09	3.35	3.61	4.08	4.12	2.55	11.26	15.45	16.74	18.04	20.39	20.62	2.30	10.18	13.97	15.13	16.31	18.43	18.64
5. Net domestic expenditure	29.73	32.96	34.08	35.35	36.63	39.03	39.97	61.76	73.14	76.38	79.65	83.46	91.48	94.32	66.94	77.72	80.48	83.80	87.72	96.03	99.09
6. Depreciation	1.02	1.33	1.47	1.59	1.65	1.94	2.04	2.19	3.26	3.66	4.03	4.27	5.20	5.48	1.98	2.95	3.31	3.64	3.86	4.70	4.95
7. Gross domestic expenditure	30.75	34.29	35.55	36.94	38.28	40.97	42.01	63.95	76.40	80.04	83.68	87.73	96.68	99.80	68.92	80.67	83.79	87.44	91.58	100.73	104.04

NOTE: [a] No breakdown can be made in personal consumption in 1957 prices because the deflators for individual items are unavailable.
SOURCES: Chapter V, Tables 71, 72, 78, 79, 88, and the discussion in the text following Tables 74 and 92; and Appendix I.

jectural estimate of domestic product by industrial origin for 1958–59, presented in Table 8, will be explained in Chapter III and Appendix K.

The relative magnitudes of "hard" and "soft" components for the different years are compared below. Although the percentage of "hard" components increases slightly from 1952 to 1957, it is not significantly different from that in 1933. It should be noted that the dividing line between "hard" and "soft" components is even less clear cut in postwar data than in prewar. For example, extensive adjustments had to be made in postwar data on such "hard" components as agricultural and industrial production to achieve reasonable reliability.[46]

Table 11

EMPLOYMENT BY INDUSTRIAL SECTORS, 1933 AND 1952–57
(millions of workers)

	1933	1952	1953	1954	1955	1956	1957
Agriculture	204.91	199.89	203.59	208.26	210.76	214.89	215.76
Factories, mining, and utilities	1.94	3.54	4.12	4.20	4.44	4.81	5.50
Handicrafts	15.74	13.50	14.03	15.19	14.56	13.78	14.51
Construction	1.55	1.29	1.82	1.90	1.95	2.44	2.40
Modern transportation and communications	0.44	0.73	0.79	0.96	1.13	1.32	1.43
Old-fashioned transportation	10.86	10.90	10.08	9.67	9.63	10.20	10.00
Trade	14.88	13.59	13.78	11.85	10.95	10.90	11.40
a. Trading stores and restaurants	7.49	6.59	6.44	5.79	5.56	5.86	6.36
b. Peddlers	7.39	7.00	7.34	6.06	5.39	5.04	5.04
Government	5.12	7.59	8.24	8.54	8.62	9.02	9.31
Finance	0.14	0.54	0.59	0.62	0.66	0.70	0.75
Personal services	3.63	3.63	3.60	3.58	3.55	3.35	3.33
Work brigades		4.08	2.52	2.88	4.92	5.31	5.56
Total nonagricultural	54.30	59.39	59.57	59.39	60.41	61.83	64.19
Total	259.21	259.28	263.16	267.65	271.17	276.72	279.95

SOURCES: Chapter IV, the discussion under employment by industrial sectors; Tables 57 through 63.

[46] One should not be misled by the generally high proportions of the hard components in all the years. The description "hard" is given to a large sector as a whole (for instance, agriculture), whereas relatively good data are available only for certain parts (for instance, food crops) of that sector.

	1933	1952	1953	1954	1955	1956	1957
Percentage of "hard" components in total net domestic product[47]	85	84	85	86	87	88	88

Domestic expenditure by end use is presented in Table 10. Again, this estimate is given in 1933, 1952, and 1957 prices. Our estimate of employment in the different sectors of the economy, a subsidiary result of our product estimate, is presented in Table 11.

[47] Computed from data given in Table 2.

CHAPTER III

PATTERN OF ECONOMIC DEVELOPMENT: PRELIMINARY ANALYSIS OF FINDINGS

PRODUCT, expenditure, and employment estimates are analyzed in this chapter to compare prewar and postwar development, to examine the magnitude and cost of the Communist investment program, to measure the rate and pattern of growth, and to study the problems of unemployment and inflation. The analyses cannot be firmer than the estimates on which they are based, and the estimates themselves are admittedly rough approximations. A great many of our findings are tentative because the six years analyzed cover only a short period; nevertheless, an image of the economy does emerge.

Although the Great Leap Forward in 1958 brought about radical changes, certain basic economic policies that had been in force during 1952–57 were still part of the core of the Communist program during 1958–59. Particular emphasis was still given to producers' goods and the strict control of personal consumption, for example. In addition to the comparison of the prewar and postwar economies, therefore, we have attempted a conjectural estimate of domestic product in 1958–59.

THE PREWAR SCALE OF ECONOMIC VALUES AND THE ALLOCATION OF MANPOWER

The picture of the Chinese economy sketched in Chapter I and the estimate of national product in Chapter II both point to the predominance of agriculture, handicrafts, and old-fashioned transportation in the economy; yet it is precisely in these fields that output per worker was lowest. In Table 12, the relative magnitudes of value added per worker in these sectors are given, and the percentages of total employment in the different industrial sectors in 1933 are presented in a more aggregated manner than was the national product estimate in Chapter II. The aggregated presentation is better suited to the way in which the breakdown data on investment and capital stock are available.[1]

[1] See Table 23 and the discussion later in this chapter.

Table 12

NET VALUE ADDED PER WORKER AND DISTRIBUTION OF EMPLOYMENT IN DIFFERENT INDUSTRIAL SECTORS, 1933

	Net value added per worker (base index number = 100)	Distribution of employment (per cent)
Finance	297	0.1
Modern transportation and communications	193	0.2
Factories, mining, and utilities	100	0.7
Trading stores and restaurants	46	2.9
Construction	43	0.6
Government administration	32	2.0
Peddlers	26	2.8
Handicrafts	26	6.1
Old-fashioned transportation	22	4.2
Personal services	19	1.4
Agriculture	18	79.0

SOURCE: Computed from data in Tables 8 and 11.

The index of value added per worker in Table 12 is computed in terms of 1933 prices. Since there was no government allocation of resources in 1933, and indirect taxation and government subsidies were very small in relation to the national product, the figures on output per worker reflect the valuation of the services of different categories of workers as determined by market supply and demand under the then-existing social setting. Indirectly the figures show the relative scarcities of the outputs of different sectors of the economy.

The lack of industrialization and modernization of the economy is quite plain. Net value added by agricultural workers was less than a fifth of the average contributed by workers in the aggregate sector of factories, mining, and utilities; yet there were more than 100 times as many workers in agriculture. A worker in old-fashioned transportation contributed only one-ninth as much to the total product as his counterpart in modern transportation, but there were more than 20 times as many old-fashioned transportation workers. Whatever differences of opinion there might be about the best way to achieve the goal, there can be no doubt that more Chinese workers needed to be trained for the sectors with higher outputs per worker. Furthermore, the output per worker in the traditional sectors had to be increased.

THE COMMUNIST INVESTMENT DRIVE

Underlying the tremendous disparity in output per worker among the various industrial sections is the differing amounts of capital invested. There is no systematic information on capital per worker in the more advanced sectors in the prewar period, but the Communists have released information on fixed capital in a few important fields for 1955. These figures, divided by our data for employment, give the following results for capital per worker in 1952 yuan: modern transportation and communications, 8,100; factories, mining, and utilities, 3,800; construction, 700; trading stores and restaurants, 300; and agriculture, 110.[2]

A large amount of capital is needed in areas where net value added per worker is high, and any attempt to hasten the development of these fields requires a high rate of capital investment. To accomplish this, the Communists have made a relentless and, after 1957, a ruthless effort. The relation of their investment program to output and employment is examined later in this chapter. Investment in the economy as a whole and its relation to total domestic expenditure will be discussed first.

The Magnitude of the Communist Investment Program

Our estimate of the aggregate gross domestic investment for each year of the period 1952–57 is presented in Table 13. On the basis of Communist data, total investment can be classified as follows: fixed

[2] The first four figures are rounded from those given in Table 77. An explanation of the differences between these figures and certain Communist data is made in the text preceding the table. The figure for agriculture is a rough estimate obtained from the prewar data given in Buck, *Farm Economy*, p. 57, adjusted for price changes and augmented by data on postwar investment as follows: Fixed capital per farm, excluding land, is assumed to be equal to one-fifth of the value of buildings, two-thirds of the value of livestock, and the value of all trees and all equipment (*ibid.*). The result is 178 (1933) yuan per farm. The number of workers per farm is estimated at 3.3, that is, 205 million (from Table 11) divided by 62 million, the number of farms. The total number of farms is the sum of farms in 25 provinces, 58.6 million, given in Chang, *Crop Estimates*, p. 13; those given in *Kwangsi Yearbook*, p. 180; and those in other areas, roughly estimated at 2 million. Capital per worker therefore amounted to 54 (1933) yuan or roughly 99 (1952) yuan (54 yuan times a price index of 183; see Appendix I). It is assumed that fixed capital per agricultural worker is the same in 1952 as in the 1930s. If the total number of agricultural workers is 200 million, fixed capital in 1952 is estimated at 19.8 billion yuan. Adding 3.91 billion yuan, the amount of net fixed investments in agriculture in 1952–55 (from Table 76), to this 19.8 billion yuan, we obtain an estimate of fixed capital in 1955 of 23.7 billion yuan. The result is then divided by 211 million agricultural workers to obtain a per capita figure of 112 yuan per worker, rounded to 110 yuan. This is a very crude estimate, but any error it contains would not appreciably affect the relative magnitudes given.

Table 13

DOMESTIC INVESTMENT, 1952–57
(billions of 1952 yuan)

	1952	1953	1954	1955	1956	1957	1953–57
Gross domestic investment	14.52	19.11	20.77	22.31	25.59	26.10	113.88
Fixed investment covered in state investment plan	3.88	6.54	7.91	9.65	15.13	16.81	56.04
Net:	2.63	5.01	5.92	7.32	11.63	13.04	42.92
Four modern sectors combined[a]	1.85	3.58	4.58	5.66	8.79	9.99	32.60
Agriculture[b]	0.38	0.51	0.32	0.52	1.02	1.12	3.49
Others[c]	0.40	0.92	1.03	1.14	1.81	1.93	6.83
Depreciation	1.25	1.53	1.99	2.33	3.50	3.77	13.12
Fixed investment outside state investment plan	2.94	4.33	4.51	3.67	3.33	3.95	19.79
Net:	0.92	2.20	2.47	1.73	1.63	2.23	10.26
Four modern sectors combined	0.40	0.41	0.63	0.84	0.84	1.19	3.91
Agriculture[d]	0.12	0.13	0.06	0.10	0.06	0.24	0.59
Others	0.40	1.66	1.78	0.79	0.73	0.80	5.76
Depreciation	2.01	2.13	2.04	1.94	1.70	1.72	9.53
Changes in work in progress and in inventory	7.08	7.86	7.91	8.24	6.32	4.49	34.82
Investment by work brigades	0.62	0.38	0.44	0.75	0.81	0.85	3.23

NOTES: [a] These four sectors are factories, mining, and utilities; trading stores, restaurants, and finance; modern transportation and communications; and construction.
[b] Including investment in irrigation and forestation.
[c] Social, cultural, and miscellaneous investment, and a small item on geological survey.
[d] Investment by the state only.
SOURCES: Tables 72 and 76. For estimates of changes in work in progress and in inventory, see Chapter V, under Domestic Investment. For estimates of depreciation, see Appendixes E through H. For each sector, depreciation in the state investment plan is calculated on the basis of percentages of output in the state and nonstate enterprises.

investment covered in the state investment plan; fixed investment outside the state investment plan; changes in work in progress and in the stock of inventory; and an estimate of investment by work brigades. Fixed investment in a given year, as defined by the Communists, includes only the value of construction and equipment completed during that year.[3]

Investment during 1953–57 was presumably governed by the First Five Year Plan. As shown in Table 13, net fixed investment covered in the state investment plan amounted to about 43 billion yuan in 1952 prices. This is quite close to the 42.74 billion yuan of basic construction investment originally given in the First Plan for these

[3] See Chapter V under Fixed Investment, Investment in Working Capital, and Fixed Capital in Four Industries, 1952–57.

years.[4] The Communist concept of basic construction investment is fixed investment plus certain ancillary expenses. Although the amount given in the Plan is lower than the 49.27 billion yuan of basic construction investment actually completed, the difference is accounted for by the ancillary expenses in the definition.[5] There is also not much difference from the 41.1 billion yuan of total fixed investment reported during these five years.[6] The similarity of all these figures indicates that Table 13 might actually present what the Communists believed to be the rates of increase of net fixed investment in the state investment plan.

The increase from 1952 to 1957 is not surprising. The hard core of the Communist investment program during the First Plan were the 156 development projects to be built with the aid of the Soviet Union.[7] Fifty of these projects were started during the rehabilitation period, 1949–51.[8] The majority of them were to be completed after 1952. Another 91 projects were started in 1953 and 15 more in 1954.[9] These additional projects helped to increase both fixed investment completed and work in progress throughout the period. Net fixed investment within the state plan also increased at different rates during different years. The largest annual increments were in 1953 (90 per cent) and 1956 (59 per cent). Communist sources have often attributed the greater capacity to invest in these years to the good harvests they had in 1952 and 1955,[10] but, as was pointed out in Chapter II, the data on agricultural output do not show sufficiently large increases to support this position.

The rate of increase of net fixed investment within the state investment plan from 1956 to 1957 was the smallest of the entire First Five Year Plan. The Communists accounted for this in two ways. First, they admitted that their investment in 1956 was excessively high, leading to shortages of many industrial materials and consumers' goods and to inflationary pressure on commodity prices.[11] This is confirmed by certain Communist price indexes, as will be shown

[4] *First Five Year Plan*, p. 23.
[5] *Great Ten Years*, p. 47.
[6] *FFYP Communique*, p. 48.
[7] *First Five Year Plan*, p. 30.
[8] Li Fu-chun, "Report on the First Five Year Plan," *HHYP*, No. 8, August 1955, p. 2.
[9] *People's Daily*, October 12, 1954.
[10] Li Chien, "Arrange the Basic Construction Plan for 1957 Properly on the Basis of the Nation's Financial and Resource Capability," *CHCC*, No. 3, March 1957, p. 4.
[11] *HHPYK*, No. 3, February 1957, p. 48; *TCKT*, No. 7, April 1957, p. 31, and No. 11, June 1957, p. 26.

later in this chapter. Second, the Communists claimed that the poor harvest in 1956 resulted in a reduction of government revenue and hence in funds available for investment.[12] This explanation is questionable; although receipts of agricultural taxes did decrease slightly from 1956 to 1957, total government revenue increased, as will be shown in Table 25. It is probably true, however, that total investment in 1956 was high.

Fixed investment in agriculture covered in the state investment plan amounted to only about one-tenth of the sum invested in the four modern sectors during 1953–57. This confirms that agriculture was accorded low priority in Communist planning.

Outside the state plan, investments were mainly in plants and equipment in private factories, a part of residential housing and other construction (such as those built with union and other welfare funds), and agriculture. The Communists were not interested in these investments, and they are small for all categories for which data can be found. Investment in agriculture outside the state investment plan amounted to only 0.59 billion yuan. The amount of private fixed investment by farmers during 1953–57 is unknown. However, it does not seem likely that the amount could have reached the 6 billion yuan expected by the Communists.[13] The relatively high depreciation charges on capital outside the state investment plan reflected the prime importance of agriculture and, in the early years, of private enterprise in the economy.

Changes in work in progress and in inventory would be fairly large, because investment in plants and equipment in the process of being built are included. The increase in the stock of military equipment and supplies probably belongs in this category as well. There was a substantial reduction in changes in work in progress and in inventory from 1955 to 1957 when fixed investment increased greatly, so that total domestic investment increased by a smaller proportion than fixed investment during the same period.

Unfortunately, it is impossible to separate changes in work in progress from changes in inventory. There is also no way to estimate the extent to which changes in inventory were planned. There have been accusations of unnecessary accumulations,[14] but other

[12] Li Chien, *op. cit.*
[13] *First Five Year Plan,* p. 25, footnote 4.
[14] *HHPYK,* No. 5, March 1957, pp. 55–57.

Communist sources have stated that these increases were exaggerated.[15]

The estimates of investment by work brigades given in the table cannot be regarded as anything but the crudest approximations. They are included here primarily as a reminder of the existence of this item.

The following data derived from Table 13 summarize the distribution of net fixed investment among the different fields during the First Five Year Plan, both within and outside the state investment plan:

	Amount (billions of 1952 yuan)	Distribution (per cent)
Four modern sectors	36.5	68
Other nonagricultural sectors	12.6	24
Agriculture (investment by state only)	4.1	8

The emphasis on the nonagricultural sectors and especially on the four modern sectors is unmistakable.

Investment in Relation to Total Expenditure

As shown in Table 13, the absolute amount of gross domestic investment increased consistently during 1952–56. Gross domestic investment as a percentage of gross domestic expenditure is presented in Figure 4 for 1933 and 1952–57, computed on the three bases of valuation. Most of the investment goods passed through factories at one stage or another. The 1952 price structure gives higher weights to factory output than to other outputs, and as a result investment is a higher percentage of total expenditure in 1952 prices than it is in 1933 and 1957 price weights. The downward revision of industrial prices in 1957 lowers the percentage of total expenditure devoted to investment when computed in 1957 prices, but compared with the estimate in 1933 prices, the percentage is still high.

In 1933, 5 per cent of total expenditure was devoted to gross investment. This percentage just about doubled from 1933 to 1952.

[15] *Shih-yu kung-yeh t'ung-hsin* (Petroleum Industry Bulletin), Peiping, No. 5, March 1957, p. 4.

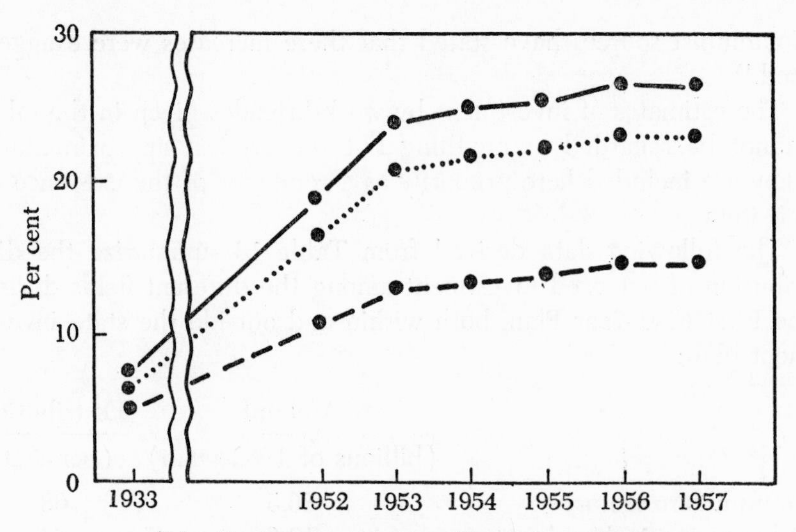

(a)—Percentage of gross domestic expenditure devoted to gross domestic investment

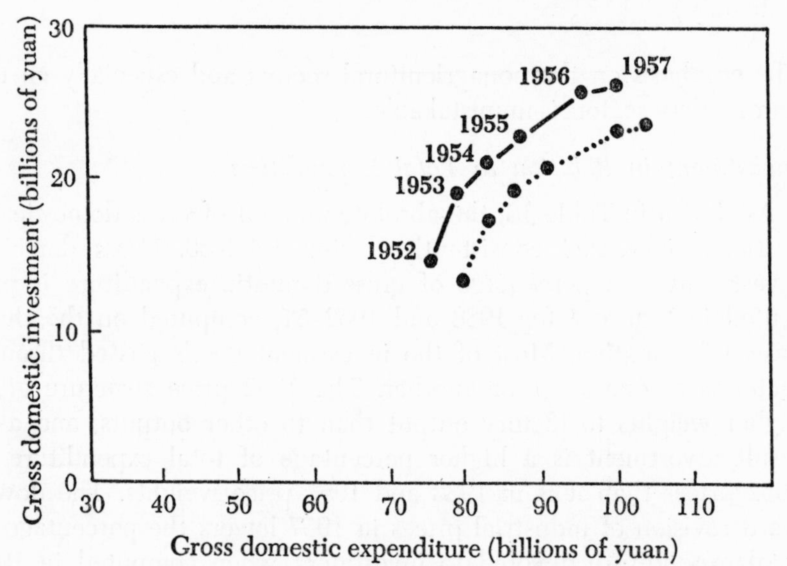

(b)—Scatter diagram of postwar gross domestic investment versus gross domestic expenditure

Key
- - - - 1933 yuan
——— 1952 yuan
.... 1957 yuan

Figure 4. Gross domestic investment and domestic expenditure

In terms of postwar prices, the increase in this percentage is even greater. Gross domestic investment in 1952 was 19 per cent of gross domestic expenditure in 1952 prices and 16 per cent in 1957 prices; each is two and a half times as high as in 1933.

As a result of the "five-anti-movement" in 1952 and the "three-anti-movement" in 1951, as well as other regulations, the Communists gained control of the modern sectors of the economy. By 1952, the only sectors not tightly organized were agriculture and the various traditional urban sectors. The amount of investment for the economy as a whole was largely a matter of government decision. The financing of investment will be discussed in detail later in this chapter.

Figure 4 indicates that the percentage of total expenditure devoted to gross investment increased steadily, but at a decreasing rate, during 1952–57. In terms of 1952 prices, this was from about 19 per cent in 1952 to 26.5 per cent in 1956. There was a slight decline to 26.2 per cent in 1957. In 1957 prices, gross investment stood at about 23 per cent in 1956 and somewhat lower in 1957. Given the nature of Mainland Chinese economic institutions before 1958, probably no more than one-fourth of total expenditure (in 1952 prices) could have been devoted to gross domestic investment. The increasing difficulty of the Communist economy in channeling resources to investment is also indicated by the declining slope of the curve in the scatter diagram given in Figure 4(b).

THE REAL COST OF THE COMMUNIST INVESTMENT PROGRAM: THE DEPRESSED STANDARD OF LIVING

The investment program resulted in a considerable industrialization of the economy. Ideally, an analysis of this program would include a comparison of alternative policies to reach the same goal, but this difficult task will not be attempted here. The forced and collectivized industrialization on the scale attempted by the Chinese Communists involved costs in terms of freedom and other human values, and a discussion of these would take us far beyond the scope of this study.

Our estimate of domestic expenditure by end use enables us to measure the cost of industrialization by the extent to which the standard of living was affected by the allotment of large shares of output to nonconsumption purposes. Table 14 presents gross domestic expenditure for the years 1933, 1952, and 1957 in terms of

Table 14

GROSS DOMESTIC EXPENDITURE AND ITS PERCENTAGE DISTRIBUTION BY MAJOR CATEGORIES, 1933, 1952, AND 1957

	Constant 1933 yuan			Constant 1952 yuan			Constant 1957 yuan		
	1933	1952	1957	1933	1952	1957	1933	1952	1957
Gross domestic expenditure (billions)	31	34	42	64	76	100	69	81	104
Percentage distribution									
Personal consumption	91	80	75	88	72	65	89	74	68
Communal services	1	2	3	1	2	3	1	3	3
Government consumption	3	7	7	4	7	6	4	7	6
Gross domestic investment	5	11	15	7	19	26	6	16	23

SOURCE: Table 10.

the three different price structures, together with the percentage distribution for personal consumption, communal services, government consumption, and gross domestic investment. Communal services includes public health, education, and cultural activities. It is obvious that much of what the Communists call education and cultural activities can properly be considered propaganda, indoctrination, and, most probably, measures of coercion.

From 1933 to 1957 the substantial increase in total domestic expenditure is partly a result of the industrialization program and will be discussed in detail later in this chapter. Our present interest is the way in which total expenditure is distributed for consumption and investment purposes. The allocation of resources for end use was drastically changed by the Communist regime in a relatively short period of time. From 1933 to 1952, government consumption increased from about 4 per cent of gross domestic expenditure to about 7 per cent. This increase, together with the increase in investment described above, naturally resulted in a sharp reduction in the proportion of gross domestic expenditure allotted to personal consumption.

In 1933 about 91 per cent of the total expenditure was for individual consumption. Since the 1952 price structure undervalues consumers' goods, personal consumption in 1933 is about 88 per cent in 1952 yuan. The share devoted to personal consumption fell sharply from 1933 to 1952; in 1952 it was only 80 per cent of total expenditure in terms of 1933 yuan, and only 72 per cent in 1952 yuan. From 1952 to 1957, there was a further increase in the ratio of investment to total expenditure but government expenditure changed only slightly and had no further adverse effect on consumption. Personal consumption accounted for no more than 68 per cent in 1957 in the prices of that year, and even less in 1952 yuan.

The severe effect of the reduction in consumption on the standard of living can be seen more clearly when we put the distribution of domestic expenditure on a per capita basis. In Table 15, per capita expenditure and its distribution by personal consumption, communal service, government consumption, and gross domestic investment are given in three bases of valuation.

A note of warning is in order here. The per capita consumption figure in 1933 yuan should not be converted on the basis of the then prevailing exchange rate to 16 (1933) U.S. dollars per person per year, nor should this figure be compared directly with the corresponding U.S. figure. In terms of comparable price weights, and when full values are imputed to economic activities rendered outside the market, the 1933 per capita consumption figure would be about 32 (1933) U.S. dollars.[16] When differences in the industrial structure between the U.S. and prewar China are taken into consideration, the figure could be revised upward again by 1.8 times.[17] Even when all these adjustments are made, the level is still extremely low.

As shown in Table 15, total per capita expenditure in 1952 had almost regained the prewar level in terms of 1933 prices, and exceeded it by a small margin in 1952 or 1957 price weights. However, per capita personal consumption in 1952 was only about 85 per cent of that in 1933—a substantial reduction. Some of the impressive increase in communal service from 1933 to 1952 may perhaps have represented genuine improvement in welfare, but the rest is of dubious value.

On all bases of valuation, per capita consumption increased from 1952 to 1957; but even in 1957 it was still substantially below the 1933 level, in spite of the fact that per capita output exceeded the

[16] Liu, *Income,* p. 72.

[17] Simon Kuznets, *Economic Change,* New York, W. W. Norton, 1953, p. 189. Both this and the preceding reference dealt with the comparison of gross national products of the Chinese Mainland and the United States rather than with consumption alone. However, the proportions discussed in the text can be applied to a comparison of consumption alone without any great error.

Table 15

PER CAPITA TOTAL EXPENDITURES AND CONSUMPTION, ABSOLUTE AND RELATIVE MAGNITUDES

	Absolute magnitudes									Relative magnitudes[a]					
	Constant 1933 yuan			Constant 1952 yuan			Constant 1957 yuan			Constant 1933 yuan		Constant 1952 yuan		Constant 1957 yuan	
	1933	1952	1957	1933	1952	1957	1933	1952	1957	1952	1957	1952	1957	1952	1957
Gross domestic expenditure	62	60	66	128	134	157	138	142	163	98	107	105	122	103	118
Personal consumption	56	48	50	113	96	101	123	105	110	86	88	85	90	85	90
Communal services	(b)	1	2	1	3	5	1	4	6	467	733	567	867	529	800
Government consumption	2	4	5	5	9	9	5	10	10	195	219	200	198	200	198
Gross domestic investment	3	6	10	9	26	41	9	23	37	203	313	268	432	269	430

NOTES: [a] Per cent: 1933 per capita magnitude = 100.
[b] Less than 0.5 yuan.
SOURCE: Table 10.

prewar amount by 7 per cent in 1933 prices and by as much as 22 per cent in terms of 1952 prices. The economic situation at the end of the First Five Year Plan is indicated by the per capita data for 1957 in Table 15. On the average, one Chinese produced 163 yuan of goods and services in terms of 1957 prices; of these 163 yuan, 10 were submitted to the Communist regime to defray public expenditure, 37 yuan were set aside for capital formation, 6 yuan were spent on communal service, and there were 110 yuan left over for consumption—13 yuan below the consumption standard endured in 1933.

SPEED OF DEVELOPMENT AND CHANGES IN THE STRUCTURE OF PRODUCTION

The Communist investment program and the resulting sacrifices by the Chinese people were presumably intended to increase the total product at the greatest possible speed and to expand those sectors of the economy that the government considered most important. The relative importance of the different sectors of the economy and the success of the Communists in achieving their purposes will be discussed in this section on the basis of the estimates of domestic product given in Tables 8 and 9. These tables present annual figures of net value added by several industrial sectors in terms of the 1933, 1952, and 1957 prices. First, we compare the levels of production in the years 1933, 1952, and 1957. Second, we discuss the rates of growth of the different sectors during the First Five Year Plan and the fluctuations in these rates. Finally, we draw some conclusions as to the degree of industrialization and modernization brought about by the Communists. While this analysis is limited to the data on domestic product, the employment data will also be used to examine the change in the structure of production in the last section of this chapter.

Levels of Production: 1933, 1952, and 1957

The levels of production will be compared in two steps: 1952 (the year immediately preceding the First Five Year Plan) with 1933; and then 1957 (the last year of the First Plan) is compared with 1952. The total domestic product and the value added by the different industrial sectors will be examined.

As shown in Table 16, net domestic product is between 13 and 20 per cent greater in 1952 than in 1933, depending on the basis of

Table 16

NET DOMESTIC PRODUCT COMPARED, 1952 AND 1957

(in constant prices)

	1952 (1933 = 100)				1957 (1952 = 100)			
	Net product		Per capita product		Net product		Per capita product	
	Billions of yuan	Index number	Actual amount	Index number	Billions of yuan	Index number	Actual amount	Index number
In 1933 yuan	33	113	57	99	40	124	63	111
In 1952 yuan	71	120	126	105	95	134	150	119
In 1957 yuan	76	118	133	103	100	132	157	118

SOURCES: Tables 8 and 9.

valuation. On a per capita basis, however, there is no significant difference; the increase in production merely reflects the increase in population.

As 50 of the 156 big development projects were started during 1949–51, some of them must have been completed before 1952. It is natural to expect that the output in some sectors of the economy would be a great deal higher in 1952 than in 1933; as shown in Table 17, this is the case. It is interesting to observe that during the early years of the Communist regime (1949–52), the highest priorities outside the finance sector and government administration were given to the expansion of mining and utilities (primarily coal and electric power). Factories and construction were then of secondary importance. This is perhaps logical; the development of the sources of power had to precede industrial expansion. The growth of modern transportation and communications was relatively modest. The lack of progress in the traditional sectors and in agriculture merely confirms the expected result, given the Communist emphasis on other sectors.

The 1957 price structure data are much more limited than for 1933 and 1952. Sector comparisons in constant 1957 prices can therefore be made only in an aggregated manner, but this limited comparison gives us a more concise view of the overall picture. Net value added by factories, mining, and utilities was 54 per cent higher in 1952 than in 1933; and in the other nonagricultural sectors combined, 33 per cent higher; whereas the contribution by agriculture to the total product was virtually the same in 1952 as in 1933.

Table 16 indicates that by 1957 a substantial increase had taken place in the per capita output—about 10 per cent in constant 1933 prices, and about 20 per cent in constant 1952 or 1957 prices. In

Table 17 it is seen that differing from the 1952 ranking, construction and factories now topped utilities and mining on the priority list. Modern transportation and communications still lagged behind utilities and mining. Handicrafts, agriculture, and old-fashioned transportation again expanded the least, but the increases in the first two fields were not inconsequential. The aggregated comparison in constant 1957 prices indicates that the modern sectors expanded by 94 per cent, far more than the 36 per cent increase in the other nonagricultural sectors combined. The nonagricultural sectors in turn expanded more than agriculture, which increased by only 9 per cent from 1952 to 1957.

The Annual Rates of Growth and Their Variability, 1952–57

The preceding comparison shows the increase in production during the First Five Year Plan as a whole; but it does not show whether the rate of increase was steady throughout the period. Table 18 is designed to indicate the pattern of growth in the different sectors. The average annual rate of growth is presented first for the net domestic product and then for the different industrial sectors. Net domestic product grew at an average annual rate of about 4.4 per cent in constant 1933 prices, but at 6 per cent in constant 1952 prices and 5.7 per cent in constant 1957 prices. The average rates of growth of the different sectors are arranged according to their orders of magnitude. The ranks are nearly the same as in Table 17.

The rates of growth fluctuated greatly in all sectors. This can be seen in two ways. First, the standard deviations of the average rates of growth are computed. In five of the fifteen sectors, the standard deviation is greater than the rate itself; and in six other sectors, it is at least half the rate. Second, the highest and the lowest rates of growth are given for each sector, together with the years in which they took place. The range between the highest and the lowest rates is great in all cases. In six sectors, including construction and mining, the lowest rates are negative. The highest rates did not all occur in the same year; in fact, every year in this period saw the highest rate of growth in some sectors and the lowest rate in others.

In this study we cannot offer explanations for all these fluctuations. However, the growth of output in the modern sectors will be related to some important economic variables—capital stock, employment, and such other factors as can be dealt with in a limited analysis.

Table 17

NET VALUE ADDED BY SECTORS, 1952 AND 1957
(in constant prices)

Sector	1952 (1933 = 100)						1957 (1952 = 100)					
	1933 yuan		1952 yuan		1957 yuan[a]		1933 yuan		1952 yuan		1957 yuan[a]	
	Rank	Index number	Rank	Index number	Rank	Index number	Rank	Index number	Rank	Index number	Rank	Index number
Factories	7	170	5	194			2	236	2	248		
Handicrafts	10	105	10	107			10	114	10	114		
Mining	2	300	2	294	1	154	4	208	4	209	1	194
Utilities	3	238	4	221			3	232	3	229		
Construction	6	178	7	178			1	252	1	252		
Modern transportation and communications	5	193	6	193			5	182	5	182		
Government administration	4	224	3	229			6	159	6	154		
Work brigades[b]	—	—	—	—			7	139	7	137		
Finance	1	374	1	374	2	133	8	135	8	135	2	136
Trading stores and restaurants	9	113	8	125			9	130	9	130		
Rent	8	114	9	114			11	112	11	112		
Old-fashioned transportation	12	100	11	102			13	92	14	92		
Personal services	11	100	13	100			14	91	13	93		
Peddlers	14	95	14	97			15	72	15	72		
Agriculture	13	98	12	101	3	101	12	108	12	109	3	109

NOTES: [a] The 1957 figures are aggregated.
[b] There were no work brigades in 1933.
SOURCES: Tables 8 and 9.

Table 18

RATES OF GROWTH OF NET DOMESTIC PRODUCT AND 15 INDUSTRIAL SECTORS, 1952–57

	Average annual rate of growth (per cent per year)	Standard deviation of the average annual rate	Highest rate of growth in the period (per cent)	Lowest rate of growth in the period (per cent)
Net domestic product				
In constant 1933 prices	4.4	1.9	8.0 (1955–56)	2.7 (1956–57)
In constant 1952 prices	6.0	3.1	11.9 (1955–56)	3.5 (1956–57)
In constant 1957 prices	5.7	3.1	11.8 (1955–56)	3.5 (1956–57)
Industrial sector[a]				
Construction	22.8	25.7	69.6 (1955–56)	−7.0 (1956–57)
Factories	20.5	12.0	40.0 (1955–56)	8.1 (1954–55)
Utilities	18.1	3.9	22.9 (1955–56)	11.6 (1954–55)
Mining	16.6	12.9	29.0 (1956–57)	−0.7 (1952–53)
Modern transportation and communications	12.8	5.1	21.4 (1952–53)	6.9 (1954–55)
Work brigades	12.1	34.8	70.4 (1954–55)	−38.7 (1952–53)
Government administration	9.1	5.1	16.9 (1955–56)	3.0 (1954–55)
Finance	6.2	3.0	11.8 (1955–56)	3.4 (1954–55)
Trading stores and restaurants	5.5	2.5	8.5 (1953–54)	2.7 (1952–53)
Handicrafts	2.6	0.5	3.5 (1953–54)	1.9 (1952–53)
Rent	2.3	0.2	3.0 (1954–55)	1.6 (1955–56)
Agriculture	1.7	0.9	3.2 (1955–56)	1.0 (1954–55)
Personal services	−1.5	2.2	0 (1952–53)	−5.6 (1955–56)
Old-fashioned transportation	−1.6	4.5	6.0 (1955–56)	−7.6 (1952–53)
Peddlers	−6.0	8.0	5.0 (1952–53)	−17.6 (1953–54)

NOTE: [a] Computed in constant 1952 prices.
SOURCE: Table 8.

The Shift Toward Industry and Modern Methods of Production

During the First Five Year Plan the average annual rates of growth of the modern sectors were substantially higher than those of the traditional sectors, but this does not indicate the degree of industrialization and modernization achieved at the end of the period. Much depends upon the relative positions of the various sectors at the beginning of the period. Tables 19, 20, and 21 present a picture of the changes that occurred in the structure of production. Table 19 shows the shifting importance of the different industrial

Table 19

INDUSTRIAL SECTORS RANKED BY THEIR PERCENTAGE CONTRIBUTION TO NET DOMESTIC PRODUCT

Industrial sector[a]	1933 Rank	1933 Per cent	1952 Rank	1952 Per cent	1957 Rank	1957 Per cent
Agriculture	1	56.9	1	47.9	1	39.0
Trading stores and restaurants	2	10.3	2	10.7	3	10.5
Handicrafts	3	7.4	4	6.6	4	5.6
Factories	4	5.6	3	9.0	2	16.8
Old-fashioned transportation	5	4.4	6	3.7	10	2.6
Peddlers	6	3.5	9	2.8	12	1.5
Rent	7	3.4	7	3.2	9	2.7
Government administration	8	2.4	5	4.6	5	5.3
Modern transportation and communications	9	1.8	8	2.9	7	4.0
Construction	10	1.7	10	2.6	6	4.8
Personal services	11	0.9	14	0.8	15	0.5
Mining	12	0.8	11	2.1	8	3.2
Finance	13	0.6	12	1.8	11	1.9
Utilities	14	0.2	15	0.4	14	0.7
Work brigades[b]			13	0.9	13	0.9

NOTES: [a] Net value added (computed in constant 1952 prices) by a given sector is taken to represent the sector's contribution to net domestic product.

[b] There were no work brigades in 1933.

SOURCE: Table 8.

Table 20

PERCENTAGE DISTRIBUTION OF NET DOMESTIC PRODUCT BY SEVEN INDUSTRIAL DIVISIONS, 1933, 1952, AND 1957

(per cent)

Industrial division	Computed in constant 1933 prices			Computed in constant 1952 prices			Computed in constant 1957 prices		
	1933	1952	1957	1933	1952	1957	1933	1952	1957
Agriculture	65.0	56.6	49.3	56.9	47.9	39.0	55.8	47.9	39.4
Industry[a]	10.5	12.8	17.5	14.1	18.1	26.4	11.7	15.3	22.6
Construction	1.2	1.9	3.8	1.7	2.6	4.8			
Transportation	5.6	6.2	6.5	6.2	6.6	6.6			
Trade	9.4	8.9	8.0	13.8	13.5	12.0	32.5	36.8	38.0
Government administration	2.8	5.7	7.3	2.4	4.6	5.3			
Others[b]	5.6	8.0	7.7	4.9	6.7	6.0			

NOTES: [a] Including factories, handicrafts, mining, and utilities.

[b] Including finance, personal services, rent, and work brigades.

SOURCES: Tables 8 and 9.

sectors ranked according to their percentage contributions to the total domestic product.

Among the traditional sectors, agriculture retained its leading position in the economy, but its relative importance declined significantly. In spite of a slow rate of growth, handicrafts descended from the third position in 1933 only to fourth in 1957, whereas old-fashioned transportation and peddlers came down considerably. Factories ascended from the fourth position in 1933 to the second in 1957 and tripled their percentage contribution to the total product. Both construction and modern transportation and communications substantially increased their percentage contribution to the total product, but they still ranked lower than handicrafts. Utilities had expanded a great deal but stayed at the bottom throughout. Although more advanced forms of manufacturing and more up-to-date methods of production were on the way, agriculture and handicrafts remained outstandingly important.

Table 21

PERCENTAGE DISTRIBUTION OF NET DOMESTIC PRODUCT BY MODERN AND TRADITIONAL SECTORS

(per cent)

Sector	In constant 1933 prices			In constant 1952 prices		
	1933	1952	1957	1933	1952	1957
Agriculture	65.0	56.6	49.3	56.9	47.9	39.0
Modern nonagricultural sectors[a]	12.6	18.1	26.9	20.9	28.8	41.2
Traditional nonagricultural sectors[b]	19.6	19.6	16.5	19.8	18.7	14.5
Government administration	2.8	5.7	7.3	2.4	4.6	5.3

NOTES: [a] Including factories, mining, utilities, construction, modern transportation and communications, trading stores, restaurants, and modern financial institutions.

[b] Including handicrafts, old-fashioned transportation, peddlers, traditional financial institutions, personal services, rent, and work brigades.

SOURCES: Tables 8 and 9. For value added by modern financial institutions in 1933 (banks, trust companies, insurance and savings institutions), see Appendix H, Table H-11. The percentage of value added attributable to modern financial institutions in the total in 1933 is assumed to be the same in both 1933 and 1952 prices. The breakdown of value added by financial institutions into modern and traditional in 1952 and 1957 is based on the percentage of the total number of workers in finance that were employed by the state and joint state and private financial institutions in 1955, given in the notes to Table 63.

In Table 20 the percentage distributions of net value added by the industrial sectors are again consolidated into seven major functional divisions for the three years, but this time three sets of price weights are used. The declining importance of agriculture and the increasing contribution by industry to the total product are unmistakable. The basis of valuation used in computing the percentage naturally has a strong effect on the degree of change in position. This effect is particularly noticeable on the shares originated in industry and trade. In 1957, value added by industry amounted to more than 25 per cent of the national product in 1952 prices, but to only 17.5 per cent in 1933 prices. The relative importance of industry in the economy in terms of 1957 prices is just about the average (23 per cent) of the two preceding measurements. The fact that value added by the trading sector was higher in 1952 prices than in 1933 prices reflects almost entirely the greatly increased business taxes and profits of trading enterprises owned by the government. The agricultural share of total product, even in 1957 price weights, is still substantially below that expressed in 1933 prices in each of the three years.

In Table 21 we examine the structural changes of the economy by cutting across the functional classifications and grouping the nonagricultural part of the economy, except government administration, into modern and traditional sectors. The contribution of the modern sectors can then be compared with the value added by traditional workers in all the nonagricultural sectors. The increase in the importance of the modern sectors is quite impressive; their contribution to the total product doubled from 1933 to 1957 in both 1933 and 1952 prices. (The data do not permit the separation of the modern from the traditional nonagricultural sectors in constant 1957 prices.) It should be noted that the difference between modern and traditional is a matter of degree only. Some of the trading stores and mining establishments are by no means modern except by comparison.

Progress was being made in modernizing the economy, but the degree depends very much on the price structure used. In 1952 prices, net value added by the modern sectors was 41 per cent of the total product in 1957; in 1933 prices it was only about 27 per cent. The 1952 and 1957 price structures affect the valuation of the agricultural and the modern nonagricultural sectors much more than they affect the traditional nonagricultural sectors and government administration. The declining importance of agriculture in the economy is clearly indicated.

OUTPUT, CAPITAL, AND LABOR IN FOUR MODERN SECTORS

We shall now examine the extent to which expansion of output through time can be explained on economic grounds and attempt to identify the effects of noneconomic factors. The importance of political, military, and social influences cannot be overemphasized, especially for the Chinese Mainland during the past decade. Productive enterprises in all fields were gradually taken over by the Communist regime, and the efficiency of these enterprises depended to a large measure upon the competence and discipline of Communist Party workers attached to them. Artificial emergencies might have speeded up production temporarily, but a general slowdown probably followed each drive. Although the Communists claimed that they had accomplished vast irrigation and flood control work, natural disasters had not really been brought under control to any significant degree, and the economy suffered from frequent droughts and floods. The changes in social relationships that took place with the collectivization of agriculture and handicrafts certainly affected productivity in these and other fields. All of these factors must have influenced the growth of the different industrial sectors at one time or another.

Economic variables were also undoubtedly important. The amount of capital invested, utilization of capacity, the number of workers employed, the hours worked per day, the amount of raw materials available, the technological improvements introduced—all must have had direct effects on production. We have a fairly large body of data on capital and employment at our disposal but not to the same extent for the different industrial sectors. Investment and capital stock can be estimated only in a more aggregated manner than output and employment, and data on investment and capital stock are not available for some of the traditional sectors. Data on capital stock are used here merely for observing certain trend relationships, and the figures on investment are used in the computation of certain incremental capital-output ratios. The more detailed analysis of the relationships between output, capital, and employment is therefore limited to the following sectors: (1) factories, mining, and utilities; (2) trading stores and restaurants; (3) modern transportation and communications; and (4) construction. These four modern nonagricultural sectors occupy a position of unique importance in the economy. They comprise six of the nine sectors that expanded most during the First Five Year Plan as was shown in Tables 17 and 18. (The other sectors are government administration, work brigades, and finance.)

The position of these four sectors in the economy can be further indicated by comparing (a) the output, investment, and employment in the four sectors combined, with (b) the output, investment, and employment in the rest of the economy as given in Table 22.

Table 22
A COMPARISON OF THE FOUR MODERN SECTORS WITH THE ECONOMY AS A WHOLE, 1952–57

	1952	1953	1954	1955	1956	1957
	(billions of 1952 yuan)					
Output (net value added)						
The four modern sectors combined	19.8	22.8	26.0	28.1	35.7	38.2
Other nonagricultural sectors combined	17.4	17.7	17.8	18.3	19.4	20.0
Agriculture	34.2	34.8	35.5	35.8	37.0	37.1
Net fixed investment						
The four modern sectors combined	2.4	4.1	5.3	6.6	9.8	11.3
Other nonagricultural sectors combined; Agriculture	1.8	3.5	3.5	3.2	4.3	4.9
	(millions of workers)					
Employment						
The four modern sectors combined (except trading stores and restaurants)	5.6	6.7	7.1	7.5	8.6	9.3
Trading stores and restaurants	6.6	6.4	5.8	5.6	5.9	6.4
Other nonagricultural sectors combined	43.2	43.9	43.7	42.4	42.1	42.9
Agriculture	199.9	203.6	208.3	210.8	214.9	215.8

SOURCES: Tables 8, 11, and 13.

Net value added by these four sectors increased much faster than agricultural output; net value added by the other nonagricultural sectors merely kept pace with agricultural output. In 1957, investment in these four sectors was about five times as high as in 1952, whereas investment in the rest of the economy (including agriculture) was only about two and a half times as high. The data on employment indicate a situation similar to that represented by the figures on output, except that employment in trading stores and restaurants declined somewhat from 1952 to 1955, and for this reason they are treated separately in Table 22. Employment in the traditional nonagricultural sectors also declined slightly.

The Data and the Nature of the Relationships

The data on net value added, capital stock at the beginning of the year and net of depreciation, and employment for the four modern nonagricultural sectors are given separately for each industry in Table 23. These data should not be used to make statistical estimates

Table 23

NET VALUE ADDED, CAPITAL STOCK, AND EMPLOYMENT IN THE FOUR MODERN SECTORS, 1952–57
(billions of 1952 yuan, millions of workers)

	1952	1953	1954	1955	1956	1957
Factories, mining, and utilities						
Output	8.2	10.1	11.8	13.2	17.5	19.8
Capital stock	7.4	8.7	11.2	14.2	18.1	23.9
Employment	3.5	4.1	4.2	4.4	4.8	5.5
Trading stores and restaurants						
Output	7.7	7.9	8.5	9.0	9.7	10.0
Capital stock	0.9	1.0	1.2	1.6	1.9	2.6
Employment	6.6	6.4	5.8	5.6	5.9	6.4
Modern transportation and communications						
Output	2.1	2.6	2.9	3.1	3.5	3.8
Capital stock	5.1	5.9	7.1	8.7	10.7	13.4
Employment	0.7	0.8	1.0	1.1	1.3	1.4
Construction						
Output	1.8	2.3	2.7	2.9	5.0	4.6
Capital stock	0.6	0.7	1.0	1.3	1.6	2.2
Employment	1.3	1.8	1.9	2.0	2.4	2.4

SOURCES: Tables 8, 11, and 77.

of the production relationships. The pitfalls of the statistical production function are too well known to be repeated here.[18] Technological and institutional changes were introduced so rapidly during the First Five Year Plan that any statistical functions obtained mechanically by fitting the data on output, capital, and employment to equations would have no resemblance to the production function as commonly understood in economic theory. The coefficients obtained, regardless of the type of function fitted, essentially reflect

[18] A rather nontechnical source of references to the literature on this subject is Phelps E. A. Brown, "The Meaning of the Fitted Cobb-Douglas Function," *Quarterly Journal of Economics*, Vol. LXXI, No. 4, November 1957, pp. 546–550.

the relations among the historical rates of growth of output, capital, and employment. The statistical function cannot indicate the output from alternative combinations of capital and employment at any point of time, and the marginal productivity of capital and employment cannot be derived from the regression coefficients. The inclusion of a time trend usually makes matters worse because of the high correlation between time and both capital and labor. Moreover, capacity utilization and the length of the working day probably varied greatly. Information on these variables is not sufficiently comprehensive or reliable to estimate labor and capital inputs on the basis of our data.

Although meaningful production functions cannot be derived from our data, it is still legitimate to observe whether output tended to move with capital or employment in some discernible pattern. The patterns, if any, represent trends or purely empirical relationships in the sense that they were the result of the working of numerous variables in addition to capital and employment. Projections from such relationships could be meaningless unless it could be assumed that all the important variables not represented in the relationships will change in the future as in the past, relative to one another and to capital and employment. Although the usefulness of such relationships is limited, they can throw some light on the pattern of growth if care is exercised in interpreting them.

The trend relationships are analyzed in two ways. Net output, net capital stock, and employment are examined first. Annual increments in gross output are then compared with gross investment during the preceding year and with increases of employment during the same year.

The Trend Relationships

Scatter diagrams of net value added in a given year and net capital stock at the beginning of the same year are presented in Figure 5 for the four modern sectors. Increase in output through time was generally accompanied by increase in capital in all four sectors, as expected. However important the other factors may have been, they did not change the fundamental relationship between capital and output.

In three of the diagrams in Figure 5, the 1952–54 points lie quite close to a straight line through the origin, which represents a unity-elasticity relationship between output and capital in the sense that

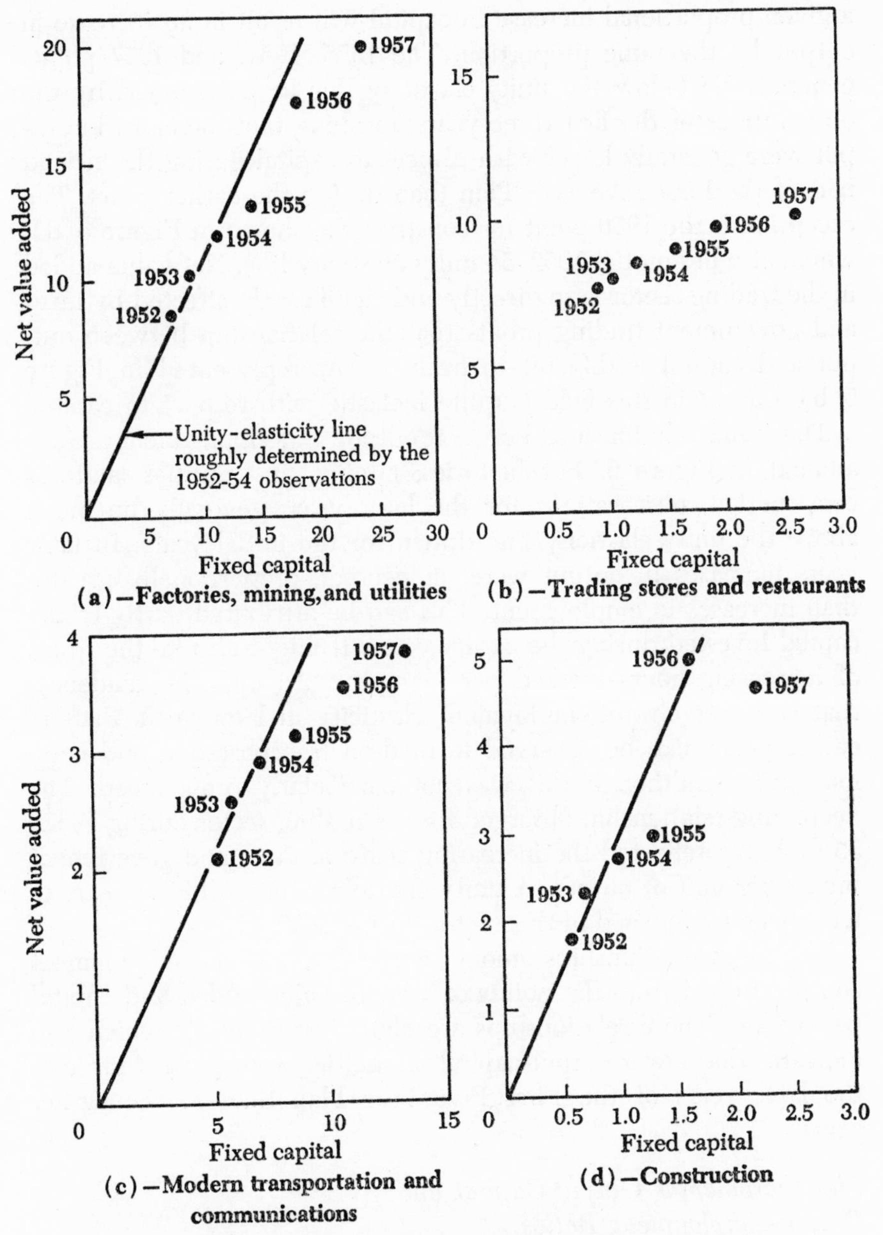

Figure 5. Output (net value added) versus fixed capital in billions of 1952 yuan

a given proportional increase in capital will result in an increase in output by the same proportion. The 1955, 1956, and 1957 points generally lie below the unity-elasticity line as determined by the observations of the first three years, meaning that increases in output were generally lower with respect to capital during the second half of the First Five Year Plan than during the earlier years. The exception is the 1956 point for construction, shown in Figure 5(d), which also lies on the 1952–54 unity-elasticity line. Net value added in the trading sector is so directly and significantly affected by taxes and government trading profits that the relationship between output and capital is difficult to evaluate. As represented in Figure 5(b), output in this field is quite inelastic with respect to capital.

The trend relationships between output and employment are examined in Figure 6. For factories, mining, and utilities, and for construction, observations for the later years generally lie much above the unity-elasticity line drawn for the initial years. In later years increases in output were, in general, proportionally greater than increases in employment. This can be attributed partly to the capital invested during the earlier years. It might also be the result of increasing hours worked per man-year. An opposite tendency, that is, lower output-employment elasticity in later years than in earlier years, can be observed in modern transportation and communications, although this was not particularly pronounced. The decreasing relationship observed for the trading sector during 1952–55 probably reflected the increasing share of taxes and government profits per unit of output. A unity-elasticity relationship appears to have been established in this sector during 1955–57.

The trend relationships among output, capital, and employment can be studied from the points of view of value added and capital per worker. These relationships are plotted in Figure 7, which also indicates that lower output-capital elasticities were present more in the later years of the First Five Year Plan than in the earlier years.

The Incremental Output-Capital and Output-Employment Ratios

The relationship between output and capital will now be examined with regard to their year-to-year increases. The incremental output-capital ratio is defined as the increase in gross value added in yuan in a given year over the preceding year divided by gross

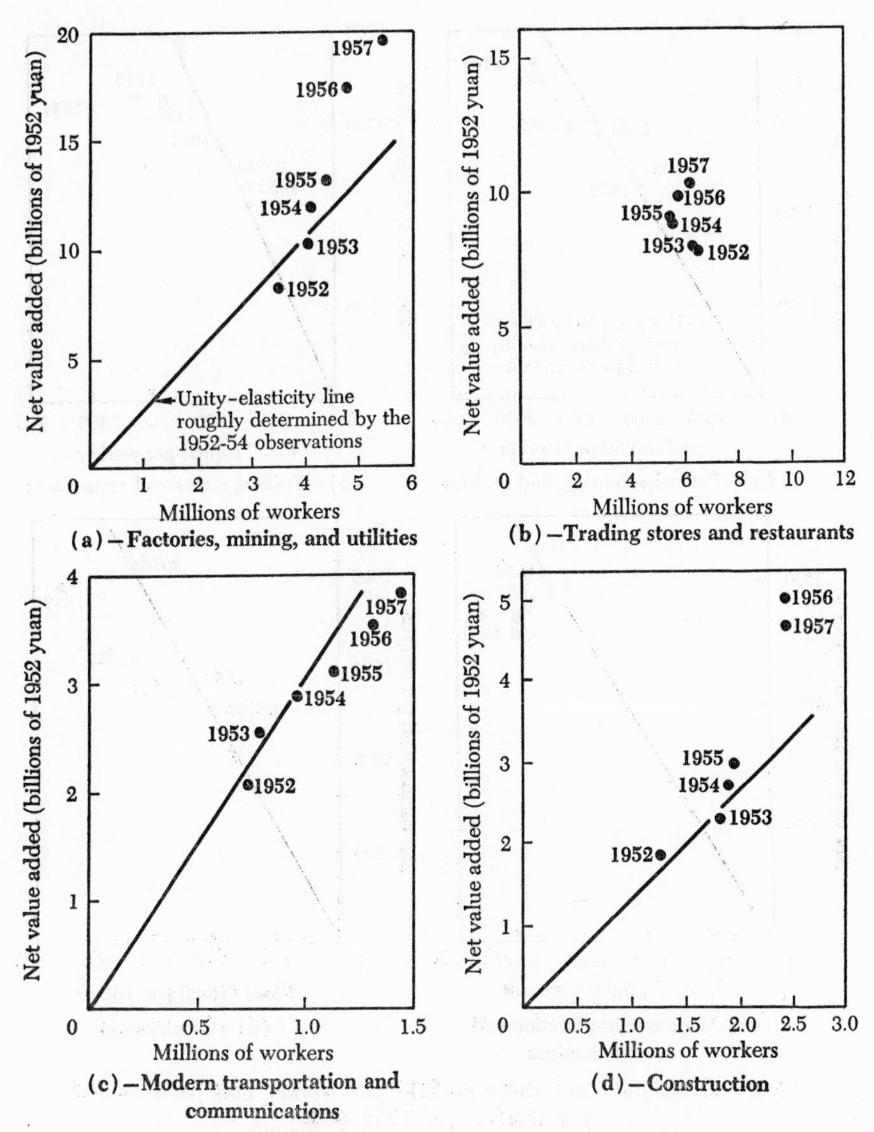

Figure 6. Output (net value added) and employment

investment in yuan in the preceding year. The ratios are plotted in Figure 8 for the four modern sectors. The incremental output-capital ratios for trading stores and restaurants are so strongly subject to government policies on taxation and profits that they do not reflect the more basic input-output relationships in which we are interested. From 1952 to 1957, except for 1956, the incremental output-capital

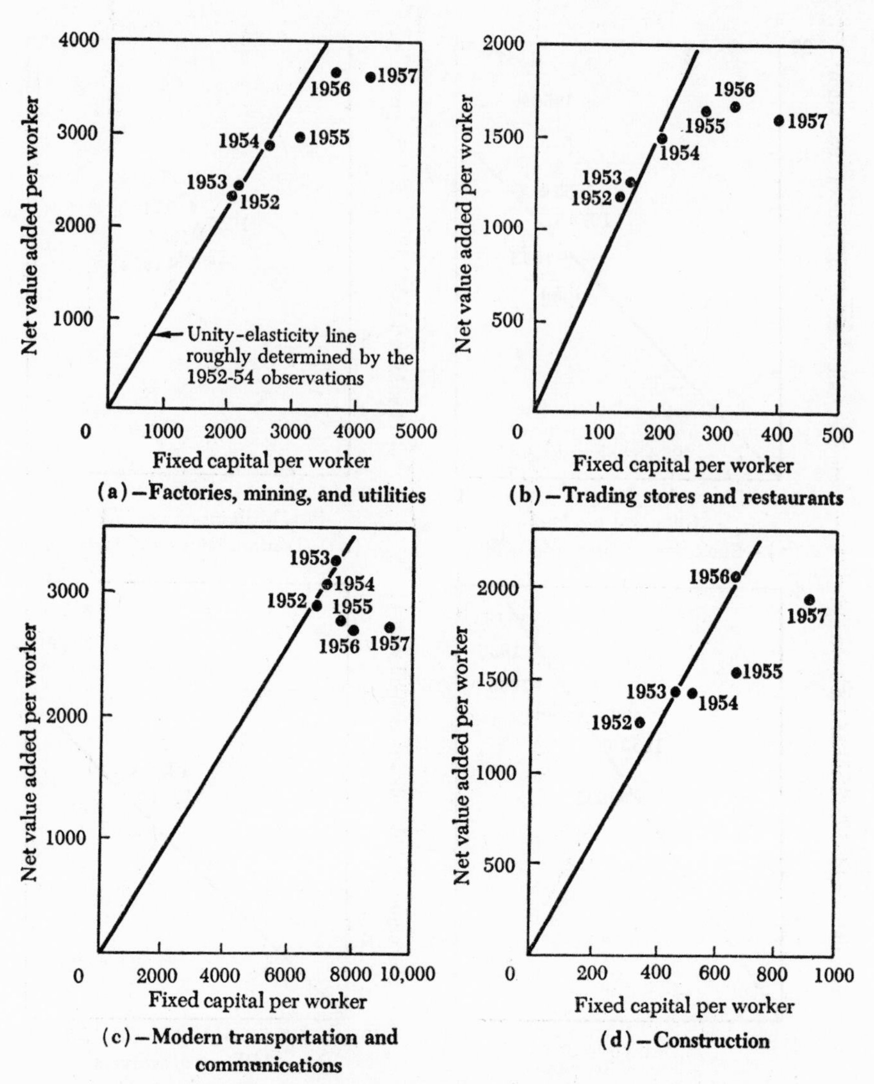

Figure 7. Output (net value added) per worker and fixed capital per worker (in 1952 yuan)

ratios in the other three sectors declined consistently and the 1957 ratios are either the same or lower than those of 1955.

According to the Communists, the industrial sectors, as well as investment, were greatly influenced by the harvest conditions during the preceding year. Some manufacturing, mainly the textile and food processing industries, depended upon agricultural products for raw materials. The volume of business done by the transporta-

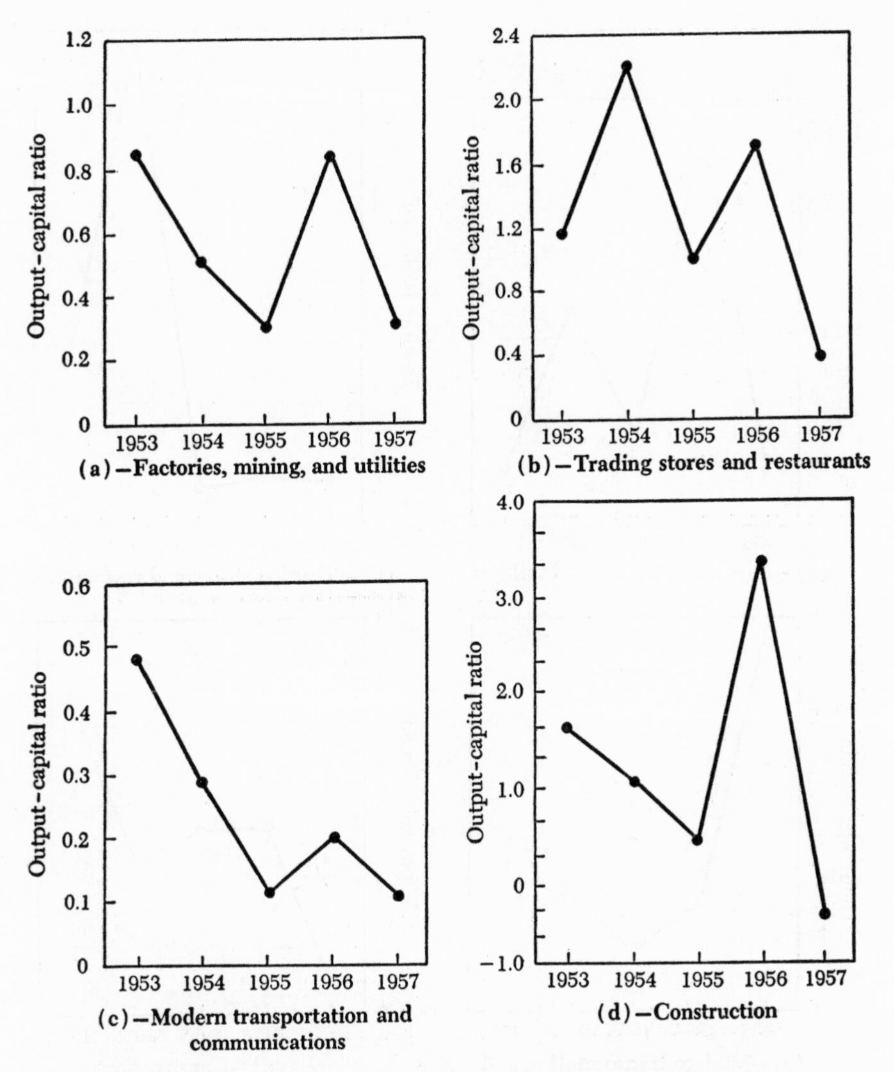

Note: The incremental output-capital ratio is the increase in gross value added in yuan in a given year over the preceding year divided by gross investment in yuan in the preceding year

Figure 8. Incremental output-capital ratios

tion and trading sectors would also have been affected by agricultural output. It has been reported by the Communists that 1952 and 1955 had good harvests, that 1953 was an average year, and that 1954 and 1956 were poor agricultural years. On the assumption that there was a one-year lag in the industrial utilization, transportation,

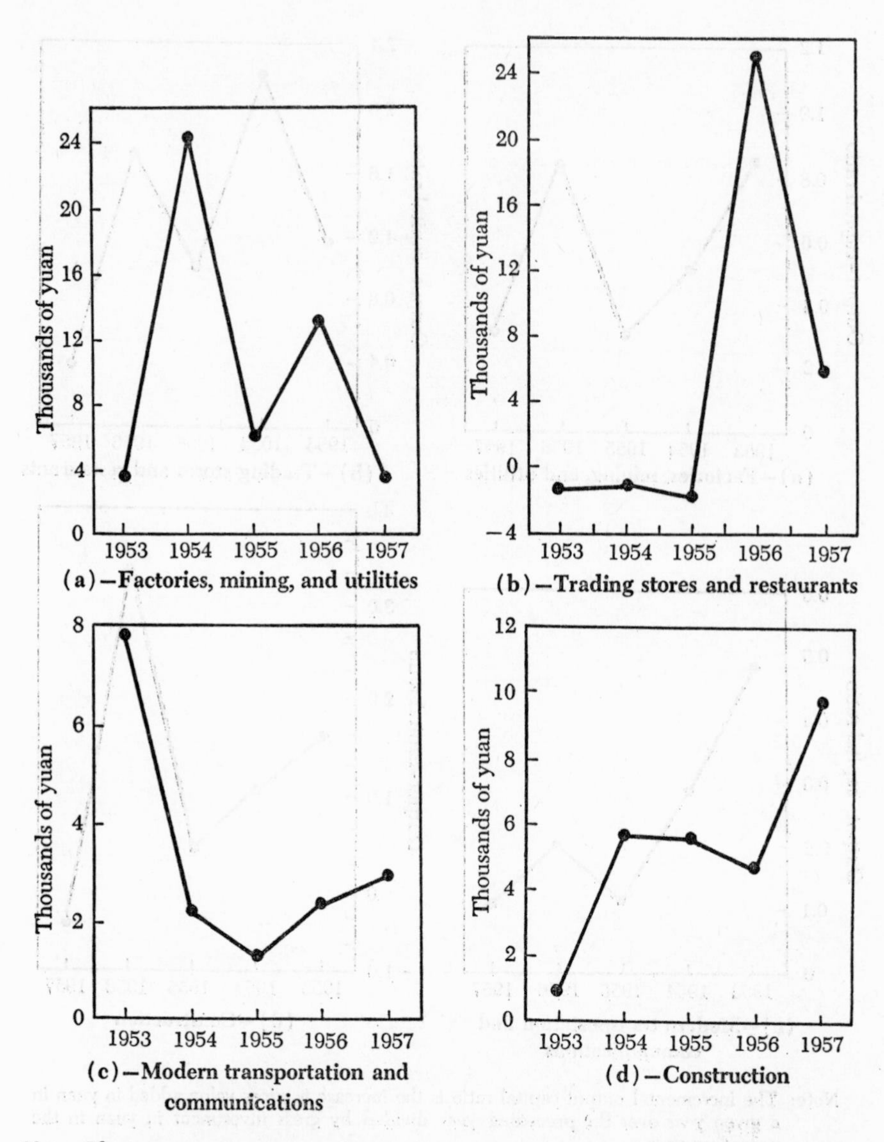

Note: The incremental output-employment ratio is the increase in gross value added in yuan in a given year over the preceding year divided by the corresponding increase in employment

Figure 9. Incremental output-employment ratios (thousands of yuan per worker)

and trading of agricultural products, productive capacity in these nonagricultural sectors should have been more fully utilized in 1953 and 1956 than in 1955 and 1957. Figure 8 confirms this conclusion, but it is difficult to accept it as the main explanation of the fluctuations in the output-capital ratios. First, harvest conditions would not have affected most of the producers' goods industries, such as the iron and steel industry, mining, and utilities. Second, the Communist statement on the harvests was not entirely borne out by their data on agricultural output as given in Chapter II under The "Hard" Components of the Product Estimate, 1952–57. Perhaps a more valid reason is that much of the increase in industrial output during the First Five Year Plan came from a more intensive utilization of the productive capacity already in existence.[19] It is quite likely that the general decline in the output-capital ratios represents the gradual exhaustion of the margin for intensification.

The incremental output-employment ratios in the four modern industrial sectors are plotted in Figure 9, in which output is represented by gross value added. These marginal ratios do not display as clear a pattern as the incremental output-capital ratios.

LABOR FORCE AND UNEMPLOYMENT

The Chinese economy was plagued by chronic unemployment in both rural and urban areas before the war. The figures for 1933 are given in Table 24. There were 347 million people having agriculture as their main occupation, and a great deal of unemployment and disguised idleness.[20] The extent of unemployment among the nonagricultural population was great. Of the 53 million males in the age range from 12 to 65 years (except students), 12 million, or more than 20 per cent, were unemployed. The age of 12 may appear to be too young as the lower age limit of the labor force, but the corresponding limit of the U.S. labor force is only 14.[21] The estimate of nonagricultural employment also includes a large number of apprentices in handicrafts and trade, many of whom were much younger than 12. Unemployment among nonagricultural females was probably equally serious, although no estimate is given because

[19] Li Fu-chun, *op.cit.*, p. 10.

[20] See Chapter V for a discussion of occupational distribution of the agricultural population.

[21] U.S. Department of Commerce, *Business Statistics*, Washington, D.C., 1957, p. 222.

Table 24

POPULATION, LABOR FORCE, AND UNEMPLOYMENT, 1933 AND 1952–57
(millions)

	1933	1952	1953	1954	1955	1956	1957
Total population	500	569	581	595	608	621	637
Agricultural population	347	350	356	363	367	379	381
Nonagricultural population	153	219	225	232	241	242	256
Rural		150	150	152	159	156	167
Urban		69	75	80	82	86	89
Nonagricultural population, age 12–64	102	144	144	153	159	160	168
Rural		99	99	100	105	103	110
Urban		45	45	53	54	57	58
Nonagricultural students, age 12 and over	1	3	4	5	5	6	7
Rural		1	1	2	2	3	3
Urban		2	3	3	3	3	4
Nonagricultural labor force	101	141	144	148	154	154	161
Rural		98	98	98	103	100	107
Urban		43	46	50	51	54	54
Male	53	73	75	77	80	80	84
Female	48	68	69	71	74	74	77
Nonagricultural workers	54	59	59	59	60	62	64
Male	41	48	48	48	49	50	52
Female	13	11	11	11	11	12	12
Unemployed male nonagricultural workers	12	25	27	29	31	30	32
Rural		18	18	19	21	20	21
Urban		7	9	10	10	10	11

NOTES: *Total population:* For the 1933 figure, see the discussion under Total Population in Chapter IV. The figures for 1952–56 are given in SSB, *Population Statistics*, p. 25. The 1957 figure is the average of the year-end totals for 1956 (627.80 million) and 1957 (646.53 million). (See *ibid.*, p. 24, and *Great Ten Years*, p. 9.)

Agricultural population: For 1933, total agricultural population, including those in agricultural pursuits only and those who also had subsidiary work, has been estimated at 365 million (Table 54). From this total we deduct 18.5 million, the number of man-labor units engaged in farm subsidiary work, to arrive at the total agricultural population of 346.5 million. The number of man-labor units in subsidiary pursuits is derived as follows: The number of males engaged in nonagricultural farm subsidiary work has been estimated at 7.8 million (5.9 million given in Table 54 plus the number of farmers selling their produce in market towns, roughly estimated at 1.9 million; see notes to Table 54). In subsidiary work there are 42 adult males for every 8 male children (Buck, *Land Utilization*, Vol. I, Table 2, p. 291). The total of 7.8 million is therefore broken down to 6.6 million adult males and 1.2 million male children. The number of male children is then converted to 0.6 million man-labor units at the ratio of 0.5 children per adult male (*ibid.*, p. 408). Similar calculations for the number of women engaged in nonagricultural farm subsidiary work yield a figure of 1.0 million man-labor units. A total of 8.3 million man-labor units is obtained. This total is divided by the number of working man-labor units per farm household, given at 2.5 (*ibid.*, p. 289), and that figure is multiplied by the average size of farm household, given at 5.57 persons per household (*ibid.*, p. 370), yielding the total

(Continued)

population engaged in nonagricultural farm subsidiary work in 1933—18.5 million. For 1952, agricultural population is estimated at 350.7 million on the assumption that it increased from 1933 to 1952 in proportion to agricultural output over the same period, 101 per cent for 1952 with 1933 = 100. (For agricultural output in 1933 and 1952, see Table 8.) For 1953–57, agricultural population is also derived on the assumption that it increased at the same rate as agricultural production.

Nonagricultural population: Total nonagricultural population is obtained by deducting agricultural population from total population. For 1952–56, urban nonagricultural population is taken from SSB, *Population Statistics*, p. 25. The figure for 1957 is derived on the assumption that urban population was 14 per cent of the total population (637 million), slightly higher than in 1956 when urban population was 13.8 per cent. The estimate of rural nonagricultural population was derived by deducting agricultural population and urban nonagricultural population from total population.

Nonagricultural population, age 12–64: The figure for 1933 is derived by multiplying the total nonagricultural population by the percentage of persons 12–64 years old in the total nonagricultural population (66.66) given in "Future Growth of Chinese Population During Industrialization," May 1946 (unpublished). For 1952–57, the percentage of nonagricultural population 12–64 years old in the total population given for 1953 (65.8) is used. For the 1953 figure see Chen Ta, *New China's Population Census of 1953 and Its Relations to National Reconstruction and Demographic Research*, Stockholm, International Statistical Institute, 1957.

Nonagricultural students, age 12 and over: The total number of nonagricultural students age 12 and over represents the total number of middle school, college, and graduate students. The figure for 1933 is given in Ministry of Education, National Government, *The Second Chinese Education Yearbook*, 1948. The annual totals for 1952–57 are the average of the two corresponding academic years given in *1956 Statistical Abstract*, p. 62, and *Great Ten Years*, p. 170. According to a Communist source, about 50 per cent of the middle school students and 25 per cent of college and graduate students in 1955 are from rural families (Fung Chi-hsi, "Growth of China's Economy as Viewed from the State Budget," *TCKT*, No. 12, June 1957, p. 30). It is assumed that the percentages of middle school students are 35, 40, and 45 for 1952–54 and 50 for both 1956 and 1957; the percentages for college students are assumed to be 10, 15, and 20 for 1952–54 and 25 for both 1956 and 1957.

Rural and urban nonagricultural labor force: These figures are the residuals after the figures for nonagricultural students are deducted from the figures for nonagricultural population age 12–64.

Nonagricultural labor force—male: For 1933, the figure is derived by applying the percentage of males in the total population, given at 52.83 in "Future Growth of Chinese Population During Industrialization," to the total nonagricultural labor force. For 1952–57, the sex ratio for population aged 12–64 is derived at 108.3 males per 100 females on the basis of sex ratios for five age groups between 12 and 64 years, and the relative size of each group (Tai Shih-kuang, *1953 Population Census of China*, Calcutta, Indian Statistical Institute, 1956). This sex ratio is applied to the total nonagricultural labor force to obtain the estimate of the male nonagricultural labor force.

Nonagricultural labor force—female: The sum of rural and urban nonagricultural labor force, less the male nonagricultural labor force.

Nonagricultural workers—total: See Table 11.

Nonagricultural workers—male: Total nonagricultural workers, less nonagricultural female workers.

Nonagricultural workers—female: The figure for 1933 is the sum of nonagricultural female workers given in Tables 54 and 55; for 1952–57, see Table 64.

Rural and urban unemployed male nonagricultural workers: The number of total unemployed male nonagricultural workers is first derived by deducting the figures for nonagricultural male workers from those for nonagricultural male labor force. These totals are then segregated into rural and urban areas on the basis of the ratios of rural to urban nonagricultural labor force.

it is impossible to distinguish between idle and unemployed housewives.

With the large-scale investment program the Communists put into effect it might seem that there would have been labor shortages, at least in the nonagricultural sectors. However, the Communist data on population and our estimate of employment indicate that this was not the case before the radical changes in social institutions in 1958.[22]

In Table 24, a rough estimate is made of unemployed males in nonagricultural sectors in the postwar years. First, nonagricultural population is obtained by deducting agricultural population from the total. The Communists have not published data on the number of workers engaged in agriculture,[23] but it is possible to make a rough estimate. As explained in Appendix E, the increased use of machinery and fertilizers in agriculture during 1952–57 was extremely limited, and whatever increase there might have been in output per worker would have been more or less cancelled out by the cultivation of formerly submarginal land. On the assumption that output per worker was the same in postwar years as in 1933, the number of agricultural workers can be computed from our estimate of agricultural production.[24] The postwar agricultural population is then estimated by assuming that it bore the same relation to agricultural workers as in 1933.

With the estimate of nonagricultural population now easily obtained as the difference between total population and agricultural population, the next step is to derive the nonagricultural labor force. We define the nonagricultural labor force as the total number of people outside the agricultural population from 12 to 65 years of age, and not attending school. This total is divided into males and females on the basis of Communist figures, including distribution of population by age and sex, for the year 1953. (This estimate in-

[22] For a judgment of the reliability of the Communist data on population see the discussion pertaining to Table 52.

[23] See Chapter V for a discussion of the difference between our idea of agricultural population and the Communist concept of rural population. The Communists occasionally refer to agricultural population as such, but we suspect they include many who did not have agriculture as their main occupation. Our estimate is in terms of full-time agricultural employment with subsidiary work excluded. This calculation was made on the basis of Buck's prewar data. Similar data are not available for postwar years.

[24] See Table 11. If output per worker had been higher in postwar years than in 1933, unemployment would also have been even higher than our estimate.

cludes many who lived in rural areas but did not belong to families with agriculture as their main occupation.) Nonagricultural employment has been estimated elsewhere (see Table 11). Nonagricultural unemployment is then computed by subtracting nonagricultural employment from the labor force.

As shown in Table 24, the number of unemployed nonagricultural male workers increased from 25–27 million in 1952–53 to approximately 31 million during 1955–57. An unemployment figure of 31 million out of a total nonagricultural labor force of 80 million might appear to be high, but it seems more reasonable if it is recalled that two-thirds of these unemployed were residents of rural areas, and only 11 million were in urban areas.

Very little Communist information is available on unemployment. There are scattered figures for a few of the larger cities at various times, and it has been reported that unemployment in 1952 was more than 3 million; but this number, about one-half of 1 per cent of the total population and less than 3 per cent of the total nonagricultural labor force, is probably too small.[25] In all likelihood, this was a rough estimate of unemployment in the large cities. The seriousness of the situation is better indicated by the discussions in the mainland press of the problem of "idle people" and the measures that the Communists have undertaken to stop migration from rural to urban areas.[26]

EXPENDITURE GAPS AND INFLATIONARY PRESSURE

If one must name a single bottleneck inhibiting growth in nearly all fields and at all times during the First Five Year Plan, that factor is the supply of capital, which was severely limited by the low capacity to save and inability to borrow from abroad. The financing of the ambitious Communist investment program would have been a difficult endeavor in itself, and investment was by no means the only item to be financed. As shown in Table 14, government consumption increased from 4 per cent of the gross domestic expenditure in 1933 to 7 per cent in 1952. To avoid price inflation, the population had to be deprived of purchasing power approximately equal to investment expenditure and government consumption. Until 1956, there had always been an import surplus in the balance of

[25] *People's Daily,* August 2, 1952, p. 1.
[26] *People's Daily,* April 17, 1953.

international trade. This became a small export surplus which was as inflationary as investment or government consumption so far as its effect on the domestic price level was concerned.

One obvious way to judge whether the Communists were successful in financing their industrialization program without inflation is to look at their own price indexes. To bring out the year-to-year change in the price level, we express the retail price index in eight cities in a given year as a percentage of the index of the preceding year.

	1951	1952	1953	1954	1955	1956	1957
(1) Communist retail price index in eight cities (March 1950 = 100)	94.6	93.7	98.3	100.2	101.1	101.0	102.2
(2) First index of inflationary pressure: index number for a given year in line (1) divided by index number for the preceding year in line (1)		99.0	104.9	101.9	100.9	99.9	101.2
(3) Communist cost-of-living index for workers in 12 leading cities (1952 = 100)		100	105.6	106.9	107.3	107.1	109.2
(4) Second index of inflationary pressure: index number for a given year in line (3) divided by the index number for the preceding year in line (3)			105.6	101.2	100.4	99.8	102.0

The same computation is made for the cost-of-living index for workers in 12 leading cities. The results, shown above, are designated the first and the second indexes of inflationary pressure. These indexes are plotted in Figure 10 together with the third and fourth indexes which will be explained later in this chapter. Inflationary pressure is said to exist when the index is greater than 100, and most of these are somewhat greater than 100. Inflationary pressure, then, existed to some extent in almost every year. It was greatest during 1953, declined to practically nothing during 1954–56, and again occurred during 1957, especially if judged by the second index. On the whole, however, price changes were minor.

If the price indexes are trustworthy, the Communists have been successful in financing industrialization without serious inflation. It is possible, of course, that the indexes were constructed largely on the basis of official prices charged in state-operated stores. Prices

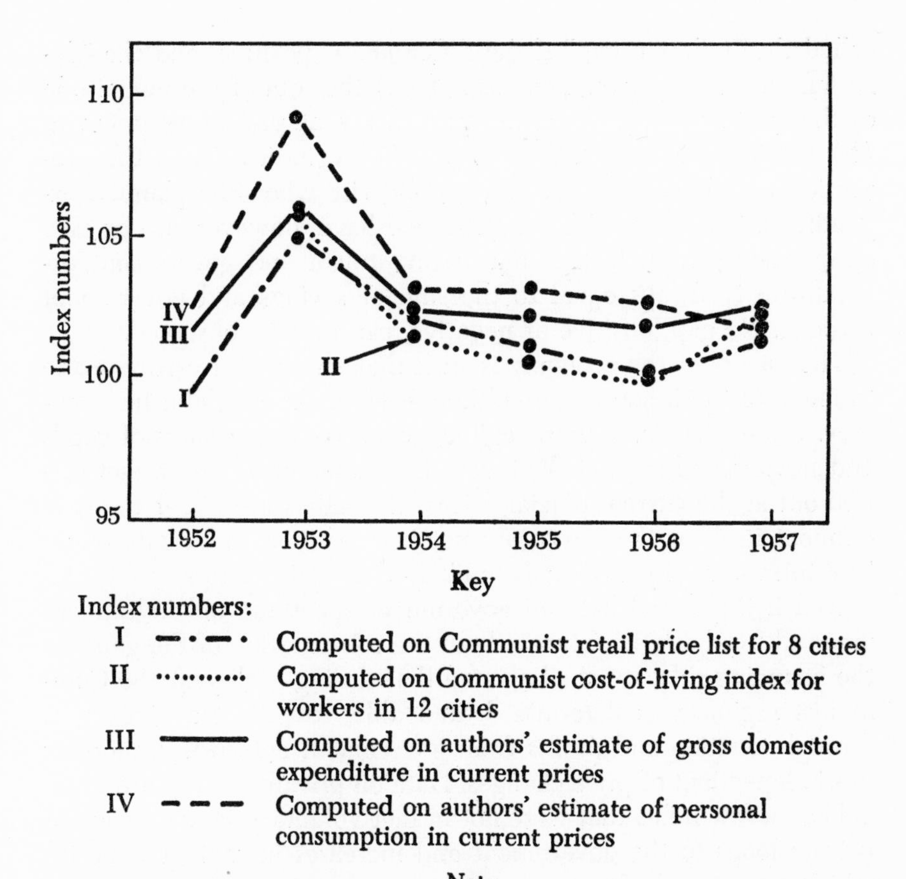

Figure 10. Four indexes of inflationary pressure

charged in private transactions may have been quite different. There is also the possibility that there were clandestine transactions, even in state-operated stores. It is doubtful that all these unofficial prices have been given proper weights. Moreover, with rationing in force, inflationary pressure might be latent in the economy in the form of excess purchasing power but never reveal itself in price changes.

It is extremely difficult, if not impossible, to estimate the magnitude of inflationary pressure. Ideally, given the prevailing prices, if both the total amount of planned (*ex ante*) expenditure to be financed (investment and government consumption) and the total volume of planned financing (savings, taxes, and other government revenues) are known, then the difference between the two can be called the "inflation gap" if the difference is positive, and the "deflation gap" if negative. The ratio of (a) the sum of the magnitude of this gap and total domestic expenditure at prevailing prices to (b) the domestic expenditure would be an indication of the proportion by which the price level would rise when the planned expenditure is incurred. The statistics we have, however, are *ex post* observations; as such, the sum of investment and government expenditure is always equal to the sum of savings and government revenue. No gap, positive or negative, can ever be observed.

The nature of the economy is such that an attempt can be made to measure the inflation gap, although we make no claim for accuracy. Under the Communist regime, government purchases of goods and services and most of the investment expenditure are in fact carried out at the current official prices: the sellers are either the government itself or those who are not in a position to bargain or refuse to sell. In any case, it is unlikely that major errors will be involved if the actual data on government spending and investment are used for the expenditure side of the computation of the gap. On the financing side, we shall assume that during each year the Communist regime was determined, and able, to collect a given sum through taxation and profits from government enterprises, more or less independent of price changes. Data on private savings are available on a few items that were not in fact voluntary savings, such as private loans to the government and increases in savings deposits, which were largely frozen.

The most important item for which the *ex ante* and actual figures would be different as a result of price changes is the reduction in consumption because of higher prices. This involuntary saving is the result of the inflation gap itself. Another major item in the gap is the forced reduction in consumption through rationing. To the extent that savings occurred because of rationing and were not transferred to the state through taxes and loans, the increased purchasing power in the hands of the people represents latent inflationary pressure. These two elements are the most important in the gap, and information is not available on them. In Table 25 we piece together the expenditures to be financed and the financial resources or savings on which some data are available. The difference will be considered to be the expenditure gap. The estimated gaps are subject to unknown margins of error that might be larger, in proportion to the gaps themselves, than the percentage errors of the data on the

Table 25

GOVERNMENT SAVINGS AND THE EXPENDITURE GAPS, 1952–57

(millions of current yuan)

	1952	1953	1954	1955	1956	1957
Government savings available to offset expenditures						
Government receipts						
Tax receipts	9,769	11,967	13,218	12,745	14,088	15,439
Agriculture	2,704	2,711	3,278	3,054	2,965	2,931
Others	7,065	9,256	9,940	9,691	11,123	12,508
Profits from public enterprise	5,728	7,669	9,961	11,194	13,426	14,221
Other receipts	1,870	1,634	1,264	904	505	369
Total	17,367	21,270	24,443	24,842	28,019	30,029
Current government expenditure						
Government and communal consumption	7,280	9,490	8,450	9,010	9,070	10,040
Certain transfer payments	451	485	618	512	575	583
Total	7,731	9,975	9,068	9,522	9,645	10,623
Government savings available to offset expenditures	9,636	11,295	15,375	15,320	18,374	19,406
Expenditures						
Expenditures to be offset						
Gross domestic investment minus investment by work brigades	13,900	19,950	20,740	20,850	22,400	22,830
Export surplus	−980	−1,050	−370	−1,160	270	440
Total	12,920	18,900	20,370	19,690	22,670	23,270
Known financial resources						
Government savings	9,636	11,295	15,375	15,320	18,374	19,406
Government loan receipts from domestic sources		54	910	704	607	650
Depreciation charges in nonstate sectors	2,014	2,267	2,083	1,875	1,534	1,550
Increase in savings deposits	223	320	225	−56	472	389
Total	11,873	13,936	18,593	17,843	20,987	21,995
Estimated expenditure gap	1,047	4,964	1,777	1,847	1,683	1,275

NOTES:

Government savings available to offset expenditures

Government receipts. Ts'ai-cheng, No. 8, 1957, p. 32; and Li Hsien-nien, "Report on the Final Accounting of the 1957 State Budget and the Draft Budget for 1958," *HHPYK*, No. 5, March 1958, pp. 3, 6.

Current government expenditure: Government and communal consumption. The estimates are derived separately as follows: Government consumption in 1952–57 in current prices is obtained by multiplying the corresponding estimates in constant 1952 prices given in Table 78 by the Communist retail price index for 1952–57 with 1952 as 100 (*Great Ten Years*, p. 153). Government consumption of services (including communal services) is obtained by multiplying the corresponding estimates in constant 1952 prices (also given

(Continued)

Table 25 (continued)

in Table 78) by the Communist cost-of-living index for 1952–57 with 1952 as 100 (SSB, "Changes in Market Prices in 1957 and Its Effect on People's Living Conditions," *TCYC*, No. 4, April 1958, p. 25, and *FFYP Communique*, p. 51).

Certain transfer payments. Ts'ai-cheng, No. 8, 1957, p. 32. The figure for 1957 is the planned target.

Government savings available to offset expenditures. Total government receipts minus total current government payments.

Expenditures

Expenditures to be offset: Gross domestic investment minus investment by work brigades. The estimates of gross domestic investment in current prices are derived by multiplying those in 1952 prices, given in Table 72, by the price index of investment for 1952–57, with 1952 as 100. See the discussion in Chapter V under Domestic Investment. The estimates of investment by work brigades in current prices are similarly derived. For data on investment by work brigades in 1952 prices, see Table 72.

Export surplus. ECAFE, *Economic Survey of Asia and the Far East, 1957*, Bangkok, 1958, p. 103.

Known financial resources: Government savings. See Government savings available to offset expenditures, above.

Government loan receipts from domestic sources. For 1952–56, see *Ts'ai-cheng*, No. 8, 1957, p. 32. The figure for 1957 is derived by deducting foreign loan receipts (Li Hsien-nien, "Report on the Final Accounting of the 1956 State Budget and the Draft Budget for 1957," *HHPYK*, No. 14, July 1957, p. 21) from total domestic and foreign loan receipts (Li Hsien-nien, "Report on the Final Accounting of the 1957 State Budget and the Draft Budget for 1958," *HHPYK*, No. 5, March 1958, p. 6).

Depreciation charges in nonstate sectors. The estimates of depreciation in nonstate sectors in 1952 prices, given in Table 13, multiplied by the price index for 1952–57 with 1952 as 100. See Chapter V under Domestic Investment.

Increase in savings deposits. For total personal bank deposits at the end of each year for 1951–57, see *TKP*, Peiping, March 19, 1958, p. 2. According to an estimate given in *People's Daily*, September 29, 1957, p. 3, savings deposits accounted for 70 per cent of the total. When this percentage is applied to total personal bank deposits, we can derive estimates of savings deposits for 1951–57. The annual increases in savings deposits for 1952–57 are then obtained from the differences between the figures in two consecutive years.

Estimated expenditure gap

Total expenditures to be offset, less total known financial resources.

expenditures and financial resources. But it is also possible that the errors cancel each other to some extent. The results given in Table 25, in any case, are tentative.

The most important financial resource is government savings, which is the excess of revenue over current government consumption (including communal services). To bring out the importance of this item, Table 25 is divided into two parts. In the first part the amount of government savings available to offset investment is derived. The major items of revenue are given first. It is seen that profits from public enterprises increased about 150 per cent from 1952 to 1957. This rate of increase was even higher than the rate of increase of tax revenue, which in 1957 was about 50 per cent higher than in 1952. Actually, the difference between taxes and profits from public enterprises is more nominal than real; these two items can be combined without resulting in much loss of information. Who actually carried the burden of these charges is an interesting question. For instance, the burden shouldered by the peasants was surely greater than is shown by the agricultural taxes because of the low prices they received and the high prices they had to pay. No attempt will be made here to analyze the nature and the incidence of the various kinds of taxes and state profits. Government consumption was very much greater in 1952 than in 1933, but the rate of increase during 1952–57 was modest. The figures on transfer payments are taken from government accounts; they are fairly small and quite stable over a period of time. With these data it is easy to obtain government savings.

In transfer payments, only relief payments are included. Other expenditures, such as foreign aid, circulating funds for local governments, and appropriations to banks for making loans, should not be included here because they are accounted for under other items. Expenditures for foreign aid, when they became effective as a source for demand for domestic output, were included under expenditures to be offset through export surplus. Funds allocated to local governments and banks, when they were actually paid out by these institutions, were included in government consumption and investment expenditures. The only expenditure that should be included here but is not included because of lack of information is services on domestic loans. (Services on domestic and foreign loans are given as one aggregate item in the Communist government budget.) Services on foreign loans are accounted for under other items. The omission of services on domestic loans will result in underestimating the expenditure gaps in Table 25.

In the second part of this table, the expenditures to be offset include gross domestic investment, less work done by work brigades and the credit balance of international trade. To be exact, the latter should have been replaced by foreign investment. The difference between the two is net income from abroad, which consisted mainly of remittances from overseas Chinese. Information on this item is not available, but it was probably very small compared with the other expenditures to be offset. The omission of this item would result in a further underestimation of the expenditure gap.

In addition to government savings, government loan receipts from domestic sources are an important financial resource. Government loan receipts from abroad (Soviet loans) were taken into consideration under export surplus. Although domestic loans were not government revenue, they nevertheless reduced the purchasing power in the hands of the public. These loans were received from individuals and private business, and no credit creation was involved. Depreciation charges in the nonstate sectors represented the only item of private savings that can be reasonably estimated. Increases in savings deposits, mostly involuntary, must also be included. The Communists have often stated that there was a significant amount of private investment, and hence savings, by the peasants. (Farmers' investment has been included in gross domestic investment.) However, government loans to peasants were also reported to be very large, as follows (in millions of current yuan): 1952, 438; 1953, 570; 1954, 760; 1955, 1,000; 1956, 3,000.[27] It is extremely doubtful that farmers had any significant amount of private savings that should be included in Table 25.

The difference between the total expenditure to be financed and the sum of the financial resources is called the "expenditure gap." The estimated gaps given in Table 25 are taken as a rough indication of the extent to which supply of goods was short of effective demand. From this table, two indexes indicating inflationary pressure in the economy have been constructed, in addition to those computed on the basis of Communist price data. The third index of inflationary pressure is the ratio of (a) the sum of gross domestic expenditure and the expenditure gap, in current prices, to (b) gross domestic expenditure. The computation (in millions of current yuan) is as follows:

	1952	1953	1954	1955	1956	1957
(1) Gross domestic expenditure in current prices	76,400	84,580	88,380	91,730	99,250	104,060
(2) Expenditure gaps	1,047	4,964	1,777	1,847	1,683	1,275
(3) Sum of lines (1) and (2)	77,447	89,544	90,157	93,577	100,933	105,335
(4) Third index of inflationary pressure: Line (3) divided by line (1)	101.4	105.9	102.0	102.0	101.7	101.2

In the computation of this index, it is implicitly assumed that inflationary pressure, as measured by the gaps, fell on all categories

[27] Li Choh-ming, *Economic Development of Communist China,* University of California Press, Berkeley and Los Angeles, 1959, Table XXX, p. 132.

of goods, but it is unlikely that this was the case. Most investment goods were allocated by the Communist regime; in the great majority of cases, prospective buyers of investment goods who were unable to obtain allotments probably had to do without them, whatever prices they might have been willing to pay. It is more realistic to assume that the inflationary gaps fell entirely on consumption goods and services.

The fourth index of inflationary pressure is the ratio of (a) the sum of personal consumption expenditure and the expenditure gaps, in current prices, to (b) consumption expenditure. The computation (in millions of current yuan) is as follows:

	1952	1953	1954	1955	1956	1957
(1) Personal consumption in current prices	54,600	54,740	58,750	61,150	67,040	70,420
(2) Expenditure gaps	1,047	4,964	1,777	1,847	1,683	1,275
(3) Sum of lines (1) and (2)	55,647	59,704	60,527	62,997	68,723	71,695
(4) Fourth index of inflationary pressure: Line (3) divided by line (1)	101.9	109.1	103.0	103.0	102.5	101.8

Both indexes of inflationary pressure (III and IV) are plotted in Figure 10 for comparison with Indexes I and II, computed directly from the Communist official price indexes. All four show the greatest increase in 1953. Indexes I and II show much weaker inflationary pressure than III and IV. However, all reveal a sharp decline from 1953 to 1954. For 1954 and 1955, there is no evidence to indicate that the forces of inflation have been underestimated in Indexes III and IV. On the other hand, the Communists have released many reports about the shortage of industrial materials and consumers' goods and the existence of pressure on commodity prices toward the end of 1956 and early in 1957.[28] Although Indexes III and IV show that inflationary pressure was present in 1956 and 1957, the index numbers are very slightly over 100, lower than in the preceding years. The expenditure gaps given in Table 25 for these years have probably underestimated the actual excess of effective demand over the supply of goods. We have not been able to locate the causes of this underestimate except for the two omissions mentioned previously in this section. At least for 1957, there is an increase in the Communist indexes, even though it is small.

[28] *HHPYK*, No. 3, February 1957, p. 48; *TCKT*, No. 7, April 1957, p. 31, and No. 11, June 1957, p. 26.

The gradual tightening of economic control during 1949–57 was discussed briefly in Chapter I. The measures of regulation and control introduced during these years were moderate indeed compared with the severe measures taken in 1958. At the peak of the development of the communes, everyone in the countryside lived the life of a soldier-peasant-laborer. People ate in mess halls instead of at home, and young children were put in nurseries away from their mothers. Work started at daybreak and lasted until late into the evening—either in the fields or in village industries. The aim was to integrate agriculture and industry in such a way that the available manpower (including housewives) would be utilized to the absolute maximum.[29]

Before 1958, the emphasis of the development plan was on modern, large-scale, capital-intensive industrial projects. The Communists took much pride in the development of power and in the up-to-date machinery and techniques of production that had been introduced in some of the factories and mines. In 1958, however, there was a sudden drive for the large-scale utilization of labor-intensive techniques to increase agricultural production and to produce industrial goods with the use of crude equipment. The importance of modern factories was never played down; the massive effort to employ crude equipment and methods was merely to be superimposed on the development of modern, capital-intensive plants. The most famous of these attempts was the backyard blast furnaces, made of crude clay and bricks. These furnaces used as raw materials all kinds of ore, coal, and scraps, including still-usable cooking pots and pans. The purpose was to double steel output from about five million tons in 1957 to ten million tons in 1958. In agriculture, such techniques as deep plowing and close planting were used, with the purpose of doubling agricultural output in one year. All these efforts were intended to bring about the Great Leap Forward.

With the announcement of the Great Leap Forward in December 1957, the central Communist regime in Peiping exerted tremendous pressure on local party members, directors of communes, and man-

[29] For a more detailed description of the institutional changes accompanying the Great Leap Forward see A. Doak Barnett, *Communist Economic Strategy: The Rise of Mainland China,* Washington, D.C., National Planning Association, 1959; and Cheng Chu-yuan, *The People's Communes,* Hong Kong, Union Press, 1959.

agers of local enterprises to expand production at a pace practically impossible to achieve. The accomplishments of a few pilot projects using concentrated technical skill and scarce resources under the most favorable conditions and closest supervision were expected to be duplicated by producers all over the country. Soon enthusiastic reports were pouring into Peiping from one locality after another claiming that the targets were being fulfilled and overfulfilled. When the *Communique on Economic Development in 1958* was issued in April 1959, the regime announced that the output of such important products as food crops, cotton, iron, and steel had more than doubled during 1958, and that the gross value of agriculture and industry had increased about 65 per cent.

It soon became apparent that these announced increases could not be true, as there was neither improvement in the food rations nor evidence of sufficient increases in the supply of industrial goods to sustain the claims. A drastic downward revision of the claims was announced in August 1959, reducing the estimated production of food crops and cotton in 1958 by one-third. The claimed increase in iron and steel production was scaled down in a more subtle way. It was admitted that roughly 30 per cent of the iron and steel produced in 1958 was "native" and not really usable for modern industrial purposes. It is difficult to say what the native iron and steel were good for, but it is significant that the backyard blast furnaces were soon abandoned. As the quantity of iron and steel was not really reduced in the revised announcement, the total value of industrial production remained unchanged. The increase in agricultural production announced for 1959 was more restrained, but the increase claimed for steel and industrial production in general was high. Communist production statistics for 1957–59, including the reported percentage increases in national income, are summarized in Table 26.

In dealing with the earlier Communist data for 1952–57, we detected certain apparent biases, and made some adjustments to correct them. A 9 per cent average annual rate of growth claimed by the Communists was reduced to 6 per cent in our calculations. The extraordinarily high increases in the official statistics in 1958 and the unprecedentedly radical revision of these statistics in 1959 indicate the confusion in the Communist data. Bolder adjustments than the limited modifications we relied on in the earlier years have had to be made in the statistics to obtain any reasonable estimate

Table 26

COMMUNIST PRODUCTION DATA FOR 1957–59

	1957[a]	1958: Announcement of April 1959[b]	1958: Announcement of August 1959[c]	1959[d]
Food crops (millions of piculs)	3,700	7,500	5,000	5,400
Cotton (millions of piculs)	33	66	42	48
Gross value of agricultural production (billions of 1957 yuan)	54	88	67	78
Pig iron (millions of tons)				
Modern	5.9	13.7	9.5	20.5
Native			4.2	
Steel (millions of tons)				
Modern	5.4	11.1	8.0	13.4
Native			3.1	
Gross value of industrial production (billions of 1957 yuan)	70	117	117	163
Percentage increase of national income over the preceding year	+5.4	+34		+22

NOTES: [a] *1957:* Gross value of agricultural and industrial production, pig iron, steel, food crops, and cotton from *Great Ten Years*, pp. 14, 84, and 105. The percentage increase in national income in 1957 over 1956 is based on data given in Table 70.

[b] *1958 Announcement of April 1959:* See *1958 Communique.*

[c] *1958 Announcement of August 1959:* Except for the percentage increase in national income, all figures are taken from Chou En-lai, "Report on the Adjustment of Major Targets in the 1959 National Economic Plan and the Launching of the Campaign To Increase Production and To Economize," *HHPYK*, No. 17, 1959, p. 22. The figure for national income is given in *Great Ten Years*, p. 18.

[d] *People's Daily*, January 23, 1960, p. 1.

SOURCE: Appendix K.

of the national income for 1958 and 1959, for which the Communists claimed increases of 34 per cent and 22 per cent, respectively. The results are of more doubtful significance, and the best that can be said for our conjectural estimate is that it is, in all likelihood, nearer to the actual figures than the highly inflated Communist claims. Only the principal adjustments we have made in the Communist data are described here; a detailed description is given in Appendix K.

Food crop production in 1958–59 is estimated by the same method used to obtain estimates for the earlier years. It is assumed that food crop production increased from 1957 to 1958 and from 1958 to 1959 at rates equal to the rate of growth of population during these years. However, reports of food shortages in the cities during 1958 and 1959 became more numerous than before. Food consumption in rural areas was also more tightly controlled after the advent of communes. Therefore our assumption may still overestimate the actual rate of increase in agricultural production.

Exports of cotton cloth and knitted goods were much greater in 1958 and 1959 than in 1957. Since there is no evidence that rations of cotton cloth were increased, domestic consumption of cotton cloth and knitted goods is assumed to have increased from 1957 to 1959 at rates equal to the rate of growth of population. Total production is then assumed to be equal to the sum of exports and domestic consumption. This procedure leads to a substantial downward adjustment in the data on cotton cloth and clothing. Proportionate reductions are applied to the data on cotton and cotton yarn production.

It will be recalled that we used Communist data on producers' goods without modification in deriving our income estimates for 1952–57, but the data on the production of steel and pig iron for 1958 and 1959 are so confused that a closer scrutiny is necessary. The output of steel for 1958 was first announced as 11.1 million tons. The Communists later admitted that of this total 3.1 million tons were native steel, probably produced from backyard furnaces. Even the 8 million tons of so-called modern steel amounted to a 50 per cent increase over 1957. In 1959 modern steel further increased by 67 per cent to 13.4 million tons. It was pointed out in a Communist source, however, that of the 13.4 million tons of modern steel, about 4.8 million tons were produced by "middle- and small-size converters." It was further explained that these medium and small converters had become important between 1958 and 1959.[30] The demarcation between the small converters and the backyard furnaces was probably not too clearly drawn during the enthusiastic "leaping" years. In making national income estimates, it is important to distinguish the part of steel output that was, in fact, steel, from the part that was produced by the small converters and backyard blast furnaces from still-usable scrap pots and pans and then returned to the people as new pots and pans.

Rates of increase of steel production as high as 50 and 67 per cent per year remain unconvincing without some corroborating

[30] "Press Communiqué on Economic Development in 1959," *People's Daily*, January 23, 1960, p. 1.

evidence in the form of comparable increases in modern steel products. The only category of such products for which a continuous series of data is available for all the years 1952–58 is the value of machinery produced, in constant 1952 prices. This series is plotted together with steel production in Figure 11. The 1952–57 observa-

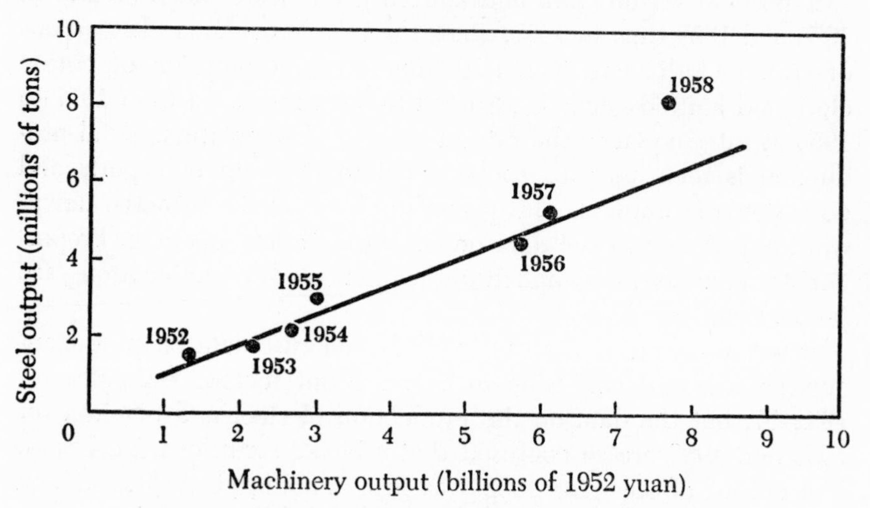

Figure 11. The relationship between machinery output and steel output, 1952–58

tions display a near-linear relationship, but the 1958 point is located well above the line. With the choice between (a) accepting an unusually large increase of steel production in a year when steel was being produced in every city and village, and (b) inferring the quantity of steel output from a six-year relationship of products requiring bona fide steel as input, we are inclined to choose the latter. The production of modern steel in 1958 is therefore roughly estimated at 6.3 million tons, following the linear relationship shown in Figure 11. The difference between the Communist figure for modern steel in 1958 and our estimate is assumed to be steel from small converters or backyard blast furnaces. We have classified this excess as handicraft output. As yet there is no Communist report on the value of machinery produced in 1959 so an adjustment cannot be made for that year. The Communist figure for modern steel for 1959 is tentatively divided into two parts, one (modern industrial steel) corresponding to our estimate for 1958, and the other corresponding to handicraft output, based on the estimated ratio for 1958, discussed above. Table 26 indicates that the Communist data on pig iron for 1958 and 1959 follow much the same pattern as their data on steel, and are adjusted downward in the same way.

The gross value of output of factories in 1958 and 1959 is separated into identified and unidentified portions with no difference in the rate of growth. The method used is the same as that applied to the 1952–57 data.

After these major and some minor adjustments have been made, the conjectural estimates of domestic product for 1958 and 1959 are obtained in essentially the same way as the 1952–57 estimates; they are presented together in Table 8. The rates of growth of domestic product so estimated are 14 per cent for 1957–58 and 15 per cent for 1958–59. Although our figures are much lower than the 35 and 22 per cent reported by the Communists, we are inclined to believe that they are still too high.

CONCLUDING REMARKS

Much of this chapter is a summary analysis of the economic growth of the Chinese Mainland under Communist control. Table 27 focuses on some key areas of interest. Because of the conjectural nature of our 1958–59 estimates, this table presents the average growth rates of certain key magnitudes for only 1952–57. The Communist figures and the estimates of W. W. Hollister of some of the items are presented together with our own.[31]

The three estimates of the average annual rate of growth of national income are based on different concepts. Our estimate is for net domestic product; the Communist estimate is made on their concept of national income; and Hollister's estimate is for gross national product. The difference in concepts has little effect on the relative rates of growth. On the other hand, the different price weights used make a significant difference in the estimates. Our rates are computed on both the 1933 and 1952 price weights, whereas Hollister's and the Communist figures are in terms of 1952 prices.[32]

Our estimate of the average annual rate of growth of net domestic product during 1952–57, from 4.4 per cent (in 1933 prices) to 6

[31] The Communist data on national income are discussed in the last section of Chapter IV, and our estimates are reconciled with these figures and the figures in the last section of Chapter V.

See also W. W. Hollister, *China's Gross National Product and Social Accounts, 1950–57*, Glencoe, Ill., The Free Press, 1958.

[32] See Table 8.

Table 27

A COMPARISON OF ESTIMATES OF GROWTH RATES OF KEY MAGNITUDES, 1952–57

	Average annual rate of growth, 1952–57 (per cent per year)		
	Our estimate	Hollister's estimate	Communists' estimate
National income			
In constant 1933 prices	4.4[a]		
In constant 1952 prices	6.0[a]	8.7[b]	9.0[c]
Per capita national income			
In constant 1933 prices	2.1[d]		
In constant 1952 prices	3.6[d]	6.1[e]	6.4[d]
Personal consumption			
In constant 1933 prices			
Including communal service[f]	3.1[g]		
Excluding communal service	2.7[g]		
In constant 1952 prices		6.3[h]	6.7[i]
Including communal service	3.8[g]		
Excluding communal service	3.5[g]		
Per capita consumption		4.2[e]	4.4[d]
In constant 1933 prices			
Including communal service	0.8[d]		
Excluding communal service	0.5[d]		
In constant 1952 prices			
Including communal service	1.5[d]		
Excluding communal service	1.2[d]		
Gross value of agricultural production	1.7[j]		4.5[k]
Gross value of producers' goods			29[m]
Gross value of machinery produced			38[n]
Output of electric power			22[p]
Output of steel			32[p]
Output of cement			20[p]
Postwar per capita consumption compared with prewar (index numbers)	90[q]		140[r]

NOTES: [a] Net domestic product. Computed from data given in Tables 8 and 9. The average annual rate of growth of gross domestic product is practically identical to that of net product.

[b] Gross national product. See W. W. Hollister, *China's Gross National Product and Social Accounts, 1950–57*, Glencoe, Ill., The Free Press, 1958, p. 2.

[c] National income as defined by the Communists. See the last section of Chapter IV.

[d] For population data, see Table 32.

[e] Hollister has assumed a rate of increase of population of 2 per cent, slightly lower than the Communist estimate of about 2.4 per cent.

[f] For communal service, see the discussion earlier in this chapter under The Real Cost of the Communist Investment Program.

[g] Computed from data given in Table 10.

[h] W. W. Hollister, *op. cit.*, p. 133.

[i] See Chapter V under Government Consumption and Communal Service.

(Continued)

Table 27 (continued)

[j] Computed from data in Appendix E.
[k] *Great Ten Years*, p. 17.
[m] See Chapter IV under Total Gross Value of the Output of Factories.
[n] See Table 39.
[p] *Great Ten Years*, p. 90.
[q] Per capita consumption in 1957 with 1933 = 100 in constant 1952 or 1957 prices. See Table 15.
[r] Per capita consumption in 1956 with 1936 = 100 (*HHPYK*, No. 6, March 1957, pp. 57–59).

per cent (in 1952 prices) per year, is lower than the Communist or Hollister's estimates, both of which are about 9 per cent per year. When the estimates are put on a per capita basis, the difference becomes greater. Our estimate of the average annual rate of growth of per capita product, somewhere between 2.1 and 3.6 per cent per year, is approximately one-third to a little over one-half of the other estimates.

A comparison of the rate of growth of the Chinese Communist economy with that of other countries has not been attempted here. It cannot be made without at least weighting the outputs of the different sectors of the two economies by the price weights used in deriving the national incomes of both countries. The hazard involved in any attempt at a comparison is vividly brought out by our own estimates. On the basis of the same set of data on physical output, the average annual rate of growth of net domestic product is 6 per cent in 1952 prices, but only 4.4 per cent in 1933 prices. The effects of the price structures of different countries on international comparisons are also likely to be great.

The Chinese people paid heavily for the Communist program of industrialization. As shown in Table 27, per capita consumption at the end of the First Five Year Plan was 10 per cent lower than in 1933. During 1952–57, according to our estimate, per capita consumption increased at the annual rate of only 0.5 to 0.8 per cent in 1933 prices, or 1.2 to 1.5 per cent in 1952 prices. This contrasts sharply with the Communist estimate of a 4.4 per cent annual increase in per capita consumption during the same period and their claim that per capita consumption in 1956 was 40 per cent higher than in 1936. If their claims were true, they would have succeeded in working out a solution for their basic economic problems—scarce resources and widespread poverty. The Communists claim that nine years after they gained control of the mainland, they had increased national income by 9 per cent per year, expanded the output of producers' goods by nearly 30 per cent per year, and, at the same time, raised the standard of living by 4.4 per cent per year, or 40 per cent higher than the prewar level. Since rationing of most daily necessities is still strictly enforced, the estimates presented in Table 27 appear more convincing.

It seems reasonably clear that neither the expansion in heavy industries during the First Five Year Plan nor the lowered standard of living prevailing in 1957 (lower than in 1933) can be seriously disputed, even though there might be some disagreement about the precise rate of expansion of the former and the degree of reduction of the latter. From the point of view of economic analysis, an interesting question is whether the same rate of growth could be achieved at a lower price. A conclusive answer cannot be given on the basis of an analysis covering only six years; but the estimates given here for production and employment are part of the data necessary for an evaluation of this question.

Of special interest would be a comparison of the scale of economic values and the allocation of manpower at the beginning and end of the First Five Year Plan. Table 12 shows the great disparity between net value added per worker in the different sectors of the economy and the corresponding percentage distribution of employment in 1933. The value added per worker in the modern sectors was anywhere from five to ten times as high as in such fields as handicrafts and agriculture. Yet it was precisely in sectors where net value added was high that few people were employed. The number of workers in the modern sectors was a mere 1 per cent of total employment.

How much this picture has been changed by the ambitious investment program and the extensive changes in economic institutions put through by the Communists during 1952–57 is shown in Table 28, where the data for 1957 are presented with net value added per worker computed in both 1933 and 1952 yuan. The total number of workers employed in sectors with high productivity per worker (that is, modern transportation and communications, factories, mining, and utilities) increased from 1 per cent of the total in 1933 to 2.5 per cent in 1957. The number of people employed in these modern fields increased by no more than 1.5 per cent of the total number of people employed. In spite of the small percentage of increase, millions of workers are represented (and hence many more millions of tons of steel, cement, and so on). And it is

Table 28

NET VALUE ADDED PER WORKER AND DISTRIBUTION OF EMPLOYMENT IN DIFFERENT INDUSTRIAL SECTORS, 1957

	Net value added per worker (basic index numbers = 100)		Distribution of employment (per cent)
	Computed in 1933 yuan	Computed in 1952 yuan	
Finance	172	66	0.3
Modern transportation and communications	125	74	0.5
Factories, mining, and utilities	100	100	2.0
Trading stores and restaurants	48	44	2.3
Construction	76	54	0.9
Government administration	37	15	3.4
Peddlers	16	8	1.8
Handicrafts	20	10	5.3
Old-fashioned transportation	13	7	3.6
Personal services	11	4	1.2
Agriculture	11	5	77.1

SOURCES: Computed from data given in Tables 8 and 11.

because of the increase in industrial power potential, both in absolute terms and relative to other Asian nations, that the Chinese Communist economy deserves careful attention.

Achievement in industrializing an economy should be assessed in terms of the scale of the economy and the increase (relative to the total labor force) of skilled workers trained in modern industrial techniques. A large population is usually considered an obstacle to industrialization; but personal consumption has been strictly controlled on the Chinese Mainland, and a large labor force would make it easier to equip a given number of industrial workers, so long as the marginal product of labor is greater than the consumption.

Considering the total investment actually made by the Chinese Communists, many economists will no doubt feel that the program could have been planned so that a greater percentage of the labor force could have been trained and equipped by the end of 1957. For example, more fertilizer plants could have been built at the expense of some of the steel mills because of the higher labor-capital ratio in the former. More industrial workers would have been employed, and it is possible that the rate of growth of the national product would have been higher. Under such a program, food rationing might not even have been necessary. A better fed population might have been able to achieve a higher level of production in all fields than the program of forced industrialization, which apparently has given little attention to the basic needs of the population.

Since, proportionally speaking, employment in the modern fields did not increase greatly, the reduction in employment in the traditional sectors was also small. A comparison of Tables 28 and 12 will show that the percentage of workers engaged in agriculture in 1957 is little different from that in 1933. The percentages of workers in handicrafts and old-fashioned transportation did decrease somewhat, but they are not substantially lower.

The ratio of the net value added per worker in agriculture to that in factories, mining, and utilities is 18 to 100 for 1933 and 11 to 100 for 1957 in terms of 1933 price weights. In terms of 1952 price weights, the 1957 ratio is only 5 to 100. The greater disparity in 1957 than in 1933 might seem surprising at first glance, but investment in agriculture was relatively small during the postwar years, and capital per worker increased substantially in factories, mining, and utilities.[33] We have the impression that not only did capital per worker in industry increase faster than in agriculture, but also that investment in agriculture during the same period relative to the amount of capital in agriculture in 1933 was smaller than the corresponding proportion of increase of capital in industry. This point cannot be demonstrated quantitatively because there is no information on the amount of nonagricultural capital in 1933.

The ratio of value added per worker in handicrafts to that in factories, mining, and utilities also declined from 1933 to 1957. It is true that the product per worker in such fields as traditional rice milling would always be quite low, but value added by highly skilled artisans in embroidery and ceramics is much higher. If the low-value handicrafts had been replaced by factories that could produce the same types of goods more efficiently, and if handicraft efforts had been concentrated in the highly skilled fields, then the value of the product per worker in handicrafts would have been a great deal higher. But the Communists concentrated their investment in producers' goods factories, and net value added per worker remained low in handicrafts.

[33] See Table 23.

CHAPTER IV

ESTIMATE OF DOMESTIC PRODUCT BY INDUSTRIAL ORIGIN

THE DETAILED figures on domestic product and employment by industrial origin are presented in this chapter together with an explanation of the source data and the methods of derivation. Estimates of value added by individual sectors are described in the first three sections. For agriculture, factories, part of handicrafts, mining, utilities, and modern transportation and communications the estimate is made on the basis of commodity output; raw materials and intermediate products used in production are deducted from the gross value of output. For such other sectors as the service industries, the number of people employed are roughly estimated, and their contributions to the domestic product are approximated by use of data on employment and estimated per capita earnings. There are a few sectors for which data are totally unavailable for 1933, and for these, crude approximations are made through a rough estimate of the total population and its occupational distribution. For those sectors for which specific data are not available in the postwar years, value added has been roughly estimated by another method.

In our calculation of domestic product by industrial origin, we have attempted to correct observed biases in the Communist data for agricultural production and manufactured consumers' goods on the basis of what we believe to be reasonable evidence and assumptions. Our estimates are made on the basis of Communist data, corrected for accuracy and adjusted to conform to the standard Western concept of domestic product. In the last section, they are compared with another set of estimates, called the adjusted estimates, which we have derived from Communist data. They are uncorrected for accuracy but adjusted to conform to the same concept of domestic product. The adjusted estimates are in turn compared with the Communists' own estimates. Unless specified as adjusted or Communist, the estimates referred to are the authors' estimates.

AGRICULTURE

For the purposes of this study, agriculture refers to activities for the production of plant, animal, forest, and fishery products. Estimates of output, price, and value of production are made for individual products so far as the available data permit; and a miscellaneous category, relatively low in value, is added to allow for products that were not included in the four main categories. Subsidiary work done by farmers is allocated to other sectors as dictated by the type of activity. For example, value added by hand-milled rice can be more or less accurately estimated, but it would not be possible to estimate as accurately what part of the hand-milling was done by workshops set up for the purpose and what part was done as subsidiary work by the farmers. The Communist classification of subsidiary work done by farmers is different from the concept used in this study, and this raises a problem in reconciling the two estimates. We have estimated net value added by agriculture in a straightforward way: gross value of output less deductible costs of production and depreciation equals net value added. Data on gross value of output are obtained for most products by multiplying statistics on physical output with farm prices.

Output of Agricultural Products[1]

PLANT PRODUCTS, 1933 [2]

The National Agricultural Research Bureau was the only organization that released estimates of crop production on an annual basis before the war.[3] The basic data on total cultivated area in the 22 provinces, the "average" (normal) percentage of cultivated area and yield per mow in each of the major crops were collected during 1929–31. In the following years, field observers were asked to report the percentage of total cultivated area planted in each crop, and the yield for each crop as a percentage of the average yield during 1929–31. The total output of each crop was obtained by simply multiplying the relevant figures.

In spite of the Bureau's efforts to check the accuracy of the data collected, it is well known that the figures are underestimates. The

[1] Appendix A presents the details of the basic data and methods used in deriving the estimates discussed in this section.

[2] The basic output data are acquired from *Agricultural Estimates,* and Buck, *Land Utilization.*

[3] For a detailed discussion of the Bureau's crop-reporting system, see *Food Crops.*

total cultivated area reported for the 22 provinces (about 1,000 million mow) is the sum total of the cultivated acreages reported by the various hsien governments on the basis of their land tax records, and, as mentioned previously, farmers purposely understated the acreages under cultivation to avoid taxation.[4] There is, however, no evidence to suggest bias in the estimates of crop yields or of the percentages of the total cultivated area in the various crops.

Buck's survey of land utilization provides an independent set of data from which the output of the major crops can be computed.[5] Buck also started with figures on the total cultivated area in roughly the same territory covered by the Bureau. He divided this territory into eight agricultural areas on the basis of different types of farming. These areas are somewhat smaller than the territory covered by the Bureau's survey, but the excluded areas are such that, according to Buck, "their elevation put them outside the main areas of cultivation." [6] Buck's group collected data on the percentage of total cultivated area for each crop and the yield per unit area for the principal crops. Most important, Buck specifically recognized that the Bureau's figures understated the extent of the cultivated area, and he attempted to correct the bias. On the basis of his surveys, he made five different estimates for the cultivated area in approximately the same territory as the 22 provinces.[7] These estimates ranged from 1,160 million to 1,410 million mow. Even though he himself considered the highest estimate to be the most accurate, Buck used the second highest, 1,317 million mow, as his estimate.[8] This estimate of 1,317 million mow was also used in our preliminary estimate of food crops for the prewar period, to avoid the probable upward bias in Buck's highest estimate.[9] Some of Buck's samples were undoubtedly taken from the more accessible regions with high ratios of cultivated land to total area.[10]

[4] C. C. Chang, "Statistical Estimation of Agriculture by Hsien," *T'ung-chi yueh-pao* (Statistical Monthly), Nanking, July 1930, p. 8.

[5] For a detailed description of Buck's data, see *Food Crops*.

[6] Buck, *Land Utilization*, Vol. I, p. 24.

[7] Buck's surveys are Farm Survey, Locality Survey, Hsien Survey, Agricultural Survey, Food Survey, and Population Survey (*ibid.*, Vol. I, pp. viii–x; Vol. III, pp. 429–443). Data collected by the first five surveys were used in his estimates of cultivated area.

[8] *Ibid.*, Vol. I, pp. 165, 167. These 5 estimates are 1,410, 1,317, 1,251, 1,245, and 1,160 million mow.

[9] *Food Crops*, pp. 11–16.

[10] Buck, *Land Utilization*, Vol. I, p. ix.

The Bureau's estimate of the output of 14 principal crops for the 22 provinces has been compared in a previous study with the amount estimated on the basis of Buck's data.[11] The data on total cultivated area are the Bureau's underestimated figure of 998 million mow and Buck's second highest estimate of 1,317 million mow. The discrepancies between these two sets of data are striking for a number of crops. Buck's estimate of total output of the 14 crops is 55 per cent higher than the Bureau's; and for nonglutinous paddy rice, Buck's estimate is about 2.4 times the estimate of the Bureau. Since the output estimate is obtained by multiplying together the data on total cultivated area, percentages planted in different crops, and unit yields, each of the three sets of data should be examined separately. The difference between these two sets of estimates lies mainly in cultivated area, the percentage of total cultivated area planted in rice, and the unit yield of rice.

A detailed study of the Bureau's and Buck's data at the provincial level would be helpful in detecting the biases in the data on total cultivated area and would yield a more reliable estimate. Four sets of estimates of the cultivated area for each province were derived on the basis of Buck's locality data and his various corrective methods. The average of these four sets of estimates will be called Buck's estimate for the province.[12] Buck's figures by province were then compared with the corresponding figures estimated by the Bureau and a number of independent estimates by other scholars familiar with the cultivation conditions of the particular regions. For some of the provinces, one of the estimates is judged to be more reasonable than the others on the basis of known topography, climate, and other agricultural conditions. For others, an average of two or more plausible estimates is used. These provincial estimates are shown in Table 29.

Our estimated cultivated area for the 22 provinces of China proper is 1,277 million mow. This figure lies between Buck's second and third highest estimates. The estimated total cultivated acreage for the mainland for 1933, 1,534 million mow, is 85 million mow lower than the 1952 Communist figure of 1,619 million mow.[13]

The percentages of cultivated area devoted to seven principal crops and the yields per mow given in, or derived from, the Bureau's

[11] *Food Crops,* Table 2, p. 10.
[12] See Appendix A, Table A-1.
[13] *1954 Statistical Abstract,* p. 183.

Table 29

CULTIVATED AREA OF THE CHINESE MAINLAND BY PROVINCE, 1933
(million mow)

Province	Area
Anhwei	70.6
Chahar	18.8
Chekiang	51.1
Fukien	23.3
Honan	123.0
Hopei	118.0
Hunan	79.3
Hupeh	84.0
Kansu	29.2
Kiangsi	43.0
Kiangsu	92.0
Kwangsi	43.0
Kwangtung	50.0
Kweichow	22.4
Ningsia	2.5
Shansi	55.8
Shantung	120.0
Shensi	54.0
Suiyuan	24.0
Szechwan	129.0
Tsinghai	7.8
Yunnan	36.0
22 provinces, total	1,276.8
Sikang	4.6
Sinkiang	16.0
Manchuria	235.0
Mongolia	0.2
Tibet	0.7
Special municipalities and districts	0.4
Mainland total	1,533.7

SOURCE: Appendix A, Table A-1.

and Buck's studies are presented in Table 30. These seven principal food crops accounted for 86 per cent of the gross value of total food crops and soybeans produced in 1933.[14] The percentage and yield figures were reported by the field observers of the two surveys independently of the information on the total cultivated area.

As shown in Table 30, the most important discrepancies between the two sets of data occur in the figures on nonglutinous paddy rice. The differences in the figures for soybeans are also important, but soybeans accounted for less than 7 per cent of the total gross value

[14] For the gross value of these crops, see Appendix E, Table E-1.

Table 30

PERCENTAGE OF TOTAL CULTIVATED AREA IN PRINCIPAL CROPS AND UNIT YIELDS: A COMPARISON OF DATA IN THE TWO PREWAR ESTIMATES

Crop	Per cent of each crop in total cultivated area		Ratio of Bureau's to Buck's (per cent)	Unit yield (catties per mow)		Ratio of Bureau's to Buck's (per cent)
	Bureau's estimate[a]	Buck's estimate[b]		Bureau's estimate[a]	Buck's estimate[b]	
Nonglutinous paddy rice	24.9	35.5	70	343	436	79
Wheat	29.8	24.8	120	144	134	107
Millet	8.0	10.0	80	165	162	102
Kaoliang	7.6	7.8	97	182	164	111
Corn	6.9	6.2	111	183	190	96
Sweet potatoes	3.4	4.2	81	1,064	1,074	99
Soybeans	7.7	5.8	133	155	122	127

NOTES: [a] The Bureau's data are the averages for the 1931–37 period, computed from data given in *Agricultural Estimates*.

[b] The percentage and unit yield (most frequent yield) estimates are the weighted national averages of Buck's regional (Agricultural Area) figures, the weights being the regional crop acreages and output figures. Buck's data are for the 1929–33 period, given in *Land Utilization*, Vol. III, pp. 192–199, 209–210.

of food crops and soybeans in 1933.[15] Buck's data on both the percentage and yield for rice are substantially higher than those of the Bureau. Because of the importance of rice crops in agricultural production and the great difference in the data on rice in the Bureau's and Buck's estimates, a study of rice production by province is discussed in Appendix A. When the provincial data are examined, discrepancies not attributable to sampling errors are found in only a few provinces. In those provinces for which the differences between Buck's and the Bureau's data are small, the averages are used as our estimate. For some of the southwestern provinces, the two sets of data differ widely but are believed to represent observations in the high and low extremes, and averages are again taken to approximate the mean figures. In a few cases, either independent regional figures or data on neighboring provinces are used in place of, or in combination with, the two main sources of data. This study at the provincial level is then compared with a previous study of rice consumption in the important rice producing and consuming

[15] *Ibid.*

Table 31

PREWAR PRODUCTION OF RICE BY PROVINCE
(millions of piculs)

Provinces	Output
Major producing provinces	
Anhwei	72
Chekiang	98
Fukien	53
Hunan	244
Hupeh	126
Kiangsi	89
Kiangsu	132
Kwangsi	79
Kwangtung	194
Kweichow	48
Szechwan	311
Yunnan	75
Minor producing provinces	32
Total	1,553[a]
Other estimates	
Our preliminary study	1,519[b]
Buck's estimate	1,903[c]
Bureau's estimate	1,105[d]
Our estimate for 1933	1,600[e]

NOTES: [a] The estimates for the major and minor producing provinces are taken from Appendix A, Table A-4.

[b] The sum of our preliminary estimate of rice production for the 22 provinces (1,505 million piculs, given in *Food Crops*, p. 16) and the output of rice in Manchuria and Sinkiang (14 million piculs, given in Appendix A, Table A-4).

[c] Buck's data on the percentage of cultivated area in rice (35.5 per cent) and on the yield of rice (436 catties per mow, both given in Table 30) for the 22 provinces applied to our estimated cultivated area in the 22 provinces (1,277 million mow, given in Table 29), plus output in Manchuria and Sinkiang.

[d] The Bureau's data on the percentage of cultivated area in rice (24.9 per cent) and on the yield of rice (343 catties per mow, both given in Table 30) for the 22 provinces applied to our estimated cultivated area in the 22 provinces, plus output in Manchuria and Sinkiang.

[e] Our estimated rice output for 1933 is extrapolated from the estimated 1929–37 average annual output of 1,553 million piculs on the basis of an index number of rice production for 1933, that is, 103 with 1931–37 average = 100. This index number is computed from the Bureau's 1933 figure of rice output of 879 million piculs and its 1931–37 average figure of rice output of 854 million piculs (*Agricultural Estimates*, p. 41). Annual data for 1929–30 are not available, but the average of 1929–37 should not be significantly different from the average of 1931–37.

provinces.[16] The estimates obtained are consistent with the generally known patterns of rice surplus or deficiency. Several estimates of rice production are presented in Table 31. Our figures are quite

[16] *Food Crops.*

Table 32

PRODUCTION OF FOOD CROPS, 1952–57

	1957	1956	1955	1954	1953	1952
Production and consumption						
1. Total production (millions of piculs)	3,700	3,686	3,728	3,690	3,607	3,533
2. Consumption as percentage of total production	83.7	81.9	79.3	78.4	78.3	78.3
3. Consumption for food (millions of piculs)	3,097	3,019	2,956	2,893	2,825	2,766
4. Total population (million)	637	621	608	595	581	569
5. Per capita consumption (piculs)	486	486	486	486	486	486
Production by major categories (millions of piculs)						
Paddy rice	1,736	1,666	1,666	1,631	1,638	1,565
Wheat	473	501	488	535	422	417
Miscellaneous	1,053	1,080	1,170	1,133	1,165	1,176
Potatoes[a]	438	439	403	391	382	374

NOTES: [a] At grain-equivalent weight, that is, one-fourth natural weight.

Production and consumption

Line 1. The figure for 1957 is taken from *Great Ten Years*, p. 105. Figures for 1952–56 are estimated by the procedure described in the text.

Line 2. Percentages for calendar years are not available. The average percentage for two consecutive "grain years" is used. (A grain year begins on July 1 of a given calendar year and ends on June 30 of the next calendar year (*TCKT*, No. 19, October 1957, p. 31). For instance, the percentage for 1954 is the average of percentages for the grain years 1953–54 and 1954–55 (*ibid.*, p. 28). For lack of information, the percentage for 1952 is assumed to be the same as that for the grain year 1952–53, and for 1957, the same as that for 1956–57. Exports and food crops used for industrial and agricultural production are not included.

Line 3. The 1957 figure for total consumption of food crops used for food can be calculated from the 1957 figures given in lines 1 and 2.

Line 4. The figures for 1952–56 are the annual averages given in SSB, *Population Statistics*, p. 25. The figure for 1957 is the average of the year-end total for 1956, 629 million (*ibid.*, p. 24), and that for 1957, estimated at 646 million on the data given in *Great Ten Years*, pp. 6 and 9.

Line 5. Per capita consumption in 1957 is computed from the total consumption figure and the population figure given in line 4. It is assumed that per capita consumption remained constant for all the years from 1957 back to 1952.

Production by major categories

The figures for 1957 are taken from *Great Ten Years*, p. 105. Those for the other years are derived by splitting total production on the basis of the percentage of the major categories in the total, computed from the Communist data on crop production (*ibid.*). Total consumption figures for 1952–56 are derived from the per capita consumption figures and the population data for these years. Total production figures are then obtained by dividing the total consumption by the percentage given in line 2.

close to the preliminary estimate that we obtained by averaging Buck's and the Bureau's data at the national level—20 per cent lower than Buck's and 40 per cent higher than the Bureau's.

For the other principal food crops, the differences between the percentage and yield figures in Buck's and the Bureau's estimates are probably within the margin of sampling errors, which must be rather high for both sets of figures. It should be noted that the differences between these two sets of data are much greater for some of the minor crops. It is our belief that a combination of these data gives us a sample of a larger number of observations and is more representative of the true situation than either of the two original sources.

In combining the Bureau's and Buck's observations for crops other than rice, arithmetic averages are taken of the percentages of total cultivated area in each crop and of the yields of each crop. (For a group of minor crops, data on percentages and yields are available in only one source and are used without adjustment.) These averages are then applied to our estimate of the total cultivated area in the 22 provinces given in Table 29. Since the acreage and yield data (shown in Table 30) are for the years 1929–37, the output so computed is in the nature of an average annual output during this period. The 1933 output is then estimated from this figure on the basis of an index of output for each crop, computed on the Bureau's data for three years. Estimated output in the areas outside the 22 provinces is added to obtain the national total. The results are presented in Table 32.

ANIMAL PRODUCTS, 1933 [17]

The value added by livestock and poultry consists of their increase in number and weight, the number used, and special products, such as wool and eggs. Based on Buck's and the Bureau's data on the number of livestock and poultry per farm and the total number of farms, the total number of livestock and poultry is estimated. The number used as well as the quantities of special products produced during the year are derived from the total number on the basis of rates of utilization and unit output per animal. There is no indication of any significant change in numbers at this time; therefore the value added by increase in number and weight of livestock is assumed to be nil for 1933.

[17] See Appendixes A and E.

FOREST, FISHERY, AND MISCELLANEOUS PRODUCTS, 1933[18]

Of these three categories, estimates of physical output can be made only for fishery products and tung nuts. For timber and general forest products, the gross value of output has been given in Appendix E. The gross value of miscellaneous agricultural products is estimated at 5.8 per cent of the aggregate value of the four major categories of products. Estimates of the output of agricultural products by different categories are given in Table 33.

FOOD CROPS, 1952–57

The principle by which our estimate of food crop production is made was discussed in Chapter II. The detailed procedure of computation is given in the notes to Table 32.

OTHER PRODUCTS, 1952–57

With the exception of the 1957 data on hogs, Communist statistics on the output of plant products other than food crops, animal products, forest products, and fishery products are used directly. Some cases have been found where the statistical coverage is definitely incomplete. The adjustment we have made on Communist figures of hog products in 1957 was explained in Chapter II, and the computation is given in Appendix C. The output figures for all categories of agricultural products are presented in Table 33.

FARM PRICES, 1933[19]

Data on prices received by farmers in 1933 are from two major sources. Quotations of farm prices were collected by mail inquiries in 22 provinces of China proper in the 1930s, and some farm prices are available in *Industrial Handbooks of China*.[20] Fragmentary information is obtained from scattered sources as well. Our estimated farm prices for rice, wheat, millet, kaoliang, corn, soybeans, peanuts, rapeseed, sesame, cotton, and tobacco are national averages weighted by regional output. For a number of minor products, including potatoes, cottonseed, the hemp crops, sugar cane, sugar beets, tea, vegetables, fruits, animal products, tung nuts, and fishery products,

[18] *Ibid.*
[19] See Appendix B.
[20] *Survey;* Bureau of Foreign Trade, National Government, *Industrial Handbooks of China,* 1933–37.

Table 33

OUTPUT OF AGRICULTURAL PRODUCTS, 1933 AND 1952–57

Product	1933	1952	1953	1954	1955	1956	1957
Plant products (millions of piculs)							
Food crops	3,914	4,656	4,755	4,863	4,934	5,002	5,014
Paddy rice	1,600	1,565	1,638	1,631	1,666	1,666	1,736
Wheat	534	417	422	535	488	501	473
Miscellaneous food crops	1,169	1,176	1,165	1,133	1,170	1,080	1,053
Potatoes[a]	611	1,498	1,530	1,564	1,610	1,755	1,752
Soybeans	236	190	199	182	182	205	201
Oil-bearing crops							
Peanuts	67	46	43	55	59	67	51
Rapeseed	42	19	18	18	19	19	18
Sesame	19	11	11	11	12	9	6
Cottonseed	38	52	47	43	63	58	65
Plant fibers							
Cotton	19	26	24	21	30	29	33
Hemp crops	7	10	5	5	8	9	10
Other industrial crops							
Sugar cane	79	142	144	172	162	173	208
Sugar beets	5	10	10	20	32	33	30
Tobacco	20	11	11	12	15	21	13
Tea	5	2	2	2	2	2	2
Vegetables	300	—	—	—	—	—	—
Fruits	120	49	59	60	51	62	65
Animal products							
Increase in number of livestock (millions)							
Cattle	—	4.0	3.6	2.9	1.5	−0.9	−1.8
Horses	—	0.4	0.4	0.4	0.3	−0.1	−0.1
Mules	—	0.2	0.1	(b)	(b)	(b)	(b)
Donkeys	—	0.8	0.5	0.1	−0.5	−0.6	−0.1
Sheep and goats	—	10.1	9.8	6.1	5.1	6.8	3.8
Hogs	—	9.1	5.9	−4.1	−8.8	13.0	2.6
Livestock and poultry used (millions)							
Cattle	6.0	8.5	9.0	9.5	9.9	10.0	9.6
Horses	0.8	0.6	0.6	0.7	0.7	0.7	0.7
Mules	0.5	0.2	0.2	0.2	0.2	0.2	0.2
Donkeys	1.3	1.1	1.2	1.3	1.2	1.2	1.1
Sheep and goats	28.9	24.7	28.8	32.5	33.7	36.7	39.1
Hogs	56.2	71.8	76.9	81.4	70.3	67.2	69.0
Chickens	269	265	—	—	—	—	—
Ducks	50	64	—	—	—	—	—
Geese	8	10	—	—	—	—	—
Other animal products							
Eggs (billions)							
Chicken	12	12	—	—	—	—	—
Duck	2.0	2.6	—	—	—	—	—
Goose	0.3	0.4	—	—	—	—	—
Wool (thousands of piculs)	1,150	943	1,100	1,241	1,287	1,395	1,467
Silkworm cocoons (thousands of piculs)							
Domesticated	3,600	1,244	1,186	1,302	1,340	1,448	1,360
Wild	600	1,222	246	514	1,276	1,236	890
Forest products (millions of piculs)							
Tung nuts	10.7	11.8	10.4	10.4	10.4	10.4	10.7
Fishery products (millions of piculs)	29.4	33.3	38.0	45.9	50.4	52.9	62.4

NOTES: — Not available.
[a] Output of potatoes in natural weight.
[b] Less than 0.05 million.
SOURCES: See Appendix A for the output in 1933 and Appendix C for the output in 1952–57.

Table 34

FARM PRICES OF AGRICULTURAL PRODUCTS, 1933 AND 1952

Product	1933 price	1952 price
Plant products (yuan per picul)		
Paddy rice	3.5	5.3
Wheat	4.6	8.0
Miscellaneous food crops[a]	3.4	6.0
Potatoes	1.0	2.0
Soybeans	3.9	7.0
Peanuts	5.2	10.5
Rapeseed	5.9	11.0
Sesame	8.0	14.4
Cottonseed	2.0	3.6
Cotton	31.4	84.9
Hemp crops	20.2	40.0
Sugar cane	0.6	1.0
Sugar beets	0.6	2.0
Tobacco	17.0	34.6
Tea	25.8	70.0
Animal products (yuan per head)[b]		
Cattle	50.0 (35.0)	75.0 (52.5)
Horses	48.0 (19.2)	110.0 (44.0)
Mules	70.0 (28.0)	160.0 (64.0)
Donkeys	26.0 (10.4)	59.2 (23.7)
Sheep and goats	3.5	8.0
Hogs	17.4	46.0
Chickens	0.4	1.1
Ducks	0.5	1.3
Geese	1.1	2.9
Eggs (yuan per thousand)		
Chicken	15.0	30.0
Duck	20.0	40.0
Goose	20.0	40.0
Wool (yuan per picul)	22.0	135.0
Silkworm cocoons (yuan per picul)		
Domesticated	30.0	65.0
Wild	20.0	43.6
Forest products (yuan per picul)		
Tung nuts	4.0	7.6
Fishery products (yuan per picul)	14.6	19.0

NOTES: [a] Including millet, kaoliang, corn, barley, glutinous rice, peas, broad beans, proso millet, mung beans, black beans, buckwheat, and oats.

[b] Prices in parentheses are "discount prices." See Appendix B.

SOURCES: See Appendixes B and D.

the national prices are simply the arithmetic averages of scattered local farm prices. The results are presented in Table 34.

Available wholesale prices of five agricultural products in four leading cities in different parts of the mainland are given in Table

35, together with our estimates of farm prices for the provinces in which the four cities are located. Except in Hupeh, where the wholesale price of paddy rice seems to be quite high in relation to the farm price, wholesale prices of these products are from 10 to 40 per cent higher than farm prices. This differential is reasonable and supports our estimates.

FARM PRICES, 1952

Data on prices received by farmers in 1952 are collected mainly from various mainland newspapers and periodicals. Local or regional prices are then averaged to get the prices for the nation as a whole. For a number of important crops, such as rice, wheat, and cotton, detailed regional prices are available, and average national prices are computed with the prewar regional output as weights. Prices of millet, kaoliang, corn, soybeans, cottonseed, and tung nuts are either completely unavailable or too meager to be used to derive the national averages. The farm prices of these products are derived indirectly from their 1952 wholesale prices or from the

Table 35

COMPARISON OF FARM PRICES AND WHOLESALE PRICES, 1933
(yuan per picul)

Product	Farm price[a]	Province	Wholesale price[b]	City	Ratio of wholesale price to farm price (per cent)
Paddy rice	3.5	Hupeh	6.4	Hankow	183
	3.5	Kiangsu	4.0	Nanking	114
	6.4	Hopei	8.7	Tientsin	136
Wheat	4.3	Shantung	4.8	Tsingtao	112
	4.5	Hupeh	5.6	Hankow	124
Soybeans	4.0	Shantung	5.1	Tsingtao	128
	4.9	Hupeh	6.7	Hankow	137
Corn	3.6	Hopei	5.0	Tientsin	139
Millet	5.1	Hopei	6.9	Tientsin	135

NOTES: [a] Farm prices are our estimated provincial average prices. See Appendix B.

[b] Wholesale prices are the annual average prices for each city. For Hankow, Nanking, and Tsingtao: Ministry of Industry, National Government, *Shih-yeh t'ung-chi tzu-liao* (Industrial Statistical Data), Nanking, Vol. 1, No. 6, September 1936. For Tientsin: Nankai Institute of Economics, *Quarterly Journal of Economics and Statistics*, Tientsin, Vol. 2, No. 4, December 1933.

ratios of prewar farm prices to other products. The detailed methods used in deriving individual prices are explained in Appendix D; the results are presented in Table 34.

Table 34 shows that farm prices in 1952 yuan are generally higher than in 1933 yuan, and that the increases differ among the various groups of agricultural products. The index of farm prices in 1952 with 1933 = 100, computed by Fisher's Ideal Index, is 183.[21] This index number is supported by a Communist statement that the farm prices in the early 1950s were not yet twice as high as those of the prewar years.[22]

FARM PRICES, 1957

Quotations of farm prices for 1957 are even more scarce than for 1952. No attempt has been made to estimate the prices of individual products, but two different indexes of 1957 prices are available, both with 1952 as the base year. The government procurement price index of agricultural products for 1957 is 122.4.[23] The second index is derived from figures on the total value of agricultural production in an article by Po I-po, the Communist Vice Premier and Chairman of the State Economic Commission, who gave the gross value of agricultural production in 1957 at 64.87 billion in 1957 prices and 60.35 billion in 1952 prices.[24] The price index in 1957 is therefore 107.5 with 1952 as 100. This index indicates that government procurement prices may not have been used for products consumed by farm households and that the prices of agricultural products not under the government procurement program rose less than those covered in the program. As Po's index presumably includes all agricultural products, it is used to convert our estimated gross value of agricultural output in 1952 prices to 1957 prices. A second estimate of the gross value of agricultural production for 1957 is given at 53.70 billion 1957 yuan.[25] However, no price index can be derived

[21] See Appendix I, Table I-1.

[22] Tien Chi, "Several Problems in the Revision of Constant 1952 Industrial Prices," *TCKT,* No. 1, January 1957, p. 15. The original text indicates that the 1952 farm prices were less than double those of 1936. There were no great differences in farm prices between 1933 and 1936.

[23] *People's Daily,* April 14, 1959.

[24] Po I-po, "Report on the Draft 1958 National Economic Plan," *HHPYK,* No. 5, March 1958, pp. 13, 15.

[25] *Great Ten Years,* p. 14.

from this figure on the basis of 1952 prices because of the difference in coverage. The former figure does not include the value of agricultural subsidiary production.[26]

Deductible Costs of Production, Depreciation, and Value Added[27]

The percentage of the gross value of production attributable to deductible costs for each category of agricultural products is estimated and applied to the corresponding gross value of production to arrive at the costs in money terms. Deductible costs include expenses for seeds, feeds, fertilizers, repairs of farm buildings, and tools. Scattered information is available for 1933. For plant products, these expenses are estimated at 8 per cent of the gross value. The same percentage is also assumed to be applicable to miscellaneous products. Feed expenses for livestock and poultry are estimated at 10 per cent of the gross value of animals. Deductible costs of the gross value of production of forest and fishery products are assumed to be 3 per cent and 5 per cent, respectively.

For the postwar years, the costs of plant production are estimated at 11 per cent of the gross value of plant products during 1953–57. The same percentage is also used to derive the costs of producing miscellaneous agricultural products. For animal, forest, and fishery products, the prewar percentages are used. Depreciation in agricultural production is assumed to be 2 per cent of the gross value of production for both 1933 and 1952–57.

The output figures for each year covered in this study are multiplied by both the 1933 and 1952 prices to arrive at the gross value of production in terms of the two price weights. The net value added by agricultural production is obtained by deducting production costs and depreciation charges from the gross value. The results are presented in Table 36.

FACTORIES

As defined in this study, factories are manufacturing establishments using power-driven machinery, regardless of the number of workers employed. This is essentially the definition used in the most important sources of statistical data on which our estimate of value

[26] *Ibid.*, note to Table, p. 14.
[27] See Appendix E.

Table 36

VALUE ADDED BY AGRICULTURE, 1933 AND 1952–57

	1933	1952	1953	1954	1955	1956	1957	1933	1952	1953	1954	1955	1956	1957
	(billions of 1933 yuan)							(billions of 1952 yuan)						
Gross value of output														
Plant products	17.12	16.54	16.70	17.10	17.67	17.79	17.76	29.81	29.57	29.79	30.45	31.71	32.06	32.04
Animal products	1.84	2.59	2.63	2.53	2.18	2.40	2.23	4.48	6.11	6.22	5.98	5.11	5.83	5.51
Forest products	0.62	0.60	0.71	0.80	0.79	0.79	0.93	1.29	1.19	1.49	1.73	1.68	1.69	2.04
Fishery products	0.43	0.49	0.55	0.67	0.74	0.77	0.91	0.56	0.63	0.72	0.87	0.96	1.00	1.18
Miscellaneous products	1.16	1.17	1.19	1.22	1.24	1.26	1.27	2.10	2.18	2.22	2.26	2.29	2.35	2.36
Total	21.17	21.38	21.78	22.32	22.62	23.01	23.10	38.24	39.68	40.44	41.30	41.76	42.94	43.15
Deductible costs of production														
Plant products	1.39	1.84	1.85	1.90	1.96	1.97	1.97	2.41	3.28	3.31	3.38	3.52	3.56	3.56
Animal products	0.47	0.55	0.59	0.62	0.61	0.61	0.60	0.97	1.10	1.17	1.25	1.20	1.19	1.19
Forest products	0.02	0.02	0.02	0.02	0.02	0.02	0.03	0.04	0.04	0.04	0.05	0.05	0.05	0.06
Fishery products	0.02	0.02	0.03	0.03	0.04	0.04	0.04	0.03	0.03	0.04	0.04	0.05	0.05	0.06
Miscellaneous products	0.09	0.13	0.13	0.14	0.14	0.14	0.14	0.17	0.24	0.25	0.25	0.25	0.26	0.26
Total	1.99	2.56	2.62	2.72	2.77	2.79	2.79	3.62	4.69	4.81	4.97	5.08	5.11	5.13
Gross value added														
Plant products	15.73	14.70	14.85	15.20	15.71	15.82	15.79	27.40	26.29	26.48	27.07	28.19	28.50	28.48
Animal products	1.37	2.04	2.04	1.90	1.57	1.78	1.63	3.51	5.01	5.04	4.73	3.91	4.64	4.32
Forest products	0.60	0.58	0.69	0.78	0.76	0.77	0.90	1.25	1.15	1.45	1.68	1.63	1.64	1.98
Fishery products	0.41	0.46	0.53	0.64	0.70	0.73	0.86	0.53	0.60	0.68	0.83	0.91	0.95	1.13
Miscellaneous products	1.07	1.04	1.06	1.09	1.10	1.12	1.13	1.93	1.93	1.97	2.01	2.04	2.09	2.10
Total	19.18	18.82	19.16	19.60	19.84	20.22	20.32	34.62	34.99	35.63	36.32	36.68	37.82	38.02
Depreciation	0.42	0.43	0.44	0.45	0.45	0.46	0.46	0.77	0.79	0.81	0.83	0.84	0.86	0.86
Net value added	18.76	18.39	18.73	19.16	19.39	19.76	19.85	33.86	34.19	34.82	35.50	35.84	36.97	37.16

SOURCE: Appendix E.

Table 37

VALUE ADDED BY FACTORIES, 1933 AND 1952–57
(billions of yuan)

	1933	1952	1953	1954	1955	1956	1957
In 1933 prices							
Gross output	2.65	5.27	6.53	7.46	7.85	10.36	11.07
Producers' goods	0.50	1.63	2.27	2.75	3.29	4.89	5.78
Consumers' goods	2.15	3.64	4.26	4.71	4.56	5.47	5.29
Gross value added	0.74	1.35	1.72	1.97	2.09	2.87	3.12
Producers' goods	0.18	0.54	0.76	0.91	1.08	1.63	1.92
Consumers' goods	0.56	0.81	0.96	1.06	1.01	1.24	1.20
Depreciation	0.11	0.26	0.33	0.37	0.39	0.52	0.55
Net value added	0.63	1.09	1.39	1.60	1.70	2.35	2.57
In 1952 prices							
Gross output	9.46	20.27	25.54	29.40	31.56	42.54	46.32
Producers' goods	2.40	8.08	11.26	13.63	16.29	24.21	28.59
Consumers' goods	7.06	12.19	14.28	15.77	15.27	18.33	17.73
Gross value added	3.71	7.46	9.56	11.05	11.94	16.64	18.31
Producers' goods	0.94	3.55	4.93	5.93	7.06	10.65	12.50
Consumers' goods	2.76	3.91	4.63	5.12	4.88	5.99	5.81
Depreciation	0.38	1.01	1.28	1.47	1.58	2.13	2.32
Producers' goods	0.10	0.40	0.56	0.68	0.81	1.21	1.43
Consumers' goods	0.28	0.61	0.71	0.79	0.76	0.92	0.89
Net value added	3.33	6.45	8.28	9.58	10.36	14.51	15.99
Producers' goods	0.84	3.15	4.37	5.25	6.25	9.44	11.07
Consumers' goods	2.48	3.30	3.92	4.33	4.12	5.07	4.92

added by factories is based.[28] Specifically, the scope of the activities covered in this sector can be seen from the list of products in Table 38.

Table 37 summarizes the estimates of net value added by factories for 1933 and 1952–57, in 1933 and 1952 prices. For convenience of discussion, only the estimates of net value added by factories and other nonagricultural sectors in constant 1933 and 1952 prices are presented in this chapter. The estimates in 1957 prices are explained in Appendix I.

1933

Gross value of output and number of workers in factories covering 61 product groups have been estimated separately for the following three groups: Chinese-owned factories in China proper, foreign-owned factories in China proper, and factories in Manchuria.[29] The national totals are given in Table 38. For later com-

[28] See Appendix F, Table F-2. The classification of manufacturing activities is essentially the same as the standard classification set out in United Nations Statistical Office, *International Standard Industrial Classification of All Economic Activities,* Statistical Papers, Series M, No. 4, Lake Success, New York, 1949.

[29] See Appendix F.

Table 38

GROSS VALUE OF OUTPUT AND GROSS VALUE ADDED BY FACTORIES, 1933
(millions of 1933 yuan)

Products	Gross value of output	Deductible cost	Gross value added
Producers' goods			
Lumber	21.6	19.6	2.0
Machinery, including transportation equipment			
Machine parts	6.3	4.3	2.0
Machine manufacture and repair	36.8	19.8	17.0
Cart and carriage manufacture and repair	31.5	18.5	13.0
Ship and boat building and repair	16.0	10.0	6.0
Others	1.8	1.0	0.8
Ferrous metals and metal products			
Pig iron	30.9	12.4	18.5
Steel	2.5[a]	1.1	1.4
Metal products	15.5	11.0	4.5
Small electrical appliances	2.1[a]	1.2	0.9
Stone, clay, and glass products			
Bricks and shingles	8.3	3.9	4.4
Glass and glass products	10.7	5.0	5.7
Cement	27.1	13.2	13.9
Others	9.7	5.4	4.3
Chemicals and chemical products			
Chemicals	17.3	7.4	9.9
Coke	5.9	4.6	1.3
Dyes and paints	17.7	10.2	7.5
Nonedible oils	45.2	35.4	9.8
Other chemical products	1.5	1.3	0.2
Textile products			
Ginned cotton	15.3	14.1	1.2
Gunny sacks	1.6	1.2	0.4
Leather	46.1	33.2	12.9
Paper, paper products, and printing			
Paper	14.7	8.0	6.7
Printing	71.4	43.6	27.8
Metal coins	41.0	30.8	10.2
Total producers' goods	498.5	316.2	182.3
Consumers' goods			
Wood products	2.6	1.8	0.8
Metal products	15.6	11.0	4.6
Small electrical appliances	19.2	11.1	8.1
Chinaware and pottery	2.2	1.0	1.2
Chemicals and chemical products			
Matches	37.3	17.5	19.8
Soap and paraffin products	15.2	10.5	4.7
Enamel	6.9	4.7	2.2
Plastic products	4.1	2.8	1.3
Pharmaceutical products	13.4	11.9	1.5
Cosmetics	9.4	5.7	3.7
Other chemical products	0.6	0.5	0.1

(Continued)

Table 38 (continued)

Products	Gross value of output	Deductible cost	Gross value added
Textile products			
Cotton yarn	520.1	386.2	133.9
Cotton cloth	260.4	198.1	62.3
Silk	44.9	34.0	10.9
Silk piece goods	79.5	47.1	32.4
Woolen textiles	26.2	17.6	8.6
Linen and hemp products	1.1	0.9	0.2
Dyed cloth	23.7	17.3	6.4
Clothing and attire	85.5	52.3	33.2
Leather and rubber products			
Rubber footwear	33.7	24.6	9.1
Other rubber products	4.2	3.0	1.2
Glue	0.2	0.1	0.1
Leather products	0.3	0.2	0.1
Food products			
Milled rice and other husked grain	172.4	160.0	12.4
Wheat flour	194.9	175.9	19.0
Edible vegetable oils	155.5	139.8	15.7
Tea	8.9	8.1	0.8
Soybean sauce	2.0	1.8	0.2
Table salt	17.2	3.3	13.9
Sugar	7.7	7.4	0.3
Egg products	30.7	28.2	2.5
Nonalcoholic beverages	13.4	8.2	5.2
Ice	1.6	0.8	0.8
Other food products	29.8	23.4	6.4
Tobacco products, wine, and liquor			
Tobacco products	267.9	142.1	125.8
Wine and liquor	9.9	8.6	1.3
Paper products	11.3	7.9	3.4
Miscellaneous	17.1	10.2	6.9
Total consumers' goods	2,146.6	1,585.6	561.0
Total	2,645.1	1,901.8	743.3

NOTE: [a] The breakdown of metal products and small electrical appliances into producers' goods and consumers' goods is based on D. K. Lieu, *Industry Survey*. According to this survey, about 50 per cent of the total gross value of metal products and 10 per cent of the gross value of small electrical appliances belong to the producers' goods category, and the rest to the consumers' goods category. Total deductible costs and gross value added are split between the two groups by the same ratio.

SOURCE: Computed from data in Appendix F, Tables F-1 and F-4.

parisons with Communist data, these products are also grouped into producers' and consumers' goods according to the Communist system of classification.[30]

[30] The detailed classification adopted officially by the Communists is not available. The system used here is based mainly on that given in Li Hui-hung, Shung Chi-ren, and Wang Hua-hsin, "The Problem of Classifying Light and Heavy Industries," *TCKT*, No. 18, September 1957, pp. 13–15; and discussions in SSB, "The Problem of Classifying Producers' and Consumers' Goods," *TCKT*, No. 3, February 1957, pp. 1–4. A comparison of the figures of gross output of producers' and consumers' goods for 1953 and 1955, given in Li Hui-hung, *et al.*, *op. cit.*, and the official figures in *Great*

Gross value added is obtained by deducting the costs of raw materials, fuels and electricity, and miscellaneous expenses from the gross value of output. The total deductions are shown in Table 38. Depreciation is roughly estimated at 105 million yuan, 4 per cent of the gross value of output for factories as a whole in 1933. Gross value added by factories is 739 million yuan; therefore, net value added is 634 million yuan.

In principle, the gross value of output in 1952 prices is derived by multiplying the physical output in 1933 by the 1952 market price for each product. The gross value added is derived by deducting 1933 nonprimary input, weighted by the 1952 price, from the gross value of output for each product. This procedure, however, can be used for only 6 producers' goods and 10 consumers' goods for which data on 1952 prices are available. The 6 producers' goods are pig iron, steel, cement, coke, machinery, and gunny sacks; the 10 consumers' goods are cotton yarn, cotton cloth, silk, silk piece goods, woolen textiles, sugar, milled rice, wheat flour, edible vegetable oils, and cigarettes.

For the sake of convenience, gross value of output and gross value added for the 6 producers' goods and 10 consumers' goods and for "other" producers' and consumers' goods are given as shown below.

	Billions of 1952 yuan
Gross value of output	
6 producers' goods	0.72
10 consumers' goods	5.62
"other" producers' goods	1.68
"other" consumers' goods	1.44
Total gross value of output	9.46
Gross value added	
6 producers' goods	0.34
10 consumers' goods	2.08
"other" producers' goods	0.61
"other" consumers' goods	0.68
Total gross value added	3.71
Less: Depreciation (4%)	
Total net value added	3.33

Ten Years, p. 76, shows that the two sets of 1952 figures are identical and the 1955 figures are very close. Any differences between the classification used here and the Communist official system must, therefore, be very small.

The gross value of output of these 16 products was 70 per cent of the total gross value of output, and their gross value added was 65 per cent of the total gross value added.[31] This calculation yields the following implicit price deflators: For gross value of output and gross value added by producers' goods, the index numbers are 482 and 520 per cent for 1952 with 1933 as 100. For gross value of output and gross value added by consumers' goods, the index numbers are 329 and 497 per cent.[32]

For other producers' and consumers' goods, for which data on 1952 prices are unavailable, gross values of output in 1933 prices are first derived at 0.35 and 0.44 billion yuan by deducting the figures for the 6 producers' goods and 10 consumers' goods from the totals (0.50 and 2.15 billion yuan).[33] Gross value added is similarly derived. It was assumed that prices for other producers' and consumers' goods increased from 1933 to 1952 in proportion to prices for the 6 producers' and 10 consumers' goods.

1952–57

The 1952–57 estimates of net value added by factories are given in Table 37. They were derived from estimating gross output and value added on the basis of available data on output and prices of individual products and total gross value of industrial production. We have made an attempt to correct the upward bias noted in Chapter II.

ESTIMATE OF VALUE ADDED BY FACTORIES DERIVED FROM UNCORRECTED COMMUNIST DATA

PRODUCTS FOR WHICH DETAILED INFORMATION IS AVAILABLE. For 12 groups of producers' goods and 14 groups of consumers' goods, data on value of output are available, or data on output and prices have been published by the Communists from which value of output can be computed.[34] The results are given in Table 39 together with the comparable items for 1933.

Data are almost entirely lacking on deductible costs of production, which are necessary for the calculation of gross value added in the 26 product groups. Clearly, it would be unsatisfactory to use

[31] For details of the calculations, see Appendix F, Table F-5.
[32] The price index numbers given here are *not* those given in Chapter II, which are the geometric mean of the index numbers given here and those given in Table 42.
[33] See Appendix F, Table F-7.
[34] For details, see Appendix F under Value Added in 26 Product Groups, 1952–57.

Table 39

GROSS VALUE OF OUTPUT AND VALUE ADDED BY 26 FACTORY PRODUCTS, 1933 AND 1952–57

	Gross value of output[a]							Gross value added[a]						
	1933	1952	1953	1954	1955	1956	1957	1933	1952	1953	1954	1955	1956	1957
Producers' goods	221	5,901	7,868	9,445	11,140	17,695	19,923	105	2,769	3,711	4,422	5,208	8,307	9,376
Pig iron	31	380	435	592	759	955	1,180	18	152	174	237	304	382	472
Steel	3	809	1,064	1,335	1,701	2,679	3,210	1	486	639	801	1,021	1,607	1,926
Rolled steel	—	1,312	1,754	1,965	2,505	3,921	4,262	—	485	649	727	927	1,451	1,577
Machinery	92	1,401	2,157	2,643	3,030	5,764	6,177	39	644	992	1,216	1,394	2,651	2,841
Cement	27	243	330	391	383	543	583	14	90	122	145	142	201	216
Sheet glass	11	63	72	93	86	91	136	6	36	41	53	49	52	78
Other construction materials	18	315	518	510	540	856	907	9	239	393	388	410	650	689
Coke	6	126	158	200	256	401	480	1	65	82	104	133	209	249
Chemicals	17	298	360	479	560	702	824	10	110	133	177	207	260	305
Paper	15	655	711	844	983	1,318	1,663	7	321	348	414	482	646	815
Gunny sacks	2	135	118	118	105	157	156	(*)	90	79	79	70	105	105
Auto tires	—	164	191	275	232	307	345	—	49	57	82	70	92	103
Consumers' goods	1,726	9,054	10,606	11,706	11,338	13,612	13,158	472	2,968	3,528	3,900	3,704	4,569	4,442
Cotton yarn	520	2,605	2,955	3,311	2,857	3,777	3,348	134	1,329	1,507	1,688	1,457	1,926	1,708
Cotton cloth	260	2,365	2,678	3,002	2,592	3,426	3,038	62	449	509	570	492	651	577
Silk	45	199	246	253	292	369	294	11	58	72	73	85	107	85
Silk piece goods	80	116	133	141	169	214	190	32	29	33	35	42	53	47
Woolen textiles	26	157	238	261	317	458	544	9	75	114	125	152	220	261
Grass cloth	1	2	4	4	5	5	6	(*)	1	1	1	2	2	2
Clothing and knitted goods	86	84	130	157	182	206	183	33	39	60	72	84	95	84
Sugar	8	274	328	382	451	570	614	(*)	134	161	187	221	279	301
Milled rice	12	310	330	360	370	390	410	1	22	23	25	26	27	29
Wheat flour	195	927	1,051	1,153	1,404	1,336	1,308	19	102	116	127	154	147	144
Edible vegetable oils	156	360	371	389	425	392	403	16	65	67	70	76	71	73
Cigarettes	267	1,298	1,740	1,827	1,748	1,914	2,183	126	545	731	767	734	804	917
Matches	37	109	96	124	136	139	123	20	39	35	45	49	50	44
Rubber footwear	34	247	305	343	390	414	515	9	81	101	113	129	137	170
Total producers' and consumers' goods	1,947	14,955	18,474	21,151	22,478	31,307	33,081	577	5,737	7,239	8,322	8,912	12,876	13,818

NOTES: — No comparable data on these items can be segregated from the industrial data for 1933.
(*) Less than 0.5 million yuan.
[a] 1933 in millions of 1933 yuan, 1952–57 in millions of 1952 yuan.
SOURCE: Appendix F.

the 1933 proportions implied in Table 38, for substantial changes must have taken place in the industrial structure and price relationships.

For most of the producers' goods, cost deductions of comparable industries in Manchuria for 1939 are adjusted for changes in relative prices of output and nonprimary input. For most of the consumers' goods, cost deductions of comparable industries in North China in 1943 are used, or a combination of these data with items in the adjusted 1939 Manchuria cost deductions. For the rest, deductions are based upon various applicable sources. Gross values added by these products can then be easily calculated and are given in Table 39, together with the corresponding information for 1933.[35]

TOTAL GROSS VALUE OF FACTORY OUTPUT. The Communists have not released a figure on the total value of the industries covered in Table 38. The 26 items of producers' and consumers' goods given in Table 39 for 1952–57 fall short of the total factory output in those years. To estimate the remainder, we must derive the total gross output of all factories. We first take the Communist estimates of the value of industrial production of producers' and consumers' goods industries for 1952–57. Although industrial production has not been precisely defined, we know that it includes the gross value of output of mining, utilities, lumbering, and part of the fishery industry.[36] Because these industries do not come under manufacturing as we define it, their gross value of output is deducted from the value of industrial production.

The Communist figure on the value of industrial production is gross in the sense that interenterprise purchases for production are counted twice, but net in that intra-enterprise uses of raw materials or intermediate products for further production in the same enterprise are not counted twice. At least two important intermediate products, pig iron and cotton yarn, are usually consumed in the enterprise in which they were produced. In order to compare the Communist figure on industrial production with the gross value figures given in Table 39, the gross value of output of pig iron and part of the cotton yarn output are added to the Communist figures of industrial production to obtain the gross value of output of producers' goods and consumers' goods in factories for 1952–57. The results are presented in Table 40.

[35] For details, see Appendix F under Costs of Production for 22 Product Groups, 1952–57.

[36] See Appendix F under Gross Value of Output of All Factories.

Table 40

GROSS VALUE OF FACTORY OUTPUT, PRODUCERS' AND CONSUMERS' GOODS, 1952–57
(billions of 1952 yuan)

	1952	1953	1954	1955	1956	1957
Gross value of industrial production, producers' goods	10.73	14.67	17.58	20.58	29.17	34.33
Deduct:						
Modern mining, producers' goods sector	1.27	1.43	1.73	2.02	2.49	2.92
Electric power	0.44	0.55	0.66	0.74	0.99	1.16
Lumber	0.08	0.18	0.27	0.37	0.36	0.56
Handicraft workshop output	1.24	1.69	1.88	1.92	2.08	2.28
Add: Pig iron	0.38	0.44	0.59	0.76	0.96	1.18
Equals: Gross value of manufactured producers' goods	8.08	11.26	13.63	16.29	24.21	28.59
Gross value of industrial production, consumers' goods	16.28	20.91	23.94	24.17	29.50	30.69
Deduct:						
Modern mining: salt	0.61	0.42	0.57	1.02	0.67	1.12
Water supply and gas	0.25	0.28	0.31	0.33	0.36	0.45
Natural fishery products	0.49	0.56	0.68	0.75	0.78	0.92
Handicraft workshop output	3.72	5.08	5.64	5.75	6.24	6.83
Add: Part of cotton yarn	0.98	1.13	1.31	1.21	1.60	1.42
Equals: Gross value of manufactured consumers' goods	12.19	15.70	18.05	17.53	23.05	22.79
Gross value of factory output	20.27	26.96	31.68	33.82	47.26	51.38

SOURCE: Appendix F, under Gross Value of Output of All Factories.

Not all the factories producing pig iron are parts of steel mills. Errors in not having made allowances for the independent pig iron factories in this estimate should be balanced by the errors introduced because of the absence of any adjustment for possible dependency in the manufacture of other goods. No adjustment is made for the intra-enterprise relationship between steel products and steel because there is a fairly clear indication that the gross values of both are included in the Communist figure on the value of industrial production.

PRODUCTS FOR WHICH DETAILED INFORMATION IS NOT AVAILABLE. When the gross value of factories as a whole and the gross value of the 26 product groups are known, the gross value of products for which detailed information is not available can be calculated as a residual. The results are shown in Table 41. The part of the 1952–57 output under consideration roughly corresponds to products in Ta-

Table 41

RESIDUAL GROSS VALUE OF PRODUCERS' AND CONSUMERS' GOODS, 1952–57
(billions of 1952 yuan)

	1952	1953	1954	1955	1956	1957
Producers' goods						
Total gross value of factory output	8.08	11.26	13.63	16.29	24.21	28.59
Deduct: gross value of identified goods	5.90	7.87	9.44	11.14	17.69	19.92
Equals: gross value of unidentified producers' goods	2.18	3.39	4.19	5.15	6.52	8.67
Unidentified portion as percentage of total	27	30	31	32	27	30
Consumers' goods						
Total gross value of factory output	12.19	15.70	18.05	17.53	23.05	22.79
Deduct: gross value of identified goods	9.05	10.60	11.71	11.34	13.61	13.16
Equals: gross value of unidentified consumers' goods	3.14	5.10	6.34	6.19	9.44	9.63
Unidentified portion as percentage of total	26	32	35	35	41	42

SOURCES: Tables 39 and 40.

ble 38 not covered in Table 39. The producers' goods in this group are lumber, certain metal products, some small electrical appliances, dyes and paints, nonedible oils and other chemical products, ginned cotton, printing, and leather. The consumers' goods are wood products, certain metal products, some electrical appliances, pottery and chinaware, soap and paraffin products, enamel, cosmetics, plastics, pharmaceuticals and other chemical products, dyed cloth, leather products, glue, rubber products other than footwear, food products (except sugar, milled rice, wheat flour, and edible vegetable oils), tobacco (except cigarettes), wine and liquor, paper products, and miscellaneous. The gross value and gross value added by these 1933 products are as follows:

	Gross value (billions of 1952 yuan)	Gross value added (billions of 1952 yuan)	Ratio of gross value added to gross value (per cent)
Producers' goods	1.37	0.50	36
Consumers' goods	1.41	0.43	30

These figures are derived by deducting the corresponding figures in 1933 prices for the identified portion given in Table 39 from the total figures given in Table 38. The residuals are then multiplied by the price indexes for gross value of output and gross value added in 1952, with 1933 as 100, to arrive at estimates in 1952 prices.[37]

In the absence of a better alternative, we apply the ratios of gross value added to gross value of output to the gross values of the two groups of unidentified products for 1952–57 in 1952 prices. The estimates of gross value added by the unidentified products are as follows:

	1952	1953	1954	1955	1956	1957
	(billions of 1952 yuan)					
Producers' goods	0.78	1.22	1.51	1.85	2.34	3.12
Consumers' goods	0.94	1.53	1.90	1.86	2.83	2.89

Table 42

NET VALUE ADDED BY FACTORIES, 1952–57
(billions of yuan)

	1952	1953	1954	1955	1956	1957
In 1933 prices						
Gross value of output	5.27	6.96	8.14	8.52	11.77	12.58
Producers' goods	1.63	2.27	2.75	3.29	4.89	5.78
Consumers' goods	3.64	4.69	5.39	5.23	6.88	6.80
Gross value added	1.35	1.81	2.11	2.23	3.16	3.44
Producers' goods	0.54	0.76	0.91	1.08	1.63	1.92
Consumers' goods	0.81	1.05	1.20	1.15	1.53	1.52
Depreciation	0.26	0.35	0.41	0.43	0.59	0.63
Net value added	1.09	1.46	1.70	1.80	2.57	2.81
In 1952 prices						
Gross value of output	20.27	26.96	31.68	33.82	47.26	51.38
Producers' goods	8.08	11.26	13.63	16.29	24.21	28.59
Consumers' goods	12.19	15.70	18.05	17.53	23.05	22.79
Gross value added	7.46	9.99	11.73	12.62	18.05	19.83
Producers' goods	3.55	4.93	5.93	7.06	10.65	12.50
Consumers' goods	3.91	5.06	5.80	5.56	7.40	7.33
Depreciation	1.01	1.35	1.58	1.69	2.36	2.57
Net value added	6.45	8.64	10.15	10.93	15.69	17.26

SOURCES: See Tables 39, 40, and 41. Figures are based on uncorrected Communist data.

SUMMARY. The estimate of gross value added by factories in 1952–57 in 1952 prices is summarized in Table 42. There is very little information on capital consumption. We estimate it at 5 per

[37] See Appendix F, Table F-15.

cent of gross value of output on the basis of fragmentary data.[38] Estimates of net value added are obtained by deducting the rough estimates of depreciation from gross value added.

The derivation of net value added for 1952–57 in 1933 prices follows the same approach used for deriving the 1933 estimate in 1952 prices. For 6 producers' goods and 10 consumers' goods, gross value added in 1933 prices is calculated on the basis of the output and nonprimary input of these products in 1952–57 and their 1933 market prices. The price indexes obtained from this calculation for producers' goods are 495 per cent for the gross value of output and 652 per cent for the gross value added for 1952, with 1933 as 100. The corresponding figures for consumers' goods are 335 and 483 per cent.[39]

For the other products in the producers' and consumers' goods industries, gross value and gross value added are derived on the assumption that the prices increased from 1933 to 1952 in proportion to prices for the 6 producers' goods and 10 consumers' goods over the same period. Estimates of net value added are the residuals obtained by allowing 5 per cent of gross value of output for depreciation.

THE AUTHORS' ESTIMATE OF VALUE ADDED BY FACTORIES

As pointed out in Chapter II, the rather high proportion of unidentified goods in the total gross value of consumers' goods output in the postwar years in relation to 1933 indicates a considerable amount of padding in these figures. The estimate of gross value of the unidentified portion of consumers' goods for 1952–57 given in Table 42 is therefore adjusted as follows. We assume, first, that any padding in the adjusted estimate for 1952 is relatively unimportant since the ratio of this item to total gross value of output for that year is only slightly higher than the corresponding figure for 1933. We then assume that the gross value of the unidentified portion increased in 1952–57 at the same rate as the gross value of the 14 identified consumers' goods. On these assumptions, the authors' estimates of gross value of the unidentified portion for 1952–57 are calculated. Gross value added is given above at 30 per cent of gross output, and this percentage is applied to obtain gross value added by the unidentified consumers' goods. The corresponding estimates

[38] See Appendix F under Depreciation.
[39] See Appendix F, Table F-15.

in 1933 prices are then derived on the basis of price indexes given above. These estimates are presented in Table 43.

Table 43

GROSS VALUE OF OUTPUT AND GROSS VALUE ADDED, CONSUMERS' GOODS, 1952–57: THE AUTHORS' ESTIMATE
(billions of yuan)

	1952	1953	1954	1955	1956	1957
In 1933 prices						
Gross value of output	3.64	4.26	4.71	4.56	5.47	5.29
Identified portion	2.70	3.16	3.49	3.38	4.06	3.93
Unidentified portion	0.94	1.10	1.22	1.18	1.41	1.36
Gross value added	0.81	0.96	1.06	1.01	1.24	1.20
Identified portion	0.61	0.73	0.81	0.77	0.95	0.92
Unidentified portion	0.20	0.23	0.25	0.24	0.29	0.28
In 1952 prices						
Gross value of output	12.19	14.28	15.77	15.27	18.33	17.73
Identified portion	9.05	10.60	11.71	11.34	13.61	13.16
Unidentified portion	3.14	3.68	4.06	3.93	4.72	4.57
Gross value added	3.91	4.63	5.12	4.88	5.99	5.81
Identified portion	2.97	3.53	3.90	3.70	4.57	4.44
Unidentified portion	0.94	1.10	1.22	1.18	1.42	1.37

SOURCE: For estimates for the identified portion, see Table 39. All others are explained in the text.

OTHER NONAGRICULTURAL SECTORS

Handicrafts

For the purposes of this study, handicrafts are defined to include all manufacturing activities performed by workers who use no mechanical power. Table 44 summarizes the estimates of value added by this sector for 1933 and 1952–57 in both 1933 and 1952 prices. These estimates are derived by using "controlling totals." A total figure for a sector (for example, the total wage bill for a given industry) is often derived as the sum total of the individual parts in the sector. In order to check whether all the parts are covered and whether some have been covered more than once, a second total, closely related to the first, but independently estimated and more reliable and comprehensive in statistical coverage, can be used for comparison. This second total is called the controlling total. For example, total employment in an industry may be used as the controlling total for the total wage bill in that industry.[40]

[40] For a more detailed explanation of this concept and its use, see Simon Kuznets, *National Income and Its Composition, 1919–1938,* New York, National Bureau of Economic Research, 1941, p. 112.

Table 44

VALUE ADDED BY HANDICRAFTS, 1933 AND 1952–57
(billions of yuan)

	1933	1952	1953	1954	1955	1956	1957
In 1933 prices							
Gross value added	2.22	2.33	2.39	2.46	2.54	2.61	2.66
Depreciation	0.18	0.19	0.20	0.20	0.21	0.22	0.22
Net value added	2.04	2.14	2.19	2.26	2.33	2.39	2.44
Identified	1.24	0.66	0.75	0.72	0.74	0.84	0.86
Unidentified	0.80	1.48	1.44	1.54	1.59	1.55	1.58
In 1952 prices							
Gross value added	4.81	5.14	5.24	5.43	5.58	5.72	5.86
Depreciation	0.40	0.42	0.43	0.45	0.46	0.47	0.48
Net value added	4.41	4.72	4.81	4.98	5.12	5.25	5.38
Identified	2.67	1.45	1.65	1.58	1.62	1.86	1.90
Unidentified	1.74	3.27	3.16	3.40	3.50	3.39	3.48

SOURCES: See the text and Tables 45 and 46.

The choice of this approach is dictated by the fact that the data on handicraft output are too meager and incomplete for a comprehensive estimate of value added by the industry as a whole. For the prewar period, the sample surveys cover only a few scattered localities, but even then there are numerous products for which data are nonexistent.[41] Although there are data on total gross output of individual handicraftsmen, handicraft cooperatives, and handicraft workshops for the postwar period, the Communists themselves have admitted that such data are incomplete.[42] The handicraft workers are scattered all over the country, and a great variety of items are produced. It would be difficult for any survey to cover all the goods and services, and, indeed, the missing portion might well be substantial. Under the circumstances, an estimate based on a controlling total would probably have a smaller margin of error than one based on fragmentary data. The fragmentary data, however, are used to build up the estimates for individual products so far as possible for several purposes: to determine the identified products for which we have relatively firm statistical bases, to compute a price index of handicraft products, and to provide the basic data for estimating

[41] This can be seen by a rough comparison of the list of products given in such surveys as the *Industrial Handbooks* for the five provinces published by the Bureau of Foreign Trade of the National Government, and the list of products that entered into interport trade in these provinces in the various issues of *The Trade of China*.
[42] Wei Yi, "The Problem of Developing Rapidly the Light Industry," *HHPYK*, No. 19, October 1956, p. 53.

investment and consumption expenditures by the commodity flow method. As can be seen from Table 44, net value added by the identified sector obtained from specific data constitutes the greater part of the total in 1933 and a smaller but still sizable part in 1952–57. The derivation of the estimates for these periods is described below.

1933

For 1933, the controlling total is provided by the number of people gainfully employed in handicrafts, derived as follows. From our estimate of the occupational distribution of the population in 1933 given in Table 53, the total number of people in industry—factories, handicrafts, mining, utilities, and construction—is estimated at 19.2 million. As shown in Table 55, there were 3.5 million people working in factories, mining, utilities, and construction. These figures were obtained from estimates of these sectors, and we believe them to be fairly accurate. The residual, about 15.7 million people, can therefore be assumed to be in handicrafts. Net value added per handicraftsman has been estimated at 130 yuan on the basis of two extensive surveys of handicrafts in Hunan and Shantung.[43] Total net value added by handicrafts is thus calculated at 2.04 billion yuan. Of this amount, 1.24 billion, or 60 per cent, is derived from detailed statistical data covering 45 products. The summary figures for these products are given in Table 45. Depreciation is very roughly calculated by applying the ratio of (a) depreciation to (b) net value added by the identified sector, as given in Table 45, to total net value added for the industry as a whole.

Estimates of value added in 1952 prices are derived by deflating value added in 1933 prices by a price index of 216 per cent for 1952 (1933 = 100). This price index was computed on the basis of the prices of nine products in 1933 and 1952 weighted by their 1933 outputs. The nine products are wheat flour, tea, sugar, soybean sauce, wine and liquor, edible vegetable oils, paper, cotton yarn, and cotton cloth. The details of the computation are given in Appendix I. Since neither the input-output coefficients for handicrafts nor the relative prices of output and input are likely to have changed during the period concerned, it is assumed that the price indexes for the gross value of output and value added are the same.

[43] Ou, *National Income*, Vol. I, pp. 73–74.

Table 45

NET VALUE ADDED BY 14 HANDICRAFT PRODUCT GROUPS, 1933
(millions of 1933 yuan)

Product	Gross value of output	Gross value added	Depreciation	Net value added
Lumber and wood products	294	60	3	57
Machinery, except electrical	16	9	1	8
Metal products	12	4	1	4
Electrical appliances	1	(*)	(*)	(*)
Transportation equipment	115	43	2	42
Stone, clay, and glass products	108	62	1	61
Chemical products	82	18	1	17
Textile goods	958	219	12	208
Clothing and knitted goods	188	66	4	62
Leather and allied products	122	30	2	28
Food products	8,905	703	80	624
Tobacco, wine, and liquor	307	55	6	50
Paper and printing	107	48	1	47
Miscellaneous	66	30	(*)	30
Total	11,280	1,349	112	1,236

NOTE: (*) Less than 0.5 million.
SOURCE: Appendix G.

1952–57

It is possible to compute net value added for only 12 products. The computation is made on the assumption that the cost deductions for each of these products have the same relation to gross value of output in 1952–57 as in 1933. The results are presented in Table 46. Estimates of total net value added are derived on the assumption that net value added by handicrafts varied from 1933 to 1952–57 in proportion to changes in the sum of the gross value of agricultural and mining output in real terms during the same period. Since the raw materials and fuels for handicrafts consist almost entirely of agricultural and mineral products and since the demand for handicraft products depends primarily on the income of the peasants, which is related to agricultural production, it appears reasonable to assume that the output of handicrafts varied with agricultural and mineral production. Net value added in 1933 (4.41 billion yuan) is given in Table 44, and gross value of agricultural and mineral output is from Tables 36 and 47. Adjusted estimates of agricultural output for 1952–57 are given in Table 68.

The adjusted estimates of net value added by handicrafts in

Table 46

NET VALUE ADDED BY 12 HANDICRAFT PRODUCTS, 1952–57
(millions of 1952 yuan)

Product	1952	1953	1954	1955	1956	1957
Milled rice	313	329	326	332	332	344
Wheat flour	290	286	380	319	340	318
Tea	21	21	23	28	32	29
Sugar	14	23	23	20	19	20
Soybean sauce	105	112	110	105	112	117
Wine and liquor	74	100	126	152	178	204
Edible vegetable oils	100	103	108	118	109	112
Paper	52	54	74	60	61	70
Cotton yarn	222	292	174	222	309	320
Cotton cloth	237	295	196	223	319	320
Silk piece goods	23	26	28	34	43	38
Pig iron	3	6	15	8	5	4
Total	1,454	1,647	1,582	1,621	1,859	1,896

SOURCE: Appendix G.

1952–57 can be derived from these data at 4.41, 4.45, 4.49, 4.94, 5.20, and 5.73 billion 1952 yuan.

The derivation of net value added for 1952–57 in 1933 prices follows the same procedure used to derive the 1933 estimate in 1952 prices. The price index in this calculation is computed at 220 per cent for 1952 with 1933 as 100.[44] The estimates of depreciation are calculated on the assumption that the ratio of depreciation to net value added for the entire industry is the same as for the group of 12 products computed from data in Table 46.

Mining[45]

A summary of estimates of value added by mining is included in Table 47. For 1933 and 1952, the estimates are derived on the basis of output, nonprimary input, and price data for 30 mineral products and a miscellaneous group. The major source of data on mineral production and prices in 1933 is the *Chinese Geological Survey.* The output data used in computing the 1952 values of production

[44] See Appendix I, Table I-2.

[45] *Geological Survey of China,* Special Bulletin, No. 5, quoted in Ou, *National Income,* Vol. I, Table 3, pp. 53–54; *1956 Statistical Abstract,* p. 32; SSB, *Industry Survey,* pp. 11, 90; *First Five Year Plan,* p. 38; International Tin Study Group, *Statistical Yearbook, 1956,* The Hague, 1956, p. 110; and U.S. Bureau of Mines, "Mineral Resources of China," *Foreign Minerals Survey,* Washington, D.C., Vol. II, No. 7, January 1948; and *Metal Statistics, 1956,* New York, American Metal Market, 1956, pp. 58, 518.

Table 47

VALUE ADDED BY MINING, UTILITIES, AND CONSTRUCTION, 1933 AND 1952–57
(billions of yuan)

	Mining							Utilities							Construction						
	1933	1952	1953	1954	1955	1956	1957	1933	1952	1953	1954	1955	1956	1957	1933	1952	1953	1954	1955	1956	1957
In 1933 prices																					
Gross value of output	0.30	0.93	0.90	1.12	1.45	1.46	1.90	0.23	0.53	0.65	0.75	0.83	1.05	1.25	1.17	1.50	—	—	—	4.74	—
Gross value added	0.23	0.68	0.66	0.84	1.06	1.09	1.40	0.16	0.39	0.46	0.54	0.60	0.74	0.89	0.38	0.67	0.84	0.99	1.08	1.84	1.71
Depreciation	0.02	0.05	0.04	0.06	0.07	0.07	0.09	0.03	0.07	0.08	0.10	0.12	0.14	0.17	0.04	0.07	0.09	0.11	0.12	0.20	0.19
Net value added	0.21	0.63	0.62	0.78	0.99	1.02	1.31	0.13	0.31	0.38	0.44	0.48	0.60	0.72	0.34	0.60	0.75	0.88	0.96	1.64	1.52
In 1952 prices																					
Gross value of output	0.73	2.17	2.10	2.63	3.39	3.41	4.45	0.32	0.69	0.83	0.97	1.07	1.36	1.61	3.13	4.56	—	—	—	14.40	—
Gross value added	0.54	1.58	1.56	1.95	2.49	2.55	3.29	0.19	0.41	0.49	0.57	0.63	0.79	0.94	1.14	2.06	2.56	3.01	3.29	5.59	5.20
Depreciation	0.04	0.11	0.10	0.13	0.17	0.17	0.22	0.04	0.10	0.12	0.14	0.16	0.20	0.24	0.11	0.23	0.28	0.33	0.36	0.62	0.58
Net value added	0.50	1.47	1.46	1.82	2.32	2.38	3.07	0.14	0.31	0.37	0.43	0.48	0.59	0.71	1.03	1.83	2.28	2.68	2.93	4.97	4.62

Note: — Not available.
Source: Appendix H.

are taken from various sources. Coal, iron ore, manganese ore, crude petroleum, and salt are from official Communist sources; tin, tungsten ore, and antimony regulus are estimates of the British International Tin Study Group and the U.S. Bureau of Mines. Output of sulfur is assumed to be the same as in 1947. The data on the following are pre-1949 peak year outputs: metals—crude antimony, copper, gold, mercury, and zinc; ores—antimony oxide, lead, magnesite, molybdenum, and talc. Limestone output is assumed to have changed in proportion to cement output from 1933 to 1952. We assume that outputs in 1952 are the same as in 1933 for the following minor items: silver, lead, bismuth, arsenic, clay and kaolin, alum, saltpeter, natural soda, pyrites, asbestos, dolomite, barite, turquoise, feldspar, gypsum, and miscellaneous.

The 1952 prices of coal, crude oil, gold, silver, copper, zinc, tin, antimony regulus, and salt are estimated on the basis of Communist price quotations. The prices of iron ore and pyrite, zinc ore, and antimony oxide and ore are assumed to have increased from 1933 to 1952 in proportion to the prices of their related products pig iron, zinc, and antimony regulus. The prices of the remaining minor products in 1952 are assumed to have increased from 1933 to 1952 in proportion to the average price of the following six products for which price data are available: coal, copper, zinc, tin, antimony, and crude oil. The price index of these products (234 per cent in 1952 with 1933 as 100) is derived on the basis of the individual prices of these products in 1933 and 1952, with their outputs in 1952 as weights.[46]

For 1953–57, data are available on the output of only the six major products coal, crude oil, salt, iron ore, limestone, and manganese ore. For other mined products, it is assumed that gross value in 1952 prices changed during the same period in proportion to the total gross value of coal, crude oil, iron ore, limestone, and manganese ore together. Deductible costs of production for 1933 are based on miscellaneous financial reports of mining companies; and, for lack of a better alternative, the same set of percentage deductions is applied to the gross value of output in 1952–57 to obtain net value added.

Gross value of output and value added in constant 1933 and 1952 prices are derived by applying the price indexes (242 and 234 per

[46] See Appendix I, Table I-3.

cent in 1952, with 1933 as 100), computed from the price quotations for the six major products, to the corresponding estimates for 1933 and 1952–57. The output of the six products in 1933 and 1952 are used as weights.[47]

Utilities[48]

Utilities as defined in this study cover enterprises supplying electric power, water, and gas. Net value added for each of these industries has been estimated for 1933 and 1952 from data on output, prices, and deductible costs. Estimates for 1953–57 are extrapolations from the 1952 estimates on the basis of output.

The output of electric power in 1933 is taken from surveys of the National Construction Commission of the Nationalist Government, and for 1952–57 from Communist reports. Price data are available from both prewar and Communist sources. For cost deductions, estimates by P. S. Ou are used for 1933, and estimates for the postwar years are based on miscellaneous Communist data.

For water supply, the 1933 estimate is primarily from data compiled by P. S. Ou. Data on output and prices are drawn from scattered Communist sources for 1952–57. The cost deductions for 1952–57 are the same percentages as for 1933, with adjustments for changes in the relative prices of output and input.

For gas, data compiled by P. S. Ou are used for 1933 and 1952–57. This industry was located mainly in Shanghai and Manchuria, and there was no evidence of any substantial expansion during 1933. These figures, in any case, would be small compared with those for electric power and would not have any noticeable effect on the national income estimate as a whole.

Estimates of gross value of output and value added by electric power and water for 1933 in 1952 prices are derived on the basis of the 1933 output and nonprimary input of these two industries and their corresponding prices in 1933 and 1952.[49] With 1933 as 100, the 1952 price indexes (140 per cent for gross value of output and 109 per cent for value added) are applied to the gross value of output and value added by gas in 1933 prices to arrive at the estimate in 1952 prices. Estimates for 1952–57 in 1933 prices are derived simi-

[47] *Ibid.*
[48] See Appendix H under Utilities.
[49] See Appendix H, Table H-4.

larly. The price index for gross value of output is 129 per cent and for net value added is 99 per cent in 1952 with 1933 as 100. The results of these calculations are included in Table 47.

Construction[50]

Construction includes the building of residences and business plants, the installation of equipment, road building, and all other work involving civil engineering except that done by work brigades. The Communist definition of value added by construction includes wages given to work brigades, but actual payments either in cash or in kind are not likely to be important. Generally, labor contributed to such work as local community projects and emergency dike building is considered voluntary and involves no payment. To allow for payments that might have been made, we have reduced by 20 per cent our estimate of work done by work brigades.

A summary of estimates of value added by construction is included in Table 47. The figure for 1933 in 1933 prices is estimated primarily on the basis of the volume of construction materials (mainly bricks, limestone, cement, and lumber) and the relationship between output and material inputs. We assume that the price deflator for net value added by construction varies from 1933 to 1952 in proportion to that for construction materials over the same period (304 per cent for 1952 with 1933 as 100). Net value added for 1933 in 1952 prices is derived by multiplying the 1933 figure by this price index.

Estimates of net value added for 1952 and 1956 are given in the Communist national income estimate. For the others years, net value added is derived from the 1956 figure and an index computed from Communist data on basic construction. The price index given above is used to obtain estimates for 1952–57 in constant 1933 prices. Depreciation for this industry is assumed to be 5 per cent of the gross value of output.

Transportation and Communications[51]

Net value added by transportation and communications is calculated separately for the modern and traditional sectors. Included in the modern sector are railroads, motor and steam boats, trucks, municipal transportation systems, civil air transport, communications

[50] See Appendix H under Construction.
[51] See Appendix H under Transportation and Communications.

systems, and postal service. The traditional sector includes all means of transportation that do not use mechanical power: hand-drawn or animal-drawn carts, wheelbarrows, boats and junks, pedicabs, and sedan chairs. A summary of estimates of value added by these two sectors is given in Table 48.

Table 48

VALUE ADDED BY TRANSPORTATION AND COMMUNICATIONS, 1933 AND 1952–57
(billions of yuan)

	1933	1952	1953	1954	1955	1956	1957
In 1933 prices							
Modern transportation and communications							
Gross receipts	0.71	1.54	1.74	2.01	2.18	2.53	2.75
Gross value added	0.46	0.88	1.06	1.21	1.29	1.46	1.59
Depreciation	0.03	0.05	0.06	0.07	0.07	0.08	0.09
Net value added	0.43	0.83	1.00	1.14	1.22	1.38	1.50
Old-fashioned transportation							
Gross receipts	1.33	1.33	1.23	1.19	1.18	1.26	1.22
Gross value added	1.21	1.21	1.12	1.08	1.07	1.14	1.11
Depreciation	0.01	0.01	0.01	0.01	0.01	0.01	0.01
Net value added	1.20	1.20	1.11	1.07	1.06	1.13	1.10
Total							
Gross receipts	2.04	2.87	2.97	3.20	3.36	3.79	3.97
Gross value added	1.67	2.09	2.18	2.29	2.36	2.60	2.70
Depreciation	0.04	0.06	0.07	0.08	0.08	0.09	0.10
Net value added	1.63	2.03	2.11	2.21	2.28	2.51	2.60
In 1952 prices							
Modern transportation and communications							
Gross receipts	1.80	3.90	4.42	5.10	5.55	6.42	6.99
Gross value added	1.15	2.23	2.70	3.07	3.29	3.73	4.05
Depreciation	0.06	0.13	0.15	0.17	0.19	0.21	0.23
Net value added	1.09	2.10	2.55	2.90	3.10	3.52	3.82
Old-fashioned transportation							
Gross receipts	2.90	2.94	2.72	2.61	2.60	2.76	2.70
Gross value added	2.64	2.68	2.48	2.38	2.37	2.51	2.46
Depreciation	0.03	0.03	0.03	0.03	0.03	0.03	0.03
Net value added	2.61	2.65	2.45	2.35	2.34	2.48	2.43
Total							
Gross receipts	4.70	6.84	7.14	7.71	8.15	9.18	9.69
Gross value added	3.79	4.91	5.18	5.45	5.66	6.24	6.51
Depreciation	0.09	0.16	0.18	0.20	0.22	0.24	0.26
Net value added	3.70	4.75	5.00	5.25	5.44	6.00	6.25

SOURCE: Appendix H.

Value added by the modern sector is estimated from data on gross receipts and cost deductions. The basic data for 1933 are those compiled by P. S. Ou for each of the following: railroads; ships; trucks, taxis, and buses; trolleys; civil air transport; communications; and postal services.[52] For 1952–57, gross receipts are calculated from data on the physical volume of freight and passenger transport carried by the railroads, trucks, and ships; average freight and passenger rates; and the gross receipts from communications. Gross and net value added are derived on the assumption that the percentage of deductible costs for each branch of this industry is the same as in 1933. Net value added for 1933 in 1952 prices and for 1952–57 in 1933 prices is calculated by applying a price deflator to the estimates. The price deflator is assumed to be 254 per cent for 1952 with 1933 as 100, the same as the wholesale price index for fuel in the same period.

The estimates of net value added for 1952–57 are based primarily on Communist statistics of the volume of freight, and their reliability is questionable. As in manufacturing, the managers probably pressured the cadres to fulfill and overfulfill their quotas; and the freight quotas were undoubtedly as difficult to fulfill as those in other sectors. There are reports that because of poor planning and other factors the freight volume often failed to make full use of the total transportation capacity, so that freight cars were only half filled or even left idle for long periods.[53] Under the circumstances it is not surprising that the cadres resorted to manipulation of statistics. Such a practice was apparently quite widespread, for it was serious enough to cause alarm in an editorial in the *People's Daily*.[54] Methods of inflating the gross output statistics vary. Some workers double count the same output; others include products of substandard quality as regular output; still others have the goods hauled over longer distances than necessary.[55] According to Communist statistics, the volume of freight carried by modern transport increased by 112 per cent from 1952 to 1956,[56] almost double the

[52] Ou, *National Income,* Vol. I, pp. 85–87, 90–91, 95–97. Ou's estimates of depreciation have been adjusted.

[53] *TKP,* Tientsin, April 6, 1954; and *People's Daily,* February 28, 1955.

[54] *People's Daily,* September 12, 1953.

[55] *TCKT,* No. 23, November 1958, p. 20; Wen Liang, "General Conditions in Railroad Transport on the Mainland," *Tsu-kuo* (China Weekly), Hong Kong, No. 11, March 16, 1953, p. 11.

[56] Freight carried by railroads, trucks, and ships in 1952 is given as 71.84 billion ton-kilometers, and in 1956 as 152.06 billion ton-kilometers. The index is calculated at 212 per cent for 1956 with 1952 as 100 (*Great Ten Years,* p. 131).

percentage increase in net value added by commodity transportation over the same period.[57]

It should be noted that the net value added figures include both the modern and traditional sectors. However, a constant proportion of the freight volume was carried by the traditional means of transport.[58] This implies an equal rate of increase for both the modern and traditional sectors, so that the percentage increase in net value added by the entire industry would be the same as for the modern sector. Communist data indicating a rapid increase in freight carried by the traditional sector does not contradict our estimate of net value added by this sector, which implies that the total volume of freight was more or less the same in 1952 and 1956. The Communist concept of the traditional sector is presumably much narrower in scope than ours. It includes only the full-time transportation workers, and even within this limited scope the statistical coverage is quite likely to be incomplete. To a considerable extent the traditional sector complements the modern; it generally handles short hauls between the small market towns and the railroad stations, whereas the railroads and inland and coastal shipping carry freight over longer distances. Thus the two can be expected to move together. That the traditional sector as defined above increased just as rapidly as the modern can also be explained in part by the deployment of workers formerly engaged in part-time transportation into transportation work within the agricultural cooperatives, or simply into other kinds of work, thus shifting the demand for services to the full-time transportation workers.[59]

Since there are no *a priori* grounds for suspecting that the Communist net value added figures were underestimates, and since the relation of value added to gross receipts at constant prices and

[57] Total national income at constant prices in 1952 is reported at 61.13 billion yuan, and for 1956, 88.75 billion yuan. The percentages of value added by commodity transportation in these two years is 4.0 and 4.4 per cent. (See SSB, "A Preliminary Analysis of the Production and Distribution of China's National Income," *TCYC*, No. 1, January 1958, p. 11.) Net value added by commodity transportation in 1952 and 1956 is computed at 2.44 and 3.90 billion yuan; the figure for 1956 represents a 60 per cent increase over 1952.

[58] *People's Daily*, May 11, 1957, p. 3.

[59] For a report on such deployment, see Huang Hsiao-chuan, "Actively Raise the Local Highway Transportation Capacity," *CHCC*, No. 3, March 1957, p. 11.

hence to the physical volume of freight could not have changed so drastically, it appears that the volume of freight was exaggerated, and the estimates of net value added based on Communist figures of freight volume given in Table 48 must be adjusted downwards. The margin of reliability is assumed to be the same as in the factory consumers' goods industry. The margins are 100, 92, 88, 88, 81, and 79 per cent of the adjusted estimates for 1952–57, computed from Tables 42 and 43. We apply these figures to the adjusted estimate given in Table 48 to derive the following estimate of net value added by modern transportation and communications for 1952–57.

Year	Billions of 1933 yuan	Billions of 1952 yuan
1952	0.83	2.10
1953	1.00	2.55
1954	1.14	2.90
1955	1.22	3.10
1956	1.38	3.52
1957	1.50	3.82

For the traditional sector, net value added in 1933 is derived from an estimate of the number of workers and the average earnings per worker. The total number of workers in transportation and communications, obtained from the occupational distribution given in the next section, was 11.3 million; the number of people employed in modern transportation and communications has been estimated at 0.4 million.[60] The 10.9 million difference between these two figures represents handlers of carts, sampans, rickshas, and draft animals, or simply human carriers. The earnings of these people are assumed to be the same as the average earnings per worker in handicrafts and agriculture. The net value added is then derived by multiplying the total number of old-fashioned transportation workers by the average annual earnings.

Net value added by old-fashioned transportation in 1957 is obtained on the basis of the number of laborers and the assumption that earnings per worker in real terms were the same as in 1933. Estimates of net value added by both the modern and traditional sectors for 1952–56 are then derived by extrapolation from the 1957

[60] Djang Gee-hung, "An Estimate of the Working Population of China," *Quarterly Review of Social Sciences*, Shanghai, Vol. IX, No. 2, December 1947, p. 78.

figure by an index of growth of net value added by agriculture, manufacturing, and mining. The net value added by the modern sector is deducted from total net value added to obtain the estimates for the traditional sector.

It is interesting to note that the Communists set their target for transportation by a procedure similar to ours. It was reported by Po I-po that the 1957 plan for transportation was drawn on the basis of the expected rate of agricultural and industrial production and the planned scale of basic construction.[61] Using the procedure described above and an index calculated from the adjusted estimates of net value added by agriculture and manufacturing, and mining as summarized in Table 47, we derived adjusted estimates of net value added by old-fashioned transportation for 1952–57 at 2.69, 2.31, 2.08, 2.22, 2.26, and 2.43 billion yuan in 1952 prices.

Trade[62]

For 1933, statistics on the ratio of the number of stores (including restaurants) to the total population are available for 790 hsien and municipalities scattered around the country. Data are also available for computing the average wage rate and the average profit rate in relation to invested capital. With these data and our estimate of 500 million for the total population, the net value added by trading stores is estimated at 1.75 billion yuan, and the number of workers at 7.5 million.

Net value added by trading stores falls short of total value added by the trading sector because of the large number of peddlers who

[61] Po I-po, *1956–57 Plan,* p. 34. It may be noted that our estimate of the trends in modern transportation is lower than that in heavy industrial production. There is no inconsistency here for the following two reasons. (1) Modern transportation was not engaged in moving heavy industrial products alone. It undoubtedly was involved in the movement of grains. Even if only a small portion of the total grain output was shipped by modern means of transportation, the volume of such freight would be large relative to that of other goods. Moreover, there was a high degree of concentration of heavy industry in Manchuria. A considerable portion of the heavy industrial materials and products were produced and consumed in Manchuria so that relatively little modern transportation was required. Furthermore, the movements of troops and military supplies by rail must have accounted for a sizable part of the modern transportation services during the Korean War. Hence, the moving of heavy industry products by modern transportation could have, and probably had, increased very sharply, while total modern transportation need not have increased as fast because of the reduction of military traffic after the Korean War and the large volume of freight other than heavy industry products. (2) Some heavy industry products could have been transported by traditional means. To the extent this was the case, modern transportation need not have increased as fast as heavy industrial output.

[62] See Appendix H under Trade.

do not have fixed locations of business and whose services have not been covered in the estimate. The number of peddlers can be calculated at 7.4 million by deducting the number of workers in trading stores from the total number of workers in trade obtained from the occupational distribution in the next section. On the assumption that net value added per worker for trade is the same as for handicrafts, total net value added by peddlers is calculated at 0.96 billion yuan.

Net value added by trading stores and restaurants in constant 1952 prices is derived by multiplying the estimates in 1933 prices by a price index of 350 per cent for 1952 with 1933 as 100; this is the arithmetic mean of the price indexes for agriculture and factories over the same period. The price index numbers for agriculture and factories are 180 and 520 per cent for 1952 with 1933 as 100, computed from value added by these two industries in 1933 with constant 1933 and 1952 prices given in Tables 36 and 37. For value added by peddlers, the price index for handicrafts is used (216 per cent in 1952 with 1933 as 100).[63] Net value added by trading stores and restaurants is 6.12 billion 1952 yuan, and net value added by peddlers is 2.07 billion 1952 yuan.

For 1952 and 1956, net value added by trade as a whole can be derived at 9.66 and 13.76 billion 1952 yuan from Communist estimates of total national income and proportions of income originating in trade. But again there are miscellaneous reports indicating that these figures might be high. For instance, in some cases data on total retail sales are actually sales by wholesale units to retail stores.[64] Therefore, except when goods are purchased and sold by retail stores in the same period, the retail sales figures are inflated; and it is on the basis of these figures that the estimates of value added are made.[65] We therefore adjust the Communist estimates downward by a margin equal to the ratio of the authors' estimate to the adjusted estimate of value added by manufactured consumers' goods in these two years (100 per cent for 1952 and 51 per cent for 1956). On the basis of our estimates of value added by trade, and by agriculture, manufacturing, and mining as a whole for 1952

[63] For computation of this index, see Appendix I.

[64] *TKP*, Peiping, July 1, 1959, p. 5.

[65] Yueh Wei, "The Method of Computing National Income," *CCYC*, No. 3, June 1956, p. 53. For the Communists' lack of confidence in their own trade statistics, see Tseng Shan, "Report Before the Conference on the Census of Private Trade and Restaurants," *TCKTTH*, No. 8, April 1955, pp. 12–15.

and 1956, a linear regression between the two is approximated. By using this relationship and our estimates of value added by the three industries already obtained for 1953–55 and 1957, we derive the value added by trade for 1952–55 and 1957.[66] By the same procedure and the adjusted data on net value added by trade for 1952 and 1956 and net value added by the three industries for 1952–57 given in Table 47, we obtained the adjusted estimates of value added by trade as 9.66, 10.57, 11.30, 12.10, 13.76, and 14.41 billion 1952 yuan for 1952–57.

The results of our calculations are shown in Table 49. The total is split into net value added by trading stores and restaurants, and

Table 49

NET VALUE ADDED BY TRADING STORES AND RESTAURANTS, AND BY PEDDLERS: AUTHORS' ESTIMATE, 1933 AND 1952–57
(billions of yuan)

	1933	1952	1953	1954	1955	1956	1957
In 1933 prices							
Trading stores and restaurants	1.75	1.97	2.02	2.20	2.30	2.50	2.57
Peddlers	0.96	0.91	0.95	0.79	0.70	0.66	0.66
Total	2.71	2.88	2.97	2.99	3.00	3.16	3.23
In 1952 prices							
Trading stores and restaurants	6.12	7.66	7.87	8.54	8.95	9.71	10.01
Peddlers	2.07	2.00	2.10	1.73	1.54	1.44	1.44
Total	8.19	9.66	9.97	10.27	10.49	11.15	11.45

by peddlers, as follows: The number of peddlers is roughly estimated in Table 61. The nature of the peddling and catering business

[66] The linear function so obtained is $Y = 0.12X + 3.98$, where X represents the value added by the three industries and Y the value added by trade. For data used in this computation, see Tables 36, 37, 47. It may be noted that the trend implied in this regression line is less steep than that of the output of light industry or that for government purchase of agricultural and subsidiary products (*Great Ten years,* p. 168). So far as the trend for light industry output is concerned, there need not be any inconsistency, because the increase in such output does not necessarily result in an increase in the total volume of trade for two reasons: some stages of distribution were eliminated as more and more commodities were brought under the centralized distribution system; and more and more products of light industries were exported at prices below costs (*HHPYK,* No. 16, 1957, p. 90). As for government purchases of agricultural and subsidiary products, these purchases are quite misleading as an indicator of the total agricultural products marketed. The increase is due partly to the displacement of private trade and partly to the increase in the government purchase prices (*ibid.,* p. 173). For at least one major product, food grain, the Communist data on government purchase show no steep rising trend in 1953–57 (*TCKT,* No. 19, 1957, p. 31).

is such that any significant change in the productivity of the workers is not likely. It can therefore be assumed that net value added per worker in the postwar years is at the same level as in 1933. Total net value added by peddlers can now be calculated, and then deducted from net value added by this sector as a whole to obtain the contribution of trading stores and restaurants. The estimates for 1952–57 in constant 1933 prices are found by deflating the 1952 estimates by 389 per cent for trading stores and 220 per cent for peddlers, with 1933 as 100. The index number for trading stores is the average of the price index numbers for agriculture and factories, and the index for handicrafts is used for peddlers.[67]

Government, Finance, and Personal Services[68]

Net value added by the government sector in 1933 is calculated as 0.82 billion yuan by adding wage payments to government employees and military subsistence estimated from budgetary data for the central and local governments. Income originating in government services in 1952–57 is derived by the same procedure. Total wage payments are estimated from data on the numbers of government employees and Communist estimates of average wage rates adjusted for fringe benefits and price level changes. Subsistence provisions for the armed forces are roughly estimated at 1.02 billion yuan for each of these years. Income originating in government services totals 3.27, 3.70, 3.95, 4.07, 4.76, and 5.03 billion 1952 yuan for 1952–57.

The price index used to derive the estimate of the income of government employees for 1933 in 1952 prices and the estimate for 1952–57 in 1933 prices is 163 per cent for 1952 with 1933 as 100. The price index for the estimates of military pay is assumed to be the same as for handicraft products, that is, 216 and 220 per cent for 1952 with 1933 as 100, with the 1933 and 1952 handicraft outputs as weights.[69]

Included in the finance sector are the modern banks, traditional money shops, trust companies, savings and insurance companies, pawn shops, and other money lenders. Net value added by the Chinese-owned modern banking institutions in 1933 has been estimated

[67] For data used in the computation of these two index numbers, see Appendix I.
[68] See Appendix H under Government, Finance, and Personal Services.
[69] See Appendix I, Table I-1.

at 71 million yuan.[70] Net value added by foreign-owned banks and by traditional money shops are roughly calculated on the ratio of the capital of these organizations to that of the Chinese-owned modern banks. By a similar procedure, crude estimates are also obtained for the relatively few insurance companies.

The number of people engaged in finance in 1952 has been derived from Communist data as 0.54 million.[71] Net value added per worker is assumed to be the same as in 1933 in real terms; it is expressed in 1952 prices by use of the price index for net value added by government civilian employees. The 1953–57 estimates are obtained by extrapolating from the 1952 figure on an index of the movement of the total net value added in agriculture, factories, mining, and trade in real terms during this period. These are the four major branches of the economy to which the financial institutions provide their services. Adjusted estimates of net value added by finance in 1952–57, corresponding to adjusted estimates for other sectors, can be derived similarly from the 1952 estimate and from an index of extrapolation based on the adjusted estimates of net value added by agriculture, factories, mining, and trade summarized in Table 68. The results are 1.31, 1.41, 1.51, 1.61, 1.89, and 2.04 billion yuan for 1952–57.

It should be noted that interest payments are not included in cost deductions in the derivation of net value added by agriculture, factories, mining, and trade. Inclusion of value added by the financial sector in the national product total, therefore, involves double counting to the extent that services rendered to the other industries for production purposes are represented. However, it seems better to count part of the net value added by the financial sector twice than to omit it completely.

The number of people who served as doctors, teachers in private schools, lawyers, accountants, domestic servants, etc., in 1933 are estimated in Appendix H. This number is somewhat less than the number for other nonagricultural occupations obtained from the occupational distribution. The per worker earnings of the people in the specified occupations and the residual are roughly estimated. Net value added as a whole is then obtained for 1933, and it is assumed that it is the same in real terms in 1952. This figure is then

[70] Liu, *Income*, p. 53.
[71] *First Five Year Plan*, pp. 128–130.

expressed in 1952 prices by use of the price index for net value added by government employees. For 1953–57, net value added is obtained by extrapolation from the 1952 estimate on an index of employment in these services during the period 1952–57.

Residential Rent

Residential rent is an imputed value derived as follows: for 1933, gross annual rent per person in cities and towns is estimated at 4.50 yuan and in farm areas at 2.10 yuan on the basis of sample studies of urban and farm rentals. With the proportions of total population attributable to the nonagricultural and agricultural populations as weights, an average for the total population is calculated at 2.75 yuan per person. The average per capita gross rent is multiplied by the total population of 500 million, and 25 per cent is allowed for deductible costs to obtain total residential rent, 1.02 billion yuan. A price deflator for residential rent is roughly estimated at 194 per cent in 1952, with 1933 as 100, from information on rentals in Tientsin. Residential rent for 1952–57 is derived on the assumption that per capita rent in real terms during this period is the same as in 1933, that is, 2.06 yuan in 1933 prices, and 4.00 yuan in 1952 prices. The total population in 1952–57 is estimated at 569, 581, 595, 608, 621, and 637 million; therefore, residential rent for those years is calculated at 1.17, 1.19, 1.22, 1.25, 1.28, and 1.31 billion 1933 yuan, and 2.28, 2.32, 2.37, 2.44, 2.48, and 2.55 billion 1952 yuan.

Work Brigades

Work brigades consist largely of unskilled and inexperienced workers whose activities are limited primarily to earth work in connection with the building of railroads, highways, and water conservation projects; that is, digging, moving, and filling. The volume of earth work done in each of those categories can be roughly estimated. Work done by paid engineers, technicians, and other regular construction workers has been included under construction. An arbitrary reduction of 20 per cent is allowed for work done by paid unskilled workers. Earth work done by work brigades in physical units is then multiplied by a rough estimate of value added per unit of earth work to arrive at total value added. Productive work done by members of the militia, a service contributed to the state, is also roughly estimated and added to the total. The results are given in Table 50.

Table 50

NET VALUE ADDED BY WORK BRIGADES, 1952–57
(billions of yuan)

	1952	1953	1954	1955	1956	1957
1952 prices						
Railway construction	0.03	0.02	0.03	0.03	0.05	0.03
Highway construction	0.01	0.01	0.01	0.01	0.02	0.02
Water conservation projects	0.44	0.22	0.26	0.57	0.60	0.66
Militia service	0.14	0.14	0.14	0.14	0.14	0.14
Total	0.62	0.38	0.44	0.75	0.81	0.85
1933 prices						
Total	0.28	0.17	0.20	0.34	0.37	0.39

Source: Appendix H.

THE CHINESE POPULATION AND ITS OCCUPATIONAL DISTRIBUTION

It is not the major purpose of this study to make an extensive review of the existing Chinese demographic statistics or to make a definite estimate of the population. As has been explained, however, the available production statistics on specific sectors of the economy do not exhaust the contributions to national income by all the working population. There is little or no information on the services rendered by a fairly large number of handicraftsmen, old-fashioned transportation workers, and peddlers. For 1933, only an estimate of the total population and its occupational distribution will yield the missing information. Although the estimate of the traditional sectors for the postwar years was made through other sources than occupational distribution, data on postwar population have been used to obtain our estimate of the per capita consumption of food crops, which, as we have seen, is an important factor in obtaining our estimate of food crop production.[72] Our estimate of population for 1933 is derived first. The reliability of the postwar Communist data on population is then discussed.

Total Population, 1933

There is a great deal of corroboration for our belief that the total Chinese population in 1933 was roughly 500 million. First, the fig-

[72] See the discussion in Chapter II under The Hard Components of the Product Estimate, and under Output of Agricultural Products, 1952–57, in this chapter.

ure of 500 million is obtained by projecting Willcox's estimate of the 1912 population, with some adjustments, to the early 1930s. Willcox estimated that there was a total of 73,485,000 households in China proper (excluding Manchuria) and 76,122,000 households in all China.[73] When the estimated 2,367,000 households in the six outlying districts of Kirin, Heilungkiang, Mongolia, Tibet, Jehol, and Tsinghai are added to his estimate, the total number would be 78,489,000.[74]

Students of Chinese population are agreed that the reported number of households is more reliable than the number of persons per household. By using the round figure of five persons per household, Professor Willcox estimated the population at 367 million for China proper and 381 million for all China.[75] When the population in the six outlying districts is included, the total population would be 392 million.

Willcox believed that the reported ratios of males to females were all unreasonably high, including the one of 120 males to 100 females implied in his own estimate. The number of males was believed to be more reliable, and that of females underreported. He then adjusted his population estimate on the basis of Buck's data on sex ratio, and raised his estimate for China proper to 386 million.[76] If he had made the adjustment for all China on the same principle, his estimate would have been 401 million; if the six outlying districts were also included, his estimate would have been 412 million.

Willcox made no adjustment for the underreporting of infants and young children, but his estimate can now be corrected on the basis of later data. In 1946, Professor Simon Kuznets went to China at the invitation of the National Government to advise on economic research and the compilation of economic statistics. In one of the studies made under Kuznets' supervision, estimates of survival rates

[73] W. F. Willcox, "The Population of China and Its Modern Increase," *Studies in American Demography*, Ithaca, N.Y., Cornell University Press, 1940, Table 222, p. 525.

[74] Figures for Kirin (739,000) and Heilungkiang (241,000) are the 1910 data (*ibid.*, Table 219, p. 521). Those for Mongolia (360,000) and Tibet (400,000) are derived from the 1910 population figures given by Willcox and his assumption of 5 persons per household. Those for Jehol (560,000) and Tsinghai (67,000) are the 1912 official Minchangpu figures taken from *She-hui ko-hsueh tsa-chih* (Quarterly Review of Social Sciences), Nanking, Vol. III, No. 3, 1932, p. 315, and Vol. IV, No. 1, 1933, p. 104.

[75] Willcox, *op. cit.*, Table 222, p. 525.

[76] *Ibid.*, p. 527.

by age groups, fertility rates, and age and sex composition were worked out on the best data available.[77] The male-to-female ratio for the early 1930s is about 112 to 100. The population in the age range from 0 to 4 years is about 15 per cent of the total. The percentages in the 1910, 1912, and 1928 censuses from which Willcox derived his estimate are not known. However, in the population data published by the National Government in 1947 for the provinces of Hunan, Shensi, and Fukien, the age range from 0 to 4 years includes about 10 per cent of the total.[78] It is probable that the long established tradition of underreporting the number of children in this age range resulted in an understatement of the total population of about 5 per cent. If we make a 5 per cent increase in Willcox's estimate of 412 million for 1912, the result is approximately 434 million.

In the study made under Kuznets' direction, two projections of the rate of growth of the Chinese population are made, representing situations that can be described as less and more favorable (that is, higher and lower mortality rates).[79] The projected annual rate of growth under the less favorable condition, about 7.8 per thousand, is used to obtain an approximate estimate of the increase of population from about 434 million in 1912 to about 500 million in 1933.[80]

Our opinion that Chinese population increased from 1912 to the 1930s differs from that held by Willcox. He believed that the population had been more or less stationary and that from 1901 to 1937 it was about the same as in 1850, the year before the Tai-ping Rebellion. To quote Willcox:[81]

[77] "Future Growth of Chinese Population During Industrialization," May 1946, p. 33 (unpublished).

[78] *China Yearbook 1948,* Nanking, Vol. I, pp. 97–98.

[79] "Future Growth of Chinese Population During Industrialization," May 1946 (unpublished).

[80] The less favorable condition assumes that the survival rates at the starting point are the average of two sets of data, one representing a situation in more or less peaceful and calamity-free regions in 1929–37 and another during 1931–35 in a region where flood and drought were followed by pestilence. This condition is then assumed to improve and to reach the more or less normal condition represented by the first situation at the end of 30 years.

By applying this projection to the period 1912–33, we merely used the *average* yearly rate of increase computed for the first 20 years of the 30-year period; it is not implied that there was necessarily a gradual improvement in the rate of increase of the population during 1912–33, as is assumed on the projection (*ibid.,* Table X, pp. 10–11, 35–36). The rate was obtained by weighing the male and female rates of growth by the ratio of 112 to 100 (*ibid.,* pp. 2, 28–29).

[81] Willcox, *op. cit.,* pp. 528–529.

"This conclusion finds support in the testimony of Dr. Hu Shih, who wrote me in 1930 supporting the view that the population of China today is about the same as it was before the Tai-ping Rebellion (1850–1864).

"His father left an autobiography written in 1881 in which he described the devastation of the Highlands in Southern Anhwei during the Tai-ping Rebellion and its effect on population. In 1840, when the clan temple was built, the population of the clan was about 6,000. In 1861 the temple was destroyed and for five years the region was devastated. In 1865 a census of the clan taken preparatory to rebuilding its temple showed only a few more than 1,200 survivors, men, women, and children either in the native village or in Shanghai; the figures are exhaustive and exact. Those 5 years had carried off four-fifths of the clan.

"The Tai-ping Rebellion devastated almost all of South China; when Dr. Hu Shih visited the sites of ruined towns and villages around his old home, he realized that China had never recovered from the effects of that rebellion. He thought of the people in the provinces of the north, northwest, and southwest which during the 15 years prior to his visit almost constantly suffered from war and famine. During the preceding 65 years his own district had not suffered from war or banditry, and yet its population had been decreasing for three decades. Counting the males for five generations from his great-great-grandfather there were in the third generation seven, all born before the Tai-ping Rebellion, and when he wrote there were only eight. He had seen scores of families related to his own which 30 years before were prosperous and populous but were then without a male heir, although the region had been for 65 years free from civil war."

Dr. Hu Shih's impression of his home district is undoubtedly accurate. The question is whether the situation in his district was typical of the country as a whole. The position taken by the two distinguished scholars is that the Chinese population had not been growing even during years of comparative peace and order. Our opinion is the contrary. Many of the merchants in Dr. Hu's home district were engaged in interregional trade and did business far away from their homes; the stationary trend of the population in that district would not be typical of the whole country. The basic data used in this work to estimate the rate of growth of the Chinese population were not available to either Professor Willcox or Dr. Hu when they wrote, and the regional coverage of these data is much broader than the observations of one person, however accurate. Signs indicating growth of population before the 1930s were reported by Buck.[82]

> "The rate of growth of the Chinese population during the past fifty years is still a disputed matter, and one concerning which this study yields no direct information. During the enumeration years the Population Survey records indicate that there were 38.3 births and 27.1 deaths . . . per 1,000 inhabitants. Superficially this rate of natural increase, which would double the population in less than 65 years, suggests that the population of China has increased rapidly. Unfortunately, the problem is not so simple. Since the birth and death rates are not completely trustworthy, their difference is still less trustworthy even though the bias in the rates is in the same direction. Nevertheless, during the survey years there undoubtedly was a substantial excess of births over deaths. This does not necessarily mean that there has been a long period of population growth, because the figures relate, as has been repeatedly indicated, to a relatively uneventful period. The population increase coming from such periods may have been wiped out entirely in other years of famine, war and pestilence.
>
> "Other evidence suggests that the increase has not been entirely cancelled by such catastrophes. Inquiries concerning population growth during the past few decades were made of local people in connection with the Agricultural Survey of 137 hsien. In 58 per cent of the communities it was stated that there had been an increase in population. The chief evidence was the increased number of buildings. A decrease was reported in 35 per cent of the communities, usually as the result of bandit activity, disease, famine, or drought. . . . In seven per cent of the communities no change was reported. While such evidence is not entirely conclusive, when coupled with the observed excess of births over deaths in the survey period, *it strongly suggests that the rural population has been increasing in recent years* [italics ours]."

Moreover, the thesis of a stationary population in a more or less normal period is inconsistent with the picture of population change

[82] Buck, *Land Utilization*, Vol. I, p. 395.

which Willcox and Dr. Hu gave for the period after the Tai-ping Rebellion. Willcox estimated the Chinese population at 350 million for 1850. If it were typical of the country as a whole that the "Tai-ping Rebellion had carried off four-fifths of the clan," and if the population in 1912 was around 400 million as Willcox estimated it, then the rate of growth from 1850 to 1912 would have been very rapid indeed. (The Chinese population apparently grew from the remaining 70 million, or one-fifth of 350 million, at the end of the Tai-ping Rebellion to about 400 million in 1912.) It is more likely that the country as a whole did not suffer as drastic a reduction. It is nevertheless true that the population was reduced greatly below 350 million by the Tai-ping Rebellion, and that it did grow even in the backward conditions of the 19th century—when sanitation, transportation, and economic development were inferior to what they became by the period from 1912 to the 1930s.

Since Willcox published his well-known criticism of the early Chinese official censuses, many scholars have made efforts to improve the population statistics. In 1935, S. T. Wang, a noted Chinese demographer, attempted to pool the various census data available and estimate the population during 1932–33 by making the following corrections in the official data:[83] (1) to accept only the *de facto* population figures and to eliminate duplications because of confusion with the *de jure* population; (2) to eliminate the part of the population that had been reported in individual households and also included in public institutions and organizations; (3) to eliminate duplications in the "alien" and "religious" categories; (4) to adjust the population returns in provinces and administrative districts in accordance with the latest changes in provincial and district boundaries; and (5) to make up the incomplete returns in certain provinces on the basis of available data on population density or the complete returns for other years in these provinces.

Wang's adjustments, however, are incomplete with regard to the two most important errors in Chinese censuses; the high male-to-female ratios and the underreporting of young children and infants. His data by province are presented in Table 51 and are then corrected for these defects. Other adjustments are made on the basis of a comparison with Willcox's estimate and the concurrent esti-

[83] Wang Shih-ta, "A New Estimate of Recent Chinese Population," *She-hui ko-hsueh tsa-chih* (Quarterly Review of Social Sciences), Vol. VI, No. 2, June 1935, pp. 191–266.

mates by Buck and C. C. Chang. The total population obtained also comes to roughly 500 million.

We have now probably worked the prewar Chinese statistics to the point of diminishing returns. A rather detailed comparison of our estimate of the population with estimates of food crop production and consumption in 1933, obtained independently of the population estimate, was presented in Chapter II. Although the check is not conclusive, the orders of magnitude of the three sets of figures appear to be roughly consistent.

Communist Population Statistics, 1952–57

The Communists claimed that they had taken a carefully planned and executed census in 1953 which showed a total population of 580 million. The important data are presented in Table 52. This census has been criticized unfavorably by both Chinese and Western students of population.[84] It is certain that this first comprehensive census ever attempted by the Communists is not as accurate as the censuses of modern, industrially advanced countries. Moreover, figures of higher than 600 million have been so loudly heralded by Communist leaders since 1953 that there is a natural suspicion of exaggeration. From a propaganda point of view, however, it is doubtful whether the world would be much more impressed by 600 million than by 500 million.

The Communist census data are likely to be less unreliable than most of their other economic statistics. It is probable that they knew more accurately what their population was than how much handwoven cotton cloth or how many cattle and hogs they had. Needless to say, no conclusive grounds can be found either to confirm or to reject the Communist population data within a narrow margin. The few indications show that the Communists' population data are fairly plausible. The male-to-female ratio given in the Communist data is 107.7, the smallest ever given in a Chinese census, and demographers would be inclined to support it.[85] The percentage of young children under 4 years of age, 15.6 per cent, comes close to the 15 per cent estimated in the study done under the supervision of Professor Kuznets.

[84] Chen Ta, *TCKT*, No. 12, 1957, pp. 1–2; Lawrence Krader and John S. Aird, "Sources of Demographic Data on Mainland China," *American Sociological Review*, Vol. 24, No. 5, October 1959, pp. 623–630.

[85] Willcox, *op.cit.*, p. 526.

Table 51

ESTIMATE OF POPULATION BY PROVINCE, EARLY 1930s

Province	Wang's estimate 1932–33		Adjustment for six provinces on the basis of other data			Adjustment for biases in sex and age distribution						Adjustment for minority population	Total population
	Households	Population	Households	Population	Preliminary adjusted population	Wang's data on sex ratios	Male population	Buck's data on sex ratios	Female population	Total population	Estimated infants and children ages 0–4		
	(thousand) (1)	(million) (2)	(thousand) (3)	(million) (4)	(million) (5)	(Female = 100) (6)	(million) (7)	(Female = 100) (8)	(million) (9)	(million) (10)	(million) (11)	(million) (12)	(million) (13)
Anhwei	3,833	22.0	—	—	22.0	121	12.0	111	10.8	22.8	1.2	—	24.0
Chahar	394	1.9	—	—	1.9	134	1.1	111	1.0	2.1	0.1	—	2.2
Chekiang	4,704	20.3	—	—	20.3	123	11.2	115	9.7	20.9	1.1	—	22.0
Fukien	1,907	9.6	2,265	11.8	11.8	136	6.8	120	5.7	12.5	0.6	—	13.1
Honan	6,041	32.6	—	—	32.6	117	17.6	104	16.9	34.5	1.8	—	36.3
Hopei	5,019	28.5	—	—	28.5	116	15.3	111	13.8	29.1	1.5	—	30.6
Hunan	5,759	30.3	—	—	30.3	127	16.9	114	14.8	31.7	1.7	—	33.4
Hupeh	5,443	25.7	—	—	25.7	116	13.8	114	12.1	25.9	1.4	—	27.3
Kansu	1,001	6.0	—	—	6.0	120	3.3	113	2.9	6.2	0.3	—	6.5
Kiangsi	3,143	14.2	—	—	14.2	135	8.0	104	7.7	15.7	0.8	—	16.5
Kiangsu	6,267	32.1	—	—	32.1	111	16.9	104	16.3	33.2	1.7	—	34.9
Kwangsi	2,324	11.9	—	—	11.9	127	6.7	108	6.2	12.9	0.7	3.0	16.6
Kwangtung	5,648	30.7	—	—	30.7	121	16.8	108	15.5	32.3	1.7	—	34.0
Kweichow	1,601	6.9	2,002	10.4	10.4	102	—	—	—	10.4	0.5	1.7	12.6
Ningsia	74	0.4	—	1.0	1.0	—	—	—	—	1.0	—	—	1.0
Shansi	2,197	11.1	—	—	11.1	122	6.1	107	5.7	11.8	0.6	—	12.4
Shantung	6,685	36.8	—	—	36.8	117	19.8	107	18.5	38.3	2.0	—	40.3
Shensi	1,911	9.0	—	—	9.0	121	4.9	113	4.3	9.2	0.5	—	9.7
Sikang	93	0.4	—	3.8	3.8	—	—	—	—	3.8	—	—	3.8
Suiyan	408	2.3	—	—	2.3	159	1.4	113	1.2	2.6	0.1	—	2.7
Szechwan	7,672	37.4	9,727	50.6	50.6	120	27.6	112	24.6	52.2	2.7	0.5	55.4
Tsinghai	207	1.2	—	—	1.2	120	0.6	113	0.6	1.2	0.1	—	1.3
Yunnan	2,338	11.8	—	—	11.8	107	—	—	—	11.8	0.6	3.5	15.9
Sinkiang	545	2.5	—	—	2.5	122	1.4	113	1.2	2.6	0.1	—	2.7
Manchuria	5,347	31.9	—	—	31.9	123	17.6	111	15.9	33.5	1.8	—	35.3
Mongolia	179	0.9	—	—	0.9	160	0.6	111	0.5	1.1	(*)	—	1.1
Tibet	142	0.8	—	1.4	1.4	—	—	—	—	1.4	—	—	1.4
Special municipalities and districts	—	10.1	—	—	10.1	—	—	—	—	10.1	—	—	10.1
Total:		429.3											503.1

NOTES: — No adjustment made.

(*) Less than 0.05 million.

Columns (1) and (2). Estimate by Wang for 1932–33. See Wang Shih-ta, "A New Estimate of Recent Chinese Population," *She-hui ko-hsueh tsa-chih* (Quarterly Review of Social Sciences), Vol. VI, No. 2, June 1935, pp. 208–210.

Columns (3), (4), and (5). Wang's estimates of the number of households have been compared with Willcox's estimate for 1912 (W. F. Willcox, "The Population of China and Its Modern Increase," *Studies in American Demography*, Ithaca, N.Y., Cornell University Press, 1940, Table 220, p. 523); Buck's estimates for the early 1930s (*Land Utilization*, Vol. III, pp. 416–419; Chang, *Crop Estimates*, Table 3, p. 13); and the official estimates given in *Statistical Abstract, 1940*, Table 5, p. 4, for 1936–37. Wang's figures on the number of households appear to be reasonable with the following exceptions:

(a) Fukien, Kweichow, and Szechwan: Wang's estimates for these provinces for 1932 are even smaller than the corresponding Willcox figures for 1912. These are replaced by the latest prewar official figures for 1936–37 given in *Statistical Abstract, 1940*, p. 4. This figure for the number of households is then multiplied by Wang's number of persons per household for all provinces, 5.2, to arrive at the population figures given in column (4).

(b) The outlying districts Ningsia, Sikang, and Tibet: the population in these districts is very small; any correction would not change the total population appreciably. Wang's figures, however, are replaced by the following, more recent estimates. Ningsia: *Statistical Abstract, 1940*, p. 4; Sikang: Chen Chung-wei, *Sikang wen-ti* (Problems of Sikang), Shanghai, 1930, p. 90, and Mei Hsui-ju, *Sikang*, Nanking, 1934, p. 14; Tibet: Kao Chang-chu, *Hsi-tsang kai-kwang* (General Conditions in Tibet), Taipeh, 1953, p. 98.

Columns (6) through (11). This adjustment corrects the biases in the sex and age distributions of Wang's data. The sex ratios given in Wang's estimate are reproduced in column (6). An estimate of male population in each province is then computed from the total population figures of these sex ratios used as given in column (7). The male population so obtained is believed to be more reliable than an estimate for female population obtained in a similar way. The more reliable estimates of sex ratio by Buck (quoted and used by Willcox, *op. cit.*, p. 526) are given in column (8).

In those provinces for which Buck's data are not available, the figure for the adjacent province is used instead. (For instance, the figure for Shensi is used for Kansu, and the figure for Kwangtung is used for Kwangsi.) No adjustment of the sex ratio has been made for Kweichow, Ningsia, Sikang, Yunnan, Tibet, and the special municipalities and districts. For Kweichow and Yunnan, Wang's original sex ratios for these two provinces are lower than 110. For Ningsia, Sikang, and Tibet, Wang's original population estimates have been replaced by more reliable estimates; no further adjustment is believed to be necessary. For the special municipalities and districts the population figures are believed to be fairly accurate.

The estimate of male population and Buck's data on sex ratio are used to compute estimates for number of females and total population. These figures are given in columns (9) and (10).

Underreporting of infants and young children has been estimated at 5 per cent of the total population, as previously discussed. This omission is therefore estimated at 0.05/0.95 of the figures given in column (10), and the results are given in column (11).

Column (12). This adjustment concerns the population of the minority nationals in the southwestern provinces of Kwangsi, Kweichow, Szechwan, and Yunnan. Numerous minority groups lived mostly in the remote mountainous regions and jungles of these provinces. The exact size of their population was never known during the prewar period because of their semi-isolation, and a large part of their population must have been excluded from population estimates. For the lack of a better alternative, it is assumed that the data have underestimated the population of these groups by an amount equal to 50 per cent of the Communist 1953 data given in *Chung-hua jen-min kung-ho-kuo fen-sheng ching-tu* (Detailed Provincial Maps of the People's Republic of China), Shanghai, Ti-tu chu-pan-she, 1953, notes to maps 28, 29, 31, 32. The estimates are given in column (12).

Column (13). The sum of columns (10), (11), and (12).

Table 52

POPULATION CENSUS OF 1953

Total Population by Province

Province	Population (millions)
Anhwei	30.3
Chekiang	22.9
Fukien	13.1
Honan	44.2
Hopei	36.0
Hunan	33.2
Hupeh	27.8
Kansu	12.9
Kiangsi	16.8
Kiangsu	41.3
Kwangsi	19.6
Kwangtung	34.8
Kweichow	15.0
Shansi	14.3
Shantung	48.9
Shensi	15.9
Sikang	3.4
Szechwan	62.3
Tsinghai	1.7
Yunnan	17.5
Sinkiang	4.9
Manchuria (Heilungkiang, Liaoning, Kirin, and part of Jehol)	46.8
Tibet	1.3
Inner Mongolia (Chahar, Suiyuan, Ningsia, and part of Jehol)	6.1
Municipalities (Shanghai, Peking, and Tientsin)	11.7
Mainland total	582.6

Sex Ratio by Age

Age groups	Sex ratio (females = 100)
All ages	107.7
Under 1 year	104.9
1–2 years	106.2
3–6 years	110.0
7–13 years	115.8
14–17 years	113.7
18–35 years	111.5
36–55 years	106.8
56 years and over	86.7

(Continued)

Table 52 (continued)

Age Composition

Age groups	Per cent of total population
All ages	100.0
Under 1 year	3.3
1–4 years	12.3
5–14 years	20.3
15–24 years	17.3
25–34 years	14.6
35–44 years	12.0
45–54 years	9.3
55–64 years	6.5
65–74 years	3.4
75 years and over	1.0

SOURCES: *Total Population by Province: Handbook on People's China*, Peiping, Foreign Language Press, 1957, pp. 13–14.

Sex Ratio by Age: Tai Shih-kuang, *1953 Population Census of China*, Calcutta, Indian Statistical Institute, December 20, 1956, p. 21.

Age Composition: Chen Ta, *New China's Population Census of 1953 and Its Relations to National Reconstruction and Demographic Research*, Stockholm, International Statistical Institute, August 8–15, 1957, p. 23.

Occupational Distribution, 1933

A summary of our estimate of the occupational distribution of the population in percentages and in number of people is presented in Table 53. The estimates of numbers of people are based on the percentage distributions by occupation, the 1933 total population estimated at 500 million, and a sex ratio of 112 males to 100 females.[86] The percentage distributions are obtained by piecing together estimates made by various organizations and scholars for different geographical areas and sectors of the economy; these are not necessarily for the year 1933. The procedure involves first, estimation of the percentages of the total population attributable to agricultural and nonagricultural population; second, the percentage distribution by occupation of the agricultural population; and third, the percentage distribution by occupation of the nonagricultural population. The details for these steps are discussed in the following three sections.

[86] For our estimate of the total population in 1933 see the preceding section of this chapter. The sex ratio was derived from "Future Growth of Chinese Population During Industrialization," May 1946 (unpublished).

Table 53

OCCUPATIONAL DISTRIBUTION, 1933

	Male	Female	Male	Female	Total
	(per cent)		(millions)		
Working population, age 7–64	62.9	39.3	166.3	92.9	259.2
Agriculture	47.2	34.0	124.6	80.3	204.9
Industry[a]	4.7	2.8	12.6	6.6	19.2
Trade	5.3	0.4	14.0	0.9	14.9
Transportation	2.9	1.5	7.7	3.6	11.3
Other nonagricultural occupations	2.8	0.6	7.4	1.5	8.9
Children under 7	19.7	19.3	52.0	45.6	97.6
Students, age 7 and over	2.7	1.5	7.2	3.6	10.8
Age 65 and over	2.5	3.7	6.3	8.8	15.1
Unemployed or idle, age 7–64[b]	12.2	(c)	32.2	(c)	(c)
Total	100.00	100.00	264.0	236.0	500.0

NOTES: [a] Includes manufacturing, utilities, mining, and construction.
[b] See discussion on following pages of the low age limit for the working population.
[c] Although it is possible to calculate the number of women in this category, the figure would be misleading because it includes not only housewives but also those who sought but could not find gainful employment. In all likelihood, the latter group would be just as large if not larger than the corresponding male segment.
SOURCES: Tables 54 and 55.

PERCENTAGE OF TOTAL POPULATION ATTRIBUTABLE TO AGRICULTURAL POPULATION

Agricultural population comprises farm households engaged solely in agricultural pursuits and those engaged jointly in agricultural and subsidiary occupations.[87] The relative size of the agricultural population used in this study is C. C. Chang's estimate of 73 per cent.[88] This figure is obtained on the basis of reports of local governments on the numbers of farm households and total households in 25 provinces in the early 1930s.

There are no figures for three entire provinces (Sikang, Tsinghai, and Kwangsi), 10 hsien in Sinkiang, 4 in Yunnan, and one each in Heilungkiang and Kweichow. Two attempts have been made to broaden the statistical coverage of Chang's estimate by including the missing figures. Buck's estimate is 74.5 per cent, very close to Chang's even after the data for Kwangsi were in-

[87] In prewar years, farmers engaged in agriculture and other occupations jointly derived their income primarily from agriculture. Hence they should be included as agricultural population (Buck, *Land Utilization*, Vol. I, p. 298).
[88] Chang, *Crop Estimates*, p. 13.

cluded in the calculation.[89] P. S. Ou arrived at a figure of 75.5 per cent by adding rough estimates for the three missing provinces.[90] Since the data for Kwangsi do not materially affect the original average, and since the estimates for the sparsely populated and remote provinces of Tsinghai and Sikang are in all likelihood much less reliable than those included in Chang's sample, it seems doubtful that Ou's adjustment could have improved upon Chang's estimate. In any event, the difference between the two is small.

Although Chang's figures on acreage of cultivated land and crop production are well known to be underestimates, there is no evidence to indicate that his figures for farm household and total households are biased in either direction. They are probably more reliable than his population figures or crop statistics since there is less possibility of such errors as underreporting of females and infants, or of farm acreage and output. In using Chang's estimate, we assume, of course, the same number of persons per household in the agricultural and nonagricultural sectors.

Rough estimates derived from Communist data for the postwar years are approximately of the same order of magnitude as the prewar estimates—73–77 per cent; the prewar figure is 73 per cent. To explain the derivation of these estimates, it is necessary to begin with the Communist concept of agricultural population, which is different from the one used here. In Communist terminology, agricultural population is defined as that part of the population supported primarily by agricultural income. It includes, among others, those who perform preliminary processing of agricultural products as a sole or an auxiliary occupation.[91] The Communist definition of agricultural population thus covers (a) those engaged in agricultural occupations only, (b) those engaged in agricultural and subsidiary occupations jointly, and (c) those engaged in subsidiary occupations only. The Communist concept is broader in scope than our definition, which excludes those engaged solely in subsidiary occupations.

Several Communist estimates of agricultural population are

[89] Buck, *Land Utilization,* Vol. III, Chapter XI, Table 1, p. 416.

[90] Ou, *National Income,* Vol. I, Table I, p. 151.

[91] Financial and Economic Commission, State Council, "Tentative Regulations on Agricultural Tax for Newly Liberated Areas," *Chung-yang ts'ai-ching cheng-tse fa-ling hui-pien,* Vol. II, June 1951, p. 303.

available. Assuming that the proportions of the three groups are the same for the postwar years as in Buck's survey, we derive the following rough estimates of agricultural population comparable in scope to our figure for 1933:[92]

	Agricultural population			
	Communist figures	Our estimate	Total population	Agricultural population in total population
Year	(million)		(million)	(per cent)
1949	470	414	536	77
1952	492	433	569	76
1953	485	427	581	73
1956	517	455	621	73
	528	465	621	75
	532	468	621	75

Occupational Distribution of the Agricultural Population

Table 54 presents an estimate of the occupational distribution of the agricultural population, derived as follows: First, the total population in agriculture is apportioned into those engaged in agriculture only, those engaged in agricultural and subsidiary occupations jointly, those not working (students, the aged, and the unemployed), and children under 7 years of age.

Buck's field study figure of age 7 as the borderline between children and the working population is used because that study is our basic statistical source; it is therefore not possible to raise the upper limit of the age group to, say, 12 or 16. Children help

[92] Sources of the Communist data on agricultural population are as follows: for the 1949 and second 1956 figures, Tan Chun-lin, "A Preliminary Analysis of the Income and Standard of Living of the Chinese Peasants," *HHPYK*, No. 11, June 1957, p. 105; for 1953 and the first 1956 figure, Ma Yin-chu, "A New Theory of Population," in his *My Economic Theory, Philosophy and Political Stand,* Peiping, Ts'ai-cheng chu-panshe, 1958, p. 161; for the 1952 and third 1956 figure, Li Shu-teh, "Peasants' Burden in 1956: Conditions and Problems," *Public Finance*, Peiping, No. 8, August 1957, p. 4. Our estimates of the agricultural population are derived by multiplying the Communist figures by 88 per cent, the percentage of all employed persons in farm areas engaged in farm work only and in farm and subsidiary work jointly given in Buck, *Land Utilization,* Vol. I, p. 290. The total population figures are from SSB, *Population Statistics,* p. 25.

Table 54

OCCUPATIONAL DISTRIBUTION OF THE AGRICULTURAL POPULATION, 1933

	Male	Female	Male	Female	Total
	(per cent)		(millions)		
Working population, age 7–64					
Agriculture only	33.16	13.24	87.54	31.25	118.78
Joint agriculture and subsidiary occupations	16.27	21.43	42.95	50.57	93.52
Agriculture	14.03	20.80	37.04	49.09	86.13
Industry[a]	0.84	0.59	2.22	1.39	3.61
Trade[b]	0.63	(*)	1.66	(**)	1.66
Transportation	0.43	(*)	1.14	(**)	1.14
Other nonagricultural occupations[c]	0.34	0.04	0.89	0.09	0.98
Children under 7	14.38	14.09	37.96	33.25	71.21
Students, age 7 and over[d]	1.30	0.72	3.43	1.70	5.13
Age 65 and over	1.75	2.70	4.62	6.37	10.99
Unemployed or idle, age 7–64	6.14	20.82[e]	16.22	49.14[e]	65.36[e]
Total	73.00	73.00	192.72	172.28	365.00

NOTES: (*) Less than 0.01 per cent.

(**) Less than 0.01 million.

[a] The sum of those in manufacturing and home industries in Buck's classification; it also includes mining, utilities, and construction.

[b] In prewar China, 45 per cent of farm products were held for sale after the harvest season (Buck, *Land Utilization*, Vol. I, p. 348). In addition, nonagricultural products manufactured by the farm households for sale were generally marketed by household members. Under the circumstances, it would be natural for any survey to include farmers engaged in these types of marketing, and those engaged in trade *per se* as farmers with subsidiary occupations. For our purpose, it is necessary to exclude those who were not actually traders. Lacking the information, we arbitrarily deduct one-half of the figure of farmers apparently engaged in trade (derived from the original survey) to allow for this item.

[c] The sum of those in professional service, public service, and others. However, the man-labor units for domestic service derived from Buck's survey are not included here because domestic service as a subsidiary occupation presumably means taking care of one's own household chores and is not considered gainful employment. See Chapter I for a definition of man-labor unit.

[d] Assumes: (1) one-sixth of the total number of students in elementary schools to be under 7. This amount is deducted from the total; (2) one-half of the number of students 7 and over to have come from the agricultural sector; and (3) the ratio of male to female students is 2:1.

[e] Including housewives.

SOURCES: Chang, *Crop Estimates*, p. 13; Buck, *Land Utilization*, Vol. I, Table 9, p. 372; Ministry of Education, National Government, *Ti-erh-tsi chung-kuo chiao-yu nien-chien* (The Second Chinese Education Yearbook), Shanghai, Commercial Press, 1948, pp. 1400, 1433, and 1457.

> with all kinds of work on farms so they should properly be included as part of the agricultural labor force.[93]

The apportionment is separate for the male and female population. Male children under age 7 are assumed to be 14.38 per cent of total males in the agricultural sector, the same percentage as for the entire male population.[94] The sum total for the working and nonworking male agricultural population age 7 and over can therefore be calculated at 58.62 per cent of the total male population by deducting the percentage for children from the total (73 per cent). To break down this total into agricultural occupations only, joint agricultural and subsidiary occupations, and those not working, we rely on Buck's data on occupational distribution of the male farm population age 7 and over. The estimates for the female agricultural population are similarly derived.

> For the male population age 7 and over, those engaged in agriculture only are calculated at 56.57 per cent, those in joint occupations at 34.29 per cent, and those not working at 9.13 per cent. For the female population age 7 and over, the corresponding figures are 22.48, 49.88, and 27.64 per cent.[95] Those in the nonworking category include all persons not gainfully employed.

Second, for the purpose of estimating the total number engaged in agriculture, it is necessary to separate joint occupations into man-labor units in agricultural and nonagricultural pursuits. Nonagricultural workers include government employees; civil servants; domestic servants; bank, finance, and school administration employees; and teachers. The separation is made on the basis of Buck's estimates of the proportions of farm population who worked in (1) agriculture alone, (2) agriculture and nonagricultural pursuits jointly, and (3) nonagricultural pursuits alone. The ratio of the people in group (3) to those in group (1) is used to split group (2) into the two categories.

Finally, the total nonworking agricultural population is segregated into the aged (65 and over), students age 7 and over, and persons

[93] For the sizable percentage of children in total agricultural workers, see Buck, *Land Utilization*, Vol. I, pp. 289–292.

[94] "Future Growth of Chinese Population During Industrialization," May 1946 (un-

[95] Buck, *Land Utilization*, Vol. I, Table 9, p. 372.

published).

between 7 and 64 who are not gainfully employed. From data on age distribution, the number of persons 65 and over can be calculated. The number of students in the agricultural sector is roughly known. The idle or unemployed between 7 and 64 can then be derived as a residual. It should be noted that idle means idle for the entire year. By this definition, there were only 16 million unemployed males between 7 and 64 in agriculture, or 3 per cent of the total population. There can be little doubt that most of the 87 million male agricultural workers were actually working part time. According to the sample study by Buck, only 35 per cent of the total number of able-bodied and working men (ages 15–60) had full-time work.[96] If the number of part-time workers is converted to man-labor units, the figure for unemployed males might well be considerably higher.

OCCUPATIONAL DISTRIBUTION OF THE NONAGRICULTURAL POPULATION

The occupational distribution of the nonagricultural population is given in Table 55. These figures are derived by estimating the percentage of (1) those gainfully employed and allocating them to the different nonagricultural occupations; and (2) those not gainfully employed and allocating this total into children, students, the aged, and the unemployed or idle. Again this is done separately for the male and female populations.

The percentage of people gainfully employed in nonagricultural occupations is first derived separately for males and females. The basic data used are the occupational censuses of Chekiang province for 1932, or Yunnan province for 1932, and of Kiangning hsien for 1933. The distribution in each of the other provinces is assumed to be the same as one or a combination of these three distributions. Kiangsu and Liaoning are assumed to have the same distribution as the average of Kiangning and Chekiang; Kwangtung and Hopei, the same as Chekiang; Hunan, Hupeh, Szechwan, and Shantung, the same as the average of Chekiang and Yunnan; Anhwei, Fukien, Kwangsi, Kweichow, Kiangsi, Sikang, Tsinghai, Sinkiang, Kansu, Shensi, Shansi, Honan, Kirin, Heilungkiang, Jehol, Chahar, and Suiyuan, the same as Yunnan. Each distribution is then weighted by the population of the province given in Table 51 to derive a distribution for the mainland as a whole.

The occupational distribution must be adjusted in one important

[96] *Ibid.*, Table 6, p. 294.

Table 55

OCCUPATIONAL DISTRIBUTION OF THE NONAGRICULTURAL POPULATION, 1933

	Male	Female	Male	Female	Total
	(per cent)		(million)		
Working population, age 7–64[a]	13.53	4.74	35.72	11.19	46.91
Industry	3.93	2.22	10.38	5.24	15.62
Factories	—	—	—	—	1.13
Handicrafts	—	—	—	—	12.13
Mining	—	—	—	—	0.77
Utilities	—	—	—	—	0.04
Construction	—	—	—	—	1.55
Trade	4.65	0.40	12.28	0.94	13.22
Transportation	2.49	1.52	6.57	3.59	10.16
Other nonagricultural occupations	2.46[b]	0.60[b]	6.49	1.42	7.91
Children					
Under 7	5.32	5.21	14.04	12.29	26.33
Under 12	8.99	8.53	23.72	20.13	43.86
Students					
Age 7 and over	1.45	0.81	3.83	1.91	5.74
Age 12 and over	0.15	0.08	0.40	0.20	0.60
Age 65 and over	0.65	1.00	1.72	2.36	4.08
Unemployed or idle					
Age 7–64	6.05	15.24[c]	15.97	35.97[c]	51.94[c]
Age 12–64	3.68	12.65[c]	9.71	29.85[c]	39.56[c]
Total	27.00	27.00	71.28	63.72	135.00

NOTES: — Not available.

[a] We take age 7 as the lower age limit of the working population merely for the convenience of grouping on the same basis as the agricultural working population. Actually the age of the working nonagricultural population falls mostly within the range of 12–64 rather than 7–64.

[b] Included in the original data on persons engaged in education are students. On the assumption that there were, on the average, 40 students to one teacher or administrator, we can estimate and deduct the number of students from the total number of persons in education.

[c] Including housewives.

SOURCES: *Statistical Abstract, 1935*, p. 259; *Shen Pao Yearbook, 1935*, pp. B87–88, B91–92; *Industrial Handbook: Kiangsu*, p. 13; Ministry of Education, National Government, *Ti-erh-tsi chung-kuo chiao-yu nien-chien*, 1948, pp. 1400, 1433, and 1457; Appendixes F and H; and text of this chapter.

respect. In the three surveys, the nonagricultural occupations include subsidiary nonagricultural occupations. For example, a hand-drawn cart in a village might have been operated by a professional carrier or by a part-time farmer. In either case, the person handling the cart would be engaged in transportation according to the provincial and county surveys. In order to estimate the number of people engaged solely in nonagricultural occupations, we must deduct those subsidiary nonagricultural workers from the provincial and hsien survey totals. Before we make this adjustment, those in industry and transportation combined must be separated into their individual categories. For this purpose, the proportions of these two categories of workers for Kiangsu province in 1932 are used.[97] From the estimates based on provincial and hsien surveys, we can now subtract the estimates for man-labor units in industry, transportation, trade, and "other" given in Table 54, to arrive at the estimates for those engaged in nonagricultural occupations only.

For the purpose of deriving value added by handicrafts, the estimate of employment in industry as a whole is subdivided into factories, handicrafts, mining, utilities, and construction. The number of workers in factories is the sum of workers in China proper and in Manchuria, given in Appendix F.[98] The number of workers in mining, utilities, and construction are estimated in Appendix H. The number in handicrafts can be derived as a residual by deducting the number of workers in factories, mining, utilities, and construction from the number of workers in industry as a whole.

Since the percentage of total population attributable to nonagricultural population is known, the percentage for the unemployed nonagricultural population can be obtained by subtracting the estimate for the employed nonagricultural population from the total. This percentage is then subdivided into the four separate groups. The numbers of people over 65, under 7, and under 12 years of age are calculated from information on prewar age distribution. It is assumed that age distribution is the same in the nonagricultural population as in total population. It was noted that in rural areas children between 7 and 12 years of age usually participated in many kinds of farm work, but probably very few children under 12 were actually employed in urban areas. In fact, one can reasonably assume that workers in the nonagricultural sector ranged between 12 and 64 years of age.

In order to present a clearer picture of the size of the labor force and the idle share in the nonagricultural sector, it seems desirable

[97] *Industrial Handbook: Kiangsu,* pp. 18–19. Kiangsu is a relatively industrialized province, and it might be argued that it is not representative of the nation as a whole. However, the data for this province are used only for the proportions of the two categories, not to separate the industrial population from the total.

[98] Lieu, *Industry Survey;* Wang Fu-shun, *op. cit.;* and South Manchurian Railway, *op. cit.*

to calculate two sets of figures, one with 7 years and the other with 12 years as the lower age limit for the labor force. Since the number of students is roughly known, the residual represents the unemployed or idle, obtained by subtracting estimates for the number of workers, the aged, children, and students from the total nonagricultural population. The results are given in Table 55.

An indirect way of judging the reliability of the occupational distribution figures given in Table 53 is to compare the nonagricultural segment of the national distribution with the occupational distribution in the large cities on the one hand, and the subsidiary occupational distribution of the agricultural population on the other. Such a comparison is made in Table 56. The percentages of males in industry and trade decrease more or less by the same proportion from

Table 56

COMPARATIVE PREWAR OCCUPATIONAL DISTRIBUTION, EARLY 1930s
(per cent)

Occupation	Total males			Total females		
	Twelve leading cities[a]	Other nonagricultural population[b]	Agricultural population[c]	Twelve leading cities[a]	Other nonagricultural population[b]	Agricultural population[c]
Manufacturing, mining, utilities, and construction	20.3	14.1	1.2	5.1	8.4	0.8
Transportation and communications	6.2	9.5	0.6	0.5	5.9	(*)
Trade	19.5	17.0	0.9	1.3	1.5	(*)
Others	54.0	59.4	97.3	93.1	84.2	99.2
Total	100.0	100.0	100.0	100.0	100.0	100.0

NOTES: (*) Less than 0.01 per cent.

[a] The twelve largest cities are Nanking, Shanghai, Tientsin, Peiping, Tsingtao, Canton, Hankow, Taiyuan, Changsha, Weihaiwai, Hwaining, and Wuhu.

Bureau of Statistics, National Government, *Chung-kuo jen-kou wen-ti chih t'ung-chi fen-hsi* (A Statistical Analysis of China's Population Problems), Chungking, 1944, p. 42; Shanghai Civic Association, *Shanghai-shih ti-fang t'ung-chi* (Statistics of Shanghai), 1933, Population, p. 5; *Shen Pao Yearbook, 1933*, pp. B93–94; and *Industrial Handbook: Shansi*, pp. C8–9. The figures are the weighted averages (the weights being the population of the twelve cities in *Shen Pao Yearbook, 1935*, and *Industrial Handbook, op. cit.*) expressed in percentages of total male and female population in the twelve cities on the basis of the sex ratio of the different groups in industry, transportation, trade, other nonagricultural occupations, and the residual for Nanking and Hankow (*Statistical Abstract, 1935*, p. 259; *Shen Pao Yearbook, 1935*, p. B94).

[b] Derived from figures for the total nonagricultural population in Table 55, and those for the twelve cities as cited above.

[c] Based on Table 54.

the leading cities, through the other nonagricultural population, to the agricultural population. Transportation has a greater percentage in the Other nonagricultural column than in the Twelve leading cities column because more manpower is required in old-fashioned transportation than in modern means of transport. Similarly, because a majority of the handicraft workers outside of the leading cities were females, a higher proportion of females are in manufacturing in the Other nonagricultural column than in the Twelve leading cities column.

The following tabulation compares our estimates of the relative shares of employment in the major industrial sectors in the 1930s with the average figures for countries with low per capita income in the 1950s. The average figures are those for countries with the lowest per capita income.[99] The figures given here are those including unpaid family labor and are more comparable to our figures than those excluding this item. Buck's data, which provide the primary basis of our estimate for the agricultural sector, also include unpaid family labor.[100] With due allowance for the roughness of the estimates and for other problems of international comparison, the two sets of figures exhibit a striking similarity in over-all pattern.

	Relative shares of major sectors in total employment (per cent)	
	Average for countries with low per capita income, 1950s	China, 1930s
Agriculture	79.9	79.0
Manufacturing, mining, utilities, and construction	6.6	7.4
Trade	4.6	5.7
Transportation	2.3	4.3
Others	6.5	3.6
Total	100.0	100.0

[99] Simon Kuznets, *Quantitative Aspects of the Economic Growth of Nations,* Supplement to *Economic Development and Cultural Change,* Vol. V, No. 4, July 1957, Tables 10, 13, pp. 23, 27. The classification of the various income groups is explained on p. 7.

[100] The figures given for China in the 1930s are computed from Table 53.

Employment, 1952–57

The estimates of employment for 1952–57 were presented in Table 11. The procedure used for each industrial sector is discussed below, and the results of our calculations are then compared with the Communist figure for nonagricultural employment.

As distinguished from the rather narrow Communist definition of a worker as a wage earner engaged in occupations involving physical labor, the term "worker" is used in this study to include all those who are gainfully employed. Thus all laborers, office employees, wage and salary earners, and self-employed persons are included.

Because the primary purpose of deriving the employment estimates is to study their relation to our output figures, we have estimated the average number (instead of the year-end total) of full-time workers in a given year. In some cases the figure is drawn directly from Communist sources. In others, the arithmetic mean of the figures at the beginning and end of a period is taken to be the average for the period. According to the Communist standard, full-time means eight hours per day and 306 days per year.[101] Actual working time generally exceeds the official standard, however, because of constant pressure to overfulfill production quotas.[102] Long working hours appear to be fairly common among all industries and at all times, so interindustry and intertemporal comparisons of the number of workers in the period concerned would not be appreciably affected. In a comparison of prewar and postwar output per worker, however, the longer hours in the postwar period might result in a misleading impression of higher labor productivity.

The employment estimates are made primarily on the basis of Communist data. As the Communists themselves openly admitted, their employment figures were rather poor.[103] Our employment figures, therefore, are somewhat less reliable than our output estimates.

[101] Ma Wen-ray, "A Decade of Struggle To Develop Productivity Rapidly and To Improve the Living Conditions of the Workers," *People's Daily*, September 25, 1959, p. 10; Hsu Kang, "On the Problem of Comparing the Standard of Living of the Workers and Peasants," *TCKT*, No. 16, August 1957, p. 33.

[102] One Communist official conceded that working hours averaged 10 hours a day, and a foreign observer noted that even a 14-hour day was not uncommon (Robert Guillain, *The Blue Ants*, London, Secker and Warburg, 1957, p. 93). Other miscellaneous reports also indicate rather long hours; for example, 60 per cent of the workers in a retail store in Peiping worked 9–10 hours daily and the rest more than 9 hours. See *Chung-kuo kung-jen* (Chinese Worker), Peiping, No. 6, 1956, p. 12.

[103] Hsieh Mu-ch'iao, "Summary Report to the Fourth Conference on Statistical Work," *HHYP*, No. 6, June 1955, p. 148.

In the employment estimates, the margin of error again varies from sector to sector. The estimates for the four modern sectors given in Table 23 are probably the least unreliable.

AGRICULTURE

The number of agricultural workers in 1952–57 is derived on the assumption that net value added per worker in real terms was the same as in 1933. Net value added by agriculture in 1933 was given at 18.76 billion yuan in Table 36 and the number of workers can be derived at 204.92 million from data in Tables 53 and 54. Net value added per worker can be calculated at 18,760/204.92 = 92 yuan. Total net value added by agriculture was estimated in Table 36 at 18.39, 18.73, 19.16, 19.39, 19.76, and 19.85 billion 1933 yuan for 1952–57. The number of agricultural workers can be calculated by dividing each of these figures by 92 yuan. Using the same assumption, a set of adjusted estimates of agricultural workers, corresponding to the adjusted estimates of net value added in agriculture given in Table 68, can be derived at 183.15, 185.65, 189.89, 201.96, 213.48, and 228.26 million yuan for 1952–57.

FACTORIES, MINING, AND UTILITIES

The number of workers in factories, mining, and utilities is derived by adjusting the Communist data on industrial workers to conform to our classification. In Communist terminology, industry includes not only factories, mining, and electric power, but also handicraft workshops, lumbering, and a part of fishery. On the other hand, those using native methods in coal and salt mines, and those working in water and gas supply are not classified as industrial workers by the Communists. Hence, the number of workers in handicraft workshops, lumbering, and a part of fishery must be subtracted from, and those in water and gas supply and in native coal and salt mining added to, the Communist estimate of industrial workers to find the number of workers in factories, mining, and utilities. These calculations are shown in Table 57.

HANDICRAFTS

The total number of handicraft workers includes those in handicraft workshops and cooperatives, individual handicraftsmen, and such others as the full-time equivalent of housewives and farmers

Table 57

WORKERS IN FACTORIES, MINING, AND UTILITIES, 1952–57
(millions)

	1952	1953	1954	1955	1956	1957
1. Industrial workers, Communist estimate	5.41	6.05	6.18	6.25	6.59	7.32
2. Deduct:						
a. Lumbering	0.20	0.25	0.30	0.28	0.28	0.36
b. Part of fishery	(*)	(*)	(*)	(*)	(*)	(*)
c. Handicraft workshops	1.98	2.00	2.00	2.00	2.00	2.00
3. Add:						
a. Native mining	0.29	0.29	0.29	0.45	0.47	0.51
b. Water and gas utilities	0.02	0.02	0.02	0.03	0.03	0.04
4. Equals: Factories, mining, and utilities	3.54	4.12	4.20	4.44	4.81	5.50

NOTES: (*) Less than 0.01 million.

Line 1. Industrial workers, Communist estimate. The 1952 figure is given in *First Five Year Plan*, pp. 128–129. No annotation is given as to whether it refers to year-end or average for the year, but we assume that the estimate is the average. The figures for 1953–55 are obtained by summing (i) the numbers of workers in state and cooperative industrial enterprises (3.55, 3.85, and 4.15 million), (ii) workers in joint state and private industrial enterprises (0.27, 0.53, and 0.78 million), and (iii) workers in private industrial enterprises (2.23, 1.80, and 1.31 million).

The average number of state and cooperative industrial workers in 1953, 3.55 million, is the arithmetic average of the beginning and end of the year (3.21 and 3.89 million) given in *1953 Communique*. The 1954 figure, 3.85 million, is interpolated from the 1953 and 1955 estimates. The 1955 figure, 4.15 million, is the total number of state and cooperative industrial workers at the end of the third quarter given in SSB, *1955 Employment*, p. 89. The number of workers in joint state and private industrial enterprises in 1952–55 are given in SSB, "Development of State Capitalism in China's Industry," *HHPYK*, No. 2, January 1957, p. 68. The numbers of workers in private industrial enterprises in 1953–55 are taken from Ching Hua, Liang Sze-ta, *et al.*, *Chi-nien-lai wor-kuo sze-ying kung-shang-yeh ti pien-hua* (*1949–56*) (Changes in China's Private Industry and Trade in the Past Seven Years), Peiping, 1957, p. 8. Industrial workers for the economy as a whole in 1956 are derived by adding to our 1955 estimate the increase in the average number of industrial workers in the period 1955–56 given in State Planning Commission, "Labor and Wages in 1956," *CHCC*, No. 3, March 1957, p. 14. The figure for 1957 is the average of the numbers of workers at the beginning and end of the same year, given at 7.17 and 7.47 million, in SSB, "Statistical Materials Concerning Improvements in the Workers' Living Conditions," *TCKT*, No. 14, July 1957, p. 13; and Su Chung, "Facts About China's Population," *Peking Review*, Peiping, No. 18, July 1, 1958, p. 10.

Line 2. a: Lumbering. Workers in lumbering in 1952 and 1955–57 are derived from data on the output of raw timber and output per worker. For the output of raw timber in 1952–57 see *Great Ten Years*, p. 85. Average output per worker in 1952 is given at 56 cubic meters in Kung Chung-hua and Li Yuan, "A Balance Sheet for the Timber Industry," *TCKT*, No. 14, July 1957, p. 30. Average output per worker for 1957 is calculated at 77 cubic meters on the basis of information in *TKP*, Peiping, October 1, 1957, p. 2. Output per worker in 1955 is assumed to be the same as that of 1954, 74 cubic meters, which is derived from output and employment in 1954. The figure for 1956 is assumed to be the average of those for 1954 and 1957. Total employment in 1954 is given in *NCNA*, Peiping, September 24, 1954. Total employment for 1953 is the average of 1952 and 1954.

(Continued)

Table 57 (continued)

Line 2. b: Part of fishery. Included in this category are the wage earners in the state-owned fishing enterprises. For 1952 and 1957 they are roughly estimated on the basis of the numbers of modern fishing boats in 1952 and 1957 given in *HHPYK*, No. 6, 1958, p. 98, and the assumption of ten workers per boat. The results for 1953–56 are interpolations from the 1952 and 1957 figures and a linear time trend.

Line 2. c: Handicraft workshops. Workers in 1952 and 1956 are derived by dividing the gross value of output of handicraft workshops (given in Appendix F, Table F-16) by the gross output per worker, estimated at 2,500 yuan for 1952 and 4,150 yuan for 1956. Gross output per worker in 1956 is the arithmetic average of that for handicraft cooperatives and handicraftsmen with some mechanized equipment in 1956, given in *People's Daily*, February 15, 1957, p. 2. The figure for 1952 is derived on the assumption that gross output per worker increased during the period 1952–56 in proportion to income per worker in the handicraft cooperatives, given at 166 per cent, with 1952 as 100, in *TKP*, Peiping, December 17, 1957, p. 3. We assume that for 1953–55 and 1957 the number of workers in handicraft workshops remained at the 1952 and 1956 level, 2 million.

Line 3. a: Native mining. Native mining refers to mining by indigenous methods. This generally means mining without the use of mechanical power. Coal and salt are perhaps the only two important minerals produced on a large scale by primitive methods. The employment figures for native coal mining in 1952–57 are derived by dividing the output of coal produced by native methods, given in Appendix H, Table H-2, by the output per worker, estimated at 150 tons on the basis of data given in Appendix H, Tables H-1 and H-3. The output of salt in 1952–57 fluctuated rather widely because of weather conditions. It does not seem likely that employment also varied so drastically. For the relatively normal years (1952, 1955, and 1957), the number of workers is derived by dividing the output of salt, given in Appendix H, Table H-2, by the output per worker in 1933, computed from data given in Tables H-1 and H-3. The number of workers in 1953–54 is assumed to be the same as in 1952, and for 1956, the average of 1955 and 1957.

Line 3. b: Water supply and gas utilities. The number of workers in these two industries in 1952–57 is assumed to have increased from 1933 in proportion to the physical quantities of output of water and gas over the same period. For the output estimates for 1933 and 1952–57 and the employment estimates for 1933, see Appendix H under Utilities.

engaged in part-time handicrafts. The number of workers in handicraft workshops is estimated in Table 58. The figures for handicraft cooperatives and individual handicraftsmen are primarily Communist estimates, presumably including those engaged in native mining (without the use of mechanical power). The number of handicraftsmen in the "Others" category in 1952 is estimated on the basis of net value added by those workers and a rough estimate of net value added per worker. The figures for 1953–57 are extrapolations from the 1952 figure using an index of agricultural output in 1952–57, derived from data in Table 36. Using the same method and the adjusted estimates of agricultural output given in Table 68, we can derive a second set of figures for "other" handicraftsmen at 3.14, 3.17, 3.23, 3.42, 3.64, and 3.99 million for 1952–57. The sum total of these four groups of handicraftsmen, minus the number of native miners, represents the number of workers in handicrafts. The results of these calculations are given in Table 58.

Table 58

WORKERS IN HANDICRAFTS, 1952–57
(millions)

	1952	1953	1954	1955	1956	1957
Handicraft workshops	1.98	2.00	2.00	2.00	2.00	2.00
Individual and cooperative handicraftsmen	7.36	7.79	8.91	8.20	7.30	8.00
Individual	7.13	7.49	7.70	6.00	4.90	—
Cooperative	0.23	0.30	1.21	2.20	2.40	—
Others	4.18	4.26	4.30	4.39	4.51	4.56
Less: native miners	0.02	0.02	0.02	0.03	0.03	0.05
Total	13.50	14.03	15.19	14.56	13.78	14.51

NOTES: — Not available.

Handicraft workshops. See Table 57.

Individual and cooperative handicraftsmen. For the 1952–55 figures, see *Great Ten Years*, p. 30. The 1956 figure is the sum of the numbers of handicraftsmen who were organized into cooperatives by the Central Handicraft Administration Bureau or were to be so organized by the Ministries of Agriculture, Commerce, and Local Industry. The total number of handicraftsmen in the first group is computed at 4.9 million on the basis of 4.3 million total handicraftsmen already in cooperatives and 88 per cent of the latter figure in the total as given in *TCKTTH*, No. 9, 1956, p. 1. The number of those in the second group, 2.4 million, is given in the same source. The figure for 1957 is taken from *TKP*, Peiping, December 17, 1957, p. 1.

Others. The 1952 figure is obtained as follows: Net value added by the handicraft workshops in 1952 is first derived at 1.42 billion yuan by multiplying the total number of workers, 1.98 million, by the net value added per worker. This figure, 715 yuan, is obtained on the assumption that the ratio of net value added per worker in handicraft workshops to that for the individual handicraftsman and handicraft cooperatives is 2.5, which is the same ratio as gross output per worker in workshops to gross output per worker in individual and cooperative handicrafts. Gross output per worker for the two groups of handicraftsmen is computed from data on employment and gross output given in this table and in Appendix F, Table F-16. The net value added per individual and cooperative handicraftsman is assumed to be the same as in 1933, 286 yuan. We deduct the net value added by the workshop handicraftsmen in 1952 yuan (1.42 billion) from total net value added by handicrafts as a whole (4.72 billion), given in Table 44, to arrive at the net value added by individual, cooperative, and other handicraftsmen, 3.30 billion. Dividing 3.30 billion by the net value added per worker we obtain the total number of individual, cooperative, and other handicraftsmen. Since the number of the first two groups is known, the number of other handicraftsmen can be calculated as a residual at 4.18 million yuan. For 1953–57, the estimates of other handicraftsmen are extrapolations from the 1952 figure on the basis of an index of agricultural output derived from data in Table 36.

CONSTRUCTION

The Communist estimates in 1952–57 for this industry are adjusted to include both the regular and temporary workers. The details are given in Table 59.

Table 59

WORKERS IN CONSTRUCTION, 1952–57
(millions)

	1952	1953	1954	1955	1956	1957
Regular workers	1.04	1.50	—	1.70	—	—
Temporary workers	0.25	0.32	—	0.25	—	—
Total	1.29	1.82	1.90	1.95	2.44	2.40

NOTES: — Not available.

1952: The number of workers in the state-owned construction enterprises in 1952 is given at 1.021 million, 98.3 per cent of the total number of construction workers (*First Five Year Plan*, p. 129; SSB, "Basic Conditions in China's Construction Industry," *TCKTTH*, No. 24, 1956, p. 31). The total is therefore calculated at 1.039 million. This figure presumably does not include the temporary workers, roughly estimated on the basis of the following considerations: The number of temporary workers at the end of 1953 is reported at 0.63 million, and at the end of the third quarter of 1955, 0.52 million (*1953 Communique;* and SSB, *1955 Employment*, p. 89). We assume a year-end figure of 0.50 million for 1952. In general, the volume of construction work is much heavier in the fourth quarter than in the first three quarters. For 1953 the average volume of work per quarter is approximately one-half of that of the fourth quarter ("Certain Problems in Basic Construction Planning," *CHCC*, No. 6, June 1957, pp. 8–9, 33). On the assumption that the number of temporary workers changes in proportion to the volume of construction work, the average number of temporary workers is derived at 0.25 million, one-half of the year-end total.

1953: The number of regular workers in 1953 is estimated at 1.50 million by multiplying the year-end figure of 1.54 million, given in the *1953 Communique*, by a factor equal to the ratio of the annual average to year-end total for state-owned construction enterprises in 1952 given in *First Five Year Plan*, p. 129; and SSB, "Statistical Materials Concerning Improvements in the Workers' Living Conditions," *TCKT*, No. 14, July 1957, p. 13. The average annual number of temporary workers is assumed to be one-half of the year-end total of 0.63 million, given in the *1953 Communique*.

1954: The 1954 figure is based on a report that the total number of construction workers, presumably including temporary workers, reached over 2 million (*NCNA*, Peiping, April 28, 1954). Applying the 1953 ratio of average to year-end figures to the reported figure of 2 million and rounding, we obtain a total of 1.90 million.

1955: The 1955 figure is derived from the percentage distribution of total employment by industries (including government) given in Chen Ta, "New China's Population Census of 1953 and Its Relation to National Reconstruction and Demographic Research" (a paper presented at a conference of the International Statistical Institute, Stockholm, August 8–15, 1957); and the number of workers in government administration given in SSB, *1955 Employment*, p. 87.

1956: The figure for 1956 is derived by adding to the 1955 figure of 1.95 million the increase in the average number of workers in 1955–56 given at 0.49 million in State Planning Commission, "Labor and Wages in 1956," *CHCC*, No. 3, March 1957, p. 14.

1957: The 1957 figure is the rounded arithmetic average of the two year-end figures, 2.95 million for 1956 and 1.91 million for 1957. The 1956 year-end estimate is given in SSB, "Statistical Materials Concerning Improvements in the Workers' Living Conditions," *TCKT*, No. 14, July 1957, p. 13. The 1957 year-end estimate is computed on the basis of an estimate of 2.33 million for August 1958, a 22 per cent increase over the figure for the end of 1957 (SSB, "The Big Leap Forward in Basic Construction Work," *TCYC*, No. 9, September 1958, p. 10).

TRANSPORTATION AND COMMUNICATIONS

The estimates of the number of workers in this industry are made separately for (a) the modern sector, which includes the railroads, coastal and inland water transport by steamships and motor barges, civil air transport, motor transport, postal and telecommunications, and municipal transit service; and (b) the traditional sector, which

Table 60

WORKERS IN TRANSPORTATION AND COMMUNICATIONS, 1952–57
(millions)

	1952	1953	1954	1955	1956	1957
Modern sector	0.73	0.79	0.96	1.13	1.32	1.43
Transportation and communications	0.72	0.78	0.95	1.12	1.30	1.41
Municipal transit	0.01	0.01	0.01	0.02	0.02	0.02
Traditional sector	10.90	10.08	9.67	9.63	10.20	10.00

NOTES: *Modern sector: transportation and communications.* The total number of workers in state-owned and joint state and private enterprises is given at 0.716 million in *First Five Year Plan*, p. 129. No information is available on the number of workers in the modern private sector, but since this sector consists of only a small number of privately owned motor transport companies, the figure above is rounded to 0.72 million to allow for those workers. The 1953 figure is the total for the end of the year given in the *1953 Communique*, and the 1955 figure is the end of September estimate for that year given in SSB, *1955 Employment*, p. 89. It is assumed that these two figures are the same as the annual averages for the two years. The 1954 figure is an interpolation from the estimates for 1953 and 1955. The 1956 figure is the sum of the 1955 figure and the increase in 1955–56 given in State Planning Commission, "Labor and Wages in 1956," *CHCC*, No. 3, March 1957, p. 14. The 1957 figure is obtained as follows. The total number of workers in industry, construction, and modern transportation and communications in November 1957 is given at 12 million in *People's Daily*, November 30, 1957, p. 1. From this total, we deduct the number of workers in industry (7.91) and construction, and 2.40 million, given in Table 59 and in SSB, "Rapid Development in China's Industrial Construction," *TCYC*, No. 9, September 1958, p. 5, to arrive at the year-end total of 1.69 million for modern transportation and communications. This figure is then multiplied by the ratio of the annual average to year-end total for 1956 to obtain the average number of workers in 1957. For the 1956 average figure see the explanation above, and for the 1956 year-end total, 1.56 million, see SSB, "Statistical Materials Concerning Improvements in the Workers' Living Conditions," *TCKT*, No. 14, July 1957, p. 13.

Municipal transit. The number of vehicles in municipal transit service is 3,500 in 1952 and 6,100 in 1957 (*Great Ten Years*, p. 69). We arbitrarily assume a figure of three workers per vehicle and derive the total number of workers at 10,000 for 1952 and 18,000 for 1957. The figures for 1953–56 are then interpolated from those for 1952 and 1957 and a linear time trend.

Traditional sector. The number of old-fashioned transportation workers is derived by dividing the net value added in 1952–57 (in 1952 prices) given in Table 48, by the net value added per worker, estimated at 243 yuan in Appendix H. The same procedure and the adjusted estimate of net value added by old-fashioned transportation given in Table 68 are used to derive the corresponding adjusted estimates of the number of old-fashioned transportation workers.

includes coolies, human or animal-drawn carts, wheelbarrows, boats, pedicabs, and rickshas. The estimates for the modern sector are derived from Communist figures with minor adjustments for the differences in the annual average and year-end totals. The estimates for the traditional sector are derived on the assumption that net value added per worker in real terms in 1952–57 is the same as in 1933. The results are given in Table 60. The corresponding estimates based on the adjusted estimate of net value added by old-fashioned transportation are 11.07, 9.51, 8.56, 9.14, 9.30, and 10.00 million.

TRADE

Table 61 summarizes our estimates of the numbers of workers in trading stores and restaurants (including food stalls), and peddlers, for 1952–57. The figures for trading stores are derived primarily from Communist data on workers in stores classified by types of ownership. For restaurants, only the data for 1952, 1955, and 1956 are available. The figures for 1953–54 are arbitrarily assumed to be the average of those for 1952 and 1956, and the figures for 1957 are assumed to be the same as for 1956.

For peddlers, estimates are made separately for urban and rural areas, although total figures are available. There are reasons to believe that these "totals" are not the national totals but are for urban areas only. In one Communist source it is clearly noted that the number of peddlers and private trading stores (which check well with the State Statistical Bureau's total figures for the comparable years) represent only a part of the national total.[104] A statement by Hsu Ti-hsin, the Director of the Central Administration of Industry and Commerce, indicates that the number of workers in the private trading sector *in the urban areas* in 1952 totalled 6.7 million, which again comes very close to the State Statistical Bureau's "total" of 6.768 million.[105] In short, peddlers in the rural areas have been omitted. The reasons are fairly obvious. Statistical information on a group of people scattered over an area of over 4 million square

[104] Ching Hua, Liang Sze-ta, *et al.*, *Chi-nin-lai wor-kuo sze-ying kung-shang-yeh ti pien-hua* (Changes in China's Private Industry and Trade in the Past Seven Years), Peiping, 1957, p. 3. Total numbers of workers in trading stores plus part of the number of peddlers in 1952–55 are 6.768, 6.079, 4.464, and 3.901 million (*ibid.*, p. 123). SSB, *Commercial Network,* pp. 81–82, gives 6.768 million for 1952 and 3.642 for 1955.

[105] Hsu Ti-hsin, *Chung-kuo kuor-tu she-chi kuo-min ching-chi ti fen-hsi* (An Analysis of the National Economy During China's Transition Period), Ko-hsueh chu-panshe, Peiping, 1959, p. 46.

Table 61

WORKERS IN TRADING STORES AND RESTAURANTS, AND PEDDLERS: YEAR-END TOTALS AND ANNUAL AVERAGES, 1952–57

(millions)

Activity	1952	1953	1954	1955	1956	1957
(*a*) *Year-end totals*						
1. State and cooperative stores	1.40	1.50	1.85	2.57	—	—
2. Private stores	4.01	3.16	2.26	1.64	—	—
3. Urban peddlers	2.76	2.92	2.20	2.27	—	—
4. Total in urban areas	8.17	7.58	6.31	6.47	6.81	7.69
5. Rural peddlers	4.24	4.50	3.50	2.67	2.80	2.80
6. Restaurants	1.45	1.40	1.40	1.40	1.35	1.35
7. Total	13.86	13.48	11.21	10.54	10.96	11.84
(*b*) *Annual averages*						
1. State and cooperative stores	1.13	1.45	1.68	2.21	—	—
2. Private stores	4.01	3.59	2.71	1.95	—	—
3. Trading stores total	5.14	5.04	4.39	4.16	4.51	5.01
4. Restaurants	1.45	1.40	1.40	1.40	1.35	1.35
5. Urban peddlers	2.76	2.84	2.56	2.24	2.24	2.24
6. Rural peddlers	4.24	4.50	3.50	3.15	2.80	2.80
7. Total	13.59	13.78	11.85	10.95	10.90	11.40

Notes to part (*a*): — Not available.

Line 1. The figures for 1952–53 are given in the *1953 Communique*. The figure for 1954 is the sum of workers in state-owned stores (0.88 million) and in cooperatives (0.97 million). The figure for state-owned stores is derived by multiplying 0.66 million, the number of workers in state-owned stores in 1953 given in *1953 Communique*, by 1.33, the ratio of the number of state-owned stores in 1954 to that in 1953 or 50,228/37,587, given in SSB, *Commercial Network*, p. 82. The number of workers in cooperatives in 1954 (0.97 million) is the average of 0.84 million, given in *1953 Communique* for 1953, and 1.101 million for 1955 given in SSB, *Commercial Network*, p. 82. The 1955 total is 2.57 million (*ibid.*).

Lines 2 and 3. Ching Hua, Liang Sze-ta, *et al.*, *Chi-nien-lai wor-kuo sze-ying kung-shang-yeh ti pien-hua* (Changes in China's Private Industry and Trade in the Past Seven Years), Peiping, 1957, p. 123. Although it is not specified, we assume the figures are year-end totals.

Line 4. The figures for 1952–55 are the sums of lines 1 through 3. The 1956 figure is derived by adding the increase of 0.34 million in 1955–56 given in State Planning Commission, "Labor and Wages in 1956," *CHCC*, No. 3, March 1957, p. 14, to the 1955 estimate of 6.47 million. The figure for 1957 is obtained as a residual by deducting the number of workers in finance (0.75 million given in Table 63) from the total number of workers in trade and finance (8.44 million) given in Ma Ming-fang, "Workers at the Financial and Commercial Front Advancing Vigorously," *People's Daily*, June 23, 1958, p. 3.

Line 5. A total figure of 7 million for all peddlers is given in Liao Kai-lung, "Certain Tasks of Reforming Capitalist Trade in the First Five Year Plan," *Hsueh-hsi ti-yi-ke wu-nien chi-hua tsarn-kow wen-chi* (A Collection of Reference Materials for Studying the First Five Year Plan), Peiping, 1955, Vol. I, p. 33. The number of urban peddlers, 2.76 million (given in line 3), is deducted from the total to obtain the number of rural peddlers. The 1953 figure is given in Chu Ching and Chu Chung-chien, "Variations in Our Rural Market Commodity Turnover," *CCYC*, No. 3, June 1957, p. 104. The figures for 1954–56

(Continued)

Table 61 (continued)

are taken from *HHYP*, No. 3, 1955, p. 149; Ching Hua, Liang Sze-ta, *et al.*, *op. cit.*, p. 145; and *People's Daily*, April 14, 1956, p. 1. The figure for 1957 is assumed to be the same as for 1956.

Line 6. The only available data are those for 1952, 1955, and 1956 given in Ching Hua, Liang Sze-ta, *et al.*, *op. cit.*, p. 52; Wu Cheng-ming, "Socialist Transformation of Private Trade," *People's China*, Peiping, No. 10, May 1956, pp. 11–15; and *People's Daily*, April 14, 1956, p. 1. For 1953–54, we assume the totals to be the same as the average of those for 1952 and 1956, and for 1957, the same as the total for 1956.

Line 7. Sum of lines 4 through 6.

Notes to part (b): — Not available.

Line 1. The 1952 figure is given in *First Five Year Plan*, p. 129. The figures for 1953–55 are the averages of the year-end totals for 1952–55 given in line 1, part (a).

Line 2. The figure for 1952 is assumed to be the same as in part (a); those for 1953–55 are the averages of the year-end totals for 1952–55 given in line 2, part (a).

Line 3. The figures for 1952–55 are the sum of lines 1 and 2. The figure for 1956 is obtained by adding the increase in the average number of workers of 0.35 million in 1955–56 given in State Planning Commission, "Labor and Wages in 1956," *CHCC*, No. 3, 1957, p. 14, to the 1955 estimate of total workers of trading stores (4.16 million). The 1957 figure of 5.01 million is derived as a residual by deducting the number of urban peddlers in 1957 given in line 5 from the total number of workers in trade in the urban areas, 7.25 million, the average of the year-end totals for 1956 and 1957 given in line 4, part (a).

Line 4. We assume that the annual averages are the same as the year-end totals given in line 6, part (a).

Line 5. The figure for 1952 is assumed to be the same as in part (a), and those for 1953–55 are the averages of the year-end totals given in line 3, part (a). Those for 1956–57 are assumed to be the same as for 1956.

Line 6. The figures for 1952–54 and 1956–57 are assumed to be the same as the corresponding year-end totals given in line 5, part (a). The 1955 figure is the average of 1954 and 1956.

Line 7. Sums of lines 3 through 6.

miles understandably must be hard to come by. It is not an uncommon practice for the Communists to separate two branches of an industry because of different qualities of the statistical data; for example, the gross output of individual handicraftsmen and handicraft cooperatives is separately listed rather than included in industrial production.[106] Another plausible explanation is that the rural peddlers and others are to be socialized under the direction of two different organizations. Thus, the rural peddlers have often been singled out as an individual group so far as their socialist transformation is concerned.[107]

There are three separate arguments in support of our contention that the Communist "totals" are not actually totals. First, the number of rural traders at the end of 1955 is given at 2.67 million,

[106] Wei Yi, *op. cit.*

[107] *People's Daily*, February 4, 1955 and April 14, 1956; Tang Fay, "The Present Conditions in the Transformation of Rural Private Traders and Comments on Future Work," *HHPYK*, No. 17, September 1956, pp. 65–68.

more than the "total number of peddlers" given at 2.4 million in early 1956.[108] Rural traders include both peddlers and storekeepers, but the number of rural storekeepers is traditionally small.[109] The total number of rural traders can be taken as the total number of peddlers without much risk. If the figures for "total peddlers" were the total for the economy as a whole, there would be no peddlers in the urban areas at all, a situation that hardly seems likely since the number of peddlers in Shanghai alone was reported to be 0.16 million in 1957.[110] When 0.16 is multiplied by the ratio of total urban population (91 million, as given in Table 67) to the population of Shanghai (6.9 million),[111] we obtain a rough estimate of 2.1 million urban peddlers, very close to our estimate of 2.2 million given in Table 61.

Second, at least two figures exceed the "totals" by a sizable amount—6 to 7 million peddlers in 1952, and 7 million private traders in 1954.[112] These two figures and their corresponding "totals" can be reconciled if the gaps are taken to represent the rural peddlers.

Third, a rough comparison of the State Statistical Bureau's "total" number of workers, 9.4 million for 1952 (8 million in trade plus 1.4 million in restaurants), and our estimate of 15 million for 1933 shows a drastic decline of more than one third.[113] It is not likely that our estimate for 1933 could be off by as wide a margin as 30 per cent. The most probable explanation is incomplete statistical coverage in the State Statistical Bureau's "total" figures.

GOVERNMENT

Included in this category are workers in (1) central and local government administration; (2) social, cultural, and public health

[108] *TKP*, December 1, 1955, p. 1; Chen Yun, "Concerning the Problem of Socialist Transformation of Private Industry and Trade," *HHPYK*, No. 14, July 1956, p. 52.

[109] Sidney D. Gamble, *Ting Hsien*, New York, Institute of Pacific Relations, 1954, pp. 277, 279.

[110] E. Faure, *The Serpent and the Tortoise*, London, Macmillan, 1958, p. 165.

[111] *Great Ten Years*, p. 9.

[112] Liao Kai-lung, "Certain Tasks of Reforming Capitalist Trade in the First Five Year Plan," *Hsueh-hsi ti-yi-ke wu-nien-chi-hua tsarn-kow wen-chi*, 1955, Vol. I, p. 33; Wu Chiang, "The Transition from a Capitalist Economy to a National Capitalist Economy," *CCYC*, No. 2, April 1956, p. 66. The "totals" were given at 2.8 million and 4.14 million (Ching Hua, Liang Sze-ta, *et al.*, *op. cit.*, p. 123). The figures in this source are apparently the same as those given by the State Statistical Bureau for the economy as a whole.

[113] For the figure on trade, see SSB, *Commercial Network*, p. 81; for restaurants, Table 61 (b); for the 1933 estimate, Table 53.

institutions operated by the state; (3) agricultural, forestry, water conservation, and meteorological departments; (4) communal services; (5) military services; and (6) party and other organizations. The estimates for the first four groups for 1952 and 1955–57 are drawn from Communist sources, and those for 1953–54 are rough approximations obtained by interpolating from the 1952 and 1955 figures on the basis of a linear trend. No specific information on the size of the military force is available. As indicated in Appendix H, rough estimates by observers vary from 2.5 to 3.4 million. We assume the total to be 3 million in the period under study. The figures for party and other organizations are residuals derived by deducting the number of salary and wage earners in nonproductive occupations already accounted for (including government administration; cultural, social, and public health services; communal services; and finance) from the total number of nonproductive workers. Presumably this residual group includes workers in the various political organizations, unions, and the like. Table 62 summarizes the estimates for the six groups.

FINANCE, PERSONAL SERVICES, AND WORK BRIGADES

Statistical data on the number of employees in financial institutions are available only for state and joint enterprises in 1952–53 and 1955, and for private enterprises in 1952. The numbers in the private sector for 1953 and 1955 are assumed to have remained unchanged since 1952. The totals in the other years are extrapolations from the data for 1952–53 and 1955 on the basis of a linear trend.

There is almost no information on the number of workers in personal services. In the absence of a better alternative, we assume that the total number in 1952, including those in communal services, is the same as the prewar total of 3.61 million. In the period 1952–57 it seems unlikely that per capita consumption of personal services other than domestic service could have changed appreciably. To a considerable extent, the increase in the number of teachers and medical personnel merely represented the absorption of private school teachers, tutors, and herb doctors into the state sector. Such professions as religious service would presumably decline in number so that any net increase in other professions would be offset and reduced. Furthermore, it is not likely that there have been significant changes in the output per worker in this period. We therefore assume that the number of employees (excluding domes-

Table 62

WORKERS IN GOVERNMENT AND COMMUNAL SERVICES, 1952–57
(millions)

	1952	1953	1954	1955	1956	1957
1. Administration	1.52	1.54	1.56	1.58	1.61	1.64
2. Social and cultural services	2.28	2.39	2.49	2.60	2.88	3.00
3. Agriculture, forestry, water conservation, and meteorological departments	0.14	0.21	0.28	0.34	0.37	0.39
4. Communal services	0.01	0.02	0.03	0.03	0.04	0.04
5. Military service	3.00	3.00	3.00	3.00	3.00	3.00
6. Party and other organizations	0.63	1.07	1.18	1.07	1.12	1.24
7. Total	7.59	8.23	8.54	8.62	9.02	9.31

NOTES: *Line 1.* The figure for 1952 is given in *First Five Year Plan*, p. 129; and for 1955 in SSB, *1955 Employment*, p. 87. The figures for 1953–54 are interpolations based on the 1952 and 1955 figures and the assumption of a linear time trend. The figure for 1957 is reported to be 6 per cent higher than the 1953 total (*NCNA*, Peiping, November 28, 1957). The figure for 1956 is the average of estimates for 1955 and 1957.

Line 2. The 1952 figure is taken from *First Five Year Plan*, p. 129. The figure for 1955 is derived from data given in Chen Ta, *TCKT*, November 12, 1957, pp. 1–2; and SSB, *1955 Employment*, p. 87. The figure for 1956 is the sum of the 1955 estimate and the increase in 1955–56 reported in State Planning Commission, "Labor and Wages in 1956," *CHCC*, No. 3, March 1957, p. 14. The 1953, 1954, and 1957 figures are approximations on the basis of the 1952 and 1955 figures and a linear time trend.

Line 3. The figures for 1952, 1955, and 1957 are derived by deducting the numbers of workers in state farms (0.10, 0.13, and 0.42 million) from the total numbers of workers in these departments, including state farm workers (0.24, 0.48, and 0.81 million). The numbers of state farm workers in 1952 and 1955 are taken from *1955 Statistical Abstract*, p. 44, and that for 1957, from *People's Daily*, February 1, 1958, p. 2. The total numbers of workers in these departments are obtained from data given in *First Five Year Plan*, p. 129; Chen Ta, *op. cit.;* SSB, *1955 Employment*, p. 87; and *Workers' Daily*, Peiping, January 1958, p. 1. The estimates for 1953–54 and 1956 are interpolations based on the 1952, 1955, and 1957 figures and the assumption of a linear time trend.

Line 4. Total numbers of workers in communal services in 1952 and the planned figure for 1957 (0.04 and 0.10 million) are taken from *First Five Year Plan*, p. 129. Those for 1953–56 are interpolations based on the 1952 and 1957 figures and a linear time trend. From these totals we deduct the corresponding estimates for numbers in water and gas utilities and in municipal transit service given in Tables 57 and 60.

Line 5. See Appendix H.

Line 6. The total numbers of workers in party organizations and government workers are derived as residuals as follows. The year-end totals of nonproductive workers in 1951–57 are given at 36.2, 33.9, 32.3, 31.3, 31.5, 27.8, and 27.1 per cent of total workers in *Great Ten Years*, p. 164. The Communist data on total workers for this period are 12.82, 15.80, 18.26, 18.81, 19.08, 24.23, and 24.51 million for 1951–57 (*ibid.*, p. 159). The year-end totals of nonproductive workers are derived at 4.64, 5.36, 5.90, 5.89, 6.01, 6.74, and 6.64 million. The annual average numbers of nonproductive workers are then obtained at 5.00, 5.63, 5.89, 5.95, 6.37, and 6.69 million by averaging the year-end totals for each year. We deduct the numbers in government administration, social, and cultural services (lines 1 and 2 of the table), those in finance given in Table 63, those in communal services given in line 4 of the table, and those in municipal transit service given in Table 60. The results are the numbers in party organizations and other government services not yet accounted for.

Line 7. Sum of lines 1 through 6.

tic servants) increased at the same rate as population in 1952–57, derive the totals, and deduct from them the corresponding number of employees in the state sector given in Table 62 to arrive at the number of employees in the private sector.

We assume the number of domestic servants to be the same as in 1933. The rapid increase in the number of women workers in urban areas and the disintegration of the large family into small units since 1949 might have increased the demand for domestic servants. One foreign observer reported that the authorities even encouraged the employment of domestic servants.[114] On the other hand, the rather restrictive policy of the government toward the inflow of rural labor into cities, the reduction of the income of the formerly wealthy middle-class families, and the establishment of child care centers would tend to reduce both the supply of and demand for domestic service. There is not enough information for us to judge whether the actual development has turned out to be in one direction or the other. On balance, any net change in the period under study should be rather small.

The number of workers in work brigades are rough estimates obtained by dividing the total income originating in this sector, given in Table 50, by the annual earnings per worker. The results are presented in Table 63.

WOMEN WORKERS

For estimating the number of employed and unemployed male workers, rough estimates of the total number of women workers are derived.[115] Table 64 summarizes the estimates for the following six groups: handicrafts, old-fashioned transportation, personal services, peddlers, work brigades, and others. Included in the "others" group are mainly the salary and wage earners, the figures for which are taken from Communist sources. The estimates for remaining groups are derived on the basis of fragmentary information.

Comparison of the Adjusted Estimate of Total Nonagricultural Employment with the Communist Estimate

Because there are two sets of estimates of net value added (our estimate and the adjusted estimate), there are also two estimates

[114] William Stevenson, *The Yellow Wind,* Boston, Mass., Houghton Mifflin Co., 1959, pp. 286–287.

[115] See the discussion in Chapter III under Labor Force and Unemployment.

of employment for handicraftsmen and old-fashioned transportation workers. Our estimate of employment is based on our estimate of net value added. The other estimate will be designated the adjusted estimate of employment. It is of interest to compare the Communist estimates with the adjusted estimates, which are built up from miscellaneous Communist data on employment in individual sectors. In Table 65 we present the total figures drawn from various

Table 63

WORKERS IN FINANCE, PERSONAL SERVICES, AND WORK BRIGADES, 1952–57
(millions)

	1952	1953	1954	1955	1956	1957
Finance	0.54	0.59	0.62	0.66	0.70	0.75
Personal services	3.63	3.60	3.58	3.55	3.35	3.33
Work brigades	4.08	2.52	2.88	4.92	5.31	5.56

NOTES: *Finance*. The figure for 1952 is derived as follows. The number of employees in government administration and finance is 2.06 million, 9.8 per cent of the Communist total of 21.02 million (*First Five Year Plan*, pp. 128–130). The number of government administration workers, 1.52 million (*ibid.*), is deducted from 2.06 million, to obtain the total number of workers in finance, 0.54 million. Of this total, 0.31 million are in the state-owned and joint state and private financial institutions (*ibid.*, p. 129), leaving 0.23 million in the private sector. The figures for 1953 and 1955 (0.59 and 0.66 million) are derived by adding those in the private and nonprivate sectors. The number of those in the private sector in 1953 is assumed to be the same as that for 1952, 0.23 million; that for 1955 (0.27 million) is the average of the figures for 1953 and 1956, the figure for 1956 being the average of the year-end totals for workers in credit cooperatives in 1955–56 given in *Chung-kuo chin-yung* (China's Finance), Peiping, No. 3, 1958, p. 22. For the state and semi-state sector, the 1953 figure (0.36 million) is the average of the year-end totals in 1952–53 computed from data given in Chen Ta, *TCKT*, No. 12, 1957, pp. 1–2; and SSB, *1955 Employment*, p. 87. The totals for 1954 and 1956–57 (0.62, 0.70, and 0.75 million) are interpolations and extrapolations on the basis of the figures for 1953 and 1955 and a linear time trend.

Personal services. The total number of workers in both communal and personal services (excluding domestic service) for 1952–57 are first derived at 3.61, 3.69, 3.77, 3.85, 3.93, and 4.03 million. The figure for 1952 is the sum of the number of workers in communal services, excluding domestic servants, which is assumed to be 1.33 million, the same as in 1933, given in Appendix H under Personal Services. For 1953–57, the figures are derived on the assumption that the total number of workers in communal and personal services increased in proportion to total population over the same period. To arrive at the number of workers in personal services, we deduct the number of workers in communal services given in Table 62 from the totals and add 2.30 million, the number of domestic servants, assumed to be the same as in 1933.

Work brigades. The total numbers of workers in work brigades are derived as follows. Man-days of work done by the work brigades in 1952–57 are obtained by dividing net value added by work brigades, given in Table 8, by the earnings per worker per day of 0.50 yuan given in Appendix H under Work Brigades. The total number of man-days are then divided by 306 working days to arrive at total full-time equivalent workers: 4.08, 2.52, 2.88, 4.92, 5.31, and 5.56 million for 1952–57.

Table 64

WOMEN WORKERS IN THE NONAGRICULTURAL SECTOR, 1952–57
(millions)

	1952	1953	1954	1955	1956	1957
Handicrafts	3.40	3.50	3.80	3.70	3.50	3.60
Old-fashioned transportation	3.60	3.40	3.20	3.20	3.40	3.30
Personal services	1.50	1.50	1.40	1.50	1.50	1.50
Peddlers	0.40	0.40	0.40	0.30	0.30	0.30
Work brigades	0.40	0.20	0.30	0.50	0.50	0.50
Others	1.85	2.13	2.43	2.47	3.27	3.29
Total	11.15	11.13	11.53	11.67	12.47	12.49

NOTES: *Handicrafts.* The figures are the sums of those in individual or cooperative handicrafts and the full-time equivalent of those engaged in handicrafts as a subsidiary occupation. The totals in the former category are derived by multiplying the total numbers of individual and cooperative handicraftsmen for 1952–57 given in Table 58 by the proportion of women workers in the total, assumed to be 27 per cent, the same as for 1956, given in *HHPYK*, No. 21, November 1956, p. 82. The total number of women workers in the second category is derived on the assumption that the figure for 1952 is the same as that for 1933 given in Table 54. It is also assumed that for 1952–57 the total increases in proportion to the total "other" handicraftsmen given in Table 58.

Old-fashioned transportation. According to our estimate for 1933, roughly one-third of the workers in old-fashioned transportation were women. (The number of female transportation workers, given at 3.6 million in Table 53, is assumed to be entirely in the traditional sector. Appendix H gives the total number of old-fashioned transportation workers at 10.9 million.) For 1952–57 the same ratio is applied to the total number of old-fashioned transportation workers given in Table 60, yielding the number of women workers.

Personal services. For lack of information, we assume that the number of women workers for 1952–57 is the same as the figure for 1933 given in Table 53.

Peddlers. These figures are derived on the assumption that the proportion of women peddlers to total peddlers in 1952–57 is the same as in 1933, that is, 6 per cent. (See Table 53.) For the total in 1952–57, see Table 61 (b).

Work brigades. These figures are derived on the assumption that 10 per cent of work brigades, which usually do rather heavy physical labor, were women. (See Table 63.) The figures are rounded to the nearest tenth of a million.

Others. Included in this category are the women workers and employees reported in *Great Ten Years,* p. 161.

Communist sources together with the adjusted estimate. The comparison shows a rather wide divergence among the Communist estimates themselves and an even wider divergence between the Communist figures and the adjusted estimates. To a large extent, these can be explained in terms of known differences of scope and concept.

A sector-by-sector comparison of the adjusted estimate with the Communist estimate for 1952, the only year for which detailed Communist statistical data on employment by individual sectors are available, is presented in Table 66. There are several discrepancies.

Table 65

COMPARISON OF THE COMMUNIST ESTIMATE AND THE ADJUSTED ESTIMATE OF TOTAL NONAGRICULTURAL EMPLOYMENT, 1952–57
(millions of workers)

	1952	1953	1954	1955	1956	1957
Communist estimate	21.02[a]	17.52[b]		15.36[c]	24.73[b]	22.17[d]
	15.11[e]			22.49[b]	22.31[e]	23.97[f]
	15.80[g]			18.73[e]	24.17[g]	24.51[h]
					24.40[i]	
					21.18[j]	
The adjusted estimate[k]	58.52	57.91	57.21	58.95	60.06	63.63

NOTES: [a] *First Five Year Plan*, p. 128.

[b] *People's Daily*, February 5, 1957, p. 1. The 1956 figure refers to the total number of workers in September 1956. The 1955 figure is calculated from data given in State Planning Commission, "Labor and Wages in 1956," *CHCC*, No. 3, March 1957, p. 14.

[c] SSB, *1955 Employment*, p. 87. Included in this figure are the workers in state, cooperative, and joint state and private enterprises, and in government organizations in September 1955. Those in the party organizations, military services, other political and civil organizations, and private enterprise are not included.

[d] *TKP*, Peiping, October 20, 1957, p. 2.

[e] SSB, "Statistics on the Improvements in the Workers' Living Conditions," *TCKT*, No. 14, July 1957, p. 13. These figures are annual averages. Apparently, the workers in cooperatives have not been included.

[f] Calculated from data given in Po I-po, *1958 Plan*, p. 19.

[g] *Ibid.* Represents the numbers of workers at the end of the year, including those covered in the state plan but excluding the workers in cooperatives.

[h] *FFYP Communique*, p. 51.

[i] Po I-po, *1956–57 Plan*, p. 30. This figure includes only those covered in the state plan, that is, workers in state, cooperative, joint state and private enterprises, government and civil organizations; and cultural, educational, scientific, and public health departments.

[j] *Ibid.* Annual average number of workers covered in the state plan.

[k] For 1952, see Table 66. 1953–55 are sums of estimates for (1) all nonagricultural sectors (except handicrafts and old-fashioned transportation) given in Table 11, and (2) handicrafts and old-fashioned transportation given in Table 58 and in the text.

First, a significant number of handicraftsmen, old-fashioned transportation workers, peddlers, and people in personal services and work brigades have been left out of the Communist total. Second, the Communist total figures include neither the employees in the private financial enterprises nor the temporary workers in construction. Third, the Communist statistics on total employment refer to total civilian employment. In short, the global figures generally cover only the wage and salary earners. They do not include all those gainfully employed. For this reason, any inferences drawn on the basis of these figures must be made with caution. For instance, the reported rapid increase in total employment does not necessarily

Table 66

RECONCILIATION OF THE ADJUSTED ESTIMATE OF NONAGRICULTURAL EMPLOYMENT IN 1952 WITH THE COMMUNIST ESTIMATE
(millions of workers)

Sector	Communist estimate	Adjustment: Difference in concept	Adjustment: Difference in classification	Adjustment: Undercoverage in Communist data	Adjustment: Entire category missing from Communist data	Adjusted estimates
Industry	5.41	—	—	—	—	3.54
Factories, mining, and electric power	3.23[a]	—	—	—	—	3.23
Lumbering	0.20[b]	−0.20	—	—	—	—
Handicraft workshops	1.98[c]	—	−1.98	—	—	—
Native mining	—	—	+0.02[d]	—	+0.27[e]	0.29
Water and gas utilities	—	—	+0.02[f]	—	—	0.02
Handicrafts	6.04	—	—	—	—	12.46
Handicraft workshops	—	—	+1.98[c]	—	—	1.98
Handicraft cooperatives	—	—	—	—	+0.23[g]	0.23
Individual handicraftsmen	6.04[h]	—	—	+1.11[i]	—	7.13[j]
Other handicraftsmen	—	—	−0.02	—	+3.14[k]	3.12
Construction	1.02	—	—	—	—	1.29
Regular workers						
State enterprises	1.02	—	—	—	—	1.02
Nonstate enterprises	—	—	—	—	+0.02[m]	0.02
Temporary workers	—	—	—	—	+0.25[m]	0.25
Transportation and communications	0.72	—	—	—	—	11.80
Modern	0.72	—	+0.01[n]	—	—	0.73
Traditional	—	—	—	—	+11.07[p]	11.07
Trade	3.45	—	—	—	—	13.59
Trading stores	3.45	—	—	+1.69[q]	—	5.14[r]
Restaurants	—	—	—	—	+1.45[r]	1.45
Peddlers	—	—	—	—	+7.00[r]	7.00
Government	4.08	—	—	—	—	7.59
Administration	1.52	—	—	—	—	1.52
Social and cultural services	2.28	—	—	—	—	2.28
Agricultural, forestry, water conservation, and meteorological departments	0.24	−0.10[s]	—	—	—	0.14
Municipal services	0.04	—	−0.03[n]	—	—	0.01
Military services	—	—	—	—	+3.00[t]	3.00
Party organizations and others	—	—	—	—	+0.63[u]	0.63
Finance	0.31	—	—	—	—	0.54
State enterprises	0.30	—	—	—	—	0.30
Joint state and private enterprises	0.01	—	—	—	—	0.01
Private enterprises	—	—	—	—	+0.23[v]	0.23
Personal services	—	—	—	—	+3.63[v]	3.63
Work brigades	—	—	—	—	+4.08[v]	4.08
Total	21.02	−0.30	—	+2.80	+35.00	58.52

NOTES: — No estimate or adjustment made.

[a] Derived by deducting the number of workers in lumbering and handicraft workshops from the total number of workers in industry.

[b] Represents workers in lumbering included by the Communists under industrial workers but classified as agricultural workers according to our definition. See notes to Table 57.

[c] Represents workers in handicraft workshops included under industrial workers by the Communists but as handicraftsmen in our classification. See notes to Table 57.

[d] Represents workers in primitive coal mining presumably included in total handicraftsmen according to the Communist definition but classified as workers in mining in the adjusted estimate. See notes to Table 57.

(Continued)

Table 66 (continued)

[e] Represents workers in salt manufacturing or salt mining not in the state enterprises. See notes to Table 57.

[f] Represents workers in the water and gas utilities classified as workers in municipal services by the Communists but as workers in utilities in the adjusted estimate. See notes to Table 57.

[g] See notes to Table 58.

[h] Represents the sum of (1) apprentices and assistants employed by individual handicraftsmen, and (2) other workers, including laborers and porters in the transportation industry. *First Five Year Plan*, footnote, p. 129.

[i] Represents the difference between the total number of individual handicraftsmen derived from one set of Communist sources and the number of handicraftsmen in another. See notes h and j.

[j] See Table 58.

[k] Represents handicraftsmen not working in workshops or cooperatives or as individual handicraftsmen. See text of this chapter under Handicrafts.

[m] Represents the number of regular workers in private construction enterprises and total temporary workers omitted from Communist data. See Table 59.

[n] Of the total number of workers in communal services, 0.02 million are reallocated to water and gas utilities, 0.02 million to municipal transit services, and 0.01 to administration and other services.

[p] Represents old-fashioned transportation workers omitted from the Communist data. See preceding section under Transportation and Communications.

[q] Represents workers not covered in the total figure given in *First Five Year Plan*, derived by deducting that figure from the estimate based on Communist data given in notes to Table 61 (b).

[r] See notes to Table 61 (b).

[s] Represents workers in state farms included under Communist agricultural departments but excluded in the total number of agricultural workers according to our definition. See notes to Table 62.

[t] See discussion in Appendix H under Government, 1953–57.

[u] See notes to Table 62.

[v] See Table 63.

SOURCES: Except as otherwise noted, the Communist estimates are taken from *First Five Year Plan*, pp. 128–130. The sources of the adjusted estimate are given in the text.

imply an equally rapid increase in total employment for the economy as a whole nor even in total agricultural employment. For the increase in the Communist total includes the transfer of farm labor and the formerly self-employed into the wage earner group, which does not represent additional employment.

> For example, in 1956, a total of 2.8 million self-employed workers become wage earners in government owned or operated organizations. Of a total of 1.78 million new workers and employees, 43 per cent were formerly farmers; 36 per cent were formerly unemployed, idle, or housewives; 13 per cent were recently graduated from schools and colleges; and 7 per cent were discharged military personnel.[116]

The reconstructed Communist estimate of nonagricultural employment helps to clarify some of the confusion arising from the misuse of several ambiguous terms relating to agricultural population. At least two terms, agricultural population and rural population, are generally used interchangeably.[117] In both cases, the Com-

[116] *KJJP*, January 19, 1957, p. 1.

[117] Po I-po, "Report Before the National Conference of Model Agricultural Workers," *HHYPK*, No. 6, March 1957, p. 58; Liao Lu-yen, "Explanation of the Plan for Agricultural Development, 1956–67," *HHPYK*, No. 4, February 1956, p. 9; and Wang Kuang-wei, "On the Allocation of Agricultural Labor," *CHCC*, No. 8, August 1957, p. 6.

munist concepts are much broader in scope than the conventional definition of agricultural population. The difference between the Communist and our definition of agricultural population was explained earlier in this chapter. Only the Communist concept of rural population need be discussed here.

Because of the rather restrictive scope of the Communist definition of an urban area, the Communist figure for rural population far exceeds the actual number of people engaged in agricultural pursuits. In Communist terminology, an urban area is any of the following: (1) the seat of the local state organ, (2) an industrial or mining center with population over 1,000 of which more than 75 per cent are engaged in nonagricultural pursuits, and (3) an area with population over 2,000, of which more than 50 per cent are engaged in nonagricultural pursuits.[118] By this definition, a sizable portion of the population who live in villages and small towns with a population below 2,000 but who make their living by nonagricultural pursuits would fall into the rural category. Since the Chinese economy has been made up predominantly of small, localized, and more or less self-sufficient villages even in the postwar period, the nonagricultural population in areas defined as rural in Communist terms must be considerable—in all likelihood, far more than the number working in agriculture but included in urban population because of the definitions. The absolute numbers and percentages of rural and urban populations for 1949–57 according to the Communist population estimates are given in Table 67.

That the Communist data on urban (rural) population cannot be taken to represent the nonagricultural (agricultural) population can be clearly seen in a comparison of the number of nonagricultural workers and urban population. For example, total nonagricultural employment in 1952, 59 million as given in Table 65, turns out to be greater than the urban labor force. As was noted in Table 24, total urban population in that year was reported at 69 million; the labor force from 12 to 64 years of age (including housewives and unemployed, but excluding students) was 43 million. Even if we subtract the 3 million "other" handicraftsmen, one-third of those in peddling and old-fashioned transportation (6 million), and the 4 million in work brigades to make a liberal allowance for those peo-

[118] Directive of State Council, "On the Classification of Rural and Urban Areas," *HHPYK*, No. 3, February 1956, p. 7.

Table 67

RURAL AND URBAN POPULATIONS, COMMUNIST ESTIMATES, 1949–57

Year	Rural (millions)	Urban	Rural (per cent)	Urban
1949	480.7	55.6	89.6	10.4
1950	487.2	59.7	89.1	10.9
1951	493.5	64.0	88.5	11.5
1952	499.9	69.0	87.9	12.1
1953	506.7	74.6	87.2	12.8
1954	515.2	79.6	86.6	13.4
1955	526.0	82.2	86.5	13.5
1956	535.2	86.0	86.2	13.8
1957	546.6	90.6	85.8	14.2

SOURCES: The figures for 1949–56 are given in SSB, *Population Statistics*, p. 25. Urban population at the end of 1957 is reported at 92 million in Wang Kuang-wei, "On the Allocation of Agricultural Labor," *CHCC*, No. 8, August 1957, p. 7. The 90.6 million average for the year is obtained by taking the arithmetic mean of 92 million and the year-end total for 1956 given at 89.2 million in SSB, *Population Statistics*, p. 24. The figure for the rural population in 1957 is the residual derived by deducting total urban population from total population, 637.2 million, given in Table 32.

ple with nonagricultural subsidiary occupations who might possibly be part of the agricultural population, the adjusted estimate, 46 million, still exceeds the total urban labor force.

COMPARISONS OF THE AUTHORS', THE ADJUSTED, AND THE COMMUNIST ESTIMATES OF DOMESTIC PRODUCT

The Authors' and the Adjusted Estimates

In deriving our estimate of domestic product, we made several major adjustments in the Communist data. First, data on food crop output for 1952–56 are replaced by our own estimate. Second, data on factory-produced consumers' goods in 1953–57 have been revised downward. Similar revisions are made in Communist data on modern transportation and communications and trade. Another estimate of domestic product (called the adjusted estimate), obtained on the basis of Communist data without these corrections but after adjustments to conform to the Western concept of domestic product, is presented in Table 68 with our estimate.

The Adjusted and Communist Estimates

In addition to our two sets of calculations, we present the Communist estimate of national income for 1952–57. We shall first briefly

Table 68

A COMPARISON OF THE AUTHORS' ESTIMATE AND THE ADJUSTED ESTIMATE OF DOMESTIC PRODUCT BY INDUSTRIAL ORIGIN, 1952–57
(billions of 1952 yuan)

	1952	1953	1954	1955	1956	1957
Agriculture						
Adjusted	31.60	32.06	32.66	34.49	36.76	40.18
Our estimate	34.19	34.82	35.50	35.84	36.97	37.16
Factories						
Adjusted	6.45	8.64	10.15	10.93	15.69	17.26
Our estimate	6.45	8.28	9.58	10.36	14.51	15.99
Handicrafts						
Adjusted	4.41	4.45	4.59	4.94	5.20	5.73
Our estimate	4.72	4.81	4.98	5.12	5.25	5.38
Mining	1.47	1.46	1.82	2.32	2.38	3.07
Utilities	0.31	0.37	0.43	0.48	0.59	0.71
Construction	1.83	2.28	2.68	2.93	4.97	4.62
Transportation and communications						
Modern						
Adjusted	2.10	2.77	3.29	3.52	4.35	4.83
Our estimate	2.10	2.55	2.90	3.10	3.52	3.82
Traditional						
Adjusted	2.69	2.31	2.08	2.22	2.26	2.43
Our estimate	2.65	2.45	2.35	2.34	2.48	2.43
Trade						
Stores and restaurants						
Adjusted	7.66	8.47	9.57	10.56	12.32	12.97
Our estimate	7.66	7.87	8.54	8.95	9.71	10.01
Peddlers	2.00	2.10	1.73	1.54	1.44	1.44
Government	3.27	3.70	3.95	4.07	4.76	5.03
Finance						
Adjusted	1.31	1.41	1.51	1.61	1.89	2.04
Our estimate	1.31	1.39	1.47	1.52	1.70	1.77
Personal services	0.55	0.55	0.54	0.54	0.51	0.51
Residential rent	2.28	2.32	2.37	2.44	2.48	2.55
Work brigades	0.62	0.38	0.44	0.75	0.81	0.85
Net domestic product						
Adjusted	68.55	73.27	77.81	83.34	96.41	104.22
Our estimate	71.41	75.33	79.28	82.30	92.08	95.34
Depreciation						
Adjusted	3.18	3.67	4.06	4.35	5.48	5.93
Our estimate	3.26	3.66	4.03	4.27	5.20	5.48
Gross domestic product						
Adjusted	71.73	76.94	81.87	87.69	101.89	110.15
Our estimate	74.67	78.99	83.31	86.57	97.28	100.82

NOTE: Where only one set of figures is given there is no difference between our estimate and the adjusted data.

describe the conceptual framework and the statistical methodology underlying the Communist estimate;[119] second, we shall tabulate or reconstruct the Communist calculations of national income by industrial origin; and third, we shall compare these figures with the adjusted estimate.

Communist Concepts and Methods of Deriving National Income

Two different concepts of national income are commonly used in the Communist literature. The first, "kuo-min shou-ju" (national income) or "kuo-min shou-ju sheng-chan" (national product), is defined as the net material product, that is, the net value produced by agriculture, industry, construction, freight transportation, the part of communications serving other productive sectors, and trade and restaurants.[120] In principle, only that part of trade in the service of other material sectors is counted as material production. However, for practical purposes the Communists have included the entire value added by trade in national income.[121] This definition of national income follows the Marxian concept of "productive" and "nonproductive" economic activities. The following sectors are con-

[119] Although the concept, method, and data used by the State Statistical Bureau have not been explained officially, the summary given here is based on a number of publications and can be considered the official interpretation. See Hsu Chien, Tai Shih-kuang, and Yu Tao, *Ching-chi t'ung-chi-she chian-hua* (Lectures on Economic Statistics), Peiping, 1957, pp. 269–285; Yueh Wei, "The Method of Computing National Income," *CCYC*, No. 3, June 1956, pp. 48–66; Chu Cheng-ping, "Some Questions Concerning National Income," *CCYC*, No. 3, June 1957, pp. 129–140; Lung Hua-yung, Chi Hsi-yung, and Chen Ming-hsi, "Several Problems Concerning the Computation of Value Added by the Construction Industry," *TCKT*, No. 8, April 1957, pp. 14–16; *Kuo-min shou-ju lun-wen-chi* (Collection of Essays on National Income), Peiping, 1956; Fang Fa, "Tabulation Forms for Industrial Production Planning," *CHCC*, No. 1, January 1957, pp. 26–31; Sun Tze-fang, "Planning Schedule for Commerce," *CHCC*, No. 2, February 1957, pp. 27–31; Chan Tieh-chang, "Tabulation Forms for Transportation Planning," *CHCC*, No. 3, March 1957, pp. 29–33. For the definition and scope of the value of agricultural production, see *TCKTTH*, No. 12, June 1956, p. 33, and No. 22, 1956, pp. 1–2; *TCKT*, No. 4, February 1957, p. 3; No. 7, 1957, pp. 15–17; No. 10, 1957, p. 10, and No. 11, 1957, pp. 11–12; *CHCC*, No. 4, April 1957, pp. 30–31; and Editorial Committee of the Statistical Press, *Handbook of Agricultural Statistical Work*, Peiping, 1956 (English translation), pp. 31–32.

[120] SSB, "A Preliminary Analysis of the Production and Distribution of China's National Income," *TCYC*, No. 1, January 1958, p. 11. See also Po I-po, "On the Correct Handling of the Problem of the Relationship Between Accumulation and Consumption," *HHPYK*, No. 20, October 1956, p. 76, footnote 1; Po I-po, "How Much To Invest and How Much To Consume," *People's China*, Peiping, No. 21, November 1956, p. 17 (the translation of the last source errs in the definition).

[121] Yueh Wei, "The Method of Computing National Income," *CCYC*, No. 3, June 1956, p. 52.

sidered nonproductive, and therefore their services are excluded from the calculation of national income: government administration; military and police forces; cultural, educational, and social organizations; and people rendering personal services.

Apart from its rather restrictive scope, there are several other features of the Communist definition. First, national income is apparently measured at market price instead of factor cost; there are indications that indirect taxes are included in national income.[122] No information can be found on how government subsidies to business enterprises are handled, but it is probable that the Soviet practice is followed and subsidies are treated as negative indirect taxes.[123] Second, national income is apparently net of depreciation allowances, for depreciation charges are listed among the costs deducted from gross value to arrive at value added.[124] However, depreciation includes only the depreciation charges in the material sectors. Third, it is not clear how factor payments from abroad are treated in the national income accounting, nor are there any statistical data available on whether their inclusion or exclusion would fit in better with Communist estimates. It is therefore uncertain whether national income in the Communist terminology refers to national product or domestic product. The amount of factor payments from abroad during the period under study is likely to be rather small relative to total national income, so that for the purpose of reconciling the two estimates, the Communist figures can be interpreted as those of domestic product. To sum up, the Communist concept of national income appears to be essentially the same as that of net domestic product at market prices as defined by the U.S. Department of Commerce, except for the narrower scope of economic activities covered in the Communist definition.

The second Communist concept of national income is "kuo-min shou-ju shih-yung" (domestic expenditures), which refers to the sum of personal, government, and communal consumption, and net domestic investment. This definition approximates net domestic expenditure as used in standard international practice, except that the Communist definition includes only expenditures on material prod-

[122] *Ibid.*, p. 58.

[123] A. Bergson, *Soviet National Income and Product, 1937*, New York, Columbia University Press, 1953, p. 143.

[124] Yueh Wei, "The Method of Computing National Income," *CCYC*, No. 3, June 1956, pp. 61–63; Po I-po, "On the Correct Handling of the Problem of the Relationship Between Accumulation and Consumption," *HHPYK*, No. 20, October 1956, p. 76.

uct; and depreciation charges for the use of capital goods in the service industries and on residential housing are included as part of social and personal consumption expenditures.[125]

Among the various methods of estimating national income, the basic approach adopted by the Communist State Statistical Bureau appears to be the value added method, and it is described below for the different productive sectors. They have also computed national income by the distributive shares method, that is, by summing up the income received by, or accruing to, the individuals and enterprises in the productive sector. The results, however, have not been released. The incomes of individuals comprise (a) wages of productive workers including fringe payments such as bonuses, labor insurance funds, union fees, and allowances for medical and other welfare expenses; (b) payments in cash or in kind to agricultural cooperative members on a labor day basis; (c) income of individual producers such as farmers not in cooperatives, handicraftsmen, peddlers, and old-fashioned transportation workers. The incomes of productive enterprises include (a) profit from productive activities; (b) direct and indirect taxes on the productive sectors such as the commodity turnover tax, business tax, customs duties, salt tax, license fees, and slaughtering tax; (c) interest receipts; (d) insurance receipts; (e) charges for workers' training; and (f) miscellaneous net incomes.

AGRICULTURE AND FARM SUBSIDIARY PRODUCTION

The gross value of agricultural production is usually given by the Communists together with the value of farm subsidiary production. This aggregate value is called the total value of agricultural and farm subsidiary production. All the plant, animal, forest, fishery, and miscellaneous products included in our estimate of agricultural output, except lumbering and some fishery products, are also included by the Communists in total value of agricultural production. Appendix C, Table C-1, lists the products in our estimate. Lumbering is included by the Communists in industry. Their classification of fishery products is complicated. "Natural" fishery products are considered part of industry.[126] Fishery products, presumably cultured, appear both in agricultural production and as part of farm subsidi-

[125] Yueh Wei, "The Method of Computing National Income," *CCYC*, No. 3, June 1956, pp. 61–63.

[126] *CHCC*, No. 1, January 1957, p. 26.

ary income.[127] The dividing line is not clear. The Communists have also counted as output green and animal manures, which we have omitted from our estimate, and fodder crops, stalks, and straws, which are included in our category of miscellaneous plant products.

Classified as farm subsidiary production are such activities as collecting wild plants, hunting wild animals, producing cultured fishery products, and the following: preliminary processing for farm household consumption—cotton ginning (included in our agricultural production), rice husking, preserving of vegetables, farm slaughtering, etc.; handicrafts for farm household consumption—spinning, weaving, tailoring, shoemaking, etc.; and processing of farm products for consumers. Much of the value of agricultural and farm subsidiary production is therefore imputed in the Communist usage. The Chinese rural economy is, to a large extent, not market-oriented, so that it is both proper and necessary to include a good part of the imputed income from farm home work in agricultural production. Net value added by agricultural production is obtained by deducting from the gross value of output the usual cost items: seeds, fertilizers (including the green and animal manures referred to as output by the Communists), insecticides, repair of farm tools, animal feed, veterinary medicines, and depreciation of fixed assets used in production.

INDUSTRY

This sector, according to the Communists, comprises manufacturing, mining, utilities, lumbering, and a part of fishery. The gross value of industrial production is computed on the basis of the factory method, that is, as the sum of the value of output of industrial enterprises.[128] Output of the nonindustrial units attached to the industrial enterprises, such as construction done by the employees of the industrial enterprises, are classified under other items. The products of the industrial enterprises are valued at factory prices.

The deductible cost items are the same as in standard non-Communist practice. They include raw materials, fuels and electricity, depreciation charges, and miscellaneous expenses such as transportation costs and allowances for wastes in storage. Depreciation allowances for nonproductive fixed assets such as dining halls and living quarters for industrial workers, and poor quality raw mate-

[127] Editorial Committee of the Statistical Press, *Handbook of Agricultural Statistical Work* (English translation), p. 31; *TCKT*, No. 4, 1957, p. 3.

[128] See Appendix F under Gross Value of Output of All Factories.

rial purchases that cannot be used for input are not considered to be deductible costs. There is no evidence that the value of inferior materials is excluded from the value of output of the enterprises that produced them.

CONSTRUCTION

Construction, in Communist usage, includes the building of productive and nonproductive structures and houses, the installation of equipment, major repairs of buildings, and geological surveying and prospecting connected with construction work. Value added by construction is computed by summing up the following types of incomes: wage payments in cash or in kind to construction workers, transportation workers, and party cadres attached to the construction unit (this does not include workers or employees engaged in nonproductive work such as the medical and educational staff of the enterprises); payments to drafted labor such as military servicemen, civilians, and criminals being "reformed" through labor; income of individual laborers (for example, members of agricultural cooperatives and individual farmers); net profit of construction enterprises; business taxes (since 1954, business taxes on the gross receipts of state construction enterprises have been abolished, amounting, in effect, to calling this item profit instead of taxes); and special charges such as contributions to labor insurance, trade unions, welfare activities, and training and education of workers.

TRANSPORTATION AND COMMUNICATIONS

Gross value of the transportation sector, according to Communist usage, includes gross receipts from the shipment of goods by railroads, coastal and inland shipping, air transport, motor transport, and carts drawn by animals or humans; and charges for loading and unloading. The gross value of the communications industry includes business receipts from its services to other productive sectors. The segregation of business receipts into productive and nonproductive services is based on sample studies. Value added is computed by deducting the usual cost items, including depreciation, from gross receipts.

TRADE

Included by the Communists in this sector are the services of government procurement agencies, wholesale and retail commercial or noncommercial enterprises, and catering. The gross value of trade is calculated as the difference between total sales and cost of purchases, and net value added by trade is derived as a residual after depreciation and material costs, if any, are deducted.

Communist Estimates of National Income

On the basis of the concepts and methods just described, the State Statistical Bureau began to make trial estimates in 1953; by 1956 a preliminary estimate for 1952–54 was completed and brought up to date.[129] These figures were available in 1956, and this probably accounts for the fact that gross value of industrial and agricultural production, rather than national income, provided the major aggregate target in the First Five Year Plan. Toward the end of 1956, Po I-po made the first specific reference to national income estimates in his speech before the Eighth Congress of the Chinese Communist Party. Absolute figures were not disclosed, but the ratios of the "state budget revenue" to national income were given in percentage terms for 1952–56.[130] In another source, government expenditures on basic construction as a percentage of national income for 1952–55 were also released.[131] Revisions of these estimates have apparently been made, and early in 1958 the State Statistical Bureau published national income estimates in absolute figures for 1952–56 for the first time. The major Communist statistics on national income are assembled and presented in Table 69.

[129] Wang Si-hua, "The Role of Statistics in Our Economic Construction and Questions Pertaining to Some Statistical Indicators," *CCYC*, No. 5, May 1958, p. 27; Yueh Wei, "The Method of Computing National Income," *CCYC*, No. 3, June 1956, p. 48.

[130] Since the revenue figures are readily available, it is possible to derive the Communist estimate of national income implied in Po's statement. However, there are two ambiguities in the same statement. First, at least three different sets of revenue figures have been published for 1952–55: Fung Chi-hsi, "Growth of China's Economy as Viewed from the State Budget," *TCKT*, No. 12, June 1957, p. 28; Ko Chih-ta, "The Nature of China's National Budget and Its Role in the Transition Period," *CCYC*, No. 3, June 1956, p. 72; and "Government Receipts and Expenditures in the First Five Year Plan Period," *Ts'ai-cheng* (Public Finance), No. 8, August 1957, p. 32. It is not known which of these figures were used by Po. Second, whether Po's figures were in current or constant prices is not clear. These ambiguities have resulted in several widely divergent estimates: Y. L. Wu, "Communist China's Economic Challenge," *Current History*, January 1957, p. 21; S. Ishikawa, "An Analysis of Economic Growth in China," *Asian Affairs*, Vol. II, No. 1, March 1957, pp. 21–46; United Nations Economic Commission for Asia and the Far East, *Economic Survey of Asia and the Far East, 1957*, Bangkok, 1958, p. 107. Because of the ambiguities and the fact that Po's figures are trial estimates, we have not used these indirect estimates.

[131] Yu Tien, "On the Proportion of Consumption and Accumulation in China's National Income," *TKP*, Peiping, March 24, 1957, pp. 1, 3.

Table 69

COMMUNIST ESTIMATES OF NATIONAL INCOME, 1952–57

	1952	1953	1954	1955	1956	1957
Net domestic product (billion yuan)						
In 1952 prices	61.13	70.04	73.88	78.80	88.75	93.53
In current prices	61.13	74.04	77.35	82.04	93.00	96.50
Net domestic product by industrial origin (per cent)						
Agriculture	59.2	52.8	52.3	52.8	48.1	48.4
Industry	18.0	21.0	23.2	23.4	26.4	27.6
Construction	3.0	3.2	3.6	3.7	5.6	4.9
Transportation and communications	4.0	4.3	4.3	4.4	4.4	4.6
Trade	15.8	18.6	16.5	15.7	15.5	14.4
Total	100.0	100.0	100.0	100.0	100.0	100.0
Net domestic product by social sectors (per cent)						
State-owned	19.3	—	—	—	32.1	33.0
Cooperative	1.6	—	—	—	53.3	56.0
Joint state and private	0.7	—	—	—	7.4	8.0
Private	7.0	—	—	—	0.1	(*)
Individual	71.4	—	—	—	7.1	3.0
Total	100.0	100.0	100.0	100.0	100.0	100.0

NOTES: (*) Less than 0.05 per cent.

— Not available.

Net domestic product in 1952 prices: TCYC, No. 1, January 1958, pp. 6, 11.

Net domestic product in current prices. 1952: *ibid.*, p. 11. 1953–55: based on data on percentages of state budget expenditures on basic construction in national income (*ibid.*, p. 15). State budget expenditures on basic construction are given in Fung Chi-hsi, "The Growth of China's Economy as Viewed from the State Budget," *TCKT*, No. 12, June 1957, p. 32. 1956: based on per capita national income data at current prices in 1956 given in *TCYC*, No. 1, January 1958, p. 12, and total population in 1956 given in *TCKT*, No. 11, June 1957, p. 25. 1957: SSB, "Great Achievements in China's Economic Construction in the Past Nine Years," *TCYC*, No. 9, September 1958, p. 2. No annotation was given for the price basis of this estimate; presumably it is in current prices.

Net domestic product by industrial origin. 1952 and 1956: *TCYC*, No. 1, January 1958, p. 11. 1953–55 and 1957: based on reconstructed Communist absolute figures given in Appendix J.

Net domestic product by social sectors. 1952 and 1956: *TCYC*, No. 1, January 1958, p. 11. 1957: *FFYP Communique.*

Comparison of Communist Figures and Adjusted Estimate

A comparison of the Communist figures with the adjusted estimate is made in Table 70. First, there are basic differences in concept. The Communists have included as farm income certain family services that are excluded from the adjusted estimate; such activities as food processing (other than the husking of food crops), slaughtering, clothmaking, and manufacture of home furnishings.

Table 70

RECONCILIATION OF THE ADJUSTED ESTIMATE AND THE COMMUNIST ESTIMATE OF NET DOMESTIC PRODUCT, 1952–57

(billions of 1952 yuan)

Year and Industry	Reconstructed Communist figures[a]	Adjustment because of differences in— Concept	Classification	Unexplained balance	Adjusted estimate
1952					
Agriculture					
Agriculture proper	27.72		+0.09[b]	+1.49	31.60
			+0.53[c]		
			+1.77[d]		
Subsidiary	8.47	−5.19[e]	−0.09[b]		0
			−1.77[d]		
			−1.42[f]		
Manufacturing					
Factories	6.45				6.45
Handicrafts	2.24		+1.42[f]		4.41
Utilities	0.31				0.31
Mining	1.47				1.47
Lumbering and fishing	0.53		−0.53[c]		0
Construction	1.83				1.83
Transportation and communications	2.45	+2.34[g]			4.79
Trade	9.66				9.66
Government	—	+3.27[h]			3.27
Finance	—	+1.31[h]			1.31
Services	—	+0.55[h]			0.55
Imputed rent	—	+2.28[h]			2.28
Work brigades	—	+0.62[h]			0.62
Net domestic product	61.13	+5.18[j]		+2.24	68.55
1953					
Agriculture					
Agriculture proper	27.77		+0.08[b]	+1.69	32.06
			+0.68[c]		
			+1.84[d]		
Subsidiary	9.18	−5.70[e]	−0.08[b]		0
			−1.84[d]		
			−1.56[f]		
Manufacturing					
Factories	8.64				8.64
Handicrafts	3.60		+1.56[f]	−0.71	4.45
Utilities	0.37				0.37
Mining	1.46				1.46
Lumbering and fishing	0.68		−0.68[c]		0
Construction	2.28				2.28
Transportation and communications	3.04	+2.04[g]			5.08
Trade	13.02			−2.45	10.57
Government	—	+3.70[h]			3.70
Finance	—	+1.41[h]			1.41

(Continued)

Table 70 (continued)

Year and Industry	Reconstructed Communist figures[a]	Adjustment because of differences in— Concept	Classification	Unexplained balance	Adjusted estimate
Services	—	+0.55[h]			0.55
Imputed rent	—	+2.32[h]			2.32
Work brigades	—	+0.38[h]			0.38
Net domestic product	70.04	+4.70[j]		−1.47	73.27
1954					
Agriculture					
Agriculture proper	29.29		+0.07[b] +0.87[c] +1.95[d]	+0.48	32.66
Subsidiary	9.38	−5.77[e]	−0.07[b] −1.95[d] −1.59[f]		0
Manufacturing					
Factories	10.15				10.15
Handicrafts	3.88		+1.59[f]	−0.88	4.59
Utilities	0.43				0.43
Mining	1.82				1.82
Lumbering and fishing	0.87		−0.87[c]		0
Construction	2.68				2.68
Transportation and communications	3.20	+2.17[g]			5.37
Trade	12.18			−0.88	11.30
Government	—	+3.95[h]			3.95
Finance	—	+1.51[h]			1.51
Services	—	+0.54[h]			0.54
Imputed rent	—	+2.37[h]			2.37
Work brigades	—	+0.44[h]			0.44
Net domestic product	73.88	+5.21[f]		−1.28	77.81
1955					
Agriculture					
Agriculture proper	31.49		+0.10[b] +1.03[c] +2.53[d]	−0.66	34.49
Subsidiary	10.16	−5.88[e]	−0.10[b] −2.53[d] −1.65[f]		0
Manufacturing					
Factories	10.93				10.93
Handicrafts	3.68		+1.65[f]	−0.39	4.94
Utilities	0.48				0.48
Mining	2.32				2.32
Lumbering and fishing	1.03		−1.03[c]		0
Construction	2.93				2.93
Transportation and communications	3.43	+2.31[g]			5.74
Trade	12.35			−0.25	12.10

(Continued)

Table 70 (continued)

Year and Industry	Reconstructed Communist figures[a]	Adjustment because of differences in— Concept	Adjustment because of differences in— Classification	Unexplained balance	Adjusted estimate
Government	—	+4.07[h]			4.07
Finance	—	+1.61[h]			1.61
Services	—	+0.54[h]			0.54
Imputed rent	—	+2.44[h]			2.44
Work brigades	—	+0.75[h]			0.75
Net domestic product	78.80	+5.84[j]		−1.30	83.34
1956					
Agriculture					
Agriculture proper	32.02		+0.10[b]	+0.93	36.76
			+0.05[c]		
			+2.66[d]		
Subsidiary	10.67	−6.17[e]	−0.10[b]		0
			−2.66[d]		
			−1.74[f]		
Manufacturing					
Factories	15.69				15.69
Handicrafts	3.72		+1.74[f]	−0.26	5.20
Utilities	0.59				0.59
Mining	2.38				2.38
Lumbering and fishing	1.05		−1.05[c]		
Construction	4.97				4.97
Transportation and communications	3.90	+2.71[g]			6.61
Trade	13.76				13.76
Government	—	+4.76[h]			4.76
Finance	—	+1.89[h]			1.89
Services	—	+0.51[h]			0.51
Imputed rent	—	+2.48[h]			2.48
Work brigades	—	+0.81[h]			0.81
Net domestic product	88.75	+6.99[j]		+0.67	96.41
1957					
Agriculture					
Agriculture proper	34.22		+0.11[b]	+1.73	40.18
			+1.37[c]		
			+2.75[d]		
Subsidiary	11.04	−6.39[e]	−0.11[b]		0
			−2.75[d]		
			−1.79[f]		
Manufacturing					
Factories	17.26				17.26
Handicrafts	3.46		+1.79[f]	+0.48	5.73
Utilities	0.71				0.71
Mining	3.07				3.07
Lumbering and fishing	1.37		−1.37[c]		
Construction	4.62				4.62
Transportation and communications	4.33	+2.93[g]			7.26

(Continued)

Table 70 (continued)

Year and Industry	Reconstructed Communist figures[a]	Adjustment because of differences in— Concept	Classification	Unexplained balance	Adjusted estimate
Trade	13.45			+0.96	14.41
Government	—	+5.03[h]			5.03
Finance	—	+2.04[h]			2.04
Services	—	+0.51[h]			0.51
Imputed rent	—	+2.55[h]			2.55
Work brigades	—	+0.85[h]			0.85
Net domestic product	93.53	+7.52[j]		+3.17	104.22

NOTES: — Not available.

[a] The Communist totals were not broken down. We have attempted to reconstruct the figures by sector.

[b] Net value added by cotton ginning is classified by the Communists as income from farm subsidiary production but is included in the adjusted estimate as agriculture.

[c] Net value added by lumbering and fishing is classified by the Communists as part of the value of industrial production but is included in the adjusted estimate as agriculture.

[d] Net value added by hunting and collecting is classified by the Communists as part of farm subsidiary production but is included in the adjusted estimate as agriculture.

[e] Net value added by that part of the Communist estimate of farm subsidiary production (including preliminary processing for farm household consumption, handicraft products for farm household consumption and processing of farm products for consumers) not included in the adjusted estimate.

[f] Net value added by that part of the Communist estimate of farm subsidiary production included in the adjusted estimate.

[g] Net value added by passenger transportation and a part of old-fashioned transportation whose services, it is believed, the Communists failed to include in their estimate. The figure represents the discrepancy due to differences in both concept and coverage, but the exact amounts cannot be segregated.

[h] Net value added by those components of the service industries and the government sector included in the adjusted but not in the Communist figures.

[j] The figure represents the discrepancy due to differences in both concept and coverage, but the exact amounts cannot be segregated.

SOURCE: Appendix J.

On the other hand, we included in our calculation income originating in the nonmaterial production sectors such as passenger transportation, government services, finance, personal services, and imputed rent, all of which were excluded from the Communist estimate. Second, the Communist data on old-fashioned transportation appears to be deficient. Finally, there are differences in industrial classification that would affect only the allocation of net product to the different sectors but not the total national income figures themselves. These differences are shown in Table 70. After adjustment is made, the unexplained discrepancy between the adjusted estimate and the Communist estimate turns out to be minor.

The close correspondence between the two indicates that the Communists computed their national income more or less on the basis of the concepts and methods described above. It also suggests that there is a fair degree of internal consistency in the Communist national income estimates and published output statistics. But as is well known, consistency of this kind does not necessarily imply accuracy or reliability.

CHAPTER V

ESTIMATE OF DOMESTIC EXPENDITURE BY END USE

DETAILED estimates of domestic expenditure by end use are presented in this chapter. The first three sections are discussions of the derivation of domestic investment, government consumption and communal services, and personal consumption, in constant 1933 and 1952 prices. (The derivation of estimates in 1957 prices is explained in Appendix I.) In addition to the authors' estimate, an estimate of domestic expenditure can be derived for 1952–57 by using Communist data adjusted to conform to Western concepts. This estimate is compared with our own and the Communist estimates.

As will be shown below, estimates of domestic investment and investment in fixed and working capital in 1952–57 are derived primarily from Communist figures on accumulation and basic construction. A possible alternative definition of investment in basic construction is described in Appendix L. The redefinition includes changes in unfinished construction as well as ancillary expenses and new fixed assets. Appendix L also includes an estimate of working capital and fixed capital based on the percentage share of working capital in accumulation rather than on accumulation and basic construction.

DOMESTIC INVESTMENT

Investment estimates for 1933 and 1952–57 are derived from a great many statistical sources. For 1933, we rely mainly on production statistics and foreign trade returns. For 1952–57, Communist data on accumulation, basic construction, and national income are used. In compiling the investment estimate for the postwar years, several by-products are obtained: Estimates of investment in fixed assets and working capital, fixed investment both within and outside the state investment plan, and fixed capital in four selected industries in 1952–57. The derivations of these estimates are discussed in turn.

1933

Net domestic investment in 1933 in 1933 prices is derived by the commodity flow method. Essentially, the procedure involves (a) estimating the value of capital goods at manufacturers' prices (capital goods are defined to include all machinery and parts, tools, metal and electrical products, and transportation equipment); (b) adding net imports of capital goods; (c) allowing for transportation and distribution markup and installation costs, if any, to derive total value of capital goods at final cost to consumers; (d) adding the gross value of construction; and (e) allowing for capital consumption. The individual steps in deriving investment expenditure in 1933 are summarized in Table 71.

The total supply of capital goods at cost to distributors is derived by adding the gross values of factory-produced capital goods and imported capital goods. Gross value of domestically produced factory capital goods was estimated on the basis of the prewar surveys by Lieu and the South Manchurian Railway, supplemented by an estimate of production in foreign-owned factories in China proper.[1] Imports of capital goods are simply those recorded in the trade returns of the Chinese Maritime Customs and the Manchurian Government. The fairly comprehensive coverage of these sources and the relative reliability of these data are distinct advantages and make the commodity flow method preferable to other approaches. However, this method does require certain refinements in the data that have not been made because of the lack of information. We have not been able to segregate some items that should be classified as consumers' durables rather than capital goods—certain imported automobile parts and office equipment, for example. We have not been able to eliminate the possibility of duplication resulting from the sales of imported capital goods to the domestic machine industry for further fabrication. We have not included in our calculation a small amount of miscellaneous nonmetal products—for example, office furniture and fixtures—the costs of which constituted part of investment expenditure. None of these items is likely to be of any sizable amount, however, and whatever bias there may be in our figure is probably small.

To the sum total of domestic and imported modern capital goods we add the transportation and distribution margin and installation costs to derive the total value at prices paid by the final consumers. Information is not available on these cost items and a crude estimate

[1] A summary of results was presented in Table 38. For a detailed discussion of these surveys and estimates, see Appendix F under Gross Value of Output and Number of Workers for 1933; and Lieu, *Industry Survey*.

Table 71

DOMESTIC INVESTMENT, 1933
(millions of 1933 yuan)

Factory-produced capital goods[a]	
Machine parts	6
Machinery	31
Small electrical appliances	2
Metal products	16
Transportation equipment	47
Total factory-produced capital goods	102
Add: imported capital goods	
Imports by China proper[b]	99
Imports by Manchuria[c]	25
Total imported capital goods	124
Equals: total supply of modern capital goods at manufacturers' prices	226
Add: distribution and transportation margin[d]	68
Equals: total supply of modern capital goods at prices to final users	294
Add: handicraft capital goods[e]	
Machinery	11
Metal products	6
Transportation equipment	115
Total handicraft capital goods	132
Add: construction[f]	1,170
Equals: gross investment	1,596
Less: depreciation[g]	−1,086
Equals: net investment	510

NOTES: [a] See Table 38. It is assumed that machine manufacture accounts for 80 per cent of the gross value of machine manufacture and repair.

[b] *The Trade of China, 1933.* Imported capital goods included machinery and tools, metal, electrical products, transportation equipment, and rails.

[c] Far East Yearbook Co., *The Far East Yearbook, 1941*, Tokyo, 1941, p. 824.

[d] Assumed to be 30 per cent of the value of modern capital goods at manufacturers' prices.

[e] See Appendix G, Table G-1. It is assumed that 70 per cent of the gross value of machinery is from the manufacture of machines and 50 per cent of the gross value of metal products is capital goods.

[f] Total net value of construction in 1933 has been estimated at 1,134.7 million yuan (see Appendix H under Construction). We assume depreciation to be 3 per cent of gross value. Our estimate of the gross value of construction is 1,170 million yuan.

[g] See the discussion on depreciation in Appendixes E through H.

has to be made. In the prewar period, both producers and consumers of modern capital goods were in the coastal cities, and capital goods were usually distributed by the manufacturers directly to the final consumers. The transportation and distribution margin for domestically produced capital goods was quite small, probably lower than the estimated 31 per cent margin for commodities distributed through the market for the economy as a whole.[2] On the other hand, imported capital goods, which accounted for more than 50 per cent of total modern capital goods, generally went through more stages of distribution than did domestic goods, and involved installation costs. Imported capital goods therefore yield a transportation and distribution margin somewhat higher than the average for all commodities. On the basis of these rather general considerations, we assume a margin of 30 per cent for capital goods as a whole.[3]

In prewar China, many capital goods—farm tools, carts, waterwheels, etc.—were produced by handicraftsmen. Data on the gross value of these products have been compiled in connection with our estimate of income originating in handicrafts.[4] Since these handicrafts were generally sold directly to the final consumers, no markup for distribution and transportation costs need be added to the gross value at producers' prices. The costs to consumers of manufactured and imported capital goods and of handicraft capital goods together make up the total value of capital equipment.

The volume of construction, net of depreciation, has been estimated at 1.17 billion yuan.[5] Two limitations in this estimate should be noted. First, it is based on data on consumption of construction materials, and does not include construction that did not require their purchase. Second, because construction materials were also used for repairs and maintenance, our figure includes a certain

[2] See Table 87.

[3] It might be of interest to compare our figures with the following percentage markups on imported equipment in other underdeveloped countries in Southeast Asia: Burma, 50; Ceylon, 30; Indonesia, 20; and the Philippines, 50 (William I. Abraham, "Investment Estimates of Underdeveloped Countries: An Appraisal," *Journal of the American Statistical Association,* Vol. 53, No. 283, September 1958, p. 674). Although these figures refer to the distribution margin of imported capital goods alone, the comparison is not entirely meaningless because of the predominance of imported capital goods in China. Our estimate falls within the range of these estimates and comes close to the lower limit, which indicates that we might not be very far off.

[4] The commodity content of handicraft output cannot be completely identified. Presumably, a large part of the unidentified portion consisted of repair work and miscellaneous consumers' goods (for instance, herb medicine, straw hats and sandals, and articles used in religious or local cult practices). We therefore assume that none of the handicrafts in this sector belongs to the capital goods category. See Appendix G.

[5] See Table 47.

amount that was not new construction. Unfortunately, there is no data on these two items whatsoever, and no reasonable estimate can be made for them. It is clear that they would tend to cancel each other out to some extent.

We have made no allowance for changes in inventory holdings in 1933. In all likelihood, the error introduced here will not be serious because there were only minor changes in the output of the different sectors of the economy between 1932 and 1933.[6]

Net domestic investment in 1933 derived by the commodity flow method amounts to 0.51 billion yuan. From our estimate of net domestic product and personal and government consumption in both 1933 and 1952 prices, a price index for investment in 1952 with 1933 as the base year has been calculated at 500 per cent on the assumption that the implicit price deflators for net domestic product and net domestic expenditure are the same.[7] If we apply this price index to our figure for net domestic investment in 1933 prices, the estimate in 1952 prices is 2.55 billion yuan.

1952–57

Estimates of net domestic investment for 1952–57 are derived primarily from Communist information on accumulation with only minor modifications. In Communist terminology, accumulation is defined as additions to productive and nonproductive fixed assets and increases in working capital and stockpiling.[8] Productive fixed assets include factory buildings, mineshafts, open hearth furnaces, dykes, power plants, machinery and equipment, tools, transportation equipment, draft animals, and so on. Nonproductive fixed as-

[6] Liu, *Income,* Table 3, p. 12.

[7] See Appendix I, Table I-4.

[8] Yueh Wei, "The Method of Computing National Income," *CCYC,* No. 3, June 1956, p. 63. These are three related concepts: basic construction, economic construction expenditure, and budgeted funds for basic construction. Basic construction refers to the sum of fixed investment and certain ancillary expenses. See *First Five Year Plan,* p. 23. Economic construction expenditure refers to funds allocated to the various economic departments of the government for the purpose of financing basic construction, repairs and maintenance, working capital and current operating expenses of some departments. Budgeted funds for basic construction are funds from the state budget. They differ from economic construction expenditures in the inclusion of capital expenditures of noneconomic departments, and exclusion of noncapital expenditures. They differ from basic construction in two respects. Whereas basic construction is work actually carried out in the period, budgeted funds for basic construction represents funds earmarked for basic construction for the period, but not necessarily spent. Furthermore, some basic construction is financed from sources other than the state budget.

sets include residences, office buildings, schools, clubs, and so on. Also included in the value of fixed assets are certain ancillary items such as expenditures on geological surveys, engineering design, scientific research, personnel training, and compensation to occupants removed from construction sites. Working capital and stockpiling comprise inventories of all productive departments, such as raw materials, fuels, goods in the process of production, construction in process, etc.; inventories held by commercial enterprises; and stockpiling by the government. The additions to fixed assets are net of depreciation.[9] Except in two minor aspects, this definition is apparently identical to that of net domestic investment as used in standard national income accounting.[10] First, the ancillary expenditures included in the Communist concept are not generally considered investment expenditures in standard practice. Second, the Communist national income estimates do not include the services of passenger transportation and finance nor the greater part of the contribution of work brigades. Some of these services must have been rendered in connection with investment, but the Communists have not taken them into account.

In recent publications, percentages of net domestic expenditure accumulated in 1952–57 have been released by the Communists.[11] Inasmuch as the Communist national income statistics are known, estimates of accumulation can be calculated and then adjusted for ancillary expenses, service expenditures, and depreciation to arrive at our estimates of net domestic investment. (Except for minor adjustments, then, our estimates of investment are essentially Communist data.) The results of the calculations are shown in Table 72.

The Communist estimates of net domestic product in 1952–57 in constant 1952 prices are presented in Table 69. We add the import surplus to arrive at net domestic expenditure. For 1952 and 1956–57, the estimates of import surplus are derived by a rather roundabout procedure. Consumption, accumulation, and net domestic expenditure in these years in 1952 prices are calculated from Communist data, and net domestic product is subtracted from net do-

[9] Yueh Wei, *op. cit.*, pp. 63–64.

[10] United Nations Department of Economic Affairs, *A System of National Accounts and Supporting Tables*, New York, 1953, pp. 29–31.

[11] For definitions of the Communist concepts of net domestic expenditure, net domestic product, and consumption, see Chapter IV under Comparisons of the Authors', the Adjusted, and the Communist Estimates of Domestic Product.

Table 72

DOMESTIC INVESTMENT, 1952–57
(billions of 1952 yuan)

	1952	1953	1954	1955	1956	1957
Net domestic product	61.13	70.04	73.88	78.80	88.75	93.53
Add: import surplus	1.73	1.05	0.37	0.16	−0.60	−1.02
Equals: net domestic expenditure	62.86	71.09	74.25	78.96	88.15	92.51
Percentage of accumulation in net domestic expenditure (per cent)	18.2	22.4	23.5	22.9	26.1	24.0
Accumulation	11.44	15.92	17.45	18.08	23.01	22.20
Deduct: ancillary expenses	1.25	1.35	1.67	1.32	4.03	1.01
Add: items omitted from Communist data						
Investment by work brigades	0.62	0.38	0.44	0.75	0.81	0.85
Passenger transportation	0.13	0.15	0.15	0.15	0.18	0.18
Finance	0.33	0.35	0.37	0.38	0.42	0.44
Equals: net domestic investment	11.26	15.45	16.74	18.04	20.39	22.66
Add: depreciation	3.26	3.66	4.03	4.27	5.20	5.48
Equals: gross domestic investment	14.52	19.11	20.77	22.31	25.59	28.14

mestic expenditure for each of these years to yield the following estimates of import surplus in billions of 1952 yuan:

	1952	1956	1957
Consumption	51.42	65.15	70.34
Accumulation	11.44	23.00	22.17
Net domestic expenditure	62.86	88.15	92.51
Net domestic product	61.13	88.75	93.53
Import surplus	1.73	−0.60	−1.02

Consumption, accumulation, and net domestic expenditure in 1952 and 1956 are derived from the following Communist data: indexes of consumption and accumulation in 1956, with 1952 as the base year, 126.7 and 201.0 per cent; the increase in net domestic expenditure in 1952–56, 25.3 billion yuan; and percentages of consumption and accumulation in net domestic expenditure in 1952, 81.8 and 18.2 per cent.[12] Some of the data are not sufficiently annotated in the source to indicate the price basis. From their context, however, they appear to be in 1952 prices.[13]

[12] SSB, "Preliminary Analysis of Production and Distribution of China's National Income," *TCYC*, No. 1, January 1958, p. 12.

[13] If C_o, C_1, I_o, I_1 denote the Communist estimates of consumption and accumulation in 1952 and 1956, the information given above can be expressed in four simple relations: $C_1 = 1.267\ C_o$; $I_1 = 2.011\ I_o$; $I_1 + C_1 - I_o - C_o = 25.3$; $C_o/I_o = 818/182$.

For 1957, consumption and accumulation are derived on the basis of the corresponding 1952 figures and their indexes in 1957 with 1952 as the base year, given at 136.8 for consumption and 193.8 per cent for the accumulation in 1952 prices.[14] For 1953–55, data on import surplus are estimates based on Communist foreign trade statistics.[15] In the absence of any information on import and export prices, we assume that the import surpluses in current prices are the same as in 1952 prices.

Table 73 summarizes the Communist estimates of percentages of accumulation in net domestic expenditure in 1952–57. The figures

Table 73

SUMMARY OF ACCUMULATION ESTIMATES, 1952–57
(percentage of national income)

Estimates of accumulation	1952	1953	1954	1955	1956	1957
1. In current prices (SSB)	18.2	21.4	22.3	20.9	22.5	21.0
2. In 1952 prices (Niu)	16.1	17.4	21.9	20.4	22.8	
3. In 1952 prices (Hsu)	18.2	22.4	23.5	22.9	26.1	24.0
4. Price basis unspecified (Po)	15.7	18.3	21.6	20.5	22.8	
5. Price basis unspecified (Yen)	19.7	22.4	22.7	21.6	24.4	23.7
6. Price basis unspecified (Li)	19.8					24.3

NOTES: *Line 1.* SSB, "A Preliminary Analysis of the Production and Distribution of China's National Income," *TCYC*, No. 1, January 1958, pp. 6, 12.

Line 2. Niu Chung-huang, *Wo-kuo kuo-min-shou-ju ti chi-lai ho hsiao-fei* (Accumulation and Consumption in China's National Income), Peiping, Chung-kuo ching-nien chu-pan-she, 1957, p. 51.

Line 3. Hsu Ti-hsin, *Chung-kuo kuo-tu she-chi kuo-min ching-chi ti fen-hsi* (An Analysis of the National Economy During China's Transition Period), Peiping, 1959, p. 262.

Line 4. Po I-po, "On the Correct Handling of the Problem of the Relationship Between Accumulation and Consumption," *HHPYK*, No. 20, October 1956, p. 74.

Line 5. Yen I-sheng, "My View Points on the Production of Means of Production and Materials for Consumption in Relation to Government Revenue and Expenditure," *CCYC*, No. 7, July 1959, p. 8.

Line 6. Li Lin-ku, "The Structure of Socialism and the Population Problems," *Hsin chien she* (New Construction), No. 4, February 1960, p. 51.

are somewhat different. In some cases the difference can be explained in terms of differing price bases or revisions of preliminary

Solving, we obtain: $C_0 = 51.42$; $I_0 = 11.44$; $C_1 = 65.15$; $I_1 = 23.00$ billion yuan. Note that accumulation for 1956 and this estimate for 1957 are slightly different from the figures given in Table 72, probably due to rounding.

[14] Wang-Si-hua, "The Role of Statistics in Our Economic Construction and Questions Pertaining to Some Statistical Indicators," *CCYC*, No. 5, May 1958, p. 26.

[15] United Nations, *Economic Survey of Asia and the Far East, 1957*, Bangkok, 1958, p. 103.

estimates, but in other cases no explanations can be found. The percentages in 1952 prices given by Hsu are used in our calculation because they are consistent with the official estimates in current prices for 1952 and because the figures in current prices for later years (particularly for 1956–57) are lower than the corresponding figures in 1952 prices.[16] This implies that the price index for net domestic product for these years, with 1952 as 100, is higher than the price index for investment in the same period, a conclusion consistent with miscellaneous Communist reports on price changes. When these percentages are applied to the total of net domestic product and import surplus given above, we obtain the Communist estimates of accumulation for 1952–57 in 1952 prices.

The Communist figures of accumulation include expenses of certain items ancillary to fixed investment but not considered investment in standard practice. To estimate net domestic investment, it was necessary to deduct these expenses from the Communist data. The calculations of ancillary expenses are presented in Table 74. The derivation of the price index for basic construction is as follows: A price index for basic construction in 1953–56 with each preceding year as 100 can be computed at 95.8, 94.8, and 93.5 per cent for 1954–56.[17] Price indexes of accumulation for 1956–57 with 1952 as the base year can be calculated at 90.4 per cent for both years from the estimates of accumulation in 1952 and in current prices. Accumulation in 1956 and 1957 in 1952 prices was estimated as 23.01 and 22.20 billion 1952 yuan in Table 72. The corresponding figures for 1956 and 1957 in current prices (20.79 and 20.06 billion yuan) are derived on the basis of the Communist estimate of national income (93.00 and 96.50 billion yuan as given in Table 69), import surplus (−0.60 and −1.02 billion yuan), and the percentages of accumulation in net domestic expenditure (22.5 and 21.0 per cent, all given earlier in the chapter). These figures yield the 1956–57 price index for accumulation as 90.4 with 1952 as 100.

Since fixed investment constitutes a great part of total accumula-

[16] Hsu Ti-hsin, *Chung-kuo kuo-tu she-chi kuo-min ching-chi ti fen-hsi* (An Analysis of the National Economy During China's Transition Period), Peiping, Ko-hsueh chu-pan-she, 1959.

[17] Yang Pong-chieh, "A Proposal To Use Constant Prices in Drawing Up the Basic Construction Plan and Budget," *CHCC*, No. 2, February 1958, p. 30. The price index for 1956 is given. For 1954–55, only the indexes of basic construction in current prices and in constant (comparable) prices are given. The price indexes for these years are obtained by dividing the index in current prices by the corresponding figure in constant prices.

Table 74

BASIC CONSTRUCTION, FIXED INVESTMENT, AND ANCILLARY EXPENSES, 1952–57, AND THE PRICE INDEX FOR BASIC CONSTRUCTION, 1953–57
(billions of yuan)

	1952	1953	1954	1955	1956	1957
In current prices						
1. Basic construction	4.36	8.00	9.07	9.30	14.80	13.83
2. Fixed investment	3.11	6.56	7.37	8.02	11.16	12.92
3. Ancillary expenses	1.25	1.44	1.70	1.28	3.64	0.91
In 1952 prices						
4. Basic construction	4.36	7.51	8.89	9.61	16.37	15.30
5. Fixed investment	3.11	6.16	7.22	8.29	12.34	14.29
6. Ancillary expenses	1.25	1.35	1.67	1.32	4.03	1.01
Price index						
7. Basic construction (per cent)	100.0	106.5	102.0	96.7	90.4	90.4

NOTES: *Line 1. Great Ten Years*, p. 46.

Line 2. Ibid., p. 55.

Line 3. Line 1 less line 2.

Lines 4 and 5. Lines 1 and 2 divided by the price index for basic construction for 1952–57 with 1952 as 100.

Line 6. Line 4 less line 5.

Line 7. This is the linked index whose derivation is described in the text; it is based on a price index for basic construction for 1953–56 and a price index of accumulation for 1956–57 with 1952 as 100.

tion, and a substantial portion of investment in working capital represents changes in basic construction in progress and in the inventory of producers' goods, the prices would most likely move together with those for basic construction. It therefore seems reasonable to assume that the price indexes of basic construction and of accumulation would move together. On this assumption we link together these two indexes. The linked index is given in Table 74, and will be referred to as the price index for basic construction.

The final step in deriving net domestic investment consists of adding to accumulation three items that have not been included in the Communist estimate: investment by work brigades, passenger transportation, and financial services rendered in connection with investment. Investment by work brigades was estimated in Table 50. Passenger transportation and financial services are arbitrarily assumed to account for one-fourth of the total net output of these two industries. Net value added by passenger transportation is derived by summing the estimates for the modern and the old-fashioned sector.[18] If the adjusted estimates of net value added by passenger transportation and finance given in Table 68 are used, we obtain the adjusted estimates of net domestic investment for 1952–57 as 11.26, 15.45, 16.75, 18.06, 20.44, and 22.73 billion 1952 yuan. Estimates of net domestic investment for 1952–57 in 1933 prices are derived by deflating the figures in 1952 prices by the price index of 500 per cent in 1952 with 1933 as the base year.[19]

In the derivation of net income originating in different industrial sectors, rough estimates have been made of depreciation in 1933 and 1952–57 in 1933 and 1952 prices.[20] The total amounts of depreciation in 1952–57 are added to the figures for net domestic investment in the same period to obtain estimates of gross domestic investment.

As noted in Chapter II, the reported rate of increase in the number of hogs in 1956–57 is unreasonably high. Accordingly, a downward adjustment in hog production in 1957 is made amounting to 2.04 billion 1952 yuan. There is a corresponding upward bias in expenditure, presumably in changes in working capital. We therefore deduct 2.04 billion yuan from the preliminary estimate of net domestic investment of 22.66 billion yuan in 1957 to arrive at our estimate of 20.62 billion yuan. Our estimate of gross domestic investment in 1957 thus amounts to 26.10 billion yuan.

Fixed Investment, Investment in Working Capital, and Fixed Capital in Four Industries, 1952–57

Estimates of fixed investment and changes in working capital in 1952–57 are again derived on the basis of Communist data on accumulation and basic construction. Net domestic expenditure in current prices is first obtained by adding net domestic product in current prices to import surplus.[21] The percentages of accumulation are then applied to the corresponding figures for net domestic expenditure to arrive at the Communist estimates of accumulation for 1952–57 in current prices: 11.44, 16.07, 17.03, 17.39, 20.79, and 20.05 billion yuan. Deducting basic construction from accumulation, we obtain investment in working capital in 1952–57 as 7.08, 8.07, 7.96, 8.09, 5.99, and 6.22 billion current yuan.[22] There is no information

[18] For total net value added in the modern sector, see Appendix H, Table H-9.
[19] For the derivation of this price index see Appendix I.
[20] See Appendixes E through H under Depreciation.
[21] For the Communist estimate of net domestic product in current prices, see Table 69; for data on import surplus, see Table 72.
[22] For data on basic construction, see Table 74.

for calculation of a price deflator for changes in working capital. In the absence of a better alternative, the unweighted average of the price index for basic construction and the wholesale price index is used to derive investment in working capital at 7.08, 7.86, 7.91, 8.24, 6.32, and 6.53 billion 1952 yuan for these years.[23] The estimate of investment in working capital for 1957 must again be adjusted downward by 2.04 billion yuan to take care of the upward bias in the hog statistics. Our estimate for 1957 is 4.49 billion yuan. Total net fixed investment is then derived as a residual by deducting investment in working capital from total net domestic investment given in Table 72. The results are 4.18, 7.59, 8.83, 9.80, 14.07, and 16.13 billion 1952 yuan for 1952–57.

Centralized investment planning by the government was effectively carried out only in the state sectors during 1952–57, and the sectors not covered in the state investment plan can be expected to yield statistics of lower reliability. It is of interest to separate the components of total fixed investment on the basis of Communist data on completed basic construction.[24] We start with total basic construction by industries at current prices and that part of basic construction covered in the state plan, and first reduce these figures by a factor equal to the percentage of fixed investment in basic construction. They are then deflated by the price index for basic construction given in Table 74, to arrive at fixed investment by the state in 1952 prices. Subtracting state fixed investment from total fixed investment, we obtain estimates of fixed investment not covered in the state investment plan. The calculations are presented in Tables 75 and 76.

We can roughly compute the total amount of fixed capital in factories, mining, and utilities; modern transportation and communications; trade; and construction on the basis of the Communist estimate of fixed capital in these industries at the end of 1955. The procedure consists of successively deducting fixed investment in 1952–55 from fixed capital in 1955 and adding fixed investment in 1956 to fixed capital in 1955. The estimates so derived are then divided by the corresponding numbers of workers to arrive at rough

[23] The wholesale price index is given in *Great Ten Years*, p. 153.

[24] See the note to the table of basic construction estimates in *1955 Statistical Abstract*, p. 42; and Hsu Chien, Tai Shih-kuang, and Yu Tao, *Ching-chi-t'ung-chi-she chian-hua* (Lectures on Economic Statistics), Peiping, T'ung-chi chu-pan-she, 1957, p. 129. Changes in the volume of basic construction in progress are included in investment in working capital. Yueh Wei, *op. cit.*, p. 63.

Table 75

BASIC CONSTRUCTION, 1952–57
(billions of current yuan)

	For the economy as a whole[a]					
	1952	1953	1954	1955	1956	1957
Factories, mining, and utilities	1.75	2.92	3.91	4.37	6.94	7.36
Industry	1.69	2.84	3.83	4.30	6.82	7.24
Water supply	0.06	0.08	0.08	0.07	0.12	0.12
Construction	0.09	0.36	0.36	0.32	0.65	0.46
Trade	0.12	0.27	0.39	0.35	0.76	0.37
Modern transportation and communications	0.87	1.24	1.66	1.91	2.84	2.33
Railroads	0.51	0.65	0.95	1.22	1.76	1.34
Municipal transport	0.11	0.17	0.16	0.15	0.23	0.26
Others	0.25	0.42	0.55	0.54	0.85	0.73
Agriculture	0.60	0.77	0.42	0.62	1.19	1.19
Water conservation	0.41	0.48	0.22	0.41	0.71	0.73
Others	0.19	0.29	0.20	0.21	0.48	0.46
Other sectors	0.93	2.44	2.33	1.73	2.42	2.12
Education and social services	0.28	0.62	0.68	0.59	1.00	0.92
Health and welfare	0.06	0.15	0.15	0.11	0.11	0.13
Geological survey	0.07	0.19	0.29	0.25	0.40	0.30
Administration	0.02	0.28	0.21	0.14	0.16	0.18
Miscellaneous	0.50	1.20	1.00	0.64	0.75	0.59
Total	4.36	8.00	9.07	9.30	14.80	13.83

	In the state investment plan[b]					
	1952	1953	1954	1955	1956	1957
Factories, mining, and utilities	1.61	2.84	3.71	4.28	6.60	6.68
Industry	1.55	2.76	3.63	4.20	6.48	6.55
Water supply	0.06	0.08	0.08	0.07	0.11	0.13
Construction	0.09	0.34	0.36	0.29	0.63	0.46
Trade	0.08	0.23	0.26	0.24	0.67	0.37
Modern transportation and communications	0.87	1.23	1.60	1.87	2.81	2.32
Railroads	0.50	0.64	0.92	1.20	1.74	—
Municipal transport	0.11	0.17	0.16	0.15	0.23	—
Other transportation	0.23	0.35	0.44	0.45	0.69	—
Communications	0.03	0.07	0.08	0.07	0.15	—
Agriculture	0.52	0.66	0.38	0.61	1.18	1.03
Water conservation	0.33	0.38	0.22	0.40	0.70	—
Others	0.19	0.28	0.16	0.21	0.48	—
Other sectors	0.54	1.20	1.20	1.34	2.10	1.78
Education, social service, health and welfare	0.32	0.77	0.77	0.69	1.09	—
Geological survey	0.05	0.12	0.29	0.15	0.40	—
Miscellaneous	0.17	0.31	0.14	0.50	0.61	—
Total	3.71	6.51	7.50	8.63	13.99	12.64

NOTES: — Not available.

[a] *Great Ten Years*, pp. 48–49. Basic construction in water supply is assumed to constitute one-third, and in municipal transport, two-thirds of basic construction in municipal utilities.

[b] For 1952–56, see *1956 Statistical Abstract*, p. 36. Basic construction in water supply is assumed to constitute one-third, and in municipal transport two-thirds, of basic construction in municipal utilities. For 1957, total basic construction is given in *Great Ten Years*, p. 47. Basic construction in industry in 1957 is given in Po I-po, *1958 Plan*, p. 12. Basic construction in water supply, construction, trade, and modern transportation and communications covered in the state investment plan is assumed to be the same as for the economy as a whole. Basic construction in agriculture is derived by deducting the total figure for 1952–56 from the sum total of state basic construction in agriculture, 1952–57, given in Han Po, "Economize Current Expenditure on Agriculture," *CHCC*, No. 2, February 1958, p. 17. Basic construction in the other sectors is derived as a residual.

Table 76

FIXED INVESTMENT BY INDUSTRIAL SECTORS, 1952–57
(billions of 1952 yuan)

Sector	For the economy as a whole[a]						In the state investment plan[b]					
	1952	1953	1954	1955	1956	1957	1952	1953	1954	1955	1956	1957
Factories, mining, and utilities	1.34	2.43	3.03	3.94	5.79	7.58	1.08	2.33	2.75	3.51	4.75	5.94
Construction	0.08	0.30	0.32	0.32	0.58	0.52	0.07	0.28	0.31	0.24	0.49	0.45
Trade	0.10	0.22	0.35	0.35	0.68	0.42	0.06	0.19	0.22	0.20	0.52	0.36
Modern transportation and communications	0.84	1.13	1.62	2.00	2.72	2.76	0.65	1.01	1.39	1.53	2.19	2.28
Agriculture	1.01	0.93	0.71	1.26	1.75	2.08	0.38	0.54	0.33	0.50	0.92	1.01
Others	0.81	2.58	2.80	1.93	2.55	2.77	0.40	0.98	1.05	1.10	1.64	1.74
Total	4.18	7.59	8.83	9.80	14.07	16.13	2.63	5.34	6.04	7.08	10.52	11.78

NOTES: [a] The derivation of fixed investment for the economy as a whole is as follows: First, fixed investment in the six sectors in current prices is derived. For industry and the economy as a whole, fixed investment is given in *Great Ten Years*, p. 57. From these figures and the corresponding figures for basic construction given in Table 75, fixed investment in basic construction for all sectors other than industry can be derived at 74, 82, 87, 90, 78, and 98 per cent for 1952–57. These percentages are then applied to basic construction in these sectors in Table 75 to derive fixed investment in current prices. The price index for basic construction, given in Table 74, is then used to deflate the figures in current prices to arrive at fixed investment in 1952 prices. We then add the services rendered by passenger transportation and finance in connection with investment but omitted in Communist data. The amount of these services, given in Table 72, is allocated among the six sectors on the basis of the percentage composition of fixed investment. Investment by work brigades in water conservation and transportation projects, given in Table 50, is also added to fixed investment. It is assumed that one-half of the work done by the militia is for water conservation projects and the other half for transportation projects.

[b] Fixed investment covered in the state investment plan is derived as follows: Fixed investment in factories, mining, and utilities in current prices is obtained by multiplying basic construction in the same industry, given in Table 75, by the ratio of fixed investment to basic construction computed from data given in *Great Ten Years*, pp. 48 and 57. Fixed investment in the other five sectors is derived similarly. The ratios of fixed investment to basic construction used here are the same as those given in Note (a) for all sectors other than industry. Fixed investment in current prices is then deflated by the price index for basic construction, given in Table 74, to arrive at fixed investment in constant 1952 prices.

estimates of fixed capital per worker. The results of this calculation appear in Table 77.

Table 77

NET FIXED CAPITAL AND NET FIXED CAPITAL PER WORKER IN FOUR INDUSTRIES, 1952–57
(at beginning of the year, in 1952 yuan)

	1952	1953	1954	1955	1956	1957
Net fixed capital (billions)						
Factories, mining, and utilities	7.40	8.74	11.17	14.20	18.14	23.93
Modern transportation and communications	5.10	5.94	7.07	8.69	10.69	13.41
Trade	0.92	1.02	1.24	1.59	1.94	2.62
Construction	0.60	0.68	0.98	1.30	1.62	2.20
Net fixed capital per worker (thousands per worker)						
Factories, mining, and utilities	2.09	2.12	2.66	3.20	3.77	4.35
Modern transportation and communications	6.99	7.52	7.36	7.69	8.10	9.38
Trade	0.14	0.16	0.21	0.29	0.33	0.41
Construction	0.46	0.37	0.52	0.67	0.66	0.92

NOTES: Estimates of net fixed capital in the four industries at the beginning of 1956 are derived on the basis of data on net fixed capital in factories, mining, and utilities, and on the percentage of total fixed assets attributable to fixed capital of factories, mining, and utilities and the other three industries, given in SSB, "A General Survey of National Industrial Capital," *TCKT*, No. 1, January 1957, p. 31. It should be noted that the fixed capital of factories, mining, and utilities includes a small amount of fixed capital in handicraft workshops. However, handicraft workshops are mostly small enterprises and accounted for less than 1 per cent of total fixed capital for these industries (*ibid.*). Hence, no adjustment is made to deduct the fixed capital of handicraft workshops in our estimate. The Communist figures are not fully annotated with regard to the method of estimate and the basis of valuation, but it is assumed that they are in 1952 prices. Estimates of fixed capital for 1952–55 are obtained by subtracting the fixed investment in 1952–55 given in Table 76 from fixed capital in 1956. The figure for 1957 is the sum of fixed capital and fixed investment in 1956. Estimates of fixed capital per worker are derived by dividing the total fixed capital by the number of workers given in Table 11.

Available Communist data on fixed capital per worker are considerably higher than our estimates.[25] There are several reasons for these differences. First, our figures cover state, joint state and private, and private enterprises, whereas the Communist figures cover only the state sector. As the private sector consists almost entirely of light industry, and as capital per worker in light industry is generally less than in heavy industry, the inclusion of the private sector would most likely yield a lower estimate of capital

[25] SSB, *Technological Level,* p. 30; and Ma Yin-chu, *op. cit.,* p. 163.

per worker. Second, in the derivation of capital per worker, the total number of workers and employees is used as the denominator in our estimate, whereas only the number of productive workers is used in the Communist estimate.[26] Our denominator is larger than the Communists' by an amount equal to the total number of technicians, engineers, administrators, and all others who are not directly involved in the production process. In addition, in our computation, fixed capital refers to the beginning of the year. It is not clear whether the Communists use the same concept. If fixed capital at the middle or the end of the year is used (and this is not unlikely), the Communist estimates are bound to be higher, since net fixed capital in the industries concerned has been increasing throughout the period under study. However, there is little likelihood of significant differences in the numbers of workers.

GOVERNMENT CONSUMPTION AND COMMUNAL SERVICES

Government consumption comprises the current purchases of goods and services by the central and local government bodies, including compensation of employees and military subsistence but excluding purchases on capital account and transfer payments. Communal services include current (as distinguished from capital) expenditures of all government agencies on education, health, welfare, and other social services. Table 78 summarizes estimates of government consumption and communal services for 1933 and 1952–57 in constant 1933 and 1952 prices.[27] The derivations of estimates for these two periods are described separately.

Total government consumption and communal services in 1933 are derived as 1.20 billion 1933 yuan by summing up expenditures on these items incurred by (1) the national government, provincial and special municipal governments, and hsien governments in China proper,[28] and (2) the Manchurian government and the local governments under the Foreign Settlement Administration.[29] On the basis of data given in the same two studies, 12 per cent of current expenditure is on communal services.[30] This percentage is applied to total government consumption, 1.2 billion yuan, to derive the expenditure on communal services at 0.14 billion yuan, and

[26] Ma Yin-chu, *op. cit.*, p. 164.
[27] Estimates in 1957 prices are derived in Appendix I.
[28] Liu, *Income,* pp. 54–55.
[29] Ou, *National Income,* Vol. I, p. 134; Vol. II, p. 291.
[30] Liu, *Income,* p. 54; Ou, *National Income,* p. 134.

Table 78

GOVERNMENT CONSUMPTION AND COMMUNAL SERVICES, 1933 AND 1952–57
(billions of yuan)

	1933	1952	1953	1954	1955	1956	1957
In 1933 prices							
Government consumption	1.06	2.35	2.87	2.59	2.79	2.66	2.92
Services	0.72	1.40	1.63	1.74	1.76	1.99	2.09
Goods	0.34	0.95	1.24	0.85	1.03	0.67	0.83
Communal services	0.14	0.80	0.97	1.00	0.97	1.36	1.40
Services	0.10	0.69	0.75	0.81	0.86	1.10	1.17
Goods	0.04	0.11	0.22	0.19	0.11	0.26	0.23
In 1952 prices							
Government consumption	2.36	5.34	6.64	5.49	6.11	5.23	5.92
Services	1.26	2.15	2.48	2.63	2.66	2.97	3.13
Goods	1.10	3.19	4.16	2.86	3.45	2.26	2.79
Communal services	0.32	1.94	2.45	2.46	2.32	3.26	3.29
Services	0.17	1.12	1.22	1.32	1.41	1.79	1.90
Goods	0.15	0.82	1.23	1.14	0.91	1.47	1.39

government consumption is calculated as 1.06 billion yuan as a residual. Total wage and salary payments, estimated in Appendix H at 0.82 billion yuan, are allocated to government and communal services as 0.72 and 0.10 billion yuan on the basis of the ratio of total income originating in government to total income originating in communal services.[31] Purchases of goods by government administration and communal services are then computed as residuals at 0.34 and 0.04 billion yuan by deducting income payments from total expenditure for each sector.

Expenditures on goods for both sectors in 1952 prices are derived by multiplying the estimate in 1933 prices by the price index of factory-produced consumers' goods, given at 329 per cent for 1952 with 1933 as 100.[32] Total income payments to the two sectors in 1952 prices were estimated at 1.43 billion yuan in Appendix H. On the assumption that payments were the same percentage of the total as in 1933 prices, income originating in communal services is computed at 0.17 billion yuan, and in government administration at 1.10 billion yuan.

For the postwar period, communal services and government consumption are derived separately. Total communal services in current prices in 1952–57 are first obtained by deducting basic construction

[31] Ou, *National Income,* Vol. I, p. 141.
[32] See Appendix F, notes to Table F-7.

in education and social projects from total current and capital expenditures incurred by the government on education and social services. Government expenditures on education and social services in 1952–57 are given at 2.28, 3.36, 3.46, 3.19, 4.60, and 4.64 billion yuan, and basic construction in the same sector at 0.34, 0.77, 0.83, 0.70, 1.11, and 1.05 billion yuan.[33] Expenditures on communal services thus amount to 1.94, 2.59, 2.63, 2.49, 3.49, and 3.59 billion current yuan. The cost-of-living index for 1952–57, with 1952 as 100, is then used to obtain the following estimates in 1952 prices: 1.94, 2.45, 2.46, 2.32, 3.26, and 3.29 billion yuan.[34] The numbers of employees in communal services in 1952–57 are estimated in Table 62. Income payments to these employees are then calculated at 1.12, 1.22, 1.32, 1.41, 1.79, and 1.90 billion 1952 yuan for 1952–57 by multiplying the number of employees by the average wage for all workers and employees.[35] Purchases of goods for communal services are derived as a residual.

Government consumption expenditure on services in 1952 prices is derived by deducting income payments to those in communal services from total income originating in government services given in our product estimate.[36] Government consumption of goods is indirectly derived from Communist data on total and personal material consumption as follows: From the Communist estimate of net domestic expenditure given in Table 72, we deduct accumulation to arrive at total material consumption (which includes personal material consumption, material consumption expenditure for communal services, and government material consumption). Accumulation is derived by deflating the estimate in current prices by the price index for basic construction given in Table 74. Total material consumption in 1952–57 amounts to 51.42, 56.00, 57.26, 61.98, 65.15, and 70.34 billion 1952 yuan. Personal material consumption is derived on the basis of the total urban and rural population, given in Chapter IV, and per capita material consumption. Per capita personal material consumption in the urban and rural areas in 1952–56 in constant 1952 prices is 167.7, 176.6, 177.9, 179.9, and 199.8 yuan for the urban population, and 72.8, 74.7, 76.8, 82.5, and 84.2 yuan

[33] *Great Ten Years,* pp. 21, 49.

[34] SSB, "Changes in the Market Prices in 1957 and Their Effects on People's Living Conditions," *TCYC,* No. 4, April 1958, p. 25; *FFYP Communique,* p. 51.

[35] See Appendix H under Government.

[36] For income payments to people in communal services, see this chapter; for total income originating in government services, see Chapter IV.

for the rural population.[37] Rough estimates for 1957 are derived at 200 yuan for the urban and 89 yuan for the rural population by extrapolating from the 1952–56 figures on the basis of a straight line trend. Multiplying these figures by the corresponding figures of urban and rural population and adding, we obtain estimates of personal material consumption for 1952–57 at 47.87, 51.11, 53.78, 58.15, 62.02, and 66.78 billion 1952 yuan. Government material consumption can now be derived as a residual. To these Communist estimates we add the services rendered by passenger transportation and finance in connection with government consumption. The results are presented in Table 78. An adjusted estimate of government consumption can be obtained similarly by using the adjusted estimate of passenger transportation and finance.[38] It is assumed that one-fourth of the total net value added by passenger transportation and finance is rendered to the government. The results are 5.34, 6.46, 5.50, 6.13, 5.28, and 5.99 billion 1952 yuan for 1952–57.

The estimates of communal services and government consumption for 1952–57 in 1933 prices are derived by separately deflating the estimates for the purchases of goods in 1952 prices by the price index of manufactured consumers' goods, given at 335 per cent in 1952 with 1933 as 100, and the estimates for the purchases of services by the price index for net value added by government services, given at 163 per cent in 1952 with 1933 as 100.[39]

PERSONAL CONSUMPTION

Personal consumption expenditures comprise the market or imputed value of goods and services (excluding housewives' services) purchased or consumed by the ultimate consumers. For convenience we have grouped these expenditures into five categories: food, clothing, fuel and light, housing, and miscellaneous. The commodity flow method is used to derive the estimates of personal consumption of food and clothing, which together made up over 70 per cent of total personal consumption expenditure for all the years. For the other items in the consumers' budget, cruder methods must be used. The summary results of our estimate were presented in Chapter II.[40]

[37] SSB, "A Preliminary Analysis of the Production and Distribution of China's National Income," *TCYC*, No. 1, January 1958, p. 13.

[38] See Table 68 and Appendix H, Table H-9.

[39] For computation of the price index of manufactured consumers' goods, see Appendix F, Table F-15; for computation of the price index for net value added by government services, see Appendix H under Government.

[40] See Table 10.

Food Consumption

In broad outline, the commodity flow method involves (a) ascertaining total domestic output at producers' prices through various stages of manufacturing; (b) allowing for net imports of food; and (c) adding the transportation and distribution margin to find the final cost to consumers. Although in principle changes in inventory holdings form part of the process of commodity flow, they are unlikely to be important in our case and have not been allowed for in our calculation.

Information on changes in the inventory of food is extremely scarce. While some data on changes in the stock of food held by the state-owned trading stores are available, they are too fragmentary to be of any use for calculating changes in total inventory of food. For instance, the stock of food held by state commercial enterprises is reported to have increased in 1957 over 1956 by 0.85 billion yuan at current prices.[41] The year 1957 was by no means a better than average crop year. Total output of food crops was at about the same level as in 1956. Total consumption in 1957 increased slightly over 1956. In all likelihood, the increase in government holdings probably meant a reduction in the holdings of food by the nonstate sector, particularly the agricultural cooperatives. Hence, for the economy as a whole, inventory changes might well have been negligibly small.

The individual steps in deriving personal consumption of goods in 1933 and 1952–57 are summarized in Table 79. The figures presented in the table are based on our estimates of agricultural production. Following the same procedure to be described but using Communist data, including those on food crops and manufactured consumers' goods, we obtain adjusted estimates of personal consumption of food at 30.38, 30.82, 33.71, 35.62, 37.71, and 41.18 billion 1952 yuan for 1952–57.

DOMESTIC FOOD PRODUCTION AT PRODUCERS' PRICES

This item is obtained first by adding the gross value of output, at prices received by farmers, of all agricultural products used directly for food or as raw materials for further processing of food products. Gross value of these products in 1933 and 1952–57 is estimated in

[41] SSB, "General Conditions of Commodity Circulation in the Domestic Market in 1957," *TCYC*, No. 4, April 1958, p. 24.

Table 79

FOOD CONSUMPTION, 1933 AND 1952–57
(billions of yuan)

	In 1933 prices							In 1952 prices						
	1933	1952	1953	1954	1955	1956	1957	1933	1952	1953	1954	1955	1956	1957
1. Domestic production at producers' prices	16.54	16.48	17.04	17.85	18.03	18.46	18.93	29.56	30.75	31.70	33.39	33.84	34.39	35.62
a. Agricultural products	15.71	15.42	15.95	16.60	16.74	17.17	17.56	27.56	28.06	29.08	30.29	30.26	31.08	31.73
Crops	11.20	11.02	11.24	11.61	11.87	12.21	12.40	18.63	18.71	19.04	19.71	20.16	20.77	21.01
Tea	0.13	0.04	0.04	0.05	0.06	0.06	0.06	0.35	0.11	0.12	0.13	0.15	0.17	0.15
Vegetables and fruits	1.44	1.00	1.07	1.09	1.07	1.14	1.15	2.52	2.22	2.43	2.46	2.36	2.58	2.64
Livestock, poultry, and fishery products	2.04	2.44	2.65	2.90	2.78	2.78	2.97	4.42	5.33	5.76	6.22	5.80	5.72	6.08
Miscellaneous	0.90	0.91	0.93	0.96	0.97	0.98	0.99	1.64	1.70	1.73	1.77	1.78	1.84	1.84
b. Value added by manufacturing	0.77	0.97	1.03	1.16	1.16	1.21	1.22	1.48	1.90	2.06	2.33	2.39	2.53	2.59
c. Salt	0.06	0.09	0.06	0.09	0.13	0.09	0.15	0.52	0.78	0.56	0.77	1.19	0.78	1.30
2. Import balance	0.03	−0.73	−0.96	−0.70	−0.88	−0.94	−0.83	0.05	−1.36	−1.79	−1.31	−1.64	−1.76	−1.56
3. Food supply for domestic consumption	16.56	15.75	16.08	17.15	17.16	17.52	18.10	29.60	29.38	29.91	32.08	32.22	32.62	34.07
4. Food consumption at producers' prices	11.53	11.54	11.65	11.89	12.12	12.37	12.62	20.64	21.52	21.74	22.17	22.62	23.07	23.53
5. Food supplied through the market at producers' prices	5.04	4.21	4.43	5.26	5.03	5.15	5.49	8.97	7.86	8.18	9.91	9.60	9.56	10.54
6. Transportation and distribution margin	1.56	1.60	1.64	1.95	1.81	1.96	2.08	3.59	3.70	3.68	4.36	4.13	4.01	4.32
7. Food consumption at prices to consumers	18.13	17.36	17.72	19.10	18.97	19.48	20.19	33.19	33.08	33.59	36.44	36.35	36.64	38.39

NOTES: *Line 3.* Line 1 plus line 2.
Line 5. Line 3 minus line 4.
Line 7. Sum of lines 4 through 6.
SOURCES: Compiled from data given in Tables 80 through 87.

Appendix E. A tabulation of these figures and the estimated amount used for human consumption in 1933 and 1952 prices are given in Tables 80 and 81. Gross values of agricultural products in 1952–57, in billions of 1952 yuan, are calculated from Communist data as follows:

	1952	1953	1954	1955	1956	1957
Food crops	14.84	15.06	15.58	17.10	18.52	19.09
Oil bearing crops	0.91	0.86	0.96	1.07	1.10	0.94
Other crops	0.86	0.89	0.86	0.88	0.98	0.98
Tea	0.11	0.12	0.13	0.15	0.17	0.15
Vegetables and fruits	2.10	2.30	2.33	2.29	2.57	2.64
Livestock, poultry, and fishery products	5.33	5.76	6.22	5.80	5.72	7.08
Miscellaneous	1.57	1.89	1.63	1.72	1.83	1.98
Total	25.71	26.57	27.70	29.01	30.88	32.87

To the total value of agricultural food products we now add the gross value of salt and manufactured food products (minus raw materials) to arrive at the value of domestic food supply at producers' prices. The estimates for processed food products are presented in Table 82. The amount of salt consumed in 1933 has been estimated at 90 per cent of the total salt output in that year.[42] The same percentage is used to derive the amount of salt in the postwar years.[43]

On the basis of Communist data on food crops output, the adjusted estimate of the gross value of manufactured food products and salt are calculated at 2.54, 2.47, 2.93, 3.50, 3.30, and 3.91 billion yuan in 1952 prices for 1952–57. We add these figures to the amount of agricultural food products to obtain the following adjusted estimates of domestic production of food in 1952 prices for 1952–57: 28.25, 29.04, 30.63, 32.51, 34.18, and 36.77 billion yuan.

The total output of manufacturing includes an unidentified portion. Since our computation of the gross value of processed food products (minus raw materials) is based on the identified products, it is possible that our figures are slightly low because some food products in the unidentified section have been excluded. From the

[42] Pei Yu-lin, "National Income, Consumption and Investment of China," *Shih-yeh jin-yung* (Journal of Finance and Industry), Vol. I, No. 1, May 1948, p. 71.

[43] For the output of salt in 1933 and 1952–57, see Appendix H, Tables H-1, H-2.

Table 80

AGRICULTURAL FOOD PRODUCTS AT PRODUCERS' PRICES, 1933

Product	Gross value of output		Amount used for food	Value of food products	
	(billion 1933 yuan) (1)	(billion 1952 yuan) (2)	(per cent) (3)	(billion 1933 yuan) (4)	(billion 1952 yuan) (5)
Food crops	12.67	20.98		9.92	16.24
Paddy rice	5.60	8.48	90	5.04	7.63
Wheat	2.46	4.27	84	2.07	3.59
Potatoes	0.63	1.22	66	0.42	0.81
Miscellaneous	3.98	7.01	60	2.39	4.21
Oil bearing crops	0.83	1.58		0.74	1.41
Peanuts	0.35	0.70	88	0.31	0.62
Rapeseed	0.25	0.46	97	0.24	0.45
Sesame	0.15	0.28	83	0.13	0.23
Cottonseed	0.08	0.14	84	0.06	0.12
Other crops	0.97	1.74		0.54	0.98
Soybeans	0.92	1.65	55	0.51	0.91
Sugar cane	0.05	0.08	73	0.03	0.06
Sugar beets	(*)	0.01	95	(*)	0.01
Tea	0.13	0.35	100	0.13	0.35
Vegetables and fruits	1.48	2.59		1.44	2.52
Vegetables	0.75	1.31	95	0.71	1.24
Fruits	0.73	1.28	100	0.73	1.28
Livestock, poultry, and fishery products	2.09	4.53		2.04	4.42
Hogs	0.98	2.58	98	0.96	2.53
Cattle	0.21	0.32	90	0.19	0.28
Sheep	0.10	0.23	90	0.09	0.21
Poultry	0.14	0.38	100	0.14	0.38
Eggs	0.23	0.45	100	0.23	0.45
Fishery products	0.43	0.56	100	0.43	0.56
Miscellaneous agricultural products	1.16	2.10	78	0.90	1.64
Total	19.33	33.87	—	15.71	27.56

NOTES: — Not applicable.

(*) Less than 5 million yuan.

Columns (1) and (2). See Appendix E.

Column (3). Paddy rice output used for food is assumed to be 90 per cent on the following basis: The National Agricultural Research Bureau estimate of 81 per cent appears to be too low (quoted in Pei Yu-lin, "National Income, Consumption and Investment of China," *Shi-yeh jin-yung* [Journal of Finance and Industry], Vol. 1, No. 1, May 1948, p. 70). Buck (in *Land Utilization*, Vol. I, p. 236) shows that only 4 per cent was used for seeds, and that the amount used for industrial purposes and animal feed was negligible. The rest, roughly 96 per cent, was probably used mainly for human consumption. T. H. Shen (*Agricultural Resources*, p. 201) made an estimate of 93 per cent. Our own observations tend to confirm a high percentage of human consumption and we arbitrarily used the round figure of 90 per cent. For the percentage of wheat, see the discussion of wheat

(Continued)

Table 80 (continued)

flour in Appendix G. The percentage of soybean output used for food is given by the National Agricultural Research Bureau (Pei Yu-lin, *op. cit.*, p. 70). The percentage of potatoes used for food is the average of the figures for Irish potatoes and sweet potatoes weighted by the output of these two crops given in Appendix A. The percentage of Irish potatoes is given and that of sweet potatoes is the average of two estimates (*ibid.*; and W. Y. Swen, "A Study of the Consumption of Staple Food Products in China," *Crop Reports*, Vol. 2, No. 8, August 1, 1934). The percentage of miscellaneous food crops used for human consumption is the weighted average of the percentage for 12 miscellaneous crops: millet, kaoliang, corn, glutinous rice, barley, buckwheat, oats, broad beans, mung beans, peas, black beans, and proso millet. The weights are the respective gross values of output given in Appendix E. The percentages for all these miscellaneous food crops except proso millet are given in Pei Yu-lin, *op. cit.* The percentages for proso millet, peanuts, and cottonseed are derived from data given in *Food Balance Sheets*, pp. 237–238. For the percentage of rapeseed used for food, see Appendix G, Table G-4. The percentages of sugar cane and sugar beet are derived from data given in Pei Yu-lin, *op. cit.* For vegetables, we arbitrarily allow 5 per cent for seed and other minor nonfood uses. We also allow 2 per cent of the gross value of hogs for the value of bristles, and 10 per cent of the gross value of cattle and sheep for miscellaneous nonfood uses such as bones and hides. Except for miscellaneous agricultural products (tea, fruits, poultry, eggs, and fishery products), we assume that the remaining minor items are used entirely for food. The percentage of miscellaneous agricultural products is assumed to be the same as for food crops.

Columns (4) and (5). Column (3) times columns (1) and (2).

list of products in Table 82, it can be seen that the most important processed food items in the Chinese diet have already been covered.[44] The assumption that all the processed food products have been included in the identified sector would not, in all likelihood, result in any serious error in our estimate.

NET IMPORT AND EXPORT OF FOOD

To derive estimates of total food supply available for domestic consumption, we now add the net import of food to, and deduct the net export of food from, total domestic food production. Table 83 presents the import and export figures for 1933, and Table 84 for 1952–57. Net import of food in 1933 totalled 0.47 billion yuan and net export, 0.44 billion yuan, and the import balance was 0.03 billion yuan. For 1952–57, only rough estimates can be made for the export of food grain, soybeans, meat products, and processed food products, and for the import of sugar. Information on other food items is available only for trade with countries outside the Soviet bloc. In the absence of a better alternative, rough approximations of the total exports and imports of these miscellaneous food products are made by multiplying the figures for exports to nonbloc countries by the ratio of total exports to nonbloc exports. Total im-

[44] For the items that made up the Chinese diet, see Buck, *Land Utilization*, Vol. III, pp. 86–121.

Table 81

AGRICULTURAL FOOD PRODUCTS AT PRODUCERS' PRICES, 1952–57
(billions of yuan)

	In 1933 prices						In 1952 prices					
	1952	1953	1954	1955	1956	1957	1952	1953	1954	1955	1956	1957
Food crops	10.07	10.30	10.64	10.83	11.11	11.37	16.94	17.30	17.89	18.21	18.69	19.09
Oil bearing crops												
Peanuts	0.21	0.19	0.25	0.27	0.30	0.24	0.43	0.39	0.51	0.54	0.62	0.48
Rapeseed	0.11	0.10	0.10	0.11	0.11	0.10	0.20	0.19	0.19	0.21	0.20	0.19
Sesame	0.07	0.08	0.08	0.08	0.06	0.04	0.13	0.14	0.14	0.14	0.11	0.07
Cottonseed	0.09	0.08	0.07	0.10	0.10	0.11	0.16	0.14	0.13	0.18	0.18	0.18
Other crops												
Soybeans	0.41	0.43	0.39	0.39	0.44	0.43	0.73	0.76	0.70	0.70	0.79	0.77
Sugar cane	0.06	0.06	0.08	0.07	0.08	0.09	0.10	0.10	0.13	0.12	0.13	0.15
Sugar beets	0.01	0.01	0.01	0.02	0.02	0.02	0.02	0.02	0.04	0.06	0.06	0.06
Tea	0.04	0.04	0.05	0.06	0.06	0.06	0.11	0.12	0.13	0.15	0.17	0.15
Vegetables and fruits												
Vegetables	0.70	0.71	0.73	0.75	0.76	0.76	1.24	1.24	1.27	1.34	1.34	1.34
Fruits	0.30	0.36	0.36	0.31	0.38	0.40	0.98	1.19	1.19	1.02	1.24	1.30
Livestock, poultry, and fishery products												
Hogs	1.22	1.31	1.39	1.20	1.15	1.18	3.24	3.47	3.67	3.17	3.03	3.11
Cattle	0.27	0.28	0.30	0.31	0.32	0.30	0.40	0.42	0.45	0.47	0.47	0.45
Sheep	0.08	0.09	0.10	0.11	0.12	0.12	0.18	0.21	0.23	0.24	0.26	0.28
Poultry	0.15	0.16	0.17	0.17	0.16	0.18	0.40	0.43	0.46	0.44	0.44	0.48
Eggs	0.24	0.25	0.27	0.26	0.26	0.28	0.48	0.51	0.54	0.52	0.51	0.57
Fishery products	0.49	0.56	0.67	0.74	0.77	0.91	0.63	0.72	0.87	0.96	1.00	1.19
Miscellaneous agricultural products	0.91	0.93	0.96	0.97	0.98	0.99	1.70	1.73	1.77	1.78	1.84	1.84
Total	15.42	15.95	16.60	16.74	17.17	17.56	28.06	29.08	30.29	30.26	31.08	31.73

NOTES: These figures are derived by applying the percentages of output used for human consumption to the gross value of output in 1933 and 1952 prices given in Appendix E. Except for food crops and miscellaneous agricultural products used for foods, the percentages of all other products are assumed to be the same as those in 1933 given in Table 80. The percentages for food crops are Communist estimates. (SSB, "The Basic Situation of Planned Purchase and Planned Supply of Food Grains in China," *TCKT*, No. 19, October 1957, p. 28.) The same percentages are applied to miscellaneous agricultural products.

Table 82

GROSS VALUE OF PROCESSED FOOD PRODUCTS (MINUS RAW MATERIALS), 1933 AND 1952–57
(millions of yuan)

	1933[a]	1952	1953	1954	1955	1956	1957
In constant 1933 prices[b]							
Milled rice							
Factory	17	22	23	26	26	28	29
Handicrafts	168	271	285	282	288	288	298
Wheat flour							
Factory	34	58	65	72	87	83	81
Handicrafts	149	228	226	301	252	268	251
Sugar							
Factory	1	12	14	16	19	24	26
Handicrafts	14	7	11	12	10	9	10
Edible vegetable oils	101	72	74	78	85	78	80
Tea	47	16	16	17	21	23	21
Soybean sauce	57	61	65	64	61	65	68
Wine and liquor	39	40	54	68	82	96	110
Others	142	183	198	224	230	244	249
Total	769	970	1,031	1,160	1,161	1,206	1,223
In constant 1952 prices[c]							
Milled rice							
Factory	24	31	33	36	37	39	41
Handicrafts	253	408	429	425	433	433	449
Wheat flour							
Factory	93	158	179	196	239	227	222
Handicrafts	255	391	387	515	432	459	430
Sugar							
Factory	13	153	184	214	252	319	344
Handicrafts	46	22	37	38	33	31	33
Edible vegetable oils	202	144	148	156	170	157	161
Tea	127	43	43	47	57	63	58
Soybean sauce	101	109	116	114	109	116	121
Wine and liquor	90	92	124	157	189	221	253
Others	273	352	381	431	443	469	478
Total	1,477	1,903	2,061	2,329	2,394	2,534	2,591

NOTES: [a] For 1933, data on gross value of output are found in Appendix F, Table F-1, and Appendix G. Data on raw materials are found in Appendix F, Table F-4, and Appendix G. Figures in 1933 prices are derived by subtracting the amount for raw materials from the gross value of output. Figures in 1952 prices are derived from data in Appendixes F and G. The value of "Others" in 1952 prices is derived by multiplying the 1933 value by a price index equal to the ratio of (1) the value of milled rice, wheat, flour, sugar, edible vegetable oils, tea, soybean sauce, and wine and liquor in 1952 prices to (2) the value of the same products in 1933 prices.

[b] For 1952–57, figures in constant 1933 yuan are derived by deflating those in 1952 yuan by price indexes calculated from the 1933 data on the value of food products in both 1933 and 1952 prices.

[c] For 1952–57, the figures in 1952 prices are derived from data on gross value of output and raw materials given in Appendixes F and G. Our estimates are based on the corrected figures of food crop production. If the Communist data on food crop production are used, estimates of processed food products (minus raw materials) for 1952–57 are 1.76, 1.90, 2.16, 2.32, 2.52, and 2.60 billion 1952 yuan.

Table 83

IMPORTS AND EXPORTS OF FOOD PRODUCTS, 1933
(millions of yuan)

Imports	
China proper	375.5
Cereals, fruits, seeds, spices, vegetables	291.9
Sugar	41.9
Processed fish and fish products	23.1
Animal products, canned goods, groceries	14.9
Miscellaneous, including beverages	3.8
Manchuria	93.3
Wheat flour	58.7
Sugar	16.0
Rice and paddy rice	4.1
Tea	3.3
Miscellaneous	11.2
Total	468.8
Exports	
China proper	185.7
Animals and edible animal and fishery products	57.4
Tea	34.2
Seeds	32.0
Cereals and cereal products	18.0
Vegetables	9.0
Fresh, dried, and preserved fruits	8.7
Miscellaneous vegetable products	7.0
Edible vegetable oils	6.3
Spices	4.8
Beans and peas	4.8
Processed fish and fish products	2.7
Sundries	0.8
Manchuria	256.2
Soybeans	169.1
Bean oil	18.5
Millet	14.7
Other beans	9.2
Ground nuts	8.8
Kaoliang	7.2
Cereals	6.4
Sesame seed	4.7
Miscellaneous	17.6
Total	441.9
Net imports	26.9

SOURCES: *The Trade of China, 1933*, Vol. II, pp. 81–93, 125–151; Japan-Manchoukuo Yearbook Company, *Japan-Manchoukuo Yearbook, 1936*, Tokyo, 1936, pp. 581–857.

ports are derived in a similar way. Admittedly this procedure is rather crude, but in view of the predominance of trade with the Soviet-bloc countries, even a very rough estimate is perhaps better than complete omission of the items for these countries.

Table 84

IMPORTS AND EXPORTS OF FOOD PRODUCTS, 1952–57
(billions of 1952 yuan)

	1952	1953	1954	1955	1956	1957
Exports						
Food grains	2.21	2.52	2.24	2.80	3.70	2.18
Soybeans	1.20	1.33	1.90	2.47	2.66	1.90
Meat products	3.17	3.40	3.62	3.17	2.94	2.26
Processed food products	2.43	3.10	2.91	3.57	4.05	3.18
Miscellaneous	5.88	9.43	5.86	8.35	6.87	8.12
Total	14.89	19.78	16.53	20.36	20.22	17.64
Imports						
Sugar	0.77	0.77	0.98	0.92	1.32	0.79
Miscellaneous	0.52	1.13	2.49	3.06	1.26	1.29
Total	1.29	1.90	3.47	3.98	2.58	2.08
Net exports	13.60	17.88	13.06	16.38	17.64	15.56

NOTES: *Food grains.* Exports are derived by multiplying the amount of food grains exported by the export price. The quantities exported in 1953–57 are given at 0.90, 0.80, 1.00, 1.32, and 0.78 million tons, in Yeh Chi-chuang, "Report before the Fourth Session of the People's Congress," *HHPYK*, No. 16, August 1957, p. 93. (The figure for 1957 is a planned figure.) The figure for 1952 is derived at 0.79 million tons on the assumption that the quantity increased from 1952–53 in proportion to food grain production from 1951–52 given in *TCKT*, No. 14, July 1957, p. 10. The export price is given at 560 rubles per ton in 1957 in Yeh Chi-chuang, *op. cit.* This figure is converted to 280 yuan per ton at the official rate of exchange of 0.5 per ruble.

Soybeans. The exports of soybeans in 1953–57 are given at 0.70, 1.00, 1.30, 1.40, and 1.00 million tons in N. Ivanov *et al.*, *Razvitie ekonomiki stran narodnoi demokratii*, Moscow, 1958, p. 145. The figure for 1952 is derived by a procedure similar to that for food grain. The export price of soybeans is given at 380 rubles per ton (1.90 yuan per ton) in Yeh Chi-chuang, *op. cit.*

Meat products. Exports of meat products are estimated by multiplying the quantity of meat exported by its export price. The quantities of meat exported in 1955–56 are given in N. Ivanov, *op. cit.*, and in 1957 in *TKP*, October 29, 1957, p. 1. The figures for 1952–54 are derived on the assumption that the percentage of the total number of hogs exported in these years is the same as in 1955. For data on the total number of hogs in 1952–55, see *HHPYK*, No. 16, August 1956, p. 43. The export price of meat is the average of the prices given in Li Pei-fang, "Actively Strengthen the Organization of Sources of Supply for Exports," *CHCC*, No. 2, February 1958, p. 30.

Processed food products. The estimates for 1952–55 are derived from an index of exports of processed food products and total receipts from these exports in the same period, given in Chao Yi-wen, *Hsin-chung-kuo ti kung-yeh* (New China's Industry), T'ung-chi chu-pan-she, Peiping, 1957, p. 58. The figures for 1956–57 are derived on the assumption that the percentage of total exports attributable to processed food product exports in these years is the same as in 1955. For total exports in 1955–57, see United Nations, *Economic Survey of Asia and the Far East, 1957*, Bangkok, 1958, p. 103.

Sugar. The amounts of sugar imported in 1953–56 and 1957 are taken or derived from information given in N. Ivanov, *op. cit.*, p. 143; and Sung Tzu-yung, "Develop the Production of Sugar To Ensure Market Supply," *TKP*, Peiping, January 1, 1958, p. 3. The figure for 1952 is assumed to be the same as for 1953.

Miscellaneous imports and exports of food. Included in the miscellaneous group are such products as oil seeds (other than soybeans), fruits and vegetables, and fish and fish prod-

(Continued)

Table 84 (continued)

ucts. Total miscellaneous exports are derived by adding exports to Soviet-bloc countries and to the rest of the world. The former figures are given at 97.8, 120.1, 56.0, 79.8, 87.5, and 88.6 million U.S. dollars for 1952–57, given in U.S. Department of State reports to the Congress, *Soviet Bloc Economic Activities in the Free World*, 1955, p. 100; *The Strategic Trade Control System, 1948–1956*, 1957, p. 114; *The 1958 Revision of East-West Trade Controls*, 1959, p. 46; and *Summary of East-West Trade in 1958*, 1960, p. 46. No comparable information for the Soviet-bloc countries is available. We assume that the proportion of total trade with Soviet-bloc countries devoted to miscellaneous food exports is the same as that for the nonbloc countries. Miscellaneous food exports and imports can be roughly estimated on the basis of miscellaneous exports to nonbloc countries and the percentages of Mainland China's trade with the Soviet-bloc and nonbloc countries given in "Fraternal Economic Cooperation," *People's Daily*, October 2, 1956 and November 28, 1957, and *HHPYK*, No. 16, August 1957, p. 93. For miscellaneous food imports from nonbloc countries, see U.S. Department of State, *Soviet Bloc Economic Activities in the Free World*, 1955, p. 99; *The Strategic Trade Control System, 1948–1956*, 1957, p. 112; *Survey of East-West Trade in 1955*, 1956, p. 97; *The 1958 Revision of East-West Trade Controls*, 1959, p. 44; and *Summary of East-West Trade in 1958*, 1960, p. 44.

There is not enough information on prices of food imports and exports in 1933 and 1952 to compute a price index for the purpose of expressing the estimates of the import balance in constant 1933 and 1952 prices. We arbitrarily assume that the export and import prices for food products vary from 1933 to 1952 in proportion to the implicit deflator for domestic food production. On this assumption, the import balance for 1933 in 1952 prices is derived at 0.05 billion yuan, and that for 1952–57 in 1933 prices, 0.73, 0.96, 0.70, 0.88, 0.94, and 0.83 billion yuan. The price index numbers used here are 179 and 187 per cent for 1952 with 1933 as 100, derived from data in Table 79.

FOOD CONSUMPTION AT PRODUCERS' PRICES

Many food products are consumed in kind or sold directly by the producers to the consumers. This consumption is estimated separately for 1933 and 1952–57. Food consumption at producers' prices in 1933 is derived by adding (a) farm consumption in kind, (b) food products sold by farmers directly to consumers, and (c) processed food products sold by producers directly to consumers. Farm consumption of agricultural products in kind is roughly estimated on the basis of gross value of agricultural output and the percentage retained on farms and used for food. The figures are based on Buck's field survey. The details are shown in Table 85. By a similar procedure, the amount of food sold to consumers at producers' prices is derived at 0.67 billion yuan, as shown in Table 86.

For processed food products, there is no information on the

Table 85

CONSUMPTION OF AGRICULTURAL FOOD PRODUCTS IN KIND, 1933
(billions of 1933 yuan)

Product	Gross value of output (1)	Percentage consumed on farm (2)	Consumption in kind (3)
Food crops	12.67		6.86
Paddy rice	5.60	56	3.14
Wheat	2.46	54	1.33
Potatoes	0.63	63	0.40
Miscellaneous food crops	3.98	50	1.99
Oil bearing crops	0.83		0.22
Peanuts	0.35	28	0.10
Rapeseed	0.25	36	0.09
Sesame	0.15	23	0.03
Cottonseed	0.08	(*)	(**)
Other crops	0.97		0.43
Soybeans	0.92	47	0.43
Sugar cane	0.05	8	(**)
Sugar beets	(**)	(*)	(**)
Tea	0.13	(*)	(**)
Vegetables and fruits	1.48		0.57
Vegetables	0.75	66	0.50
Fruits	0.73	10	0.07
Miscellaneous agricultural products	2.09	30	0.63
Animal products	1.16	—	0.34
Total	19.33	—	9.05

NOTES: (*) Less than 1 per cent.
(**) Less than 0.01 billion yuan.
— Not available or not applicable.

Column (1). See Appendix E.

Column (2). Except for miscellaneous food crops, fruits, and miscellaneous agricultural products, the percentages are given in Buck, *Land Utilization*, Vol. I, Table 23, p. 236. For miscellaneous food crops, the figures given by Buck range from 36 to 77 per cent for the individual crops. We assume a figure of 50 per cent. Buck gives 23 per cent for peaches and 5 per cent for pears. The average for fruits is probably closer to the lower figure and we assume it to be 10 per cent. For miscellaneous agricultural products, the percentage is assumed to be 30 per cent.

Column (3). Except for animal products, the figures are derived by multiplying those in column (1) by the corresponding figures in column (2). Per capita meat consumption in rural areas is supposedly about 10 catties a year. (Hsu Kang, "Have the Living Conditions of the Workers and Peasants Improved Since Liberation?" *TKP*, Peiping, August 9, 1957, p. 2.) This figure is probably an overestimate; however, there is no satisfactory way of correcting the bias. We have not enough information to be able to estimate the consumption of other animal products such as eggs or fishery products. The omission of these minor items would compensate to some extent for the overestimate in the Communist figure. On the assumption that per capita consumption was the same in 1933 as in 1952, total consumption of animal products in 1933 can be roughly calculated at 3.65 billion catties by multiplying the per capita consumption by the total agricultural population of 365 million. According to Buck, 37 per cent of food calories from animal products consumed by the farmers were supplied by the farm (Buck, *Land Utilization*, Vol. I, Table 1, p. 401). Farm consumption of animal products in kind is therefore computed at 1.35 billion catties. Since pork is the most important animal product, the quantity of farm consumption is multiplied by the price of pork, estimated at 0.25 yuan per catty in 1933 on the basis of data given in Nankai Economic Research Institute, *Nankai chih-shu tzu-liao chun-pien* (Source Materials on Nankai Indices), Peiping, T'ung-chi chu-pan-she, 1958, p. 277.

Table 86

FOOD SOLD AT PRODUCERS' PRICES, 1933

Product	Output (billions of yuan)	Amount sold by farms directly to consumers (per cent)	Amount sold to consumers (billions of yuan)
Paddy rice	5.60	3.6	0.20
Wheat	2.46	7.0	0.17
Potatoes	0.63	5.5	0.03
Miscellaneous food crops	3.98	2.4	0.09
Other agricultural products, excluding animal products	4.57	3.9	0.18
Total	17.24	—	0.67

NOTES: — Not applicable.

For data on output, see Appendix E. Rice, wheat, and potatoes sold by farmers are given at 15, 29, and 23 per cent in Buck, *Land Utilization*, Vol. I, Table 23, p. 236. Miscellaneous food crops are assumed to be 10 per cent, the same percentage as millet (*ibid.*). Of the total farm produce farmers put on the market, 24 per cent was purchased directly by consumers. The percentage of total output sold by farmers directly to consumers is therefore equal to 24 per cent of the percentage of total output sold. The percentage for "other agricultural products" is assumed to be the same as for food crops as a whole.

amount consumed by producers or sold directly to consumers. However, it is believed that these direct sales were small. We arbitrarily assume that one-fifth of the total gross value of processed food products was sold directly to consumers. Total gross value is estimated at 9.05 billion 1933 yuan from data in Appendixes F and G; therefore direct sales amount to 1.81 billion yuan. The three categories of food consumption at producers' prices amount to 11.53 billion yuan, about 70 per cent of total domestic food production.

For 1952, we assume that food consumption at producers' prices is the same percentage of total domestic food production as in 1933, and that food consumption at producers' prices increased from 1952–57 in proportion to rural population over the same period. The assumption seems reasonable, for rough calculations for several postwar years indicate that the proportion of food crop output consumed in kind by farmers, the most important item for food consumption at producers' prices, comes close to the prewar figure. For 1955–57 the proportions can be roughly calculated at 52, 54, and 55 per cent, which agree closely with our prewar figure of 54 per cent. In deriving the postwar figures, it is assumed that farm consumption in kind is 75 per cent of total national consumption of food crops, the same as the percentage of total population ascribed to agricultural population.[45] Estimates of total consumption of unprocessed grain (with potatoes at grain-equivalent weight) in 1955–57 are given as 2,576, 2,630, and 2,695 million piculs in Table 5. Farm consumption in kind therefore amounts to 1,936, 1,972, and 2,021 million piculs for 1955–57. The total food crop output for the same period was given at 3,728, 3,686, and 3,700 million piculs in Table 32, and the percentage of total food crop output consumed in kind by farmers can be calculated. The 1933 output of food crops and consumption in kind (12.67 and 6.86 billion yuan) are given in Table 85.

On these assumptions, food consumption at producers' prices is derived as 21.52, 21.74, 22.17, 22.62, 23.07, and 23.53 billion 1952 yuan for 1952–57. Estimates for 1933 in constant 1952 prices and for 1952–57 in constant 1933 prices are derived by the same method. Following the same procedure but using the adjusted estimate of domestic food production given earlier in this chapter, we can derive adjusted figures of food consumption at producers' prices as 19.78, 19.97, 20.37, 20.78, 21.20, and 21.62 billion 1952 yuan for 1952–57.

FOOD CONSUMPTION AT RETAIL PRICES

The residual obtained by deducting consumption at producers' prices from the total supply represents food sold to consumers through various distribution channels. We add a transportation and distribution margin to derive the estimate of food supplied through the market and sold at consumers' prices. In principle, this margin should be computed on the basis of transportation costs, indirect taxes, and distribution markups relating specifically to the marketing of food, but such data are not available. A margin for all commodities can be estimated, however, and we can apply it to food on the assumption that the distribution margin per monetary unit of food is the same as for commodities as a whole. Admittedly, such an estimate is at best a rough approximation. However, it may be a reasonably good one, for the food that went through distribution channels constituted a large part of the total volume of all goods distributed through the market. For example, in 1933 food products accounted for almost 40 per cent of the total commodities marketed.[46] On the other hand, because only about one-third of total

[45] See Chapter IV.
[46] For data used in computing this figure, see Tables 79, 80.

food supply went through distribution channels (over two-thirds of total food supply was sold to consumers at producers' prices), the distribution margin, only a fraction of the marketed food supply, was even smaller in relation to the total value of food consumption.[47] Any error in the estimated margin would have only a minor effect on the total value of food consumption.

The transportation and distribution margin for all commodities (except food and clothing at producers' prices) is defined as the share that transportation and distribution costs represent in total gross value. It is equal to the sum of gross revenue from commodity transportation and value added by trade, divided by the algebraic sum of (a) the gross value of output in agriculture and mining, (b) the gross value of output in manufacturing after costs of raw materials and fuels are deducted, and (c) the net balance of trade, minus (d) the value of food and clothing consumed at producers' prices. Most of these items have been or can be computed from our product estimate. The results are shown in Table 87. When these distribution margins are applied to the corresponding figures of food supplied through marketing channels in 1933 and 1952–57, we obtain estimates of transportation and distribution costs. Total food consumption is then derived by adding food consumed at producers' prices to food supplied to consumers at retail prices.

If the Communist data on food crop production are used, the distribution and transportation margin can be calculated for 1952–57 at 49, 49, 49, 47, 47, and 44 per cent in 1952 prices. On the basis of these figures and the adjusted estimates of total food supply and food consumption at producers' prices given earlier in this chapter, food supply through the marketing channels can be calculated at 7.12, 7.28, 8.95, 10.10, 11.23, and 13.59 billion yuan, and transportation and distribution costs at 3.49, 3.56, 4.39, 4.74, 5.28, and 5.98 billion yuan for 1952–57.

Other Personal Consumption Expenditures

CLOTHING

Results of the following calculations are shown in Tables 88 through 92. The derivation of personal consumption expenditures on clothing in 1933 and 1952–57 follows the general approach outlined above for food. The basic data on domestic production of clothing and clothing materials are drawn from product estimates presented

[47] See Table 79.

Table 87

THE TRANSPORTATION AND DISTRIBUTION MARGIN, 1933 AND 1952–57

(billions of yuan)

	In 1933 prices							In 1952 prices						
	1933	1952	1953	1954	1955	1956	1957	1933	1952	1953	1954	1955	1956	1957
1. Gross revenue from freight	1.53	2.74	2.85	3.08	3.25	3.66	3.85	3.44	6.55	6.87	7.45	7.89	8.90	9.42
2. Net income from trade	2.71	2.88	2.97	2.99	3.00	3.16	3.23	8.19	9.66	9.97	10.27	10.49	11.15	11.45
3. Gross value of agricultural output	21.17	21.38	21.78	22.32	22.62	23.01	23.11	38.24	39.68	40.44	41.30	41.76	42.94	43.15
4. Gross value of mineral output	0.30	0.93	0.90	1.12	1.45	1.46	1.90	0.73	2.17	2.10	2.63	3.39	3.41	4.45
5. Gross value of manufactured products minus raw material and fuel costs	3.08	4.09	4.63	5.05	5.28	6.39	6.79	8.95	14.22	16.88	18.99	20.13	26.09	28.31
6. Import balance of trade	0.87	0.26	0.28	0.11	0.32	−0.05	−0.09	2.27	0.98	1.05	0.37	1.16	−0.27	−0.44
7. Food consumption at producers' prices	11.53	11.54	11.65	11.89	12.12	12.37	12.62	20.64	21.52	21.74	22.17	22.62	23.07	23.53
8. Clothing consumption at producers' prices	0.24	0.29	0.40	0.32	0.24	0.34	0.33	0.85	1.04	1.45	1.15	0.89	1.25	1.20
9. Total transportation and distribution costs	4.24	5.62	5.82	6.07	6.25	6.82	7.08	11.63	16.21	16.84	17.72	18.38	20.05	20.87
10. Total value of commodities distributed through the market	13.65	14.83	15.54	16.39	17.31	18.10	18.76	28.70	34.49	37.28	39.87	42.93	47.85	50.74
11. Transportation and distribution margin (per cent)	31	38	37	37	36	38	38	40	47	45	44	43	42	41

NOTES: *Line 1. 1933.* Derived by summing up the estimates for the modern and traditional sectors. Total gross receipts of the three major branches of the modern sector (railroads, shipping, and highway transportation) amounted to 369, 137, and 95 million 1933 yuan respectively. (See Appendix H under Modern Transportation and Communications.) The percentages of total receipts from freight in these three branches are estimated at 56, 80, and 15 per cent, in Pei Yu-lin, "National Income, Consumption and Investment of China," *Shi-yeh jin-yung* (Journal of Finance and Industry), Vol. I, No. 1, Shanghai, May 1948, p. 72. Gross revenue from freight therefore amounted to 207, 110, and 14 million yuan, totalling 331 million yuan. Gross revenue from civil air transport is derived mainly from passenger transportation, and no allowance is made for the minor revenue from air freight. For the traditional sector, we arbitrarily allow one-tenth of the total receipts for such items as repairs, feeding of draft animals, and depreciation of carts and boats; the rest is net income of the carriers, which was estimated in Appendix H under Old-fashioned Transportation. Total receipts can then be calculated. Of the total receipts, the portion from passenger transportation is presumably small. Allowing 10 per cent of the total for this item, we obtain a rough estimate of gross revenue from freight in the traditional sector at 1.20 billion yuan. Total gross revenue from freight in 1933 therefore amounted to 1.53 billion yuan. The estimate in 1952 prices is derived by multiplying the corresponding estimates for the modern and old-fashioned sectors in 1933 prices by the price index numbers given at 254 and 216 per cent in 1952 with 1933 as 100 in Appendix I, Table I-1.

1952–57. Gross revenue from freight in 1952 prices is derived by summing up the estimates for the modern and the traditional sectors for 1952–57. For estimates for the modern sector, see Appendix H, Table H-9. The estimates for the traditional sector are derived on the same assumptions as those used in obtaining the estimate for 1933. For the data on net income in this sector in 1952–57, see Appendix H under Old-fashioned Transportation. The estimates in 1933 prices are derived by deflating the corresponding estimates by the price index numbers for the two sectors, given at 254 and 220 per cent in 1952, with 1933 as 100, in Appendix I, Table I-1.

(Continued)

Table 87 (continued)

Line 2. See Table 49.

Line 3. See Appendix E.

Line 4. See the discussion on Mining in Chapter II.

Line 5. 1933. The figure given in this table is the sum of those for factories and handicrafts. The figure for factories in 1933 prices is derived on the basis of gross output and the percentages of raw materials and fuel costs in gross output of factories given in Appendix F, Tables F-1 and F-4. The corresponding estimate in 1952 prices is derived by multiplying the estimate in 1933 prices by a price index of 488 per cent in 1952 with 1933 as 100, which in turn is derived from data on gross output, raw material, and fuel costs for 16 products in constant 1933 and 1952 prices given in Appendix F, Table F-5. For handicrafts, gross output of the identified products minus raw material and fuel costs in 1933 prices is derived from data given in Appendix G. The figure for the unidentified products is roughly estimated by multiplying their net value added (given in Table 44) by a factor equal to the ratio of gross output minus raw material and fuel costs to net value added by the identified handicraft products. The total for handicrafts amounted to 2.24 billion yuan. The corresponding figure in 1952 prices is derived at 4.84 billion yuan by multiplying 2.24 billion yuan by the price index for handicraft products, given at 216 per cent in 1952, with 1933 as 100, in Appendix I, Table I-1.

1952–57. The figures are the sums of estimates for factories and handicrafts. For factories, the ratios of gross output minus raw materials and fuel costs to net value added by 16 products in 1952 both in constant 1933 and 1952 prices are first calculated from data given in Appendix F, Table F-14. These ratios are then applied to total net value added by factories in 1952–57 in 1933 and 1952 prices, given in Table 37, to obtain gross output minus raw material and fuel costs for factories as a whole. The estimates for handicrafts are derived by the same procedure. The data used in this computation are given in Appendix G and Table 44.

Line 6. For 1933, data on imports and exports of China proper in 1933 prices are given in Liu, *Income*, p. 69; those of Manchuria are given in *Japan-Manchoukuo Yearbook, 1936*, Tokyo, 1936, p. 844. Imports and exports in 1933 in 1952 prices are derived on the basis of two price index numbers. The price index for imports is arbitrarily assumed to be the unweighted average of those for gross output of agricultural and manufactured products given in Appendix I, that is, 255 per cent in 1952 with 1933 as 100. The price index for exports is assumed to be the unweighted average of those for the gross output of agricultural, mineral, and manufactured products also given in Appendix I, that is, 251 per cent in 1952 with 1933 as 100. For 1952–57, imports and exports in 1952 prices are assumed to be the same as those, presumably in current prices, given in United Nations, *Economic Survey of Asia and the Far East, 957*, Bangkok, 1958, p. 103. Imports and exports in 1933 prices are computed on the basis of 1952 prices and the price index numbers given above.

Line 7. See Table 79.

Line 8. See Table 88.

Line 9. Sum of lines 1 and 2.

Line 10. Sum of lines 3 through 6 minus lines 7 and 8.

Line 11. Line 9 divided by line 10.

Table 88

CLOTHING CONSUMPTION, 1933 AND 1952–57
(billions of yuan)

	In constant 1933 prices							In constant 1952 prices						
	1933	1952	1953	1954	1955	1956	1957	1933	1952	1953	1954	1955	1956	1957
1. Domestic production at producers' prices	1.66	1.86	2.23	2.17	2.09	2.83	2.73	5.47	5.88	7.02	6.92	6.57	8.86	8.42
2. Import balance	0.05	−0.06	−0.16	−0.22	−0.26	−0.37	−0.40	0.17	−0.18	−0.51	−0.71	−0.84	−1.17	−1.25
3. Clothing supply for domestic consumption	1.71	1.80	2.07	1.94	1.83	2.46	2.33	5.64	5.70	6.51	6.21	5.74	7.69	7.17
4. Clothing consumption at producers' prices	0.24	0.29	0.40	0.32	0.24	0.34	0.33	0.85	1.04	1.45	1.15	0.89	1.25	1.20
5. Clothing supplied through the market at producers' prices	1.48	1.51	1.67	1.63	1.59	2.12	2.01	4.80	4.66	5.06	5.05	4.85	6.44	5.97
6. Transportation and distribution margin	0.46	0.58	0.62	0.60	0.57	0.80	0.76	1.92	2.19	2.28	2.22	2.09	2.71	2.45
7. Clothing consumption at consumers' prices	2.17	2.38	2.69	2.54	2.40	3.27	3.09	7.56	7.89	8.79	8.43	7.82	10.40	9.62

NOTES: *Line 1.* See Table 89.
Line 2. See Tables 90 and 91.
Line 3. Sum of lines 1 and 2.
Line 4. See Table 92.
Line 5. Line 3 minus line 4.
Line 6. Line 5 multiplied by the corresponding transportation and distribution margins given in Table 87.
Line 7. Sum of lines 4 through 6.

Table 89

PRODUCTION OF CLOTHING AND RELATED PRODUCTS AT PRODUCERS' PRICES, 1933 AND 1952–57
(billions of yuan)

	In 1933 prices							In 1952 prices						
	1933	1952	1953	1954	1955	1956	1957	1933	1952	1953	1954	1955	1956	1957
1. Agricultural products														
a. Cotton	0.54	0.65	0.82	0.74	0.67	0.95	0.91	1.47	1.75	2.21	1.99	1.81	2.57	2.45
b. Ramie	0.09	0.03	0.04	0.04	0.04	0.05	0.04	0.18	0.06	0.08	0.08	0.09	0.10	0.08
c. Silkworm cocoons	0.12	0.06	0.04	0.05	0.07	0.07	0.06	0.26	0.13	0.09	0.11	0.14	0.15	0.13
d. Wool	0.02	0.01	0.02	0.02	0.02	0.02	0.02	0.10	0.08	0.10	0.11	0.12	0.13	0.13
2. Value added by manufacturing														
a. Textile industry														
Cotton yarn	0.18	0.24	0.28	0.28	0.26	0.35	0.32	1.18	1.66	1.93	2.00	1.80	2.40	2.18
Cotton cloth	0.22	0.29	0.33	0.33	0.30	0.41	0.37	0.69	0.81	0.94	0.91	0.84	1.14	1.05
Silk	0.03	0.02	0.02	0.02	0.03	0.03	0.03	0.12	0.09	0.10	0.10	0.12	0.15	0.12
Silk piece goods	0.14	0.01	0.01	0.01	0.02	0.02	0.02	0.64	0.07	0.08	0.08	0.10	0.12	0.11
Woolen textiles and grass cloth	0.02	0.02	0.03	0.04	0.05	0.06	0.08	0.07	0.10	0.15	0.16	0.20	0.28	0.33
b. Clothing industry	0.12	0.12	0.14	0.13	0.12	0.17	0.16	0.41	0.42	0.50	0.49	0.46	0.62	0.58
c. Leather and rubber industry														
Leather goods	0.15	0.26	0.30	0.29	0.29	0.43	0.43	0.27	0.44	0.52	0.50	0.50	0.74	0.74
Rubber goods	0.04	0.15	0.19	0.22	0.23	0.27	0.30	0.07	0.25	0.33	0.38	0.40	0.46	0.52
3. Total	1.66	1.86	2.23	2.17	2.09	2.83	2.73	5.47	5.88	7.02	6.92	6.57	8.86	8.42

NOTES: *Line 1.a.* Gross values of cotton in 1933 and 1952–57 in constant 1933 and 1952 prices are derived by multiplying the quantity of cotton available for consumption in 1933 and 1952–57 (given in the discussion on Textile Products in Appendix G) by the farm price of cotton in 1933 and 1952 given in Table 34.

Line 1.b. Gross value of ramie in constant 1933 and 1952 prices is obtained by multiplying the 1933 and 1952–57 outputs by the corresponding prices. The output of ramie in 1933 is assumed to be one-third of the total hemp crop, the same as in 1952. (For 1952, see the discussion under Hemp Crops in Appendix C.) Since output of hemp crops was 6.8 million piculs in 1933 (Appendix A, Table A-9), output of ramie is calculated at 2.3 million piculs. Output in 1952–57 is derived at 0.78, 0.98, 0.98, 1.09, 1.19, and 1.05 million piculs on the basis of information given in *CCTP*, Hong Kong, No. 520, May 27, 1957, p. 12, and No. 604, January 26, 1959, p. 8; Chi Chung-wei, "China's Industry Should Support and Spur the Development of Agriculture," *CCYC*, No. 2, February 1958, p. 2; and *TCKT*, No. 15, 1957, p. 4. The price of ramie in 1933 is derived at 40 yuan per picul on the assumption that it increased from 1933 to 1952 in proportion to the price of hemp crops over the same period, that is, 198 per cent in 1952 with 1933 as 100, computed from data given in Table 34. The price of ramie in 1952 is estimated at 80 yuan per picul as follows: The government procurement prices of ramie in 1955 and 1957 are reported at 68 and 120 yuan per picul in *TKP*, Tientsin, July 19, 1955; and *People's Daily*, January 17, 1957. On the basis of a price index for all agricultural products procured by the government (113 per cent in 1955 and 121 per cent in 1957, with 1952 as 100) given in *TCKT*, No. 17, 1957, p. 5, the procurement price of ramie in 1952 is computed at 60 and 100 yuan per picul. For our calculation, the arithmetic mean of these two figures is used.

Line 1.c. See Appendix E.

(Continued)

Table 89 (continued)

Line 1.d. We arbitrarily allow one-third of the output of wool for uses other than the manufacture of clothing. For the total output of wool, see Appendix E.

Line 2.a. 1933. Value added by the five product groups in 1933 prices is derived by deducting the raw material costs already included in the agricultural products (given in Appendix F, Table F-4, and Appendix G, Table G-1) from gross value of manufactured products (given in Appendix F, Table F-1, and Appendix G, Table G-1). The estimates in 1952 prices are separately calculated for factory and handicraft products. Gross output and raw material costs for all products in 1933 in 1952 prices, except factory-produced grass cloth, are given in Appendix F, Table F-5. Value added by grass cloth in 1952 prices is derived by multiplying the estimate in 1933 prices by the price index of ramie given in the note to line 1.b. above. Value added by all handicraft products in 1952 prices is also derived by multiplying the estimate in 1933 prices by the appropriate price index. The price index numbers for cotton yarn and cotton cloth are 396 and 351 per cent in 1952 with 1933 as 100 derived from data given in Appendix I, Table I-2. Index numbers for silk, silk piece goods, and woolen textiles are 475, 475, and 424 per cent, which are the implicit deflators for value added by the corresponding factory products. The price index for ramie is the deflator for grass cloth.

1952–57. Value added is derived separately for the various factory and handicraft products as follows: The estimates for all the factory products (except grass cloth) for 1952 in 1952 prices are obtained by deducting raw material costs from gross output given in Appendix F, Table F-14. The estimates for 1953–57 are derived by applying the ratio of value added to gross output for each product in 1952 to the gross output of the corresponding product in 1953–57 given in Table 39. The estimates for the same products in 1952 in 1933 prices are derived similarly from data on gross output and raw materials given in Appendix F, Table F-14. The estimates for 1953–57 in 1933 prices are derived by deflating the corresponding estimates in 1952 prices by the appropriate price index calculated from the estimates for 1952 in both 1933 and 1952 prices. Values added by handicraft cotton yarn, cotton cloth, and silk piece goods in 1952–57 in 1952 prices are obtained by deducting raw materials from gross output, given in Appendix G, under Cotton Yarn and Silk Piece Goods. Estimates for the same products in 1933 prices are derived by deflating the estimates in 1952 prices by the appropriate price index numbers given above. For both factory and handicraft grass cloth, value added in 1952–57 in 1933 prices is derived by extrapolating from the 1933 estimate on an index of output of ramie in 1933 and 1952–57 given above. The estimates for 1952–57 in 1933 prices are then derived by applying the price index of ramie in 1952, with 1933 as 100, to the estimates in 1933 prices. For silk and woolen textiles, values added by both factory and handicraft products in 1952–57 in 1933 prices are first derived on the basis of the corresponding estimates for 1933 in 1933 prices and indexes of silk cocoon output and wool output in 1933 and 1952–57, given in Appendix A under Other Animal Products (*Great Ten Years*, p. 110); and Appendix C, Table C-5. Value added by factory products is then deducted from the corresponding totals to obtain value added by handicraft products. The estimates in 1952 prices are calculated by applying the price index numbers for the two products (475 and 424 per cent in 1952 with 1933 as 100) already obtained, to the estimates in 1933 prices.

Line 2.b. 1933. Value added in 1933 prices is derived from data on gross output and raw materials given in Appendix F, Tables F-1 and F-4, and Appendix G, Table G-1. The estimate in 1952 prices is derived by multiplying the figure in 1933 prices by the price index of cotton cloth, given at 352 per cent for 1952 with 1933 as 100 in Appendix F, Table F-6.

1952–57. It is assumed that value added by the clothing and knitted goods industry increased from 1933 to 1952–57 in proportion to that of agricultural and textile products over the same period given in lines 1.a. through 1.d. and 2.a. of this table.

Line 2.c. For 1933, estimates for the leather and rubber goods in 1933 prices are the gross output of these two industries given in Appendix F, Table F-1, and Appendix G under Leather Goods. The raw material costs need not be deducted here because they have not been included elsewhere. Estimates in 1952 prices are calculated by multiplying the figures in 1933 prices by a price index of 182 per cent in 1952 with 1933 as 100, computed from data on the gross value of cattle, sheep, and goats for 1933, in 1933 and 1952 prices as given in Appendix E. For 1952–56, gross outputs of the two industries in 1952 prices are given in Chao Yi-wen, *Hsin-chung-kuo ti kung-yeh* (New China's Industry), T'ung-chi chu-pan-she, Peiping, 1957, p. 59. Gross output of leather goods in 1957 is an extrapolation from the 1956 figure on an index of livestock used in 1956–57, computed from data given in Appendix E. Gross output of rubber goods is assumed to have increased in 1957 over 1956 in proportion to leather goods over the same period. The estimates for 1952–57 in 1933 prices are derived on the basis of 1952 prices and a price index of 172 per cent in 1952, with 1933 as 100, computed from data on cattle, sheep, and goats used in 1952, in 1933 and 1952 prices, also given in Appendix E.

in Chapter IV and the related appendixes. Detailed statistical data on imports and exports of clothing and clothing materials in 1952–57 are again extremely scarce, and only rough estimates can be made. The transportation and distribution margins for clothing are assumed to be the same as for all commodities. If the adjusted

Table 90

IMPORT AND EXPORT OF CLOTHING AND RELATED PRODUCTS, 1933
(millions of 1933 yuan)

Imports into China	
China proper	229.1
Raw cotton, cotton thread, cotton yarn, and cotton products	111.5
White or dyed cotton piece goods	33.4
Wool and wool products	33.4
Printed cotton piece goods	15.5
Silk and silk products	13.8
Flax, ramie, hemp, jute, and related products	6.8
Miscellaneous cotton piece goods	6.3
Hides, leather, skins (furs), and related products	5.4
Gray cotton piece goods	2.9
Manchuria	117.2
White or dyed cotton piece goods	28.1
Gray cotton piece goods	27.1
Cotton yarn	20.9
Raw cotton	11.0
Printed cotton piece goods	10.3
Silk piece goods	8.1
Woolen piece goods	7.8
Miscellaneous cotton piece goods	3.8
Total	346.3
Exports from China	
China proper	273.1
Textile fibers	114.1
Yarn, thread, plaited and knitted goods	63.8
Piece goods	47.3
Hides, leather, and skins (furs)	31.9
Straw hats, braid	7.9
Other textile products	7.8
Others	0.3
Manchuria	21.1
Raw silk	9.6
Cotton yarn	7.0
Skins (furs)	2.1
Hides and leather	1.2
Wool	1.2
Total	294.2
Net imports	52.1

SOURCES: *The Trade of China, 1933*, Vol. II, Shanghai, 1934, pp. 48–65, 104–105, 127, 140–153; Japan-Manchoukuo Yearbook Company, *Japan-Manchoukuo Yearbook, 1936*, Tokyo, 1936, pp. 851–855.

Table 91

IMPORT AND EXPORT OF CLOTHING AND RELATED PRODUCTS, 1952–57

(millions of 1952 yuan)

	1952	1953	1954	1955	1956	1957
Exports[a]						
Silk piece goods	145	182	201	243	281	—
Woolen piece goods	(*)	11	31	82	141	—
Cotton cloth	20	48	66	119	177	—
Rugs	8	5	5	5	8	—
Knitted goods	1	4	39	57	93	—
Semifinished and finished textile products	30	46	76	99	162	—
Subtotal	204	296	418	605	862	862
Silk	125	155	159	184	232	185
Miscellaneous[b]	121	190	343	448	472	537
Total	450	641	920	1,237	1,566	1,584
Imports[c]						
Raw cotton	200	29	109	225	114	52
Miscellaneous[d]	69	105	102	178	282	285
Total	269	134	211	403	396	335
Net exports	−180	−507	−710	−835	−1,169	−1,248

NOTES: — Not available.

(*) Less than 0.5 million yuan.

[a] Exports of silk piece goods, woolen piece goods, cotton cloth, rugs, knitted goods, and semifinished and finished textile products in 1952–56 are given in SSB, *Industry Study*, p. 173. The 1957 exports of these commodities are assumed to be the same as in 1956. Export of silk in 1954 is given at 63 per cent of output in Yeh Chi-chuang, "Report Before the Second Session of the First People's Congress," *HHYP*, No. 8, August 1955, p. 169. For the other years we assume the same percentage of output exported. For data on output, see Table 39. It is assumed that the export price of silk is the same as the factory price.

[b] Includes raw cotton, wool and other animal hair, furs, skins, feathers, flax, clothing, and footwear.

For miscellaneous exports, only exports to the countries outside of the Soviet bloc are available. They are given in the U.S. Department of State reports to the Congress, *Soviet Bloc Economic Activities in the Free World*, 1955, pp. 98, 100; *The Strategic Trade Control System 1948–56*, pp. 114–115; *The 1958 Revision of East-West Trade Controls*, 1959, pp. 46–47. The original data given in U.S. dollars are expressed in yuan at the official rate of exchange of one U.S. dollar to 2.617 yuan. No comparable information on miscellaneous exports to the Soviet-bloc countries is available. We assume that miscellaneous exports to the bloc countries are the same proportion of total trade as in the nonbloc countries. On the basis of miscellaneous exports to the nonbloc countries and the ratio of trade with Soviet-bloc countries to that with nonbloc countries (see notes to Table 84), miscellaneous exports to the Soviet-bloc countries can be roughly estimated.

[c] Imports of raw cotton are derived by multiplying the quantity of raw cotton imported by the import price. For data on the quantity of cotton imports in 1952–57, see Appendix G, Table G-8. For the import price of cotton, see Li Pei-fang, "Actively Strengthen the Organization of Sources of Supply for Exports," *CHCC*, No. 2, February 1958, p. 31.

(Continued)

Table 91 (continued)

[d] Includes raw wool and animal hair; unspecified textile fibers and related products; hides, skins, and fur skins; synthetic fibers; other textile fibers and wastes; textile yarns and related products; cotton yarn, fabrics, and related products; synthetic yarn, fabrics, related products; clothing; and footwear.

Miscellaneous imports are derived by adding the imports from nonbloc and Soviet-bloc countries. Miscellaneous imports from nonbloc countries are taken from the U.S. Department of State reports to the Congress, *Soviet Bloc Economic Activities in the Free World*, 1955, p. 99; *The Strategic Trade Control System 1948–56*, 1957, pp. 112–113; *The 1958 Revision of East-West Trade Controls*, 1959, pp. 44–45. Data on miscellaneous imports from the bloc countries are lacking. Available information on Sino-Soviet commodity trade indicates that imports of capital goods are much larger than the imports of clothing and related products. It may not be far wrong to assume that miscellaneous imports from the bloc countries are less than miscellaneous imports from the nonbloc countries. In our calculation we arbitrarily assume that they amounted to one-half of the miscellaneous imports from nonbloc countries.

estimate of the transportation and distribution margin is used, adjusted estimates of clothing consumption are obtained for 1952–57 as 7.98, 8.99, 8.68, 8.02, 10.72, and 9.80 billion 1952 yuan.[48]

FUEL AND LIGHT

Personal consumption expenditure on fuel and light in 1933 is derived from an estimate of per capita consumption given at 4.32 yuan on the basis of a study of prewar family budget data and our estimate of total population at 500 million.[49] The statistical sources used in the estimation of the per capita figure consist of 14 sample studies of family budget data for 25 localities in 1926–33. The per capita consumption figure is a weighted average of the 14 samples, the weights being the size of the total Chinese population broadly classified into 12 groups according to geographical region, occupation, and relative income level.

Briefly, the method of deriving this weighted average is as follows. The mainland is first divided into the Southeastern and Lower Yangtze Valley regions (consisting of eight provinces), and all parts of the mainland outside the eight provinces.[50] The agricultural and nonagricultural populations in each region are segregated on the basis of the percentages of agricultural population estimated by C. C. Chang.[51] The agricultural and nonagricultural populations in each region are grouped into three categories according to their

[48] For data used in deriving these figures, see Tables 87, 88.

[49] Ou, *National Income*, Vol. I, pp. 151, 171.

[50] The total populations in these two regions are those given in *The Chinese Yearbook, 1935–36*.

[51] Chang, *Crop Estimates*.

Table 92

CLOTHING CONSUMPTION AT PRODUCERS' PRICES, 1933 AND 1952–57
(millions of yuan)

	In 1933 prices							In 1952 prices						
	1933	1952	1953	1954	1955	1956	1957	1933	1952	1953	1954	1955	1956	1957
Cotton consumption in kind	118	140	196	154	117	167	159	319	380	529	417	316	450	429
Value added by cotton clothing manufacture	112	139	194	152	116	165	157	494	627	873	688	521	742	708
Wool consumption in kind	3	3	3	4	4	4	4	21	17	20	22	23	25	27
Value added by woolen clothing manufacture	2	5	5	6	6	5	6	12	20	24	26	27	30	32
Total	235	287	398	316	243	342	326	846	1,044	1,446	1,153	887	1,247	1,196

NOTES: Cotton consumption in kind is roughly estimated by multiplying the gross value of cotton given in Table 89 by the percentage of cotton output retained by the farmers. The percentages for 1952–55 are given in Chu Ching and Chu Chung-chien, "Variations in Our Rural Market Commodity Turnover," *CCYC*, No. 3, June 1957, p. 108. The percentage for 1933 is assumed to be the same as in 1952, and for 1956–57, the same as in 1955.

Value added in cotton clothing manufacturing is derived by multiplying the figures of cotton consumption in kind by a factor equal to the ratio of value added by cotton yarn, cotton cloth, and clothing to the gross value of cotton output given in Table 89.

Wool consumption in kind is estimated at 20 per cent of wool output by the Nationalist Chinese Northwest Wool Improvement Bureau (U.S. Department of Agriculture, *Report of the China-U.S. Agricultural Mission*, Washington, D.C., 1947, p. 221). Amounts of wool consumption in kind in 1933 and 1952–57 are derived by applying this percentage to estimates of wool production given in Table 89.

Value added by the manufacture of woolen clothing is derived by multiplying the amount of wool consumption in kind by a factor equal to the ratio of value added by woolen textiles to gross value of wool output given in Table 89.

relative income levels. The consumption pattern of each group is then assumed to be identical to another group or an average sample of family budget data.[52]

For 1952–57, information on fuel and light consumption is even scarcer than for the prewar years. In the absence of a better alternative, we assume that the per capita consumption of fuel and light in real terms in 1952–57 remained the same as in 1933. Total expenditures on fuel and light in 1952–57 can be derived at 2.46, 2.51, 2.57, 2.63, 2.68, and 2.75 billion yuan in 1933 prices by multiplying the per capita consumption expenditure on fuel and light by the population figures for 1952–57 as given in Chapter IV. On the basis of the prices of fuel wood, coal and coal briquettes, grain stalks, and vegetable oils in 1933 and 1952, a price index for fuel and light is computed as 208 per cent in 1952 with 1933 as 100.[53] Estimates of consumption expenditure on fuel and light for 1933 and 1952–57 in 1952 prices are then calculated by applying this price index to the estimates in 1933 prices.

Urbanization, increase in the number of households as indicated by a decrease in the number of persons per household, and migration to colder regions such as Manchuria and the northwest in 1952–57 might have raised the per capita consumption of fuel in these areas. However, it is doubtful whether these changes could have been important enough to have a perceptible effect on the per capita figure for the population as a whole.

RESIDENTIAL HOUSING

Estimates of expenditures on residential housing for 1933 and 1952–57 are derived by the same procedure and from the same sources of data as the estimates for net income from residential rent given in Chapter IV.

MISCELLANEOUS ITEMS

Our estimate of net domestic expenditure by end use is complete except for the category of miscellaneous personal consumption which can be obtained by deducting other expenditures from our estimate of domestic product adjusted for import balance. The result of this calculation is shown in Table 10. Using the same procedure and data on adjusted estimates of net domestic product, net domestic investment, government consumption, and personal consumption

[52] Ou, *National Income*, Vol. I, pp. 147–172.
[53] See Appendix I, Table I-4.

(except miscellaneous) given above, we can derive the adjusted estimate of miscellaneous consumption for 1952–57 at 5.23, 1.65, 2.58, 5.66, 8.57, and 9.98 billion 1952 yuan.[54]

Table 93

A COMPARISON OF THE ADJUSTED ESTIMATE WITH THE AUTHORS' ESTIMATE OF DOMESTIC EXPENDITURE, 1952–57
(billions of 1952 yuan)

	1952	1953	1954	1955	1956	1957
Personal consumption						
Adjusted	51.74	49.78	53.48	58.01	66.88	71.26
Authors'	54.60	51.84	54.96	56.99	62.60	64.49
Food						
Adjusted	30.38	30.82	33.71	35.62	38.70	42.36
Authors'	33.08	33.59	36.41	36.35	36.64	38.39
Clothing						
Adjusted	7.98	8.99	8.68	8.02	10.72	9.80
Authors'	7.89	8.79	8.43	7.82	10.40	9.62
Fuel and light	5.11	5.22	5.35	5.46	5.58	5.72
Housing	3.04	3.10	3.16	3.25	3.31	3.40
Miscellaneous						
Adjusted	5.23	1.65	2.58	5.66	8.57	9.98
Authors'	5.48	1.14	1.61	4.11	6.67	7.36
Communal services	1.94	2.45	2.46	2.32	3.26	3.29
Government consumption						
Adjusted	5.34	6.64	5.50	6.13	5.28	5.99
Authors'	5.34	6.64	5.49	6.11	5.23	5.92
Net domestic investment						
Adjusted	11.26	15.45	16.75	18.06	20.44	22.73
Authors'	11.26	15.45	16.74	18.04	20.39	20.62
Net domestic expenditure						
Adjusted	70.28	74.32	78.19	84.52	95.86	103.27
Authors'	73.14	76.38	79.65	83.46	91.48	94.32
Depreciation						
Adjusted	3.18	3.67	4.06	4.35	5.48	5.93
Authors'	3.26	3.66	4.03	4.27	5.20	5.48
Gross domestic expenditure						
Adjusted	74.36	77.99	82.25	88.87	101.34	109.20
Authors'	76.40	80.04	83.68	87.73	96.68	99.80

SOURCES: For our estimates, see Table 10. Adjusted estimates for personal consumption, communal services, government consumption, and net domestic investment are given in this chapter. The adjusted estimate of depreciation is given in Table 68.

COMPARISONS OF THE ADJUSTED ESTIMATE OF NET DOMESTIC EXPENDITURE WITH OUR ESTIMATE AND THE COMMUNIST ESTIMATE

The adjusted estimate of net domestic expenditure and our own estimate are presented together in Table 93. Since the adjusted

[54] See Table 72.

estimates are derived from Communist data, they are reconciled with the Communist estimates of net domestic expenditure by specifying difference in concepts and in coverage of basic data in Table 94. Differences in the investment and government consumption estimates have already been noted above. Differences in the consumption estimates are mainly two. The Communists include in their estimate depreciation on residential housing and value added by the production of certain consumers' goods for farm home consumption, which are not included in our estimate. Some items belonging to the category of consumers' goods and services are in our estimate but not in the Communist estimate. These include services rendered by modern passenger transportation, old-fashioned transportation, peddlers, finance, personal services, and imputed rent.

Table 94

RECONCILIATION OF THE ADJUSTED ESTIMATE AND THE COMMUNIST ESTIMATE OF NET DOMESTIC EXPENDITURE, 1952–57
(billions of 1952 yuan)

	1952				1953			
	Communist estimate (1)	Adjustments because of differences in concept (2)	Unexplained difference (3)	Adjusted estimate (4)	Communist estimate (1)	Adjustments because of differences in concept (2)	Unexplained difference (3)	Adjusted estimate (4)
1. Personal consumption	47.87	−0.69	+4.56	51.74	51.11	−3.41	+2.08	49.78
a. Processing for farm consumption		−5.19				−5.70		
b. Passenger transportation		+0.26				+0.38		
c. Trade						−2.45		
d. Finance		+0.65				+0.71		
e. Personal services		+0.55				+0.55		
f. Imputed rent		+3.04				+3.10		
2. Communal services	0.82	+1.12		1.94	1.23	+1.22		2.45
a. Salary and wage payments		+1.12				+1.22		
3. Government consumption	2.73	+2.61		5.34	2.83	+2.98	+0.83	6.64
a. Salary and wage payments		+2.15				+2.48		
b. Passenger transportation		+0.13				+0.15		
c. Finance		+0.33				+0.35		
4. Net domestic investment	11.44	−0.17		11.26	15.92	−0.47		15.45
a. Ancillary expenses		−1.25				−1.35		
b. Work brigades		+0.62				+0.38		
c. Passenger transportation		+0.13				+0.15		
d. Finance		+0.33				+0.35		
5. Net domestic expenditure	62.86	+2.87	+4.56	70.28	71.09	+0.32	+2.91	74.32

(Continued)

Table 94 (continued)

	1954				1955			
	Communist estimate (1)	Adjustments because of differences in concept (2)	Unexplained difference (3)	Adjusted estimate (4)	Communist estimate (1)	Adjustments because of differences in concept (2)	Unexplained difference (3)	Adjusted estimate (4)
1. Personal consumption	53.78	−1.92	+1.62	53.48	58.15	−1.25	+1.11	58.01
a. Processing for farm consumption		−5.77				−5.88		
b. Passenger transportation		+0.28				+0.28		
c. Trade		−0.88				−0.25		
d. Finance		+0.75				+0.81		
e. Personal services		+0.54				+0.54		
f. Imputed rent		+3.16				+3.25		
2. Communal services	1.14	+1.32		2.46	0.91	+1.41		2.32
a. Salary and wage payments		+1.32				+1.41		
3. Government consumption	1.88	+3.16	+0.46	5.50	1.82	+3.21	+1.10	6.13
a. Salary and wage payments		+2.63				+2.66		
b. Passenger transportation		+0.15				+0.15		
c. Finance		+0.38				+0.40		
4. Net domestic investment	17.45	−0.70		16.75	18.08	−0.02		18.06
a. Ancillary expenses		−1.67				−1.32		
b. Work brigades		+0.44				+0.75		
c. Passenger transportation		+0.15				+0.15		
d. Finance		+0.38				+0.40		
5. Net domestic expenditure	74.25	+1.86	+2.08	78.19	78.96	+3.35	+2.21	84.52

(Continued)

Table 94 (continued)

	1956				1957			
	Communist estimate (1)	Adjustments because of differences in concept (2)	Unexplained difference (3)	Adjusted estimate (4)	Communist estimate (1)	Adjustments because of differences in concept (2)	Unexplained difference (3)	Adjusted estimate (4)
1. Personal consumption	62.02	−1.06	+5.92	66.88	66.78	+0.12	+4.36	71.26
a. Processing for farm consumption		−6.17				−6.39		
b. Passenger transportation		+0.34				+0.38		
c. Trade						+0.96		
d. Finance		+0.95				+0.51		
e. Personal services		+0.51				+3.40		
f. Imputed rent		+3.31				+1.02		
2. Communal services	1.47	+1.79		3.26	1.39	+1.90		3.29
a. Salary and wage payments		+1.79				+1.90		
3. Government consumption	1.65	+3.62	+0.01	5.28	2.14	+3.82	+0.03	5.99
a. Salary and wage payments		+2.97				+3.13		
b. Passenger transportation		+0.18				+0.18		
c. Finance		+0.47				+0.51		
4. Net domestic investment	23.01	−2.57		20.44	22.20	+0.53		22.73
a. Ancillary expenses		−4.03				−1.01		
b. Work brigades		+0.81				+0.85		
c. Passenger transportation		+0.18				+0.18		
d. Finance		+0.47				+0.51		
5. Net domestic expenditure	88.15	+1.78	+5.93	95.86	92.51	+6.37	+4.39	103.27

(Continued)

Table 94 (continued)

NOTES: *Column* (*1*). Communist estimate: See Tables 72 and 78, and the text following Table 78.

Column (*2*). The adjustments are as follows:

Line 1.a. This item comprises mainly the imputed value of processed farm products mostly for home consumption (other than grain husking and making of clothing). See Table 70.

Line 1.b. Total value added by passenger transportation minus passenger services rendered in connection with investment and government consumption. See text of this chapter.

Line 1.c. See Table 70.

Line 1.d. Total value added by finance given in Table 68, minus those portions of finance in the service of investment and government consumption given earlier in this chapter.

Line 1.e. This item represents all the personal services rendered to consumers which have been included in the adjusted estimate but not the Communist estimate. See Table 68.

Line 1.f. See Table 93.

Line 2. See Table 78.

Lines 3.a.–3.c. See Table 78 and text following.

Lines 4.a.–4.d. See Table 72.

Line 5. Total adjustments represent the algebraic sum of figures in lines 1 through 4.

Column (*3*). The unexplained balance is the residual obtained by deducting the Communist estimate and total adjustments from the adjusted estimate.

Column (*4*). See Table 93.

PART II

Appendix A

OUTPUT OF AGRICULTURAL PRODUCTS, 1933

This appendix presents in detail the basic data and the methods used in deriving the estimates given in Chapter IV on the 1933 output of agricultural products. We first estimated the cultivated area of prewar China by province in Table 29. In the first section of this appendix, we shall present the basic data and the method used in deriving this estimate. The next three sections explain our estimate of rice output for 1933; estimates of the 1933 output of the other plant products; and our estimate of the 1933 output of animal, forest, and fishery products.

CULTIVATED AREA BY PROVINCE

The basic data used in our estimate of cultivated area are presented in Table A-1. The last column gives the estimate obtained. The estimates presented in columns (1) - (6) are those made by recognized scholars. As can be seen, for some of the provinces the estimates differ substantially. If there are no reasons for believing any particular estimate to be more reliable than the others, the arithmetic average of all available estimates is used in our own estimate. For others, some particular estimates are given more weight on the basis of farming and other conditions of the provinces concerned.

PRODUCTION OF RICE BY PROVINCE

The greatest difference between the estimates of the Bureau and Buck in food crop production is in rice.[1*] A comparison of Buck's and the

---

[*] Footnotes are found at the end of each appendix.

Table A-1

ESTIMATES OF CULTIVATED AREA BY PROVINCE, 1928-37

(million mow)

Province	Buck (1)	Chang (2)	Chen (3)	Chiao (4)	Lieu (5)	Ma (6)	Our Estimate (7)
1. Anhwei	76.4	49.3	53.5	85.6	93.9	70.6	70.6
2. Chahar	-	15.5	16.8	15.5	-	22.1	18.8
3. Chekiang	58.7	38.0	56.7	52.2	46.1	54.6	51.1
4. Fukien	35.7	21.5	23.3	21.5	29.8	29.1	23.3
5. Honan	125.2	104.1	133.6	104.1	129.0	142.0	123.0
6. Hopei	159.4	95.3	103.4	95.3	-	137.0	118.0
7. Hunan	79.3	42.0	45.6	113.1	125.0	84.0	79.3
8. Hupeh	84.2	56.2	61.0	127.0	142.4	95.6	84.0
9. Kansu	49.9	21.7	23.5	21.7	24.6	30.8	29.2
10. Kiangsi	47.3	38.4	41.6	75.7	89.3	75.7	43.0
11. Kiangsu	87.4	84.5	93.1	107.9	68.2	103.0	92.0
12. Kwangsi	43.0	-	43.9	40.9	72.3	40.9	43.0
13. Kwangtung	61.2	39.1	42.5	39.1	85.6	57.1	50.0
14. Kweichow	44.3	21.5	23.3	21.5	7.6	29.1	22.4
15. Ningsia	4.2	1.8	2.1	1.8	-	2.6	2.5
16. Shansi	77.4	55.8	60.6	55.8	-	80.1	55.8
17. Shantung	139.5	102.0	110.7	102.0	103.0	140.6	120.0
18. Shensi	76.9	30.9	33.5	33.9	48.4	58.5	54.0
19. Sikang	-	-	-	-	-	-	4.6
20. Suiyuan	14.4	17.2	24.0	17.2	-	24.6	24.0
21. Szechwan	206.2	88.7	96.5	88.7	140.7	127.1	129.0
22. Tsinghai	-	-	2.1	7.8	-	7.8	7.8
23. Yunnan	46.4	26.0	29.6	27.3	24.0	35.9	36.0
24. Sinkiang	-	16.7	14.6	14.9	9.9	18.0	16.0
25. Manchuria	-	190.9	259.3	235.2	151.2	268.7	235.0
26. Mongolia	-	-	-	-	-	-	0.2
27. Tibet	-	-	-	-	-	-	0.7
28. Special municipalities and districts	-	-	-	-	-	-	0.4
Totals							
23 provinces[a]		998.2[b]					1,276.8
All mainland							1,533.7

(Notes to this table are on the following pages.)

Notes:

- Not available.

[a] Sum of the cultivated area in the first 23 provinces (excluding Sikang) listed in this table.

[b] Estimates of cultivated area for Kwangsi and Tsinghai have not been made by Chang. Chiao's estimates for these two provinces are used instead. See note to column (4) below.

Column (1). As mentioned in Chapter IV, the figures in this column are averages of four sets of estimates based on Buck's data, derived as follows: (a) The difference between the "cultivation index," reported in Buck's survey for certain hsien, that is, percentage of total area under cultivation, and the corresponding percentages reported in the official statistics. This difference is assumed to indicate the extent of the bias in the official statistics for these hsien. A corrected estimate of the cultivated area for a province is then obtained by assuming that the bias in the surveyed hsien in a province is representative of that in the official statistics for the whole province. (b) Another estimate is obtained on the assumption that this correction applies only to the official figures for the surveyed hsien, while the official data for the other hsien in that province need no corrections. (c) A third estimate is obtained by multiplying the average size of farms obtained in Buck's survey by the official data on the number of farms in each province. (d) A fourth estimate is based on the direct estimates of Buck's investigation of the bias in the official statistics of the cultivated areas in the surveyed hsien and an application of an average of such correction factors to the official figure of the total cultivated area of the province. Buck's original data used in deriving these four sets of estimates can be found in Land Utilization, Vol. III, pp. 21-29, 37, 186. These data were collected during 1929-33. As mentioned in Chapter V under Plant Products, Buck's original data are for localities that have been grouped into Agricultural Areas. In using these data, we have reaggregated the locality figures to derive our estimates for the various provinces.

Column (2). C. C. Chang was the chief planner of the crop reporting system. Original figures were given in old mow which have been converted to shih mow at the rate of one old mow to 0.9216 shih mow. Corrections for Chang's incomplete coverage for Kweichow, Sinkiang, and Yunnan have been made on the assumption that the cultivated areas of the "no report" hsien in these provinces are of the same sizes as the averages of the reporting hsien in the respective provinces. Chang's data were collected in 1929-31, and are available in Chang, Crop Estimates, p. 11.

Column (3). Chen Chang-heng, a member of the Legislative Yuan (Parliament) of the National Government before 1949, published a study of China's population problems in relation to farmland in 1935. His estimate of the cultivated area by province was based on his correction of Chang's data, data given in Manchoukuo Yearbooks, and some new data supplied by the Ministry of Interior. See Chen Chang-heng, "A Preliminary Comparison of China's Land and Population and Discussion on Policies

Notes (continued):

Concerning the National Economic Reconstruction," Ti-li hsueh-pao (Journal of the Geographical Society of China), Nanking, Vol. II, No. 4, December 1935, pp. 1-44.

Column (4). Professor Chiao Chi-ming, of the University of Nanking, and his assistant Chiang Chieh, made extensive corrections to Chang's data on the cultivated area in eight provinces (Anhwei, Chekiang, Hunan, Hupeh, Kiangsi, Kiangsu, Shensi, and Yunnan) and Manchuria. New estimates of the cultivated acreage were made for Kwangsi and Tsinghai that were not included in Chang's estimate. For the other provinces, Chang's estimates were accepted. The basis for their correction was the data supplied by the Kwangsi Provincial Government, Kwang-si nien-chien (Kwangsi Yearbook), 1934, Japan-Manchoukuo Yearbooks, published by the Japan-Manchoukuo Yearbook Company, Tokyo, and other private studies. Chiao and Chiang's data, collected in 1936, were given in Chung-k'uo jen-kou yu shih-liang wen-ti (China's Population and Food Problems), Shanghai, Chung-hua Book Company, 1939, pp. 27-28.

Column (5). This column refers to figures given by D. K. Lieu and C. M. Chen, members of the Institute of Economic and Statistical Research in Shanghai. Basic information for their estimates was obtained from Nung shang tung-chi (Agricultural and Commercial Statistics), published annually from 1914 to 1924 by the old Peking Government, and other land records in various provinces. These are cited in Lieu and Chen, "Statistics of Farm Land in China," Chinese Economic Journal, Peiping, Vol. II, No. 3, March 1928, pp. 181-213.

Column (6). Ma Li-yuan, a member of the Institute of Social Sciences, Academia Sinica, made his estimate by province largely on the basis of the unpublished results of the land registration conducted by the National Government before the war. These results indicated that the old official data on cultivated acreage in a large number of localities were below those reported in land registration by varying proportions. These "ratios of underestimation" were used by Ma to correct Chang's data on cultivated areas for the various provinces. Ma's figures are for the prewar period (years unspecified), given in "Another Estimate of China's Farm Area," Ching-chi chien-she chi-k'an (Economic Reconstruction Quarterly), Chungking, Vol. III, No. 2, October 1944, pp. 157-164.

Column (7). Our estimates for the respective provinces are derived as follows:

1. Anhwei. Ma's estimate, roughly the mean of all other estimates, is used.
2. Chahar. Average of estimates by Chiao and Ma.
3. Chekiang. Average of all estimates.
4. Fukien. Buck's figures for this province may not be reliable as his survey covered only two localities of the province. Chen's estimate, close to a special estimate made by the Fukien Provincial Government, is used. For the Provincial Government's estimate, see Tu Tsun-tung, "Production and Consumption of Food Crops in Fukien," Fu-kien hsien-cheng pan-yueh k'an (Fukien Local Administration Semimonthly), Foochow, Vol. II, No. 1, March 1937, pp. 6-17.
5. Honan. Average of all estimates.
6. Hopei. Average of all estimates.

Notes (continued):

7. Hunan. Chang's extremely low estimate and Lieu's extremely high estimate are both discarded. Buck's estimate, close to the average of all the other estimates, is used.

8. Hupeh. Land registration completed in eight hsien of the province showed that the actual cultivated acreage was 43 per cent higher than officially reported. (Kwan Chi-yu, Tien-fu cheng-shih li-lun yu shih-wu (Theory and Practice of Land Taxation in Kind), Chungking, 1944, pp. 95-96.) If the official figures for cultivated acreage, that is, Chang's estimate of about 56 million mow, is raised by this percentage, it comes to approximately 80 million mow. We therefore use Buck's estimate of 84 million mow, which is quite close to this figure as well as to the average of the other estimates.

9. Kansu. Buck's estimate appears too high, considering the topography of this province. His survey covered mainly the fertile valleys along the tributaries of the Yellow River, and his estimate is likely to be too high. Both Lieu and Ma reported that about 5 per cent of the total area is cultivated. This percentage is applied to the total area of this province of 584 million mow to obtain our estimate of the cultivated area. See Bureau of Statistics, National Government, Chung-kuo tu-ti wen-ti chih t'ung-chi fen-hsi (Statistical Analysis of China's Land Problems), Chungking, 1941, p. 9.

10. Kiangsi. Chiao's, Lieu's, and Ma's estimates appear to be too high, considering the rugged topography over most parts of this province. The average of Buck's and Chang's estimates is used.

11. Kiangsu. Both Chiao's extremely high estimate and Lieu's extremely low estimate are discarded. The average of the other estimates is used.

12. Kwangsi. Lieu's estimate, amounting to 23 per cent of the total area, appears to be too high, considering the fact that most of the province consists of rolling hills and rough mountain ranges. Buck's estimate, being very close to the average of all other estimates, is used.

13. Kwangtung. The average of Buck's and Chang's estimates is used.

14. Kweichow. Buck's estimate is almost six times higher than Lieu's estimate, and both appear to be extreme. The average of Chang's and Chen's estimates is used.

15. Ningsia. We have used Chu Lien-tsing's estimate based on a survey he conducted under the auspices of the Chinese National Geological Survey. (Chu, "Suggestion on the Utilization and Amelioration of the Soils in Ningsia," Tu-jang chi-k'an (Soil Quarterly), Chungking, Vol. V, No. 2, April 1946, pp. 63-74.)

16. Shansi. Since Chiao is a native of this province and did extensive social and economic studies there, his figure is used.

17. Shantung. The available estimates cluster in two groups: a higher estimate represented by Buck's estimate and a lower one represented by Chang's estimate. The average of these two is used.

18. Shensi. The average of Buck's and Chang's figures is used.

19. Sikang. The cultivated acreage was roughly estimated by the Ministry of Agriculture and Forestry at 0.6 per cent of the total area.

Notes (continued):

(Nung-lin t'ung-chi shou-t'se (Handbook of Agricultural and Forestry Statistics), Nanking, 1948, p. 1.) On the basis of the total area of 760 million mow, the cultivated acreage is computed to be 4.6 million mow. (Chen Chung-wei, Si-kang wen-ti (Problems of Sikang), Shanghai, 1930, p. 43.)

20. Suiyan. Buck's, Chang's, and Chiao's estimates, amounting to less than 4 per cent of the total area of 456 million mow, appear to be too low. Chen's estimate, which is very close to Ma's, is used.

21. Szechwan. Buck's estimate for this province is more than double Chang's estimate. Neither is believed to be correct. Land registration in 20 hsien of the province revealed that the registered farm land was 45 per cent higher than the old official estimate. (Kwan Chi-yu, Tien-fu cheng-shih chih li-lun yu shih-wu (Theory and Practice of Land Taxation in Kind), Chungking, 1944, pp. 95-96.) Chang's estimate is then raised by this ratio to 129 million mow, which is found to be very close to Ma's estimate. Chang's estimate thus raised is used.

22. Tsinghai. Chiao's estimate, based on a rural economic survey made by Chiu Hsien-chu is believed to be the best figure available and is therefore used. (Chiao Chi-ming and Chiang Chieh, Chung-kuo jen-k'ou yu shih-liang wen-ti (China's Population and Food Problems), Shanghai, Chung-hua Book Company, 1939, p. 26)

23. Yunnan. The average of Buck's and Chang's estimates, being about the same as Ma's estimate, is used.

24. Sinkiang. Lieu's estimate, being made on the basis of incomplete official land records, is too low. All the other estimates vary within a narrow range. The average of all estimates, except Lieu's, is used.

25. Manchuria. Taken from Manchoukuo Yearbook Company, Manchoukuo Yearbook, 1934, Hsinking, 1934, p. 13.

26. Mongolia. Taken from Pan Kung-chao, Jin-jih chih Mung-ku (Mongolia Today), Shanghai, 1947, pp. 93-94.

27. Tibet. No dependable information on the cultivated acreage is available. Our rough estimate is derived from our estimate of Tibet's prewar population of 1.4 million (see Table 51) and an estimate of the cultivated area that is required to produce the food crops for a population of this size. After taking into consideration the diet of the Tibetans, which consists mainly of meat and dairy products, the per capita annual consumption of food crops is assumed to be 100 catties. Thus, the total requirement of food crops is estimated to be 1.4 million piculs. Assuming that unit yield of food crops from Tibet's cultivated area to be 200 catties per mow, in view of the short growing season, high altitude, and low rainfall, we deduced the required cultivated acreage to be 0.7 million mow.

28. Special municipalities and districts. Included in this group are Shanghai, Nanking, Peiping, Tientsin, Tsingtao, Dairen, Harbin, Sian, Mukden, Hankow, Canton, Kwantung Leased Territory in Manchuria, Weihaiwei Special District in Shantung, and a number of other cities, which at one time or another were under the direct administrative control of the Executive Yuan (Cabinet) of the National Government. The cultivated area in these districts is not included

Notes (continued):

in the provincial statistics and has to be separately estimated. The given estimate of the total area in these districts is 7.24 million mow (Shen Pao Yearbook, 1935, pp. B9-10). It is then roughly estimated (ibid, p. 94) that 5 per cent of this area is cultivated (this is the ratio of farming population to the total population in Shanghai, Nanking, and Peiping). Multiplying these two figures gives our estimate of total cultivated area at 0.4 million mow.

Bureau's data at the provincial level is made here to facilitate understanding of the discrepancies.

In Table A-2, the Bureau's and Buck's data on the percentage of cultivated area in rice in the different provinces are presented together with the ratio of the former to the latter. The differences between these two sets of data for the major producing provinces of Anhwei, Chekiang, Hupeh, Kiangsi, and Kwangtung are probably within reasonable margins of sampling errors, which must be fairly large. We use the averages of these two sets of data, which are taken to represent the means of a sample of a larger number of observations. The differences for Kiangsu and for the Southwestern provinces of Kweichow, Szechwan, and Yunnan are much greater; Buck's figures are higher than the Bureau's. Our judgment is that Buck's estimates are biased substantially upward and the Bureau's substantially downward. Although the sizes of these biases are not known, we use the averages of the two estimates as they are probably near the true magnitudes. In the case of Fukien, Buck's figure is definitely too high. An independent estimate given in a Fukien Provincial Government report is used. Hunan is the famous "rice bowl" of China, and Buck's figure, the higher of the two, is accepted. For Kwangsi, Buck's percentage was collecte from two localities only. To obtain a broader geographical coverage, the average of the Bureau's figure and an estimate given in a Kwangsi Provincial Government study is used. For the minor producing provinces, the Bureau's data are accepted for those provinces for which Buck has given no data, and the averages of the two are used where both figures are available.

Data on unit yields are presented in Table A-3. For the major producing

Table A-2

PERCENTAGE OF CULTIVATED AREA IN RICE IN

DIFFERENT PROVINCES

Province	Bureau's estimate	Buck's estimate	Ratio of Bureau's to Buck's	Percentage used in this study
	(1)	(2)	(3)	(4)
Major producing				
Anhwei	30.2	35.4	85	32.8
Chekiang	61.6	60.5	102	61.1
Fukien	53.4	128.3	42	59.0
Hunan	59.8	76.0	79	76.0
Hupeh	41.1	33.4	123	37.3
Kiangsi	51.3	68.7	75	60.0
Kiangsu	26.9	45.2	60	36.0
Kwangsi	78.0	107.3	-	56.0
Kwangtung	117.1	134.3	87	125.7
Kweichow	34.4	81.2	42	57.8
Szechwan	42.0	66.1	64	54.1
Yunnan	39.1	74.5	52	56.8
Minor producing				
Chahar	1.3	-	-	1.3
Honan	1.9	7.1	27	4.5
Hopei	1.3	0.7	186	1.0
Kansu	0.1	-	-	0.1
Ningsia	5.5	-	-	5.5
Shansi	0.2	-	-	0.2
Shantung	0.2	-	-	0.2
Shensi	3.6	0.3	1,200	2.0

Notes:

- Not available.

Column (1). The percentage for each province is obtained by dividing the Bureau's provincial cultivated acreage (given in column (2), Table A-1) with its provincial rice acreage. The Bureau's rice acreage figures are the 1931-37 averages, taken from Agricultural Estimates, p. 39.

Column (2). The percentage for each province is the weighted average of Buck's locality percentages, the weights being the locality cultivated areas. Buck's percentage data are taken from Land Utilization, Vol. III, pp. 194-199, and his cultivated acreage figures are taken from pp. 21-29.

Column (4). The percentage for each province is the average of the Bureau's and Buck's percentages given in column (1) and (2), except those

Notes (continued):

for Fukien, Hunan, and Kwangsi. For Fukien, it is the Fukien Provincial Government's estimate, given in Tu Tsun-tung, "Production and Consumption of Food Crops in Fukien," Fu-kien hsien-cheng pan-yueh-k'an (Fukien Local Administration Semi-monthly), Foochow, Vol. II, No. 1, March 1937, pp. 6-17. For Hunan, Buck's estimate is used. For Kwangsi, it is the average of the Bureau's percentage and an estimate of 34 per cent derived from data given by the Kwangsi Provincial Government in Kwang-si nien-chien (Kwangsi Yearbook), 1934, pp. 23 and 177.

Table A-3

UNIT YIELD OF RICE IN DIFFERENT PROVINCES

(catties per mow)

Provinces	Bureau's estimate (1)	Buck's estimate (2)	Ratio of Bureau's to Buck's (3)	Yield data used in this study (4)
Major producing				
Anhwei	290	325	89	308
Chekiang	334	294	114	314
Fukien	373	407	92	390
Hunan	388	420	92	404
Hupeh	304	569	53	404
Kiangsi	332	359	92	346
Kiangsu	371	429	86	400
Kwangsi	309	349	89	329
Kwangtung	342	274	125	308
Kweichow	290	812	36	369
Szechwan	383	595	64	445
Yunnan	317	420	75	369
Minor producing				
Chahar	136	-	-	136
Honan	252	143	176	198
Hopei	196	352	56	274
Kansu	169	-	-	169
Ningsia	106	-	-	106
Shansi	72	-	-	72
Shantung	94	-	-	94
Shensi	280	343	82	312

Notes:

- Not available.

Column (1). The yield figure for each province is obtained by dividing the Bureau's output by the acreage planted in rice in the province. The Bureau's rice output and acreage data are the average annual figures for the 1931-37 period, given in Agricultural Estimates, pp. 39 and 41.

Column (2). The yield figure for each province is the weighted average of Buck's "most frequent yields" in localities of the province, the weights being Buck's locality rice acreages. Buck's yield data are for the 1929-33 period, given in Land Utilization, Vol. III, pp. 209-210.

Column (4). The yield figure for each province is the average of the Bureau's and Buck's estimates given in columns (1) and (2), except those

Notes (continued):

for Hupeh, Kweichow, and Szechwan. For Hupeh, the average yield for Hunan is used. For Kweichow, the average yield for Yunnan is used. For Szechwan, Buck's estimate for this province is first averaged with his estimate for Yunnan (595 + 420)/2; the resultant figure (507 catties) is then averaged with the Bureau's estimate (507 + 383)/2 to arrive at the yield figure of 445 catties.

provinces, the two sets of estimates are fairly close except those for Hupeh, Kweichow, and Szechwan. For Hupeh, the Bureau's figure is too low and Buck's too high. It is unlikely that the unit yield in Hupeh is much different from that in the neighboring province of Hunan. The Bureau's and Buck's figures for Hunan are very close, and the average of these two is used as the average yield in Hupeh. Buck's figure for Kweichow is unreasonably high, therefore the yield in the neighboring province of Yunnan is used. In the case of Szechwan, Buck's figure again appears to be excessively high, even though the yield in this province should be higher than in the neighboring province of Yunnan. The mean of Buck's figures for these two provinces is then averaged with the Bureau's figure for Szechwan, and the result is used as the yield for Szechwan. The percentage and unit yield data given in Tables A-2 and A-3 are then used to obtain the production estimate by province given in Table A-4.

As a check for our estimate of rice production, rice consumption by province is estimated in Tables A-5 through A-7. The two major sources are again the Bureau's and Buck's studies. The derivation of per capita consumption of rice used for food from the Bureau's and Buck's data is explained in detail in Tables A-5 and A-6. The results are compared in the first two columns of Table A-7. They must be considered as fairly close. We have accepted the averages of those two sets of data as the per capita consumption of rice in this study.

The Bureau's and Buck's data on the percentage of rice used for food, however, differ very widely. Buck's percentages vary from a low of 85 per cent for Ningsia to a high of 100 per cent for Shansi.[2] In the Bureau's data, the highest percentage was 89 for Hopei and the lowest

Table A-4

ESTIMATE OF RICE PRODUCTION BY PROVINCE

Province	Total cultivated area (million mow)	Cultivated area in rice (per cent)	Rice acreage (million mow)	Unit yield (catties per mow)	Output (million piculs)
	(1)	(2)	(3)	(4)	(5)
Major producing					
Anhwei	70.6	32.8	23.2	308	71.5
Chekiang	51.1	61.1	31.2	314	98.0
Fukien	23.3	59.0	13.7	390	53.4
Hunan	79.3	76.0	60.3	404	243.6
Hupeh	84.0	37.3	31.3	404	126.4
Kiangsi	43.0	60.0	25.8	346	89.3
Kiangsu	92.0	36.0	33.1	400	132.4
Kwangsi	43.0	56.0	24.1	329	79.3
Kwangtung	50.0	125.7	62.9	308	193.7
Kweichow	22.4	57.8	12.9	369	47.6
Szechwan	129.0	54.1	69.8	445	310.6
Yunnan	36.0	56.8	20.4	369	75.3
Minor producing					
Chahar	18.8	1.3	0.2	136	0.3
Honan	123.0	4.5	5.5	198	11.0
Hopei	118.0	1.0	1.2	274	3.3
Kansu	29.2	0.1	0.1	169	0.2
Ningsia	2.5	5.5	0.1	106	0.1
Shansi	55.8	0.2	0.1	72	0.1
Shantung	120.0	0.2	0.2	94	0.2
Shensi	54.0	2.0	1.1	312	3.4
Sinkiang	16.0	-	-	-	5.2
Manchuria	235.0	-	-	-	8.3
Total					1,553.2

Notes:

- Not available.

Column (1). Taken from column (7), Table A-1.

Column (2). Taken from column (4), Table A-2.

Column (3). Column (1) times column (2).

Column (4). Taken from column (4), Table A-3.

Notes (continued):

Column (5). Column (3) times column (4). Output for Sinkiang is from Chang, Crop Estimates, p. 15. For Manchuria, it is an average annual output for 1931-37 computed from data given in Manchoukuo Yearbook Co., Manchoukuo Yearbook, 1942, Hsinking, 1942, p. 425.

Table A-5

PER CAPITA RICE CONSUMPTION BY PROVINCE:

ESTIMATED ON THE BUREAU'S DATA

Province	Per capita food consumption requirement of rice (glutinous and nonglutinous) (catties)	Nonglutinous rice as a percentage of total rice (per cent)	Per capita food consumption of nonglutinous rice (catties)
	(1)	(2)	(3)
Major producing			
Anhwei	406	91.0	369
Chekiang	545	87.0	474
Fukien	532	91.2	485
Hunan	594	93.6	556
Hupeh	430	91.1	391
Kiangsi	581	88.7	515
Kiangsu	351	85.5	300
Kwangsi	518	92.8	481
Kwangtung	528	95.8	506
Kweichow	451	84.5	381
Szechwan	498	92.7	462
Yunnan	495	92.1	456
Minor producing			
Chahar	6	100.0	6
Honan	43	79.8	34
Hopei	12	70.1	9
Kansu	6	62.8	4
Ningsia	99	66.7	66
Shansi	3	60.9	2
Shantung	4	44.4	2
Shensi	56	82.5	46

Notes:

Column (1). Taken from Crop Reports, Vol. 6, No. 10, 1938, Table 1, p. 115. The Bureau's original figures were collected in 1936-37. They were given in terms of polished rice which have been converted into paddy rice at the rate of 0.7 picul of polished rice to one picul of paddy rice.

Column (2). These are the Bureau's 1931-37 average ratios of nonglutinous rice production to the total rice production, computed from data given in Agricultural Estimates, pp. 41 and 45.

Column (3). Column (1) times column (2).

Table A-6

PER CAPITA RICE CONSUMPTION BY PROVINCE: ESTIMATED ON BUCK'S DATA

Province	Intake of calories per adult-male unit[a]: Per day (calories)	Per year (thousand calories)	Percentage of calories supplied by polished rice (per cent)	Annual intake of calories supplied by polished rice per adult-male unit (thousand calories)	Annual food consumption of rice per adult-male unit: Polished rice (catties)	Paddy rice (catties)	Ratio of adult-male unit to single person (per cent)	Annual per capita food consumption of paddy rice (catties)
	(1)	(2)	(3)	(4)	(5)	(6)	(7)	(8)
Major producing								
Anhwei	3,235	1,181	47.7	563	319	456	77.0	351
Chekiang	3,404	1,242	76.1	945	535	764	76.5	585
Fukien	2,906	1,061	66.2	702	398	568	76.4	434
Hunan	4,228	1,543	82.5	1,273	721	1,030	73.7	759
Hupeh	3,810	1,391	28.8	401	227	324	78.7	255
Kiangsi	3,936	1,437	81.9	1,177	667	952	75.5	719
Kiangsu	3,543	1,293	44.6	577	327	467	78.0	364
Kwangsi	2,584	943	86.0	811	459	656	77.6	509
Kwangtung	3,647	1,331	88.1	1,173	665	950	78.8	748
Kweichow	3,633	1,326	83.3	1,104	625	893	73.7	658
Szechwan	2,874	1,049	62.0	650	368	526	76.5	403
Yunnan	3,334	1,217	70.6	859	487	696	76.6	533
Minor producing								
Honan	2,589	945	9.8	93	53	76	77.0	58
Hopei	4,457	1,627	1.8	29	16	23	78.9	18
Ningsia	3,005	1,097	0.1	1	b	b	79.2	b
Shansi	2,642	964	0.7	7	4	6	77.1	5
Shantung	2,848	1,040	0.2	2	1	1	76.9	1
Shensi	3,106	1,134	2.0	23	13	18	78.0	14

(Notes to this table are on the following page.)

Notes:

[a]The "adult-male unit" was used by Buck as a standard for estimating the calorie intake of the people. Any male or female of 17 or older was considered as one "adult-male unit." Those under 17 were counted as various fractions of one "unit" (the younger, the smaller). Land Utilization, Vol. I, pp. 406-408.

[b]Less than 0.05.

Column (1). The figure for each province is the weighted average of locality figures in the province, the weights being the number of adult-male units in the localities. Locality calorie data are taken from Land Utilization, Vol. III, p. 73.

Column (2). Column (1) times 365.

Column (3). The percentage for each province is the weighted average of locality percentages (ibid., p. 75), the weights being the calorie intake figures for the localities.

Column (4). Column (2) times column (3).

Column (5). Column (4)/1,765. 1,765 is the number of calories produced by one catty of polished rice. Ibid., p. 67.

Column (6). Column (5)/0.7. 0.7 is the ratio of polished rice to paddy (by weight). For this conversion ratio, see Chiao Chi-ming and Chiang Chieh, Chung-kuo jen-kou yu shih-liang wen-ti (China's Population and Food Problems), Shanghai, Chung-hua Book Co., 1939, p. 38, and Food and Agriculture Organization of the United Nations, Report of the Second Session of International Rice Commission, Bangkok, 1950, p. 40.

Column (7). Ratio for each province is the weighted average of locality ratios in the province, the weights being the locality population figures. Locality ratios are taken from Land Utilization, Vol. III, p. 66.

Column (8). Column (6) times column (7).

Table A-7

ESTIMATE OF RICE CONSUMPTION BY PROVINCE

Province	Per capita consumption for food purpose: Estimate based on Bureau's data (catties)	Per capita consumption for food purpose: Estimate based on Buck's data (catties)	Per capita consumption for food purpose: Average of the Bureau's & Buck's (catties)	Per capita consumption for all purposes (catties)	Population (million)	Food consumption (million piculs)	Total consumption (million piculs)
	(1)	(2)	(3)	(4)	(5)	(6)	(7)
Major producing							
Anhwei	369	351	360	400	24.0	86.4	96.0
Chekiang	474	585	530	589	22.0	116.6	129.6
Fukien	485	434	460	511	13.1	60.3	66.9
Hunan	556	759	657	730	33.4	219.4	243.8
Hupeh	391	255	323	359	27.3	88.2	98.0
Kiangsi	515	719	617	686	16.5	101.8	113.2
Kiangsu	300	364	332	369	34.9	115.9	128.8
Kwangsi	481	509	495	550	16.6	82.2	91.3
Kwangtung	506	748	627	697	34.0	213.2	237.0
Kweichow	381	658	520	578	12.6	65.5	72.8
Szechwan	462	403	432	480	55.4	239.3	265.9
Yunnan	456	533	494	549	15.9	78.5	87.3
Minor producing							
Chahar	6	-	6	7	2.2	0.1	0.2
Honan	34	58	46	51	36.3	15.6	18.5
Hopei	9	18	13	14	30.6	4.0	4.3
Kansu	4	-	4	4	6.5	0.3	0.3
Ningsia	66	(*)	33	37	1.0	0.3	0.4
Shansi	2	5	3	3	12.4	0.4	0.4
Shantung	2	1	1	1	40.3	0.4	0.4
Shensi	46	14	30	33	9.7	2.9	3.2

Notes:

- Not available.

(*) Less than 0.5.

Column (1). Taken from column (3), Table A-5.

Column (2). Taken from column (8), Table A-6.

Column (3). Averages of the figures given in the two preceding columns.

Column (4). Figures in column (3) divided by 0.9.

Column (5). Data taken from Table 51.

Column (6). Column (3) times column (5).

Column (7). Column (4) times column (5).

was 74 for Kwangsi and Hunan.[3] No convincing explanation can be found for the wide variance in the percentages in the different provinces. We have therefore decided to take the mean of Buck's national figure of 95 per cent, T. H. Shen's estimate of 93 per cent, and the Bureau's national average of 82 per cent as our estimate.[4] The mean is 90 per cent, and is applied to all provinces to obtain rice consumption for all purposes. Total rice consumption in the different provinces is then estimated and the result shown in Table A-7.

Production and consumption of rice in the major rice producing provinces are compared in Table A-8. Because of the very rough nature of the estimate of rice consumption for nonfood purposes, more weight should be given to the production of rice for food. Hunan, Hupeh, Kiangsu, and Szechwan are found to have substantial surpluses. Kwangtung is a major deficit province. All these figures are quite consistent with common knowledge of rice supply in these provinces. Anhwei is a major rice distribution center. It is rather surprising that it has been found to be a major deficit province. The deficit found for Chekiang is also difficult to explain. On the whole, however, the picture is reasonably acceptable. When nonfood use of rice is added to consumption, the picture becomes less satisfactory. The total deficit of supply is unlikely to be as large as 7 per cent of total production. It is more likely that nonfood use of rice has been overestimated rather than that production has been underestimated. The estimate of provincial distribution of nonfood use of rice is also rather unsatisfactory.

Table A-8

COMPARISON OF PRODUCTION AND CONSUMPTION OF RICE

BY MAJOR RICE-PRODUCING PROVINCES

(million piculs)

		Comparison with:			
		I. Food Consumption		II. Total Consumption	
Province	Rice production	Consumption	Surplus(+) or Deficit(-)	Consumption	Surplus(+) or Deficit(-)
	(1)	(2)	(3)	(4)	(5)
Anhwei	71.5	86.4	- 14.9	96.0	- 24.5
Chekiang	98.0	116.6	- 18.6	129.6	- 31.6
Fukien	53.4	60.3	- 6.9	66.9	- 13.5
Hunan	243.6	219.4	+ 24.2	243.8	- 0.2
Hupeh	126.4	88.2	+ 38.2	98.0	+ 28.4
Kiangsi	89.3	101.8	- 12.5	113.2	- 23.9
Kiangsu	132.4	115.9	+ 16.5	128.8	+ 3.6
Kwangsi	79.3	82.2	- 2.9	91.3	- 12.0
Kwangtung	193.7	213.2	- 19.5	237.0	- 43.3
Kweichow	47.6	65.5	- 17.9	72.8	- 25.2
Szechwan	310.6	239.3	+ 71.3	265.9	+ 44.7
Yunnan	75.3	78.5	- 3.2	87.3	- 12.0
Total	1,521.1	1,467.3	+ 53.8	1,630.6	-109.5

Notes:

Column (1). Taken from column (5), Table A-4.

Column (2). Taken from column (6), Table A-7.

Column (3). Column (1) minus column (2).

Column (4). Taken from column (7), Table A-7.

Column (5). Column (1) minus column (4).

OUTPUT OF OTHER PLANT PRODUCTS

The national output of other plant products for 1933 is the sum of the output in the 22 provinces of China proper, Manchuria, and Sinkiang.[5] For 15 principal crops on which data are available,[6] our estimates of the output in the 22 provinces are obtained by first multiplying our estimated total cultivated area of the 22 provinces by the averages of Buck's and the Bureau's data on the percentages of cultivated area devoted to the respective crops to obtain the crop acreages. The latter are then multiplied by Buck's and the Bureau's average figures on unit yield to obtain the estimates for total output. For 8 less important crops,[7] the data given in Buck's and the Bureau's estimates are not as complete as those for the principal crops. Chang's data are used to supplement the two main sources. Production estimates for these 23 crops are explained below. Only fragmentary data are available for plant products other than food crops (namely, cottonseed, sugar beets, tea, vegetables, and fruit). Estimates for these products are derived by *ad hoc* methods; they are explained separately in subsections below.

Output of 23 Crops

The estimates obtained are presented in Table A-9. The method of derivation is explained in detail in the notes to that table.

In Communist sources, the output figures of miscellaneous food crops and of potatoes are given in aggregates without breakdowns for each individual crops. In order to compare our estimate for 1933 with the postwar figures, we have summed up our 1933 output estimates of these two groups of products and have presented the totals in Table 33. The "miscellaneous food crops" group includes millet, kaoliang, corn, barley,

Table A-9

OUTPUT OF 23 CROPS, 1933

Crop	China Proper: Percentage share of each crop in total cultivated area (per cent): Bureau's	Buck's	Average	Yield per mow (catties): Bureau's	Buck's	Average	Prewar average annual output (million piculs)	1933 output as percentage of prewar annual average (per cent)	1933 output (million piculs)	Manchuria (million piculs)	Sinkiang (million piculs)	Mainland total (million piculs)
	(1)	(2)	(3)	(4)	(5)	(6)	(7)	(8)	(9)	(10)	(11)	(12)
Wheat[a]	29.8	24.8	27.3	144	134	139	484.6	105	508.8	13.0	12.2	534.0
Millet	8.0	10.0	9.0	165	163	164	188.4	101	190.3	63.7	0.7	254.7
Kaoliang	7.6	7.8	7.7	182	164	173	170.1	99	168.4	80.4	2.5	251.3
Corn	6.9	6.2	6.5	183	190	187	155.2	91	141.2	35.2	9.5	185.9
Barley[a]	9.9	6.3	8.1	156	138	147	152.0	96	145.9	4.1	1.6	151.6
Glutinous paddy rice	2.4	0.7	1.5	309	409	359	68.6	118	80.9	-	0.7	81.6
Peas	5.2	2.3	3.7	118	171	145	68.4	94	64.3	-	1.0	65.3
Broad beans	4.1	2.1	3.1	144	180	162	64.2	94	60.3	-	-	60.3
Proso millet[a]	2.3	1.9	2.1	129	119	124	33.2	100	33.2	5.0	-	38.2
Sweet potatoes	3.4	4.2	3.8	1,064	1,074	1,069	518.5	102	528.9	-	-	528.9
Soybeans	7.7	5.8	6.7	155	122	139	119.0	121	144.0	92.0	0.3	236.3
Peanuts	2.2	2.0	2.1	242	196	219	58.7	113	66.3	0.6	-	66.9
Rapeseed	5.7	2.9	4.3	87	92	90	49.4	85	42.0	-	-	42.0
Lint cotton	5.6	4.3	5.0	29	26	28	17.9	103	18.4	0.3	0.3	19.0
Tobacco	0.8	1.2	1.0	153	147	150	19.2	100	19.2	0.6	(*)	19.8
Irish potatoes	(0.5)	0.4	0.4	(1,001)	852	926	47.2	-	47.2	35.1	-	82.3
Oats	1.5	0.6	1.0	113	-	113	14.5	92	13.3	-	-	13.3
Buckwheat	-	1.1	1.1	-	87	87	12.2	-	12.2	6.8	-	19.0
Black beans	(0.4)	2.0	1.2	(155)	110	132	20.2	-	20.2	-	-	20.2
Mung beans	-	2.1	2.1	-	102	102	27.3	-	27.3	-	-	27.3
Sesame	2.2	0.9	1.6	78	-	78	15.9	115	18.3	1.0	-	19.3
Hemp crops[b]	(0.1)	0.5	0.3	(146)	-	146	5.5	-	5.5	1.3	(*)	6.8
Sugar cane	(0.3)	0.4	0.3	(2,068)	-	2,068	78.6	-	78.6	-	-	78.6

(Notes to this table are on the following pages.)

Notes:

- Not available.

(*) Less than 0.05 million piculs.

[a]The figures for wheat, barley, and proso millet include those for spring wheat, hull-less barley, and nonglutinous proso millet.

[b]This group includes jute, hemp, flax, ramie, and other plant fibers. As there are no individual acreage and yield figures, the aggregate figures for the whole group are estimated.

Column (1). Derived from the total cultivated acreage of 998 million mow (see column (2), Table A-1) and the prewar average acreages of these crops in 22 provinces. The crop acreage data are taken from the Bureau's Agricultural Estimates. Figures in parentheses are estimates computed from crop acreages given in Chang, Crop Estimates, pp. 15-20.

Column (2). These are the weighted averages of percentages in eight Agricultural Areas, the weights being the cultivated area in each Area, computed from data given in Land Utilization, Vol. III, pp. 192-199.

Column (3). Average of the Bureau's and Buck's estimates given in columns (1) and (2).

Column (4). Computed from the prewar average annual output and acreages of these crops given in the Bureau's Agricultural Estimates. Figures in parentheses are taken from Chang, Crop Estimates.

Column (5). These are the weighted averages of Buck's most frequent yields in eight Agricultural Areas, the weights being the crop acreage in each Area, computed from data given in Land Utilization, Vol. III, pp. 209-210.

Column (6). Average of the Bureau's and Buck's estimates given in columns (4) and (5).

Column (7). Output figures are obtained by multiplying together our estimated cultivated area for 22 provinces (1,277 million mow in Table A-1), the percentage figures given in column (3), and the yield figures given in column (6). Since the basic data used refer to various years around 1933, the output estimates are estimates of the average annual output for those years, roughly 1929-37.

Column (8). Ratios of the Bureau's estimates of 1933 output to annual averages of its estimates of 1931-37 output, based on data in Agricultural Estimates. They are used to derive our estimates of 1933 output from figures in column (7). Although part of the basic data for the latter are for 1929-31, the use of the 1931-37 average as a

Notes (continued):

base to extrapolate the 1933 output should not result in any serious error, as the average output of the 1929-37 period does not differ significantly from that of 1931-37.

Column (9). Products of column (7) and column (8). Also see note to column (8) above.

Column (10). Output figures for Manchuria are taken from Manchoukuo Yearbook Co., Manchoukuo Yearbook, 1941, Hsinking, 1941, p. 430; Manchoukuo Yearbook, 1942, Hsinking, 1942, p. 425; and Ou, National Income, Vol. I, p. 25.

Column (11). Output figures for Sinkiang are taken from Chang, Crop Estimates. Two adjustments in Chang's data have been made: (a) Chang's data were given in old piculs, which have been converted into Chinese standard weight of shih piculs on the basis of one old picul to 1.2096 shih piculs. (b) Chang's original figures covered only 50 of the 66 hsien in the province. Output for the other 16 hsien is estimated by assuming that the average output in these 16 hsien was equal to the average output in the 50 hsien for which data are available. Chang's data refer to 1929-31 average output. They are used on the assumption that changes in the output between 1929-31 and 1933 are not significant.

Column (12). Sum of the output figures for China proper, Manchuria, and Sinkiang, given in columns (9), (10), and (11).

glutinous paddy rice, peas, broad beans, proso millet, oats, buckwheat, black beans, and mung beans. The potato group includes sweet potatoes and Irish potatoes.

Cottonseed

Data on the 1933 output of cottonseed are not available. Our estimate is based on the information that the weight of cottonseed was normally twice that of lint cotton.[8] Since the 1933 output of lint cotton has been estimated at 19 million piculs (see Table A-9), that of cottonseed is 38 million piculs.

Sugar Beets

This crop was produced chiefly in Manchuria and the northern provinces of Honan, Shansi, and Shantung during the prewar period. The only available record of the output of sugar beets is a 1939 figure of 4.8 million piculs for Manchuria.[9] The 1933 output probably was smaller, in view of the generally increasing trend of total crop production from 1933 to 1939 in that region. However, this probable overestimation is more or less offset by the missing output figure for China proper. The estimate of 4.8 million piculs is taken to be the total output for the whole nation in 1933.

Tea

The output of crude tea leaves in 1933 and adjacent years was estimated by both the Directorate of Statistics and the Central Planning Board of the National Government at around 5 million piculs per year.[10] We use this figure.

Vegetables

The vegetable acreage in China proper is estimated at 26.3 million mow on the basis of Buck's data.[11] To this we added our roughly estimated acreages of 3.7 million mow for Manchuria, Sinkiang and other border provinces to obtain the national total of 30 million mow.

Various estimates of the unit yield of vegetables are available. In this study we use an estimate of 10 piculs per mow derived from a nation-wide survey by the Ministry of Agriculture and Commerce in the 1920s.[12] The Economic Yearbook, 1934, gives the average yield of cabbage, turnips, spinach, onion, celery, and eggplant for Anhwei, Chekiang, Kiangsu, and Shantung provinces in 1933 as 12 piculs per mow.[13] The yields in other provinces should have been lower because of the less favorable agricultural environments. Therefore, a national average yield of 10 piculs per mow appears to be reasonable.

By multiplying the total acreage planted in vegetables, 30 million mow, by the estimated unit yield of 10 piculs per mow, we estimate the national vegetable output to be 300 million piculs in 1933. This is supported by an estimate of prewar vegetable consumption made by the Food and Agriculture Organization of the United Nations (FAO).[14] The FAO study, based on the intake of calories supplied by vegetables, shows that about 268 million piculs of vegetables were consumed annually in China proper. The sum of this amount and the consumption in Manchuria, Sinkiang, and other bordering provinces would be very close to our production figure.

Fruits

An estimate of fruit acreage for China proper at 17.7 million mow is derived from Buck's figures for total "crop-mow area" (total sown acreage of 1,962 million mow)[15] and a share of 0.9 per cent in fruits.[16] The acreage in Manchuria, Tibet, Mongolia, and Sinkiang is estimated at 0.8 million mow on the basis of our estimated cultivated area of 252 million mow in these areas[17] and the assumption that 0.3 per cent of the cultivated area was in fruits. Total fruit acreage for the whole nation is thus 18.5 million mow.

The average yield of fruit in the four eastern-central provinces was reported by the Economic Yearbook, 1934, at about 13 piculs per mow in 1933.[18] It is common knowledge that this average yield is much higher than in other provinces because of the more advanced techniques used in fruit growing and the more favorable natural environment in the four eastern-central provinces. For lack of any quantitative information on the difference between the yields in the four eastern-central provinces and in the others, the average yield in the nation as a whole is simply assumed at 6.5 piculs per mow, or one-half of the higher figure.

Multiplying the estimated total fruit acreage of 18.5 million mow by the estimated unit yield of 6.5 piculs per mow, we estimate the national fruit output in 1933 at 120 million piculs.

OUTPUT OF ANIMAL, FOREST AND FISHERY PRODUCTS

Animal Products

The total value of livestock and poultry and their related products produced in a year consists of the value added during the year by (1) increases in their total numbers and average weights; (2) the numbers utilized; and (3) special products, such as wool, eggs, and silkworm cocoons. There are no reliable data by which changes in the total numbers and the average weights of the various livestock and poultry from 1932 to 1933 can be estimated. In fact, there are no indications that the total numbers and the average weights changed significantly during the early 1930s. We therefore assume that value added during 1933 by increases in the total numbers and average weights of the various livestock and poultry to be negligible. We shall consider only the value added by livestock and poultry utilized and by special products.

Number of livestock and poultry utilized. The numbers utilized are estimated by multiplying the total numbers of the various categories of livestock and poultry and their rates of utilization. Although the Bureau published annual data on livestock and poultry for the early 1930s, the figures for the years prior to 1934 are extremely unreliable. For 1931-33, an annual estimate of animal population was obtained by multiplying the total number of farm households in China proper by the reported average number of livestock and poultry raised in typical "medium farms" during the year. These "medium farms," the meaning of which was not clearly defined, were selected at the discretion of the crop reporters in a few localities.

Having realized that the "medium farms" approach was not reliable, the Bureau decided in 1934 to make sample surveys of 100 randomly chosen farms per locality. Data were collected by crop reporters. By multiplying the total number of farms in a locality by the average number of livestock and poultry per farm in the sample, the total number of livestock and poultry in this locality was estimated. The locality estimates were added to obtain provincial estimates, which in turn were summed up to obtain national figures. From 1934 on, the estimates of the livestock and poultry population were made by this method. The same method had already been used by Buck and his investigators in studying farm conditions during 1929-33. The average number of livestock and poultry in samples of 100 farms in different localities and in all Agricultural Areas are given in Land Utilization.[19] Since the methods used in deriving these two sets of data are similar, an average of these two would yield a better estimate for two reasons. A larger number of observations are thus taken into consideration and the geographical coverage is extended.

Our estimate of the average number of livestock and poultry per farm is obtained by taking the average of Buck's data for 1929-33 and the Bureau's data for 1934 and multiplying by Buck's total number of farm households in China proper, 56.6 million,[20] to obtain the total number of livestock and poultry in China proper. The estimated number of livestock for Manchuria, Sinkiang, and Mongolia in 1933 (or the nearest year) are then added to the figure for China proper to obtain the total number of livestock and poultry in the whole country.

The basic data used in deriving the total number of livestock and poultry covered the prewar years (1929-34). The estimates obtained in Table A-10 are therefore in the nature of annual average figures during these years. These estimates are considered as rough approximations to the 1933 numbers on the assumption that 1933 was about an average year in that period insofar as the size of the animal population is concerned.

We must now estimate the rate of utilization. In addition to the slaughtering of livestock and poultry raised specifically for food, the sale of the bodies of draft animals that died of old age, sickness, or other causes also produced some income to the farmers. To estimate

Table A-10

LIVESTOCK AND POULTRY, 1933

Livestock and poultry	China proper		Manchuria (millions)	Sinkiang (millions)	Mongolia (millions)	Mainland total (millions)
	Number per 100 farms (head)	Total number (millions)				
	(1)	(2)	(3)	(4)	(5)	(6)
Cattle		36.2	1.3	1.2	1.4	40.1
Buffalos	22.7	12.8	-	-	-	-
Oxen	41.3	23.4	-	-	-	-
Horses	7.1	4.0	1.8	1.0	1.6	8.4
Mules	7.1	4.0	0.6	0.1	-	4.7
Donkeys	20.8	11.8	0.6	0.2	-	12.6
Sheep	43.6	24.7	1.7	9.4	15.6	51.4
Goats	28.2	16.0	0.8	-	4.0	20.8
Hogs	113.6	64.3	5.9	-	-	70.2
Chickens	457.7	259.0	9.9	-	-	268.9
Ducks	87.5	49.5	-	-	-	49.5
Geese	14.1	8.0	-	-	-	8.0

Notes:

- Not available.

Column (1). Averages of Buck's and the Bureau's estimates. For Buck's data, see Land Utilization, Vol. III, Table 1, p. 122; for the Bureau's data, see Crop Reports, Vol. 3, No. 10, October 1935.

Column (2). Buck's number of farm households in China proper (56.6 millions) multiplied by figures given in column (1).

Columns (3), (4), and (5). From Ralph W. Phillips, Livestock Improvement in China, Chungking, 1944, and R. W. Phillips, R. G. Johnson, and R. T. Moyer, The Livestock of China, Washington, D. C., U.S. Government Printing Office, 1945.

Column (6). The sum of columns (2), (3), (4), and (5).

the total value so produced, we have to know the number of livestock and poultry slaughtered and the number of those that died of natural causes in a year. Some estimates of the slaughtering rate of each kind of animal are available and are given in Table A-11. There are no data on sales of the bodies of draft animals that died of sickness and other natural causes. Taking into consideration the slaughtering rates and estimated average lengths of life of these animals, we have made our own estimates of the utilization rates in column (2) of Table A-12. By multiplying our estimated utilization rates by the corresponding total number of each kind of animal in 1933, given in column (1) of Table A-12, the numbers of livestock and poultry utilized in the year are obtained. They are given in the last column of Table A-12.

Other animal products. Products in this category are those obtained from livestock and poultry such as eggs, wool, and silkworm cocoons. Because of the meagerness of basic data, only the output of a few major products could be estimated.

(a) Eggs. Briefly, the number of eggs produced by chickens, ducks, and geese in 1933 is estimated in this manner: Number of eggs produced by each kind of poultry = our estimated number of that poultry X percentage that laid eggs X average number of eggs laid annually by each bird. The data are given in Table A-13.

(b) Wool. The procedure for estimating the output of wool, including sheep's wool and goats' hair, is as follows: Wool (hair) output = total number of sheep (goats) X percentage of the total that were producing wool X annual average quantity of wool clipped per head.

Table A-11

SLAUGHTER RATES BASED ON TOTAL ANIMAL POPULATION
(per cent)

Livestock	Ministry of Agriculture and Forestry (1)	Chang and Hwang (2)	Hsu (3)
Water buffalos	5	5	-
Oxen	12	10	-
Yaks and bison	20	20	-
Horses, mules, donkeys	5	-	-
Sheep	30	30	50
Goats	40	40	45
Hogs	70	80	-

Notes:

- Not available.

Column (1). Ministry of Agriculture and Forestry, National Government, Nung-lin t'ung-chi shou-t'se (Handbook of Agricultural and Forest Statistics), Nanking, 1948, p. 59.

Column (2). Chang Chung-wan and Hwang Wei-yi, Tsu-kuo ti hsu-mo yu hsu-chan tzu-yuan (Animal Husbandry and Animal Products of Our Fatherland), Shanghai, Yung-hsiang Book Co., 1953, p. 207.

Column (3). Hsu Cheng-ying, Chung-kuo chih hsu-mo (Animal Husbandry in China), Shanghai, Yung-hsiang Book Co., 1950, p. 41.

Table A-12

LIVESTOCK AND POULTRY UTILIZED, 1933

Livestock and Poultry	Total number (millions)	Per cent utilized	Number utilized (millions)
	(1)	(2)	(3)
Cattle	40.1	15	6.0
Horses	8.4	10	0.8
Mules	4.7	10	0.5
Donkeys	12.6	10	1.3
Sheep and goats	72.2	40	28.9
Hogs	70.2	80	56.2
Chickens	268.9	100	268.9
Ducks	49.5	100	49.5
Geese	8.0	100	8.0

Notes:

Column (1). Taken from the last column in Table A-10.

Column (2). The utilization rates are estimated as follows:

Cattle. The slaughtering rate of this group has been estimated by the various sources listed in Table A-11 to be around 12 per cent. This probably did not include cattle that died of natural causes. Assuming that the average length of life of cattle was somewhat higher than six years (including cattle slaughtered and those that died of natural causes), we adjusted the utilization rate upward to 15 per cent of cattle population each year.

Horses, mules, and donkeys. The slaughtering rate of this group of draft animals was estimated to be 5 per cent by the various sources listed in Table A-11. When those that died of natural causes are also included, the percentage would be much higher. We thus assumed the utilization rate of this group to be 10 per cent of their total population.

Sheep and goats. The slaughtering rate of this group of animals was estimated in Table A-11 from 30 to 50 per cent of their total population in

Notes (continued):

a year. As a large part of this group were slaughtered before they reached old age, the average slaughtering rate of 40 per cent is accepted as our utilization rate.

Hogs. Since hogs are raised primarily for meat and other products, their slaughtering rate, 80 per cent of their total population in a year, is also considered to be their utilization rate.

Poultry. As most poultry are utilized within one year of birth, the utilization rate is assumed to be 100 per cent of the poultry population in each year.

Column (3). Column (1) times column (2).

Table A-13

PRODUCTION OF EGGS, 1933

Poultry	Total number of poultry (millions) (1)	Number of egg-laying poultry (millions) (2)	Annual number of eggs laid (per head) (3)	Total number of eggs produced (millions) (4)
Chickens	268.9	134.4	90	12,096
Ducks	49.5	24.8	80	1,984
Geese	8.0	4.0	70	280

Notes:

Column (1). Taken from the last column of Table A-10.

Column (2). Column (1) times 50 per cent. Egg-laying birds are assumed to be 50 per cent of the total. See Chang Chung-ko and Hwang wai-yi, *Tsu-kuo ti hsu-mo yu hsu-chan tzu-yuan* (Animal Husbandry and Animal Products of Our Fatherland), Shanghi, Yung-hsiang Book Co., 1953, p. 213.

Column (3). Estimated on the basis of information from the following sources: *Ibid.*, pp. 143-149 and 213; Hsu Cheng-ying, *Chung-kuo chih hsu-mo* (Animal Husbandry of China), Shanghai, Yung-hsiang Book Co., 1950, pp. 29-31; and U.S. Department of Agriculture, *Report of the China-United States Agricultural Mission*, Washington, D. C., Government Printing Office, 1947, p. 265.

Column (4). Column (2) times column (3).

Total number of sheep in 1933 was estimated to be 51.4 million head,[21] of which 70 per cent, or 36 million head, were sheared; on the average, 2.5 catties of wool were obtained per sheep.[22] The wool output so computed is 0.9 million piculs.

Of the total number of goats in 1933 (20.8 million head),[23] an estimated 60 per cent, or 12.5 million head, were sheared. With each goat producing two catties of hair,[24] the total hair output comes to 0.25 million piculs. The aggregate output of wool and hair is therefore estimated to be 1.15 million piculs.

(c) Silkworm cocoons. Production of cocoons consists of those produced by domesticated silkworms and "wild" silkworms.[25] The output of cocoons is derived indirectly from the prewar data on raw silk production.

The average annual output of raw silk in the 1930s has been estimated at around 320,000 piculs.[26] According to reports based on field studies, about 13 piculs of fresh cocoons are required to reel one picul of raw silk.[27] The total cocoon output is thus estimated to be 4.2 million piculs.

Wild silk was produced primarily in Liaoning province of Manchuria. The 1933 output of wild cocoons in Manchuria was estimated to be about 0.5 million piculs.[28] A small number of wild cocoons was also produced in Shantung and Honan provinces of China proper, and the annual output was estimated to be 0.1 million piculs.[29] Deducting the sum of these two, 0.6 million piculs, from the national total cocoon output of 4.2 million piculs, we estimate the output of domesticated cocoons to be 3.6 million piculs.

Forest Products

Since the gross value of timber and general forest products in 1933 was directly estimated, their output figures are not presented here.[30] The only output that needs to be separately estimated is that of tung nuts. No information is available on the 1933 output of tung nuts in China, but it can be derived indirectly from the data on the production of tung oil.

The prewar average annual production of tung oil has been estimated to be about 3.0 million piculs.[31] Based on an extraction ratio of 100 piculs of tung nuts to 28 piculs of tung oil,[32] a total quantity of 10.7 million piculs of tung nuts was required to produce the 3.0 million piculs of tung oil. This 10.7 million piculs is accepted as the output of tung nuts for 1933. Since the tung oil plant is a perennial, no allowance is made for seeds.

Fishery Products

Our estimate of output of fishery products for China proper in 1933 amounted to 29.4 million piculs. Since this estimate was obtained partially from the data on total value of fishery production and an estimated unit price, the explanation of this estimate will be presented in Appendix E.

FOOTNOTES TO APPENDIX A

1. See Table 30 and the discussion following the table.

2. Land Utilization, Vol. III, p. 238. Buck's original data were given at the locality level, which have been aggregated by province.

3. See Crop Reports, Vol. II, No. 8, 1934, and Vol. 6, No. 10, 1938.

4. Land Utilization, Vol. III, p. 238; Shen Tsung-han, Agricultural Resources, Ithaca, N.Y., Cornell University Press, 1951, p. 201; and Crop Reports, Vol. II, No. 8, 1934.

5. Crop output in Sikang, Mongolia, Tibet, and the special municipalities and districts are not separately estimated because of the lack of data. However, as agricultural production in these areas is very small, it is included in our estimate of the miscellaneous products.

6. Wheat, millet, kaoliang, corn, barley, glutinous rice, peas, broad beans, proso millet, sweet potatoes, soybeans, peanuts, rapeseed, cotton, and tobacco.

7. Irish potatoes, oats, buckwheat, black beans, mung beans, sesame, hemp crops, and sugar cane.

8. Bureau of Foreign Trade, National Government, Mien-tze-yu (Cottonseed Oil), Changsha, 1940, p. 6; and Shen, p. 248.

9. Japan-Manchoukuo Yearbook Co., Japan-Manchoukuo Yearbook, 1941, Tokyo, 1941, p. 688; and Manchoukuo Yearbook Co., Manchoukuo Yearbook, 1941, Hsinking, 1941, pp. 435-438.

10. The Directorate of Statistics' estimate of the 1933 tea output is 4.9 million piculs. The Central Planning Board's figure is the prewar average annual output for the whole nation. Central Planning Board, National Government, Wu-tse chien-she wu-nien chi-hua tsao-an ti-yao (Draft Five Year Plan for Economic Reconstruction), Chungking, 1945, Chapter 5, Table 3.

11. Buck estimated that the vegetable acreage was 2 per cent of his figure for total cultivated area, 1,317 million mow. (Land Utilization, Vol. III, pp. 192-199.)

12. Quoted in Tsou Hsu-pu and Chang Hsiao-mei, Chung-kuo chan-hou nung-yeh chien-she chi-hua kang-yao (Outline of Postwar Agricultural Reconstruction Plan in China), Chengtu, 1944, p. 117.

13. Economic Yearbook, 1934, pp. F141-F142.

14. Food Balance Sheet, pp. 239-241.

15. This is obtained by multiplying Buck's total cultivated area of 1,317 million mow by the double cropping index, 1.49. (Land Utilization, Vol. I, p. 216.)

16. Ibid., p. 209.

17. See Table A-1.

18. Economic Yearbook, 1934, pp. F141-142.

19. Land Utilization, Vol. III, p. 122.

20. Buck's total number of farm households is two million more than C. C. Chang's estimate of 54.6 million for the same territory. (Chang, Crop Estimates, p. 13.)

21. Table A-10, column (6).

22. Chang Chung-wan and Hwang Wei-yi, Tsu-kuo ti hsu-mo yu hsu-chan tzu-yuan (Animal Husbandry and Animal Products of Our Fatherland), Shanghai: Yung-hsiang Book Co., 1953, pp. 127, 199, and 209.

23. Table A-10, column (6).

24. Chang and Hwang, pp. 127 and 209.

25. Production figures of silkworm cocoons are computed by weight of fresh (not dried) cocoons only.

26. Basic information is obtained from the following estimates: T. H. Shen - 330,000 piculs (Shen, p. 319); C. Y. W. Meng - 304,600 piculs (C. Y. W. Meng, "Our Silk, Tung Oil, and Tea," China Trade Monthly, March 1947, Shanghai, pp. 161-162); Central Planning Board - 302,000 piculs (Central Planning Board, Chapter 5, Table 3).

27. This is the finding of five different surveys made on the Chinese silk reeling industry. Ou, National Income, Vol. II, p. 102.

28. This figure is derived from a total value of wild cocoons produced in Manchuria at 10 million (1933) yuan with the price of wild cocoons at 20 yuan/picul in 1933. See Manchoukuo Yearbook Co., Manchoukuo Yearbook, 1934, Hsinking, p. 277, and Appendix B.

29. Industrial Handbook: Shantung, pp. H68-H69.

30. For the gross value produced by timber and general forest products, see Appendix E.

31. The following estimates of the prewar average annual output of tung oil are available: China Vegetable Oil Corporation, 2.0 million piculs (Shen, p. 252); China-United States Agricultural Mission, 2.4 million piculs (U.S. Department of Agriculture, Report of the China-U.S. Agricultural Mission, Washington, D.C., Government Printing Office, 1947, p. 131); Foreign Trade Commission, 2.7 million piculs (Yen Kuang-kuo, Tung-yu (Tung Oil), Shanghai, Cheng-chung Book Co., 1947, p. 21); Tsou and Chang, over 3.0 million piculs (Tsou, p. 130); Central Planning Board, 3.2 million piculs (Central Planning Board, Chapter 5, Table 3).

32. Tsou Hsu-pu, Chung-kuo yu-tung yu tung-yu (China's Tung Plant and Tung Oil), Shanghai, Chung-hua Book Co., 1944, p. 109.

Appendix B

FARM PRICES IN 1933

This appendix presents detailed information on our estimates of the 1933 farm prices of individual agricultural products, given in Table 34. The first section explains the sources of the data used and is followed by a section on the method used in arriving at the estimates. The next section contains an evaluation of the reliability of the estimates by comparing our farm prices for 1933 with those estimated in previous studies and with the average farm prices for 1933-35. Detailed data and the procedure of estimating the farm prices of each individual product are presented in the last section.

SOURCES OF DATA

Systematic collections of data on prices received by farmers in the early 1930s were made by the National Agricultural Research Bureau and other research institutions. The results of these studies were published mostly in the form of price indexes without showing the original price quotations.[1] We therefore could not use their findings to estimate absolute prices. Also, the lack of many local newspapers for 1933 prevented us from piecing together the primary price quotations to arrive at average prices for the nation as a whole.

The main source of our data is a Post Office Administration publication, which provides detailed information on the prices of major products in a large number of townships and marketing places along mail routes all over the nation.[2] Data were gathered from 22 provinces of China proper, Sikang, and Sinkiang. The four Manchurian provinces -- Heilungkiang, Jehol, Kirin, and Liaoning -- were excluded because the Japanese occupied these regions during that time. General information was collected by mail inquiry and by mail carriers directly from rural communities, mainly in 1934 and 1935. The reported prices presumably represent average prices for the 1933-35 period.

Because of the wide geographical coverage of this Post Office survey, its price data are believed to include all major producing areas. While the survey might not have covered some remote regions where mail routes had not been established, it did cover most of the rural areas. In the remote and inaccessible areas, farm prices were almost entirely governed by local harvest conditions because of limited marketability of their farm products and the absence of supply from outside sources. These prices might have been somewhat different from the prices in the more accessible areas along the mail routes, but there is no reason to believe that they were consistently higher or lower than the national level.

The second source of our data is a set of Industrial Handbooks of China,[3] published by the Bureau of Foreign Trade of the Ministry of Industry during 1933-37. The set consists of five volumes, each of which is devoted to the survey of the economy of a particular province: Chekiang, Hunan, Kiangsu, Shansi, and Shantung. These volumes contain some data on the prices of agricultural products in rural producing areas.

Most of the prices obtained from the two sources mentioned above are for the years 1933-35. We feel that estimates obtained from these data can be taken to represent 1933 prices; the evaluation of our estimates shows that the average prices of the 1933-35 period were about the same level as the 1933 prices.

Farm prices in Manchuria are obtained from the Economic Handbook of Northeast China.[4] Figures obtained from this source are not very satisfactory, but the paucity of price data in this area leaves us with no other choice. In 1933 Manchuria was under Japanese occupation. Very little is known about whether any field study of farm prices was made. The price data used are prices of principal farm products sold in Agricultural Produce Exchanges in 1933 in the cities of Harbin, Dairen, Changchun, and Shenyang (Mukden). These prices, assumed to be the prices paid to the farmers at the Exchange, might have included some freight and handling expenses. As the farmers themselves customarily transport most of their produce by using their own draft animals and wooden carts, freight costs should have been very small. On the other hand, these prices are much lower than the farm prices then prevailing in China proper. Therefore, it is uncertain whether they are biased upward or downward. However, any such bias should be small, and should not materially affect the estimates arrived at in this appendix.

In addition, scattered price quotations for certain products in 1933 are taken from other official and private studies. Reference will be made to these miscellaneous sources later in this appendix.

METHOD OF ESTIMATE

The methods used in computing the national average prices are generally as follows: For those products for which price data are abundant, an arithmetic average price for each producing province is calculated from local prices in that province. The provincial average prices are then weighted by their respective quantities of prewar output of the product in question to obtain a national average price. For those products for which available price data are scanty, a simple average price is computed, or a representative price is chosen from local prices to indicate the national price of each product.

In arriving at the price data used in our estimation, local measurements of weights and volumes have been converted into standard units. So far as practical, only prices directly received by farmers, or prices quoted in rural markets of the producing areas, have been used. Consideration was also given to the seasonal patterns of the prices.

EVALUATION OF OUR ESTIMATES

A comparison of our estimated 1933 farm prices in certain regions with the corresponding city wholesale prices in those regions was made in Chapter IV, and the result appears to be fairly reasonable.[5] A further support of the validity of these estimates is a comparison with other published estimates and with the average farm prices for the 1933-35 period made in this section.

Our Estimates Compared with Previous Estimates

Farm prices for 1933 were previously estimated by the Bureau, P. S. Ou, and T. C. Liu. Although all three of these estimates are believed to have been carefully made, they are not used in the present study for the reasons explained below.

During the years 1931-36, the Bureau engaged in the compilation of indexes of prices received by farmers. Price data were collected from more than 1,000 localities in 22 provinces of China proper. Most of the important producing areas of major agricultural products were represented, especially in the data for 1933-35. These index numbers were published in Crop Reports. However, the original price data in absolute figures were never given, except in the case of tea, livestock, and poultry. Some of the Bureau's farm prices of principal crops were quoted by Ou in his income study, although he did not give the source of these absolute figures; nor did he use these price data in arriving at his own estimates.[6] Ou did not accept the Bureau's farm prices because the Bureau's prices were higher than the wholesale prices of the same products in the two seaports of Shanghai and Tientsin. He believed that the wholesale prices were more reliable. The Bureau's data might have their shortcomings, but Ou's reasoning is not well founded.

Ou's estimates were based almost entirely upon the wholesale prices of agricultural products in Shanghai (Eastern Central China) and North China (presumably Tientsin). The sources of his information were not given. By deducting 25 per cent for shipping, processing, and marketing costs from the wholesale prices, Ou obtained his "producers' prices." Whether a flat 25 per cent reduction on wholesale prices of all products can be used to arrive at the farmers' realized prices is questionable. The main defect, however, is that the wholesale prices in Shanghai and Tientsin are far from being representative of national wholesale prices. The wholesale prices of agricultural products in such large seaport cities as Shanghai and Tientsin were often lower than in inland cities. This was especially true of rice and wheat, as they were highly affected by the quantities and prices of imported grains.

One of the present authors derived his 1933 farm prices by discounting 20 per cent of the unit value of domestic agricultural products moved between inland ports in that year.[7] Data on unit values, that is, the total value divided by the corresponding total quantity, were reported by the Inspector General of Customs of the National Government. Since the Customs Offices were established in only a very limited number of inland ports, the geographical representation of these unit values, and hence that of the resultant farm prices, is quite restricted.

These three sets of estimates are reproduced in Table B-1 for comparison with our own estimates. It is seen that the present estimates lie within the wide range set by the previous ones.

Comparison of 1933 Farm Prices with the Average Prices for 1933-35

It was mentioned earlier that most of the data we used refer to prices for the years 1933-35. In this subsection we shall show that the average farm prices of major agricultural products in this three-year period were about the same as in 1933. The evidence consists of two price indexes, one compiled by the Bureau and the other by the Farmer's Bank of China.

The Bureau's index numbers of farm prices were given by quarter at the hsien level. Before using them, annual average indexes for each product at the national level were computed. Then the average

Table B-1

FARM PRICES IN 1933: AUTHORS' ESTIMATES COMPARED WITH PREVIOUS ESTIMATES

(yuan per picul)

Product	Our Estimate[a]	Bureau's Estimate[b]	Ou's Estimate[c]	Liu's Estimate[d]
Paddy rice	3.5	3.64	2.02	3.76
Wheat	4.6	5.14	3.08	2.56
Millet	3.6	6.37	3.00	-
Kaoliang	2.8	3.85	1.89	-
Corn	2.9	3.20	2.00	-
Soybeans	3.9	4.72	2.79	-
Rapeseed	5.9	6.06	4.47	3.62
Peanuts	5.2	9.67	3.82	4.34
Cotton	31.4	39.83	24.90	26.89
Tobacco	17.0	16.94	16.95	19.38

Notes and Sources:

- Prices of these individual products were not given.

[a] See text of this appendix.

[b] Taken from Ou, National Income, Vol. I, p. 26.

[c] Ibid., p. 38.

[d] Liu, Income, p. 22.

indexes for the 1933-35 period, with 1933 as the base year, were obtained. The results are summarized in Table B-2.

It is seen that the three-year average prices of these products are at levels close to those of the 1933 prices. This is especially true for the most important products, such as paddy rice, wheat, cotton, and wool. With regard to millet, kaoliang, and soybeans, some differences did exist between the 1933-35 average prices and the 1933 prices. However, we do not believe that proper adjustments can be made on the basis of these price indexes. Since the Bureau's original price data for these crops did not cover all major producing areas for each of the years under investigation, the margin of error of the Bureau's indexes might have been substantial. Adjustments made on the basis of these indexes would not result in any improvement in the accuracy of the estimates. Hence average prices for 1933-35 are taken as approximations of those in 1933.

Another index of farm prices was prepared by the Research Department of the Farmer's Bank of China. The Farmer's Bank published some figures for the general price level of farm products by province without breakdowns by commodities. The original absolute prices and method of compilation are not given. From these provincial indexes, the national indexes for each year and the average index for the three-year period have been computed and are presented in Table B-3. The 1933-35 national average index, with 1933 as the base year, is 100. This again supports our contention that the use of the 1933-35 average prices to represent the prices in 1933 is an acceptable approximation.

Table B-2

THE BUREAU'S INDEX OF FARM PRICES, 1933-35

(1933 = 100)

Product	1933	1934	1935	1933-35 average
Paddy rice	100	97	104	100
Wheat	100	90	105	98
Millet	100	90	99	96
Kaoliang	100	78	94	91
Proso millet	100	89	105	98
Soybeans	100	89	97	95
Cotton	100	99	98	99
Wool	100	102	100	101

Source:

Based on data from Crop Reports, Vol. 4, Nos. 5 to 9, and 11; Vol. 5, Nos. 1, and 7 to 11; Vol. 6, Nos. 1, 2, and 4 to 6, Nanking-Chungking, May 15, 1936 to June 15, 1938.

Table B-3

FARMER'S BANK INDEXES BY PROVINCE, 1933-35

(1933 = 100)

Province	1933	1934	1935
Fukien	100	97	97
Hupeh	100	127	170
Kiangsi	100	100	106
Kwangsi	100	92	83
Kwangtung	100	102	110
Kweichow	100	88	95
Shansi	100	65	67
Szechwan	100	106	106
National average:			
Annual	100	97	104
1933-35 average		100	

Source:

Chung-nung ching-chi t'ung-chi (Economic Statistics of the Farmers' Bank of China), Chungking, Vol. 2, No. 7, July 31, 1942.

ESTIMATION OF FARM PRICES OF INDIVIDUAL PRODUCTS

The detailed procedures for estimating the national prices of individual products (summarized in Table 34) and the basic data used for their derivation are described below.

Paddy Rice

The farm prices of nonglutinous paddy rice for 102 hsien in 19 provinces are available in the *Survey*. Except for the prices in Szechwan and Sinkiang provinces, which had to be discarded because of the difficulty involved in converting the local weight and currency into standard units, the average prices in the various provinces are computed and are given in the first column of Table B-4.

From the *Industrial Handbooks*, average prices of paddy rice can be computed for Hunan and Kiangsu provinces. As presented in the second column of Table B-4, they are fairly close to the *Survey* figures in the corresponding provinces.

The average price received by farmers in Szechwan province is derived from data collected by the Szechwan Agricultural Improvement Bureau in 15 hsien of the province and is given in the third column of Table B-4.

From the above sources, an average price for each rice producing province is computed.[8] These average prices are then weighted by our estimated prewar rice output in each province to obtain a national average price of paddy rice at 3.5 yuan/picul. This price represents the average price of 96 per cent of the nation's total paddy rice output.

Table B-4

FARM PRICES OF PADDY RICE, 1933

Province	Price (yuan/picul) Survey[a]	Industrial Handbook[b]	Szechwan[c]	Our estimate	Weight (per cent)[d]
Anhwei	3.3			3.3	4.64
Chahar	4.8			4.8	0.02
Chekiang	4.2			4.2	6.37
Fukien	5.5			5.5	3.47
Honan	1.8			1.8	0.71
Hopei	6.4			6.4	0.21
Hunan	2.5	2.6		2.5	15.82
Hupeh	3.5			3.5	8.21
Kansu	5.3			5.3	0.01
Kiangsi	3.3			3.3	5.80
Kiangsu	3.4	3.7		3.5	8.61
Kwangsi	3.9			3.9	5.15
Kwangtung	5.1			5.1	12.58
Kweichow	3.0			3.0	3.09
Shansi	2.7			2.7	0.01
Shensi	4.9			4.9	0.22
Szechwan			2.7	2.7	20.18
Yunnan	3.3			3.3	4.90
			National average	3.5	Total 100.00

Notes:

[a] The provincial price is the average of locality prices in each province, obtained from various chapters of the Survey.

[b] Industrial Handbooks: Hunan, p. G123; Kiangsu, Chapter 5, pp. 28-31.

[c] See Szechwan Agricultural Improvement Bureau, Sze-chwan nung-tsun wu-chia chih-shu (Farm Price Index of Szechwan), Chengtu, 1942. These were originally the 1937 prices but are accepted as the 1933 prices. The farm price indexes released by the Bureau show that the 1937 rice price in the Chengtu area of Szechwan was about the same as the 1933 price. Crop Reports, Vol. 6, No. 11, November 15, 1938, p. 129.

[d] The weights are the percentage shares of the respective provinces in the total output of rice during the prewar period. See Appendix A, Table A-4.

Wheat

Farm prices of wheat in some 70 localities of 19 provinces can be found in the Survey. The average price in each of the 17 provinces is computed. (Szechwan and Sinkiang are left out because their local weight and currency units have not been defined.) Industrial Handbooks provided the provincial prices of wheat in Hunan, Shantung, and Shansi, and also hsien prices in Kiangsu and Chekiang from which provincial average prices can be calculated. An average of the two is computed for each province when both sets of prices are available. For Szechwan, the average farm price collected by the Szechwan Agricultural Research Bureau is used in this study. All the provincial prices are given in Table B-5. Using the Bureau's prewar average output of wheat in each province as the weight, the weighted average price for the nation comes to 4.6 yuan/picul. This price covers 18 provinces, where over 92 per cent of China's wheat crops were produced.

Miscellaneous Food Crops

The crops in this category, including millet, kaoliang, corn, barley, glutinous paddy rice, peas, broad beans, proso millet, mung beans, black beans, buckwheat, and oats, are treated as one group in the agricultural statistics published by the Communists. For convenience of comparison with Communist figures, a prewar average price (in 1933 yuan) of all the crops in this group is needed. We shall therefore present not only the estimates of the individual crop prices for 1933, but also the average price of the group as a whole.

Millet (Table B-6). The estimated farm price of millet in China proper, 4.0 yuan/picul, is a weighted average of provincial prices given for seven

Table B-5

FARM PRICE OF WHEAT, 1933

Province	Survey	Price (yuan/picul) Industrial handbooks[b]	Szechwan[c]	Our estimate	Weight (per cent)[d]
Anhwei	4.2			4.2	6.92
Chahar	5.0			5.0	0.61
Chekiang	5.0	4.6		4.8	2.59
Fukien	5.5			5.5	1.25
Honan	4.2			4.2	19.90
Hopei	7.1			7.1	8.92
Hunan	4.4	4.0		4.2	1.32
Hupeh	4.5			4.5	6.33
Kansu	3.8			3.8	1.83
Kiangsi	4.0			4.0	1.86
Kiangsu	3.7	5.8		4.7	14.42
Kwangsi	4.0			4.0	1.12
Kwangtung	4.3			4.3	0.61
Kweichow	2.5			2.5	1.22
Shansi	3.7	4.5		4.1	4.13
Shantung	5.0	3.5		4.3	17.53
Suiyuan	5.3			5.3	0.59
Szechwan			4.2	4.2	8.85
			National average	4.5	100.00

Notes:

[a]The Survey's provincial prices are averages of local prices in each province.

[b]Industrial Handbooks: Chekiang, pp. D76-D79; Hunan, p. G197; Kiangsu, Chapter 5, pp. 72-74; Shansi, p. D16; Shantung, p. E21.

[c]See note (c) to Table B-4.

[d]The weights are the percentage shares of the respective provinces in the total output of wheat during 1931-37. Agricultural Estimates, p. 4.

Table B-6

FARM PRICE OF MILLET, 1933

Area	Price (yuan/picul)			Weight (per cent)[b]
	Survey	Industrial Handbooks[a]	Our estimate	
Provinces - China proper				
Chahar	3.4		3.4	3.57
Honan	3.5		3.5	20.21
Hopei	5.1		5.1	26.66
Kansu	2.0		2.0	3.57
Shansi	3.0	2.8	2.9	13.41
Shantung	4.2	4.2	4.2	32.06
Yunnan	2.5		2.5	0.52
Weighted average			4.0	Total 100.00
All Mainland				
China proper			4.0[c]	74.90
Manchuria			2.5[c]	25.10
National average			3.6	Total 100.00

Notes:

[a] Industrial Handbooks: Shansi, pp. D66 and D326-27; Shantung, p. E307.

[b] The weights of the respective provinces are the percentage shares in the total output of millet in these provinces during the 1931-37 period, based upon data from Agricultural Estimates, p. 53. The weights for China proper and Manchuria are the percentage shares of the respective areas in the national output of millet in 1933. See Appendix A, Table A-9.

[c] Price for China proper from weighted average; price for Manchuria from data given in Northeast Economic Handbook, Vol. 3, Chapter 8, Table 170.

provinces in the Survey and for Shansi and Shantung in the Industrial Handbooks. The data cover about 86 per cent of the prewar millet production in China proper. In Manchuria, the 1933 price of millet is estimated at 2.5 yuan/picul. The weighted average price of China proper and Manchuria, 3.6 yuan/picul, is taken as our estimate of the national price of millet.

Kaoliang (Table B-7). The farm prices of Kaoliang are reported by the Survey and the Industrial Handbooks in nine provinces, where about 77 per cent of the kaoliang crops of China proper were produced. The provincial prices are weighted by their corresponding prewar output to arrive at an average price of 3.4 yuan/picul for China proper.

Our estimated national price of kaoliang, 2.8 yuan/picul, is the weighted average of 3.4 yuan/picul in China proper and 1.6 yuan/picul in Manchuria, the weights being our estimated prewar outputs in the respective areas.

Corn (Table B-8). The farm prices of corn are available for nine major producing provinces, which accounted for about 73 per cent of the total output of corn in China proper. By using the prewar average output of each province as the weight, the average price in these provinces is 3.2 yuan/picul. The corn price in Manchuria is estimated at 1.6 yuan/picul in 1933. The average price of corn for China as a whole comes to 2.9 yuan/picul, the weights being the respective prewar output of Manchuria and that of the rest of the nation.

Barley (Table B-9). From the Survey and the Industrial Handbooks, farm prices of barley in eight provinces were obtained. The simple average of these provincial prices, 3.8 yuan/picul, is used as the national price in 193[illegible]

Glutinous paddy rice (Table B-9). The estimated national price of 4.1 yuan/picul is obtained by taking a simple average of the three provincial prices from the Survey and the Industrial Handbooks.

Table B-7

FARM PRICES OF KAOLIANG, 1933

Area	Price (yuan/picul) Survey	Industrial Handbooks[a]	Our estimate	Weight (per cent)[b]
Provinces - China proper				
Chahar	2.8		2.8	4.70
Chekiang		3.1	3.1	0.18
Honan	3.5		3.5	21.01
Hopei	4.5		4.5	18.53
Hunan	5.5		5.5	0.55
Kiangsu	2.2		2.2	9.95
Shansi	1.7	2.4	2.1	8.76
Shantung	2.8	4.3	3.6	35.58
Yunan	1.5		1.5	0.74
Weighted average (total)			3.4	100.00
All Mainland				
China proper			3.4[c]	68.01
Manchuria			1.6[c]	31.99
National average (total)			2.8	100.00

Notes:

[a] Industrial Handbooks: Chekiang, pp. D2 and D142; Shansi, p. D53; Shantung, pp. D122-125 and E47.

[b] The weights of the respective provinces are the percentage shares in the total output of kaoliang during 1931-37. Agricultural Estimates, p. 49. The weights of China proper and Manchuria are the percentage shares in the national total output of kaoliang in 1933. See Appendix A, Table A-9.

[c] Price for China proper from weighted average; price for Manchuria computed from data given in Northeast Economic Handbook, Vol. 3, Chapter 8, Table 170.

Table B-8

FARM PRICES OF CORN, 1933

Area	Price (yuan/picul)				Weight (per cent)[c]
	Survey	Industrial Handbooks[a]	Szechwan[b]	Our estimate	
Provinces-China proper					
Anhwei	4.3			4.3	2.31
Chahar	3.6			3.6	0.52
Chekiang	5.5	6.7		6.1	1.68
Hopei	3.6			3.6	24.74
Kiangsu	2.5			2.5	13.63
Kweichow	1.1			1.1	5.45
Shansi		2.7		2.7	5.87
Shantung		3.0		3.0	16.87
Szechwan			3.7	3.7	28.93
Weighted average (total)				3.2	100.00
All Mainland					
China proper				3.2[d]	81.07
Manchuria				1.6[d]	18.93
National average (total)				2.9	100.00

Notes:

[a] Industrial Handbooks: Chekiang, p. D2; Shansi, pp. D77-78; Shantung, p. E307.

[b] See note (c) to Table B-4.

[c] The weights of the respective provinces are the percentage shares in the total output of corn during 1931-37. Agricultural Estimates, p. 61. The weights of China proper and Manchuria are the percentage shares in the national total output of corn in 1933. See Appendix A, Table A-9.

[d] Price for China proper, weighted average; price for Manchuria is computed from data given in Northeast Economic Handbook, Vol. 3, Chapter 8, Table 170.

Table B-9

FARM PRICES OF BARLEY AND GLUTINOUS RICE, 1933

(yuan per picul)

	Barley Prices			Glutinous Rice Prices		
Province	Survey	Industrial Handbooks	Average	Survey	Industrial Handbooks	Average
Anhwei	2.3		2.3			
Chekiang		3.5	3.5	4.6		4.6
Hopei	6.0		6.0			
Fukien	4.0		4.0			
Hupeh	4.1		4.1			
Kiangsi	2.3		2.3	3.7		3.7
Kiangsu	2.3	3.9	3.1	3.7	4.4	4.1
Kwangsi	5.2		5.2			
National average			3.8			4.1

Source:

Industrial Handbooks: Chekiang, pp. D76-79; Kiangsu, Chapter 5, pp. 72-74, for barley, and pp. 28-31 for glutinous rice.

Peas. The estimated national price of 3.4 yuan/picul is the average of the Survey's prices in four provinces. The provincial prices are (in yuan/picul): Hunan, 3.3; Kansu, 1.9; Kiangsi, 4.0; and Kiangsu, 4.4.

Broad beans (Table B-10). Both the Survey and the Industrial Handbooks reported the farm prices of broad beans in Chekiang and in Kiangsu. A simple average of the two price quotations for each province is taken to represent the price for that province. In addition, prices for Anhwei and Hupeh are given in the Survey. The prices of these four provinces are averaged to arrive at the national price of 4.4 yuan/picul.

Proso millet (Table B-11). Data on prewar farm prices of proso millet in Shansi, Shantung, and Suiyuan are taken from the Survey and the Industrial Handbooks. Our estimated national average price, 3.0 yuan/picul, is a simple average of these provincial prices.

Mung beans. The estimated national price of 4.4 yuan/picul is the average of seven provincial prices obtained from the Survey. The provincial prices are (in yuan/picul): Anhwei, 3.7; Honan, 3.5; Hopei, 8.5; Hupeh, 4.6; Kiangsu, 2.2; Shansi, 2.6; and Shantung, 5.7.

Black beans. By taking the average of the prices in five provinces from the Survey, the national price of black beans is estimated at 3.4 yuan/picul. The provincial prices are (in yuan/picul): Honan, 2.5; Hopei, 4.8; Kwangsi, 3.0; Shansi, 2.1; and Shensi, 4.7.

Buckwheat and oats. Data on farm prices of buckwheat and oats in 1933 are not available. These prices are believed to be approximately the same as the price of barley, one of the most important crops in this group. The estimated national price of barley, 3.8 yuan/picul, is therefore also considered as the price of both buckwheat and oats.

Table B-10

FARM PRICES OF BROAD BEANS, 1933

(yuan per picul)

Province	Survey	Industrial Handbooks	Average
Anhwei	4.5		4.5
Chekiang	3.5	5.0	4.3
Hupeh	3.5		3.5
Kiangsu	4.4	6.3	5.4
National average			4.4

Sources:

Industrial Handbooks: Chekiang, pp. D98-D99; Kiangsu, Chapter 5, pp. 97-99.

Table B-11

FARM PRICES OF PROSO MILLET, 1933

(yuan per picul)

Province	Survey	Industrial Handbooks	Average
Shansi		2.5	2.5
Shantung	3.1	4.5	3.8
Suiyuan	2.7		2.7
National average			3.0

Sources:

Industrial Handbooks: Shansi, pp. D326-D327; Shantung, p. H307.

Miscellaneous food crops as a group (Table B-12). The average price for the crops in this group amounts to 3.4 yuan/picul, the weights being our estimated 1933 output of the respective crops.

Potatoes

Sweet potatoes. The estimated national average farm price of sweet potatoes, 1.1 yuan/picul, is a simple average of seven price quotations in five provinces given in the Survey. The five provinces and their respective average prices are (in yuan/picul): Anhwei, 1.50; Chekiang, 0.85; Hunan, 1.00; Hupeh, 1.50; and Kiangsu, 0.75.

Irish potatoes. The only 1933 price of Irish potatoes available is given in the Industrial Handbook: Shansi.[9] Since Shansi was one of the largest Irish potato producing provinces in prewar China, this price, 0.6 yuan/picul, is used as an approximation to the national average price.

Potatoes as a group. For comparison with potato prices in the postwar period, an average 1933 price for sweet and Irish potatoes as a group has been computed, the weights being their respective prewar output.[10] The result is 1.0 yuan/picul.

Soybeans (Table B-13)

An average price of 4.6 yuan/picul for China proper is obtained on the basis of data for 14 provinces given in the Survey and those for four provinces given in the Industrial Handbooks.

The price of soybeans in 1933 in the nation as a whole, estimated at 3.9 yuan/picul, is the average of 4.6 for China proper and 2.7 for Manchuria, the weights being our estimated prewar output in the respective areas.

Peanuts (Table B-14)

Farm prices of peanuts are available for 11 provinces in the Industrial

Table B-12

AVERAGE PRICE OF MISCELLANEOUS FOOD CROPS AS A GROUP, 1933

Crop	Unit price (yuan/picul)	Weight (per cent)[a]
Millet	3.6	21.8
Kaoliang	2.8	21.5
Corn	2.9	15.9
Barley	3.8	13.0
Glutinous paddy rice	4.1	7.0
Peas	3.4	5.6
Broad beans	4.4	5.2
Proso millet	3.0	3.3
Oats	3.8	1.1
Buckwheat	3.8	1.6
Black beans	3.4	1.7
Mung beans	4.4	2.3
Weighted average	3.4	Total 100.00

Note:

[a] The weights are the percentage shares of the individual crops in the output of the whole group. For the outputs of the individual crops see Table A-9.

Table B-13

FARM PRICES OF SOYBEANS, 1933

Area	Price (yuan/picul)			Weig (per c
	Survey	Industrial Handbooks	Our estimate	
Province - China proper				
Anhwei	4.7		4.7	7.8
Chahar	5.5		5.5	0.6
Chekiang	5.9	5.5	5.7	3.2
Honan	3.7		3.7	14.2
Hopei	4.7		4.7	6.0
Hunan	4.4	3.0	3.7	1.6
Hupeh	4.9		4.9	4.1
Kiangsu	4.6	7.2	5.9	21.9
Kwangsi	6.2		6.2	1.9
Kwangtung	8.5		8.5	0.9
Kweichow	2.0		2.0	2.3
Shantung	3.5	4.5	4.0	30.5
Yunnan	2.5		2.5	4.4
Weighted average			4.6	Total 100.0
All Mainland				
China proper			4.6[b]	61.0
Manchuria			2.7[b]	38.9
National average			3.9	Total 100.0

Notes:

[a] The weights of the respective provinces are the percentage shares the total output of soybeans during 1931-37. Agricultural Estimates, p. The weights of China proper and Manchuria are the percentage shares in t national output of soybeans in 1933. See Appendix A, Table A-9.

[b] Price for China proper from weighted average; price for Manchuria computed from data given in the Northeast Economic Handbook, Vol. 3, Chapter 8, Table 169.

Sources:

Industrial Handbooks: Chekiang, pp. D98-99; Hunan, p. G104; Kiangs Chapter 5, pp. 97-99; and Shantung, p. E79.

Table B-14

FARM PRICES OF PEANUTS, 1933

Province	Price (yuan/picul) Survey	Price (yuan/picul) Industrial Handbooks	Our estimate	Weight (per cent)[a]
Anhwei	4.9		4.9	5.22
Fukien	4.9		4.9	3.18
Honan	4.7		4.7	12.25
Hopei	4.8		4.8	19.27
Hunan	5.9	7.0	6.5	2.49
Hupeh	4.6		4.6	4.54
Kiangsu	6.7	5.1	5.9	14.51
Kwangtung	9.8		9.8	7.48
Kweichow	9.0		9.0	2.04
Shansi	5.0		5.0	0.45
Shantung	3.7	3.8	3.8	28.57
National average			5.2	Total 100.00

Note:

[a] The weights are the percentage shares of the respective provinces in the total output of peanuts during 1931-37. *Agricultural Estimates*, p. 77.

Sources:

Industrial Handbooks: *Hunan*, p. G104; *Kiangsu*, Chapter 5, pp. 123-124; and *Shantung*, p. H175.

Handbooks and the Survey. The weighted average of these prices is 5.2 yuan/picul. These 11 provinces accounted for 80 per cent of the nation's total peanut output.

Rapeseed (Table B-15)

Farm prices of rapeseed are available for eight provinces in the Survey and the Industrial Handbooks. Our estimated national prices of 5.9 yuan/picul is a weighted average of these provincial prices.

Sesame (Table B-16)

More than 30 price quotations of sesame are available in the Industrial Handbooks and the Survey, from which 11 provincial prices have been computed. Our estimated national price of 8.0 yuan/picul is the weighted average of these provincial prices. These 11 provinces accounted for 90 per cent of the nation's sesame output.

Cottonseed

Available farm prices of cottonseed range from 1.0 to 3.0 yuan/picul.[1] The average (2.0) of these scattered data is used in this study as the national price.

Cotton (Table B-17)

Our estimated national price of cotton (ginned), 31.4 yuan/picul, is the weighted average of the provincial prices given in the Survey and the Industrial Handbooks for 11 provinces. These data cover about 90 per cent of China's cotton producing areas.

Hemp Crops (Table B-18)

In prewar sources, farm prices of jute, hemp, flax, ramie, and other plant fibers are mostly given as a group. It is thus impossible to estimate their 1933 farm prices separately. Farm prices for the group are available

Table B-15

FARM PRICES OF RAPESEED, 1933

Province	Price (yuan/picul)			Weight (per cent)[a]
	Survey	Industrial Handbooks	Our estimate	
Anhwei	7.1		7.1	12.21
Chekiang	8.3	7.7	8.0	14.62
Hunan	5.2	4.0	4.6	18.24
Hupeh	5.8		5.8	10.64
Kiangsi	5.5		5.5	20.64
Kiangsu	5.8		5.8	12.60
Kwangsi	5.3		5.3	9.20
Shantung		4.5	4.5	1.85
National average			5.9	Total 100.00

Note:

[a] The weights of the respective provinces are the percentage shares in the total output of rapeseed during 1931-37. Agricultural Estimates, p. 20.

Sources:

Industrial Handbooks: Chekiang, pp. D2-5; Hunan, p. G104; and Shantung, p. H175.

Table B-16

FARM PRICES OF SESAME, 1933

Province	Price (yuan/picul) Survey	Industrial Handbooks	Our estimate	Weight (per cent)[a]
Anhwei	8.5		8.5	10.01
Chekiang		9.3	9.3	0.84
Honan	6.6		6.6	29.97
Hopei	11.1		11.1	13.25
Hunan	11.4	8.0	9.7	1.14
Hupeh	6.9		6.9	11.18
Kiangsi	12.1		12.1	5.26
Kiangsu	6.7		6.7	11.26
Kwangsi	7.2		7.2	1.64
Shansi	6.3		6.3	2.73
Shantung	6.7	10.0	8.4	12.72
National average (Total)			8.0	100.00

Note:

[a] The weights of the respective provinces are the percentage shares in the total output of sesame during 1931-37. Agricultural Estimates, p. 81.

Sources:

Industrial Handbooks: Chekiang, p. D2; Hunan, p. G104; Shantung, p. H175.

Table B-17

FARM PRICES OF COTTON, 1933

Province	Price (yuan/picul)[a]		Weight (per cent)[b]
Anhwei	35.0		3.67
Chekiang	26.0		3.75
Honan	33.3		11.79
Hopei	28.0		19.76
Hupeh	36.0		12.24
Kiangsi	29.0		1.86
Kiangsu	30.9		23.81
Kwangsi	41.0		0.61
Shansi	32.0		4.34
Shantung	30.5		12.43
Shensi	34.0		5.74
National average	31.4	Total	100.00

Notes:

[a] Except for Shantung, these are the average local prices in each province given in the Survey. The Shantung figure is the average of the Survey's 23.0 and the Industrial Handbook's 38.0 yuan. Industrial Handbook: Shantung, p. E179.

[b] The weights are the percentage shares of the respective provinces in the total output of cotton during 1931-37. Agricultural Estimates, p. 73.

Table B-18

FARM PRICES OF HEMP CROPS, 1933

(yuan per picul)

Province	Survey	Industrial Handbooks	Average
Anhwei	20.3		20.3
Chahar	14.6		14.6
Chekiang	12.5		12.5
Hopei	20.5		20.5
Hunan	25.1	25.0	25.1
Hupeh	17.4		17.4
Kiangsi	23.0		23.0
Kiangsu	22.5		22.5
Kwangsi	16.9		16.9
Kwangtung	20.5		20.5
Kweichow	33.8		33.8
Shansi	15.0	11.5	13.3
Shantung	21.7		21.7
National average		Total	20.2

Sources:

Industrial Handbooks: *Hunan*, p. G36, and *Shansi*, p. D150.

for 13 provinces in the Survey and the Industrial Handbooks. Because of the lack of prewar output data for these provinces, a simple average of the provincial prices has been calculated. The result is 20.2 yuan/picul.

Sugar Cane

The price quotations (in yuan/picul) for the major sugar cane producing provinces are as follows: Average price in Kwangtung, Szechwan, Fukien, Kwangsi, and Kiangsi,[12] 0.6; Chekiang, 0.6; Kwangtung, 0.8; Kweichow,[13] 1.2; two prices for Szechwan[14] are given, 0.4 and 0.4 to 0.7. Since most of the prices are below 1 yuan/picul, the figure for Kweichow appears to be much too high. In most regions the price of 0.6 prevailed and since it is near the average of all other figures it is used as the national average price in this study.

Sugar Beets

The prices of sugar beets in 1933 were about 0.6 yuan/picul in Manchuria[15] and 0.85 in the Kwantung Leased Territory.[16] The price in Shansi was about 0.5 yuan/picul.[17] Since Manchuria was the largest beet producing area in China, the price there (0.6) is used as the average price in the nation as a whole.

Tobacco (Table B-19)

Data on the 1933 farm prices of tobacco, including both the flue-cured and the native varieties, are available in Survey, Industrial Handbooks, and an independent study of the Szechwan economy. From these sources the average prices in 12 provinces have been computed. The output of tobacco in these 12 provinces accounted for more than 70 per cent of China's total tobacco production in the prewar period. Our national price of 17.0 yuan/picul is the average of these provincial prices, the weights being the

Table B-19

FARM PRICE OF TOBACCO, 1933

Province	Price (yuan/picul)				Weight (per cent)[b]
	Survey	Industrial Handbooks	Szechwan[a]	Our estimate	
Anhwei	9.5			9.5	4.47
Chekiang	14.5	17.5		16.0	3.90
Fukien	18.8			18.8	2.75
Honan	25.5			25.5	14.17
Hopei	35.0			35.0	4.94
Hunan	21.0	15.3		18.1	7.63
Kiangsi	19.0			19.0	2.87
Kiangsu		18.0		18.0	1.51
Kwangsi	6.0			6.0	4.38
Kwangtung	23.8			23.8	4.25
Shantung	6.2			6.2	16.35
Szechwan			17.0	17.0	32.78
National average (Total)				17.0	100.00

Notes:

[a] Tobacco price ranged from 14.0 to 20.0 yuan/picul in Szechwan in 1933. The average is 17.0. Lu Ping-teng, Sze-chwan nung-tsun ching-chi (Rural Economy of Szechwan), Shanghai, 1936, p. 326.

[b] The weights of the respective provinces are the percentage shares in the total output of tobacco during 1931-37. Agricultural Estimates, p. 85.

Sources:

Industrial Handbooks: Chekiang, p. D2 and p. G213; Hunan, p. D177; and Kiangsu, Chapter 5, p. 241.

prewar output of tobacco in the respective provinces.

Tea

Data on tea prices are available for both crude and refined tea leaves. Only the price of crude tea is considered here, as it represents the price received by tea planters, exclusive of all processing costs. The national price of crude tea used in this study, 25.8 yuan/picul, is the average price obtained by the Bureau in a survey of 14 tea producing provinces in 1933.[18]

Vegetables and Fruits

Data on farm prices of vegetables are so scarce as to be almost non-existent. Vegetable prices must vary a great deal from province to province; nevertheless, the national average wholesale price of vegetables has been roughly estimated in an authoritative source at 3.2 yuan per picul for the prewar years.[19] Since vegetables were never shipped any distance in prewar China and there were almost no processing costs involved, the average price received by farmers may have been approximately 80 per cent of the average wholesale price, or roughly 2.5 yuan/picul. This happens to be the average farm price reported in the Survey for Kwangtung, one of the most important vegetable producing provinces.[20]

Farm prices information on fruits is as scarce as that on vegetables. The national average farm price of fruits is estimated at 6.1 yuan/picul, an average of three data: 4.9 for Chekiang, 3.0 for Hunan and 10.5 for Kiangsu.[21] While this estimate is obtained on very sketchy grounds, it appears to be fairly reasonable when compared with an estimated export price of 7.8 yuan/picul.[22]

Livestock and Poultry

Available data on farm prices of livestock and poultry are summarized in columns (1) to (4) of Table B-20. The prices given in the Survey appear to be reasonable and are accepted in this study; some of them are modified slightly in the light of data from other sources also presented in the table. Data are lacking for mules and geese in the Survey. Within the ranges given for their prices in the other sources, however, we have selected certain levels believed to be reasonable.

The prices given in Table B-20 are for live animals on the farm. However, in the case of draft animals, including horses, mules, donkeys, and the majority of oxen and buffalo, the prices would be lower when they were old, sick, or disabled and could only be sold to slaughtering houses at discount prices.

The discount price of each draft animal is obtained by applying a discount ratio to its regular price. The discount ratios are arrived at on the basis of the following considerations: (1) Next to hogs, cattle are the second largest meat supplier in China, and their hides and bones have valuable industrial uses. Hence, their discount price is assumed to be 70 per cent of their regular price. (2) The regular price of horses, donkeys, and mules is greatly reduced when they are sold to the slaughtering houses, for their meat, hides, and by-products are not highly valued. The discount price of this group is therefore assumed to be only 40 per cent of their regular price. Multiplying these discount ratios by the regular prices of cattle, horses, mules, and donkeys -- 50, 48, 70, and 26 yuan/head respectively (see column (5), Table B-20) -- we obtain the following discoun prices: 35, 19.2, 28, and 10.4 yuan/head.

Other Animal Products

Eggs. Our estimated national price of chicken eggs, 15.0 yuan thousand, is shown in Table B-21. This is a simple average of nine provincial prices

Table B-20

FARM PRICES OF LIVESTOCK AND POULTRY, 1933

(yuan per head)

Animal	Bureau		Industrial Handbooks	Survey	Our estimate
	(1)	(2)	(3)	(4)	(5)
Cattle	26.0-53.0	24.6-33.9	48.9-60.0	51.0	50.0
Horses	48.0	49.4		48.0	48.0
Mules	77.0	68.2			70.0
Donkeys	26.0	28.0		25.0	26.0
Sheep and goats	3.5	2.8-3.4	3.3-4.7	3.8	3.5
Hogs	15.0	17.2	19.3	17.4	17.4
Chickens	0.4	0.6	0.3-0.7	0.4	0.4
Ducks	0.5		0.2-1.0	0.7	0.5
Geese	1.0		1.2-1.4		1.1

Sources:

Column (1). Average prices in China proper taken from Crop Reports, Vol. 3, No. 10, October 10, 1935. Surveys were made in 1934.

Column (2). Quoted by Ou in National Income, Vol. I, p. 36.

Column (3). Industrial Handbooks: Kiangsu, Chapter 5, pp. 344, 352, 361, and 373; Chekiang, pp. D2, D4, and D345-380; Shantung, p. D129.

Column (4). National average prices computed from data given in the various chapters of the Survey.

Column (5). See text of this appendix.

Table B-21

FARM PRICE OF CHICKEN EGGS, 1933

(yuan per thousand)

Province	Survey	Industrial Handbooks	Average
Chahar	13.0		13.0
Chekiang	18.0	20.0	19.0
Honan	9.3		9.3
Hopei	15.3		15.3
Hunan	13.0		13.0
Hupeh	11.0		11.0
Kansu	10.0		10.0
Kiangsu	15.0		15.0
Kwangtung	29.0		29.0
National average			15.0

Source:

Industrial Handbook: *Chekiang*, p. D386.

reported in the Survey and the Industrial Handbooks.

Both the Survey and the Industrial Handbooks reported the price of duck eggs in Chekiang at about 20.0 yuan per thousand.[23] As Chekiang is one of the major egg producing provinces, this price is accepted as the 1933 national average price.

No data on the price of goose eggs are available but since their price was usually the same as duck eggs, we use the same estimated price of 20.0 yuan per thousand.

Wool. Our estimated national price of wool, 22.0 yuan/picul, is a simple average of seven provincial prices obtained from the Survey. The provincial prices (yuan/picul) are: Chekiang, 25.0; Honan, 22.0; Kansu, 20.3; Kiangsu, 22.5; Shansi, 26.4; Suiyuan, 21.5; and Tsinghai, 16.6.

Another source indicates that the 1933 wool price in the northwest wool producing areas was about 24.0 yuan/picul,[24] which is quite close to our average price for the whole country.

Silkworm cocoons. Domesticated. Two kinds of fresh domesticated cocoons were sold by the farmers: "improved cocoons" produced by improved breeds of silkworm, which customarily brought higher prices, and "native cocoons" produced by native breeds of silkworm. Available price data, however, do not always indicate to what breed of cocoon they refer. Hence, only a mixed average price for both groups is used.

Our national average price for all fresh domesticated cocoons is estimated at 30.0 yuan/picul, based on information gathered in the four largest silk producing provinces. The price ranges (yuan/picul) in these provinces are as follows: Chekiang, 24 to 55; Kiangsu, 23 to 60; Shantung, 33 to 60; and Szechwan, 24 to 50.[25]

We suspect that the higher prices were probably for improved cocoons and the lower prices for native cocoons. Since the output of native cocoons was overwhelmingly larger than that of the improved ones, the weighted average price should lean to the lower side. A national price of 30.0 is therefore used.

Wild cocoons. Data on farm prices of wild cocoons are available only for Shantung province, one of the two major wild silk producing areas. The average price for Shantung is 20.0 yuan/picul[26] and is used as our national average price.

Tung Nuts

Farm prices of tung nuts, ranging from 3.9 to 4.5 yuan/picul, are reported for Chekiang, Kwangsi, and Szechwan provinces from various sources.[27] The lower figure is the result of an extensive investigation on tung oil production made in Szechwan, the largest tung growing province, by the University of Nanking. We accept a round figure of 4.0 yuan/picul as the average price in the nation as a whole.

Fishery Products

The national average price of fishery products, 14.6 yuan/picul, is derived from an estimated value of fishery products of 426.0 million yuan and an estimated output of 29.1 million piculs for China proper in 1933.[28]

FOOTNOTES TO APPENDIX B

1. Indexes of farm prices are available in Land Utilization, Vol. III, but the original price data were not published. The Bureau also published many price indexes in the various issues of Crop Reports without giving the absolute figures.

2. Survey.

3. Industrial Handbooks. These handbooks were published in both Chinese and English. The Chinese versions were used because they contain more detailed information.

4. Northeast Natural Resources Control Committee, National Government, Tung-pei ching-chi hsiao ts'ung-shu (Economic Handbook of Northeast China), Shenyang, 1947, Vol. 3, "Distribution of Agricultural Products." An English translation of the Chinese text was used, since the original volume is not available.

5. See Table 35 and the discussion preceding Table 34.

6. Ou, National Income, Vol. I, pp. 26-27.

7. Liu, Income, p. 19. These unit values are, according to the customs regulations, wholesale prices.

8. These become our accepted provincial prices and are hereafter referred to as "our" prices.

9. Industrial Handbook: Shansi, p. D44.

10. 528.9 million piculs for sweet potatoes and 82.3 million piculs for Irish potatoes. See Appendix A, Table A-9.

11. The price of 1.0 yuan/picul is found in Bureau of Foreign Trade, National Government, Mien-tze-yu (Cottonseed Oil), Changsha, 1940, p. 38; 2.0 in Industrial Handbook: Shantung, p. H175; and 3.0 in Industrial Handbook: Chekiang, p. G108.

12. National Economic Commission, National Government, Shih-tang kung-yeh pao-kao-shu (Report on the Sugar Manufacturing Industry), Shanghai 1936, p. 42.

13. Industrial Handbook: Chekiang, p. D272, "Report on Surveying the Sugar Cane Plantation in Kwangtung Delta," CCYC (Economic Research), November 1938; Survey, the chapter on Kweichow.

14. 0.4 - Chang Hsiao-mei, Sze-chwan ching-chi tsan-kao tzu-liao (Reference Materials on Szechwan Economy), Shanghai, 1939, p. T111; 0.4 to 0.7 - Lu Ping-teng, Sze-chwan nung-tsun ching-chi (Rural Economy of Szechwan), Shanghai, 1936, p. 310.

15. According to the Japan-Manchoukuo Agricultural Policy Research Society, Manshu Nogyo Yoran (Brief Views on Manchurian Agriculture), 1940, pp. 365 and 725-726, the sugar beets price in Manchuria in 1938 was about 0.9 yuan/picul. The same source also gives the agricultural price index in 1938 as 150 per cent of that in 1933. Assuming that the price of sugar beets moved in proportion to general agricultural prices, the 1933 price of sugar beets may be estimated at 0.6 yuan/picul.

16. Japan Kwantung Bureau, A Thirty-Year Collection of Statistics by the Kwantung Bureau, 1937, pp. 273 and 279.

17. National Economic Commission, p. 30. This is the price in 1928.

18. Crop Reports, Vol. 2, No. 10, October 1, 1934.

19. Central Planning Board, National Government, Wu-tse chien-she wu-nien chi-hua tsao-an ti-yao (Draft Five Year Plan for Economic Reconstruction), Chungking, 1945, Chapter 5, Table 5.

20. Survey, the chapter on Kwangtung.

21. Industrial Handbooks: Chekiang, p. D267; Hunan, p. D140; and the Survey's chapter on Kiangsu.

22. Economic Yearbook, 1934, p. E144.

23. Survey chapter on Chekiang, and Industrial Handbook: Chekiang, p. D386.

24. Economic Yearbook, 1934, p. T82.

25. For Chekiang and Kiangsu: Shen Pao Yearbook, 1934, pp. 822-23, and Industrial Handbooks: Chekiang, p. D214; Kiangsu, Chapter 5, p. 191; for Shantung: Industrial Handbooks: Shantung, pp. H68-69; and for Szechwan: Lu Ping-teng, p. 333, and Chang Hsiao-mei, Sze-chwan ching-chi tsan-kao tzu-liao (Reference Materials on Szechwan Economy), p. N14.

26. Industrial Handbook: Shantung, pp. H68-69.

27. 4.5 yuan is given in Industrial Handbook: Chekiang, p. G108, and the Survey's chapter on Kwangsi. 4.3 is given in Chang Hsiao-mei, p. R73, and in Swen, Szechwan-shen chi tung-yu (Tung Oil in Szechwan), p. 119 (cited in Shen, Agricultural Resources, p. 257). 3.9 yuan was reported for Szechwan by the University of Nanking after an extensive survey of tung oil production in that province.

28. See the discussion of fishery products in Appendix E.

Appendix C

OUTPUT OF AGRICULTURAL PRODUCTS, 1952-57

This appendix explains the source data and the methods used for the derivation of the physical output of individual agricultural products in 1952-57 presented in Table 33.

PLANT PRODUCTS

Food Crops

Our own estimates of the production of food crops for 1952-57 were explained in detail in Table 32. The original Communist data on the output of food crops are reproduced in Table C-1. The sources of data on other plant products not shown in the table are as follows:

Cotton

1952-57: Great Ten Years, p. 105.

Soybeans, Peanuts, Rapeseed, Sugarcane and Sugar Beets

1952-55: 1955 Statistical Abstract.

1956: 1956 Statistical Abstract.

1957: Great Ten Years, p. 109.

Tea

1952-57: Great Ten Years, p. 110.

Sesame

1952: Total output of oil bearing crops in 1952 is given by the Communists as 75.5 million piculs.[1] The outputs of peanuts and rapeseed in 1952 have been given above at 65 million piculs.[2] The difference between the total output of oil bearing crops and the sum of the output of peanuts and rapeseed, about 11 million piculs, is assumed to be the output of sesame in 1952.

Table C-1

COMMUNIST DATA ON OUTPUT OF FOOD CROPS, 1952-57
(million piculs)

Food Crop	1952	1953	1954	1955	1956	1957
Rice	1,369	1,425	1,417	1,560	1,649	1,736
Wheat	362	366	467	459	496	473
Miscellaneous	1,030	1,014	985	1,099	1,068	1,053
Potatoes						
At grain-equivalent weight	327	333	340	378	437	438
At natural weight	1,308	1,332	1,360	1,412	1,748	1,752
Food crops, total						
Potatoes at grain-equivalent weight	3,088	3,138	3,209	3,496	3,650	3,700
Potatoes at natural weight	4,067	4,137	4,227	4,530	4,961	5,014

Source:

Great Ten Years, p. 105.

1953-55: Derived from our estimate for 1952 and a sesame output index for 1953-55 with 1952 = 100 computed from data in a British source.

1956: 1956 Statistical Abstract.

1957: CCTP, Hong Kong, No. 604, January 26, 1959, p. 8.

Cottonseed

1952-57: Estimated on the basis of lint cotton output given in Table 33 and a ratio of 1:2 for lint cotton and cottonseed by weight.[4]

Hemp Crops

Besides cotton, China produces several varieties of plant fibers, of which hemp, ramie, jute, and flax are the most important. However, only the data on the output of jute and hemp are available. For each year from 1952-57, they are 6.10, 2.76, 2.74, 5.14, 5.16, and 6.02 million piculs.[5] The other products in this group, namely ramie and other plant fibers, have to be estimated.

According to a pre-Communist source, the output of jute and hemp constituted 61 per cent of the total output of hemp crops in 1939.[6] As there is no indication of any significant change in the composition of the output of hemp crops from 1939 to postwar years, the total output of hemp crops in 1952-57 can be derived on the basis of the output given above and the proportion of the output of jute and hemp in the total output of hemp crops, that is, 61 per cent.

Tobacco

Included in this group are flue-cured, sun-cured, and other native tobacco. The outputs of flue-cured tobacco in 1951-57 are given at 5.0, 4.4, 4.3, 4.6, 6.0, 8.0, and 5.1 million piculs.[7] Total output of all tobacco crops in 1951 being 13 million piculs,[8] those in 1952-57 can be derived on the assumption that total output of all tobacco crops changed during 1951-57 in proportion to output of flue-cured tobacco over the same period.

Fruits

1952-57: Great Ten Years, p. 112.

ANIMAL PRODUCTS

The categories of annual output of animal products during 1952-57 are estimated separately: first, the increase in the number of livestock; second, the number of livestock utilized; and third, other animal products.

Increase in Number of Livestock (Table C-2)

The number of livestock given in the 1955 and 1956 Statistical Abstracts for the years 1952-55 are midyear figures.[9] The year-end figures can be estimated by taking averages of the consecutive midyear figures. Differences between two consecutive year-end numbers are then taken to represent net change of livestock inventory in each year.

The Communist data on the number of hogs in 1957 appears to be unreasonably high,[10] and we have made the following adjustment. On the assumption that the midyear and year-end numbers of hogs changed from 1956 to 1957 in proportion to total human population during the same period, the midyear and year-end numbers of hogs in 1957 can be estimated at 86.2 and 101.6 million head.[11] The adjusted estimate of the increase in the number of hogs in 1957 can thus be calculated at 2.6 million head by deducting the total year-end number of hogs in 1956 (99.0 million head) from that of 1957 (101.6 million head).

Table C-2

INCREASE IN NUMBER OF LIVESTOCK, 1951-57

(millions)

Livestock	Midyear figures							Year-end figures[a]							Increase in number of livestock, 1952-57[b]					
	1951	1952	1953	1954	1955	1956	1957	1951	1952	1953	1954	1955	1956	1957	1952	1953	1954	1955	1956	1957
Cattle	51.9	56.6	60.1	63.6	66.0	66.6	64.2	54.3	58.3	61.9	64.8	66.3	65.4	63.6	4.0	3.6	2.9	1.5	-0.9	-1.8
Horses	5.7	6.1	6.5	6.9	7.3	7.4	7.2	5.9	6.3	6.7	7.1	7.4	7.3	7.2	0.4	0.4	0.4	0.3	-0.1	-0.1
Mules	1.1	1.6	1.6	1.7	1.7	1.7	1.6	1.4	1.6	1.7	1.7	1.7	1.7	1.7	0.2	0.1	(*)	(*)	(*)	(*)
Donkeys	10.6	11.8	12.2	12.7	12.4	11.7	11.3	11.2	12.0	12.5	12.6	12.1	11.5	11.4	0.8	0.5	0.1	-0.5	-0.6	-0.1
Sheep and goats	51.9	61.8	72.0	81.3	84.2	91.7	97.7	56.8	66.9	76.7	82.8	87.9	94.7	98.5	10.1	9.8	6.1	5.1	6.8	3.8
Hogs																				
Communist data	78.1	89.8	96.1	101.7	87.9	84.0	114.0	83.9	93.0	98.9	94.8	86.0	98.0	145.9	9.1	5.9	-4.1	-8.8	13.0	46.9
Our estimate							86.2						99.0	101.6						2.6

Notes:

(*) Less than 0.05 million.

[a] Derived by averaging the midyear number for each year with that of the following year.

[b] Computed from year-end data.

Sources:

Midyear figures

1951: Absolute numbers of livestock in 1951 are not available. Numbers of cattle, horses, sheep and goats, and hogs are derived from percentage increases in 1952 over 1951 given in 1952 Communique and the 1952 figures given in 1955 Statistical Abstract. The numbers of mules and donkeys are derived from the 1949 figures given in 1955 Statistical Abstract and the ratios of the 1951 numbers to the 1949 numbers given in "The General Conditions of Animal Husbandry in New China," HHJP, Chungking, October 29, 1952.

1952-55: 1955 Statistical Abstract.

1956: 1956 Statistical Abstract.

1957: Numbers of large livestock as a group (cattle, horses, mules, donkeys), and smaller livestock (sheep and goats) are from People's Daily, December 20, 1957. Number in each category estimated on the basis of this total and the percentage share of each animal in the total number for 1956. Number of hogs is from TKP, August 17, 1957.

Year-end figures

1956: The number of hogs is given in 1956 Communique.

1957: Numbers of large livestock as a group, of sheep and goats, and of hogs, are given by Han I-chun in "Try for a Big Leap Forward in Animal Product Production,"

Livestock Utilized

Livestock (Table C-3). The number of livestock utilized in the postwar years is estimated by the same method used to derive the 1933 estimate,[12] that is, by applying the utilization rates[13] to the number of each. Since there are two estimates of the number of hogs in 1957 (the Communist figure and our estimate, Table C-2), two estimates of the number of hogs utilized are derived. Both are given in Table C-3.

Poultry. For 1952 we have the following data on the stock of poultry:[14] Chickens, 265.1 million head; ducks, 64.1 million head; and geese, 10.0 million head. We assume that these data refer to the stock at midyear and that the entire midyear stock is utilized. Because of lack of information on the numbers of poultry, only the value produced by their utilization is estimated for the years 1953-57. The value estimates are given in Appendix E.

Other Animal Products

Eggs (Table C-4). The output of eggs in 1952 is estimated by multiplying the total number of poultry given in the preceding section, the percentage of the total that produced eggs, and the average number of eggs laid per bird.[15]

Egg production in 1953-57 has not been estimated because of the lack of data on the number of poultry in these years; the value of eggs produced in these years is estimated in Appendix E.

Wool (Table C-5). The outputs of sheep's wool and goats' hair are estimated from Communist data on the numbers of these animals and certain prewar information on the wool producing capacities of sheep and goats. The detailed procedure is described in the notes to Table C-5.

Table C-3

LIVESTOCK UTILIZED, 1952-57

(millions)

Livestock	Rate of utilization[a]	1952	1953	1954	1955	1956	1957
Cattle	15	8.5	9.0	9.5	9.9	10.0	9.6
Horses	10	0.6	0.6	0.7	0.7	0.7	0.7
Mules	10	0.2	0.2	0.2	0.2	0.2	0.2
Donkeys	10	1.1	1.2	1.3	1.2	1.2	1.1
Sheep and goats	40	24.7	28.8	32.5	33.7	36.7	39.1
Hogs							
Communist data	80	71.8	76.9	81.4	70.3	67.2	91.2
Our estimate							69.0

Note:

[a] Percentage of total number. The totals are the midyear figures given in Table C-2.

Table C-4

PRODUCTION OF EGGS, 1952

Poultry	Total number of poultry (millions) (1)	Number of egg-laying poultry (millions) (2)	Annual number of eggs laid (per fowl) (3)	Total number of eggs produced (millions) (4)
Chickens	265.1	132.6	90	11,934
Ducks	64.1	32.1	80	2,568
Geese	10.0	5.0	70	350

Notes:

Column (1). See text of this appendix.

Column (2). Column (1) times 50 per cent.

Column (3). See Appendix A, notes to Table A-13.

Column (4). Column (2) times column (3).

Table C-5

PRODUCTION OF WOOL, 1952-57

(Number of animals in millions; wool output in thousand piculs)

	1952	1953	1954	1955	1956	1957
1. Total number of sheep and goats	61.8	72.0	81.3	84.2	91.7	97.7
2. Total number of sheep	36.9	42.8	48.2	50.2	53.4	53.4
3. Number of wool-producing sheep	25.8	30.0	33.7	35.1	37.4	37.4
4. Output of sheep's wool	645.0	750.0	843.0	879.0	935.0	935.0
5. Total number of goats	24.9	29.2	33.1	34.0	38.3	44.3
6. Number of hair-producing goats	14.9	17.5	19.9	20.4	23.0	26.6
7. Output of goat's hair	298.0	350.0	398.0	408.0	460.0	532.0
8. Total production, wool and hair	943.0	1,100.0	1,241.0	1,287.0	1,395.0	1,467.0

Notes:

Line 1. Aggregate midyear numbers of sheep and goats taken from Table C-2.

Lines 2 and 5. For 1952-56, the number of sheep and goats are estimated from their total number given in line 1 on the basis of their 1952 numbers given in First Five Year Plan and 1952-56 indexes given in TCKTTH, No. 23, 1956, pp. 31-32. For 1957, the number of sheep is given as 53.4 million in People's Daily, November 16, 1958, and the number of goats is computed as 44.3 (97.7 - 53.4 = 44.3).

Line 3. The number of wool-producing sheep is estimated as 70 per cent of the total number of sheep. See Appendix A. Line 3 = line 2 times 0.7.

Line 4. The output of wool is estimated on the basis of the number of wool-producing sheep given in line 3 and 2.5 catties of wool

Notes (continued):

produced annually per head. See Appendix A. Line 4 = line 3 times 2.5 catties.

Line 6. The number of hair-producing goats is estimated at 60 per cent of the total number of goats. See Appendix A. Line 6 = line 5 times 0.6.

Line 7. The output of hair is estimated on the basis of the number of hair-producing goats given in line 6 and 2 catties of hair produced annually per head. See Appendix A. Line 7 = line 6 times 2 catties.

Line 8. The sum of lines 4 and 7.

Silkworm Cocoons. 1952-57: Great Ten Years, p. 110.

FOREST PRODUCTS

Timber

1952-57: Great Ten Years, p. 85.

Tung nuts

1952: Since the Communists have never announced any increase in the acreage of tung trees, it is assumed that the output of tung nuts and tung oil in 1952 remained at the pre-1949 level. Tung oil output has been reported at 3.3 million piculs for 1946.[16] On the basis of this figure and a nut-oil extraction ratio of 100:28 by weight,[17] the output of tung nuts in 1952 is estimated at 11.8 million piculs.

1953-54: According to a British source, the output of tung oil in 1953-54 is about 88 per cent of that in 1952.[18] On the basis of this index and the output of tung nuts in 1952 given above (11.8 million piculs), the output in 1953-54 is estimated at 10.4 million piculs.

1955-56: A Communist source indicated that the output of tung nuts in 1956 was more or less the same as in the preceding years.[19] The output in 1955-56 is therefore assumed to be equal to that in 1954.

1957: Estimated on the basis of the output of tung oil given at 3 million piculs in People's Daily, December 14, 1958, and the nut-oil extraction ratio given above.

FISHERY PRODUCTS

1952-55: 1955 Statistical Abstract.

1956: 1956 Statistical Abstract.

1957: FYYP Communique.

FOOTNOTES TO APPENDIX C

1. The planned output of oil-bearing crops for 1957 is given as 116 million piculs, 53.7 per cent higher than the output in 1952. The 1952 output is thus computed at 75.5 million piculs. See HHYP, No. 11, 1954, p. 132, and the 1954 Statistical Abstract.

2. See Table 33.

3. The Economist Intelligence Unit, Ltd., Three-Monthly Economic Review of China, Hongkong, and North Korea, Annual Supplement, London, May 1957, p. 4. The index of sesame output derived from the absolute output figures given in this source, rather than the absolute figures themselves, is used in this study for the following reason. The output figures for peanuts and rapeseed for 1952-55, also given in this source, are different from the Communist figures; however, they vary more or less proportionally with the Communist figures during this period. Therefore, it seems reasonable to assume that this data on sesame also change through time in rough proportion to the Communist data, even though the absolute amounts given in the two sources are different.

4. Chung-kuo nung-pao (Chinese Agricultural Bulletin), Peiping, No. 4, 1957, p. 7, and WHP, Shanghai, November 14, 1957.

5. 1955 Statistical Abstract, 1956 Statistical Abstract, and People's Daily, September 30, 1958.

6. Ministry of Agriculture and Forestry, Nung-lin t'ung-chi shou-t'se (Handbook of Agricultural and Forest Statistics), Nanking, 1948, p. 22.

7. 1952 Communique, 1955 Statistical Abstract, 1956 Statistical Abstract, and Great Ten Years, p. 109.

8. Wu Hua-pao, Fu-yao ti chung-kuo nung-yeh tzu-yuan (The Abundant Agricultural Resources of China), Shanghai, 1951, pp. 46-47.

9. Communist statistics on livestock published in the early 1950s refer to "livestock years" (July 1 to June 30). The number of livestock registered for a particular year represents the number in existence on July 1 of that year. Starting from December 31, 1957, the livestock year became identical with the calendar year, and the numbers reported thereafter are the numbers registered on the last day of each calendar year. TCKTTH, 1956 issues, No. 12, p. 32; No. 21, p. 20; and No. 23 p. 31.

10. See Chapter II.

11. For data on total population in 1956-57, see Table 32. For the midyear and year-end total numbers of hogs in 1956, see Table C-2.

12. See Appendix A, the section on animal products output.

13. See Appendix A, Table A-12.

14. Chang Chung-wan and Hwang Wei-yi, Tsu-kuo ti hsu-mo yu hsu-chan tzu-yuan (Animal Husbandry and Animal Products of Our Fatherland), Shanghai, Yung-hsiang Book Company, 1953, p. 205.

15. See Appendix A, Table A-13. These figures are believed to be applicable in both prewar and postwar periods.

16. Ministry of Agriculture and Forestry, p. 22.

17. See the section on forest products in Appendix A.

18. Economist Intelligence Unit, Ltd., p. 4.

19. Based on a statement made by Liang Hsi, Communist Minister of Forestry. See Chung-kuo lin-yeh (China's Forestry), Peiping, No. 5, 1956, p. 8.

Appendix D

FARM PRICES IN 1952

Unlike the data on physical output, which have been more or less systematically published by the Communists, data on agricultural prices, with the exception of cotton procurement prices, have never been issued regularly by official sources for 1952 or any other year. Official indexes of procurement prices of agricultural products and of city wholesale and retail prices are available, but they are given in aggregates without breakdowns by commodities.

Direct quotations on farm prices of important commodities such as rice, wheat, soybeans, rapeseed, cotton, hemp crops, sugar cane, tea, fruits, cattle, sheep and goats, hogs, chicken eggs, wool, silkworm cocoons, and fishery products are collected from local newspapers, and national average prices are computed from these local prices. All prices discussed in this appendix are in 1952 yuan. In the majority of the less important commodities, data on farm prices are either completely lacking or are too scattered to be of any value. For most of these products, their farm prices are derived indirectly from the ratios of their wholesale prices to the known prices of other farm products. The assumption implicit in this procedure is that the margins between wholesale prices and farm prices are roughly the same.

The Communists have published a considerable amount of data on cotton procurement prices and on the cotton-food crop price ratios for many regions. It might be thought that farm prices for food crops could be estimated directly from cotton prices. However, cotton-food crop price ratios are those of cotton procurement prices paid by the government (prices received by cotton farmers from government procurement agencies) to the sale prices of food crops received by the government (prices paid by cotton farmers to government sales agencies for food crops). Since the differences between government sale prices and procurement prices of food crops are not known, it is not possible to derive the farm prices of food crops from the government procurement prices of cotton and the cotton-food crop price ratios.

PADDY RICE (Table D-1)

Some 50 price quotations for nonglutinous paddy rice in 11 provinces have been collected from 11 different newspapers. Output of rice in these provinces represents roughly 95 per cent of the nation's total rice output. The provincial prices have been obtained by averaging the local prices in the respective provinces. The national price, 5.3 yuan/picul, is the weighted average of these provincial prices, the weights being the prewar percentages of the total output of the respective provinces.

WHEAT (Table D-2)

About 70 quotations on farm prices of wheat have been collected from 13 of the provinces which accounted for nearly 90 per cent of the nation's wheat output in prewar years. The weighted average price for the mainland in 1952 is 8.0 yuan/picul.

MISCELLANEOUS FOOD CROPS

Millet, Kaoliang, and Corn

Data on farm prices of these three crops are very scarce, and the number of available price quotations for 1952 in local newspapers is too small to form an adequate basis to derive estimates of the national

Table D-1

FARM PRICE OF PADDY RICE, 1952

Province	Average price (yuan/picul)[a]		Weight (per cent)[b]
Anhwei	6.1		4.85
Chekiang	5.9		6.65
Fukien	6.4		3.62
Hunan	4.9		16.53
Hupeh	4.6		8.58
Kiangsi	5.9		6.06
Kiangsu	6.2		8.99
Kwangsi	4.0		5.38
Kwangtung	5.3		13.15
Szechwan	5.2		21.08
Yunnan	4.5		5.11
National average	5.3	**Total**	100.00

Sources:

[a] Price data (in 1952 yuan) are taken from: CKJP, Hangchow, August 24 and November 18, 1952; FCJP, Foochow, August 23 and 29, 1952; HHJP, Chungking, September 20 and October 10, 1952; HPJP, Hankow, July 21, August 6 and 19, and September 21, 1952; People's Daily, Peiping, August 26, 1952; KSJP, Nanchang, September 13, 1952; NFJP, Canton, July 12, August 12 and 27, 1952; TKP, Shanghai, September 3, 1952; TKP, August 9, 1953 (1952 price); and YNJP, Kunming, June 13, 1952.

[b] The weights are the percentage shares of the respective provinces in the total output of rice during the prewar period, as given in Appendix A, Table A-4.

Table D-2

FARM PRICE OF WHEAT, 1952

Province	Average price (yuan/picul)[a]		Weight (per cent)[b]
Anhwei	6.0		7.21
Fukien	8.5		1.30
Honan	8.8		20.75
Hopei	10.0		9.30
Hupeh	4.8		6.60
Kansu	6.5		1.91
Kiangsu	8.4		15.04
Kwangtung	7.0		0.64
Shansi	10.0		4.31
Shantung	9.1		18.28
Shensi	8.8		3.87
Szechwan	4.3		9.23
Yunnan	6.5		1.56
National average	8.0	Total	100.00

Sources:

[a] Price data (in 1952 yuan) are taken from: FKJP, Foochow, July 19 and August 10, 1952; HHJP, Chungking, September 10 and 30, 1952; HPJP, Hankow, July 4 and all issues for September 1952; NFJP, Canton, April 19, 1952; YNJP, Kunming, June 29, 1952; CCJP, Hankow, June 15 and July 6, 1952; CFJP, Shanghai, May 15, July 8, and August 8, 1952; CCJP, Sian, June 9 and September 26, 1952; HSCJP, Soochow, July 31, 1952; HNJP, Kaifeng, October 16 and December 13, 1951; and SSJP, Taiyuan, July 15, 1952.

[b] The weights are the percentages of the total output of wheat of the respective provinces during 1931-37. See Agricultural Estimates, Shanghai, 1947, p. 4.

average prices. However, data on wholesale prices in markets near the producing areas are relatively abundant. By assuming that for each crop the ratio of the farm price to the wholesale price is the same as the corresponding ratio for wheat, the farm price of each crop can be derived from the farm price of wheat and the ratios of the wholesale price of wheat to those of millet, kaoliang, and corn.

The ratios of the wholesale price of wheat to wholesale prices of millet, kaoliang, and corn are estimated at 97, 63, and 78 in Table D-3, with the wholesale price of wheat as 100. The 1952 farm price of wheat has been estimated at 8.0 yuan per picul.[1] Applying the ratios obtained to this farm price of wheat, the 1952 farm prices for millet, kaoliang, and corn are thus estimated at 7.8, 5.0, and 6.2 yuan per picul.

Other Miscellaneous Food Crops

In addition to millet, kaoliang, and corn, there are also barley, glutinous rice, peas, broadbeans, mung beans, buckwheat, proso millet, oats, and other crops in the miscellaneous food crops group. Price data are available only for buckwheat in Hupeh, broadbeans in Szechwan, and barley in North China. Since barley is the most important crop of this group, its price (5.1 yuan/picul)[2] is taken as the price for all the crops in this group.

Miscellaneous Food Crops as a Group

The average price of all miscellaneous food crops as a whole, 6.0 yuan/picul, is the weighted average price of millet, kaoliang, corn, and the other products in this group, the weights being their respective outputs in 1952.[3]

Table D-3

RATIOS OF THE WHOLESALE PRICE OF WHEAT TO THOSE OF

MILLET, KAOLIANG, AND CORN, 1952

(per cent)

Locality	Wheat	Millet	Kaoliang	Corn
Four localities in Hopei[a]	100	92	46	67
Peiping district[b]	100	108	-	83
Shihchiachwan area[c]	100	91	71	83
Tsingtao, Shantung[d]	100	95	-	80
Shanghai district[e]	100	-	69	-
Average	100	97	63	78

Note:

- Not available.

Sources:

Price ratios for each area or district are computed from the average individual wholesale prices reported in the sources indicated below:

[a] HPJP, Paoting, September 29, 1951 (in the absence of 1952 price ratios, late 1951 percentages have been used instead).

[b] People's Daily, Peiping, August 16, 1952.

[c] SCCJP, Shihchiachwan, all issues for October and November, 1952.

[d] TTJP, Tsingtao, all issues for January and November, 1952.

[e] CFJP, Shanghai, May 10, 1952.

POTATOES

Available information shows that the price of potatoes in the two important potato producing provinces, Szechwan and Kwangtung, ranged from 1.3 to 2.9 yuan/picul in 1952.[4] The average price, 2.0 yuan/picul, is used in this study.

SOYBEANS

The farm prices of soybeans in the major producing areas are not available for 1952. However, the following information is on farm prices in Honan and Manchuria where most of the soybeans are produced: 6.2 yuan/picul in Manchuria in 1953 and 7.8 yuan/picul in Honan in 1951.[5] The round figure of 7.0 is taken to represent the average farm price of soybeans for the mainland as a whole in 1952.

PEANUTS

The ratio of the wholesale price of peanuts to that of millet has been reported at 135:100 for 1952.[6] The farm price of peanuts can thus be derived from this ratio and data on the farm price of millet. The result is 10.5 yuan per picul. This falls within the range of scattered price data for peanuts reported in local newspapers.[7]

RAPESEED

A news commentary in the North Anhwei Daily stated that in 1952 "the rapeseed procurement price has been reduced to 10.0 yuan per picul, which is 'unfair' to the producers."[8] Another news item reported that the price of rapeseed sold by the East China Supply and Marketing Cooperative Association to the China Oils and Fats Company in 1952 was about 12.4 yuan/picul.[9] From these two reports, it seems reasonable to assume that farm price of rapeseed in 1952 was within the range of 10.0 to 12.4 yuan/picul. The rounded figure of 11.0 is used in this study.

SESAME

The ratio of the wholesale price of sesame to that of wheat is 180:100.[10] The farm price of sesame is estimated at 14.4 yuan/picul from this ratio and the farm price of wheat given above.[11]

COTTONSEED

On the assumption that the ratio of the farm price of cottonseed to that of sesame in 1952 was about the same as that in 1933 (1:4),[12] the farm price of cottonseed can be estimated at 3.6 yuan per picul on the basis of that of sesame.

COTTON (Table D-4)

Data on the price of lint cotton are relatively abundant. Almost all of them are government procurement prices paid to the cotton growers.[13] In 1951 and 1952, the Communists made every effort to increase cotton production. Favorable cotton procurement prices were published in most newspapers to encourage producers to sell their disposable cotton to the government. It was reported that in 1952 about 80 per cent of the marketed cotton (total output less cotton growers' own consumption) was purchased by the government.[14] Consequently, the government procurement prices were the dominating prices realized by cotton farmers.

The 1952 cotton price data used in this study covered about 80 localities in 11 cotton producing provinces, where over 90 per cent of Chinese cotton was produced. The national average price is 84.9 yuan/picul.

HEMP CROPS

As in the case of hemp prices in 1933, farm prices of jute and hemp fibers in 1952 are available mostly without breakdowns for the individual crops. Some 50 quotations are available. One source gives 41 quotations on government procurement prices of

Table D-4

FARM PRICE OF COTTON, 1952

Province	Price (yuan/picul)		Weight (per cent)
Anhwei	87		3.59
Chekiang	86		3.68
Honan	81		11.55
Hopei	85		19.35
Hunan	84		2.65
Hupeh	79		11.99
Kiangsi	83		1.82
Kiangsu	92		23.32
Shansi	81		4.25
Shantung	84		12.18
Shensi	80		5.62
National average	84.9	Total	100.00

Sources:

Provincial prices are the averages of local prices in each province. They are computed from price data given in CCJP, Hankow, August 10, 1952; CFJP, Shanghai, August 10, 1952; CCJP, Sian, August 3, 1952; HNJP, Kaifeng, October 19, 1952; HPJP, Hankow, August 4, 1952; People's Daily, Peiping, August 4, 1952; KSJP, Nanchang, September 13, 1952; SCCJP, Shihchiachwan, August 19 and September 7, 1952; and TCJP, Tsinan, August 16, 1952.

The weights are the percentage shares of the respective provinces in the total output of cotton during the prewar period. See Agricultural Estimates, p. 61.

different grades of hemp crops in Anhwei, Chekiang, Honan, Shansi, and Szechwan. The price ranged from 28.4 to 75.1 yuan/picul,[15] and the average price of the medium-grade crops was about 52.0 yuan/picul. In North China, the government procurement prices were much lower; they ranged from 14.4 to 35.0 yuan/picul.[16] The average price was about 25 yuan/picul. Another source indicated that the average price for all hemp crops in central China was about 40 yuan/picul.[17] This price, covering the major producing areas and being close to the average of all available prices, is taken as the national average price for the whole hemp group.

SUGAR CANE

The only available price quotation for sugar cane is 1.0 yuan/picul in Szechwan, one of the largest sugar producing provinces.[18] It has also been reported that the 1954 farm price of sugar cane in Kwangtung, the largest sugar cane producing province on the mainland, ranged from 1.2 to 1.4 yuan/picul,[19] and that the official procurement price of industrial crops (or technical crops) was somewhat higher in 1954 than that in 1952.[20] Hence, the 1952 price of sugar cane is assumed to be 1.0 yuan/picul.

SUGAR BEETS

Data on farm prices of sugar beets are not available. However, the ratio of the farm price of beets to that of soybeans in Manchuria, the most important sugar beet producing area in China, was about 28.4:100.[21] The farm price of sugar beets, 2 yuan/picul, can thus be derived from this ratio and the farm price of soybeans given earlier in this appendix.

TOBACCO

For flue-cured tobacco, only one quotation is available for 1952, 40.0 yuan/picul,[22] in Kweichow. It appears to be rather low when compared with the wholesale prices of tobacco in many regions.[23] As the tobacco planters usually received no less than one-half of the wholesale price, a national farm price of 50.0 yuan/picul is assumed in this study.

For native, sun-cured tobacco, the average of four price quotations[24] for Fukien and Hupeh provinces, 25 yuan/picul, is taken to represent the national average price.

By using the 1952 output of these two kinds of tobacco as weights[25] for their respective prices, the weighted average price for the whole tobacco group is computed at 34.6 yuan/picul.

TEA

Thirteen price quotations ranging from 20.0 to 130.0 yuan/picul of various grades of tea have been collected from six tea-producing provinces. The national price of 70.0 is a simple average of the following provincial prices, given in yuan/picul: Anhwei, 75.0; Chekiang, 125.0; Fukien, 60.0; Hupeh, 55.0; Szechwan, 82.0; and Yunnan, 22.0.[26]

FRUITS

Only one quotation for Kwantung province in 1951 (26.7 yuan/picul) is available.[27] Prices in Kwantung are generally much higher than those in other major producing areas. A rounded price of 20 is arbitrarily assumed.

CATTLE

Farm prices of cattle in 1952, available for four provinces and one region, are given as follows, in yuan per head: Chekiang, 105; Hupeh, 60; Sinkiang, 70; Szechwan, 50; and Northwest China, 90.[28] A simple average of these prices, 75 yuan per head, is taken as the farm price of cattle for the mainland as a whole.

SHEEP AND GOATS

A price range of 4.9 to 15.0 yuan per head has been reported for East China.[29] However, as Northwest China is a much more important producing area for sheep and goats, the price of 8 yuan per head reported for this region[30] is accepted as the national price.

HORSES, MULES, AND DONKEYS

Very little is known about the 1952 farm prices of these three animals. As these animals are produced mainly in North and West China, where most sheep and goats are also raised, their prices could be derived indirectly from the farm price of sheep on the assumption that the rates between the farm prices of these animals in 1952 were the same as those in 1933. The prewar price ratios of sheep to horses, mules, and donkeys, are 1,370, 2,000, and 740 with the price of sheep as 100.[31] These ratios have been applied to the above 1952 farm price of sheep, 8.0 yuan per head, to obtain the 1952 farm prices of horses, mules, and donkeys at 110, 160, and 59.2 yuan per head.

As explained in Appendix B, there are two kinds of prices to be considered in estimating the value of output realized from draft animals: the regular prices and the discount prices. The discount prices are for draft animals that were slaughtered or that died of natural causes and whose carcasses were sold. The discount prices for draft animals in 1952 are derived from the regular prices on the ratios of the discount prices to the regular prices in 1933.

	Regular prices in 1952 (yuan/head)	Discount rate[32] (per cent)	Discount prices[33] (yuan/head)
Cattle	75.0	70	52.5
Horses	110.0	40	44.0
Mules	160.0	40	64.0
Donkeys	59.2	40	23.7

HOGS

Available quotations of hog prices per head vary widely, from 18.0 to 69.4, according to the difference in size.[34] The extreme prices are not usable since they represented the prices of very small or very large hogs. For quantity sale in Hupeh, the average price of hogs of all sizes has been reported to be about 38 yuan[35] and the average government purchase price in Szechwan for various sizes of hogs was about 54 yuan.[36] The average of these two, 46 yuan per head, is used in this study.

CHICKENS, DUCKS, AND GEESE

Since poultry and pork are two of the three most important meats in the Chinese diet, farm prices of poultry are derived indirectly by applying the prewar hog-poultry farm price ratios to the 1952 farm price of hogs. The 1933 price ratios of chickens, ducks, and geese to hogs were 2.2, 2.9, and 6.3, with the hog price as 100.[37] The 1952 national price of hogs has been estimated at 46.0 yuan per head. The 1952 farm prices of chickens, ducks, and geese are therefore 1.1, 1.3, and 2.9 yuan per head.

EGGS

Price data are available for chicken eggs only. Prices of duck and goose eggs have to be estimated indirectly from the 1952 price of chicken eggs and the prewar price ratios of chicken eggs to duck and goose eggs.

Scattered price quotations indicate that in rural areas the price of chicken eggs in 1952 was about 28 yuan per thousand,[38] and that in urban markets, where most farmers sold eggs directly to consumers, the prices were between 26 and 40 yuan per thousand as follows: Chungking, 28;

Hankow, 26; Nanking, 28; Shanghai, 40; Shihchiachwan, 30; and Tientsin, 30. The average of these prices, 30 yuan per thousand, is taken to be the price received by farmers in 1952.

On the prewar price ratio of chicken eggs to duck and goose eggs (100:133),[40] the 1952 price of duck and goose eggs is estimated at 40 yuan per thousand.

WOOL

In the wool producing districts of Tsinghai, Inner Mongolia, and Sinkiang, the government procurement prices of wool ranged from 130 to 151 yuan/picul in 1952.[41] The types of wool to which the prices referred are not given. It is assumed that the share of improved wool in the total production was about one-fourth and that it was the higher price of 151 yuan/picul. The price of native wool, accounting for the remaining three-fourths of total production, is assumed to be the lower price of 130. The weighted average price of the two types of wool is about 135 yuan/picul in 1952.

SILKWORM COCOONS

Domesticated Cocoons

Detailed data on the prices of fresh cocoons paid by government procurement agencies are available for the four provinces of Anhwei, Chekiang, Kiangsu, and Shantung, where over 55 per cent of domesticated cocoons (usually of better quality) were produced.[42] The prices range from 55 to 95 yuan/picul (see Table D-5), the average being about 75. This estimate is very close to the basic procurement price in 1952 announced by the government (70 yuan/picul).[43]

In Szechwan, a low farm price of 42.5 yuan/picul has been reported.[44]

Table D-5

PRICES OF SILKWORM COCOONS IN EAST CHINA, 1952

(yuan per picul)

Grade	Anhwei (South)	Chekiang	Kiangsu (South)	Shantung
Super fine	-	95	95	-
1st	85	89	89	83
2nd	79	83	83	77
3rd	74	78	78	71
4th	70	74	74	65
5th	65	70	70	60
6th	62	66	66	55

Note:

- Not available.

Source:

CFJP, Shanghai, May 24, 1952.

This was probably the price paid for cocoons of inferior grades, because the average price could not have been too much lower in Szechwan than in the other four provinces. The government procurement price in Szechwan during 1950 was about 69 yuan/picul, which was very close to the price then prevailing in East China.[45] Taking into consideration the differences in the quality of silk cocoons in various parts of China and the fact that the government customarily purchases only the better quality cocoons,[46] the average farm price for all kinds of fresh domesticated cocoons would be somewhat lower than the average government procurement price. The national average price received by farmers is therefore assumed to be 65 yuan per picul.

Wild Cocoons

The 1952 farm price of wild cocoons (43.6 yuan/picul) has been derived from the above 1952 price of 65 yuan/picul for domesticated cocoons and the prewar price ratio of domesticated to wild cocoons (100:67).[47]

FOREST PRODUCTS

Timber

The prices of raw timber in 1952 are available only at the wholesale level, the average being 120 yuan/cubic meter.[48]

On the assumption that the prewar wholesale-farm price ratio (100:40)[49] for raw timber still prevailed in 1952, the 1952 farm price of timber is estimated at 48 yuan per cubic meter.

Tung Nuts

It is assumed that the prewar ratio between the wholesale price of tung oil and the farm price of tung nuts (100:20)[50] prevailed in 1952. The wholesale price of tung oil was 38 yuan/picul in 1952.[51] The 1952 farm price of tung nuts was then 7.6 yuan/picul.

FISHERY PRODUCTS

The 1952 prices of fishery products are available for East, South, and Southwest China as follows, the average being 19 yuan/picul: Fukien, 18.0; Kwangtung, 18.5; East China, 13.4; and Yunnan, 26.0.[52]

FOOTNOTES TO APPENDIX D

1. See Table D-2.

2. Farm prices (in 1952 yuan) of barley ranged from 4.8 to 13.3 yuan/picul, and the median price was 5.1. See SPJP, Yangchow, July 31, 1952, and CCJP, Sian, December 16, 1952.

3. The prices (in 1952 yuan) of these four crops are 7.8, 5.0, 6.2, and 5.1 yuan per picul. Their outputs are 230, 223, 338, and 240 million piculs, estimated on the basis of their 1952 total output and the percentages of each crop in the total as given by Wang Shou, Deputy Administrator of Agricultural Production, Communist Ministry of Agriculture, in "Conditions and Current Problems of Food Crop Production in Our Country," Ko-hsueh t'ung-pao (Science Bulletin), Peiping, No. 5, 1954, pp. 17-20.

4. HHJP, Chungking, October 28, 1952, and CCJP, Hankow, August 21, 1952.

5. TKP, Tientsin, October 14, 1953, and HNJP, Kaifeng, November 8, 1951.

6. HPJP, Paoting, August 29, 1952.

7. From 4.5 to 12.0 yuan/picul. See HHJP, Chungking, November 11, 1952, and NFJP, Canton, August 27, 1952.

8. WPJP, Hofei, May 28, 1952.

9. HWJP, Shanghai, June 7, 1952.

10. This is the unweighted average of two ratios computed from data given in CPJP, Tientsin, all issues for June-November 1952, and CKJP, Chungking, November 1952 issues.

11. Table D-2.

12. For data used in deriving this ratio, see Table 34.

13. All cotton prices are for standard medium grade lint with a staple length of seven-eighths of an inch.

14. HHJP, Chungking, April 26, 1953.

15. HWJP, Shanghai, August 28, 1952. The government procurement price ranges (in yuan/picul) of hemp crops reported by this source are: Anhwei, 39.6 - 75.1; Chekiang, 61.6 - 73.5; Honan, 28.4 - 50.8; Shansi, 56.1 - 66.0; and Szechwan, 61.6 - 73.5.

16. CPJP, Tientsin, September 4 and November 2, 1952; HPJP, Paoting, November 20, 1952.

17. WPJP, Hofei, March 13, 1952.

18. HHJP, Chungking, September 14, 1952.

19. NFJP, Canton, July 7, 1954, and WHP, Hong Kong, March 16, 1954.

20. TCKT, No. 17, 1957, p. 5.

21. Computed from data given in TPJP, Shenyang (all issues for July-September 1950). While this was the ratio of the two prices in 1950, it is unlikely that the ratio was significantly different in 1952.

22. HHJP, Chungking, December 3, 1952.

23. Wholesale prices (in yuan/picul) at 80, 90, and 120 are reported respectively by CPJP, Tientsin, January 18, 1952; NFJP, Canton, July 22, 1952; and CFJP, Shanghai, May 10, 1952.

24. 10, 18, 35, and 38 yuan/picul. See FKJP, Foochow, October 29 and September 2, 1952; and CCJP, Hankow, August 30, 1952.

25. The 1952 output figures are taken from Appendix C.

26. (Anhwei) WPJP, Hofei, May 23 and 28, 1952, and CFJP, Shanghai, May 22, 1952; (Chekiang) CKJP, Hangchow, September 30, 1952; (Fukien) FCJP, Foochow, July 17, 1952; (Hupeh) HPJP, Hankow, November 9, 1952; (Szechwan) HHJP, Chungking, September 14, 1952; (Yunnan) YNJP, Kunming, June 13, 1952, and HHJP, Chungking, October 4, 1952.

27. CCTP, Hong Kong, No. 19, 1954, pp. 12-13.

28. (Chekiang) CKJP, Hanchow, November 18, 1952; (Hupeh) CCJP, Hankow, May 5 and September 6, 1952; (Sinkiang) SKJP, Tihua, March 4, 1952; (Szechwan) HHJP, Chungking, October 8, 1952; (Northwest China) CCJP, Sian, November 13 and 16, 1952.

29. HWJP, Shanghai, June 8, 1952.

30. CCJP, Sian, December 16, 1952.

31. See Appendix B, Table B-20.

32. Obtained from the discussion on livestock and poultry in Appendix

33. Products of the corresponding figures in the two preceding columns.

34. CFJP, Shanghai, May 25, 1952, and HHJP, Chungking, August 25, 1952

35. HPJP, Hankow, July 15 and 17, 1952. The original quotation at 40 yuan per head was the average price of hogs sold by farmers through the marketing cooperatives. Deducting an assumed service fee of 2 yuan per head charged by the cooperatives, the net price received by farmers would be around 38 yuan.

36. HHJP, Chungking, August 25 and September 14, 1952.

37. See Table 34.

38. People's Daily, Peiping, June 29, 1953. Prices are given for 1952.

39. HHJP, Chungking, July 5, 1952; average of prices reported by HPJP, Hankow, September 1952 issues; HHJP, Nanking, July 18, 1952; average of prices reported by CFJP, Shanghai, May 1952 issues; average of prices reported by SCCJP, Shihchiachwan, all issues for October and November 1952; average of prices reported by CPJP, Tientsin, all issues for July and August 1952.

40. Prices of duck and goose eggs are assumed to be the same in 1933. See Appendix B.

41. Farm prices of wool in 1952 were (in yuan/picul): 130-138 in Inner Mongolia (NMKJP, Huhehot, February 10, 1952); 137-151 in Sinkiang (CCJP, Sian, July 18, 1952); and 130.3 in Tsinghai (ibid., December 16, 1952).

42. Ministry of Agriculture and Forestry, National Government. Nung-lin t'ung-chi shou-t'se (Handbook of Agricultural and Forestry Statistics), Nanking, 1948, p. 21.

43. CFJP, Shanghai, May 24, 1952.

44. HHJP, Chungking, October 29, 1952.

45. Ibid., October 26, 1950.

46. Cocoons procured by the government are used for reeling silk for export. These are mostly the better grades.

47. See Appendix B.

48. The wholesale prices in 1952 were (in yuan/cubic meter): 78 in Shenyang (TPJP, Shenyang, November 20, 1952); 112 in Tientsin (TTJP, Tientsin, October 16, 1952); 134 in Changchiakow (NMKJP, Huhehot February 5, 1952); and 156 in Kweisui (SYJP, Kuai-sui, March 2, 1952).

49. Ou, National Income, Vol. I, pp. 40-42.

50. The ratio is computed from our estimated farm price (in 1933 yuan) of tung nuts in 1933 (4 yuan/picul, Appendix B) and the average wholesale price (about 20 yuan/picul) given in Hsu Ming, Yu-tung chi tsai-pai yu kai-liang (Planting and Improvement of Tung Trees), Chungking, 1943, p. 260.

51. Average of prices obtained from CKJP, Chungking, November 1952 issues.

52. (Fukien) FKJP, Foochow, May 21, 1952, and September 8, 1952; (Kwangtung) NFJP, Canton, August 16, 1952; (East China) NFJP, Canton, April 19, 1952; (Yunnan) YNJP, Kunming, June 14, 1952.

Appendix E

GROSS AND NET VALUE OF AGRICULTURAL PRODUCTION, 1933 AND 1952-57

This appendix explains the derivation of the authors' and the adjusted estimates for the gross and net values of agricultural production presented in **Tables 36 and 68.**

The adjusted estimates were taken directly from Communist data.[1] Primary data for the authors' estimates were taken from the works of noted Chinese scholars as well as from Communist sources. The authors' estimates are unique combinations of the field studies, adjusted for bias, such as food crop and vegetable production in 1952-56, hogs in 1957, and miscellaneous products in 1952-57. In some cases, no adjustment was necessary. All estimates are given in 1933 and 1952 prices.

GROSS VALUE OF AGRICULTURAL PRODUCTION

Three different methods have been used in estimating the gross value of agricultural products.

(I) For most products, the gross values of production are obtained simply by multiplying output estimates (given in Appendixes A and C) by farm prices (given in Appendixes B and D). The agricultural products in this category are (a) food crops, oil bearing crops, fiber crops, other industrial crops, wool, silkworm cocoons, fruits, and tung nuts for all the years 1933 and 1952-57; (b) vegetables in 1933; (c) livestock in all years: (d) the utilization of poultry and poultry eggs in 1933 and 1952; and (3) timber and fishery products in 1952-57.

(II) For certain products, data on output and price are either unavailable or incomplete, but are available on gross value of output. Therefore, these gross value figures are used directly in our estimates. In this category are timber, other forest products, and fishery products in 1933.

(III) For still other products for which the data on output in certain years are not available, their gross value of production in these years is estimated indirectly on the basis of a ratio of their value to th value of the products of another group (in a year for which data on both groups are available). Included in this category are: (a) vegetables in 1952-57; (b) poultry through increase in numbers in 1952-57 and through utilization and production of eggs in 1953-57; (c) other forest products i 1952-57; and (d) miscellaneous products in 1933 and 1952-57 such as spice linseed, and dairy products; small animals such as rabbits and pigeons; a by-products such as camel hair and buckskin.

The derivation of the gross values of the products in Group (I) requi no explanation. The method of estimating the gross values of the products in the Groups (II) and (III) is described in the following subsections.

The estimated gross values of individual products are presented in Tables E-1, E-2, and E-3, and summarized in Table E-4.

Timber and Other Forest Products in 1933 and 1952-57

The value of annual production of the forest industry can be divided into three categories: (1) value added through the net increase in the forest area; (2) value added through the amount of timber logged; and (3) value added through forest products obtained without felling the trees. H ever, for the year 1933, there are no systematically collected data on the year-to-year change in the forest area; nor is there any information on th output and prices of raw timber, fuel woods, and other forest products, su as waxes, resin, barks, corks, and syrups. For 1933 the value produced by the forest industry is simply estimated by multiplying the total forest ar

ESTIMATED GROSS VALUE OF AGRICULTURAL PRODUCTS, 1933 AND 1952-57

Product[a]	Billions of 1933 yuan							Billions of 1952 yuan						
	1933	1952	1953	1954	1955	1956	1957	1933	1952	1953	1954	1955	1956	1957
Plant products, total														
Authors'	17.12	16.54	16.70	17.10	17.67	17.79	17.76	29.81	29.57	29.79	30.45	31.71	32.06	32.04
Adjusted	17.12	14.86	14.91	15.26	16.79	17.66	17.76	29.81	26.75	26.79	27.36	30.23	31.84	32.04
Food crops, total														
Authors'	12.64	12.86	13.15	13.57	13.66	13.56	13.58	20.98	21.63	22.09	22.82	22.97	22.82	22.81
Adjusted	12.64	11.27	11.45	11.81	12.82	13.43	13.58	20.98	18.95	19.23	19.87	21.56	22.61	22.81
Paddy rice														
Authors'	5.60	5.46	5.73	5.70	5.83	5.83	6.08	8.48	8.28	8.67	8.63	8.83	8.83	9.20
Adjusted	5.60	4.79	4.99	4.96	5.46	5.77	6.08	8.48	7.25	7.55	7.51	8.27	8.74	9.20
Wheat														
Authors'	2.46	1.91	1.94	2.46	2.24	2.30	2.18	4.27	3.33	3.37	4.27	3.90	4.01	3.78
Adjusted	2.46	1.67	1.68	2.15	2.11	2.28	2.18	4.27	2.90	2.93	3.73	3.67	3.97	3.78
Miscellaneous food crops														
Authors'	3.97	3.99	3.96	3.85	3.98	3.67	3.58	7.01	7.04	6.98	6.79	7.02	6.48	6.32
Adjusted	3.97	3.50	3.45	3.35	3.73	3.63	3.58	7.01	6.18	6.08	5.91	6.59	6.40	6.32
Potatoes														
Authors'	0.61	1.49	1.53	1.56	1.61	1.75	1.75	1.22	2.99	3.06	3.12	3.22	3.51	3.50
Adjusted	0.61	1.31	1.33	1.36	1.51	1.75	1.75	1.22	2.61	2.66	2.72	3.02	3.50	3.50
Soybeans	0.92	0.74	0.77	0.71	0.71	0.80	0.78	1.65	1.33	1.39	1.27	1.28	1.43	1.41
Oil-bearing crops, total	0.83	0.54	0.51	0.57	0.63	0.64	0.55	1.58	1.03	0.97	1.09	1.21	1.24	1.06
Peanuts	0.35	0.24	0.22	0.29	0.30	0.35	0.27	0.70	0.49	0.45	0.58	0.61	0.70	0.54
Rapeseed	0.25	0.11	0.10	0.10	0.11	0.11	0.10	0.46	0.20	0.19	0.19	0.21	0.20	0.19
Sesame	0.15	0.08	0.09	0.09	0.09	0.07	0.05	0.28	0.15	0.16	0.16	0.17	0.13	0.09
Cottonseed	0.08	0.10	0.09	0.09	0.12	0.12	0.13	0.14	0.19	0.17	0.15	0.22	0.21	0.24
Plant fibers, total	0.74	1.02	0.83	0.76	1.12	1.08	1.23	1.88	2.62	2.18	1.99	2.92	2.79	3.18
Cotton	0.60	0.82	0.74	0.67	0.95	0.91	1.03	1.61	2.22	2.00	1.81	2.58	2.45	2.78
Hemp crops	0.14	0.20	0.09	0.09	0.17	0.17	0.20	0.27	0.40	0.18	0.18	0.34	0.34	0.40
Other industrial crops, total	0.52	0.33	0.32	0.36	0.43	0.53	0.42	1.12	0.67	0.66	0.75	0.91	1.12	0.88
Sugar cane	0.05	0.09	0.09	0.10	0.10	0.10	0.12	0.08	0.14	0.14	0.17	0.16	0.17	0.21
Sugar beets	(*)	(*)	(*)	0.01	0.02	0.02	0.02	(*)	0.02	0.02	0.04	0.06	0.07	0.06
Tobacco	0.34	0.19	0.19	0.20	0.24	0.35	0.22	0.69	0.39	0.38	0.41	0.53	0.71	0.45
Tea	0.13	0.04	0.04	0.50	0.06	0.06	0.06	0.35	0.11	0.12	0.13	0.15	0.17	0.16
Vegetables														
Authors'	0.75	0.74	0.75	0.77	0.80	0.80	0.80	1.31	1.31	1.31	1.34	1.40	1.41	1.41
Adjusted	0.75	0.67	0.67	0.68	0.75	0.79	0.80	1.31	1.18	1.17	1.20	1.34	1.40	1.41
Fruits	0.73	0.30	0.36	0.36	0.31	0.38	0.40	1.28	0.98	1.19	1.19	1.02	1.24	1.30

Notes:
(*) Less than 0.005 billion yuan.
[a] Where the figures are the same, only one is given.

Table E-2

ESTIMATED GROSS VALUE OF ANIMAL PRODUCTS, 1933 AND 1952-57

Product[a]	Billions of 1933 yuan							Billions of 1952 yuan						
	1933	1952	1953	1954	1955	1956	1957	1933	1952	1953	1954	1955	1956	1957
Animal products, total														
Authors'	1.85	2.59	2.63	2.53	2.18	2.40	2.23	4.48	6.11	6.22	5.98	5.11	5.83	5.51
Adjusted	1.85	2.59	2.63	2.53	2.18	2.40	3.39	4.48	6.11	6.22	5.98	5.11	5.83	8.57
Increase in number, total														
Authors'		0.46	0.37	0.12	-0.06	0.19	-0.02		0.96	0.74	0.13	-0.26	0.56	0.08
Adjusted		0.46	0.37	0.12	-0.06	0.19	0.75		0.96	0.74	0.13	-0.26	0.56	2.11
Cattle		0.20	0.18	0.15	0.08	-0.05	-0.09		0.30	0.27	0.22	0.11	-0.07	-0.14
Horses		0.02	0.02	0.02	0.01	(*)	(*)		0.04	0.04	0.04	0.03	-0.01	-0.01
Mules		0.01	(*)	(*)	(*)	(*)	(*)		0.03	0.02	(*)	(*)	(*)	(*)
Donkeys		0.02	0.01	(*)	-0.01	-0.02	(*)		0.05	0.03	(*)	-0.03	-0.04	(*)
Sheep and goats		0.04	0.03	0.02	0.02	0.02	0.01		0.08	0.08	0.05	0.04	0.05	0.03
Hogs														
Authors'		0.16	0.10	-0.07	-0.15	0.23	0.05		0.42	0.27	-0.19	-0.40	0.60	0.12
Adjusted		0.16	0.10	-0.07	-0.15	0.23	0.82		0.42	0.27	-0.19	-0.40	0.60	2.16
Poultry		0.01	0.01	(*)	(*)	(*)	0.02		0.04	0.03	(*)	(*)	0.02	0.08
Livestock and poultry utilized, total														
Authors'	1.47	1.81	1.94	2.06	1.89	1.84	1.88	3.61	4.42	4.74	5.03	4.54	4.42	4.54
Adjusted	1.47	1.81	1.94	2.06	1.89	1.84	2.27	3.61	4.42	4.74	5.03	4.54	4.42	5.56
Cattle	0.21	0.30	0.32	0.33	0.35	0.35	0.34	0.32	0.45	0.47	0.50	0.52	0.53	0.50
Horses	0.02	0.01	0.01	0.01	0.01	0.01	0.01	0.04	0.03	0.03	0.03	0.03	0.03	0.03
Mules	0.01	(*)	(*)	(*)	(*)	(*)	(*)	0.03	0.01	0.01	0.01	0.01	0.01	0.01
Donkeys	0.01	0.01	0.01	0.01	0.01	0.01	0.01	0.03	0.03	0.03	0.03	0.03	0.03	0.03
Sheep and goats	0.10	0.09	0.10	0.11	0.12	0.13	0.14	0.23	0.20	0.23	0.26	0.27	0.29	0.31
Hogs														
Authors'	0.98	1.25	1.34	1.42	1.22	1.17	1.20	2.59	3.30	3.54	3.74	3.23	3.09	3.17
Adjusted	0.98	1.25	1.34	1.42	1.22	1.17	1.59	2.59	3.30	3.54	3.74	3.23	3.09	4.20
Poultry, total	0.14	0.15	0.16	0.17	0.17	0.17	0.18	0.38	0.40	0.43	0.46	0.44	0.44	0.48
Chickens	0.11	0.11						0.30	0.29					
Ducks	0.02	0.03						0.06	0.08					
Geese	0.01	0.01						0.02	0.03					
Other animal products, total	0.37	0.32	0.32	0.35	0.36	0.36	0.37	0.87	0.74	0.74	0.81	0.84	0.85	0.89
Eggs, total	0.23	0.24	0.25	0.27	0.26	0.26	0.28	0.45	0.47	0.51	0.54	0.52	0.51	0.57
Chicken eggs	0.18	0.18						0.36	0.36					
Duck eggs	0.04	0.05						0.08	0.10					
Geese eggs	(*)	(*)						0.01	0.01					
Wool	0.03	0.02	0.02	0.03	0.03	0.03	0.03	0.16	0.13	0.15	0.17	0.17	0.19	0.20
Silkworm cocoons														
Domesticated	0.11	0.04	0.04	0.04	0.04	0.04	0.04	0.23	0.08	0.08	0.08	0.09	0.09	0.09
Wild	0.01	0.02	(*)	0.01	0.03	0.02	0.02	0.03	0.05	0.01	0.02	0.06	0.05	0.04

Notes:
(*) Less than 0.005 billion yuan.

Table E-3

ESTIMATED GROSS VALUE OF FOREST, FISHERY, AND MISCELLANEOUS PRODUCTS, 1933 AND 1952-57

Product[a]	Billions of 1933 yuan							Billions of 1952 yuan						
	1933	1952	1953	1954	1955	1956	1957	1933	1952	1953	1954	1955	1956	1957
Forest products, total	0.62	0.60	0.71	0.80	0.79	0.79	0.93	1.29	1.19	1.49	1.73	1.68	1.69	2.04
Timber and general forest products	0.57	0.55	0.67	0.76	0.75	0.75	0.89	1.21	1.10	1.41	1.65	1.61	1.61	1.96
Tung nuts	0.04	0.05	0.04	0.04	0.04	0.04	0.04	0.08	0.09	0.08	0.08	0.08	0.08	0.08
Fishery products	0.43	0.49	0.55	0.67	0.74	0.77	0.91	0.56	0.63	0.72	0.87	0.96	1.01	1.18
Miscellaneous products														
Authors'	1.16	1.17	1.19	1.22	1.24	1.26	1.27	2.10	2.18	2.22	2.26	2.29	2.35	2.36
Adjusted	1.16	1.08	1.09	1.12	1.19	1.25	1.33	2.10	2.01	2.04	2.08	2.20	2.34	2.54

Note:

[a] Where the figures are the same, only one is given.

Table E-4

ESTIMATED GROSS VALUE OF TOTAL AGRICULTURAL PRODUCTION, 1933 AND 1952-57

	1933	1952	1953	1954	1955	1956	1957
			Billions of 1933 yuan				
Gross value of production[a]							
Authors' estimate	21.17	21.38	21.78	22.32	22.62	23.01	23.10
Adjusted estimate	21.17	19.61	19.90	20.38	21.68	22.87	24.33
a. Plant products, total							
Authors'	17.12	16.54	16.70	17.10	17.67	17.79	17.76
Adjusted	17.12	14.86	14.91	15.26	16.79	17.66	
b. Animal products, total							
Authors'	1.85	2.59	2.63	2.53	2.18	2.40	2.23
Adjusted	1.85	2.59	2.63	2.53	2.18	2.40	3.39
c. Forest products, total	0.62	0.60	0.71	0.80	0.79	0.79	0.93
d. Fishery products, total	0.43	0.49	0.55	0.67	0.74	0.77	0.91
e. Miscellaneous products, total							
Authors'	1.16	1.17	1.19	1.22	1.24	1.26	1.27
Adjusted	1.16	1.08	1.09	1.12	1.19	1.25	1.33
			Billions of 1952 yuan				
Gross value of production							
Authors' estimate	38.24	39.68	40.44	41.30	41.76	42.94	43.15
Adjusted estimate	38.24	36.70	37.26	38.03	40.19	42.70	46.38
a. Plant products, total							
Authors'	29.81	29.57	29.79	30.45	31.71	32.06	32.04
Adjusted	29.81	26.79	26.79	27.36	30.23	31.84	32.04
b. Animal products, total							
Authors'	4.48	6.11	6.22	5.98	5.11	5.83	5.51
Adjusted	4.48	6.11	6.22	5.98	5.11	5.83	8.57
c. Forest products, total	1.29	1.19	1.49	1.73	1.68	1.69	2.04
d. Fishery products, total	0.56	0.63	0.72	0.87	0.96	1.01	1.18
e. Miscellaneous products, total							
Authors'	2.10	2.18	2.22	2.26	2.29	2.35	2.36
Adjusted	2.10	2.01	2.04	2.08	2.20	2.34	2.54

Note:

[a]Where the figures are the same, only one is given.

Sources:

by an estimated value of output per unit area. Information, though scarce, is available for these two items.

The forest acreage has been reported at 1,443, 1,380, and 1,366 million mow for 1933, 1934, and 1935.[2] We take the round figure of 1,400 million mow as the estimate for 1933. From the information given in Table E-5, it is estimated that the value of forest products per mow of forest land in 12 provinces amounted to about 112.4/276 = 0.41 yuan. The gross value of forest products for 1933, in 1933 prices, is therefore equal to 1,400 x 0.41 = 574 million yuan. Other forest products accounted for 53 per cent of the total;[3] therefore, gross value of timber and other forest products, in 1933 yuan, amounted to 270 million and 304 million yuan. Gross values in 1952 prices are estimated at 721 million and 492 million yuan, by multiplying the estimates in 1933 prices by the price index numbers for these two products in 1952 (267 and 162, with 1933 as 100).[4]

The value of timber and tung nuts produced during 1952-57 falls under category (I) enumerated above and requires no further explanation. Only the value of other forest products has to be estimated. These forest products consisted mainly of fuel wood, and since per capita consumption of fuel wood in the postwar years is not likely to be significantly different from that in prewar years, it is assumed that forest products increased from 1933 to 1952-57 in proportion to total population over the same period. Total population in 1933 and 1952-57 being known, the value of forest products for 1952-57 can be estimated.

Gross value of timber and other forest products for 1952-57 in 1933 prices can then be easily calculated from the price index number of these two products given above.

Table E-5

VALUE OF FOREST PRODUCTS AND FOREST ACREAGE

IN 12 PROVINCES, 1933

Province	Value (million yuan) (1)	Acreage (million mow) (2)
Anhwei	1.5	107.0
Chahar	0.4	2.3
Chekiang	24.3	12.1
Honan	11.2	1.6
Hopei	7.2	1.9
Hunan	2.9	61.4
Kiangsi	2.7	30.3
Kiangsu	1.4	4.1
Kwangsi	6.8	16.5
Kwangtung	48.5	33.6
Shantung	5.4	1.6
Suiyuan	0.1	3.6
Total	112.4	276.0

Sources:

Column (1): Statistical Abstract, 1935, p. 557.

Column (2): Economic Yearbook, 1934, pp. H3-H9.

Fishery Products in 1933

The gross value of fishery products for China proper in 1933 has been estimated at 426.0 million yuan.[5] The same source also gives the 1933 output of fishery products as 29.1 million piculs. The average price is therefore 14.6 yuan per picul.

For Manchuria, the gross value of fishery products has been reported to be 4.0 million yuan.[6] On the assumption that the 1933 price of fishery products in Manchuria was the same as in China proper, the quantity of output is equal to 0.3 million piculs.

For China as a whole, the gross value of fishery products in 1933 comes to 430.0 million yuan, and the output 29.4 million piculs.

Vegetables, 1952-57

Data on vegetables are not sufficient to estimate the value of production for the postwar years. On the assumption that the ratio of the value of vegetables to that of the principal plant products (that is, food crops, soybeans, oil bearing crops, plant fibers, and other industrial crops) in the postwar years is the same as in 1933, the value of vegetables for 1952-57 can be computed on the basis of the value of the principal plant products in the same years.

Poultry, 1952-57

Since the numbers of the different categories of poultry and their respective prices in 1952 are known,[7] the value of the stock, in 1952 prices, can be derived as follows:

	Number (million head)	Price (yuan/head)	Value (million yuan)
Chickens	265.1	1.1	291.6
Ducks	64.1	1.3	83.3
Geese	10.0	2.9	29.0
Total			403.9

Value added through change in the number of poultry in 1952 is assumed to bear a ratio to the midyear 1952 stock equal to the corresponding ratio for livestock; it can then be easily estimated at 35.1 million yuan in 1952 prices or 12.5 million yuan in 1933 prices. Value added by changes in the number of poultry is then assumed to vary from 1952 through successive years to 1957 in proportion to value added by livestock. The computation in both 1933 and 1952 prices is presented in Table E-6.

The value of poultry utilized in each year is assumed to be equal to the stock in existence in midyear.[8] It is therefore equal to 404 million yuan in 1952 prices or 149 million yuan in 1933 prices. For the later years, the midyear stock of poultry (or the value of poultry utilized) is assumed to vary from 1952 through successive years to 1957 in proportion to the midyear value of livestock. The computation is given in Table E-7.

Poultry Eggs, 1953-57

Data on the number of eggs produced in 1953-57 are not available. The value of eggs is derived indirectly by applying the annual index of the value of poultry to the 1952 value of eggs.[9] The value of eggs produced in 1953-57 so computed is given as follows:

Table E-6

VALUE ADDED BY LIVESTOCK AND POULTRY THROUGH INCREASES IN NUMBER, 1952-57

(millions of yuan)

Year	Livestock (1)	Poultry (2)
In 1933 prices		
1952	448	13
1953	356	10
1954	117	3
1955	- 59	- 2
1956	185	5
1957	732	21
In 1952 prices		
1952	923	35
1953	709	27
1954	128	5
1955	-248	- 9
1956	538	21
1957	2,036	77

Notes:

Column (1): Sum of value added through increases in the numbers of cattle, horses, mules, donkeys, sheep and goats, and hogs, computed from data given in Table E-2.

Column (2): 1952 figure from text. The other figures are obtained on the 1952 ratio of the figures for livestock and poultry and the data on livestock for these years.

Table E-7

VALUE OF LIVESTOCK AND POULTRY UTILIZED, 1952-57

(millions of yuan)

Year	Livestock (1)	Poultry (2)
In 1933 prices		
1952	5,320	149
1953	5,670	159
1954	6,015	168
1955	5,916	166
1956	5,891	165
1957 (adjusted)	6,287	176
(authors')	5,803	176
In 1952 prices		
1952	10,496	404
1953	11,197	431
1954	11,881	457
1955	11,476	442
1956	11,371	437
1957 (adjusted)	12,558	483
(authors')	11,279	483

Notes:

Column (1): Obtained by summing up the products of the midyear numbers of various livestock, given in Appendix C, Table C-2, and their respective prices per head, given in Table 34.

Column (2): Value of poultry in existence at midyear. It is assumed to vary in proportion to the midyear value of livestock.

	1933 yuan (millions)	1952 yuan (millions)
1952	237	475
1953	253	506
1954	268	537
1955	264	519
1956	263	514
1957	281	568

Miscellaneous Products, 1933 and 1952-57

The estimates of the gross value of production of the four major groups (plant, animal, forest, and fishery products), have covered practically all the important products in agriculture. However, owing to the lack of data, there are still a number of minor products whose values have not yet been separately estimated. Products in this group include plant products such as taro, lotus roots, natural rubber, dye-stuff, spices, medicinal herbs, perilla, linseed, castor seed, flowers cultured for commercial purposes; other products such as honey, milk and other dairy products; and animals and animal by-products such as rabbits, pigeons, camel hair, deer, and buckskin. While the value of the output of each of these products may be negligible, the sum of their values is significant.

According to J. L. Buck, miscellaneous products contributed about 5.5 per cent of the total farm receipts in the prewar years.[10] On the assumption that this percentage is also applicable to the estimates for the postwar years, the value of miscellaneous products in 1933 and 1952-57 can be derived from the aggregate value of output in the four major groups of products given in Table E-4.

DEDUCTIBLE COSTS OF PRODUCTION

Plant Products

Among the production costs of plant products, the following items should be deducted from the gross value of output: costs of seeds, purchased fertilizers, repair and maintenance expenses of farm implements and buildings, and agricultural chemicals for killing insects and preventing diseases.[11]

1933. Our estimates of the deductible costs of plant products in 1933, expressed as percentages of the gross value of plant products, are based upon information obtained from seven studies, covering nine principal crops in ten provinces.[12] The basic data on the percentage shares of the cost items and the average percentages computed from these data are given in Table E-8. The estimates of the ratios of each cost item to the aggregate gross value of plant products varied greatly from one study to another. The discrepancies are due mainly to the differences in crops included and in the area covered by the various studies. Since there is no a priori basis for assigning weights to these estimates, a simple average of these percentage figures for each item is taken to represent the prewar ratio. However, some nondeductible costs are also included in the costs of production. To eliminate the nondeductible portions of these cost ratios, adjustments are made on the basis of information provided by the Farmer's Bank study as follows.[13]

Seed: Nearly all the seeds used were produced on the farm, and their value of output has been included in our estimate of gross value of plant products. The entire 3.7 per cent should be deducted from the gross value of production.

Table E-8

COST OF PRODUCTION: PERCENTAGES OF GROSS VALUE OF PLANT PRODUCTS, 1921-41

Investigator	Period	Province	Cost items: Seeds	Fertilizers	Repair and maintenance of: Implements	Buildings
Buck[a]	1921-25	7 provinces	1.0	1.4	1.2	1.7
Swen[b]	1924	Shantung	3.2	27.3	3.0	2.5
Hsu[c]	1926-27	Kiangsu	2.8	15.2	2.5	3.5
Chen & Chang[b]	-	Hopei	6.3	11.0	2.0	0.3
Han[b]	1934	Kwangsi	6.3	14.5	1.7	1.1
University of Chekiang[b]	1934	Chekiang	3.4	31.3	1.4	-
Farmer's Bank[d]	1940-41	Szechwan	2.8	11.7	6.3	5.4
Average	1921-41		3.7	16.1	2.6	2.4

Notes:

- Not available.

[a] Percentage share of expense items in the total receipts (including both cash receipts and imputed value of farm household consumption) from plant products, based on data in Farm Economy, Table 23, p. 65, and Table 31, p. 75. The seven provinces are Anhwei, Chekiang, Fukien, Honan, Hopei, Kiangsu, and Shansi.

[b] Original publications are not available. Data are taken from National Income, Vol. II, pp. 1, 2, 5, and 7.

[c] Hsu Fank-kan, Wang Mou-shui, and Kung Chun, "Survey of Farmers' Living Conditions in Ihsin and Wuching," Tung-fang tsa-chih (Eastern Miscellany), Shanghai, Vol. 24, No. 16, August 1927, pp. 85-89 and 105-109.

[d] Based on data from the Farmer's Bank of China, Tiao-tsa pao-kao (Report on an Agricultural Survey of Szechwan Province), Chungking, 1941, Vol. I, Appendix III, Tables 1, 4, 7, and 10, pp. 53-64.

Fertilizers: An overwhelmingly large portion of fertilizers used on farms, such as night soil, manure, and ashes, was obtained from the farm or from nearby cities. Since these items have not been included as a part of income, they should not be counted as deductible costs. Only a small portic of fertilizers, including lime, bonemeal, oil cakes, and chemical fertilize was purchased from nonagricultural industries. According to the Farmer's B study, this portion of purchased fertilizers was about 23 per cent of the total expenditure on fertilizers. This means that the deductible costs of fertilizers were 3.7 per cent (23 per cent of 16.1 per cent) of the gross value of plant production.

Repair and maintenance of implements: The agricultural implements usec on Chinese farms are mostly simple tools made of bamboo, wood, and/or iron, manually operated or pulled by draft animals. The repair and maintenance are usually done by farmers themselves without involving much paid labor or material costs. The Farmer's Bank study indicates that the deductible porti was only about 11 per cent of such repair and maintenance expenses. It mean that these deductible costs accounted for only 0.3 per cent (11 per cent of 2.6 per cent) of the gross value of plant production.

Repair and maintenace of farm buildings: According to the Farmer's Ban study, the deductible portion was about 18.5 per cent of the repair and maintenance expenses of farm buildings, or 0.4 per cent (18.5 per cent of 2.4 per cent) of the gross value of plant production. This estimate seems reasonable in view of the fact that the repair and maintenance of Chinese farm buildings are done mostly by the farmers. Besides being used as residences, the buildings are used also for the storage of plant products and farm tools, and for sheltering livestock and poultry.[14] There can be no doubt that the storage of plant products is by far the principal commercial use of farm buildings. A part of the repair and maintenance expenses should also be charged to animal and other products; it is, of course, impossible to allocate these joint costs. The entire repair and maintenance expenses are therefore included here.

The deductible costs of producing plant products in the prewar period amounted to about 8 per cent of their aggregate gross value of output. (The percentages for individual items are given in the first column of Table E-10.)

1952-57. The basic data on postwar costs of agricultural production are presented in Table E-9.

Seeds: While there are four sources of information on this product, the survey made by the State Statistical Bureau covers a much larger area than the other studies. Its estimate is used in this study.

Fertilizers: Information on the cost of fertilizers in the postwar period is not available in the State Statistical Bureau's study. Average cost of fertilizers computed from the other three studies amounted to 22 per cent of the gross value of plant production. This figure includes both farm produced and purchased fertilizers. Based on the estimate by the Farmer's Bank that purchased fertilizers accounted for about 23 per cent of all expenses on fertilizers, the deductible portion is thus computed to be 5 per cent (23 per cent of 22 per cent) of the gross value of production.

Repair and maintenance of farm implements and farm buildings: Data on the costs of these items in the postwar period are not available. It is likely, however, that such repair and maintenance are done mostly by the farmers themselves with few paid expenses. Similar to 1933, these two items are estimated at 0.3 and 0.4 per cent of the total gross value of plant output produced.

Table E-9

COST OF PRODUCTION: PERCENTAGES OF GROSS VALUE OF PLANT PRODUCTS, 1953-57

Investigator	Period	Province	Cost items: Seed	Ferti-lizers	Agricultur. chemicals
State Statistical Bureau[a]	1954	24 provinces	4.4	-	-
Chia and Chen[b]	1953-56	Chekiang	4.0	17.2	0.3
Communist Party[c]	1957	Liaoning	0.8	19.8	0
Shanghai College of Social Science[d]	1957	Kiangsu	7.2	29.6	2.3

Notes:

- Not available.

[a] SSB, "Data on the 1955 Survey of Income and Expenditures of Agricultural Cooperatives," HHPYK, Peiping, No. 24, December 1956, pp. 63-65.

[b] Chia Hung-yu and Chen Yung-ping, "Economic Survey of the Advanced Agricultural Producers' Cooperatives in Kingshan, Haining Hsien, Chekiang Province," Ts'ai-ching yen-chiu (Financial and Economic Research), Shanghai, No. 1, March 1957, pp. 49-57, and No. 2, June 1957, pp. 51-60. These are the average percentages for the four-year period, 1953-56.

[c] Computed from crop income and cost figures given in People's Daily, October 22, 1957, by the Heishan Hsien Committee, Chinese Communist Party.

[d] Prepared by the senior students of the Department of Public Finance, Trust, and Credit, "Survey of the Costs of Producing Major Agricultural Products (Rice, Cotton and Vegetables)," Ts'ai-ching yen-chiu, No. 7, October 1958, pp. 29-30. The percentages are computed from the average costs of producing rice, cotton, Irish potatoes, winter melons, and mustard greens in the total value of their production in 1957.

Equipment and chemicals for insect control and other purposes: The use of spraying and dusting equipment and chemicals for the control of insect pests and the prevention of plant diseases and the use of small motorized irrigation facilities increased during the years immediately after the Second World War.[15] Postwar studies show that these cost items accounted for, on the average, about 1 per cent of the gross value of plant production. Since they are purchased from nonagricultural industries, the total amount should be deducted from the gross value of crop production.

The deductible costs used in this study for the years 1952-57, totalling about 11 per cent of the gross value of plant production, are given in Table E-10.

The question may be raised whether it is reasonable to assume that the ratio of deductible costs to the gross value of production was constant for all the postwar years 1952-57. The answer appears to be in the affirmative. First of all, the Communists' data on the ratios of the cost of production to the gross value of production of 1952, 1953, and 1956, given in Table E-11, do not vary significantly.[16] It is indeed not surprising that the ratios remain fairly constant. In spite of the Communist claim that the production of modern farm tools and chemical fertilizers has been increasing in recent years, the supply available per unit of sown acreage was negligible throughout the period. Table E-12 shows the total numbers of tractors, improved plows, and the quantity of chemical fertilizers supplied in each year, together with the sown acreage. It is seen from this table that there were less than 5 tractors per million mow of sown acreage in 1957 (about 28 tractors per one million acres), compared with 1 tractor per 19 million mow (1 tractor per three million acres) in 1953. The amount of chemical fertilizers, including both domestic production and imports, per mow of sown

Table E-10

DEDUCTIBLE COSTS OF PRODUCING PLANT PRODUCTS

AS PERCENTAGES OF GROSS VALUE OF OUTPUT

Product	1933	1952-57
Seeds	3.7	4.4
Fertilizers	3.7	5.1
Repair and maintenance of tools	0.3	0.3
Repair and maintenance of buildings	0.4	0.4
Insecticides and others	-	0.9
Total	8.1	11.1

Note:

- Not available.

Table E-11

COMMUNIST DATA ON RATIO OF PRODUCTION COSTS TO GROSS VALUE OF AGRICULTURAL PRODUCTION

(billions of 1952 yuan)

	1952	1953	1956
Gross value of agricultural and subsidiary production[a]	48.4	49.9	58.3
Net value of agricultural and subsidiary production[b]	36.2	37.0	42.9
Cost of production[c]	12.2	12.9	15.4
Ratio of cost to gross value (per cent)	25.2	25.8	26.4

Notes:

[a] For 1952 and 1953, 1955 Statistical Abstract, p. 36; for 1956, 1956 Statistical Abstract, p. 23.

[b] The figure for 1952 is derived from the percentage of net value of agricultural production in national income (59.2 per cent of 61.13 billion yuan), given by Lu Kuang in "China's National Income," Peking Review, Peiping, No. 6, April 8, 1958, pp. 7-8. The 1953 figure is given by Ma Yin-chu in "New Population Theory," HHPYK, No. 15, August 1957, p. 40. The figure for 1956 is based on the ratio of net value to gross value in agriculture, 73.6 per cent. Ibid.

[c] Difference between gross and net values of production. The Communist cost of production includes depreciation charges.

Table E-12

SUPPLY OF FARM IMPLEMENTS AND CHEMICAL FERTILIZERS PER UNIT AREA, ESTIMATED ON THE BASIS OF COMMUNIST DATA, 1952-57

	1952	1953	1954	1955	1956	1957
Total sown acreage[a] (million mow)	2,119	2,161	2,219	2,266	2,390	2,359
Total number of tractors[b] (standard unit of 15 hp)	-	113	778	2,377	9,862	10,933
Number of tractor per million mow of sown acreage	-	0.05	0.35	1.05	4.13	4.63
Total number of improved plows[b] (thousand units of double-bladed wheel plows)	(*)	8	18	368	1,070	2,500
Number of improved plows per million mow of sown acreage	-	0.004	0.008	0.163	0.448	1.060
Total supply of chemical fertilizers[b] (million piculs)	6	11	16	23	32	40
Use of chemical fertilizers per mow (catties)	0.3	0.5	0.5	1.0	1.4	1.7

Notes:

(*) Less than 500.

- Not available.

[a] Figures for 1952-55 are taken from the 1955 Statistical Abstract; for 1956, 1956 Statistical Abstract, p. 39; for 1957, the FFYP Communique.

[b] Figures for 1952-56 are taken from Yang Pei-hsin, "The Ways of Financing for Agricultural Development," CCYC, Peiping, No. 1, January 1958, p. 33. Figures for 1957 are based on the Ministry of Agriculture, Communist Government, "China's Food Crop Production During the First Five Year Plan Period," HHPYK, No. 9, May 1958, pp. 81-82.

acreage was 1.7 catties (about 11 pounds per acre) in 1957, compared with 0.3 catty (about 2 pounds per acre) in 1952. While the relative increase in the amount of fertilizers used per unit area is substantial, if the claim is reliable, the amount per unit area in 1957 is extremely small and would not noticeably change the cost of production per unit area.[17]

Animal and Animal Products

The deductible costs of production in this category consist of expenses for foodstuff, prevention and cure of diseases, and repair and maintenance of animal shelters. Data on expenses for the prevention and cure of animal diseases are not available, but they are believed to be negligible. On Chinese farms, livestock and poultry are usually kept in the same building used for residence, crop storage, and other purposes. Barns, stables, or poultry houses specially built for animals are almost nonexistent. The repair and maintenance expenses of farm buildings have already been accounted for. This leaves only the cost of feed to be considered. According to Buck's survey of farm business in China,[18] the ratio of feed expense to the value of total animal stock was about 10 per cent. On the assumption that this ratio is applicable to all years under investigation, our estimate of feed expense is obtained by taking 10 per cent of the aggregate value of animal stock in each year. The results are given in Table E-13.

Forest Products

Logging and the production of forest products in China is done chiefly by manual and animal labor, with simple tools such as saws, axes, wooden carts, and baskets. Except at a few places in Manchuria, modern machinery has not been used extensively; therefore, the costs of repairing and maintaining logging equipment must be very small. Moreover, there has been

Table E-13

FEED EXPENSES, 1933 AND 1952-57

(billion yuan)

Year	In 1933 prices: Gross value of livestock and poultry[a]	In 1933 prices: Feed expense[b]	In 1952 prices: Gross value of livestock and poultry[a]	In 1952 prices: Feed expense[b]
1933	4.68	0.47	9.62	0.97
1952	5.47	0.55	10.90	1.10
1953	5.83	0.59	11.63	1.17
1954	6.18	0.62	12.34	1.25
1955	6.08	0.61	11.92	1.20
1956	6.06	0.61	11.81	1.19
1957 (adj.)	6.46	0.65	13.04	1.32
(authors')	5.98	0.60	11.76	1.19

Notes:

[a] See Table E-7.

[b] Obtained by multiplying the gross value of livestock and poultry by the ratio of feed expense to the value of livestock per farm (6.63:65.76 yuan). Farm Economy, pp. 57 and 75.

little reforestation expense as most of the forests in China grew naturally with little human care. The deductible costs of equipment and facilities are arbitrarily assumed at 3 per cent of the gross value of forest products.

Fishery Products

Data on the costs of repairing and maintaining fishing boats, fishing gear, and storage facilities are not available. However, most of the fishing boats and equipment in China are quite rudimentary, and the repair and maintenance work is done largely by the fishermen. The deductible costs for fishery are arbitrarily assumed at 5 per cent of the gross value of fishery products.

Miscellaneous Products

As most of the products in this group are plant products,[19] the ratio of deductible costs to their aggregate gross value of output is assumed to be the same as for plant products.

Deductible Costs in Money Value

Our estimates of the deductible costs for the production of plant, forest, fishery, and miscellaneous products are obtained simply by multiplying the cost ratios (estimated above) and the gross value of output of each group given in Table E-1. The results are presented in Table 36.

DEPRECIATION

Depreciation of agricultural production in 1933 is estimated at 2 per cent of the gross value of production on the basis of information given in Buck's study of farm business.[20] Since Buck's estimate of gross farm receipts included income from all agricultural products, this ratio is considered to be applicable to the gross value of all categories of agricultural products.

In Communist economic statistics, the depreciation of farm "fixed assets" is considered as a part of the production costs in agriculture.[21] However, despite numerous discussions on the methods of calculating depreciation costs,[22] the actual amount of depreciation deducted from the gross value of agricultural production is not known. One sample study of production costs conducted in Kiangsu shows that depreciation was about 2 per cent of the gross value of producing rice, cotton, potatoes, and vegetables in 1957.[23] Depreciation is therefore assumed also at 2 per cent of the gross value of agricultural production for 1952-57.

NET VALUE OF AGRICULTURAL PRODUCTION

The net value added by agriculture is obtained by subtracting costs of production and depreciation from the gross value of agricultural output. Our estimate of the net values so obtained for 1933 and 1952-57 is presented in Table 36, and the Communist estimate in Table 68.

FOOTNOTES TO APPENDIX E

1. Although the Communist estimates consist of figures directly computed from Communist output and price data, the total gross and net values of agricultural production are still different from the corresponding figures published by the Communists as such. For the differences between the Communist estimate referred to here and the Communist figures as such, see Chapter IV, from the discussion preceeding Table 68 to the end of the chapter.

2. 1933, Economic Yearbook, 1934, pp. H3-H9; 1934, The Chinese Yearbook, 1935-36, Shanghai, Commercial Press, 1935, p. 776; and 1935, Shen Pao Yearbook, 1936, pp. 904-905.

3. Statistical Abstract, 1935, p. 557. This percentage is obtained from a 1933 survey of forest products in 12 provinces.

4. For data used in deriving these price index numbers, see the discussion under construction in Appendix H, and the discussion under fuel and light in Appendix I.

5. Shen Pao Yearbook, 1936, pp. 915-916.

6. Manchoukuo Yearbook Company, Manchoukuo Yearbook, 1942, Hsinking, 1942, p. 474. The figure quoted was for 1934. In the absence of a figure for 1933, this figure is used.

7. For the numbers of chickens, ducks, and geese, see Appendix C, Table C-4, and for their respective prices, see Appendix D.

8. It should be noted that the assumption of a rate of utilization of poultry of 100 per cent of the midyear poultry population does not imply an unchanging poultry population through the years.

9. The value of egg production in 1952 is directly estimated by multiplying the number of eggs produced in that year by the corresponding 1933 and 1952 prices of eggs. For the number of eggs in 1952, see Appendix C, Table C-4; for the prices of eggs, see Table 34.

10. A survey of 2,866 farms made by Buck in seven provinces during 1921-25 showed that the income from miscellaneous products per farm was 20.77 yuan in a total farm receipt of 376.24 yuan. See **Farm Economy**, Table 23, p. 65.

11. The cost of agricultural chemicals is not estimated for 1933, as the quantity used during prewar years was negligible.

12. The nine crops are: rice, wheat, millet, kaoliang, corn, barley, sweet potatoes, soybeans, and tobacco. The ten provinces are: Anhwei, Chekiang, Fukien, Honan, Hopei, Kiangsu, Kwangsi, Shansi, Shantung, and Szechwan.

13. The Farmer's Bank of China, Tiao-tsa pao-kao (Report on an Agricultural Survey of Szechwan Province), Vol. I, Chungking, 1941, pp. 53-62.

14. See **Farm Economy**, p. 700, and Land Utilization, Vol. I, pp. 449-445

15. Several small plants for manufacturing agricultural chemicals and equipment were started by the Japanese in North and Central China during the war years of 1937-45. More facilities in this field were provided by the United Nations Relief and Rehabilitation Administration during the postwar rehabilitation period, 1945-49. Since then, China has produced large amounts of insecticides, fungicides, and appliances for farm use.

16. The Communist percentages of deductible costs given in Table E-11, around 25 per cent, are implausibly high. The main reason is that items such as green manures are included in both the cost of production and the

gross value of agricultural production. A less important reason is that the Communist data on agricultural production also include farm subsidiary production for which the percentage of deductible cost is relatively high. It is for these two reasons that the percentages of deductible costs used in this study are derived from sample data rather than from the Communist data on costs of agricultural production.

17. The Communists estimate that 1 catty of nitrogen fertilizer can increase the output of food crops by 3 catties, or the output of seed cotton by 1 catty, and that 1 catty of phosphate fertilizer can increase the output of food crops by 1.5 catties, or the output of seed cotton by 0.5 catty (CHCC, Peiping, No. 10, 1957, p. 11). The minimum effective requirement of chemical fertilizers, in addition to organic fertilizer, for various crops is estimated by the Communist Ministry of Agriculture at about 25 catties per mow (ibid., p. 8) which is very close to a prewar estimate of 23 catties per mow. The latter figure is obtained by dividing the total estimated requirement of chemical fertilizers of 30 billion catties by the total crop acreage of 1.3 billion mow. (T. H. Shen, Agricultural Resources, pp. 38 and 377.) Actual application of chemical fertilizers was 66 catties per mow in Taiwan in 1957 (based on an estimated sown acreage of about 200 million mow and total chemical fertilizer consumption of 1,318 million catties, given by China-U.S. Joint Commission on Rural Reconstruction, A Decade of Rural Progress, Washington, D. C., U.S. Government Printing Office, 1958, pp. 2 and 11), and 50 catties per mow in Japan (a figure for 1952 given by CHCC, Peiping, No. 10, 1957, p. 7).

18. Farm Economy, Table 13, p. 57, and Table 31, p. 75.

19. See the previous discussion of miscellaneous products.

20. One of the items in Buck's farm expenses is "decrease of capital," which is essentially depreciation of farm capital. This item was estimated to be 7.44 yuan against a total farm receipt of 376.24 yuan per farm. Ibid., Table 31, p. 75.

21. See Editorial Committee of the Statistical Press, Handbook of Agricultural Statistical Work, Peiping, T'ung-chi chu-pan-she, 1956 (English translation, pp. 33 and 35), and TCKT, No. 10, 1957, p. 11. The "fixed assets" are divided into two categories: the "productive" assets, such as tools, machines, and buildings; and the "nonproductive" assets, such as houses and furniture.

22. For example, see Chang Sun and Wang En-juen, "A Brief Discussion on the Fixed Assets of Industrial Enterprises and Their Depreciation," CCYC, Peiping, No. 5, October 1956, pp. 69-78.

23. Shanghai College of Social Sciences, "Survey of the Costs of Producing Major Agricultural Products (Rice, Cotton, and Vegetables)," TCYC, Peiping, No. 7, October 1958, p. 30.

Appendix F

DERIVATION OF VALUE ADDED BY FACTORIES, 1933 AND 1952-57

This appendix explains the derivation of value added by factories in 1933 and 1952-57 presented in Table 37. The first two sections describe the basic data and methods of deriving the estimates for the two periods. For convenience of exposition, the first section also presents an estimate of the number of workers employed in factories in 1933 for use in the derivation of the employment estimates by industrial sectors elsewhere, for example, in Table 55.

VALUE ADDED BY FACTORIES, 1933

The procedure of estimating net value added by factories in 1933 involves the following steps: (1) taking the gross value of output for a comprehensive list of products; (2) deducting costs of nonprimary inputs (raw materials, fuels and electricity, and miscellaneous items) to derive gross value added; and (3) reducing gross value added by 4 per cent of gross value of output as a rough allowance for depreciation. Each of these steps will be explained in turn.

Gross Value of Output and Number of Workers

Gross value of output of factories in 1933 given in Table 38, and the number of workers employed in these factories, are derived by summing the data for three different groups of factories: Chinese-owned factories in China proper, foreign-owned factories in China proper, and all factories in Manchuria. The basic data are presented in Table F-1. The sources of these data are explained below.

Table F-1

GROSS VALUE OF OUTPUT AND NUMBER OF

WORKERS IN FACTORIES, 1933

	Gross value of output (million yuan)				Number of workers (thousand)		
	China proper				China proper		
	Chinese -owned	Foreign -owned	Manchuria	Total	Chinese -owned	Foreign -owned	Manchuria
Lumber & wood products							
Lumber	4.4	5.6	11.6	21.6	1.2	1.5	2.3
Wood products	1.2	0.5	0.9	2.6	0.5	0.2	0.8
Machinery							
Machine parts	3.8	1.1	1.5	6.3	3.4	1.2	1.9
Machine manufacture & repair	27.6	4.7	4.1	36.3	25.5	2.4	2.6
Machinery, special			0.5	0.5			0.2
Others			1.8	1.8			1.5
Metals & metal products							
Iron and steel	16.9		16.5	33.4	11.2		11.0
Misc. metal products	25.1	2.8	3.2	31.1	8.7	0.9	1.5
Metal coins	41.0			41.0	0.2		
Small electrical appliances	13.4	8.0	0.1	21.4	6.5	3.0	
Transportation equipment, manufacture & repair							
Carts & carriages, automobiles	13.9	0.6	17.0	31.5	13.2	0.3	7.1
Ship building and repair	10.1	3.5	2.3	16.0	3.6	1.3	1.1
Stone, clay & glass products							
Bricks & shingles	5.3	0.3	1.7	7.3	16.3	0.3	5.1
Bricks, for industrial use			1.0	1.0			1.0
Pottery & chinaware	1.3	0.2	0.7	2.2	1.3		1.9
Glass & glassware	6.4	1.3	3.1	10.8	7.6	0.8	1.4
Cement	23.2		3.9	27.1	8.1		1.4
Others	9.6		0.1	9.7	2.7		

(Contin

Table F-1 (continued)

	Gross value of output (million yuan)				Number of workers (thousand)			
	China proper				China proper			
	Chinese -owned	Foreign -owned	Manchuria	Total	Chinese -owned	Foreign -owned	Manchuria	Total
Chemicals and chemical products								
Matches	28.3	5.5	3.5	37.3	27.4	4.6	4.8	36.7
Soap & paraffin products	9.7	5.2	0.2	15.2	3.1	0.8		4.0
Enamel	6.3	0.7		6.9	2.8	0.3		3.1
Plastics	4.2			4.2	1.5			1.5
Pharmaceutical products	7.4	5.8	0.2	13.4	0.9	1.6		2.6
Cosmetics	9.4			9.4	2.7			2.7
Dyes & paints	11.1	5.3	1.3	17.7	1.2	1.0	0.2	2.5
Oils, nonedible								
Tung oil		1.7		1.7		0.8		0.8
Kerosene	36.6			36.6	1.4			1.4
Mineral oil			5.7	5.7			1.2	1.2
Others			1.2	1.2			0.1	0.1
Coke	0.5		5.4	5.9	0.2		0.6	0.9
Charcoal			0.6	0.6			0.2	0.2
Other chemical products								
Explosives			1.6	1.6			0.5	0.5
Soda			0.4	0.4			0.1	0.1
Other industrial chemicals	10.3	3.0	1.5	14.8	2.7	0.6	0.2	3.5
Miscellaneous			2.1	2.1			1.3	1.3
Textile products								
Ginned cotton	14.5		0.8	15.3	4.3		0.4	4.7
Cotton yarn)			18.8	520.1			5.7	198.5
)	473.3	251.9			193.8	100.7		
Cotton cloth)			36.5	260.4			16.6	118.4
Silk	37.6	0.7	6.6	44.9	97.4	1.3	8.8	107.5
Silk piece goods	77.4		2.1	79.5	84.0		3.4	87.4
Wool textiles	17.1	4.2	4.9	26.2	4.8	2.0	2.7	9.5
Linen and hemp goods		1.0	1.7	2.7		0.7	1.6	2.3
Clothing & attire								
Dyed cloth	22.1	0.4	1.2	23.7	8.2	0.2	1.3	9.7
Clothing & attire	79.0	4.2	2.2	85.4	93.5	1.8	2.2	97.5

(Continued)

Table F-1 (continued)

	Gross value of output (million yuan)				Number of workers (thousand)			
	China proper				China proper			
	Chinese -owned	Foreign -owned	Manchuria	Total	Chinese -owned	Foreign -owned	Manchuria	
Leather & rubber products								
Leather	37.0	8.1	1.0	46.1	4.5	0.9	0.7	
Leather products	0.2	0.1		0.3	(*)		(*)	
Glue	0.2			0.2	0.1			
Rubber products	35.8	2.1		37.9	15.0	0.7		
Food products								
Milled rice & other husked grains	151.3		21.2	172.4	14.1		5.1	
Wheat flour	170.0		24.9	194.9	8.4		4.0	
Edible vegetable oils	54.6	3.6	97.3	155.5	9.5	0.6	8.7	
Tea	7.2	1.6		8.9	5.1	0.4		
Soybean sauce	0.2		1.9	2.0			0.5	
Salt	12.0		5.2	17.2	0.8		0.3	
Sugar	7.2	0.5		7.7	0.3			
Egg products	15.2	15.5		30.7	3.2	2.6		
Beverages, except wine & liquor	1.9	11.0	0.5	13.4	0.4	2.7	0.2	
Ice	1.0		0.6	1.6	0.3		0.2	
Other food products	15.7	6.9	7.2	29.8	9.0	2.2	2.5	
Tobacco products, wine & liquor								
Shredded tobacco	0.7			0.7	0.3			
Cigarettes	122.7	114.9	30.0	267.2	19.5	18.2	6.9	
Wine & liquor	1.5	2.4	6.0	9.9	0.5	0.8	1.5	
Paper manufacturing & printing								
Paper	9.8	1.8	3.1	14.7	3.6	0.6	0.6	
Paper products	2.9	0.5	7.9	11.3	1.8	0.2	4.7	
Printing	62.2	8.9	0.3	71.4	38.4	3.0	0.2	
Miscellaneous								
Apparatus and ornaments	7.4	0.6		8.0	5.0	0.4		
Others	6.4	0.9	1.8	9.1	2.9	1.0	0.6	
Total	1,771.4	497.4	376.7	2,645.5	783.2	163.1	129.5	1,

Note:

* Less than 0.05 thousand.

Chinese-owned factories in China proper. The only extensive survey of nese-owned factories in the prewar period is the one conducted by D. K. u on behalf of the National Resources Commission of the Chinese Governt.[1] This survey was made by specially trained investigators of the titute of Economic and Statistical Research under the direction of Lieu, took field trips to the factories and gathered the statistical information ectly from the managers of the factories.[2] The definition of manufacturing ivity in this survey was based on the listing of industrial classification the International Labor Office with only minor adjustments. The survey ered all the provinces in China proper[3] except Kansu, Sinkiang, Yunnan, ichow, Ningsia, Tsinghai, Tibet, and Mongolia. By and large, the statisal coverage of the results is believed to be quite comprehensive.[4] In paring the survey, the Institute adopted fairly elaborate measures to ure completeness of coverage in each locality.[5]

While there are undoubtedly some omissions, they probably consist tly of small handicraft workshops. Employment data for these shops are ered in our estimate of total employment in the manufacturing industry.[6]

For obvious reasons, no definite estimate of the margin of error in u's data can be made. Two general considerations suggest that there may l be a fair degree of reliability in these data. The first is that the a have been carefully checked for consistency, and where doubts arose, hecks with the factories concerned were made.[7] Second, the Institute not inexperienced in conducting surveys. A similar survey on a smaller le for factories in Shanghai was made by the same organization in 1931. sible errors resulting from fear of government taxation, exaggeration, or iberate falsification were taken into consideration in preparing the questionnaire.

However, because this survey was not originally designed for income and product measurement, the data collected are not wholly suitable for our purpose. Certain specific adjustments are necessary and will be made later. In addition, there are several general limitations. First, some of the data on gross value of output are actually records of total sales. How much of this was so derived has not been given. However, inventory changes probably were not important so that total sales were fair approximations of total gross value of output for the same period. Second, some data on gross value of output are estimates made by Lieu on the basis of the monthly output of the factory concerned and the average number of months during which other factories in the same industry were in operation. These estimates are therefore subject to possible errors apart from those involved in the survey. Third, the number of workers given by Lieu refers to that in December of 1932. For our present purpose, it is necessary to assume that the number of workers in 1933 was the same as that given in the survey.

Two sets of data on gross value of output and employment have been compiled by Lieu from the results of the survey. The first covers only those manufacturing establishments qualified as factories under the Chinese factory law, which defined a factory as one using mechanical power and employing 30 or more workers. The second includes all manufacturing establishments using mechanical power regardless of the number of workers in each establishment. In our study, the second set of data is used mainly because these data are more comparable in coverage to the Manchurian data for 1933 and the Communist data for the postwar years. For the Manchurian data, a factory refers to a manufacturing establishment with five or more workers.[8] The number of factories employing less than five persons being rather small, this definition is virtually the same as that for Lieu's data. On the other hand, the Communists define a factory in the "modern industry" as one using relatively modern technical equipment and machines in the major production process with no specification on the minimum number of workers.[9]

The data on gross value of output and employment for Chinese-owned factories in China proper given in Table F-1 are taken from Lieu's survey after several adjustments of the data are made. These adjustments include: (a) adding certain data omitted in Lieu's survey, (b) reclassifying several industries to make the data conform to our definition of factories, (c) correcting some minor errors, and (d) replacing some of Lieu's data with estimates believed to be more reliable.

(a) As noted above, the geographical coverage of Lieu's survey is not complete and data for factories in Kansu, Sinkiang, Yunnan, Ningsia, Tsinghai, Tibet, Mongolia, and certain parts of Hopei and other provinces are lacking. Furthermore, Lieu's survey does not cover the motion picture industry and the manufacturing of metal coins. To fill in these gaps the data shown in Table F-2 has been taken from diverse sources and added to the series.

(b) Included in Lieu's data are water supply and electric power, which we classify as utilities, and certain mineral products, which are classified as mining in this study. These figures are therefore omitted in Table F-1.

(c) Several figures given in Lieu's survey are believed to be in error or inconsistent and have been corrected as shown in Table F-3.

(d) For cotton yarn, cotton cloth, cement, pig iron and steel, data from other sources appear to be more reliable and more comprehensive and hence are used in our calculation. For convenience of exposition, the estimates of output in both China proper and Manchuria are explained here.

Table F-2

GROSS VALUE OF OUTPUT AND NUMBER OF WORKERS IN FACTORIES, BY INDUSTRY AND LOCATION, 1933

Industry	Location	Gross value of output (thousand yuan)	Number of workers (thousand)
Machinery[a]	Yunnan	80	0.06
Metal products[b]	Hopei	12	0.06
	Peiping	24	0.03
	Shantung	48	0.23
Miscellaneous metal products[c]	China Proper	5,000	1.70
Metal coins[d]	China proper	41,034	0.20
Glass[e]	Hopei	1,800	2.10
Clay and stone products[f]	Hopei	314	0.06
Plastic products[g]	Kwangtung	2,400	0.51
Woolen textiles[h]	Peiping	236	0.38
	Shanghai	90	0.45
Silk[i]	Shanghai	8,265	31.51
Leather[j]	Yunnan	128	0.02
Tea[k]	Hankow	1,260	0.89
Cigarettes[m]	Yunnan	50	0.01
Motion pictures[n]	Shanghai	2,312	1.87

(Notes to this table are on the following page.)

Notes:

[a]Gross value of output for machinery is given in Yunnan ching-chi (The Yunnan Economy) and Chung-kuo kung-chuan chien-tsa nien pao (Annual Report on the Inspection of Chinese Factories), p. 227, quoted in Ou, National Income, Vol. II, p. 37. The total number of workers is estimated on the assumption that the ratio of gross value of output to the total number of workers in the Yunnan factories is the same as that for other machinery factories in China proper computed from data given in Lieu, Industry Survey.

[b]Ibid., Vol. II, p. 261.

[c]Included in this category are the numerous metal products other than those specified in Lieu's survey. The figure for gross value of output is a rough estimate given in Ou, National Income, Vol. II, p. 42. The number of workers is estimated in a manner as described in his footnote 1.

[d]Ibid., Vol. II, p. 45, and Vol. I, pp. 70 and 72.

[e]Economic Yearbook, 1934, Vol. 2, p. K-540. The number of workers is estimated in a similar manner as described in footnote 1 in this yearbook.

[f]Lieu, Industry Survey, Vol. II, pp. 259 and 261.

[g]Ibid., pp. 274 and 646.

[h]Ibid., pp. 244 and 597.

[i]Ibid., pp. 271 and 639.

[j]Estimated by Ou, National Income, Vol. II, p. 119.

[k]T. H. Chu, Tea Trade in Central China, p. 221, quoted in Ou, National Income, Vol. II, p. 131.

[m]Yunnan ching-chi, p. 0:78.

[n]Estimated by Ou, National Income, Vol. II, p. 162, and Vol. I, p. 72.

Table F-3

ADJUSTED GROSS VALUE OF OUTPUT, 1933

Industry	Locality	Gross value of output	
		Original data	Adjusted
Lumber[a]	Chekiang	1,320	591
	Kwangtung	12	115
Metal products[b]	Anhwei		12
Glass[c]	Kiangai		27
Woolen textiles[d]		1,063	5,308
Milled rice[e]		5,144	75,730

Notes:

[a]The original figures are given in Lieu, Industry Survey, Vol. III, pp. 100-101, 338-339. Being way out of line with the others, these figures have been adjusted on the basis of the number of workers in these factories and average gross value of output per worker in all other factories in the same industry.

[b]The original figure is missing. (Ibid., pp. 142-143.) The adjusted figure is obtained by multiplying the number of workers by the average gross value of output of factories in Chekiang, Kiangsu, and Tientsin.

[c]The original figure is missing. (Ibid., pp. 147-148.) The missing item is derived on the basis of employment in this factory and the average gross value of output per worker in all other factories in the same industry.

[d]Ibid., Vol. II, pp. 272 and 641. The figures are believed to be more complete in coverage than those given in Vol. III, pp. 196 and 198. Hence, the former is used.

[e]In the original source the gross value of output for some factories refers to fees received for rice milling (ibid., Vol. III, pp. 31-192) and is not comparable to other data on gross value of milled rice. Hence, the figure is adjusted by multiplying the number of workers in these factories by the average gross value of output per worker of other factories in the same industry.

The output of cotton yarn produced in China proper in 1933 is first derived at 9.9 million piculs on the basis of the quantity of cotton consumed by these textile mills.[10] Multiplying this figure by the price of cotton yarn estimated at 50.2 yuan per picul[11] and adding the gross value of cotton waste estimated at 4.2 million yuan,[12] we derive the total gross value of output at 501.2 million yuan.

In Manchuria, the total output of cotton yarn in 1933 was 0.352 million piculs,[13] and cotton waste, 0.039 million piculs,[14] and the prices were 53.10 and 3.86 yuan per picul.[15] Gross value amounted to 18.7 and 0.1 million yuan for the two products, or a total of 18.8 million yuan.

The number of workers in the cotton spinning industry in China proper and Manchuria are derived at 192.8 thousand and 5.7 thousand, by dividing the gross value of output per worker estimated at 2,600[16] and 3,280 yuan[17] for the two regions.

Output of cotton cloth produced in China proper has been estimated at 29.20 million bolts,[18] and that in Manchuria at 4.76 million bolts,[19] totalling 33.96 million bolts. Multiplying the output figures by the 1933 price of cotton cloth of average quality (7.67 yuan per bolt)[20] we obtain the gross value of output at 223.94 and 36.51 million yuan for the two regions. The number of workers employed by the factories in China proper and Manchuria are roughly estimated at 101.8 thousand and 16.6 thousand, on the basis of gross value of output produced by these two groups of factories and the gross value of output per worker estimated at 2,200 yuan.[21]

Estimates of the gross value of output for pig iron, steel, and cement are derived by multiplying the 1933 output of these products for the Chinese Mainland as a whole, 606.7 and 25.0 million tons, and 4.4928 million barrels, respectively (Chinese Geological Survey, cited by Ou), by the prices estimated at 51 and 100 yuan per ton and 6 yuan per barrel, respectively.[22] The results are 30.94 million, 2.50 million, and 26.96 million yuan for pig iron, steel, and cement. The gross value of pig iron and steel factories in China proper is obtained at 16.93 million yuan by deducting the estimate for Manchurian factories, 16.51 million,[23] from the national total of 33.44 million. Gross value of output of cement factories in China proper is similarly derived at 23.18 million yuan.[24]

The total number of workers in the iron and steel industry and in the cement industry on the Chinese Mainland are estimates by Ou.[25] These totals are apportioned into those in China proper and in Manchuria according to the proportions of gross value of output in the two regions in the case of iron and steel, and by deducting the estimate of employment for Manchuria from the national total in the case of cement.

Foreign-owned factories in China proper. The predominant position of foreign-owned factories in prewar China's manufacturing industry was well known. Yet exactly how important they were in terms of their share in total output remains to this day an unsettled question. No comprehensive survey, let alone a census, has ever been made; and available estimates of gross value of output produced by these factories differ rather widely. A total of 432 million yuan is given by Ou, 497 million by Wang, and 3,003 by Wu.[26] The main reason for the wide discrepancies among these estimates lies both in the basic data used and in the method of estimation. The estimate by Wu was based primarily on estimates of capital in Chinese-owned and foreign-owned factories and the assumption of an identical capital-output ratio in these two groups of factories.[27] The estimate by Ou was based upon fragmentary information from miscellaneous sources,[28] and that by Wang on two Japanese surveys which were by far more comprehensive than Ou's data.[29]

While all these estimates are subject to considerable margin of error, the one by Wang appears to be the least unreliable. Wu's estimate, which is derived on the basis of capital and capital-output ratios, is unsatisfactory for two reasons. First, the reliability and comparability of the data on capital is open to serious question. Second, numerous factors, such as capital intensity, rate of utilization of equipment, and labor productivity, might well be different in the Chinese-owned and foreign-owned factories, and there is no reasonable basis for the assumption of identical capital-output ratios in these two groups of factories. On the other hand, Ou attempted to make the estimate merely by collected specific data without making up for the missing portion. His result therefore represents only that part of output by foreign factories on which there are data and would in all likelihood be an underestimate. For these reasons, Wang's estimate is used in our calculation.

Statistical data on output and employment given in the two Japanese studies were by no means complete, but the information on the number of foreign factories, their productive capacity, number of workers, and monthly or daily output is apparently quite comprehensive. The data on gross value of output are used by Wang whenever they are available. Where such data are lacking, estimates are made by Wang either by multiplying the actual output or annual capacity by estimated prices, or by multiplying the number of workers by estimated gross value of output per worker.[30] Two possible sources of error in Wang's figures may be noted. First, to the extent there was idle capacity in these factories, Wang's estimate would be high. Second, his figures do not include the output of factories with less than 30 workers. Hence, for our purposes, these figures might be underestimates. However, foreign-owned factories generally employed more than 30 workers so that any omissions in Wang's data would have only a minor effect on the total figure. Several obvious misprints in Wang's figures have been corrected and the data for the utilities have been excluded in accordance with our classification system. These adjusted figures, together with the number of workers given in the same source, are included in Table F-1.

Factories in Manchuria. Detailed statistics for 1933 are lacking. However, two rather extensive surveys by the South Manchurian Railway and the Manchurian Government are available, one covering the factories in the Kwantung Leased Territories in 1933 and the other covering all Manchurian factories (including the Kwantung Leased Territories) in 1934.[31] Both surveys give detailed data on gross value of output, raw material, fuels consumed, and number of workers in individual industries. Except for 14 products (pig iron, steel, coke, cotton yarn, cotton cloth, silk, silk piece goods, tobacco products, wheat flour, soybean oil, table salt, paper products, animal products, and footwear) gross value of output is derived on the basis of these two surveys as follows:

(a) To derive the total gross value of factory and handicraft output for Manchuria as a whole, we take the set of figures for Kwantung in 1933 given in the Kwantung survey[32] and multiply the figure for each of the products by a factor equal to the ratio of gross value of output for Manchuria to the gross value of output for Kwantung computed from data given in the 1934 Manchurian survey.[33]

(b) From the 1934 Manchurian survey,[34] the percentages of factory output in total factory and handicraft output for each product are calculated and applied to the gross value of factory and handicraft output in 1933 obtained in (a). The results represent estimates of the gross value of factory output in 1933 and are shown in Table F-1.

The gross value of output figures which we used for the 14 products mentioned above can now be given. The estimate for pig iron and steel in 1933 derived from the two surveys appears to be extremely low. The Kwantung survey gives a figure of 0.8 million yuan, which was merely 2 per cent of our estimate of 33.4 million yuan for China as a whole. Since the iron and steel works in Kwantung were the most important in China, the figure given in the survey is obviously in error. Therefore, the figure given in the Manchurian survey for 1934 is used. The gross value of coke output for the Chinese Mainland is first derived at 5.9 million yuan by multiplying the output of coke given at 536.6 thousand tons in the Chinese Geological Survey, cited by Ou, and the price of coke estimated by Ou at 11 yuan per ton.[35] From this total, the gross value of output produced by factories in China proper, given at 0.47 million yuan in Lieu's survey,[36] is deducted to arrive at 5.43 million yuan for the Manchurian factories.

The gross values of cotton yarn and cotton cloth have already been estimated above. The gross value of silk piece goods produced by Manchurian factories is estimated at 2.06 million yuan on the basis of an output of 61.7 thousand bolts,[37] and the price of 33.3 yuan per bolt.[38] Estimates for silk, wheat flour, tobacco products, soybean oil,[39] and table salt are those given in Ou.[40] For paper products, animal products, and footwear, no estimates are given in the 1933 Kwantung survey. The figures given in the 1934 Manchurian survey are used in place of the missing ones.[41] The results of these adjustments are presented in Table F-1.

It may be noted that the data on gross value of output given in the two surveys are in terms of the Manchurian yen. In 1933 and 1934, capital and goods flowed freely between China proper and Manchuria, and the exchange rates between the yuan and yen, which fluctuated freely, may be taken as a fair approximation to the purchasing power parity rates. The average exchange rates in 1933 and 1934 were roughly one to one.[42] Hence, for our present calculation, the two monetary units are assumed to be equivalent.

With the exception of the estimates for 10 industries (iron and steel, machinery, glass, bricks and shingles, cotton yarn, cotton cloth, animal products, table salt, paper products, and miscellaneous products), the numbers of workers in each industry are derived by dividing the gross value of output for Manchurian factories already obtained above, by gross value of output per worker in Kwantung factories computed from data on gross value of output and employment given in the 1933 Kwantung survey. The estimates for iron and steel, cotton yarn, and cotton cloth have already been explained. For machinery, bricks and shingles, glass, animal products, table salt, paper products, and miscellaneous, the gross value of output per worker in Manchuria 1934 is used to calculate the number of workers in these industries, either because the data given in the 1934 survey are, in our judgment, more reasonable when compared with those of the same industries in China proper, or because they are the only data available. The results are presented in Table F-1.

<u>Total number of workers</u>. In principle, the number of workers given in Table F-1 does not include supervisors, engineers, and managers. On the basis of data given in Lieu's survey, the ratio of those not included to the number of workers is calculated at 6 per cent.[43] Applying this ratio

to the total number of workers of 1.07 million given in Table F-1, we derive a rough estimate of the total number of workers and employees at 1.13 million.[44]

Deductible Costs of Production

Costs of production, which are deducted from gross value of output to obtain gross value added, have been grouped into three categories: raw materials, fuels and electricity, and miscellaneous expenses. The proportions of these items in gross value of output have been separately calculated for the two groups of factories (those in China proper and those in Manchuria) and presented in Table F-4. For the factories in China proper, including both the Chinese-owned and the foreign-owned, the basic data on gross value of output and costs of production are taken from Lieu's survey.[45] It may be noted, however, that these data cover only the Chinese-owned factories employing 30 or more workers. It is assumed that the percentages of deductible costs computed from these data are applicable to the output of foreign-owned factories and factories of smaller size.

For the factories in Manchuria, the percentages of deductible costs are computed from the data given for factories in Kwantung. We assume that these figures are the same as for other parts of Manchuria.

Data on depreciation are almost entirely lacking. The only estimate available for factories with 30 or more workers is given at 2 per cent of gross value of output.[46] When compared with Buck's figure of 2 per cent for agriculture in the prewar period,[47] this estimate appears to be too low. For the postwar years, a rough estimate of about 5 per cent is calculated on the basis of Communist data for manufacturing, mining, and utilities, as we will show later in our discussion on depreciation. In the absence of a

Table F-4

PROPORTION OF DEDUCTIBLE COSTS OF PRODUCTION IN GROSS VALUE OF OUTPUT,

CHINA PROPER AND MANCHURIA, 1933

(per cent)

	Factories in China Proper			Factories in Manchuria		
	Raw mater-ials	Fuels & electric-ity	Miscel-laneous expenses	Raw mater-ials	Fuels & electric-ity	Misce[illegible] lane[illegible] expe[illegible]
	(1)	(2)	(3)	(4)	(5)	(6
Lumber & wood products						
Lumber	76	2	10	83	(*)	1[illegible]
Wood products	60	2	10	56	(*)	1[illegible]
Bamboo and rattan products	31	3	10			
Machinery						
Machine parts	59	12	2	43	10	[illegible]
Machine manu-facture	52	12	5	70	4	[illegible]
Machine repair		12	5		4	[illegible]
Machinery, special				62	2	[illegible]
Others				49	4	[illegible]
Metals & metal products						
Iron and steel	39	4	2	30	4	[illegible]
Misc. metal products	55	10	5	72	3	
Metal coins	75	†	†			
Small electrical appliances	50	3	5	33	3	
Transportation equipment manufacture & repair						
Carts and carriages	47	1	2	62	3	
Ship & boat building & repair	49	10	5	50	2	
Stone, clay and glass products						
Bricks & shingles		40	5	14	18	
Bricks, for industrial use				41	33	
Chinaware	18	25	5	27	20	

(Continued)

Table F-4 (continued)

	Factories in China proper			Factories in Manchuria		
	Raw materials	Fuels & electricity	Miscellaneous expenses	Raw materials	Fuels & electricity	Miscellaneous expenses
	(1)	(2)	(3)	(4)	(5)	(6)
Glass & glassware	14	17	15	22	11	15
Cement	29	19	†	28	22	5
Others	46	4	5	79	1	
Chemicals & chemical products						
Matches	35	1	9	61	1	5
Soap & paraffin products	58	1	10	84	2	(*)
Enamel	56	2	10			
Plastics	55	2	13			
Pharmaceutical products	70	1	18	50	3	18
Cosmetics	42	1	18			
Dyes & paints	45	1	12	40	1	12
Oils, nonedible						
Tung oil	60	10	5			
Kerosene	80	†	†			
Mineral oil				37	26	5
Others				69	5	5
Coke	64	9	5	64	9	5
Charcoal				73	2	5
Other chemical products - explosives				85	2	(*)
Soda				88	1	(*)
Other industrial chemicals	17	5	10	87	2	
Miscellaneous				63	3	5
Textile products						
Ginned cotton	90	1	2	75	(*)	2
Cotton yarn	70	3	1	79	1	1
Cotton cloth	70	4	2	75	1	2
Silk	69	7		69	5	(*)
Silk piece goods	49	2	8	52	6	5
Woolen textiles	54	3	8	67	2	8
Linen & hemp products	70	2	8	76	1	2

(Continued)

Table F-4 (continued)

	Factories in China proper			Factories in Manchuria		
	Raw materials	Fuels & electricity	Miscellaneous expenses	Raw materials	Fuels & electricity	Misce lane exper
	(1)	(2)	(3)	(4)	(5)	(6)
Clothing & attire						
Dyed cloth	67	3	3	67	3	3
Clothing and attire	51	2	8	64	1	4
Leather & rubber products						
Leather	60	2	10	70	2	5
Leather products	72	2	5			
Glue	52	6	10			
Rubber products	60	3	10			
Food products						
Milled rice & other husked grains	90	2	1	90	(*)	1
Wheat flour	82	2	6	85	2	5
Edible vegetable oils	70	4	10	90	4	(*)
Tea	79	12	†			
Soybean sauce	78	2	10	78	2	10
Salt	10	5	5	10	5	5
Sugar	95	1	†			
Egg products	87	3	2			
Beverages, except wine & liquor	50	5	5	80	1	5
Ice	6	22	10	41	8	15
Other food products	70	3	5	72	2	7
Tobacco, wine & liquor						
Shredded tobacco	59	8	†			
Cigarettes	49	4	†	49	4	†
Wine & liquor	73	4	10	73	4	10
Paper manufacturing & printing						
Paper	34	14	5	50	6	5
Paper products	46	1	10	64	1	10
Printing	52	4	5	58	1	5
Miscellaneous						
Apparatus and ornaments	50	†	†			
Others	63	†	†	77	1	10

(Notes to this table on following pag

Notes:

(*) Less than 1 per cent.

† Included in raw materials.

Column (1). Raw materials, factories in China proper. Except for iron and steel, metal coins, machine repair, cement, cotton yarn, cotton cloth, soybean sauce, and wine and liquor, the proportions of production costs in gross value of output are calculated from data in Lieu's survey. The data on gross value of output are given in Lieu, Industry Survey, Vol. II, Table 14, and costs of raw materials in Table 13.

For iron and steel the only information on deductible costs is that of Liu-ho-kao Iron Works in Honan Province given in Kuang-yeh chou-pao (Mining Weekly), No. 290; and Chinese Geological Survey, No. 5, p. 503 which are quoted in Ou, National Income, Vol. II, p. 15. Total cost of raw materials, fuels, and miscellaneous items in the production of pig iron was roughly 45 per cent of gross value of output. According to our estimate for the factories in Manchuria, fuels and miscellaneous items amounted to about 6 per cent of gross value of output (see below). Assuming the same proportion for the iron works in China proper, we derive the proportion of raw material cost at 39 per cent. Data for steel production are completely lacking. We assume the same percentage as for pig iron. Any bias that may result from this assumption need not be serious since in 1933 over 90 per cent of the total value of iron and steel was pig iron.

The percentage of total deductible costs, including depreciation, for the manufacturing of metal coins has been estimated by Ou, National Income, Vol. II, p. 45, at 80 per cent of total gross value of output. Assuming depreciation to be 5 per cent, we obtain a rough estimate of deductible costs at 75 per cent.

About 30 per cent of total gross receipts of the machine shops in China proper was from machine repairs. We assume that the same proportion applies to this industry in Manchuria in 1933. In our calculation of cost deductions for machine repair, the small amount of material costs is assumed to have been included in the miscellaneous items.

The percentage of raw material cost for cement is taken from Ou, National Income, Vol. II, pp. 17-18.

The percentage of raw materials, fuels and electricity, and miscellaneous items in gross value of cotton yarn and cotton cloth are derived from data given in Wang Tze-chien, Report on a Survey of Chinese Textile Mills in Seven Provinces, quoted in Yen Chung-ping, Chung-kuo chin-tai ching-chi-she t'ung-chi tzu-liao shuan-chi (Selected Statistical Materials on the Contemporary Economic History of China), Peiping, 1955, p. 170.

Notes (continued):

For soybean sauce and wine and liquor, the percentages are those of Manchurian factories.

Column (2). Fuels and electricity. Except for cotton yarn and cotton cloth, total consumption of fuels and electricity by factories in China proper is derived by multiplying the daily consumption in physical quantities given in Lieu, Industry Survey, Table 3, and the average number of days of operation in a year given in Table 10 of the same source. The quantities consumed are then multiplied by the price of electricity given in Appendix H, Table H-4, and prices of fuels given in Ou, National Income, Vol. I, pp. 61-62, to obtain the total costs of fuels and electricity.

Columns (3) and (6). Miscellaneous expenses. Included in this item are mainly stationery, advertising and other selling expenses, insurance, storage, etc. The percentage deductions, except those for cotton yarn and cloth, are roughly estimated on the basis of fragmentary information compiled by Ou, National Income, Vol. II, pp. 30-169.

Column (4). Raw materials, factories in Manchuria. The percentages of raw material costs are based on data given in Manchurian Factories, 1934, pp. 2-8.

Column (5). Fuels and electricity, factories in Manchuria. Physical quantities of fuels and electricity consumed by individual industries in the Kwantung area are given in the source cited in the previous paragraph. The average prices of fuels and electricity are derived from data given in Manchurian Factories, 1934, pp. 106 and 196. Total costs of fuels and electricity are then calculated and expressed as percentages of gross value of output.

better alternative, we more or less arbitrarily assume that depreciation for the factories in 1933 amounted to 4 per cent of gross value of output.

Value Added in 1933 in Constant 1952 Prices

The method by which we derive estimates of value added for 1933 in constant 1952 prices is as follows. First, gross value of output and nonprimary input for 1933 in 1952 prices for individual products are calculated so far as available data on prices permit, and value added in 1952 prices is then obtained as a residual. Such calculations have been made for six producers' goods and ten consumers' goods. The results are presented in Table F-5. The prices of output and raw materials used in this computation are summarized in Table F-6. For pig iron, steel, cement, and coke, where coal is the most important fuel, the price index of coal, estimated in Appendix H, Table H-3, at 250 per cent for 1952, with 1933 as 100, is used. For all other products, the unweighted average of the price indexes of coal and electricity taken from Table H-4, 125 per cent for 1952, with 1933 as 100, is used. Prices of the items that made up the miscellaneous expenses are assumed to have changed from 1933 to 1952 in proportion to the prices of the products.

Second, for those products on which prices are not available, the calculation of gross output and value added in 1952 prices is made on the assumption that the prices of output and nonprimary input of these products vary in 1933-52 in proportion to the prices of the 16 products given above over the same period. The computations are shown in Table F-7.

Total gross value added so derived (in 1952 yuan) amounts to 3.71 billion. Depreciation is assumed to be 4 per cent of gross output, or 0.38 billion. Net value added is thus calculated at 3.33 billion yuan.

Table F-5

GROSS VALUE OF OUTPUT AND VALUE ADDED IN 16 MANUFACTURED PRODUCTS, 1933

	Millions of 1933 yuan[a]					Millions of 1952 yuan[a]				
	Gross value of output	Raw materials	Fuels and electricity	Miscel-laneous expenses	Gross value added	Gross value of output	Raw materials	Fuels and electricity	Miscel-laneous expenses	Gross value added
Producers' goods										
Pig iron	30.9	10.8	1.2	0.6	18.3	120.7	42.2	3.0	2.4	73.1
Steel	2.5	0.9	0.1	(*)	1.5	15.0	3.4	0.3	0.3	11.0
Cement	27.1	7.8	5.5	(*)	13.8	65.0	19.6	13.8	(*)	31.6
Coke	5.9	3.8	0.5	0.3	1.3	23.6	9.5	1.3	1.2	11.6
Machinery[b]	81.5	43.6	5.6	2.8	29.5	488.8	261.3	7.0	16.7	203.8
Gunny sacks	1.6	1.1	0.1	0.1	0.4	8.0	2.2	0.1	0.4	5.3
Total	149.5	68.0	13.0	3.8	64.7	721.1	338.2	25.5	21.0	336.4
Consumers' goods										
Cotton yarn	520.1	365.7	15.2	5.2	134.0	2,059.6	987.4	19.0	20.6	1,032.6
Cotton cloth	260.4	182.9	10.1	5.2	62.3	916.8	724.3	12.6	18.3	161.6
Silk	44.9	31.0	3.0	-	10.9	213.3	147.2	3.8	(*)	62.3
Silk piece goods	79.5	39.1	1.7	6.3	32.4	349.8	185.7	2.1	27.7	134.3
Woolen textiles	26.2	14.8	0.8	2.1	8.5	118.9	70.6	1.0	9.5	37.8
Sugar	7.7	7.3	0.1	(*)	0.3	29.9	18.2	0.1	(*)	11.6
Milled rice	151.3	136.1	3.0	1.5	10.6	207.3	186.5	3.8	2.1	14.9
Wheat flour	194.9	160.6	3.8	11.4	19.0	534.0	440.2	4.8	31.3	57.7
Edible vegetable oils	155.5	128.0	5.9	5.8	15.7	381.0	313.6	7.4	14.2	45.8
Cigarettes	267.2	130.9	10.7	(*)	125.6	807.0	267.1	13.4	(*)	526.5
Total	1,707.7	1,196.4	54.3	37.5	419.3	5,617.6	3,340.8	68.0	123.7	2,085.1

Notes:

(*) Less than 0.05 million yuan.

- Not available.

[a]Figures in 1933 prices are computed from data given in Tables F-1 and F-4. Those in 1952 prices are derived by multiplying the estimates in 1933 prices by the appropriate price indexes given in Table F-6 and in the text.

[b]For comparison with the postwar figures, gross value of output and value added for machinery repairs have been roughly estimated on the basis of figures given in Ou, National Income, Vol. II, p. 38, and then deducted from the total.

Table F-6

PRICES OF OUTPUT AND RAW MATERIALS FOR 16 MANUFACTURED PRODUCTS, 1933 AND 1952

(yuan per unit)

Product	Price of output 1933	Price of output 1952	1952 Index (1933=100)	Price of raw materials 1933	Price of raw materials 1952	1952 Index (1933=100)
Producers' goods						
Pig iron (ton)	51	200	390			390
Steel (ton)	100	600	600	51	200	390
Cement (ton)	35	85	240	2	5	250
Coke (ton)	11	44	400	5	12.5	250
Machinery			600			600
Gunny sacks (each)	0.4	2.0	500	20	40	200
Consumers' goods						
Cotton yarn (bale)	182	720	396	31.4	84.9	270
Cotton cloth (bolt)	7.67	27.0	352	182	720	396
Silk (picul)	462	2,195	475			475
Silk piece goods (bolt)	27	118.8	440	462	2,195	475
Woolen piece goods (M)	3.7	16.8	454	34.6	165	477
Sugar (ton)	280	1,100	390	0.6	1.5	250
Wheat flour (ton)	113	310	274			274
Milled rice (ton)	146	200	137			137
Edible vegetable oils (ton)	418	1,025	245			245
Cigarettes (case)	162	490	302	17	34.6	204

Notes:

Prices of output, 1933. The prices of pig iron, steel, cement, and coke are given in Ou, National Income, Vol. I, Table 3, pp. 53-54. The price of cement is given at 6 yuan per barrel and has been converted to 35 yuan per ton at the ratio of 5.85 barrels to a ton. The price of gunny sacks is derived from the gross value and quantities of output in Manchuria. (Ibid., Vol. II, Table 11, p. 111.) The price of cotton yarn has already been estimated at 50.2 yuan per picul. The price index for machinery is assumed to be the same as for steel. The price of cotton yarn is converted to 182 yuan per bale at the ratio of 3.628 picul per bale given in State Planning Commission, Ti-yi-ke wu-nien-chi-hua-ti ming-tsi chieh-hsi (Explanation of Terms Used in the First Five Year Plan), Peiping, Jen-min chu-pan-she, 1955, p. 23.

The price of cotton cloth was given earlier in this appendix. The page numbers in parentheses below refer to prices given in Ou, National Income, Vol. II. The price of silk and silk piece goods are computed from data on gross value and quantities of silk and silk piece goods (pp. 101, 104), and the price of woolen piece goods is the unweighted average of three prices quoted by Ou (p. 106). Factory-made sugar consists almost entirely of white

Notes (continued):

sugar priced at 14 yuan per picul. This is equivalent to 280 yuan per ton which is converted to 113 yuan per ton at the ratio of 20 kg per bag (pp. 128, 139). The average price weighted by output of rice mills in six provinces is 7.3 yuan per picul, which is equivalent to 146 yuan per ton (pp. 126-127). The average price of vegetable oils, 20.9 yuan per picul, is derived by dividing the gross value of output (including oil cake) by the quantity given in Ou (p. 145); this price is converted to 418 yuan per ton. The price of cigarettes is derived by dividing gross output by the quantity of output (p. 132).

Price of output, 1952. See Table F-10.

Price of raw materials, 1933 and 1952. The price of pig iron is taken as the price of raw material for steel. For cement and coke, the respective prices of limestone and coal are used. (See Appendix H for source of data.) For gunny sacks, cotton cloth, silk piece goods, sugar, and cigarettes, the prices of the following are used: jute, cotton yarn, silk, sugar cane, and cured tobacco. Prices of jute, sugar cane, and cured tobacco in 1933 and 1952 are given in Appendixes B and D. For the price of cotton in 1933 and 1952, see Appendix B, Table B-17; and Appendix D, Table D-4. For woolen piece goods, the prices of raw materials are the wholesale prices of Si-ning wool in Tientsin in 1933 and 1952. *Ibid.*, pp. 78 and 215. For the rest (pig iron, machinery, silk, wheat flour, milled rice, and edible vegetable oils), relative price changes for output and raw materials are assumed to be the same.

Table F-7

GROSS OUTPUT AND VALUE ADDED IN FACTORIES, 1933, IN 1933 AND 1952 PRICES

(million yuan)

	Gross output		Gross value added	
	in 1933 prices (1)	in 1952 prices (2)	in 1933 prices (3)	in 1952 prices (4)
Producers' goods	498	2,403	182	944
Six products	149	721	65	336
Others	349	1,682	117	608
Consumers' goods	2,147	7,062	561	2,784
Ten products	1,708	5,618	419	2,085
Others	439	1,444	142	704
Total	2,645	9,465	743	3,733

Notes:

Columns (1) and (3). For gross output of producers' and consumers' goods and the total see Table 38. For figures of the six producers' and ten consumers' goods, see Table F-5. The gross output of the other producers' and consumers' goods are derived as residuals.

Column (2). For the gross output of the six producers' and ten consumers' goods, see Table F-5. The gross output of the other producers' goods is derived by multiplying the estimate in 1933 prices, 349 million yuan, by a price index equal to the ratio of the gross output of the six producers' goods in 1952 prices (721 million) to that in 1933 prices (149 million) given in Table F-5, 482 per cent for 1952 with 1933 as 100. The gross output of the consumers' goods other than the ten products is derived similarly. The price index that results from the individual calculation for the ten products is calculated at 329 per cent for 1952 with 1933 as 100.

Column (4). The estimates for the six producers' and ten consumers' goods are given in Table F-5. Those for the other producers' and consumers' goods are derived by the same procedure as described for the figures in column (2). The price indexes computed on the basis of value added in the six producers' and ten consumers' goods in 1933 and 1952 prices are 520 for producers' and 497 per cent for consumers' goods.

VALUE ADDED BY FACTORIES, 1952-57

In this section we shall explain in detail the sources of data and method of estimating the gross output and value added by factories for 1952-57 presented in Table 37. It may be recalled that the procedure of derivation involves the following steps: (1) estimating the gross output and gross value added for 12 producers' goods and 14 consumers' goods; (2) estimating the total gross output of producers' and consumers' goods; (3) estimating the gross output of those products that have not been covered in step (1) and the share of gross value added in gross output of such products for each category of goods; and then (4) reducing the total gross value added for factories as a whole by 5 per cent of total gross output as a rough allowance for depreciation. The following two subsections will present the basic data and the calculations in each step separately. It is to be noted that all the discussions in this appendix are concerned with the preliminary estimates of value added, that is, the set of estimates that has not been corrected for the overstatement in the Communist official data on consumers' goods production.[48]

Value Added in 26 Product Groups, 1952-57

Estimates of value added in the 26 product groups are derived by subtracting the deductible costs from gross output for each product group. The results have been presented in Table 39. The derivation of gross output and deductible costs of production are discussed in turn.

Gross value of output for 26 product groups, 1952-57. Gross value of output for the 26 product groups is obtained primarily by multiplying the physical output of these products for 1952-57 by their factory prices in 1952. The estimates of output are presented in Table F-8 but do not include handicraft output. The sources of data and methods of deriving these estimates are as follows:

1. Pig iron. The figures for 1952-56 are given in the 1956 Statistical Abstract, pp. 32-33, and the 1957 figure in People's Daily, February 1, 1958, p. 3.

2. Steel. Great Ten Years, p. 84.

3. Cement. The figures for 1952-56 are given in the 1956 Statistical Abstract, pp. 32-33, and the 1957 figure in FFYP Communique, 1959, p. 49.

4. Coke. The figure for 1952 is given in First Five Year Plan, p. 36. Those for 1953-54 are computed on the basis of the 1952 figure and output indexes for 1953 and 1954 with the preceding year as 100 given in 1953 Communique and 1954 Communique. The figures for 1955-57 are not available. Since coke is used primarily for steel production, these figures are derived on the assumption that output of coke increased from 1954 to 1957 in proportion to steel output over the same period.

5. Machinery. For 1952-55, the figures are given in the 1955 Statistical Abstract, p. 41, and for 1956 in the 1956 Statistical Abstract, p. 29. Output in 1957 is given at 9.5 per cent of gross value of industrial production. (FFYP Communique.) The gross value of industrial production in 1957 being 65.02 billion yuan (Chou En-lai, "Report on Government Work," HHPYK, No. 9, 1959, p. 3), machinery output in 1957 is calculated at 6.177 billion yuan.

6. Gunny sacks. The figures for 1952-56 are given in SSB, Industry Study, p. 166. That for 1957 is the planned output given in Po, 1956-57 Plan, p. 32.

7. Paper. SSB, Industry Study, p. 209.

Table F-8

OUTPUT OF FACTORIES FOR 26 PRODUCT GROUPS, 1952-57

	1952	1953	1954	1955	1956	195
Producers' goods						
1. Pig iron (million tons)	1.900	2.175	2.962	3.795	4.777	5.9
2. Steel (million tons)	1.349	1.774	2.225	2.835	4.465	5.3
3. Cement (million tons)	2.861	3.877	4.600	4.503	6.393	6.6
4. Coke (million tons)	2.860	3.600	4.540	5.690	7.160	7.4
5. Machinery (billion yuan)[a]	1.401	2.157	2.643	3.030	5.764	6.1
6. Gunny sacks (million pieces)	67.350	59.080	59.060	52.600	78.680	78.1
7. Paper (million tons)	0.372	0.427	0.518	0.574	0.729	0.9
8. Chemicals (million tons)						
a. Ammonium sulfate	0.181	0.226	0.298	0.324	0.446	0.5
b. Caustic soda	0.079	0.088	0.115	0.137	0.156	0.1
c. Pure soda	0.192	0.223	0.309	0.405	0.476	0.5
d. Sulfuric acid	0.190	0.260	0.344	0.375	0.517	0.6
9. Sheet glass (million square meters)	21.320	24.300	31.350	29.210	30.750	46.0
10. Construction materials[b] (billion yuan)	0.315	0.518	0.510	0.540	0.856	0.9
11. Auto tires (million)	0.417	0.488	0.701	0.593	0.783	0.8
12. Rolled steel (million tons)	1.312	1.754	1.965	2.505	3.921	4.2
Consumers' goods						
13. Cotton yarn (million bales)	3.618	4.104	4.598	3.968	5.246	4.6
14. Cotton cloth (million bolts)	87.600	99.200	111.200	96.000	126.900	112.5
15. Silk (thousand tons)	4.052	5.026	5.153	5.964	7.528	6.0
Mulberry silk	3.548	4.319	4.607	5.377	6.191	-
Tussah silk	0.504	0.707	0.546	0.587	1.337	-
16. Silk piece goods (million meters)	38.820	44.280	46.950	56.380	71.170	63.1
17. Woolen textiles	13.125	18.292	21.524	23.340	40.843	46.9
Woolen yarn (thousand tons)	1.979	3.718	3.273	3.743	5.658	6.1

(Continued)

Table F-8 (continued)

	1952	1953	1954	1955	1956	1957
Woolen piece goods (million meters)	4.233	6.227	7.823	10.271	14.267	18.170
Woolen blankets (million)	0.717	0.393	0.712	0.784	0.920	0.997
Carpets and rugs (million yuan)	6.196	7.954	9.716	8.542	19.998	21.678
18. Grass cloth (million yuan)	1.820	3.485	4.345	4.824	5.405	5.469
19. Clothing and knitted goods (million yuan)	84.500	130.300	156.770	181.920	206.130	182.634
20. Sugar (million tons)	0.249	0.298	0.347	0.410	0.518	0.558
21. Milled rice (million tons)	1.550	1.650	1.800	1.850	1.950	2.050
22. Wheat flour (million tons)	2.990	3.390	3.720	4.530	4.310	4.220
23. Edible vegetable oils (billion yuan)	0.360	0.371	0.389	0.425	0.392	0.403
24. Cigarettes (million cases)	2.650	3.552	3.728	3.567	3.907	4.456
25. Matches (million cases)	9.110	8.020	10.340	11.360	11.590	10.250
26. Rubber footwear (million pairs)	61.690	76.360	85.840	97.450	103.480	128.850

Notes:

- Not available.

[a] All prices are in 1952 yuan.

[b] Includes shingles, bricks, tiles, and other construction material except lumber, cement, and glass.

8.a. Ammonium sulfate. The figures for 1952-56 are given in 1956 Statistical Abstract, pp. 32-33. The 1957 figure is the planned target for this year given in First Five Year Plan, p. 36.

8.b-d. Caustic soda, pure soda, sulfuric acid. Great Ten Years, p. 8

9. Sheet glass. The 1952 figure is given in First Five Year Plan, p. 36. The figures for 1953-54 are computed on the basis of the 1952 figure and the output indexes for 1953-54 with the preceding year as 100 given in 1953 Communique and 1954 Communique. For 1955, output is derived from the 1956 output of 31.35 million square meters given in Chao Yi-wen, Hsin-chung-ti kung-yeh (New China's Industry), Peiping, T'ung-chi chu-pan-she, 1957, p. 52, and the output indexes for 1955-56 (476.5 and 499.6 per cent with 1949 a 100) given in CCTP, Hong Kong, No. 543, November 4, 1957, p. 4. The 1957 figure is given in TKP, Peiping, January 30, 1958, p. 1.

10. Construction materials. Gross value is derived as a residual by deducting the gross values of cement and sheet glass from the total gross value of all construction materials. The gross values of cement and sheet glass are obtained by multiplying the output figures given above and the prices of these two products (given in Table F-10). The gross values of all construction materials in 1952 and 1957 are derived from data on total gross value of industrial production and the percentage of construction materials in the total given in Great Ten Years, pp. 80-81. The figures for 1953-56 are derived on the basis of the 1952 figure and indexes for 1952-56 given in Chi Chung-wei, "How to Achieve More Balanced Development in China's Industry," CHCC, Peiping, No. 7, 1957, p. 5.

11. Auto tires. The figures for 1952-56 are given in 1956 Statistical Abstract, pp. 32-33, and the figure for 1957, in TKP, Peiping, January 18, 1958, p. 3.

12. Rolled steel. The figures for 1952-56 are given in SSB, Industry Study, pp. 19-20. The 1957 figure is derived from the 1958 output target and its percentage increase over 1957 output given in NCNA, Peiping, January 25, 1958.

13. Cotton yarn. For 1952-56, the figures are given in SSB, Industry Study, p. 166, and the 1957 figures, in TKP, Peiping, February 27, 1958, p. 3.

14. Cotton cloth. In China, cotton cloth output may be classified into nine different types according to the kinds of cotton yarn used for raw material and the production unit as follows:

Cotton yarn used	Production Unit
(a) Machine-spun yarn	Factory
(b) Machine-spun yarn	Handicraft workshops
(c) Machine-spun yarn	Handicraft cooperatives
(d) Machine-spun yarn	Individual handicraftsmen
(e) Mixed machine-spun & hand-spun yarn	Handicraft workshops
(f) Mixed machine-spun & hand-spun yarn	Handicraft cooperatives
(g) Mixed machine-spun & hand-spun yarn	Individual handicraftsmen
(h) Hand-spun yarn	Handicraft cooperatives
(i) Hand-spun yarn	Individual handicraftsmen

The available Communist data on the output of various kinds of cotton cloth are presented in Table F-9. Clearly, the output of factories, that is, output of type (a), cannot be derived on the basis of these data. According to the State Statistical Bureau, about 79 per cent of the total output of cotton cloth in 1956, given at 5.878 million meters, was machine-woven. (SSB, Industry Study, p. 194.) Machine-woven cloth for 1956 is therefore estimated at 4.644 million meters. For the other years, the estimates are derived on the assumption that output of machine-woven cloth varies in proportion to that of machine-spun yarn. Output estimates of machine-spun yarn for 1952-57 being known, those of machine-woven cloth

Table F-9

COMMUNIST DATA ON OUTPUT OF COTTON CLOTH, 1952-57

Types of cotton cloth[a]	1952	1953	1954	1955	1956	1957
(Million bolts)[b]						
1. Sum of (a) through (i)	137.90	154.23	182.49	144.94	182.44	-
2. Sum of (a) through (g)	111.63	139.23	159.57	132.32	172.47	-
3. Sum of (h) and (i)	26.27	25.00	22.92	12.62	5.48	-
4. Machine-woven cloth	117.53	147.32	156.62	132.90	174.89	-
5. Sum of (a), (b), (c), (e), and (f)	89.27	107.79	122.33	103.22	136.15	-
(Million meters)[b]						
6. Sum of (a) through (i)	4,158.00	5,002.00	5,541.00	4,510.00	5,878.00	-
7. Sum of (a) through (g)	3,828.91	4,685.40	5,230.18	4,361.29	5,803.19	5,050.0
8. Sum of (h) and (i)	329.16	316.50	310.63	149.49	74.47	-

Notes:

- Not available.

[a]Types: (a) through (i) as defined in item 14 in the text.

[b]Both measurements are given because of the lack of a constant conversion factor.

Lines 1 and 6. For 1952-55, SSB, "A General Survey of China's Socialist Industrialization," HHPYK, Peiping, No. 2, 1957, p. 58. For 1956, People's Daily, October 1, 1958, p. 5, and SSB, Industry Study, p. 194.

Lines 2, 3, 7, and 8. For 1952-56, ibid., p. 166. The figure for 1957 in line 7 is given in FFYP Communique, p. 49. A slightly different figure of 5,770 million meters for the sum of (a) through (g) in 1956 is given in Great Ten Years, p. 88.

Line 4. People's Daily, April 20, 1957, p. 3. Although the Communist source refers to these figures as the output of "machine-woven cloth," it is doubtful whether they are such, for all these figures (with the exception of the 1954 figure) exceed those given for the sum of machine-woven cloth and a portion of hand-woven cloth in line 2. A plausible explanation is that these figures actually represent cotton cloth made of machine-spun yarn rather than machine-woven cloth. Cotton cloth made from machine-spun yarn is among the 71 major products for which production and consumption balance sheets are prepared. TCKT Peiping, No. 5, 1958, pp. 24-25.

Line 5. 1956 Statistical Abstract, pp. 32-33.

are computed at 3.204, 3.631, 4.168, 3.511, 4.644, and 4.114 million meters for 1952-57. These estimates are then converted to bolts at the ratio of 36.376 meters per bolt given in State Planning Commission, Explanation of Terms Used in First Five Year Plan, p. 24.

15. Silk. Figures for 1952-56 are given in SSB, Industry Study, p. 166, and that for 1957, in People's Daily, April 3, 1958, p. 2.

16. Silk piece goods. The figure for 1952, 38.83 million meters, is given in First Five Year Plan, p. 36. For 1952-57, total output of both machine-woven and hand-woven silk piece goods are given at 64.76, 73,80, 78.25, 93.97, 118.61, and 105.26 million meters. SSB, Industry Study, p. 166; and People's Daily, November 2, 1958, p. 6. Estimates of machine-woven output for 1953-57 are derived on the assumption that the proportion of machine-woven output for 1953-57 is the same as for 1952.

17. Woolen yarn, woolen piece goods, woolen blankets, carpets and rugs. Figures for 1952-56 are given in SSB, Industry Study, pp. 164-166. Figures for 1957 except that for woolen piece goods are derived on the basis of the 1956 figures and the index of wool output for 1955-56 computed from data given in Appendix D. The output of woolen piece goods in 1957 is derived from the 1958 figure and its percentage increase over 1957 given in People's Daily, November 2, 1958, p. 6.

18. Grass cloth. The figures for 1952-56 are given in SSB, Industry Study, pp. 164-165. Output in 1957 is assumed to have increased over 1956 in proportion to the output of hemp crops in 1955-56 given in Appendix D.

19. Clothing and knitted goods. Estimates of output of both factories and handicraftsmen for 1952-56 are given in SSB, Industry Study, pp. 164-165 as follows: 272.57, 420.34, 505.70, 586.86, and 664.95 million yuan for 1952-56. In 1933, factory output (85 million yuan) constituted 31 per

cent of the total output (274 million yuan). (For factory and handicraft output in 1933, see Table F-1, and Appendix G, Table G-1.) Assuming the same percentage for the postwar period, we apply this percentage to the total output for 1952-56 to derive the factory output. The estimate for 1957 is an extrapolation from the 1956 figure on the basis of machine-spun yarn output for 1956-57 given above.

20. Sugar. The figures for 1952-56 are given in the 1956 Statistical Abstract, pp. 32-33. The 1957 figure is the 1956 figure plus the amount the 1957 output increased over 1956 as reported in HHPYK, No. 2, 1958, p. 5

21. Milled rice. The quantity of paddy rice milled by factories in 1952 is assumed to have increased from 1933 in proportion to total populati 569/500 times 38.9 = 44.3 million piculs. (Total population in 1933 and 19 is discussed in Chapter IV; the quantity of paddy rice milled by factories 1933 is discussed in Appendix G.) According to a report in TKP, Peiping, December 29, 1957, p. 2, from each hundred piculs of paddy rice, an average of 69 piculs of milled rice was produced in 1952. A slightly higher figure of 74 piculs of milled rice per hundred piculs of paddy rice is given in Food Balance Sheets, p. 241. For our calculation a round figure of 70 per cent is used. The output of factory-milled rice in 1952 is thus derived at 31 million piculs. For 1953-57, output of factory-milled rice is assumed to have increased in proportion to urban population over the same period. For data on urban population, see Table 67.

22. Wheat flour. The figures for 1952-55 are given in SSB, "A General Survey of China's Socialist Industrialization," HHPYK, Peiping, No. 2, 1957, pp. 54 and 58, and for 1956, in People's Daily, January 1, 1957, p. 1. The figure for 1957 is an extrapolation from the 1956 estimate on the basis of

an index of average wheat output for 1955-56 and 1956-57 computed from data given in Table 32.

23. Edible vegetable oils. The figure for 1952 is given in Appendix G. The figures for 1953-57 are derived on the basis of the 1952 estimate and an index of total factory and handicraft output of edible vegetable oils given in Great Ten Years, p. 89.

24. Cigarettes. Ibid.

25. Matches. The figure for 1952 is given in First Five Year Plan, p. 37. Figures for 1953-54 are computed on the basis of the 1952 figure and indexes of output for 1953 and 1954, with the preceding year as 100, given in 1953 Communique and 1954 Communique. Those for 1955-57 are given in TKP, Peiping, December 30, 1956, p. 3, and April 12, 1958, p. 1.

26. Rubber footwear. Great Ten Years, p. 88.

It should be noted that the products within each group listed in Table F-8 are not always of standard quality. The rapid increase in output expansion was often achieved at the expense of the quality of the products. Consequently, substandard products accounted for sizable proportions of the total output of some items.[49] Since the prices used are prices of products of standard quality, the gross output so derived may be biased in the upward direction. Furthermore, changes over time in the percentages of inferior quality products in total output also tend to distort the rates of growth. But such distortions are probably rather minor, for available evidence does not indicate any significant change in the quality of the important products over the period concerned.[50]

The prices of 20 product groups in 1952 are summarized in Table F-10. In principle, the prices given in this table are factory prices. However,

Table F-10

PRICES OF 20 PRODUCT GROUPS, 1952

(1952 yuan)

Product	Price
Pig iron	200.00/ton
Steel	600.00/ton
Cement	85.00/ton
Coke	44.00/ton
Gunny sacks	2.00 each
Chemicals	
Ammonium sulfate	400.00/ton
Caustic soda	1,257.00/ton
Pure soda	350.00/ton
Sulfuric acid	335.00/ton
Sheet glass	2.96/square meter
Auto tires	392.00 each
Rolled steel	1,000.00/ton
Cotton yarn	720.00/bale
Cotton cloth	27.00/bolt
Silk	43,910.00/ton
Silk piece goods	3.00/ton
Woolen textiles	
Woolen yarn	30,864.00/ton
Woolen piece goods	16.80/meter
Woolen blankets	26.00 each
Sugar	1,100.00/ton
Milled rice	200.00/ton
Wheat flour	310.00/ton
Cigarettes	490.00/case
Matches	12.00/case
Rubber footwear	4.00/pair

information on factory prices is extremely scarce. Of the 25 quotations given in Table F-10, only four -- sulfuric acid, auto tires, rubber footwear, and matches -- are specifically stated in Communist sources as factory prices. For the rest, the price data used for the producers' goods are wholesale prices at the major producing centers, and those for consumers' goods are wholesale prices reduced by 10 per cent as a rough allowance for the price differential between wholesale and factory prices.

Traditionally, and probably in 1952, factories manufacturing producers' goods in China handled their own distribution to consumers and retailers. The wholesale prices, therefore, were actually the factory prices. The price structure consists mainly of transfer prices for materials allocated from one state enterprise to another, and wholesale market prices for other products not centrally allocated. The transfer prices, then, are also generally factory prices.[51] As we have said, sales of producers' goods at wholesale market prices are mostly direct sales to the users, and these prices are, in effect, factory prices. There is no evidence that in 1952 the transfer prices were different from the wholesale prices.[52] By and large, the wholesale prices of producers' goods at the major producing centers in 1952 remained fair approximations to, if not the actual, factory prices.

For consumers' goods, however, a wholesale stage did exist between the manufacturers and the retailers. The wholesale prices are not prices charged by the manufacturers (as is the case with producers' goods) but by wholesalers. To use the wholesale prices as factory prices in our calculation of gross value of manufactured products would involve double-counting of that portion of value added by the wholesalers distributing such products both in the manufacturing sector and in the trade sector. In order to arrive at factory prices, we must reduce the wholesale prices by an amount equal to the difference between the two prices. Information necessary to make such an adjustment is not available and a rough estimate has to be made. The price differential includes wholesale distribution costs, profits of the wholesalers, and taxes at the wholesale level.[53] According to a Communist source, the average distribution cost of the state trade enterprises in 1952 was 15.9 per cent of total sales.[54] Since the state trading enterprises in 1952 handled mostly the wholesale distribution of consumers' goods, it seems reasonable to assume that the distribution cost for consumers' goods would come close to this figure. However, this figure represents total distribution costs for both wholesaling and retailing. Furthermore, the wholesale prices used for our calculation are those at the major producing centers so that little or no transportation costs are involved in transferring the goods from the manufacturers to the wholesalers. For these two reasons, the distribution margin relevant to our calculation should be much lower than the 15.9 per cent given for total trade as a whole. On the other hand, profits and taxes have yet to be allowed. Taking these various factors into consideration, we arbitrarily assume a round figure of 10 per cent for the differential between the wholesale prices and factory prices of consumers' goods. While this procedure would undoubtedly introduce a margin of error, it is believed that such errors would be less than if no adjustments are made. In any event, if either an overestimate or an underestimate of the gross value of the products listed in Table F-8 does exist, because of errors in the price data, it would affect only the size of the unidentified portion of gross output but not the total gross output of factori

In selecting the price data for our purpose, greater weight is given to prices at the major production centers, prices of products whose quality represents the industry's total output (for example, the prices of 20-count cotton yarn in the cotton-spinning industry) and prices at the third quarter of 1952 which has been selected by the Communists as the base period for constant 1952 prices.

It may be noted that producers' goods, as well as consumers' goods, are all subject to indirect taxes including the commodity tax which was later incorporated in the turnover tax.[55] Consequently, in our calculations both the gross value of output and value added by these industries include indirect taxes.

The sources and method of deriving the prices given in Table F-10 are as follows:

1. Pig iron. The following eight price quotations ranging from 200 to 280 yuan/ton are available:

Locality	Price (yuan/ton)	Source
Chengchow (factory purchase price)	280	CCJP, Hankow, April 23, 1952
Shanghai (special grade)	235	HWJP, Shanghai, August 31, 1952
(No. 1 grade)	225	Ibid.
(No. 2 grade)	215	Ibid.
(No. 3 grade)	205	Ibid.
Tientsin (official wholesale)	200	CPJP, Tientsin, August 31, 1952
Shihchiachuan	200	SCCJP, Shihchiachuan, August 30, 1952
Chungking	240	HHJP, Chungking, April 23, 1952

The price quoted at Tientsin has been selected partly because it is the official wholesale price at which presumably the bulk of transactions are made, and partly because Tientsin is probably closer to the factory than the others.

2. Steel. The price of steel has to be estimated. The ratio of steel price to pig iron price was roughly 3:1 in Manchuria in 1938.[56] On the assumption that the same price ratio prevailed for the Chinese Mainland in 1952, we derive the price of steel at 600 yuan/ton.

3. Cement. Eight quotations in three cement producing centers are obtained: 69 yuan/ton at Tientsin (TTJP, Tientsin, October 18, 1952); 96 yuan/ton at Canton (NFJP, Canton, August 10, 1952); and an average of six price quotations, 91 yuan/ton, at Shanghai (CFJP, Shanghai, August 31, 1952). The arithmetic mean of the prices in these three cities, 85 yuan/ton, is used in this study.

4. Coke. The price of coke given in Table F-10 is the unweighted average of three quotations: 31.20 yuan/ton for Kailan coke in Tientsin, 48.00 yuan/ton for Chin Ching coke also in Tientsin (TTJP, Tientsin, August 30, 1952), and 52.87 yuan/ton in Chungking (HHJP, Chungking, April 19, 1952).

5. Gunny sacks. Three quotations are obtained: 2.15 yuan/piece in Shanghai for sacks 43 by 29 inches (CFJP, Shanghai, November 6, 1952); 2.30 at Tungliao, Inner Mongolia (NMKJP, Huhehot, February 2, 1952); and 1.75 in Tientsin (CPJP, Tientsin, August 31, 1952). The arithmetic average of these prices comes to 2.07 yuan/piece which is rounded off to 2.00 for use here.

6. Chemicals. Four price quotations for ammonium sulfate are obtained: 430 yuan/ton in Tientsin (CPJP, Tientsin, October 12, 1952), 390 in Wuhsi (SNJP, Wuhsi, September 4, 1952), 384 in Hangchow (CKJP, Hangchow, August 28, 1952), and 400 in Tienshui (KSJP, Lanchow, March 30, 1952). The arithmetic mean of these quotations, 400 yuan/ton, is taken as the average factory price.

For caustic soda, only three quotations are available: 1,248 and 1,280 yuan/ton in Shanghai and 1,245 yuan/ton in Tientsin (TKP, Shanghai, June 1, 1952, HWJP, Shanghai, October 8, 1952, and Nankai Economic Research Institute, Source Materials on Nankai Indices, p. 250). The unweighted average of these quotations, 1,257 yuan/ton, is used.

The price of soda ash in Shanghai was quoted at 386 yuan/ton (CFJP, Shanghai, January 3, 1952). A second quotation for soda ash produced by Yung-li Chemical Works in Tientsin puts it at 318 yuan/ton (TTJP, Tientsin, April 10, 1953). On the assumption that the price in 1952 was roughly the same as in 1953 in Tientsin, we use the average of the two quotations, that is, 350 yuan/ton, in our calculations.

Three quotations of factory prices for sulfuric acid of three different degrees of concentration are given at 193.3, 311.1, and 422.2 yuan/ton (HWJP, Shanghai, February 30, 1952). Two other quotations (TKP, Shanghai, March 20, 1952, p. 3 and December 6, 1953, p. 1), come close to these factory prices. For our calculations, the median, 311 yuan/ton, is used.

7. Sheet glass. Three quotations for Shanghai are available: 1.85, 2.96, and 6.48 yuan/square meter of sheet glass of two millimeters and five millimeters (HWJP, Shanghai, September 22, 1952). A fourth quotation puts it at 1.67 yuan/square meter at Changchiako without

specifying the type of glass. For our calculation, the median, 2.96 yuan/square meter, is used.

8. Auto tires. Seven price quotations are available. However, only two are specifically quoted as factory prices in Tientsin at 370 and 438 yuan (CPJP, Tientsin, August 31, 1952).[57] The latter figure includes the price of inner tubes, 23 yuan each. Deducting this 23 yuan, we derive the price of the tire at 415 yuan. The price given in Table F-10 is an average of these two quotations, 392 yuan.

9. Rolled steel. Prices vary widely because of differences in quality and types of products as shown as follows:

Locality	Price (yuan/ton)	Source
Shanghai (high quality steel)	2,600	TKP, Shanghai, February 1, 1952.
(steel bar)	1,806	Ibid.
(steel bar)	1,600	Ibid.
(sheet, 3 mm)	1,520	CFJP, Shanghai, January 3, 1952.
Hangyang (nickel steel)	1,500	CCJP, Hankow, June 3, 1952.
Tsingtao (steel sheet, 3 mm)	1,480	TTJP, Tsingtao, September 14, 1952.
Shanghai (medium grade)	1,350	TKP, Shanghai, February 18, 1952.
(steel rod, 25 mm)	900	HWJP, Shanghai, October 31, 1952.
(steel bar, 3 mm)	850	Ibid.
(steel bar, 5 to 6 mm)	850	Ibid.
Hankow (steel bar)	830	CCJP, Hanchow, April 23, 1952.
Shanghai (steel bar, 9 mm)	810	HWJP, Shanghai, October 31, 1952.
Canton (low carbon steel)	800	TKP, Shanghai, March 31, 1952.

Locality	Price (yuan/ton)	Source
Shanghai (steel bar, 12 mm)	790	HWJP, Shanghai, October 31, 1952
(steel bar, 16 mm)	790	Ibid.
Tientsin (steel rod)	780	TTJP, Tientsin, August 30, 1952.
(steel rod)	750	Ibid.
Shanghai (steel bar, 19mm)	730	HWJP, Shanghai, October 31, 1952.
(steel bar, 22 mm)	730	Ibid.
(steel bar, 25 mm)	700	Ibid.
(steel, 38 mm)	700	Ibid.
(steel, 50 mm)	700	Ibid.

One would expect steel products on the Chinese Mainland in 1952 to consist mainly of bars and sheets rather than tubes, structural steel, or other high grade steel. Unfortunately the limited information available does not permit weighting. Under the circumstances, a rounded arithmetic average of 1,000 yuan/ton is probably a fair approximation to the average price of steel products.

10. Cotton yarn. The price of cotton yarn also varies widely because of different degrees of fineness in the yarn. Traditionally, the 20-count yarn has always been the most common.[58] Moreover, the average fineness of the total yarn output was roughly 20-count in 1933,[59] 21.8-count in 1952, and 23.2-count in 1956.[60] Therefore, the price of 20-count yarn is taken as the average price of total cotton yarn output in our calculation. The following data on the average price of 20-count yarn in 18 localities have been compiled:

Locality	Price (yuan/bale)	Source
Foochow	908	KSHW, Canton, December 3, 1952.
Shengyang	856	Ibid.
Chungking	835	Ibid.

Locality	Price (yuan/bale)	Source
Nanchang	815	KSHW, Canton, December 3, 1952.
Sian	812	Ibid.
Tientsin	810	Ibid.
Canton	810	Ibid.
Hankow	820	KSHW, Canton, December 3, 1952; and CCJP, Hankow, August 31, 195
Nanning	800	CCJP, Hankow, February 21, 1952.
Tsinan	692	KSHW, Canton, December 3, 1952; and TCJP, Tsinan, September 1, 1
Changsha	790	CCJP, Hankow, February 2, 1952.
Chengchow	785	Ibid.
Nanchang	780	Ibid.
Shashih	770	Ibid.
Nanking	768	KSHW, Canton December 3, 1952; and HHJP, Nanking, September 2,
Hangchow	750	CKJP, Hangchow, August 28, 1952.
Wuhsi	745	SNJP, Wuhsi, September 4, 1952.
Shanghai	742	TKP, Shanghai, August 20, 1952.

Since the prices vary so widely, some kind of weighting appears desirable. Lacking the detailed information on the output of different localities, we more or less arbitrarily assign 60 per cent weight to the average price of the three most important textile centers: Shanghai, Tientsin, and Hankow, and 40 per cent to the average price for the other localities. The average price so derived amounts to 797 yuan/bale. Reducing it by 10 per cent to arrive at the factory price, we obtain an estimate of 720 yuan/bale.

11. Cotton cloth. The quality of cotton cloth differs considerably, and the price of cotton cloth also varies rather widely. For our calculation, the price of "dragon head" cloth, which is of average quality, is taken to represent the average price of the different kinds of cotton cloth for each locality.[61] For those localities where no such brand of cloth is produced, the price of cloth of similar grade is used. Altogether prices for 17 producing centers are obtained.

Locality	Price (yuan/bolt)	Source
Tsinan	36.4	TCJP, Tsinan, September 1, 1952.
Ningpo	35.0	NPJP, Ningpo, August 26, 1952.
Foochow	33.9	KSHW, Canton, December 3, 1952.
Amoy	32.4	AMJP, Amoy, August 31, 1952.
Chungking	32.3	KSHW, Canton, December 3, 1952.
Nanchang	30.8	Ibid.
Sian	30.8	Ibid.
Hankow	30.5	CCJP, Hankow, August 31, 1952; and TKP, Shanghai, September 5, 1952.
Shenyang	30.5	KSHW, Canton, December 3, 1952.
Nanking	29.9	Ibid., and HHJP, Nanking, September 2, 1952.
Canton	29.8	KSHW, Canton, December 3, 1952.

Locality	Price (yuan/bolt)	Source
Tientsin	29.2	Ibid., and TKP, Shangh[ai], September 5, 1952.
Taiyuan	28.6	Ibid.
Tsingtao	27.5	TTJP, Tsingtao, September 14, 1952.
Hangchow	26.3	CKJP, Hangchow, August 28, 1952.
Wuhsi	25.8	SNJP, Wuhsi, September 4, 1952.

The average price of the major production centers Shanghai, Tientsin, Hankow, and Tsingtao, and that of the other localities, are weighted by the same percentages as given for the prices of cotton yarn, that is, 60 and 40 per cent. The average price is derived at 29.8 yuan/bolt. Allowing 10 per cent for the price differential between wholesale and factory prices and rounding, we obtain an estimate of 27 yuan/bolt.

12. Silk. Factory-reeled silk is mostly bleached silk of higher quality than that produced by the handicraftsmen, and thus sells for a considerably higher price. The price given in Table F-10 is the average of four quotations: 40,928 yuan/ton for 40/44 denier, and 46,230 yuan/ton for 16/18 denier (HWJP, Shanghai, March 13, 1952). In computing the gross value of output, an allowance of 11.7 per cent is made for the gross value of silk waste to gross value of silk for 1933 (computed from data given in Ou, National Income, Vol. II, p. 101). Total gross value of output of the silk-reeling factories presented in Table 39, is the sum of the gross values of silk and silk waste.

13. Silk piece goods. Four quotations are given (HWJP, Shanghai, March 13 and August 31, 1952) for silk piece goods of different quality in

Shanghai where the bulk of machine-woven silk piece goods are manufactured: 91, 114, 151, and 168 yuan/bolt. Lacking the necessary data for weighting, we take the unweighted average of these quotations, 131 yuan/bolt, as an approximation. Traditionally a bolt of silk measures 40 meters. (SSB, Industry Study, p. 155.) The average price per meter is therefore equal to 3.28 yuan per meter. A 10 per cent deduction is then applied to this average price to allow for the wholesale distribution margin, giving an estimated factory price of 2.95 yuan/meter which is rounded off to 3.00 yuan/meter.

14.(a) Woolen yarn. The only quotation available is the price of Ti-yarn in Tientsin (Nankai Economic Research Institute, Source Materials on Nankai Indices, p. 205). Presumably this is the factory price and no adjustment for the wholesale distribution margin is made.

14.(b) Woolen piece goods. Three quotations of factory prices in Shanghai are available. Tientsin and Shanghai were the two most important woolen textile centers on the Chinese Mainland. The prices of woolen piece goods for civilian use are quoted at 21.87 and 20.23 yuan/meter, and for military uniforms, at 10.35 (HWJP, Shanghai, January 3, 1952). The wide range between these quotations is probably due in part to quality differences and to a possible subsidy to military personnel. In our calculation, an unweighted average of these three quotations is used.

14.(c) Woolen blankets. The price of blankets in 1933 is estimated at 5.5 yuan each on the basis of output and gross value for Hopei Province given in Ou, National Income, Vol. II, p. 106. The price in 1952 is derived on the assumption that the price of blankets increased from 1933 to 1952 in proportion to the price of Si-ning wool in Tientsin over the same period. The latter price quotations are given at 34.56 and 165.00 yuan per picul for 1933 and 1952 (Nankai Economic Research Institute, pp. 78 and 215).

15. Sugar. Machine-refined sugar consists largely of white sugar as distinguished from yellow and brown sugar produced by the native mills. Geographically, the major producing areas include the provinces of Kwangtung, Kwangsi, Fukien, Szechwan, Chekiang, and Manchuria, but some sugar refineries are also found in other localities. Altogether 14 quotations for white sugar in these areas are obtained as follows:[62]

Locality	Price (yuan/ton)	Source
Canton	1,224	CCCP, Shanghai, December 20, 1951, p.
Foochow	1,000	FKJP, Foochow, September 2, 1952.
Amoy	1,080 1,120 1,540	AMJP, Amoy, August 31, 1952.
Chungking	1,160	CCCP, Shanghai, December 20, 1951, p.
Shengyang	1,500	Ibid.
Tientsin	1,320	Ibid.
Hankow	1,000	HPJP, Hankow, September 2, 1952.
	1,240	CCJP, Hankow, August 31, 1952.
Shanghai	1,320	CFJP, Shanghai, January 3, 1952.
Tsingtao	1,200	TTJP, Tsingtao, September 14, 1952.
Hangchow	1,520	CKJP, Hangchow, August 28, 1952.
Nanchang	1,180	KSJP, Nanchang, September 2, 1952.

The rather high prices in Amoy and Hangchow are for special brands of high quality white sugar. The price in Shengyang probably refers to beet sugar. Presumably all of these would contribute a minor portion of total white sugar output. An unweighted average of the above quotations at 1,240 yuan per ton is derived. Allowing 10 per cent for the difference between the wholesale and factory price, we obtain a rough estimate of the factory price at 1,100 yuan per ton.

16. Milled rice. Twelve quotations of milled rice in cities and towns located at the rice producing areas are obtained. Milled rice comes in different grades depending on the quality of the unhusked rice and the degree of fineness in polishing. The prices given here are those of medium grades, including the "medium white kan," "medium shu san," "medium si kan," "medium huai pai," and "medium white chien."

Locality	Price (yuan/ton)	Source
Shanghai	272	CFJP, Shanghai, August 31, 1952.
Nanking	202	HHJP, Nanking, September 2, 1952; and KSHW, Canton, December 2, 1952.
Wuhsi	263	SNJP, Wuhsi, September 4, 1952.
Hangchow	210	CKJP, Hangchow, August 28, 1952.
Ningpo	218	NPJP, Ningpo, August 26, 1952.
Nanchang	175	KSHW, Canton, December 2, 1952.
Foochow	226	Ibid.
Amoy	232	AMJP, Amoy, August 31, 1952.

Locality	Price (yuan/ton)	Source
Hankow	209	KSHW, Canton, December 2, 1952.
Tsinan	210	Ibid.
Canton	226	NFJP, Canton, August 31, 1952.
Chungking	169	KSHW, Canton, December 1952; and HHJP, Chungki August 30, 1952.

The information on the regional output of factory-milled rice is totally lacking. In the absence of any better alternative, we take the unweighted average of 218 yuan/ton and deduct from it 10 per cent to allow for the wholesale distribution margin. This figure is then rounded off to 200 yuan/ton.

17. Wheat flour. Wholesale price quotations of medium grade wheat flour in 15 cities have been compiled.

Locality	Price (yuan/ton)	Source
Amoy	432	AMJP, Amoy, August 3, 1952.
Foochow	430	KSHW, Canton December 2, 1952.
Ningpo	364	NPJP, Ningpo, August 26, 1952.
Sheyang	357	KSHW, Canton, December 2, 1952.
Shanghai	345	TKP, Shanghai, March 30 1952.
Tientsin	343	TTJP, Tientsin, August 30, 1952.
Tsingtao	339	TTJP, Tsingtao, September 4, 1952.
Canton	336	KSHW, Canton, December 2, 1952.

Locality	Price (yuan/ton)	Source
Nanchang	328	Ibid.
Paoting	327	HPJP, Paoting, August 31, 1952.
Hangchow	318	CKJP, Hangchow, August 28, 1952.
Wuhsi	309	SNJP, Wuhsi, September 4, 1952.
Hankow	309	KSHW, Canton, December 2, 1952; and CCJP, Hankow, August 30, 1952.
Nanking	300	KSHW, and HHJP, Nanking, September 2, 1952.
Sian	261	KSHW, Canton, December 2, 1952.

An unweighted average of 340 yuan/ton is derived. This figure comes quite close to the price at the most important producing centers such as Shanghai, Tientsin, and Tsingtao, to which greater weight would have been attached if weighting were possible. From this figure we deduct 10 per cent and round it off to 310 yuan/ton.

18. Cigarettes. Prices of cigarettes vary widely because of different qualities and brands. Wholesale prices of medium quality cigarettes in 11 localities are obtained:

Locality	Price (yuan/case of 10,000)	Source
Foochow	144.0	KSHW, Canton, December 2, 1952.
Chungking	135.5	Ibid.
Nanchang	135.5	Ibid.
Nanking	132.5	Ibid.
Tientsin	127.5	Ibid.

Locality	Price (yuan/case of 10,000)	Source
Shanghai	109.0	CFJP, Shanghai, August 31, 1952.
Sian	108.0	KSHW, Canton, December 2, 1952.
Hankow	107.0	Ibid.
Tsinan	103.0	Ibid.
Shenyang	98.5	Ibid.
Canton	92.0	Ibid.

In the period immediately before 1949, an overwhelmingly large proportion of output in the cigarette industry was produced by factories in Shanghai.[63] This situation probably changed very little in 1952. Hence, among the price quotations it appears more reasonable to take the price of cigarettes in Shanghai as the representative price rather than an unweighted average. Allowing 10 per cent for the distribution margin, we derive a factory price of 98 yuan per case. The output of cigarettes, however, is given in cases of 50,000 cigarettes (State Planning Commission, p. 24). The average price of 98 yuan per case of 10,000 is therefore converted to 490 yuan per case of 50,000 cigarettes.

19. Matches. While matches are produced in factories scattered all over the Chinese Mainland, the most important centers are located in East, North, and Northeast China. A factory price of 17 yuan per case in Shanghai is quoted for matches of ordinary quality (HWJP, Shanghai, March 15, 1952). For North and Northeast China, we take the average price of 10 yuan per case in Tientsin given in Nankai Economic Research Institute, p. 245. The weighted average of these two quotations is computed at 12 yuan per case, the weights being 66 per cent for the Tientsin quotation

and 33 per cent for the Shanghai quotation.

20. Rubber footwear. Five quotations of factory price of rubber footwear in Shanghai are given in TKP, Shanghai, August 12, 1952.

	Price (yuan/dozen pair)
Rubber boots	32.20
Taiping boots	42.12
Rubber shoes	63.00
"A" special rubber shoes	79.70
Boots, long trunk	164.62

The most common types of rubber footwear are rubber shoes and boots, the output of which presumably constitutes the largest proportion of total output. The unweighted average price for rubber shoes and boots, 4 yuan per pair, is taken as the average price of rubber footwear. This price is believed to be fairly representative since Shanghai up to 1952 was the production center of rubber footwear on the Chinese Mainland.[64]

Costs of production for 26 product groups, 1952-57. Table F-11 summarizes the percentages of deductible costs in gross output for 26 product groups in 1952 that are used to derive estimates of gross value added for 1952-57 presented in Table 39. The derivation of these percentages is discussed below.

The basic data in the calculation of deductible costs for the 26 product groups in 1952 are drawn mainly from two Japanese surveys of Manchurian industries in 1939 and of those in North China in 1943, these being the latest cost data that are available. Of course, the technical input-output relationships in 1952 in all likelihood would be different from those in Manchuria in 1939 or China proper in 1943. However, at the

Table F-11

PERCENTAGE OF DEDUCTIBLE COSTS OF PRODUCTION IN GROSS VALUE OF OUTPUT FOR 26 PRODUCT GROUPS, 1952

Product	Raw materials	Fuels and electricity	Miscellaneous expenses	Gross value added
Producers' goods				
Pig iron	49	9	2	40
Steel	32	6	2	60
Cement	43	18	2	37
Coke	37	9	2	52
Machinery	48	1	5	46
Gunny sacks	27	1	5	67
Paper	43	3	5	49
Chemicals	54	4	5	37
Rolled steel	52	1	10	37
Sheet glass	32	6	5	57
Auto tires	59	1	10	30
Construction materials	3	16	5	76
Consumers' goods				
Cotton yarn	45	2	2	51
Cotton cloth	77	1	3	19
Silk	69	2	-	29
Silk piece goods	69	1	5	25
Woolen textiles	43	1	8	48
Grass cloth	64	1	4	31
Clothing and knitted goods	45	1	8	46
Sugar	44	2	5	49
Milled rice	90	2	1	7
Wheat flour	83	1	5	11
Edible vegetable oils	79	1	2	18
Cigarettes	22	1	35	42
Matches	53	1	10	36
Rubber footwear	56	1	10	33

Note:

- Not available.

time these surveys were made, the Japanese industrialization program in Manchuria and in North China had already begun. These industries, particularly the heavy industries, later became the backbone of the manufacturing industries on the Chinese Mainland. In any case, the latest data on Manchuria and North China that are available are the best data that can be used. As it will be shown, the cost deductions we have worked out on the basis of the Manchurian and North Chinese data, in the aggregate, checked rather closely with such Communist figures as are available.[65]

The percentages of production costs taken from the various sources are given in Table F-12. Because of wartime and postwar inflation, however, these percentage deductions cannot be applied without adjustments for the changes in input and output prices. It is difficult to make full allowance for this factor as data on the prices of individual commodities are generally not available for Manchuria in 1939 and North China in 1943. Changes in relative prices in these regions, however, probably occurred in later years. Adjustments for relative price movements are therefore made on the basis of the changes in output and input prices from 1933 to 1952. Even looking at these two years only, data on the price of output and input are by no means complete for the products included in Table 39. Relative price changes can be computed for only 12 products -- pig iron, steel, cement, coke, gunny sacks, cotton yarn, cotton cloth, silk, silk piece goods, woolen textiles, sugar, and cigarettes. In addition, it may be reasonably assumed that the output-raw material price relationships have not changed significantly for milled rice, wheat flour, and vegetable oils and that the prices of both the output and raw materials for the machinery industry have moved with that of steel.

Table F-12

PERCENTAGE OF DEDUCTIBLE COSTS IN GROSS VALUE OF OUTPUT, 26 PRODUCT GROUPS

Product	Raw materials (1)	Fuels and electricity (2)	Miscellaneous expenses (3)
Producers' goods			
Pig iron	49	14	2
Steel	49	14	2
Cement	41	17	2
Coke	59	14	2
Machinery	48	5	5
Gunny sacks	68	3	5
Paper	49	6	5
Chemicals	62	8	5
Rolled steel	60	3	10
Sheet glass	37	12	5
Auto tires	68	2	10
Construction materials	3	35	5
Consumers' goods			
Cotton yarn	72	5	2
Cotton cloth	69	1	3
Silk	69	7	-
Silk piece goods	64	2	5
Woolen textiles	41	3	8
Grass cloth	73	2	4
Clothing and knitted goods	51	2	8
Sugar	68	5	5
Milled rice	90	2	1
Wheat flour	83	1	5
Edible vegetable oils	79	1	2
Cigarettes	32	1	35
Matches	60	2	10
Rubber footwear	64	2	10

Notes:

- Not available.

Column (1). Percentage of costs of raw material for pig iron, steel products, machinery, cement, sheet glass, chemicals, and matches are derived from data given in Ministry of Economic Affairs, Manchurian Government, Manshu kojo tokei 1939 (Statistics of Manchurian Factories, 1939), Hsinking, 1940. Those for cigarettes, auto tires, and rubber footwear are

Notes (continued):

the arithmetic averages of figures for Tientsin, Tsingtao, and Peiping in 1943 given in Japanese Embassy, Kahoku kojo tokei (Statistics of Factories in North China), Peiping, 1943, Vol. 1, p. 9; Vol. 2, p. 17; and Vol. 3, p. 13.

For coke, the Tientsin percentage of costs is used. Ibid., Vol. 2, p. 11. The figures for cotton yarn and cotton cloth are the averages for Tientsin and Tsingtao. Ibid., Vols. 1-3, pp. 2-3.

For silk piece goods and gunny sacks, the averages of the figures for Manchuria and Tientsin given in Ministry of Economic Affairs, and Japanese Embassy, Vol. 5, p. 3, are used.

For woolen textiles, the percentage is the average of figures for Tientsin, Tsingtao, Peiping, and Manchuria, ibid., Vol. 2, p. 2; Vol. 3, p. 1; and Ministry of Economic Affairs.

For wheat flour and paper, the averages of the data for the following are used: Tientsin, Peiping, Tsingtao, Hopei, Shantung, and Manchuria. These data are given in Japanese Embassy, Vol. 1, p. 7; Vol. 2, p. 13; Vol. 3, p. 9; Vol. 4, p. 7; Vol. 5, p. 9; and Ministry of Economic Affairs.

In the case of milled rice and sugar, which are for the most part products of industries outside of Manchuria or North China, we use the prewar figure computed from data given in Lieu, Industry Survey, Vol. II, Tables 13 and 14, pp. 575 and 655.

For construction materials, silk, grass cloth, and clothing and knitted goods, the percentages of raw materials and fuels and electricity are assumed to be the same as those for the Chinese Mainland in 1933 given in Table F-4.

Column (2). Except for iron and steel, percentages of costs of fuels and electricity are derived from data in the same sources given for column (1). The figures for iron and steel are those taken from Ministry of Economic Affairs, A, 1940.

Column (3). The percentages for miscellaneous costs are assumed to be the same as those in 1933.

The procedure of adjustment consists of: (1) calculating price indexes for output, raw materials, fuels and electricity, and miscellaneous expenses for 1952 with 1933 as 100; (2) computing the ratio of the price index for each category of deductible costs to the price index of output; and (3) multiplying the percentages of deductible costs for each product given in Table F-12 by the corresponding ratios. The price indexes for output, raw materials, fuels and electricity, and miscellaneous expenses for the products noted above have been given earlier in this appendix. On the basis of these indexes, the input-output price index ratios shown in Table F-13 are derived.

The ratios as shown in Table F-13 are then applied to the respective percentages given in Table F-12 to arrive at the corrected figures which were shown in Table F-11. By multiplying the gross output of the 16 products for 1952, given in Table 39, by the corrected percentages, estimates of gross value added in these products for 1952, in 1952 prices, are obtained. The calculations are shown in Table F-14. The estimates of gross value of output for 1953-57 given in Table 39 are multiplied by the same percentages to arrive at gross value added for 1953-57.

For the ten products[66] for which price data are not sufficient to make the necessary adjustments individually, we use the average price indexes of output and nonprimary input calculated for the six producers' goods and nine consumers' goods on the basis of gross output and value added for the 16 products in 1952, in constant 1933 and 1952 prices. The estimates in 1952 prices have already been derived. Those in 1933 prices are computed on the basis of output of the 16 products for 1952, their respective prices in 1933, and estimates of the nonprimary input for each of the products in 1933 prices. The results of this calculation are presented in Table F-14. From

Table F-13

INPUT-OUTPUT PRICE INDEX RATIOS, 16 PRODUCT GROUPS

(per cent)

Product	Raw materials	Fuels and electricity	Miscellaneous expenses
Producers' goods			
Pig iron	100	64	100
Steel	65	42	100
Cement	104	104	100
Coke	63	63	100
Machinery	100	21	100
Gunny sacks	40	25	100
Consumers' goods			
Cotton yarn	62	73	100
Cotton cloth	112	36	100
Silk	100	26	100
Silk piece goods	108	28	100
Woolen textiles	105	28	100
Sugar	64	32	100
Milled rice	100	91	100
Wheat flour	100	46	100
Edible vegetable oils	100	51	100
Cigarettes	68	41	100

Table F-14

GROSS VALUE OF OUTPUT AND VALUE ADDED, 16 MANUFACTURING PRODUCTS, 1952, IN 1933 AND 1952 PRICES

	Millions of 1933 yuan					Millions of 1952 yuan				
	Gross value of output	Raw materials	Fuels and electricity	Miscel-laneous expenses	Gross value added	Gross value of output	Raw materials	Fuels and electricity	Miscel-laneous expenses	Gross value added
Producers' goods										
Pig iron	97	48	14	2	34	380	186	34	8	152
Steel	135	66	19	3	47	809	259	49	16	486
Cement	101	42	17	2	41	243	105	44	5	90
Coke	31	18	4	1	8	126	46	11	2	66
Machinery	234	112	12	12	98	1,401	672	14	70	644
Gunny sacks	27	18	1	1	7	135	36	1	7	90
Total	625	304	67	20	234	3,094	1,305	153	108	1,528
Consumers' goods										
Cotton yarn	658	474	33	13	138	2,605	1,172	52	52	1,329
Cotton cloth	672	464	7	20	181	2,365	1,821	24	71	449
Silk	42	29	3	-	10	198	137	4	-	58
Silk piece goods	27	17	1	1	8	116	80	1	6	29
Woolen textiles	35	14	1	3	17	157	68	2	13	75
Sugar	70	48	4	4	16	274	120	6	14	134
Milled rice	113	102	2	1	8	310	279	6	3	22
Wheat flour	378	314	4	19	42	927	769	9	46	102
Edible vegetable oils	147	116	3	3	25	360	284	4	7	65
Cigarettes	430	138	4	150	138	1,298	286	13	454	545
Total	2,571	1,714	61	214	582	8,622	5,017	120	666	2,808

Notes:

Figures for gross value of output in 1952 prices are derived by multiplying the output figures given in Table F-8 by the 1952 prices given in Table F-10. Those in 1933 prices are derived by dividing the gross output in 1952 prices by the price index for 1952, with 1933 as 100, for each of the products given in Table F-6. Gross value of output for silk includes 11.7 per cent for silk waste.

these results, the price indexes and input-output price index ratios shown in Table F-15 are computed.

Applying these ratios to the percentages for the ten products given in Table F-12, we derive the corrected percentages as presented in Table F-11. The gross value of output of these products for 1952-57 in 1952 prices, given in Table 39, are then multiplied by the corrected percentages to arrive at gross value added.

Value Added in All Factories

Having obtained the gross output of the 26 product groups, we now derive the gross output of the remaining products by subtracting the gross output of the 26 products from the total gross output of producers' and consumers' goods factories. The percentages of value added, based on roughly comparable products in 1933, are applied to the gross output of these remaining products to arrive at the gross value added. The sum of the gross value added in the 26 products and the remaining products represents total gross value added in factories. Total net value added is obtained by reducing total gross value added by 5 per cent of total gross output to allow for depreciation. The results of these calculations were presented in Table 42. The basic data, sources, and methods of derivation for all these items except total gross output and depreciation have been explained in the preceding section of this appendix or in Chapter IV. In this section, we shall explain only the derivation of total gross output of producers' and consumers' goods, and depreciation.

Gross value of output of all factories. The estimates of gross value of output of all factories for 1952-57, given in Table 40, are based on Communist data on the gross value of industrial production. According to

Table F-15

PRICE INDEXES AND INPUT-OUTPUT PRICE INDEX RATIOS, 1952, PRODUCERS' AND CONSUMERS' GOODS

(per cent)

	Producers' goods	Consumers' goods
Price indexes (1933 = 100)[a]		
Output	495	335
Raw materials	429	293
Fuels and electricity	230	198
Miscellaneous expenses	495	335
Gross value added	652	483
Input-output price index ratio[b]		
Raw materials	87	88
Fuels and electricity	46	59
Miscellaneous expenses	100	100

Notes:

[a]Price indexes for output, raw materials, fuels and electricity, and gross value added are derived by dividing the total figures in 1952 prices by the corresponding figures in 1933 prices given in Table F-14. Note that the computation is based on figures rounded to the nearest tenth of a million yuan, whereas the figures in Table F-14 are rounded to the nearest million yuan. The price indexes for miscellaneous expenses are assumed to be the same as for output.

[b]The ratio for each category of deductible costs is derived by dividing the price index for that category by the price index of output.

the Communist definition, the gross value of industrial production refers to the sum of the gross value of output produced by industrial enterprises.[67] This concept is different from our definition of gross value of output of factories in three respects.

First, the Communist concept is broader in scope in that it includes both the factory output and a portion of handicraft output. Under the Communist classification system, three types of industrial enterprises are distinguished: modern industry, handicraft workshops, and handicrafts industry, which comprises handicraft cooperatives and individual handicraftsmen. A modern industrial enterprise is one employing relatively modern technical equipment in the major production process.[68] A handicraft workshop is an industrial establishment in which production is carried on primarily by manual labor. It is distinguished from a handicraft cooperative in the form of organization, and from an individual handicraftsman by the number of workers employed. In a handicraft workshop, the total number of workers, including apprentices, exceeds three persons. Communist data on the gross output of these various types of industrial enterprises are presented in Table F-16. In common Communist usage the value of industrial production generally refers to the gross output of modern industrial enterprises and handicraft workshops.[69] The amounts of producers' goods and consumers' goods in total gross value of industrial production are generally given separately, but no further breakdown by modern industry and handicraft workshops is made. For individual handicraftsmen and handicraft cooperatives, the percentage can be calculated at 20 per cent of the total output produced by this group.[70] The proportion for the handicraft workshops would be close to this figure but probably higher since certain handicraft producers' goods,

Table F-16

COMMUNIST DATA ON INDUSTRIAL PRODUCTION

(billions of 1952 yuan)

	1952[a]	1953[a]	1954[a]	1955[a]	1956[a]	1957[b]
Gross value of industrial production	27.01	35.58	41.51	44.75	58.66	65.02
Producers' goods	10.73	14.67	17.58	20.58	29.17	34.33
Consumers' goods	16.28	20.91	23.94	24.17	29.50	30.69
Modern industry	22.05	28.81	33.99	37.08	50.34	55.92
Producers' goods	9.49	12.98	15.70	18.66	27.09	32.05
Consumers' goods	12.56	15.83	18.29	18.42	23.25	23.86
Handicraft workshops	4.96	6.77	7.53	7.67	8.32	9.10
Producers' goods	1.24	1.69	1.88	1.92	2.08	2.28
Consumers' goods	3.72	5.08	5.64	5.75	6.24	6.83
Handicrafts industry	7.31	9.12	10.46	10.12	11.70	13.37
Individual handicraftsmen	7.07	8.63	9.61	8.82	8.82	-
Handicraft cooperatives	0.25	0.49	0.86	1.30	2.88	-
Total	34.33	44.70	51.98	54.87	70.39	78.39

Notes:

- Not available.

[a] 1952-1956. All the figures except those of producers' goods and consumers' goods in modern industry and in handicraft workshops are given in the 1956 Statistical Abstract, pp. 23 and 26-29. Estimates of producers' goods in handicraft workshops are derived by multiplying total output of handicraft workshops by 25 per cent. Estimates of consumers' goods in handicraft workshops, producers' goods, and consumers' goods in modern industry are then derived as residuals.

[b] 1957. Gross value of industrial production and output of handicrafts are given in Chou En-lai, "Report on Government Work," HHPYK, No. 9, May 1959, p. 3. Proportions of producers' and consumers' goods in gross value of industrial production are given at 52.8 and 47.2 per cent, in FFYP Communique, p. 49. Data on the output of modern industry and handicraft workshops are not available. Output of handicraft workshops is derived on the assumption that it increased from 1956-57 in proportion to the gross value of industrial production over the same period. Output of modern industry is then obtained as a residual. Estimates of producers' and consumers' goods in handicraft workshops and modern industry are derived in the same manner as for 1952-56.

such as paper, pig iron, and farm tools are generally produced by workshops rather than individuals. Thus, it seems reasonable to assume that 25 per cent of the output of handicraft workshops belong to the category of producers' goods. On this assumption, the output of handicraft workshops is segregated from total industrial production in order to derive estimates of industrial output by modern industry alone, that is, factory industrial output. The calculations are given in Table F-16.

Second, the Communist definition of modern industry is much broader in industrial coverage than our definition of factories. It includes manufacturing, mining, utilities, lumbering, and fishing (which encompasses all natural marine products).[71] For our purpose, it is necessary to deduct the gross value of industries not engaged in manufacturing from the total gross value of industrial production. This adjustment is made separately for the gross value of producers' goods and consumers' goods. From the total gross value of producers' goods in modern industry, we need to deduct mineral products (excluding salt and coal produced by native methods), electric power and lumbering. Estimates of total gross value for mineral products, electric power, and lumber have been derived elsewhere.[72] In the case of lumber, the total gross value of output includes both the modern and the other sector, and only the former should enter into our calculation. The proportions of total lumber output produced in the modern sector for 1952 and 1957 are given at 17 and 42 per cent.[73] For 1953-57, the proportions are roughly approximated by interpolation from the figures for 1952 and 1957 on the basis of a linear time trend. Applying these percentages to total gross output of lumber for 1952-57, we obtain estimates of gross value of lumber that are included in the Communist data on producers' goods in the modern industry.

From the total gross value of consumers' goods we deduct the gross value of salt (excluding that portion produced by native methods), water and gas supply, and natural marine products. The first two items are derived in connection with our estimates of value added in mining and utilities, as shown in Appendix H, Tables H-2 and H-5. The total gross value of all marine products is shown in Appendix E, Table E-1. It is reported that fish hatcheries contributed some 22 per cent of the national output of marine products.[74] On the assumption that this percentage holds for 1952-57, we derive estimates of natural marine products by multiplying the total gross value of all marine products by 78 per cent. The results of these calculations are summarized in Table 40.

Third, the Communist data on gross value of industrial production are computed on the basis of the so-called "factory method," that is, total gross value is the sum of the output of industrial enterprises. Consequently, interenterprise sales of industrial output are double counted, and intra-enterprise sales are excluded. In order that the Communist data be comparable to the gross value of the 26 product groups which is computed primarily on the basis of quantities of output and prices individually, the value of the intra-enterprise consumption should be added to the Communist figures of industrial production. According to the Communist instructions for compiling industrial statistics, the gross value of the following products is included in the gross value of industrial production, even though they are generally consumed within an enterprise: iron ore, coke, steel ingots and castings, mineral ores of nonferrous metals, wood pulp, coal, fuel oil, and natural gas produced and consumed by the same enterprise.[75] Notably absent in this list are pig iron and cotton yarn.

Being more important than any of the products in the above list, they probably would have been mentioned specifically if their gross value was to be included in the total gross value of industrial production. It appears reasonable to assume that although the gross values of these two products were used as inputs in integrated cotton textile plants or steel mills, they have not been included here, and therefore should be added to the Communist figures of industrial production. Since the iron and steel works were practically all integrated enterprises, the entire amount of gross value of pig iron already estimated is added to industrial production.[76] For cotton yarn, however, only that portion which was consumed by the integrated spinning and weaving mills should be added. This portion is derived as shown in Table F-17.

The adjustment of the Communist data on industrial production is now complete. Two other problems, however, should be noted. The first has to do with the production of military hardware. It is clear that the gross output of military goods is included in that of producers' goods.[77] But the basis of valuation for such goods is not known, and to the extent that the Communists' own ratio of value added to gross output of military goods differs substantially from the one used in our calculation, it may constitute a source of error. However, the error, if it exists, will probably be minor, for as will be shown in the following section, the Communist over-all ratio of value added to gross value of output comes rather close to our estimate. There is, of course, the possibility that the bias in the estimate for military goods is sizable but offset by others in the opposite direction, so that the over-all total is not affected. But no evidence indicating such a possibility has been found.

Table F-17

COTTON YARN CONSUMED BY INTEGRATED SPINNING AND WEAVING MILLS, 1952-57

	1952	1953	1954	1955	1956	1957
1. Gross value of cotton cloth (million 1952 yuan)	2,365	2,678	3,002	2,592	3,426	3,038
2. Consumption of cotton yarn (million 1952 yuan)	1,885	2,089	2,342	2,022	2,672	2,370
3. Total number of looms (thousand units)	142	151	164	169	175	-
4. Number of looms in integrated factories (thousand units)	74	81	92	102	106	-
5. Percentage of total looms in integrated factories	52	54	56	60	60	60
6. Gross value of cotton yarn consumed by integrated factories (million 1952 yuan)	980	1,128	1,312	1,213	1,603	1,422

Notes:

- Not available.

Line 1. Taken from Table 39.

Line 2. Derived by multiplying figures in line 1 by 78 per cent. For derivation of the percentage figure, see Tables 11-13.

Lines 3 and 4. SSB, Industry Study, p. 162.

Line 5. Derived from figures in lines 3 and 4. The figure for 1957 is assumed to be the same as for 1956.

Line 6. Line 2 times line 5.

The second problem is that the average factory prices in the third quarter of 1952 for 16,000 products are used as weights by the Communists to compute the gross value of industrial production in constant prices for the First Five Year period. Presumably these prices are weighted averages for the country as a whole. In actual computation, the basic data are primarily the factory prices of state enterprises in the major production centers only.[78] In the computation of the gross value of the 26 product groups, not all of the price data used are factory prices of state enterprises. However, miscellaneous information seems to suggest that in 1952 there was probably a considerable degree of uniformity in the price levels of the output of private and state enterprises.[79]

Depreciation. Depreciation is generally estimated by the Communists by dividing the value of the fixed asset (minus estimated scrapped value, if any) by the number of years for which the asset is expected to be in use.[80] Unfortunately, available data are insufficient for us to derive depreciation by the same method. As an alternative, a rough estimate of slightly over 5 per cent of gross value of output is computed from miscellaneous Communist data,[81] and a round figure of 5 per cent of gross value of output is used in our calculation.

PROPORTION OF VALUE ADDED IN GROSS OUTPUT: A COMPARISON OF THE COMMUNIST AND OUR ESTIMATES

It may be of some interest to compare our statistics on the percentages of value added in total gross value of output with the Communist statistics in order to check the consistency of the data used in our estimates with the Communist data. Table F-18 brings together these two sets of estimates. Because the Communist data on industrial production exclude intra-enterprise sales and include handicraft workshop output, they are

Table F-18

PROPORTION OF NET VALUE ADDED IN GROSS OUTPUT: A COMPARISON OF THE COMMUNIST AND AUTHORS' ESTIMATES
(per cent)

	1952	1953	1954	1955	1956	1957
1. Communist estimates						
a. Factories, handicraftsmen, mining, utilities, lumber, and part of fisheries	32	33	33	34	33	33
Producers' goods	41	-	-	44	-	-
Consumers' goods	27	-	-	26	-	-
Heavy industry	39	-	-	44	-	-
Light industry	30	-	-	30	-	-
b. Factories, mining, and utilities adjusted for intra-enterprise sales	37	38	38	38	37	36
c. Factories	33	36	35	35	34	33
2. Our estimates						
a. Factories, mining, and utilities	36	36	36	37	38	38
b. Factories	32	32	33	33	34	34
Producers' goods	42	42	41	41	42	42
Consumers' goods	30	31	31	30	31	31

Notes:

- Not available.

Line 1.a. The figures are computed from data given in Table F-16, Table J-3, and Li Hui-hung, Shung Chi-ren, and Wang Hua-hsin, "The Problem of Classifying Light and Heavy Industries," TCKT, No. 18, September 1957, p. 15.

Notes (continued):

Line 1.b. The figures are derived on the basis of Communist data on net value added and gross output given in the sources cited above, the gross value of intra-enterprise consumption of pig iron and coal given in Table 40, the gross value of handicraft output given in Table F-16, and net value added by handicrafts roughly estimated at 19 per cent of gross output as follows: Net value added per worker in handicrafts in 1952 has been estimated at 250 yuan (Cheng Chu-yuan, "Trends in Mainland China's National Income," *Tsu-kuo* (China Weekly), Hong Kong, No. 189, August 13, 1956, p. 21), and the number of handicraftsmen at 9.34 million in Table 58. Total net value added in handicrafts in 1952, therefore, amounts to 2.34 billion yuan, or 19 per cent of gross output.

Line 1.c. The figures are derived from the data for line 1.b. after further adjustments are made to exclude the gross value of mining, utilities, and lumber given in Table 40, net value added in mining and utilities given in Tables H-2 and H-5, and net value added in lumber estimated at 95 per cent of gross output. Our estimates for factories, mining and utilities are computed from data given in Tables 37 and 47.

adjusted in order to place them on a comparable basis with our estimates. The percentages based on these adjusted Communist data are also presented in the table.

The following general observations seem warranted by the evidence in this table. First, there seems to be fair agreement in the order of magnitude between the adjusted Communist estimates and our estimates for factories, mining, and utilities. Second, the two estimates for manufacturing also come rather close to each other, except perhaps for 1953. Third, our estimates for consumers' goods in factories for 1952 and 1955 are both higher than the unadjusted Communist figures because of the exclusion of intra-enterprise sales and inclusion of handicraft products in the Communist figures for which the ratio of value added to gross output is relatively lower than factories. Finally, it may be noted that our estimate for producers' goods in factories remains more or less the same for all the years, whereas the Communist data for producers' goods in industry show a slight increase from 41 to 44 per cent in 1952-55. By assumption, our ratios for 1952 and 1955 can vary only if there are disparities in the rates of growth of the individual output with the producers' goods industries. As for the Communist estimate, not only changes in the product mix of industry but also changes in technical input-output relationships for the same product could affect the ratio. In fact, the Communists claim that because of improvement in management the ratio has been raised.[82] To the extent the increase in the Communist ratio is reliable, our figure for the producers' goods would be on the low side. However, the Communist estimate, even if accurate, is higher than ours by such a small margin (a difference of only 3 per cent) that any resultant error in our figures would be relatively minor.

FOOTNOTES TO APPENDIX F

1. The results of this survey are given in Lieu, Industry Survey.

2. Ibid., Vol. I, pp. 1-17.

3. China proper refers to all the Chinese Mainland outside Manchuria.

4. A rough comparison of the list of localities surveyed and that of cities and towns with electricity indicates that the more important manufacturing centers have been covered. For the list of localities surveyed, see Lieu, Industry Survey, Vol. III. For the list of localities with electricity, see Manchurian Electric Power Company, Chuka minkoku denki jigyo, 1933 (The Electric Power Industry of the Republic of China, 1933), 1935, pp. 9-84.

5. The list of factories surveyed in each locality is checked against information from several sources to guard against omissions. These sources include the local government, the tax bureau, the telephone company, the electric power company, and trade associations. For such important manufacturing centers as Shanghai, this survey was conducted more like a census taking. The list of factories investigated was also checked against two other surveys by the Shanghai Municipal Government and the Institute for the Promotion of Chinese Products. Of course, there may still be omissions. For example, a few factories refused to supply information and several others were not in operation at the time of the survey and no information was available. But such cases were relatively few.

6. See Chapter IV under Occupational Distribution.

7. Checks were made for the relationship between the input and output data, between output and capacity, between output of major products and by-products, and between equipment and labor.

8. Manchurian Factories, 1933, preface.

9. State Planning Commission, Ti-yi-ke wu-nien-chi-hua-ti ming-tsi chieh-hsi (Explanation of Terms Used in the First Five Year Plan), Peiping, Jen-min chu-pan-she, 1955, p. 2.

10. Mill consumption of cotton in China proper in 1933 is given at 11.0 million piculs. (The Trade of China, 1933, Vol. I, p. 47.) According to an estimate by the Cotton Textile Association, cotton waste from spinning is equal to 10.1 per cent of the cotton consumed. (Ou, National Income, Vol. II, p. 90.) The quantity of cotton waste is therefore calculated at 1.1 million piculs. Deducting this figure from total cotton input, we obtain the quantity of yarn output at 9.9 million piculs.

11. The price of cotton yarn is the weighted average of the prices of 20-count yarn produced in Chinese-owned and Japanese-owned factories, the weights being 2:1, which is roughly the ratio of the yarn output of the two groups of factories respectively. (Ou, National Income, Vol. II, p. 91. The price of yarn produced by Chinese mills is the unweighted average of Jen-chung and Chin-cheng yarn in Shanghai (52.2 and 55.5 yuan per picul) and San-lu yarn in Tientsin (49.3 yuan per picul) (ibid.) and of figures from Nankai Economic Research Institute, Nankai chih-shu tzu-liao chun-pien (Source Materials for the Nankai Indexes), Peiping, T'ung-chi chu-pan-she, 1958, p. 75. The price of the yarn produced by Japanese mills is that of Shiu-yueh yarn given at 47.5 yuan per picul in Ou, National Income, Vol. II, p. 91.

12. The gross value of cotton waste is derived by multiplying the quantity of cotton waste (1.1 million piculs given above) and the price of cotton waste estimated at 3.86 yuan per picul. Ibid., p. 92.

13. South Manchurian Railway, Manshū koku keizai teigo (Statistical Abstract of the Manchurian Economy), 1938, p. 395. The original figure

is given in bales which have been converted to piculs at 410 pounds per bale. This figure comes close to another estimate of 0.328 million piculs given in Japan Manchoukuo Yearbook Company, Japan-Manchoukuo Yearbook 1936, Tokyo, 1936, p. 835.

14. This is derived on the assumption that the ratio of yarn to cotton waste in Manchurian mills is the same as in the mills in China proper.

15. The price of cotton yarn is given in South Manchurian Railway, Manshū keizai tōkei nempo, 1933 (Manchurian Economic Statistical Yearbook, 1933), Dairen, 1934, p. 43. For cotton waste, the price in Manchuria is assumed to be the same as in China proper.

16. China Cotton Textile Regulatory Commission, Statistics of Cotton Textile Factories, pp. 29 and 45, quoted in Ou, National Income, Vol. I, p. 72, footnote 9.

17. This figure is derived on the basis of output and employment in the Kwantung textile mills given by the South Manchurian Railway and the Manchurian Government in Manchurian Factories, 1933, pp. 2-8. It is assumed that the gross value of output per worker in other Manchurian mills is the same as in the Kwantung mills.

18. This is the sum of the output of the weaving and the spinning mills. Output of the weaving mills producing cotton cloth only is given at 5.73 million bolts in Lieu, Industry Survey, Vol. II, pp. 637-638, and that of the spinning mills producing both yarn and cloth, at 23.46 million bolts in Shen-pao Yearbook, 1936, p. G:47.

19. South Manchurian Railway, Statistical Abstract of the Manchurian Economy, p. 395.

20. Ou, National Income, Vol. II, pp. 91-92.

21. Gross value per worker in Chinese-owned factories, computed from data given in Lieu, Industry Survey, Vol. II, pp. 270 and 638, is equal to 2,050 yuan per worker. However, the average for the entire industry is probably higher because of higher productivity of the workers in foreign-owned factories noted in Ou, National Income, Vol. II, p. 91. We more or less arbitrarily raise the above figure by 10 per cent and round it off to obtain an estimate of 2,200 yuan per worker.

22. Ibid., Vol. I, p. 51.

23. For the derivation of this figure, see discussion of estimates for Manchuria below.

24. Gross value of output of Manchurian factories is estimated at 3.78 million yuan. See explanation given for Manchurian figures below.

25. Ou, National Income, Vol. II, pp. 21-22 and 24-25.

26. Ibid., Vol. I, pp. 60-61; Wu Cheng-ming, Manufacturing Industries in China: A Preliminary Report, New York, 1946 (mimeographed), p. 29; Wang Fu-shun, "The Proportion of Industrial Production by Foreign-Owned Factories in Total Industrial Production in Prewar China," Chung-yang yin-hang yueh-pao (Central Bank Monthly), Shanghai, Vol. II, No. 3, March 1947, pp. 1-19. Data for the utilities have been excluded in all cases.

27. For Chinese-owned factories, the data on capital given in Lieu's survey were used. For foreign-owned factories, there were several estimates available. A summary of these estimates can be found in Hou Chi-ming, "Foreign Capital in China's Economic Development, 1895-1937," Ph.D. Thesis, Columbia University, New York, 1952 (typewritten), pp. 3-14. Wu uses the

estimate by Koh Tso-fan, Chung-kuo kung-yeh-hua tung-lun (A General Discussion of China's Industrialization), Shanghai, Commercial Press, 1947, pp. 169-177. A summary of Koh's data may be found in his paper, Capital Stock in China, China Council Paper No. 2, Part 2, Eighth Conference of the Institute of Pacific Relations, December 1942, p. 18.

28. Ou, National Income, Vol. II, pp. 30-172.

29. East Asia Research Institute, Nihon no taishi toshi (Japanese Investments in China), 1942, and Shogaikoku no taishi toshi (Foreign Investments in China), 1943.

30. Wang Fu-shun, pp. 7-19.

31. South Manchurian Railway, Manchurian Factories, 1933, and South Manchurian Railway and the Manchurian Government, Manchurian Factories, 1934. The Kwantung Leased Territories refer to that part of Manchuria outside of the puppet nation Manchoukuo.

32. Manchurian Factories, 1933, pp. 2-8.

33. Ibid., 1934, pp. 56-59.

34. Ibid., pp. 388-392.

35. Ou, National Income, Vol. I, Table 3, p. 53.

36. Lieu, Industry Survey, Vol. III, pp. 1-2, and 206.

37. Japan-Manchoukuo Yearbook Company, Japan-Manchoukuo Yearbook, 1936, Tokyo, 1936, p. 833.

38. Estimated by Ou, National Income, Vol. II, p. 104.

39. The estimate for edible vegetable oils derived from the two surveys, 68 million yuan, appears to be low when compared with the gross value of 106 million yuan for 1932. (Japan-Manchoukuo Yearbook, 1936, p. 819.) The estimate by Ou, National Income, Vol. II, p. 141,

99.3 million yuan, seems more reasonable. According to the 1934 Manchurian survey, 98 per cent of the total was produced by factories. Applying this percentage to Ou's estimate we derive a figure of 97.3 million yuan for the Manchurian factories.

40. Ou, <u>National Income</u>, Vol. II, pp. 101, 128, 132, 140, and 141.

41. Inasmuch as the 1933 survey was the first survey ever conducted in Manchuria, it seems more likely that these items were missing because of incomplete coverage rather than because they were the product of new industries in 1934.

42. The average exchange rates were 98.41 and 97.50 Chinese yuan per 100 Manchurian yen in 1933 and 1934, respectively. South Manchurian Railway, <u>Statistical Abstract of the Manchurian Economy</u>, p. 619.

43. Lieu, <u>Industry Survey</u>, Vol. II, Table 8, pp. 262 and 291.

44. In the actual surveys, engineers and managers were sometimes included in the total number of workers because it was difficult to distinguish between workers and managers in small plants. (Lieu, <u>Industry Survey</u>, Vol. I, p. 16.) Hence the total figure may be slightly on the high side.

45. <u>Ibid.</u>, Vol. II, Table 13, pp. 511-594, and Table 14, pp. 595-673.

46. Computed from data given in Ou, <u>National Income</u>, Vol. I, Table 2, following p. 64.

47. Stated in Appendix E, under the section on depreciation.

48. For a discussion of the overstatement, see Chapter II, the text preceding and following Figure 3; for the correction, see Chapter IV, the discussion following Table 42.

49. This is especially true of some consumers' goods in the earlier years of the First Five Year Plan period. Chia To-fu, "Speech Before the

People's Congress," HHYP, No. 8, August 1955, pp. 91-92; Sung Chao-wen, "Light Industry Must Maintain the Standard of Quality and Economize the Use of Raw Materials," HHYP, No. 11, November 1955, p. 150; TKP, Peiping, December 12, 1958, p. 3, July 19, 1959, p. 3; and People's Daily, Peiping, May 22, 1959, p. 2.

50. See, for example, the quality ratings of six consumers' products for 1955, 1956, and the first half of 1957 given in SSB, "A General Survey of China's Socialist Industrialization," HHPYK, No. 2, January 1957, p. 60, and "Output of China's Light Industry Under the Increase-Production Practice-Economy Drive," TCYC, No. 2, 1958, pp. 12-15.

51. Chu Chi, "The Analytical Work in Drafting Plans for Factory Prices of Producers' Goods," CHCC, Peiping, No. 3, March 1957, p. 19.

52. However, since 1953, the transfer prices were set at levels below those of the wholesale market prices. Fan Jo-i, "Further Remarks on Price Policy of the Heavy Industrial Products," CCYC, Peiping, No. 3, June 1957, p. 54; "Price Policy and the Law of Value," CCYC, No. 5, March 1958, p. 45.

53. Yueh Wei, "Problems of Computing National Income," TCKTTH, Peiping, No. 1, January 1956, p. 15.

54. Shih-shih shao-ts'e (Current Events Handbook), Peiping, May 10, 1954, p. 17.

55. SSB, "Several Problems in the Compilation of Constant 1957 Industrial Prices," TCKTTH, Peiping, No. 19, October 1957, p. 12.

56. This ratio is computed from data given in Statistical Abstract of the Manchurian Economy, pp. 2-3.

57. Other quotations are given in CCJP, Hankow, September 6, 1952, May 30, 1952; and CFJP, Shanghai, January 3, 1952.

58. The "count" measures the fineness of the yarn. According to the British system which has been adopted on the Chinese Mainland, one pound of one-count yarn stretches 840 yards in length, and one pound of 20-count yarn, 16,800 yards. In 1947, 63 per cent of the cotton consumed by the mills was used to manufacture 20-count yarn. Ching-chi-pu fang-chi kung-ye shan-charn hui-yi chi-lu (Proceedings of the Conference on Textile Producti Held by the Department of Economic Affairs), Shanghai, 1947, p. 63. The proportion in 1952 would probably be just as high if not higher because of reduced supply of imported cotton which was used mainly to produce the finer yarn. In any event, the proportion must have been rather large, for the productivity of spindles is measured by the Communists in terms of the output of 20-count yarn or its equivalent per spindle per hour. Li Liang, "Technical and Economic Norms in the Cotton Textile Industry," CHCC, Peiping, No. 5, May 1956, p. 27.

59. Ou, National Income, Vol. II, p. 91.

60. Li Liang, p. 28.

61. Probably for the same reason the price of "dragon head" cloth is used by the Communists in the computation of the commodity equivalent unit, a price index was commonly used in financial plans during 1950-54 when prices fluctuated considerably, particularly in 1950. This price index is separately computed for seven cities on the basis of price quotations for rice or wheat flour (and for some cities, corn meal and salt), edible vegetable oils, cotton cloth, and fuel.

62. Among these quotations four refer to prices in late 1951. It is assumed that no changes in these prices took place between 1951 and 1952.

63. About 82 per cent of total cigarette output in the 18 major cities in China was produced in Shanghai in 1947. "Survey of Manufacturing Industries," Chinese Yearbook, 1948, pp. 1525 and 1528.

64. It is interesting to note that the total gross value of rubber footwear estimated on the basis of this price amounts to 246 million yuan for 1952, which comes very close to the Communists' own estimate of 254 million yuan. (For the Communist source, see Chao Yi-wen, Hsin-chung-kuo ti kung-yeh (New China's Industry), Peiping, T'ung-chi chu-pan-she, 1957, p. 59. The small difference may be due to the gross value of a small number of minor products included in the Communist figure.

65. See the discussion later in this appendix on the comparison of the Communist and authors' estimates.

66. These ten products are paper, chemicals, rolled steel, sheet glass, auto tires, matches, and rubber footwear, construction materials, grass cloth, clothing, and knitted goods.

67. State Planning Commission, p. 3.

68. Ibid., p. 2. In China, modern technical equipment generally means any kind of machinery that uses mechanical power. Hence, a modern industrial enterprise amounts to a factory using mechanical power.

69. Two reasons have been given for not including the output of individual handicraftsmen and handicraft cooperatives in industrial production. First, the statistical data on the output of this group are much less reliable than the others. (Wei Yi, "The Problem of Developing Rapidly

the Light Industry," HHPYK, No. 19, October 1956, footnote 1, p. 53). Second, it is argued that the separate listing of the output of this group serves to indicate the progress in the socialization of this particular sector. (Fang Fa, "Tabulation Forms for Industrial Production Planning," CHCC, Peiping, No. 1, January 1957, p. 26.) At times, particularly after 1957, the term gross value of industrial production also refers to the output of all industrial enterprises including individual handicraftsmen and handicraft cooperatives.

70. Gross output of producers' goods for modern industry, handicraft workshops, individual handicraftsmen and handicraft cooperatives in 1952 is given at 12.20 billion yuan. (Li Hui-hung, et al., p. 15.) The figure for modern industry and handicraft workshops is given at 10.78 billion yuan. That for individual handicraftsmen and handicraft cooperatives is therefore equal to 14.90 billion yuan which amounts to 20 per cent of the total gross output of individual handicraftsmen and handicraft cooperatives. (1955 Statistical Abstract, pp. 39-40.)

71. Fang Fa, p. 26.

72. See Appendix H, Tables H-2 and H-5, and Appendix E, Table E-5.

73. TKP, Peiping, October 1, 1957, p. 2.

74. Chang Yu-tien, "Fishermen's Record Hauls," Peking Review, Peiping, No. 11, March 17, 1959, p. 13.

75. Hsu Chien, Tai Shih-kuang, and Yu Tao, Ching-chi-tung-chi-she chian-hua (Lectures on Economic Statistics), Peiping, T'ung-chi chu-pan-she, 1957, pp. 106-107.

76. See figures summarized in Table 39; source of data is discussed earlier in this appendix.

77. SSB, "The Problem of Classifying Producers' and Consumers' Goods," TCKT, Peiping, No. 3, February 1957, p. 3.

78. Tien Chi, "Several Problems in the Revision of Constant 1952 Industrial Prices," TCKT, Peiping, No. 1, January 1957, p. 16.

79. The official and market prices of wheat flour, cigarettes, and edible vegetable oils in Yangchow are given in SPJP, Yangchow, September 1, 1952, p. 4; and prices of milled rice in Nanking are from HHJP, Nanking, September 2, 1952, p. 4.

80. Central Bureau of Administrative Control of Industry and Trade, Sze-ying kung-shan-yeh ti she-hui-chu-i kai-tsao cheng-tse fa-ling hsuan-pien (A Collection of Directives and Decrees Relating to the Socialist Reclamation of Private Industry and Trade, 1949-1952), Vol. I, Peiping, Ts'ai-ching chu-pan-she, 1957, p. 189. See also the schedule of the life expectancy for different types of assets. Ibid., pp. 193-196.

81. According to a Communist source, the rate of profit in state enterprises under eight industrial ministries in 1953 was 32 per cent of total cost. Niu Chung-huang, Wo-kuo kuo-min-shou-ju ti chi-lai ho hsiao-fei (Accumulation and Consumption in China's National Income), Peiping, Chung-kuo ching-nien chu-pan-she, 1957, p. 97. Presumably, profits and total cost sum up to gross value of production. The ratio of total cost to gross output is thus calculated at 1/1.32, that is, 76 per cent. According to another source, the percentage of depreciation in total cost in Liaoning Province amounts to from 5 to 9 per cent. Statistical Bureau of the Liaoning Province, "Why is the Cost of Coal Production in Liaoning Rising?" TCKT, No. 5, March 1958, p. 22. Taking an average of 7 per cent and applying this ratio to the percentage of total cost to gross output, we derive the percentage of

depreciation in gross output of state enterprises at 5.3 per cent. We assume that the percentage for the industry as a whole is the same as that for the state enterprises.

82. Niu Chung-huang, p. 26.

Appendix G

DERIVATION OF VALUE ADDED IN CERTAIN HANDICRAFT PRODUCTS, 1933 AND 1952-57

This appendix explains the derivation of net value added in certain handicraft products for 1933 and 1952-57 presented in Tables 45 and 46. The following sections describe the data, sources, and methods used in the construction of these two tables.

1933 (TABLE 45)

Estimates of net value added by the 14 product groups shown in Table 45 are derived primarily by deducting costs of materials, fuels, miscellaneous expenses, and depreciation from gross output for individual products in each group. The results of these calculations are presented in Table G-1. The details are discussed below.

Lumber and Wood Products

Lumber. Included here are all sawed or split boards and planks produced without the use of mechanical power. The calculations of gross output and value added are set forth in Table G-2.

Wood products. Wood products include large and small items such as furniture, cupboards, trunks, barrels, coffins, boxes, combs, toothpicks, etc. Estimates for this item are taken from Ou.[1]

Rattan and bamboo products. Included in this group are the many ordinary household articles handmade with bamboo and rattan, such as chopsticks, baskets, shades, chairs, tables, beds, etc. Ou's estimates are used, with the minor adjustment of allowing 1 per cent for depreciation.[2]

Table G-1

NET VALUE ADDED IN 45 HANDICRAFT PRODUCT GROUPS, 1933

(millions of yuan)

Product	Gross value of output	Raw materials and fuels	Other costs	Gross value added	Depreciation	N va ad
Lumber and wood products						
Lumber	214.5	171.6	10.7	32.2	2.1	3
Wood products	39.6	23.8	4.0	11.9	0.4	1
Rattan and bamboo products	40.0	24.0	(*)	16.0	0.4	1
Machinery, except electrical	16.0	6.1	0.8	9.1	0.8	
Metal products	12.3	7.4	0.6	4.3	0.6	
Electrical appliances	1.0	0.6	0.1	0.3	(*)	
Transportation equipment						
Carts and carriages	57.2	26.6	1.1	29.5	1.1	2
Ships and boats	57.4	43.6	(*)	13.8	0.6	1
Stone, clay, and glass products						
Bricks and shingles	66.0	26.4	(*)	39.6	0.7	3
Glass and glass products	0.6	0.2	(*)	0.4	(*)	
Chinaware and pottery	22.9	6.9	0.2	15.8	0.2	1
Lime	17.0	11.7		5.3	(*)	
Others	1.8	0.9	0.1	0.8	(*)	
Chemical products						
Matches	3.1	1.1	0.2	1.7	(*)	1
Candles and soap	30.4	17.9	(*)	12.5	0.3	12
Enamel	0.3	0.2	(*)	0.1	(*)	(
Dyes and paint	0.2	0.1	(*)	0.1	(*)	(
Tung oil	47.3	42.8	1.2	3.3	0.3	3
Cosmetics	0.4	0.2	(*)	0.2	(*)	(
Textile products						
Cotton yarn	126.5	100.5	1.2	24.7	1.2	2
Cotton cloth	518.0	375.2	25.9	116.9	5.2	111
Silk	96.5	84.8	3.9	7.8	1.0	6
Silk piece goods	201.2	100.6	36.2	64.4	4.0	60
Woolen piece goods	7.3	4.4	0.6	2.3	0.1	2
Linen	8.3	4.6	0.4	3.3	0.2	3

(continued)

Table G-1 (continued)

Product	Gross value of output	Raw mater-ials and fuels	Other costs	Gross value added	Depreci-ation	Net value added
thing and attire	188.5	113.1	9.4	66.0	3.8	62.2
ther and allied products						
eather goods	121.3	87.3	3.6	30.4	2.4	28.0
lue	0.3	0.2	(*)	0.1	(*)	0.1
d products						
illed rice	5,071.3	4,903.2	28.0	140.1	14.0	126.1
heat flour	2,449.6	2,175.6	(*)	274.0	34.8	239.2
ea	168.1	142.7	-	25.4	1.7	23.7
dible vegetable oils	719.9	577.1	14.4	128.4	21.6	106.8
everages	2.7	1.6	(*)	1.1	(*)	1.1
ugar	47.2	32.8	4.7	9.7	0.5	9.2
ce	1.0	0.3	(*)	0.6	(*)	0.6
gg products	1.6	1.4	(*)	0.1	(*)	0.1
oybean sauce and vinegar	145.0	72.2	14.5	58.3	1.4	56.9
thers	298.4	232.8	-	65.6	6.0	59.6
acco, wine and liquor						
obacco products	129.2	80.6	11.1	37.5	3.9	33.6
ine and liquor	177.6	142.0	17.8	17.8	1.8	16.0
er and printing						
aper	56.2	28.1	(*)	28.1	1.1	27.0
aper products	50.0	30.7	(*)	19.3	(*)	19.3
rinting	0.7	0.3	(*)	0.4	0.1	0.3
cellaneous						
pparatus and ornaments	17.9	14.5	(*)	3.4	(*)	3.4
thers	48.0	21.9	(*)	26.1	(*)	26.1
al	11,280.3	9,740.6	190.7	1,348.7	112.3	1,236.4

es:

- Not available.

(*) Less than 0.05 million yuan.

Table G-2

CALCULATIONS OF GROSS OUTPUT AND VALUE ADDED, LUMBER, 1933

(million yuan)

Value of forest products at producers' prices	574.0[a]
Gross value of forest products at market prices	956.7[b]
Value of forest products other than fuel wood	449.6[c]
Value of forest products purchased by the manufacturing industry	188.8[d]
Purchased by factories	17.2[e]
Purchased by handicraftsmen	171.6[f]
Gross value of lumber produced by handicraftsmen	214.5[g]
Deduct: raw materials	171.6[e]
miscellaneous expenses	10.7[h]
Gross value added	32.2
Deduct: depreciation	2.1[i]
Net value added	30.1

Notes:

[a] Appendix E, Table E-3.

[b] According to Ou's estimate, the value of forest products at producers' prices amounts to approximately 60 per cent of gross value of output at market prices. (Ou, National Income, Vol. II, p. 31.) Gross value at market prices is therefore equal to 574/0.6 = 956.67 million yuan.

[c] Approximately 53 per cent of total value of forest products was used for fuel wood (Appendix E, Table E-5). The gross value of forest products is therefore equal to 0.47 x 956.7 = 449.6.

[d] Of the total value of forest products other than fuel wood, 42 per cent was used for finished lumber (Ou, National Income, Vol. II, p. 31; therefore, 0.42 x 449.6 = 188.8.

[e] Raw material costs constituted 76.4 per cent of gross value of output (10.05 million yuan) in China proper and 82.6 per cent of gross value of output (11.58 million) in Manchuria. See Appendix F, Table F-4.

Notes (continued):

[f] This figure is the residual from total gross value of forest products after deducting that portion consumed by the factories. We assume that there was little or no net export or import of raw timber.

[g] According to Lieu's data, the proportion of raw materials in gross value of output amounted to 76.4 per cent. (Lieu, Industry Survey, Vol. II, Table 13.) According to another source, it was 88 per cent. (Industrial Handbook, Shantung, p. H-748.) An arithmetic average of these two figures, 80 per cent, is used here. Total value of lumber output by handicraftsmen therefore comes to 171.6/0.8 = 214.5 million yuan.

[h] Estimated by Ou at 5 per cent of gross value of output. (Ou, National Income, Vol. II, p. 32.)

[i] Assumed to be 1 per cent of gross value of lumber produced.

Machinery, Except Electrical

Included in this industry are machine manufacture and repair. The basic data used in estimating the gross value of output are on manufacturers in China proper compiled by the National Economic Commission of the National Government.[3] The original data include the gross value of output of both factories and handicraftsmen. For our purpose, the gross value of output of factories should be deducted. The adjusted estimate amounts to 14.5 million yuan. The data for the individual localities are summarized in Table G-3. To allow for the handicraft output in Manchuria, we more or less arbitrarily add 10 per cent to the figure for China proper and derive a total of 16 million yuan. According to the data given for the machine industry in Shantung province gross receipts for repairs constituted about 50 per cent of total gross output.[4] This ratio is used to split up the total of 16 million yuan. Applying the percentage of deductible costs to gross output estimated by Ou (National Income, Vol. II, p. 41) to gross output (56, 10, 5, and 5 per cent for new materials, fuels, miscellaneous expenses, and depreciation), the value added in this industry is derived.[5]

Metal Products

Included in this group are mainly metal cooking and household utensils made of copper, tin, or iron, and other items such as kerosene cans, knives, farm tools, etc. A rough estimate of the gross value of output of factories and handicraftsmen has been made by Ou (National Income, Vol. II, pp. 41-44) at 43.4 million yuan. From this total we deduct our estimate for the factories, 31.1 million,[6] to obtain an estimate of 12.3 million yuan for handicrafts. The percentages of deductible costs are estimated by Ou (National Income, Vol. II, pp. 42, 43) at 52, 8, 5, and 5 per cent for raw materials, fuels, miscellaneous expenses and depreciation.

Table G-3

GROSS VALUE OF MACHINERY OUTPUT BY LOCALITY, 1933

(thousand yuan)

Locality	Gross value of output
Suchow, Kiangsu	140
Chun-hai, Chekiang	15
Hanyang, Hupei	1,846
Kao-yi, Hopeh	9
Ting-hsing, Hopeh	18
Lei-wu, Shantung	6
Hsia-tsin, Shantung	6
Taiyuan, Shansi	1,401
An-yang, Honan	19
Liuchow, Kwangsi	103
Amoy, Fukien	40
Subtotal	3,603
Tsingtao	941
Peiping	51
Canton	2,115
8 hsien in Kiangsu	4,644
Han hsien, Chekiang	668
Rey-an, Chekiang	47
Tientsin	1,295
Tsinan, Shantung	1,160
Nanning, Kwangsi	12
Subtotal	10,933
Total	14,536

Sources:

Data given in the first group are taken from the National Economic Commission, Chih-hsieh kung-yeh pao-kao-shu (Report on the Machinery Industry), summarized in Ou, National Income, Vol. II, Table 4, pp. 39-40. Those given in the second group represent the difference between those given in the National Economic Commission and those in Lieu, Industry Survey, Vol. III.

Applying these percentages to the gross value of output, we derive gross and net value added at 4.3 and 3.7 million yuan.

Electrical Appliances

Gross output of handicraftsmen in China proper is obtained at 0.5 million yuan by deducting the gross output of Chinese-owned factories, estimated at 13.3 million yuan[7] from that of Chinese-owned factories and handicraftsmen, estimated at 13.8 million yuan.[8] To arrive at a gross output figure for all handicraftsmen, we add the gross output of other handicraftsmen given by Ou (National Income, Vol. II, p. 48) as 0.5 million yuan to arrive at a total of 1.0 million yuan. The percentages of deductible costs are derived at 57 per cent for raw materials and 1 per cent for miscellaneous items and depreciation on the basis of data compiled by Ou (National Income, Vol. II, pp. 45-48). Estimates of gross and net value added are obtained as residuals by deducting those costs from gross output.

Transportation Equipment

Carts and carriages; ships and boats. These figures are Ou's estimates (National Income, Vol. II, pp. 50-54). We assume that, of the 10 per cent to be deducted for expenses other than raw material costs in the manufacture and repair of ships and boats, depreciation accounted for 1 per cent.

Stone, Clay, and Glass Products

Bricks and shingles. The total gross value of output is derived at 74.3 million yuan on the basis of fragmentary data.[9] From this total we deduct the gross output of factories given in Table F-1 at 8.3 million yuan to arrive at the gross output of 66.0 million yuan for the handicraft sector. Allowing 40 per cent for fuels and 10 per cent for the depreciation of furnaces and equipment as given by Ou (National Income, Vol. II, p. 56), we obtain estimates of gross and net value added at 39.6 and 38.9 million yuan.

Glass and glass products. Gross output is derived by summing up the gross output of handicrafts in China proper, estimated by Ou at 0.34 million yuan (National Income, Vol. II, p. 58), and our estimate for Manchuria at 0.27 million yuan.[10] From the total amount of 0.61 million yuan we deduct Ou's 40 per cent of gross output for costs of raw materials and 2 per cent for depreciation (National Income, Vol. II, p. 59), leaving gross and net value added at 0.37 and 0.35 million yuan.

Chinaware and pottery. Total gross value of output of factories and handicraftsmen has been estimated at 25.1 million yuan and of factories alone at 2.2 million yuan.[11] Gross output of handicraftsmen is, therefore, 22.9 million yuan. Allowing 10 per cent of this amount for raw materials, 20 per cent for fuels, and 1 per cent each for miscellaneous expenses and depreciation (Ou, National Income, Vol. II, p. 61), we obtain the gross and net value added at 15.8 and 15.6 million yuan.

Lime. These figures are Ou's estimates (National Income, Vol. II, pp. 61-63).

Other stone, clay, and glass products. Included in this group are stones for building material, chalk, and coal briquettes. The gross value of the first two items is estimated by Ou (National Income, Vol. II, p. 64) at 1.0 million yuan and that of coal briquettes at 3.06 million yuan. From this amount, we deduct 2.24 million yuan which has already been accounted for in factories, leaving 0.82 million yuan.[12] Estimates of value added are obtained by applying Ou's percentage of deductible costs (National Income, Vol. II, pp. 64-65) to the gross value of output.

Chemical Products

Matches. Gross value of handicraft output in China proper is estimated at 6.25 million yuan by Ou (National Income, Vol. II, p. 74). Two minor adjustments of this estimate have been made. First, Ou's figure (taken from Lieu's survey) includes that for Kwangtung province which has already been included in our factory sector. Thus the figure for this province, 3.24 million, is deducted to avoid double counting. This leaves 3.01 million yuan. Second, the handicraft output in Manchuria, estimated in Appendix F at 0.04 million yuan, is added to obtain a total of 3.05 million yuan. The percentages of deductible costs used in deriving value added are Ou's estimates (National Income, Vol. II, p. 76).

Candles and soap. Gross output of factories (excluding foreign factories in China proper) and handicraftsmen is estimated by Ou (National Income, Vol. II, pp. 78-79) at 40.36 million yuan. From this figure we deduct the estimate given in Table F-1 for Chinese-owned factories in China proper and for factories in Manchuria, totalling 9.96 million yuan, to derive the gross value of handicraft output at 30.4 million. Percentages of deductible costs are also taken from Ou (National Income, Vol. II, p. 79).

Enamel. Net value added is estimated at 0.10 million yuan by Ou (National Income, Vol. II, p. 80) on the basis of the number of workers and wage data. Assuming that the percentage of net value added in gross output is the same as that for factories (that is, 30 per cent)[13] and that of depreciation is 1 per cent, we obtain a rough estimate of gross output and gross value added at 0.33 and 0.13 million yuan.

Dyes and paint. The only available estimate of gross output is that of 0.23 million yuan given for Chekiang province.[14] The percentages of deductible costs used to derive value added are those estimated by Ou (National Income, Vol. II, p. 82).

Tung oil. The fee for processing one picul of tung oil is 1.50 yuan,[15] of which net value amounts to two-thirds. Ou estimates (National Income, Vol. II, p. 83) that deductible costs other than raw materials amount to one-third. Output of tung oil in 1933 was given in Appendix A as 3 million piculs. Net value added and deductible costs other than raw materials are therefore equal to 3.0 million and 1.5 million yuan. We assume that depreciation accounted for one-fifth of the total deductions of 1.5 million, or 0.3 million yuan. Adding together the estimates of net value added, deductible costs other than raw materials, and raw materials (3.0, 1.5, and 42.8 million yuan)[16] we obtain the gross value of output at 47.3 million yuan.

Cosmetics. These figures are Ou's estimates (National Income, Vol. II, p. 85).

Textile Products

Cotton yarn. Value added in the handicraft cotton spinning industry is estimated on the basis of the quantity of raw cotton consumed (in millions of piculs), derived as follows: Domestic output available for consumption (17.3)[17] added to net imports for China proper and Manchuria (1.6 and 0.2 respectively)[18] equals a total supply of 19.1. From this, mill consumption for China proper (11.0)[19] and Manchuria (0.4)[20] and wadding and other uses (4.5)[21] are deducted to equal the cotton used for hand-spun yarn of 3.2.

Output of hand-spun yarn is estimated at 3.04 million piculs after allowing 5 per cent of total cotton input for cotton waste, that is, 0.16

million piculs. The prices of hand-spun yarn and cotton waste have been estimated at 41.4 and 3.86 yuan per picul.[22] Multiplying the output figures by the corresponding prices and summing, we obtain the total gross output at 126.5 million yuan. From this total we deduct raw material costs estimated at 100.5 million yuan[23] and allow 1 per cent of gross output for miscellaneous expenses and another 1 per cent for depreciation to arrive at total net value added of 23.5 million yuan.

Cotton cloth. Output of hand-woven cloth is estimated at 8.1 million piculs on the basis of the quantity of cotton yarn consumed as follows. All figures are in million piculs. From the output of machine-spun yarn (9.9),[24] the amount for knitting and other uses (1.5)[25] and mill consumption (3.4)[26] is deducted to equal handicraft consumption of 5.0. To this, the output of hand-spun yarn (3.0) is added to equal the total handicraft consumption of 8.0.

According to an estimate by Yen Chung-ping, 10.8 catties of yarn are used to produce 1 bolt of cloth.[27] Dividing the total quantity of yarn consumed by handicrafts given above by this ratio, we obtain the total output of hand-woven cloth at 74 million bolts. The price of hand-woven cloth has been estimated by Ou (National Income, Vol. II, p. 100) at 7 yuan per bolt. Gross output, therefore, amounts to 518 million yuan. Costs of raw materials are derived at 375 million yuan by multiplying the quantities of machine-spun yarn and hand-spun yarn used by the corresponding prices of these two types of yarn (50.2 and 41.4 yuan per picul) and by summing up the products. Allowing 5 per cent of gross value of output for miscellaneous expenses and 1 per cent for depreciation, we obtain gross value added at 116.9 million yuan, and net value added at 111.7 million yuan.

Silk. The following computation explains the derivation of value added by handicraft silk reeling. From the total output of 320 thousand piculs,[28] we deduct the output of factories, 87 thousand piculs,[29] which equals the output of handicraftsmen, 233 thousand piculs. Using the price of 360 yuan per picul given by Ou (National Income, Vol. II, p. 103), the value is 83.9 million yuan. To this we add the cost of silk waste of 12.6 to get the gross value of silk of 96.5 million yuan.[30] We now deduct 84.8 million yuan, which is the value of silk cocoons (3,029 thousand piculs at 28 yuan per picul)[31] and 3.9 million yuan, the cost of fuels and miscellaneous,[32] to arrive at the gross value added of 7.8 million yuan. By deducting 1 per cent for depreciation, net value added is determined to be 6.8 million yuan.

Silk piece goods. Gross output is derived indirectly from the amount of new materials consumed as follows. All figures are in thousand piculs. From domestic production of silk, 320 (as given above), we deduct export of silk, 122,[33] purchases of silk weaving factories, 40,[34] and silk used for knitting, 20,[35] which equals the purchases of handicraftsmen, 138. This includes machine-spun silk (28)[36] and hand-spun silk (110). Adding an amount of artificial silk equal to that of natural silk, 138 (Ou, National Income, Vol. II, p. 105), equals 276, the total silk input of handicrafts.

The prices of machine-spun silk, hand-spun silk, and artificial silk have been estimated by Ou (National Income, Vol. II, p. 106) at 520, 360, and 270 yuan per picul. Multiplying the prices by the corresponding amounts of silk given above and summing, we obtain the total cost of silk input at 91.5 million yuan. To this amount, we add 10 per cent to allow for other minor raw materials used in silk weaving, totalling 100.6 million yuan.

According to our estimates in Table F-2 for the silk weaving factories, raw materials accounted for about 50 per cent of gross output. By applying this proportion to the total raw material costs of handicrafts, the gross output of the industry is derived at 201.2 million yuan. Deducting the raw material costs already obtained, and allowing 18 per cent of gross output for miscellaneous expenses and 2 per cent for depreciation (Ou, National Income, Vol. II, p. 107), we derive gross and net value added at 64.4 and 60.4 million yuan.

Woolen piece goods. Gross output of woolen piece goods is also derived indirectly from the value of raw materials as follows (in million yuan): Total output of wool, 25.3,[37] less export of wool estimated by Ou (National Income, Vol. II, p. 110) at 16.4, equals domestic consumption of wool of 8.9. Subtracting purchases of woolen textile factories of 5.5,[38] equals purchases of handicraftsmen, 3.4. Other raw materials are estimated by Ou (National Income, Vol. II, p. 111) at 30 per cent of the cost of wool, thus, adding 1.0 to the purchases equals the total cost of raw materials of 4.4. Ou also estimates that costs of raw materials account for about 60 per cent of gross output, miscellaneous expenses, 8 per cent, and depreciation, 2 per cent. Gross output, gross and net value added, thus amount to 7.3, 2.3, and 2.2 million yuan.

Linen. These figures are Ou's estimates (National Income, Vol. II, pp. 112-114).

Clothing and Attire

These figures are Ou's estimates (National Income, Vol. II, pp. 116-118).

Leather and Allied Products

Leather Goods. Gross output is derived indirectly from the value of raw materials (in million yuan) as follows: To domestic output of leather, given in Table F-1 as 46.1, we add net imports of leather of 2.5,[40] which equals leather for domestic consumption, 48.6. Subtracting purchases of factories, 0.1,[41] equals purchases of handicraftsmen of 48.5.

The cost of leather accounted for about 40 per cent of gross output. Gross value of output is, therefore, calculated at 121.3 million yuan.

Besides leather, a considerable amount of other raw materials such as cotton cloth, wooden boards, nails and locks, etc., are also used in the manufacture of leather goods. According to a sample survey,[42] these materials constitute 32 per cent of gross output. Allowing an additional 3 per cent of gross output for miscellaneous expenses and 2 per cent for depreciation, we obtain the gross and net value added at 30.4 and 28.0 million yuan.

Glue. Value by beef bones, hooves, and horns used to manufacture glue has been estimated by Ou (National Income, Vol. II, p. 123) at 0.3 million yuan. Of this amount, 0.1 million yuan was used as raw materials by the factories.[43] Cost of materials for handicrafts is, therefore, equal to 0.2 million yuan. According to Lieu's survey, and as shown in Table F-2, costs of raw materials constituted 52 per cent of gross value of output. On the assumption that the proportion for handicrafts was the same, we derive the gross output at 0.3 million yuan. Allowing 10 per cent of gross output for miscellaneous expenses and 1 per cent for depreciation, we obtain a rough estimate of gross (and net) value added at 0.1 million yuan.

Food Products

Milled rice. Gross value added in rice milling is derived by, first, estimating the amount of paddy rice that was milled by handicraftsmen, and second, by multiplying this amount by the processing fee per picul of paddy rice. The derivation of the quantity of paddy rice milled (in million piculs) by handicraftsmen is as follows: Output of paddy rice, 1,599.8,[44] deduct waste due to storage and transportation and amount reserved for seed, 160.0,[45] which equals amount available for milling, 1,439.8. From this deduct amount milled by factories, 38.9,[46] which equals the amount milled by handicraftsmen, 1,400.9.

The fee for processing one picul of paddy rice is estimated by Ou (National Income, Vol. II, p. 127) at 0.12 yuan of which 0.03 yuan is for miscellaneous expenses and depreciation. We assume that depreciation amou to 0.01, and miscellaneous expenses, 0.02 yuan per picul. On the basis of this information, gross and net value added (in million yuan) are derived as follows: Gross value of output, which is the sum of raw materials (4,903.2),[47] miscellaneous expense (28.0),[48] and gross value added (140.1), is given as 5,071.3. Depreciation of 14.0 is then subtracted,[50] giving a net value added of 126.1.

Wheat flour. The quantity of wheat used as raw material by handicraft is estimated (in million piculs) as follows: Output of wheat is given in Appendix A, Table A-9, as 534.0. From this deduct allowance for feed, seed waste, and industrial uses, 85.4,[51] add net imports, 21.1.[52] This equals wheat available for milling, 469.7. Deduct amount milled by factories, 34.8,[53] which equals the amount milled by handicraftsmen of 434.9.

Ou estimates (National Income, Vol. II, p. 130) that approximately 65 catties of wheat flour and 25 catties of bran can be produced from 100 catties of wheat. Applying these ratios to the quantity of wheat milled by handicraftsmen, 435 million piculs, we obtain the output of wheat flour and bran at 282.8 and 108.8 million piculs. The prices of flour and bran are estimated at 7.6 and 2.7 yuan per picul on the basis of the price of wheat given in Appendix B at 4.6 yuan per picul and the ratios of the price of flour to that of wheat (5:3) and the price of bran to that of wheat (0.61:1) given by Ou (National Income, Vol. II, p. 130). Gross value of wheat flour thus amounted to 2,149.3 million yuan, and that of bran, 300.3 million, totalling 2,449.6 million yuan.

On the basis of data compiled by Ou (National Income, Vol. II, pp. 129-130), gross and net value added in the processing of 1 picul of wheat are calculated at 0.63 and 0.55 yuan. Multiplying these estimates by the total quantity of wheat milled by handicraftsmen, we derive the gross and net value added at 274.0 and 239.2 million yuan, the difference of 34.8 representing depreciation.

Tea. Output of crude tea has been estimated at 5 million piculs.[54] Generally, as pointed out by Ou (National Income, Vol. II, p. 130), one picul of crude tea is required to produce 0.6 picul of refined tea. Applying this ratio to the total output of crude tea, we obtain the output of refined tea at 3 million piculs. The price of refined tea varies considerably because of differences in quality. An average price weighted by the output of three different grades of refined tea is estimated at 59 yuan per picul.[55] Gross output thus amounts to 177 million yuan. From this total, we deduct the gross output of factories, given in Table F-1 at 8.9 million yuan, to arrive at the gross value of handicraft output of 168.1 million yuan.

Total cost of raw materials in the production of refined tea by factories and handicraftsmen is derived at 129 million yuan by multiplying the quantity of crude tea (5 million piculs) by its price estimated at 25.8 yuan per picul.[56] This total is then divided into costs for factories and handicraftsmen according to their respective proportions in total gross output of refined tea. The figure so derived for handicrafts amounts to 122.5 million yuan. Allowing 12 per cent of gross output (168.1 million) for fuels and miscellaneous expenses given by Ou (National Income, Vol. II, p. 131), and 1 per cent for depreciation, we derive gross and net value added at 25.4 and 23.7 million yuan.

Edible vegetable oils. Included in this group are soybeans, rapeseed, peanut, cottonseed, sesame, and tea seed oils, and oils made from other seeds such as sunflower, flax, perilla, and castor seeds. The gross output of factories and handicraftsmen as a whole is first derived. The calculation of gross value of vegetable oils is shown in Table G-4. The gross value of oil cake, the by-product of oil extraction, and the value of raw materials are then derived in Table G-5. The gross value of oils and oil cakes in the tables sum up to 875.4 million yuan. From this amount we deduct the gross output of factories estimated in Table F-1 at 155.5 million yuan to obtain the gross value of handicraft output at 719.9 million yuan. Cost of raw materials is similarly derived at 577.1 million yuan by deducting the cost of seed in factories estimated at 128 million yuan[57] from the total of 705.1 million yuan given in Table G-5. Miscellaneous expenses and depreciation are assumed to be 2 and 3 per cent of gross output, that is, 14.4 and 21.6 million yuan. By subtracting these deductible costs from gross output, gross and net value added are derived at 128.4 and 106.8 million yuan.

Beverages, nonalcoholic. The figures are Ou's estimates (National Income, Vol. II, pp. 148-149).

Table G-4

GROSS VALUE OF EDIBLE VEGETABLE OILS, 1933

d	Output of seed (million piculs) (1)	Amount for oil extraction (per cent) (2)	Quantity for oil extraction (million piculs) (3)	Extraction rate (per cent) (4)	Amount for cake (per cent) (5)	Output of oil (million piculs) (6)	Price of oil (yuan/ picul) (7)	Value of oil output (million yuan) (8)
beans	236.3	25	59.1	13	80	7.7	13	100.1
eseed	42.0	97	40.7	30	60	12.2	20	244.0
nuts helled)	50.2	33	16.6	40	50	6.6	20	132.0
tonseed	34.8	60	20.9	10	30	2.1	16	33.6
ame	19.3	33	6.4	45	45	2.9	22	63.8
. seed			3.0			1.0	20	20.0
.ers						1.0	20	20.0
.al						33.5		613.5

's:

Column (1). All figures except cottonseed are taken from Appendix A, .e A-9. Total output of peanuts in 1933 totalled 66.9 million piculs. Output shelled peanuts is estimated at 75 per cent of this figure, 50.18 million ıls, according to a ratio of shelled to raw peanuts by weight given in Ou, ional Income, Vol. II, p. 143. The quantity of cottonseed used for oil raction is derived at twice the output of cotton for 1932. For the ratio of ;onseed to raw cotton, see the discussion under Cottonseed in Appendix A. output of cotton in 1932 is discussed earlier in this appendix.

Column (2). Soybean Seed. FAO estimates soybeans used for oil extraction ınted to 30 per cent of soybean production for 22 provinces in the periods 1-37 and 1947-48 (FAO, Food Balance Sheets, pp. 237-242). Ou's figure is ut 23 per cent (National Income, Vol. I, p. 28, and Vol. II, p. 142). A rd estimate puts it at 58 per cent (Oils and Fats Production and International de, Rome: International Institute of Agriculture, 1939, quoted in Shen, icultural Resources, p. 250). The first estimate is probably too high for

Notes (continued):

our purpose since data for Manchuria, the most important producing region, are not included. A considerable amount of soybeans in Manchuria were exported so that the inclusion of the Manchurian data would probably lower the percentage given by FAO. The second estimate, Ou's figure, appears to be fairly reasonable. The third estimate was obviously much too high, for besides being used for oil extraction, soybeans were used for food, animal feed, export, the manufacture of bean milk, bean curd, soybean sauce, and other foodstuffs. After carefully considering all three estimates, we use a round figure of 25 per cent.

Rapeseed. The percentage left for seed has been estimated at 2 per cent by Buck, Land Utilization, Vol. I, p. 236, and at 5 per cent in Food Balance Sheets, pp. 238, 240. Buck's estimate is used in our calculations. Export of rapeseed in 1933 amounted to 0.33 million piculs, roughly 1 per cent of total output (Ou, National Income, Vol. II, p. 142). The percentage of total output used for oil extraction thus comes to 97 per cent.

Peanuts (shelled). Two widely different estimates are available: 33 per cent as given in Ou, National Income, Vol. II, p. 143, and 55 per cent as given in FAO, Food Balance Sheets, p. 237. According to Shen, Agricultural Resources, p. 262, the crop was largely used for food rather than oil extraction. Hence, the FAO estimate appears to be too high. In our calculation, Ou's estimate is used.

Cottonseed. Feed and seed accounted for 36 per cent of total output (Land Utilization, Vol. I, p. 238). Together with an export of 1.38 million piculs in 1933 (Ou, National Income, Vol. II, p. 142), this comes to roughly 40 per cent. Proportion of output for oil extraction is, therefore, 60 per cent.

Sesame. A figure of 73 per cent is given in Food Balance Sheets, p. 238. However, this presumably includes the use of sesame butter. We use Ou's estimate of 33 per cent (Ou, National Income, Vol. II, p. 144)

Column (3). The figures in column (1) times corresponding figures in column (2). The quantity of tea seed is Ou's estimate (Ou, National Income, p. 145).

Column (4). Estimates of the extraction rates are listed below from FAO, Ou, National Agricultural Research Bureau, and Dawson, respectively, as per cents of output: Sesame, 35, 50, 41, and 40; rapeseed, 25, 35, 30 to 32, and 25 to 37; cottonseed, 10, 10, 9 to 10, and 10 to 12; peanuts (shelled), 30, 50, 33 to 40, and 28 to 39; soybeans, 12, 13, 8 to 11, and 9.5 to 11. (FAO, Food Balance Sheets, p. 242; Ou, National Income, Vol. II, pp. 141-144; and Shen, Agricultural Resources, pp. 269-270).

Notes (continued):

Since very little is known of the basic data upon which these estimates were made, there is no reason to reject or accept any particular estimate, except for soybeans. Ou's estimate for soybeans is a weighted average and appears to be a more satisfactory estimate than the others. For the rest we use the average of these four estimates: 45 per cent for sesame, 30 per cent for rapeseed, 10 per cent for cottonseed, and 40 per cent for shelled peanuts.

Column (5). These figures are based on Ou's estimates, National Income, Vol. II, pp. 141-144. Those for sesame, peanuts, and soybeans are assumed to be slightly higher than Ou's figures since our extraction rates are somewhat lower.

Column (6). Column (3) times column (4). The output for tea seed oil and others are rough estimates. Ibid.

Column (7). Soybean oil. The price of soybean oil in Manchuria is quoted at 11 yuan per picul (ibid., p. 141) and that in Shantung at 17 yuan per picul (Industrial Handbook: Shantung, p. H-200). The price given above is the average of these two quotations with a higher weight (60 per cent) given to the Manchurian quotation.

Rapeseed oil and cottonseed oil. These are the unweighted averages of prices in Chekiang and Shantung (Industrial Handbook: Chekiang, p. G-112, and Industrial Handbook: Shantung, p. H-200).

Peanut oil and sesame oil. Both figures are taken from Industrial Handbook: Shantung. Shantung was the most important producing region for peanuts. Hence, the price for this province would be a fair approximation of the average price for China as a whole. The price of sesame was generally higher than that of other oils. The quotation given here appears to be quite reasonable. For tea seed oil and other miscellaneous vegetable oils we assume that their prices were the same as that of rapeseed oil.

Column (8). Column (6) times column (7).

Table G-5

GROSS VALUE OF OIL CAKES AND OIL SEEDS USED FOR EXTRACTION, 1933

Seeds	Cake output (million piculs) (1)	Price of cake (yuan/ picul) (2)	Value of cake (million yuan) (3)	Price of seed (yuan/ picul) (4)	Value see (mill yua (5
Soybeans	47.3	3	141.9	3.9	230.
Rapeseed	24.4	2.7	67.5	5.9	240.
Peanuts (shelled)	8.3	3	24.9	6.9	114.
Cottonseed	6.3	2	18.9	2.0	41.
Sesame	2.9	3	8.7	8.0	51.
Tea seed				4.5	13.
Others					13.
Total	89.2		261.9		705.

Notes:

Column (1). Derived by multiplying the figures in column (3) of Table G-4 by the corresponding figures in column (5) of the same table.

Column (2). Estimated by Ou, National Income, Vol. II, pp. 141-144. The price of rapeseed cake seems low. We used the slightly higher price instead.

Column (3). Column (1) times column (2), except for cottonseed. A second by-product of cottonseed oil extraction is the dried shell that comes with the seed. According to a prewar study (ibid., p. 142), 60 per cent of cottonseed by weight consists of dried shell. Total output of cottonseed being 20.9 million piculs (Table G-4). total output of the shell thus comes to 12.5 million piculs. The price of the shell is estimated at 0.50 yuan per picul (ibid., p. 143). Gross value of this by-product thus amounts to 6.3 million yuan. Added to the value of cottonseed oil cake, 12.6 million yuan, this totals 18.9 million yuan.

Column (4). Taken from Table 34 except for the price of tea seed which is given in Industrial Handbook: Chekiang, p. G-108. The price

Notes (continued):

of shelled peanuts is derived by dividing the price of raw peanuts (5.21 yuan per picul) by the ratio of shelled peanuts to raw peanuts (0.75).

Column (5). Figures in column (4) multiplied by the corresponding figures in column (3) of Table G-4. The figure for other oil seeds is assumed to be the same as for tea seed.

Sugar. Total gross value of both factory and handicraft output has been estimated by Ou (National Income, Vol. II, pp. 138-139) at 54.9 million yuan. (A minor computational error in his calculation of gross output of white sugar has been corrected.) From this figure, we deduct the gross value of output of factories (7.7 million yuan as shown in Table F-1) to derive the gross value of handicraft output at 47.2 million yuan. The gross and net value added are obtained by applying the percentages of deductible costs estimated by Ou (National Income, Vol. II, p. 139) to gross output.

Ice; egg products. These figures are Ou's estimates (National Income, Vol. II, pp. 148-150).[58]

Soybean sauce and vinegar. Total output of soybean sauce is roughly estimated at 15 million piculs on the basis of per capita annual consumption of 3 catties[59] and a total population of 500 million in 1933 as given in Chapter IV. Price of soybean sauce averaged 9 yuan per picul,[60] thus giving a total gross value of output at 135.0 million yuan. From this amount we deduct the factory output of 2.0 million yuan shown in Table F-1 to derive the gross value of handicraft output at 133.0 million yuan.

Gross output of vinegar and the percentages of deductible costs for both soybean sauce and vinegar are Ou's estimates (National Income, Vol. II, pp. 136-137).

Other food products. This group includes the numerous kinds of foodstuffs not listed elsewhere, such as canned food, preserved fruits and vegetables, salted meat and fish, bean curd, etc. No data on the output of these products are available. However, there could be no doubt that these products were important items in the Chinese diet, and that the handicraft output probably constituted a rather large portion of the total. It appears reasonable to assume that the gross value of these handicraft products would amount to at least ten times that of "other food products" of the factories.[61] On this assumption we arrive at a rough figure of 298.4 million yuan. We arbitrarily allow 70 per cent of gross value for raw materials, 8 per cent for fuels and miscellaneous expenses, and 2 per cent for depreciation. Gross and net value added are thus derived at 65.6 and 59.6 million yuan.

Tobacco, Wine and Liquor

Tobacco products. Included in this group are cigars and shredded tobacco. The gross value of cigars is given at 0.3 million yuan by Ou (National Income, Vol. II, p. 134). The gross value of output of cured tobacco is derived at 128.9 million yuan indirectly from the output of cured tobacco as follows: Output of cured tobacco is estimated in Appendix A, Table A-9, at 19.8 million piculs, of which 1.8 million piculs were used for manufacturing cigarettes,[62] and 18.0 million piculs for manufacturing shredded and other types of tobacco. About 20 per cent of the 18 million piculs of cured tobacco, 3.6 million piculs, was used to make shredded tobacco. (Ou, National Income, Vol. II, p. 135.) Roughly 1 picul of cured tobacco can be manufactured into 0.9 picul of shredded tobacco,[63] thus output of shredded tobacco comes to 3.24 million piculs. At an average price of 40 yuan per picul,[64] gross value of output amounts to 129.6 million yuan. From this figure, we deduct the gross value of factory output, 0.7 million yuan, shown in Table F-1. The residual of 128.9 million yuan is the gross value of handicraft output.

The percentages of deductible costs for cigars and shredded tobacco are computed from Ou's data (National Income, Vol. II, pp. 134-135) and then applied to the respective gross output to derive the figures given in Table G-1.

Wine and Liquor. A rough estimate of the total consumption of wine and liquor at 12.5 million piculs is obtained by multiplying the per capita consumption of 2.5 catties by the total population of 500 million.[65] Assuming no net imports or exports or changes in inventories, we take this figure as the total output in 1933. The output of sediment, a by-product, is estimated at 25.0 million piculs, or twice the output of wine and liquor.[66] The average price of wine was estimated at 13 yuan per picul[67] and that of sediment estimated by Ou (National Income, Vol. II, p. 136) at 1 yuan per picul. On the basis of the above information, total gross output is derived at 187.5 million yuan. From this amount we deduct the gross output of factories, 9.9 million yuan, shown in Table F-1. The residual, 177.6 million yuan, is the gross value of handicraft output.

The raw materials used in the production of wine and liquor include kaoliang, millet, barley, potato, corn, and glutinous rice, among which kaoliang is probably the most important. The input-output ratio for the different raw materials, however, are not much different, and a rough estimate of 3 piculs of raw materials to 1 picul of output is obtained on the basis of data given for this industry in Shantung province.[68] At this ratio total quantity of raw materials comes to 37.5 million piculs, of which 35.5 million piculs were consumed by handicrafts.[69] At an average price of 4 yuan per picul, estimated by Ou (National Income, Vol. II, p. 136), cost of raw materials amounts to 142.0 million yuan. Costs of fuels and miscellaneous expenses are arbitrarily assumed to be 10 per cent, and depreciation, 1 per cent of gross value of output. Gross and net value added are then derived at 17.8 and 16.0 million yuan.

Paper and Printing

Paper. The derivation of gross value of output (in million yuan) is as follows. Gross output of Chinese-owned factories and handicraftsmen in China proper is given by Ou (National Income, Vol. II, pp. 151, 153) as 65.3. From this we deduct output of Chinese-owned factories in China proper, 9.8, given in Table F-1, to equal handicraft output in China proper, 55.5. To this we add handicraft output in Manchuria, 0.7, given by Ou (National Income, Vol. II, p. 153) to equal total handicraft output of 56.2. The percentages of deductible costs compiled by Ou (National Income, Vol. II, p. 155) are applied to, and deducted from, gross output to arrive at value added.

Paper products. Included in this group are firecrackers, paper products for ceremonial use, and miscellaneous paper products such as paper boxes, paper toys, and the like. Ou (National Income, Vol. II, p. 156) estimated the gross value of firecrackers at 5.3 million yuan. This figure is probably high because the samples used to derive the total are for the relatively prosperous provinces of Chekiang and Shantung. For our calculation a round figure of 5 million yuan is used.

For paper products to be used in ancestral worship ceremonies, the only available information is a figure of 28.6 million yuan for Chekiang, the most important producing region on the Chinese Mainland.[70] Ancestral worship and other religious ceremonies being such a common practice in China, it would seem reasonable to assume that there was some production of paper products by other provinces, though probably not as much as in Chekiang. On the assumption that the gross output of these other provinces amounts to one-half of that for Chekiang, total gross output is roughly estimated at 40 million yuan.

For the gross output of all other paper products and the percentage deductions, we use the estimates by Ou (National Income, Vol. II, p. 157)

Printing. Total gross output of factories and handicraftsmen has been estimated by Ou (National Income, Vol. II, pp. 158-159) at 72.1 million yuan, from which we deduct the gross value of factory output of 71.4 million yuan given in Table F-1 to obtain the gross value of handicraft output at 0.7 million yuan. We then allow 39 per cent of gross output for cost of raw materials,[71] 5 per cent for miscellaneous expenses and 6 per cent for depreciation, estimated by Ou (National Income, Vol. II, p. 161). Gross value added is thus derived at 0.4 million and net value added at 0.3 million yuan.

Miscellaneous

Apparatus and ornaments; miscellaneous products. These figures are Ou's estimates (National Income, Vol. II, pp. 162-164 and 166-169).

1952-57

Milled rice. Value added by handicraft rice milling is estimated on the basis of the quantity of paddy rice milled by handicraftsmen and the processing fee per picul of paddy rice milled.[72] The quantities of paddy rice milled by handicraftsmen are derived by deducting nonfood uses of paddy rice and the quantities milled by factories from total paddy rice output as shown in Table G-6. Processing fees (in 1952 yuan) for milling rice in the rural areas are quoted at 0.30 yuan per picul of paddy rice in Hupei and 0.25 in Hunan.[73] From data given in another source, a processing charge of 0.30 is computed.[74] A charge of 0.30 yuan per picul appears to be the usual fee and is used in our calculation. Included in this processing fee are the miscellaneous expenses, depreciation, and net value added. Assuming that the proportions of these three items in the

Table G-6

PADDY RICE MILLED BY HANDICRAFTSMEN, 1952-57

(million piculs)

	1952	1953	1954	1955	1956	1957
Output of paddy rice[a]	1,736	1,666	1,666	1,631	1,638	1,565
Quantity used for food[b]	1,405	1,473	1,466	1,499	1,499	1,562
Less quantity milled by factories[c]	44	48	51	53	55	58
Quantity milled by handicraftsmen	1,361	1,425	1,415	1,446	1,444	1,504

Notes:

[a]Table 32.

[b]For a percentage of output used for food, see Chapter V, notes to Table 81.

[c]Derived by dividing the raw material cost in factory rice milling given in Appendix F, Tables F-8, F-10, and F-11, by the price of paddy rice given in Appendix D, Table D-1.

total processing fee are the same as for 1933, we break down the total fee of 0.30 into 0.23 yuan per picul for net value added, 0.05 for miscellaneous expenses, and 0.02 for depreciation. Applying these figures to the total quantity of paddy rice milled by handicraftsmen shown in Table G-6, we obtain the net value added for each of the years 1952-57 as shown in Table G-7.

Wheat Flour

Gross value of wheat flour is estimated on the basis of the quantity of wheat consumed by handicrafts which is derived as follows: First, the quantity of wheat used for food is obtained on the assumption that the percentage of total wheat output used for food in 1952-57 is the same as for 1933, that is, 84 per cent. The results are 349, 354, 449, 410, 421, and 397 million piculs for 1952-57.[75] From these totals, we now deduct the quantities of wheat milled by the factories to arrive at the following quantities of wheat milled by the handicraftsmen: 271, 267, 355, 298, 316, and 297 million piculs.[76]

The extraction rate for handicraft milled flour is 65 per cent and for the by-product, wheat bran, 25 per cent, estimated by Ou (National Income, Vol. II, p. 130). Applying these percentages to the quantities of wheat milled by handicraftsmen, we derive the output of wheat flour at 176, 173, 231, 194, 206, and 193 million piculs; and the output of bran at 68, 67, 89, 74, 79, and 74 million piculs for 1952-57.

Specific data on the prices of handicraft milled flour and bran are not available. A rough estimate of the price of wheat flour per picul is derived on the assumption that the ratio of the price of flour to the price of wheat in 1952 is the same as in 1933. The ratio for 1933 and

Table G-7

NET VALUE ADDED, PADDY RICE, 1952-57

(millions of 1952 yuan)

	1952	1953	1954	1955	1956	1957
Gross output	7,621	8,003	7,926	8,079	8,079	8,384
Less: raw materials	7,213	7,574	7,502	7,646	7,646	7,935
miscellaneous	68	71	71	72	72	75
Gross value added	340	357	354	361	361	374
Less depreciation	27	29	28	29	29	30
Net value added[a]	313	329	326	332	332	344

Note:

[a] If the Communist data on paddy rice output for 1952-57 given in Great Ten Years, p. 105, are used, the corresponding adjusted estimates of net value added by rice milling are 273, 284, 281, 311, 328, and 347 million yuan from 1952-57.

the price of wheat in 1952 being known, the price of handicraft flour can be calculated at 13 yuan per picul.[77] By a similar procedure, the price of bran is derived at 4 yuan per picul.[78]

Gross output of wheat flour is now derived by multiplying the output of flour and bran by their respective prices and summing. The results are 2,558, 2,521, 3,354, 2,811, 2,990, and 2,804 million yuan for 1952-57. Raw material costs are obtained by multiplying the quantities of wheat consumed by handicrafts given above and the price of wheat estimated at 8 yuan per picul. Allowing 2 per cent of gross output for miscellaneous expenses and another 2 per cent for depreciation, we obtain gross value added at 341, 336, 448, 376, 400, and 374 million yuan, and net value added at 290, 286, 380, 319, 340, and 318 million yuan for 1952-57.

Tea

The output of crude tea in 1952-57 is given at 1.65, 1.69, 1.84, 2.16, 2.41, and 2.23 million piculs.[79] As mentioned earlier, it takes one picul of crude tea to produce approximately 0.6 picul of refined tea. Applying this ratio to the output of crude tea, we derive the output of refined tea at 0.99, 1.01, 1.10, 1.30, 1.45, and 1.34 million piculs. On the assumption that the ratio of the price of refined tea to that of crude tea for 1952 is the same as for 1933, the price of refined tea for 1952 is estimated at 160 yuan per picul.[80] The gross value of output thus amounts to 158, 162, 176, 208, 232, and 214 million yuan for 1952-57.

No information is available as to the proportion of factory output in 1952-57. Traditionally, it was rather small.[81] It would not be far wrong to assume the same percentage as for 1933, that is, 5 per cent, which is given in the first section of this appendix. On this assumption, the gross value of output of handicrafts is derived at 110, 112, 122, 144, 160, and 148 million yuan. Total raw material cost in the production of refined tea in factories and handicrafts is obtained by multiplying the output of crude tea by its price. The portion which should be allocated to the handicraft sector is derived by multiplying the total raw material cost by the percentage of handicraft output in total output. Assuming that the percentages of deductible costs for fuels and miscellaneous expenses (12 per cent) and depreciation (1 per cent) to be the same as for 1933, we derive the gross value added at 23, 23, 25, 30, 34, and 31 million yuan, and net value added at 21, 21, 23, 28, 32, and 29 million yuan for 1952-57.

Sugar

The handicraft output of sugar in 1952-57 is derived at 4.04, 6,80, 6.92, 6.14, 5.78, and 6.12 million piculs, by deducting the factory output from the total output of both factories and handicrafts.[82] Information on the proportions of the four varieties of native sugar (white, brown, yellow, and crystallized) in total output is not available, nor are their prices, except that of white sugar which was given at around 30 yuan per picul.[83] White sugar is of relatively higher quality than others and probably constitutes a minor proportion of the total output. In the absence of a better alternative, we assume that the ratio of the price of native sugar for the whole period to the price in 1952 is the same as that in 1933. On this assumption, the price of native sugar is derived at 17 yuan per picul.[84] Gross value of sugar output is then calculated at 69, 116, 118, 104, 98, and 104 million yuan for 1952-57. To these figures, we add the gross value of the by-product estimated at 3 per cent of the gross value of sugar. Total gross value of output, therefore, amounts to 71,

119, 121, 107, 101, and 107 million yuan. Allowing 69 per cent of gross output for raw materials, 10 per cent for fuels and miscellaneous expenses, and 2 per cent for depreciation (Ou, Vol. II, p. 139), we derive gross value added at 15, 25, 25, 22, 21, and 22 million yuan, and net value added at 14, 23, 23, 20, 19, and 20 million yuan for 1952-57.

Soybean Sauce

Total output of both factories and handicrafts in 1957 is given at 18 million piculs.[85] On the basis of the 1957 output and an index of soybean output for 1952-57 (with a half-year time lag) total output of soybean sauce in 1952-56 is derived at 16.2, 17.3, 17.0, 16.2, and 17.3 million piculs.[86] From these figures, we deduct rough estimates of factory output to arrive at the following estimates of handicraft output: 16.0, 17.1, 16.8, 16.0, 17.1, and 17.8 million piculs.[87] The price of soybean sauce in 1952 is assumed to have increased from 1933 in proportion to the price of soybeans over the same period.[88] On this assumption, the 1952 price of soybean sauce is estimated at 16 yuan per picul. Multiplying this price by the output of soybean sauce in 1952-57, we obtain the gross output at 256, 274, 269, 256, 274, and 285 million yuan. According to Ou's estimate for 1933 (Vol. II, pp. 136-137), raw materials accounted for 48 per cent of gross output, fuels and miscellaneous 10 per cent, and depreciation 1 per cent. Applying these percentages to gross output, we derive gross value added at 108, 115, 113, 108, 115, and 120 million yuan, and net value added at 105, 112, 110, 105, 112, and 117 million yuan for 1952-57.

Wine and Liquor

The procedure of estimation involves the derivation of gross output, deductible costs, and value added in 1952 and the extrapolation of the figures for 1952 on an output index for 1952-57. The estimates for 1952 are obtained as follows: The planned output of wine and liquor for 1957 is given at 605.59 thousand tons, 228 per cent of the output in 1952;[89] the output in 1952 is therefore calculated at 266 thousand tons, or 5.32 million piculs. The ratio of output of wine to output of sediment, a by-product of wine making, is roughly one-half by weight.[90]

The output of sediment in 1952 is obtained at 10.64 million piculs by applying this ratio to the output of wine and liquor. Data on the prices of wine and liquor are rather scarce, but weighted average price of 30 yuan per picul is derived on the basis of two quotations, the weights being the proportions of wine and liquor in total output.[91] For sediment, we assume that the ratio of the price of wine and liquor to the price of sediment for 1952 is the same as for 1933 given in the first section as 13:1. The price of wine and liquor being 30 yuan per picul, that of sediment is thus estimated at 2.3 yuan per picul.

By multiplying the outputs of wine, liquor, and the by-product, sediment, by their respective prices and summing up the products, total gross output of the wine and liquor industry is derived at 184 million yuan. Of this total, the gross output of factories constituted 12 per cent,[92] and that of handicrafts, 88 per cent, that is, 162 million yuan.

The quantity of raw materials is derived at three times the output of wine and liquor, or 14.04 million piculs.[93] The most important raw material in wine making is kaoliang, the 1952 farm price of which has been estimated in Appendix D as 5 yuan per picul. Raw material cost thus amounts to 70 million yuan. For fuels and miscellaneous expenses, and depreciation, we allow 10 and 1 per cent of gross output. Deducting these cost items from gross output, we obtain gross and net value added at 76 million and 74 million yuan.

Output of wine and liquor in 1957 is given at 14.68 million piculs.[94] On the basis of output data for 1952 and 1957 and the assumption of a linear time trend, an output index for 1952-57 is computed and is used to derive gross value added for 1953-57 at 102, 129, 156, 182, and 209 million yuan, and net value added at 100, 126, 152, 178, and 204 million yuan.

Edible Vegetable Oils

Estimates of gross and net value added in 1952 are derived as follows: the gross value of both factory and handicraft output in 1952 is obtained by summing up the estimates of gross output for vegetable oils and oil cake. The output of vegetable oils is calculated at 19.66 million piculs on the basis of the Communist planned output for 1957 given at 1.794 million tons, and its percentage increase over the 1952 output given at 82.5 per cent.[95] On the assumption that the ratio of oil output to oil cake output for 1952 is the same as for 1933, 1:2.65,[96] the output of oil cake is estimated at 52.1 million piculs.

The three most important vegetable oils are rapeseed oil, soybean oil, and peanut oil. The average of the 1952 prices of these three products, estimated at 36.7 yuan per picul, is taken to represent the average price of vegetable oils as a whole.[97] The price of oil cake is derived at 5.9 yuan per picul on the assumption that the ratio of the price of oil cake to that of oil in 1952 is the same as in 1933, that is, 0.16:1, as given in the first section of this appendix. Multiplying the output of oil and oil cake by their respective prices and summing up the products, we obtain the total gross output at 1.029 million yuan.

No information on the proportion of handicraft output in total output in 1952 is available; however, a rough estimate can be derived on the basis of the percentage of productive capacity of the handicraft establishments in total capacity. Two such percentages, 42 per cent and 60-65 per cent, are given for 1956.[98] The latter ratio is probably more reliable because oil pressing has always been done largely by the handicraft sector. Based on data in the first section, it can be seen that handicraft output in 1933 constituted 82 per cent of total gross value of output. It appears reasonable to assume that this proportion has declined but probably not to the extent of 42 per cent. We therefore use the figure of 65 per cent. Implicit in this procedure is the assumption that the percentage of handicraft oil-pressing capacity in total capacity in 1956 is the same as in 1952. This premise appears to be reasonable, for there is no evidence indicating that the Communists have invested in modern oil pressing factories during this period. On this assumption, the gross values of handicraft output and factory output are calculated at 669 million and 360 million yuan. Applying the percentages of deductible costs for 1933 given above,[99] we obtain estimates of raw material costs, fuels and miscellaneous expenses, gross value added, depreciation, and net value added at 535, 13, 120, 20, and 100 million yuan.

On the basis of the estimates for 1952 and an index computed from data on the total output of vegetable oils,[100] gross value added is computed at 124, 130, 142, 131, and 135 million yuan, and net value added at 103, 108, 118, 109, and 112 million yuan for 1953-57.

Paper

Output of native paper in 1952-57 totalled 231.7, 239.7, 323.7, 264.4, 268.6, and 308.0 thousand tons.[101] The price of native paper in 1952 is estimated at 471 yuan per ton from data on gross value of output and the physical quantities of output in 1952.[102] Multiplying the output figures for 1952-57 by the price of native paper, we derive gross output at 109, 113, 152, 124, 126, and 145 million yuan for 1952-57. Ou's estimates (Vol. II, p. 155) of the percentages of deductible costs in gross output for 1933 (raw material, 45 per cent; miscellaneous expense, 5 per cent; and depreciation, 2 per cent) are then applied to the gross output for 1952-57 to derive gross value added at 55, 56, 76, 62, 63, and 73 million yuan, and net value added at 52, 54, 74, 60, 61, and 70 million yuan.

Cotton Yarn

Estimates of the output of hand-spun yarn in 1952-57 are derived on the basis of the quantity of raw cotton used in the production of hand-spun yarn in the same period. The latter figures are, in turn, derived from data on the output and net import of raw cotton and factory consumption. The calculations are shown in Table G-8.

Data on the price of hand-spun yarn for 1952 are not available. Since machine-spun yarn and hand-spun yarn are fairly good substitutes as raw materials used for hand-weaving of cotton cloth, it seems reasonable to assume that the price of hand-spun yarn in 1933-52 varies in proportion to the price of machine-spun yarn during the same period. On this assumption, the 1952 price of hand-spun yarn is derived at 163.9 yuan per picul.[10 The price of cotton waste is similarly derived at 10.4 yuan per picul on th assumption that it increased from 1933 to 1952 in proportion to the price o raw cotton over the same period.[104]

Multiplying the output of hand-spun yarn and cotton waste by their respective prices and summing, we obtain total gross output at 508, 668, 398, 508, 709, and 734 million yuan for 1952-57. The cost of raw material

Table G-8

PRODUCTION AND CONSUMPTION OF RAW COTTON, 1952-57

(millions of piculs)

	1952	1953	1954	1955	1956	1957
Output of preceding year[a]	20.61	26.07	23.49	21.30	30.37	28.90
Add: imports[a]	1.54	0.22	0.84	1.73	0.88	0.40[b]
Total supply	22.15	26.29	24.33	23.03	31.25	29.30
Deduct: mill consumption[c]	14.40	16.13	18.25	15.29	20.44	18.12
Wadding and other uses[d]	4.50	5.89	3.53	4.49	6.27	6.48
Handicraft consumption	3.25	4.27	2.55	3.25	4.54	4.70
Output of hand-spun yarn[e]	3.09	4.06	2.42	3.09	4.31	4.46
Cotton waste	0.16	0.21	0.13	0.16	0.23	0.24

Notes:

[a] Data on domestic output for 1951-56 and imports for 1952-56, from SSB, Industry Study, p. 182.

[b] The 1957 figure of cotton imports is the planned figure for that year given in CHCC, Peiping, No. 5, 1957, p. 5.

[c] The estimates of mill consumption are derived by multiplying the output of machine-spun yarn for 1952-57 given in Appendix F, Table F-8, by the quantity of cotton input required to produce one bale of yarn for 1952-56 given in the SSB, Industry Study, p. 170. The consumption of cotton per bale of yarn for 1957 is assumed to be the same as for 1956.

[d] The quantity of raw cotton used for wadding and other uses is assumed to account for the same percentage in total cotton supply after deducting the mill consumption as in 1933. (For data used in computing this percentage, see the discussion under Textile Products in the first section of this appendix.)

[e] The output of hand-spun yarn is derived by allowing 5 per cent of the handicraft consumption of new cotton for cotton waste.

is derived by multiplying the quantity of raw cotton input given in Table G-8 by the farm price of raw cotton given at 84.9 yuan per picul in Appendix D. Miscellaneous expenses and depreciation are each assumed to amount to 1 per cent of gross output. Subtracting these deductible costs from gross output, we obtain gross value added at 227, 298, 178, 227, 316, and 327 million yuan, and net value added at 222, 292, 174, 222, 309, and 320 million yuan for 1952-57.

Cotton Cloth

The output of hand-woven cloth in 1952-57 is derived from data on the quantity of cotton yarn consumed by the hand-weaving industry. The calculation of the latter figures is shown in Table G-9.

To produce 1 bolt of cloth, a total of 12 pounds of cotton yarn, or 0.03 bales, is required. Dividing the quantity of cotton yarn used for hand-weaving by this input-output ratio, we obtain the output of hand-woven cloth at 52.03, 61.67, 44.83, 46.37, 67.97, and 66.20 million bolts.

The price of hand-woven cloth in 1952 is derived at 24.6 yuan per bolt on the assumption that the price of hand-woven cloth increased from 1933 to 1952 in proportion to the price of machine-woven yarn.[105] Gross output is then computed on the basis of the price and output at 1,280, 1,517, 1,103, 1,141, 1,672, and 1,628 million yuan for 1952-57. The total cost of raw materials is derived by multiplying the quantities of yarn input given in Table G-9 by the respective prices of machine-spun and hand-spun yarn.[10 For miscellaneous expenses and depreciation, we allow 1 per cent of gross output for each item, and then derive gross value added at 250, 310, 207, 234, 336, and 336 million yuan, and net value added at 237, 295, 196, 223, 319, and 320 million yuan for 1952-57.

Table G-9

PRODUCTION AND CONSUMPTION OF COTTON YARN, 1952-57
(millions of bales)

	1952	1953	1954	1955	1956	1957
Output of machine-spun yarn[a]	3.618	4.104	4.598	3.968	5.246	4.650
Deduct: yarn used for knitting[b]	0.304	0.469	0.564	0.625	0.712	0.631
Other uses[c]	0.181	0.205	0.230	0.198	0.263	0.232
Mill consumption[d]	2.424	2.699	3.126	2.606	3.420	3.030
Machine-spun yarn used for **hand-weaving**	0.709	0.731	0.678	0.539	0.851	0.757
Add: output of hand-spun yarn[e]	0.852	1.119	0.667	0.852	1.188	1.229
Handicraft consumption	1.561	1.850	1.345	1.391	2.039	1.986

Notes:

[a] Appendix F, Table F-8.

[b] The quantities of yarn used for knitting in 1952-56 are given in SSB, Industry Study, p. 182. For 1957, we assume that the proportion of output of machine-spun yarn used for knitting is the same as for 1956.

[c] The quantity left for other uses for 1956 is derived at 0.263 million bales by deducting the quantities used for knitting (0.712 million bales) and for weaving, 4.271 million bales (ibid., p. 190), from total output of 5.246 million bales. The estimates for other years are derived on the assumption that machine-spun yarn for other uses occupies the same proportion in total output as in 1956.

[d] Derived by multiplying the output of machine-woven cloth for 1952-57 given in Appendix F, Table F-8, by the quantity of yarn required to produce one bolt of cloth for 1952-56 (ibid., p. 170). The figure of yarn input per bolt of cloth for 1957 is assumed to be the same as in 1956.

[e] Given in Table G-8.

Silk Piece Goods

Handicraft output of silk piece goods in 1952-57 is derived at 25.94, 29.52, 31.30, 37.59, 47.44, and 42.10 million meters by deducting factory output given above from total factory and handicraft output given in Communist sources.[107]

The price of hand-woven silk in 1952 is assumed to be the same as that of machine-woven silk, given in Table F-10, that is, 3 yuan per meter. Gross value of output is then computed at 78, 88, 94, 113, 142, and 126 million yuan. Assuming that the percentages of raw material cost, miscellaneous expenses, and depreciation are the same as those given by Ou (National Income, Vol. II, p. 106) for 1955 (60, 8, and 2 per cent of gross output), we derive gross value added at 25, 28, 30, 36, 46, and 40 million yuan, and net value added at 23, 26, 28, 34, 43, and 38 million yuan for 1952-57.

Pig Iron

Output of pig iron produced by native methods in 1952-57 is derived at 29, 59, 152, 77, 49, and 36 thousand tons by deducting factory output given in Table F-8 from total output given in Great Ten Years, p. 84. Multiplying the output figures by the price of pig iron given in Table F-10 at 200 yuan per ton, we obtain gross output at 6, 12, 30, 15, 10, and 7 million yuan for 1952-57. On the assumption that the percentages of raw material and fuel cost, miscellaneous expenses, and depreciation are the same as those given by Ou (National Income, Vol. II, pp. 52-53) for 1933 (46, 2, and 2 per cent of gross output), gross value added is derived at 3, 6, 16, 8, 5, and 4 million yuan, and net value added at 3, 6, 15, 8, 5, and 4 million yuan for 1952-57.

FOOTNOTES TO APPENDIX G

1. Ou Pao-san, 1933 Chung-kuo kuo-min so-te (China's National Income, 1933), Shanghai, Chung-hua Book Co., 1947.

2. Ibid., pp. 34-35.

3. National Economic Commission, Chih-hsieh kung-yeh pao-kao shu (Report on the Machinery Industry), ibid., pp. 39-40.

4. Industrial Handbook: Shantung, p. H-644.

5. No allowance for raw materials used in repair work is made. The relatively small amount of raw materials is included in miscellaneous expenses.

6. Appendix F, Table F-1.

7. Ibid.

8. Gross output of Chinese-owned factories with 30 or more workers is given at 11.3 million yuan in Lieu, Industry Survey, Vol. II, Table 14, and that of handicraftsmen and other Chinese-owned factories at 2.5 million yuan in Ou, National Income, Vol. II, Table 2, p. 47. The total is then 13.8 million yuan.

9. According to Ou the per capita production of bricks and shingles amounted to 1.02 yuan in the cities and 0.093 in other areas (ibid., p. 55). Population in cities of 100,000 and over is roughly estimated at 30 million in 1933. (Djang Gee-hung, "An Estimate of the Working Population of China," She-hui ko-hsueh tsa-chih (Quarterly Review of Social Sciences), Shanghai, Vol. IX, No. 2, December 1947, p. 86). Since total population was 500 million in 1933 (see Chapter IV), the population outside the cities therefore was 470 million. Multiplying the total population figures by the

corresponding per capita production estimates and summing, the total gross value of output is 30.6 + 43.7 = 74.3 million yuan.

10. In deriving the gross value of output of factories in Manchuria, we have derived a total figure for factory and handicrafts and then segregated the two sectors. (See Appendix F.)

11. The 25.1 million yuan is the sum of the estimate of 24.37 million for China proper given in Ou (National Income, Vol. II, p. 61), and the estimate of 0.73 million for Manchuria as given in Appendix F.

12. The figures in Ou's estimate (taken from Lieu's survey) for Shanghai, Nanking, Chin-hsien, Hangchow, Wuhu, and Canton, totalling 2.24 million yuan, have already been included in the output of factories.

13. Appendix F, Table F-2.

14. Industrial Handbook: Chekiang, Shanghai, pp. 277-278.

15. See Szechwan-shang chih tung-yu (Szechwan's Tung Oil), p. 127, cited in T. H. Shen, Agricultural Resources in China, Ithaca, N.Y., Cornell University Press, 1951, p. 257; and Chekiang tung-yu tiao-tsa pao-kao-shu (Report on the Survey of Chekiang's Tung Oil), p. 44, cited in Ou, National Income, Vol. II, p. 83.

16. Raw material cost is obtained by multiplying the output of tung nuts of 10.7 piculs given in Appendix A, by 4.0 yuan per picul, the price of tung nuts given in Appendix B.

17. Total output of raw cotton in 1933 is given at 19.0 million piculs. (Appendix A, Table A-9.) To allow for a time lag of one year between harvesting and ginning of cotton and actual consumption, we need to derive the output for 1932. This figure is obtained at 17.3 million piculs by multiplying the 1933 figure by the output index for 1932

estimated at 91 per cent with 1933 as 100. This index is computed on the basis of cotton output in China proper given in Agricultural Estimates at 15.1 and 16.6 million piculs for 1932-33. While the index used here is based on the output of China proper only, it is a fair approximation of the one for the entire mainland, because output in Manchuria and Sinkiang is relatively small.

18. The Trade of China, 1933, Vol. I, p. 47; and South Manchurian Railway, Statistical Abstract of Manchurian Economy, p. 395.

19. The Trade of China, 1933, Vol. I, p. 47.

20. Appendix F, the discussion following Table F-3.

21. Five estimates of cotton used for wadding are available. (See Ou, National Income, Vol. II, p. 96.) Those given by Yen Chung-ping, 4.8 million piculs, and in a Japanese study, 3.6 to 4.8 million piculs, appear to be more reasonable. The figure used here is an arithmetic mean of these two estimates.

22. The percentage of cotton waste is taken from Yen Chung-ping, The Development of China's Cotton Textile Industry, p. 272, quoted in Ou, National Income, Vol. II, p. 96. The price of hand-spun yarn is also given in Ou (ibid.). For the price of cotton waste, see Appendix F, footnote 12.

23. Obtained by multiplying total cotton input, 3.2 million piculs, by the price of cotton given at 31.4 yuan per picul in Appendix B, Table B-17. The handicraftsmen engaged in cotton spinning were found largely at or near cotton producing areas so that the price of cotton for the handicraftsmen would be close to, if not actually, the farm price of cotton.

24. The ratio of yarn output to cotton input is roughly calculated at 87 per cent on the basis of data given in Appendix F. Total amount of

cotton consumed by the mills being 11.4 million piculs, total output of yarn is, therefore, 9.9 million piculs.

25. Estimated by Yen Chung-ping, The Development of China's Cotton Textile Industry, p. 273 at 15 per cent of output of machine-spun yarn.

26. Total output of power-woven cloth is estimated at 33.96 million bolts in Appendix F. 11.2 pounds of machine-spun yarn is required to produce 1 bolt of cloth. Ibid., p. 271. Total yarn input required to produce 33.96 million bolts is, therefore, equal to 380.3 million pounds or 3.45 million piculs.

27. Ibid., p. 275.

28. From the discussion of Silkworm Cocoons in Appendix A.

29. Gross value of output of the silk reeling factories in 1933 was 44.9 million yuan (Appendix F, Table F-1). The price of silk may be derive from data given in Ou, National Income, Vol. II, p. 101, at 516.4 yuan per picul. Dividing the gross value of output by the average price, we obtain rough estimate of the output of silk produced by factories at 87 thousand

30. The value of silk wasted in the production of silk has been estimated at 54 yuan per picul of output of silk (ibid.). The output of silk being 233 thousand piculs, the value of silk waste is equal to 54 x 0.233 12.6 million yuan.

31. About 13 piculs of silk cocoons are required to produce 1 picul of silk (ibid., p. 102). Total output of silk by handicraftsmen being 233 thousand piculs, the quantity of silk cocoons consumed by handicrafts is equal to 233 x 13 or 3,029 thousand piculs. The price is the weighted average of domesticated and wild cocoons, the weights being the output of the two types of cocoons. For data used in this calculation see

the discussions Silkworm Cocoons in Appendix A, and Wild Cocoons in Appendix B.

32. Fuels and miscellaneous expenses accounted for about 4 per cent of the gross value of output. Industrial Handbook: Chekiang, p. G-46.

33. Annual Foreign Trade Statistics of Manchuria, quoted in Ou, National Income, Vol. II, p. 105; and The Trade of China, 1933.

34. The quantity of silk input per million yuan of gross output of silk piece goods can be calculated at 0.5 thousand piculs on the basis of data given in Ou, National Income, Vol. II, p. 105. Gross output of factories being 79.5 million yuan (Appendix F, Table F-1), factory consumption of silk is 79.5 x 0.5 = 39.75 thousand piculs.

35. According to Ou (National Income, Vol. II, footnote 98, p. 105), roughly 10 per cent of domestic consumption of silk is used for knitting. Domestic consumption is equal to total output (320 thousand piculs) minus exports (122 thousand piculs), that is, 198 thousand piculs. The quantity of silk used for knitting, therefore, totalled 198 x 0.1 = 20 thousand piculs.

36. The quantity of machine-spun silk consumed by handicrafts amounted to 20 per cent of total silk consumption, that is, 138 x 0.2 = 28 thousand piculs. Industrial Handbook: Chekiang, p. G-52.

37. See Appendix E, Table E-1.

38. Estimated by multiplying the percentage of cost of wool in total gross value of woolen textiles given in Ou, National Income, Vol. II, p. 107, by the gross value of output of woolen textile factories given in Appendix F, Table F-1.

39. A minor adjustment of Ou's estimate for clothing and attire has been made. In estimating value added, Ou did not include the value of domestically produced straws as part of the total raw material costs

because the gross value of straw output has not been counted elsewhere. In our calculation, however, this item has already been allowed for in "miscellaneous agricultural product" and therefore is deducted from gross output.

40. Imports totalled 2.95 million, and exports, 0.43 million yuan. The Trade of China, 1933, pp. 104-105, 126-127.

41. The cost of leather is estimated at 40 per cent of gross output by Ou (National Income, Vol. II, footnote 14, p. 122) on the basis of a survey by the National Resources Commission. Gross output of leather goods factories being 0.28 million (Table F-1), the cost of leather consumed amounts to 0.28 x 0.4 = 0.11 million yuan.

42. Kwangsi Yearbook, Vol. II, p. 442.

43. This figure is derived by multiplying the percentage of raw materials in gross output (52 per cent) given in Appendix F, Table F-2, by the gross value of glue (0.25 million) given in Table F-1.

44. See discussion on production of rice in Appendix A.

45. Nonfood uses of rice are estimated at 90 per cent of output. See notes to Table 80.

46. Gross value of milled rice produced by factories is estimated at 151.26 million yuan (Appendix F, Table F-4). Multiplying this figure by the percentage of raw material costs in gross value of output (90 per cent) given in Appendix F, Table F-2, we obtain the gross value of paddy rice milled by factories at 136.13 million yuan. Dividing this amount by the average price of paddy rice, 3.5 yuan per picul, given in Appendix B, Table B-4, we derive the quantity of paddy rice milled by factories at 38.9 million piculs.

47. Total quantity of paddy rice output, 1,400.9 million piculs, multiplied by the average price of paddy rice, 3.5 yuan per picul, given in Appendix B, Table B-4.

48. Paddy rice output, 1,400.9 million piculs, multiplied by miscellaneous expenses per picul, 0.02 yuan.

49. Total quantity of paddy rice available for milling by handicraftsmen, 1,400.9 million piculs, multiplied by the gross value added per picul, 0.10 yuan.

50. Total quantity of paddy rice, 1,400.9 million piculs, multiplied by the depreciation charge, 0.01 yuan per picul.

51. The percentage of total output used for seed is the average of three estimates of 9, 11, and 10 per cent, given in Land Utilization, Vol. I, Table 23, p. 236; Crop Reports, Vol. II, No. 8, 1943; and FAO, Food Balance Sheets, p. 237. For the percentage of wheat wasted, used for food, and other industrial uses, we use the FAO figures of 6 per cent, which are the only available data.

52. The Trade of China, 1933.

53. Cost of raw materials in modern milling factories has been estimated at 82 per cent of the 195 million yuan gross output, that is, 160 million yuan. (Appendix F, Tables F-1 and F-4.) Dividing this figure by the price of wheat (4.6 yuan per picul given in Appendix B under the discussion on wheat), we obtain a rough estimate of the quantity of wheat consumed by the flour mills.

54. See the discussion on tea in Appendix A.

55. The prices of top grade, medium grade, and low grade refined teas are given at 90, 50, and 30 yuan per picul, and the proportions of

these three types of refined tea, at 30, 55, and 15 per cent. Ou, <u>Nationa</u> <u>Income</u>, Vol. II, p. 122.

56. See the discussion under Tea in Appendix B.

57. Estimated on the basis of data on gross output given in Appendix F, Table F-1, and the percentages of raw materials in gross output given in Appendix F, Table F-4.

58. A minor adjustment has been made in the gross value of manufactured ice given by Ou at 0.825 million yuan. Included in this amount is the gross value of output in 9 cities totalling 0.325 million yuan (Lieu, <u>Industry Survey</u>, Vol. III) which has already been accounted for in our estimate of factory output. This amount of 0.325 million yuan is deducted from the total of 0.825 million to avoid double counting. The residual, 0.50 million yuan, is used in our calculation.

59. This figure is derived from data on population and consumption of soybean sauce given in <u>Land Utilization</u>, Vol. III, pp. 86-121.

60. Estimated on the basis of data given in <u>Industrial Handbook: Chekiang</u>, p. G-157, and <u>Industrial Handbook: Hunan</u>, p. G-181.

61. For our estimate of the factory output of other food products, see Appendix F, Table F-1.

62. Output of cigarettes is derived at 1.7 million cases by dividing the gross output of 267.2 million yuan, given in Appendix F, Table F-1, by the average price of cigarettes, given at 161 yuan per case, in Ou, Vol. II, p. 132. About 1.5 million piculs of cured tobacco are required to manufacture one case of cigarettes. The quantity of cured tobacco consumed by the cigarette industry is, therefore, equal to 2.5 million piculs From this total, we deduct the quantity of imported cured tobacco of 0.7

million piculs (Ou, National Income, Vol. II, p. 133) to arrive at the industry's consumption of domestically produced cured tobacco of 1.8 million piculs.

63. Industrial Handbook: Hunan, pp. G-206-07.

64. Industrial Handbook: Chekiang, p. G-216.

65. Estimated on the basis of data given in Land Utilization, Vol. III, pp. 86-121.

66. Industrial Handbook: Shantung, pp. H-304-05.

67. Based on data given in Industrial Handbooks: Shantung, p. H-312; Chekiang, p. G-156; Hunan, p. G-151.

68. Industrial Handbook: Shantung, p. H-305.

69. This is derived on the assumption that the proportion of total raw materials consumed by handicrafts is the same as the proportion of handicraft output in total gross output, that is, 177.6/187.5 = 94.7 per cent.

70. Industrial Handbook: Chekiang, p. G-505.

71. Based on data given in Industrial Handbook: Shantung, p. H-760.

72. The usual procedure of estimating net value added by deducting material costs from gross value of output is not feasible here because a large portion of paddy rice output is retained in the hands of the farmers for home consumption. In 1952 the quantity of food grain held by the farmers was about 76.6 per cent of total output. (Chu Ching and Chu Chung-chien, "Variations in Our Rural Market Commodity Turnover," CCYC, No. 3, June 1957, p. 108.) This portion of paddy rice is either milled by the peasants themselves or by the rural handicraftsmen who receive a processing fee for the milling. Data on farm price of milled rice which should be used to derive the gross value of this portion of output are totally lacking. Prices of milled rice in cities and towns, which are the only available data, are not appropriate because they include a considerable

amount of taxes, transportation costs, and state trading profits. That th
amount is quite large is indicated by the following statement, "According to the statistics of 292 rice-milling factories in 8 hsien in the Soochow district, 0.274 million tons of paddy rice were processed in the fourth quarter of 1955, which not only resulted in the receipt of 1.64 million yuan as processing fees, but also increased state revenue by 5.495 million yuan." (People's Daily, September 16, 1956, p. 4.) Hence, to use the price of milled rice in the cities or towns to calculate the gross value of handicraft milled rice would simply amount to imputing a fictitious markup of taxes and profits to the value added by handicrafts.

73. TKP, Peiping, April 6, 1957, p. 2; and People's Daily, March 30, 1958, p. 1.

74. People's Daily, September 16, 1956, p. 4.

75. For output of wheat in 1952-57, see Table 32.

76. The quantities of wheat milled by the factories are derived by dividing the output of factory wheat flour given in Appendix F, Table F-8, by the extraction rate. The rates for 1952-53 and 1957 are given in TKP, December 29, 1957, p. 2; and Shih-shih shao-ts'e (Current Events Handbook), Peiping, No. 21, November 10, 1953, p. 6. The rates for 1954-56 are interpolated on the basis of the figures for 1953 and 1957 and a linear time trend.

77. The price of handicraft flour is 1.6 times that of wheat. See Ou, National Income, Vol. II, p. 130. The price of wheat is estimated at 8 yuan per picul in Appendix D.

78. The price of bran is roughly one-third of that of wheat flour. Ou, National Income, Vol. II, p. 130.

79. Great Ten Years, p. 110.

80. The prices of crude and refined tea in 1933 are 25.8 and 59.0 yuan per picul. The price of crude tea in 1952 is estimated at 70 yuan per picul. (See the discussion under Tea in Appendix D.)

81. A survey of modern factory output of the principal cities in 1947 shows that the factory output of tea was negligibly small (Chinese Yearbook, 1948).

82. Factory output of sugar is given at 4.98, 5.96, 6.94, 8.20, 10.36, and 11.16 million piculs in 1956 Abstract, pp. 32-33; and HHYP, No. 2, 1958, p. 56. Total factory and handicraft output is given at 9.02, 12.76, 13.86, 14.34, 16.14, and 17.28 million piculs in Great Ten Years, p. 89.

83. Price of white sugar is quoted at 29-34 yuan per picul in NFJP, Canton, December 12, 1952, p. 2.

84. The 1933 price of white sugar is given at 14 yuan per picul in Ou, National Income, Vol. II, p. 139. The price of native sugar is derived at 7.91 yuan per picul by dividing total gross value by output, ibid., pp. 138-139. The price of white sugar in 1952 being 30 yuan per picul, that of native sugar is calculated at 16.95 yuan per picul.

85. People's Daily, December 31, 1957, p. 3.

86. Output of soybeans is derived from data given in SSB, "Agricultural Production in the Past Seven Years," TCKT, No. 14, 1957, pp. 9-10; and Great Ten Years, p. 109 at 172.6, 190.4, 198.6, 181.6, 182.4, 204.7, and 197.5 million piculs for 1951-57.

87. According to the 1947 survey of factories, the monthly output of soybean sauce is 18.9 thousand piculs (Chinese Yearbook, 1948). Annual output is therefore about 0.23 million piculs. We assume that factory

output of soybean sauce in 1952 was the same as in 1947, and that it increased from 1952-57 in proportion to the soybean output (still considering the time lag) over the same period.

88. The prices of soybeans in 1933 and 1952 are 3.9 and 7.0 yuan per picul (Table 34). The price of soybean sauce in 1933 was estimated earlier at 9 yuan per picul.

89. TKP, Peiping, October 5, 1957.

90. Computed from data given in Industrial Handbook: Shantung, pp. H-304-305.

91. An average price (in 1952 yuan) of 24.6 yuan per picul of white wine in Hunan province for 1957 is given in TKP, Peiping, May 22, 1957, p. 2. The price of liquor (pai-kan) at Taiyuan in 1952 is quoted at 78 yuan per picul in SSJP, Taiyuan, August 31, 1952, p. 4. These two prices are then weighted by the proportions of wine and liquor outputs to derive an average price of wine and liquor. According to People's Daily, April 27, 1957, p. 3, 86 per cent of the total output, 4.6 million piculs, was white wine. This figure is rounded to 90 per cent to include other wines. Output of liquor is thus assumed to be 10 per cent of total output. With these proportions as weights, we obtain an average price of wine and liquor at 30 yuan per picul.

92. The output of wine and liquor produced by factories in the principal cities in 1947 totalled 0.644 million piculs (Chinese Yearbook, 1948). We assume that factory output in 1952 was the same as in 1947. Thus, the 1952 figure accounted for 12 per cent of total factory and handicraft output (5.32 million piculs).

93. According to a Communist source, "To increase production of wine (without increasing raw materials) by 10 thousand tons would mean the saving of 30 thousand tons of grain." (People's Daily, April 27, 1953, p. 3.) The ratio of raw materials to output is, therefore, 3:1 by weight, which checks well with the prewar ratio given earlier. The handicraft output is estimated at 88 per cent of total output (5.32 million piculs), that is, 4.68 million piculs. The quantity of raw materials is equal to 14.04 million piculs.

94. TKP, Peiping, April 12, 1958, p. 1.

95. First Five Year Plan, p. 65.

96. This ratio is calculated from data given in Tables G-4 and G-5.

97. The prices of vegetable oils produced by handicraftsmen are not available. An estimate is made by deriving the average price of vegetable oils in the cities and small towns and by allowing for the differential between this price and the one in the rural areas. The average price of rapeseed oil in eight cities was 40.9 yuan per picul. (SPJP, Yangchow, September 1, 1952; NPJP, Ningpo, August 26, 1952; NFJP, Canton, August 23, 1952; CCJP, Hankow, August 31, 1952; CKJP, Hangchow, August 28, 1952; SYJP, Kuai-sui, March 8, 1952; HHJP, Chungking, July 1, 1952; and HSCJP, Soochow, August 31, 1952.) The average price of soybean oil at three cities is calculated at 39.2 yuan per picul. (TCJP, Tsinan, September 1, 1952; TTJP, Tsingtao, September 14, 1952; and TTJP, Tientsin, August 30, 1952.) For peanut oil, an average price of 42.2 yuan per picul in five cities is computed. (TCJP, Tsinan; TTJP, Tsingtao and Tientsin; NFJP, Canton; and SCCJP, Shihchiachuan, August 30, 1952.) The unweighted average of these three prices comes to 40.8 yuan per picul. According to a

Communist source, the rural price of vegetable oils in 1952 was roughly 90 per cent of that in the cities. (Tan Chun-lin, "A Preliminary Study of Income and Standard of Living of Farmers," HHPYK, Peiping, No. 11, 1957 p. 111.) On the assumption that the ratio for 1952 is the same as for 1956, we reduce the average price in the cities (4.08 yuan per picul) by the same percentage to obtain the average price in rural areas at 3.67 yuan per picul.

98. TKP, Tientsin, September 11, 1965, p. 1; and Mung Chun-hu and Liu Fu-yuan, "On Certain Problems in the Supply of Edible Vegetable Oils," Liang-shih kung-tso (Grain Work), Peiping, No. 12, June 1956, p. 10.

99. The percentage deductions for raw materials, fuels and miscellaneous expenses, and depreciation are 79, 3, and 3 per cent of gross output. For data used in this computation, see the first section of this appendix.

100. Great Ten Years, p. 89.

101. The figures for 1952-56 are given in SSB, Industry Study, p. 216. The figure for 1957 is derived by deducting factory output (913 thousand tons) from total factory and handicraft output (1,221 thousand tons). Ibid., p. 209; and Great Ten Years, p. 88.

102. For gross value of output in 1952, see SSB, Industry Study, p. 21

103. The price of hand-spun yarn in 1933 was 41.4 yuan per picul, and of machine-spun yarn in 1933 and 1952, 182 and 720 yuan per bale. See the first section of this appendix, and Appendix F, Table F-6.

104. The price of cotton waste in 1933, 3.86 yuan per picul, was given earlier. The prices of raw cotton in 1933 and 1952, 31.4 and 84.9 yuan per picul, are from Table 34.

105. The price of hand-woven cloth in 1933 (7 yuan per bolt) is given in the first section of this appendix. The prices of machine-woven cloth in 1933 and 1952 (7.67 and 27.0 yuan per bolt) are given in Appendix F, Table F-6.

106. The 1952 price of hand-spun yarn (595 yuan per bale) was given earlier in this section. The price of machine-spun yarn (720 yuan per bale) is given in Appendix F, Table F-10.

107. For the factory output of silk piece goods in 1952-57, see Appendix F, Table F-8. For the total factory and handicraft output, see SSB, Industry Study, p. 166; and People's Daily, November 2, 1958, p. 6.

Appendix H

DERIVATION OF VALUE ADDED IN OTHER NONAGRICULTURAL SECTORS

This appendix describes in detail the basic data and the sources and methods of deriving value added in mining, utilities, construction, transportation and communications, trade, government, finance, services, residential rent, and work brigades. A summary of the results has been given in Chapter IV, under Other Nonagricultural Sectors. For convenience, the numbers of workers employed in these sectors are also derived in this appendix. The estimates for each of the sectors will be discussed separate

MINING

The derivation of gross output and value added in mining for 1933 in 1933 prices and for 1952-57 in 1952 prices given in Table 47 is explained with reference to Tables H-1 and H-2.[1] The construction of these two tables is explained below. The next subsection presents the estimates of the number of workers employed in the mining industry in 1933 and 1952.

Gross Output and Net Value Added, 1933 and 1952-57

The basic data used in the computation of gross output and net value added in 1933 and 1952 are presented in Table H-1. Estimates of gross and net value added are then obtained, amounting to 0.23 and 0.21 billion yuan for 1933 and 1.58 and 1.47 billion yuan for 1952. However, information on depreciation is extremely meager. For 1933, depreciation allowances for coal and iron ore are roughly estimated at 5 per cent of gross output on the basis of fragmentary financial reports.[2] For lack of a better alternative, the same percentage is used for the mining industry as a whole in the prewar and the postwar periods.

Table H-1

GROSS VALUE OF OUTPUT AND NET VALUE ADDED IN THE MINING INDUSTRY, 1933 and 1952

	1933				1952			
	Output (1,000 tons)	Price (yuan/ton)	Gross output (million 1933 yuan)	Net value added (million 1933 yuan)	Output (1,000 tons)	Price (yuan/ton)	Gross output (million 1952 yuan)	Net value added (million 1952 yuan)
duct	(1)	(2)	(3)	(4)	(5)	(6)	(7)	(8)
l	28,379	5	142	99	66,488	-	831	582
ative coal	-	-	-	-	2,960	12.5	37	26
ther	-	-	-	-	63,528	12.5	794	556
de oil	91	140	13	8	436	160	70	43
n ore	2,313	4	9	7	4,287	20	85	66
estone	5,220	2	10	9	19,300	5	96	86
t	3,305	20	66	41	4,940	175	865	536
ative salt	-	-	-	-	1,480	175	259	160
thers	-	-	-	-	3,460	175	606	376
ers								
lum	15	55	1	1	15	129	2	2
ntimony, crude	2	122	(*)	(*)	3	1,250	4	3
ntimony oxide	1	214	(*)	(*)	2	2,600	6	4
ntimony regulus	11	201	2	2	8	2,530	20	14
lay	944	10	9	8	944	23	22	20
opper	1	585	(*)	(*)	2	2,530	6	3
olomite	166	5	1	1	166	12	2	2
eldspar	27	10	(*)	(*)	27	23	1	1
old	112[a]	100[b]	11	8	150[a]	95[b]	14	11
ypsum	64	17	1	1	75	40	3	2
ead	4	183	1	(*)	4	428	2	(*)
ead ore	5	50	(*)	(*)	15	117	2	1
anganese ore	10	10	(*)	(*)	190	53	10	8
agnesite	71	15	1	1	604	35	21	16
ercury	(**)	3,212	(*)	(*)	(**)	7,516	1	1
atural gas			1	1			2	2
iter	5	300	2	1	5	702	4	3
yrite	1	220	(*)	(*)	45	50	2	2
oda, natural	36	22	1	1	36	51	2	2
ulfur	4	150	1	(*)	7	351	2	1
alc	65	10	1	(*)	130	23	3	3
in	8	2,327	19	14	8	3,200	26	19
ungsten ore	6	544	3	2	20	1,273	25	19
inc	(**)	210	(*)	(*)	7	3,685	25	12
inc ore	10	7	(*)	(*)	14	129	2	1
scellaneous[c]	-	-	6	3	-	-	14	7
al			301	208			2,170	1,472

es:

- Not available.

*) Less than 1 million yuan.

*) Less than 1,000 tons.

[a]The unit for the output of gold is 1,000 liang which is equivalent to 3.125 kg. (1 liang = 3.125 grams or 11 oz.).

[b]The unit is yuan per liang.

[c]Includes asbestos, florite, borite, turquoise, silver, arsenic, bismuth, and others.

Notes (continued):

Column (1). These are the estimates by the Geological Survey of China given in Special Bulletin, No. 5, December 1935, quoted in Ou, National Income, Vol. I, Table 3, pp. 53-54.

Column (2). These are the estimates by Ou on the basis of the market prices compiled by the Geological Survey. Ibid., pp. 50-51, and Table 3, pp. 53-54.

Column (3). Column (1) times column (2).

Column (4). Gross output multiplied by percentages of value added in gross output estimated by Ou. Ibid., Vol. II, pp. 12-19.

Column (5). Output of coal (excluding native coal), crude oil, and salt (excluding native salt) are given in the 1956 Statistical Abstract, p. 32. Output of native coal is obtained by deducting the above figure from total output of coal given in SSB, Industry Study, p. 90. Output of native salt is given in First Five Year Plan, p. 38. Estimates for iron ore and manganese ore are taken from SSB, Industry Study, p. 11. The output of limestone in 1952 is assumed to have increased from 1933 in proportion to the output of cement in the same period. Output of cement in 1933 is estimated at 4.5 million barrels, or 0.765 million tons. (See Appendix F for output of cement. One barrel of cement weighs 375 pounds, or 0.17 tons. For the unit weight, see U.S. Bureau of Mines, "Mineral Resources of China," Foreign Minerals Survey, Washington, D. C., Vol. 2, No. 7, January 1948, Table 3, pp. 16-17.) Output of cement in 1952 is given at 2.861 million tons (Appendix F, Table F-8), or 3.7 times that in 1933. Output of limestone for 1952 is therefore equal to 3.7 times the 1933 output from column (1), which equals 19.3 million tons. Data for tungsten ore and antimony are U.S. Bureau of Mines' estimates given in Metal Statistics, 1956, New York, American Metal Market, 1956, pp. 58 and 518; data for tin are given in International Tin Study Group, Statistical Yearbook, 1956, The Hague, 1956, p. 110. Output estimates for copper, zinc, zinc ore, lead ore, mercury, antimony oxide, crude antimony, gypsum, talc, and magnesite are pre-1948 peak-year output given in U. S. Bureau of Mines, Metal Statistics, 1956, pp. 57, 72, 78, 80, 95, 99, 129, 138, 153. Output data for gold and sulfur are assumed to be the same as the output in the peak years of 1946 and 1947, given in the Chinese Yearbook, 1948, pp. 1569-1570. For the remaining minor items, we assume that output figures for 1952 are the same as for 1933.

Column (6). The price of coal is derived by dividing the gross value of coal for 1952, 830 million yuan, by the total output of coal given at 66.49 million tons in SSB, Industry Study, p. 95. The price of manganese ore is also derived on the basis of the gross value of output and physical quantities of output given in Yeh-chin pao (Metallurgy News), Peiping, March 25, 1957, p. 31. For the price of crude oil, see CCJP, Hankow, January 28, 1952. The price of copper

Notes (continued);

is given in HWJP, Shanghai, January 8, 1952. The price of zinc is the average of four quotations given in HWJP, September 26, 1952. The price of tin is quoted in KSJP, Hong Kong, August 2, 1950. The price quotation for antimony is taken from HWJP, September 9, 1952. The price of salt is the arithmetic average of three quotations in three localities, Tsingtao, Tientsin, and Shenyang given in TTJP, Tsingtao, September 14, 1952 and CCCP, Shanghai, Vol. 13, No. 25, December 20, 1951, p. 498. The price of gold is the official purchasing price quoted in TCJP, Tsinan, September 1, 1952. The prices of iron ore and pyrite, limestone, zinc ore, and antimony oxide and ore are assumed to have increased from 1933 to 1952 in proportion to the prices of their related products pig iron, cement, zinc, and antimony regulus. The prices of pig iron and cement in 1933 and 1952 are given in Appendix F, Table F-6. On the basis of the price data for coal, copper, zinc, tin, antimony regulus, and crude oil in 1933 and 1952, a price index for mineral products weighted by the output of these six products in 1952 is computed at 234 per cent for 1952 with 1933 as 100 (see Appendix I). The prices of the sixteen remaining products are assumed to have increased from 1933 to 1952 in proportion to this price index.

Column (7). Column (5) times column (6). The gross value for the miscellaneous category is derived by multiplying the 1933 figure by 234 per cent.

Column (8). These figures are derived by applying the ratio of net value added to gross output for 1933 to the gross output for 1952.

For 1953-57, gross output and value added for six products (coal, crude oil, iron ore, manganese ore, limestone, and salt) are derived on the basis of output of these products for 1953-57 at 1952 prices. The ratio of value added to gross output is assumed to be the same for each product in 1953-57 as in 1952. Estimates of gross output and value added in the other products are obtained on the assumption that the increase during 1952-57 of these products and coal, crude oil, iron ore, manganese ore, and limestone were in proportion. The results of these calculations are given in Table H-2. For the purpose of deriving the gross output of factories[3] the estimates of gross output of the mineral products given in Table H-2 are classified into producers' goods and consumers' goods in the modern sector and in handicrafts.[4]

Number of Workers, 1933 and 1952

In estimating the occupational distribution of the Chinese population for 1933, the number of workers employed in mining must be determined.[5] The latter estimate is derived by summing up the number of productive workers who actually did the mining and the number of other workers and employees in the mining industry. The numbers of miners in the individual branches of this industry have been estimated by Ou and are summarized in Table H-3. The ratio of the number of miners to the number of other workers in 1933 is roughly estimated at 1:0.11.[6] The number of miners being 0.69 million, total number of workers in the mining industry comes to 0.77 million.

It may be of some interest to compare the number of workers in the prewar and the postwar periods. For this purpose, Table H-3 also presents rough estimates for 1952. The estimates for the coal industry are

Table H-2

GROSS OUTPUT AND VALUE ADDED IN MINING, 1952-57

	1952	1953	1954	1955	1956	1957
Output (million tons)						
Coal						
Native	2.960	3.110	3.730	4.700	4.438	6.770
Other	63.528	66.572	79.928	93.604	105.922	123.230
Crude oil	0.436	0.622	0.789	0.966	1.163	1.458
Iron ore	4.287	5.821	7.229	9.597	15.484	19.370
Manganese ore	0.190	0.195	0.172	0.276	0.524	0.655
Limestone	19.300	26.150	31.030	30.380	43.120	45.120
Salt						
Native	1.480	1.190	1.640	1.680	1.110	1.860
Other	3.460	2.380	3.250	5.850	3.830	6.420
Gross value of output (billions of 1952 yuan)						
Modern sector Producers' goods	1.27	1.43	1.73	2.02	2.49	2.92
Coal	0.79	0.83	1.00	1.17	1.32	1.54
Crude oil	0.07	0.10	0.13	0.15	.18	0.23
Iron ore	0.08	0.11	0.14	0.19	0.31	0.39
Manganese ore	0.01	0.01	0.01	0.01	0.03	0.03
Limestone	0.10	0.13	0.15	0.15	0.22	0.22
Miscellaneous	0.22	0.25	0.30	0.35	0.43	0.51
Modern sector Consumers' goods						
Salt	0.61	0.42	0.57	1.02	0.67	1.12
Handicrafts						
Coal	0.04	0.04	0.04	0.06	0.06	0.09
Salt	0.26	0.21	0.29	0.29	0.19	0.33
Total	2.17	2.10	2.63	3.39	3.41	4.45
Net value added (billions of 1952 yuan)						
Coal						
Native	0.03	0.03	0.03	0.04	0.04	0.07
Other	0.55	0.58	0.70	0.82	0.93	1.08
Crude oil	0.04	0.06	0.08	0.09	0.11	0.14
Iron ore	0.07	0.09	0.11	0.15	0.24	0.30
Manganese ore	0.01	0.01	0.01	0.01	0.02	0.03
Limestone	0.09	0.12	0.14	0.14	0.19	0.20
Salt						
Native	0.16	0.13	0.18	0.18	0.12	0.20
Other	0.38	0.26	0.35	0.64	0.42	0.70
Miscellaneous	0.16	0.18	0.22	0.25	0.31	0.36
Total	1.47	1.46	1.82	2.32	2.38	3.07

(Notes to this table are on the following page.)

Notes:

Output. The output of coal and crude oil for 1952-57 is given in 1956 Statistical Abstract, pp. 32-33; SSB, "Basic Conditions in China's Coal Industry," TCYC, No. 4, 1958, p. 22; and Great Ten Years, p. 84. For the output of iron ore, manganese ore, and salt (excluding native salt) in 1952-56, see 1956 Statistical Abstract, pp. 32-33; and SSB, Industry Study, pp. 19 and 95. The output of iron ore in 1957 is given in Peking Review, Peiping, No. 31, September 30, 1958, p. 15. The 1957 output of manganese ore is assumed to have increased in proportion to iron ore during the 1956-57 period. The output of salt (excluding native salt) is assumed to have increased in 1956-57 in proportion to total output of salt. Total salt output in 1952-57, including native salt, is given in "Proposal for the Second Five Year Plan," HHPYK, No. 20, October 1956, p. 165; Hu Ming, "Key Problems in Food Industry," TKP, Peiping, January 17, 1958, p. 3; and People's Daily, March 14, 1958, p. 3. Output of limestone in 1952-57 is assumed to have increased in proportion to cement output during the same period. The 1952 output of limestone is shown in Table H-1, and the 1952-57 output of cement in Appendix F, Table F-8,

Gross value of output. All estimates, except those for "Miscellaneous," are derived by multiplying the output figures given in this table by the 1952 prices given in Table H-1. Gross value of miscellaneous products in 1952 is derived at 0.22 billion yuan by deducting the gross output of the six products from total gross output of the mining industry given in Table H-1. For 1953-57, gross value of miscellaneous products is assumed to have increased in proportion to that of coal (including native coal), crude oil, limestone, iron ore, and manganese ore as a whole over the same period.

Net value added. All estimates, except those for miscellaneous products, are derived by multiplying the gross output for 1952-57 by the ratio of value added to gross output of each product for 1933 computed from data given in Table H-1. The derivation of net value added in the miscellaneous group follows the same procedure as that for deriving gross output.

Table H-3

WORKERS IN MINING, 1933 AND 1952

(thousands)

	1933[a]	1952[b]
Miners	694	1281
Coal	270	443
Native	-	20
Other	-	423
Crude oil	24	116
Iron ore	19	35
Limestone	35	130
Salt	186	274
Other products	160	283
Alum	3	3
Antimony, crude	(*)	3
Antimony oxide	(*)	2
Antimony regulus	12	7
Clay	32	32
Copper	2	11
Dolomite	3	3
Feldspar	1	1
Gold	19	25
Gypsum	3	3
Lead	1	1
Lead ore	(*)	1
Manganese ore	1	19
Magnesite	3	20
Mercury	(*)	8
Natural gas	(*)	(*)
Niter	3	3
Pyrite	1	1
Soda, natural	4	4
Sulfur	1	2
Talc	2	4
Tin	42	42
Tungsten ore	19	67
Zinc	(*)	3
Zinc ore	1	11
Miscellaneous	7	7
Other workers and employees	76	130
Coal	-	38
Others	-	92
Total	770	1411

(Notes to this table are on the following page.)

Notes:

- Not available.

(*) Less than one thousand.

[a]For the number of miners in 1933, see Ou, National Income, Vol. II, pp. 19-28. The number of other workers and employees for 1933 is derived by multiplying the number of miners by the ratio of the number of other workers and employees to that of miners, estimated at 11 per cent. (Ibid., Vol. I, p. 57.)

[b]The number of coal miners in 1952 is given in SSB, Industry Study, p. 90. Other figures for 1952 are derived by dividing output in 1952 by the output per worker computed from data on output and number of workers in 1933 given above and in Table H-1. The estimate of miners for other products is derived on the basis of the number of miners in this group and the prewar ratio of the number of other workers and employees to that of miners. The number of other workers and employees in coal mining is the residual obtained by deducting the number of coal miners from the total number of workers and employees. Ibid., p. 99.

Communist figures. Others are derived on the assumption that the output per worker for each product in the postwar years is the same as in 1933. For 1952, this assumption probably would not result in any serious error, since technological advances took place between 1933-52 mainly in coal mining. Even for the modern state-owned coal mines in 1952, mining was done primarily by human labor.[7] Output per worker for other industries in 1952 probably would not be far different, if at all, from that in 1933. However, the same cannot be said for the period after 1952, perhaps with the exception of native coal and salt. For these two industries, it is unlikely that labor productivity could have changed perceptibly in 1952-57.

UTILITIES

The derivation of value added in utilities for 1933 and 1952-57 is presented in Table 47. The construction of this table is described first. Workers employed in the utilities in 1933 and 1952 are then derived.

Gross Output and Value Added, 1933 and 1952

The estimates of value added for 1933 and 1952 are derived by deducting nonprimary costs from gross output. The detailed figures are presented in Table H-4. The sources and methods used in the calculation of these estimates are as follows.

With the exception of gas supply, estimates of gross output are derived by multiplying the physical quantities of output by the respective prices for each industry. The output of electric power in 1933 is the sum of the estimates for China proper given at 2.15 billion kilowatt-hours (kwh) and for Manchuria given at 0.66 billion kwh.[8] The output of electric power in 1952, 7.26 billion kwh, is taken from the 1956 Statistical Abstract, p. 32. The output of water supply in 1933 is estimated by Ou (National

Table H-4

GROSS OUTPUT AND VALUE ADDED, UTILITIES, 1933 AND 1952

(million yuan)

	Electric power (1)	Water supply (2)	Gas supply (3)	Total (4)
1933, in 1933 prices				
Output[a]	2810	199	16	-
Price[b]	0.06	0.15	-	-
Gross output	168.6	30.3	27.7	226.6
Raw materials	24.1	1.5	9.7	35.3
Fuels	-	3.0	-	3.0
Miscellaneous expenses	22.6	0.9	2.8	26.3
Gross value added	121.9	24.9	15.3	162.0
Depreciation	21.1	6.1	2.8	29.9
Net value added	100.8	18.8	12.5	132.1
1952, in 1952 prices				
Output[a]	7260	460	16	-
Price[b]	0.06	0.40	-	-
Gross output	435.6	184.0	69.2	688.8
Raw materials	144.5	9.2	24.2	177.9
Fuels	-	16.6	-	16.6
Miscellaneous expenses	65.3	11.0	6.9	83.2
Gross value added	225.8	147.2	38.1	411.0
Depreciation	56.6	36.8	6.9	100.3
Net value added	169.1	110.4	31.2	310.7
1933, in 1952 prices				
Gross output	168.6	79.6	69.2	317.4
Raw materials	55.9	4.1	24.2	84.2
Fuels	-	7.6	-	7.6
Miscellaneous expenses	25.6	4.5	6.9	37.0
Gross value added	86.9	63.5	38.1	188.5
Depreciation	21.1	15.9	6.9	43.9
Net value added	65.8	47.5	31.2	144.5
1952, in 1933 prices				
Gross output	435.6	69.0	27.7	532.3
Raw materials	62.3	3.4	9.7	75.4
Fuels	-	6.6	-	6.6
Miscellaneous expenses	57.3	2.2	2.8	62.3
Gross value added	316.0	56.7	15.3	388.0
Depreciation	56.6	13.8	2.8	73.2
Net value added	259.4	42.9	12.5	314.8

(Notes to this table are on the folowing page.)

Notes:

- Not available.

[a]The units of output for electric power, water supply, and gas supply are million kwh, million tons, and million cubic feet, respectively.

[b]The units for the price of electric power and water supply are yuan per kwh and yuan per ton.

Income, Vol. II, pp. 65-67) at 52,591 million gallons, or 199 million tons. The output of water supply in 1952 is given at 460 million cubic meters, or 460 million tons.[9]

The average price of electricity for China proper in 1933 is estimated at 0.06-0.07 yuan per kwh, and for Manchuria at 0.06 yuan per kwh on the basis of two studies of China's national income in the prewar period.[10] A national average of 0.06 yuan per kwh is used in our calculation. For 1952, the price is the constant 1952 price for the electric power industry given at 0.06 yuan per kwh.[11] According to Ou (National Income, Vol. II, p. 67), the gross value of water supply in 1933 totals 30.32 million yuan. The price is therefore computed at 0.15 yuan per ton by dividing gross value by the quantity of output. For 1952, the average price is 0.40 yuan per ton, which is the average of the quotations in Canton and Tientsin.[12]

Gross output of gas supply for 1933 in 1933 prices is compiled by Ou (National Income, Vol. II, p. 71). No information is available for 1952. We arbitrarily assume that output of this industry in 1952 remained at the prewar level. Gross output for 1933 in 1952 prices (and for 1952 in 1952 prices) is derived by multiplying the estimate in 1933 prices by the price index of coal estimated at 250 per cent for 1952 with 1933 as 100.[13]

The derivation of the cost deductions for the three industries on different price bases is explained separately in the order of the columns of Table H-4.

(1) Electric Power

(a) 1933, in 1933 prices. Costs of raw materials, miscellaneous items, and depreciation are estimates made by Ou (National Income, Vol. II, p. 70) at 14.3, 13.4, and 12.5 per cent of gross output. By applying these percentages to the gross output of 168.6 million yuan given in Table H-4, deductible costs of raw materials, miscellaneous items, and depreciation are computed at 24.1 million, 22.6 million, and 21.1 million yuan.

(b) 1952, in 1952 prices. The two items of raw material costs, fuels and electricity, are derived separately. Fuel costs are derived as follows: Output of thermoelectric power in 1952 is calculated at 6 billion kwh.[14] Consumption of coal per kwh of electricity generated in 1952 being 0.659 kg,[15] total coal consumption is, therefore, 3.954 million tons. The average price of coal in ten cities where major thermal plants are located is estimated at 23 yuan per ton.[16] Total fuel costs, therefore, amount to 90.9 million yuan. Apart from coal, the use of electricity by the power plants themselves and transmission loss also constitute part of the raw material costs. The amount of plant consumption and transmission loss in 1952 is estimated at 1.03 billion kwh.[17] At the price of 0.052 yuan per kwh,[18] this item comes to 535.6 million yuan. Total raw material costs, therefore, amount to 144.5 million yuan.

The percentage of miscellaneous items is derived at 15 per cent of gross output on the basis of the corresponding ratio for 1933 given at 13.4 per cent after allowing for changes in the relative prices of electricity and the miscellaneous items. As may be seen in Table H-4, the price of electricity in 1952 remained at the 1933 level. For miscellaneous items, which consist mainly of lubricating oils, the price index of crude oil (114 per cent for 1952 with 1933 as 100)[19] is taken as an approximation to the relative changes in the price of the miscellaneous items. The adjusted percentage for miscellaneous items is thus calculated at 15 per cent by multiplying the prewar percentage of 13.4 per cent by the price index of miscellaneous items, 114 per cent. Total deductions for miscellaneous items is derived by applying this adjusted percentage to gross output.

The percentage of depreciation in gross output is assumed to be the same as the prewar percentage, that is, 13 per cent. Depreciation is then obtained by applying this percentage to gross output in 1952.

(c) <u>1933, in 1952 prices; 1952, in 1933 prices</u>. The estimate of raw materials for 1933 in 1952 prices is derived by multiplying the corresponding estimate in 1933 prices (24.1 million yuan) by the price index for raw materials computed at 232 per cent for 1952 with 1933 as 100. This price index is derived as follows: the ratio of the value of raw materials for 1952 in 1952 prices to the corresponding estimate for 1933 in 1933 prices is equal to 144.5:24.1. On the assumption that the quantity of raw material increased from 1933 to 1952 in proportion to output in the same period, or 7.26/2.81, the price index for raw materials for 1952 with 1933 as 100 is (144.5/24.1)(7.26/2.81) = 232 per cent. The estimate of raw materials for 1952 in 1933 prices (62.3 million yuan) is obtained by dividing the estimate in 1952 prices (144.5 million yuan) by the same price index.

The estimate of miscellaneous items for 1933 in 1952 yuan (25.8 million) is derived by multiplying the estimate in 1933 prices (22.6 million) by the price index for miscellaneous items given above at 114 per cent in 1952 with 1933 as 100. The estimate for 1952 in 1933 yuan (57.3 million) is derived by dividing the estimate in 1952 prices (65.3 million) by the same price index.

Estimates of depreciation for 1933 in 1952 prices and for 1952 in

1933 prices are derived by applying the percentages given above (12.5 and 13 per cent) to the gross output for 1933 in 1952 prices (168.6 million yuan) and to the gross output for 1952 in 1933 prices (435.6 million yuan).

(2) Water Supply

(a) 1933, in 1933 prices. The percentages of raw materials, fuels, miscellaneous items, and depreciation have been estimated by Ou (National Income, Vol. II, p. 67) at 5, 10, 3, and 20 per cent of gross output. The amounts of deductions for these four items are derived by applying these percentages to the gross output of 30.3 million yuan given in Table H-4.

(b) 1952, in 1952 prices. For raw materials, which consist mainly of purifying agents, it is assumed that the percentage of raw materials in gross output is the same as in 1933, that is, 5 per cent. For fuels and miscellaneous items we also assume that the prewar percentages are applicable after adjustments are made for changes in relative prices of output and input. The price index of water supply for 1952 with 1933 as 100 is computed from Table H-4 at 267 per cent. The price indexes of coal and manufactured producers' goods are taken to represent those of fuels and miscellaneous items. The price index of coal is estimated at 250 per cent,[20] and that of manufactured producers' goods at 495 per cent[21] for 1952 with 1933 as 100. The prewar percentage of fuels being 10 per cent, the adjusted percentage is thus calculated at 9 per cent.[22] The adjusted percentage of miscellaneous items is similarly calculated at 6 per cent of gross output. By applying these percentages (5, 9, and 6) to the gross output of 184.0 million yuan, amounts of deductible costs for raw materials, fuels, and miscellaneous items are obtained. Depreciation for 1952 is derived by allowing the same 20 per cent of gross output as for 1933.

(c) 1933 in 1952 prices and 1952 in 1933 prices. Estimates of raw materials, fuels, and miscellaneous items for 1933 in 1952 prices are obtained by multiplying the corresponding estimates in 1933 prices by the price indexes of 267 per cent for water supply, 250 for fuels, and 495 for miscellaneous items.[23] Estimates for 1952 in 1933 prices are obtained by dividing the corresponding estimates in 1952 prices by the same indexes. Estimates of depreciation are derived by allowing the same percentages of gross output as for 1933 in 1933 prices.

(3) Gas Supply

(a) 1933 in 1933 prices and 1952 in 1952 prices. For the gas utilities in 1933, the percentage of fuel costs, miscellaneous items, and depreciation have been estimated by Ou (National Income, Vol. II, p. 71) at 35, 10, and 10 per cent of gross output. For lack of information on these items for 1952, we assume that the percentages are the same as those for 1933. Deductible costs are then derived by multiplying gross output in 1933 and in 1952 prices by these percentages.

(b) 1933 in 1952 prices and 1952 in 1933 prices. The gross output and deductible costs and, hence, the value added for 1933 in 1952 prices are assumed to be the same as those for 1952 in 1952 prices, and those for 1952 in 1933 prices, identical to those for 1933 in 1933 prices.

Gross Output and Value Added, 1953-57

Estimates of gross output and value added in electric power and water supply for 1953-57 in 1952 prices are extrapolations from the estimates for 1952 on the basis of output indexes of these two utilities for 1952-57. Estimates for gas for 1953-57 are assumed to remain unchanged at the 1952 level. The results are shown in Table H-5. On the basis of

Table H-5

GROSS OUTPUT AND VALUE ADDED, UTILITIES, 1952-57

(millions of 1952 yuan)

	1952	1953	1954	1955	1956	1957
Gross value of output	689	833	969	1071	1355	1608
Electric power	436	554	663	737	994	1160
Water supply	184	210	237	265	292	379
Gas supply	69	69	69	69	69	69
Gross value added	411	493	572	632	787	942
Electric power	226	287	344	382	515	601
Water supply	147	168	190	212	234	303
Gas supply	38	38	38	38	38	38
Depreciation	100	121	142	156	196	235
Electric power	56	72	87	96	130	152
Water supply	37	42	48	53	59	76
Gas supply	7	7	7	7	7	7
Net value added	311	372	430	476	591	707
Electric power	169	215	257	286	385	449
Water supply	110	126	142	159	175	227
Gas supply	31	31	31	31	31	31

Notes:

For estimates for 1952, see Table H-4. Estimates for electric power and water supply are derived on the basis of the estimates for 1952 and indexes of output of electric power and water supply in 1952-57. For output of electric power, see Great Ten Years, p. 84; and for output of water supply in 1952, 1956, and 1957, see p. 69, and People's Daily, February 16, 1957, p. 2. Estimates of output of water supply in 1953-55 are interpolated on the basis of the figures for 1952 and 1956 and a linear time trend. Estimates for gas supply for 1953-57 are assumed to be the same as for 1952.

the estimates of net value added for 1952, both in 1933 and 1952 prices, a price index of 99 per cent in 1952 with 1933 as 100 is obtained. Applying this price index to the net value added for 1953-57 in 1952 prices, we derive the corresponding estimates in 1933 prices at 376, 434, 481, 597, and 714 million 1933 yuan.

Number of Workers Employed in Utilities, 1933 and 1952

According to Ou (National Income, Vol. I, p. 72), the gross value of output per worker in the electric power industry in 1933 is about 6,000 yuan. Gross value of output in 1933 being 168.6 million yuan,[24] the number of workers is 28,000. The number of workers in the water and gas utilities in 1933 have been estimated by Ou (National Income, Vol. I, pp. 70, 72) at 5,000 for each of these industries. The number of workers in utilities in 1933 thus totals 38,000.

For 1952, only the number of workers in the electric power industry is available. The State Statistical Bureau reported figures of 61,000 and 114,000 for 1952 and 1956.[25] Assuming that output per worker in water and gas utilities for 1952 is the same as in 1933, the numbers of workers can be calculated at 15,000 in water supply and 5,000 in gas supply.[26] The number of workers in the utilities in 1952, therefore, totals 81,000.

CONSTRUCTION

The derivation of value added in construction for 1933 and 1952-57, summarized in Table 47, is explained below.

1933

Net value added in construction in 1933 is obtained by multiplying the value of raw materials used by construction, by the ratio of net value added to the value of raw materials in this industry. The estimated volume of raw materials used in construction is shown in Table H-6.

Table H-6

RAW MATERIALS USED IN CONSTRUCTION, ESTIMATED VOLUME, 1933
(millions of yuan)

	Value of materials used in construction	
Gross output of bricks, shingles, and stones at producers' prices[a]		
Factories	8	
Handicrafts	67	
Add: transportation margin[c]	8	83
Gross output of lime at producers' prices[a]	17	
Add: transportation margin[c]	8	
Less: nonconstruction uses[d]	5	20
Gross output of cement at producers' prices[a]	27	
Add: transportation margin[c]	8	35
Gross output of timber at producers' prices[b]	287	
Add: transportation margin[c]	287	
Less: nonconstruction uses[d]	57	517
Net import of construction materials		
Imports[e]	144	
Less: Exports[e]	4	140
Total		795

Notes:

[a]Estimates of gross output of bricks, shingles and stones, lime, and cement are given in Appendix F, Table F-1, and Appendix G, Table G-1.

[b]The gross output of forest products is given at 574 million yuan in Appendix E.

[c]The transportation margins for bricks, shingles and stones, lime, cement, and timber are estimated at 10, 50, 30, and 100 per cent of the gross value at producers' prices. Ou, National Income, Vol. I, pp. 79-80.

[d]Estimates of the amount of lime and timber for uses other than construction are estimated at 20 and 10 per cent of the gross value of these products at prices to users. Ibid.

[e]Ibid., p. 81.

The ratio of net value added to the value of raw materials has been estimated by Ou (National Income, Vol. I, p. 78) at 3:7. Applying this ratio to the total value of raw materials estimated at 795 million yuan, we derive net value added at 340 million yuan. Depreciation is arbitrarily assumed to be 3 per cent of gross output. On this assumption, gross value added, depreciation, and gross output in 1933 prices are computed at 375, 35, and 1,170 million yuan.

The price indexes for gross output and value added for 1952 with 1933 as 100 are assumed to vary in proportion to the price index of construction materials over the same period. The latter is computed at 304 per cent for 1952 with 1933 as 100 on the basis of the prices of cement, limestone, and lumber in 1933 and 1952[27] with the proportions of the gross output of these three products consumed by construction as weights.[28] Multiplying the estimates of value added in 1933 prices, we derive the corresponding estimates in 1952 prices.

The number of workers in construction is roughly estimated at 1.55 million on the basis of total net value added and net value added per worker. Construction in the prewar period consisted primarily of hand-built wooden structures. This is indicated by the fact that cement and imported construction materials constituted only one-fifth of the total volume of raw materials used in construction. It may not be far wrong to assume that net value added per worker in construction is close to that of handicrafts and mining which had only a small amount of modernized equipment. On this assumption, we derive a rough estimate of value added per worker in construction at 220 yuan.[29] The total net value added in 1933 already has been estimated at 340 million yuan, therefore the total number of workers employed in construction is derived at 1.55 million.

1952-57

The derivation of estimates for 1952-57 in 1952 prices is as follows. The figures of gross value of output in 1952 and 1956 are Communist estimates.[30] The figures of net value added for these two years are derived at 1.83 and 4.97 billion 1952 yuan on the basis of the percentages of net value added by construction in national income given at 3.0 and 5.6 per cent and estimates of national income given at 61.13 and 88.75 billion 1952 yuan by the State Statistical Bureau.[31] Estimates of net value added for 1953-55 and 1957 are extrapolations from the estimate for 1956 on the basis of the index of basic construction for 1953-57 in constant 1952 prices.[32] The results are 2.28, 2.68, 2.93, and 4.62 billion 1952 yuan. Depreciation allowances for construction in 1952 are assumed to be 5 per cent of gross output, that is, 0.23 billion yuan. On the assumption that depreciation charges for 1952-57 increased in proportion to net value in the same period, we derive estimates of depreciation for 1953-57 at 0.28, 0.33, 0.36, 0.62, and 0.58 billion yuan. Gross value added is then obtained at 2.06, 2.56, 3.01, 3.29, 5.59, and 5.20 billion yuan for 1952-57 by summing up net value added and depreciation. Estimates of gross output, value added, and depreciation for 1952-57 in 1933 prices are derived by dividing the estimates in 1952 prices by the price index of 304 per cent for 1952 with 1933 as 100 given above.

TRANSPORTATION AND COMMUNICATIONS

The derivation of gross receipts and value added by the modern and the traditional sector of this industry presented in Table 48 is explained below.

Modern Transportation and Communications

Total net value added for 1933 in 1933 prices is the sum of the following estimates made by Ou (National Income, Vol. I, pp. 85-87, 90-91, 95-97) for the different branches of this industry.

	Gross receipts (million yuan)	Net value added
Railroad	369	258
Shipping	137	62
Trucks, taxis, and buses	95	33
Trolleys	13	9
Civil air transport	4	1
Communications	44	33
Postal services	46	32
Total	708	428

Depreciation in these seven branches of modern transportation and communications in 1933 has also been estimated by Ou in the same source at 26 million yuan. For trucks, taxis, and buses, and for communications, the estimates include both maintenance and depreciation. We assume that depreciation accounted for one-half of the total amount. Gross value added thus amounts to 454 million yuan.

Information on the prices of the services or of the primary input in modern transportation for 1933 and 1952 is not available. It is assumed that these prices increased in 1933-52 in proportion to the price of the nonprimary input of this industry over the same period. The latter consist mainly of fuels, including coal, gasoline, and fuel oil. The price index of these items is computed at 254 per cent for 1952 with 1933 as 100 on the basis of a wholesale price index of 14 types of fuels for Tientsin calculated by the Nankai Economic Research Institute.[33] The estimate of net value added for 1933 in 1933 prices, 428 million yuan, is multiplied by this price index to obtain the estimate for 1933 in 1952 prices at

1,087 million yuan. Gross value added and depreciation in 1952 prices are similarly calculated at 1,152 million and 65 million yuan. The number of workers employed in 1933 has been estimated at 0.37 million for modern transportation and 0.07 million for communications, totalling 0.44 million.[34]

For the postwar period, estimates of gross and net value added for 1952 in 1952 prices are first derived from freight and passenger volume, rates, and deductible costs, and then extrapolated to 1953-57 on the basis of individual indexes of freight volume and passenger traffic for the different carriers over the same period. The calculations for 1952 are shown in Table H-7, the data on freight volume in 1952-57 are summarized in Table H-8, and the estimates of gross receipts and value added in 1952-57 are presented in Table H-9.

Estimates of gross receipts and value added for 1952-57 in 1933 prices are obtained by deflating the corresponding estimates in 1952 prices by the price index given above of 254 per cent in 1952 with 1933 as 100.

The estimates presented in Table H-9 are preliminary in that an overstatement in the Communist data on freight volume in 1952-57 has yet to be corrected. The estimates of net value added have been adjusted as shown in the discussion on transportation and communications in Chapter IV. For the purpose of deriving the transportation and distribution margin, we also need the corrected estimates of gross receipts of the modern sector. These figures are derived at 3.90, 4.42, 5.10, 5.55, 6.42, and 6.99 billion 1952 yuan for 1952-57 on the same assumption made in the adjustment of the estimates of net value added.

Table H-7

VALUE ADDED BY MODERN TRANSPORTATION AND COMMUNICATIONS, 1952
(billions of 1952 yuan)

	Gross receipts (1)	Gross value added (2)	Depre- ciation (3)	Net v add (4
Freight				
Railroad	2.41	1.59	0.07	1.5
Trucks	0.25	0.09	0.02	0.0
Ships	0.19	0.09	0.01	0.0
Passenger transportation				
Railroad	0.32	0.21	0.01	0.2
Others	0.19	0.07	0.02	0.0
Communications (including postal service)	0.24	0.18	(*)	0.1
Total	3.90	2.23	0.13	2.1

Notes:

(*) Less than 0.01 billion yuan.

Column (1). Gross receipts from freight and passenger transportation are derived by multiplying the volumes of freight and passenger transportation given in Table H-8 by the respective rates estimated as follows. Frei carried by the railroad cost 0.01 - 0.17 yuan/ton-kilometer for cargo varyi from Class 1 to 13 (HHJP, Chungking, November 25, 1950). Single quotations of 0.01 yuan/ton-kilometer are often given, indicating that the bulk of the cargo is of the lower class type. (See, for example, TKP, January 22, 1957 p. 1; and People's Daily, August 18, 1957, p. 5.) Hence, we arbitrarily derive an average freight rate of 0.04 yuan per ton-kilometer by assigning weights of four-fifths to the lower rate and one-fifth to the higher rate. The freight rate for trucks is estimated at 0.325 yuan per ton-kilometer by averaging the rates quoted for Szechwan, Kansu, Fukien, and Kwantung (given in HHJP, Chungking, January 20, 1952; KSJP, Lanchow, January 3, 1952 FKJP, Amoy, June 29, 1952; and NFJP, Canton, December 8, 1952). The freigh rate for ships, 0.018 yuan per ton-kilometer, is the quotation given for inland shipping (People's Daily, August 18, 1957, p. 5).

Railroad passenger rates are quoted at 0.0135 and 0.0236 yuan per passenger-kilometer for hard and soft seats, respectively (China Travel Service Gazette, Hong Kong, September 1956). Presumably, there are more hard than soft seats, and we arbitrarily assign weights of one-fifth to the soft-seat rate and four-fifths to the hard-seat rate to derive an average of 0.016 yuan per passenger-kilometer. For all other types of passenger travel, the bus fare of 0.04 yuan per passenger-kilometer quoted

Notes (continued):

in NFJP, Canton, December 5, 1952, p. 1, is used. The gross receipts from communications are given in Great Ten Years, p. 138.

Column (2). Gross value added is derived by multiplying gross receipts in column (1) by the percentage of gross value added in total receipts which is assumed to be the same as in 1933. The percentage for railroad (both for freight and passenger service) is computed at 66 per cent from data given in Liu, Income, p. 42. For trucks, ships, and communications, the percentages are 36, 50, and 73 per cent, computed from data given in Ou, National Income, Vol. I, pp. 86, 91, 97.

Column (3). Depreciation is derived by multiplying gross receipts by percentage of depreciation based on data given in Ou (ibid., pp. 86, 91, 96). The percentages used here are 3, 9, 5, and 0.5 per cent for the railroad, trucks, ships, and communications.

Column (4). Net value added figures are derived as residuals by deducting the figures in column (3) from the corresponding figures in column (2).

Table H-8

FREIGHT VOLUME, MODERN TRANSPORTATION AND COMMUNICATIONS, 1952-57

	1952	1953	1954	1955	1956	1957
Freight (billion ton-kilometers)						
Railroad	60.16	78.14	93.24	98.15	120.35	134.59
Trucks	0.77	1.30	1.94	2.52	3.49	3.9[illegible]
Ships	10.61	13.57	18.64	24.44	28.21	34.3[illegible]
Passenger service (billion passenger-kilometers)						
Railroad	20.06	28.17	29.47	26.74	34.38	36.1[illegible]
Others	4.61	6.65	7.43	8.45	12.00	13.3[illegible]
Communications (million 1952 yuan)	243.50	299.90	327.80	364.50	431.40	420.3[illegible]

Source:

Great Ten Years, pp. 131, 133, 138.

Table H-9

GROSS RECEIPTS AND VALUE ADDED,

MODERN TRANSPORTATION AND COMMUNICATIONS, 1952-57

(billions of 1952 yuan)

	1952	1953	1954	1955	1956	1957
Gross receipts	3.90	4.81	5.79	6.31	7.92	8.85
Freight: Railroad	2.41	3.13	3.74	3.93	4.82	5.40
Trucks	0.25	0.42	0.63	0.82	1.14	1.28
Ships	0.19	0.24	0.33	0.44	0.50	0.62
Passenger: Railroad	0.32	0.45	0.47	0.42	0.55	0.58
Others	0.19	0.27	0.30	0.34	0.49	0.55
Communications	0.24	0.30	0.32	0.36	0.42	0.42
Gross value added	2.23	2.85	3.51	3.78	4.69	5.20
Freight: Railroad	1.59	2.07	2.46	2.59	3.18	3.56
Trucks	0.09	0.15	0.23	0.30	0.41	0.46
Ships	0.09	0.11	0.16	0.21	0.24	0.29
Passenger: Railroad	0.21	0.29	0.31	0.28	0.36	0.38
Others	0.07	0.10	0.11	0.13	0.18	0.20
Communications	0.18	0.22	0.24	0.27	0.32	0.31
Depreciation	0.13	0.17	0.22	0.24	0.33	0.37
Freight: Railroad	0.07	0.09	0.11	0.11	0.14	0.16
Trucks	0.02	0.03	0.05	0.06	0.09	0.10
Ships	0.01	0.01	0.02	0.02	0.03	0.03
Passenger: Railroad	0.01	0.01	0.01	0.01	0.02	0.02
Others	0.02	0.03	0.03	0.04	0.05	0.06
Communications	(*)	(*)	(*)	(*)	(*)	(*)
Net value added	2.10	2.77	3.29	3.52	4.35	4.83
Freight: Railroad	1.52	1.98	2.36	2.48	3.04	3.40
Trucks	0.07	0.12	0.18	0.23	0.31	0.36
Ships	0.08	0.10	0.14	0.18	0.21	0.26
Passenger: Railroad	0.20	0.28	0.29	0.27	0.34	0.36
Others	0.05	0.07	0.08	0.09	0.13	0.14
Communications	0.18	0.22	0.24	0.27	0.32	0.31

Note:

(*) Less than 0.005 billion yuan.

Source:

Computed from data given in Tables H-7 and H-8.

Old-fashioned Transportation

Net value added for 1933 in 1933 prices is derived by multiplying the number of workers by an estimate of net value added per worker. The total number of old-fashioned transportation workers is obtained at 10.86 million by deducting the number of workers in the modern sector (0.44 million) given previously from the total numbers of workers employed in this industry as a whole (11.3 million) given in Table 53. Net value added per worker is assumed to be the average of those for agricultural workers and handicraftsmen, that is, 111 yuan.[35] Total net value added therefore is equal to 1,205 million yuan in 1933 prices.

Net value added in 1952 prices is obtained at 2,606 million yuan by multiplying the total number of workers by the net value added per worker in 1952 prices, estimated at 240 yuan. The latter figure is derived by applying the price index of handicraft products, 216 per cent for 1952 with 1933 as 100,[36] to the net value added per worker of 111 yuan in 1933 prices.

Deductible costs in old-fashioned transportation are presumably a very minor portion of the gross receipts of the workers. We assume that depreciation amounts to 1 per cent of net value added. On this assumption, depreciation for 1933 is calculated at 12 million 1933 yuan, and 26 million 1952 yuan.

Estimates of net value added for 1952-57 in 1952 prices are derived as follows: First, net value added in 1957 is obtained at 2,430 million yuan by multiplying the net value added per worker (243 yuan obtained by multiplying the estimate in 1933 prices, that is, 110.7 yuan given above, by the price index of handicraft products, that is, 220 per cent given in Appendix I), by the total number of workers, roughly estimated at 10 million, as shown in Table H-10. Next, estimates for 1952-56 are derived as residuals by subtracting estimates of net value added in the modern sector, given above

Table H-10

TRANSPORTATION WORKERS, BY CATEGORY, 1957

(millions)

Boats and junks[a]	0.5
Animal-drawn carts	
Urban areas[b]	0.2
Rural areas[c]	3.0
Hand-drawn carts[d]	0.3
Wheelbarrows[e]	2.3
Rickshas, pedicabs, and sedans[f]	0.7
Coolies and longshoremen[g]	0.7
Farmers working in transportation[h]	1.4
Others[i]	0.9
Total	10.0

Notes:

[a]The total number of boats and junks is given at 0.29 million for 1955 (Wang Shou-tao, "Carry Out the Transportation Work Well, and Support the Agricultural Cooperative Movement," HHYP, No. 2, December 1955, p. 220). The total number for 1957 is assumed to be the same as for 1955. Not all the boats were in use, however. On the basis of a sample survey for Kiangsu Province reported in People's Daily, March 14, 1957, p. 1, a utilization rate of 60 per cent is roughly calculated. Applying this percentage to the total number of boats, we derive the number of boats used for transportation at 0.17 million. The average number of workers per boat is calculated at 3 persons from data given in Wang Shou-tao, and the total number of workers is therefore 0.5 million.

[b]The total number of animal-drawn carts in urban areas is given at 0.14 million in TKP, September 2, 1957, p. 1, but the number of carts actually in use is given at 0.10 million in People's Daily, March 14, 1957, p. 1. The average number of workers per cart is calculated at 1.7 persons, based on data given in Wang Shou-tao. The total number of workers is obtained by multiplying the total number of animal-drawn carts by 1.7.

Notes (continued):

[c]The total number of animal-drawn carts in rural areas is given at 5 million in TKP, September 2, 1957, p. 1. The total number of workers handling these carts is derived on the assumption that one-half are for hire and that the percentage of carts in use and the average number of workers per cart is the same as those for animal-drawn carts in urban areas.

[d]The total number of hand-drawn carts is given at 0.3 million. Ibid. Assuming the same percentage of carts in full-time use as the animal-drawn carts and the same number of workers per cart, we derive a total number of 0.2 million hand-drawn carts operated by 0.3 million workers.

[e]The total number of wheelbarrows is estimated at 10 million. Ibid. We assume that one-third of the total are for hire and that the utilization rate is the same as for animal-drawn carts. The number of wheelbarrows in full-time use and the number of workers, therefore, both equal 2.3 million.

[f]The number of workers in this group has been estimated at 0.56 millic in 1933 by Ou, National Income, Vol. II, p. 221. On the assumption that th total number increased from 1933 to 1957 in proportion to total population over the same period, that is, 128 per cent for 1957 with 1933 as 100, the figure for 1957 is calculated at 0.7 million. (For data on total population, see Chapter IV.)

[g]The number of workers in this group in 108 cities in 1950 is estimated at 0.68 million in HHYP, No. 1, 1951, p. 537. During 1950-57 the volume of freight through the seaports declined while inland transportation expanded. It appears likely that the number of workers in this group in 1957 is roughly the same as in 1950. A round figure of 0.7 million is used.

[h]The number of farmers engaged in part-time transportation in 1933 converted to the equivalent of full-time has been estimated at 0.43 per cent of the total male population. (See Table 54.) Total male population can be calculated at 332 million on the basis of data on total population, given in Table 32, and on sex ratio given in Table 52. It is assumed that the same percentage of total males was engaged in transportation as subsidiary occupations.

[i]Other workers include those not covered above (for example, full-time coolies in rural areas) and are assumed to be 10 per cent of the total workers in the above categories.

from total net value added for the entire industry, derived by extrapolating from the estimate for the entire industry in 1957 on an index of net value added in agriculture, manufacturing, and mining for 1952-57.[37] The results are 2.65, 2.45, 2.35, 2.34, 2.48, and 2.43 billion 1952 yuan for 1952-57.[38] Deflating these figures by the price index of handicraft products given in Appendix I at 220 per cent in 1952 with 1933 as 100, we obtain net value added by old-fashioned transportation at 1.22, 1.05, 0.95, 1.06, 1.13, and 1.10 billion 1933 yuan for 1952-57.

Assuming that the ratio of depreciation to net value added for 1952-57 is the same as for 1933, we derive estimates of depreciation at 0.03 billion 1952 yuan and 0.01 billion 1933 yuan for all the postwar years.[39]

TRADE

Estimates of value added by trade in 1933 and 1952-57 were explained in Chapter IV. Only the details relating to the derivation of net value added by stores (including restaurants) for 1933 need be discussed here.

According to the statistics compiled by Ou,[40] the ratio of the number of shops to population is 3.8 per thousand. Total population in 1933 being 500 million (as estimated in Chapter IV), the total number of shops is therefore calculated at 1.9 million. Included in the total number of shops are those providing services such as hotels, theaters, bath houses, barber shops, and so on, and probably even some manufacturers. But, undoubtedly, trading stores and restaurants must occupy by far the major proportion in the total numbers of shops. In the absence of any information, we assume that one-fourth of the total number are shops other than trading stores and restaurants. The number of trading stores and restaurants thus totals 1.43 million. The average number of workers and employees in a shop has been estimated by Ou (National Income, Vol. I, pp. 103 and 105) at 5.24

persons, and the average annual wage rate at 150 yuan. Multiplying these figures by the above total, we obtain the total number of persons employed in stores and restaurants at 7.49 million and the total wage at 1,124 million yuan.

The average net profit per shop is estimated by Ou (National Income, Vol. II, pp. 104, 106) at 440 yuan. Total profit is obtained at 629 million yuan by multiplying the average profit per shop by the total number of stores. Summing up the total wage bill and total net profit, we obtain net value added at 1,753 million yuan.

GOVERNMENT

Estimates of net income originating in government services are derived separately for 1933 and 1952-57.

1933

Included in the government sector are the national, provincial, and county governments. 1933 estimates of value added (in million yuan) in these governments made by Liu and Ou are summarized here: National government, 464; provincial and municipal governments including the Manchurian government, 208; county government, 144; and total, 816.[41] For the purpose of deriving the estimate in 1952 prices, it is necessary at this point to break down the total value added into incomes of civil servants and those in military service. Total military servicemen in 1933 numbered about 3 million.[42] According to the opinions of Chinese officials, military subsistence per person in the armed forces was roughly 60 yuan, and average wage for government employees, about 300 yuan. The amount of subsistence provisions for the armed forces, therefore, totals 180 million yuan. Deducting this amount from the total salary, wage, and subsistence payments of 816 million yuan, we obtain the total wage bill for government employees at 636 million yuan. The total number of government employees is derived at 2.12 million by dividing the total wage bill by the average wage per employee. The total number of persons in government service is, therefore, 5.12 million.

The average wage rate of a worker or employee in 1952 is estimated at 490 yuan.[43] Assuming that the output per worker in real terms in 1952 is the same as in 1933, we derive total wages of government employees for 1933 in 1952 prices at 1,039 yuan by multiplying the total number of government employees in 1933 (2.12 million) by the average wage of 490 yuan per employee. For the armed forces, the price index of handicraft products, which is based mainly on the prices of food and clothing products, appears to be a fair approximation to the price index for military subsistence. This index has been computed in Appendix I, Table I-2, at 216 per cent for 1952 with 1933 as 100. Total military pay of 180 million yuan for 1933 is then multiplied by this index to arrive at the estimate in 1952 prices at 389 million yuan. Total net value added in the government sector in 1933 thus sums up to 1,428 million yuan in 1952 prices.

<u>1952-57</u>

Net income originating in the government sector in 1952-57 is derived by summing up the income of government employees in administrative organizations and cultural, educational and social institutions, and adding it to military subsistence.

The number of government employees in 1952-57 has already been estimated at 4.59, 5.23, 5.54, 5.62, 6.02, and 6.31 million.[44] The average wage rate of a government employee is assumed to be the same as that of all workers and employees. The latter figures for 1952-57 are derived at 490, 541, 566, 582, 665, and 694 yuan per person per annum, by adjusting the Communist figures to include fringe benefits.[45] Total wage payments to government employees thus amount to 2.25, 2.84, 3.14, 3.27, 4.00, and 4.38 billion current yuan for 1952-57. These figures are then deflated by the cost-of-living index for 1952-57 with 1952 as 100 to arrive at the following estimates for this period in constant 1952 prices: 2.25, 2.68, 2.93, 3.05, 3.74, and 4.01 billion yuan.[46]

Estimates of total wage payments to government employees for the same period in 1933 prices are made by deflating the estimates, which are in 1952 prices, by a price index of 163 per cent with 1933 as 100. The price index is derived by dividing the wage rate in 1952 (490 yuan) by that in 1933 (300 yuan) on the assumption that the output per worker in real terms in these two years remained unchanged.

No information on the size of the armed forces on the Chinese Mainland in 1952 is available. Estimates for the period 1952-57 made by various observers range from 2.5 to 3.4 million.[47] For our calculation, a round figure of 3 million for 1952-57 is assumed. The military pay per person is reported at 2,700 catties of millet which is roughly equivalent to 1,890 catties of rice.[48] Valued at the retail price of 0.18 yuan per catty of rice,[49] military subsistence amounts to 340 yuan per person. Multiplying this figure by the total number of military servicemen, we obtain total military pay at 1.02 billion yuan.

The corresponding estimate in 1933 prices is derived at 0.46 billion yuan for all the years by dividing the estimate in 1952 prices by the price index of handicraft products given in Appendix I at 220 per cent in 1952 with 1933 as 100.

FINANCE

1933

Included in this sector are the modern banks, traditional money shops, trust companies, savings and insurance companies, pawn shops, and miscellaneous money lenders. Estimates of 212 million yuan net value added in these institutions for 1933 in 1933 prices are summarized in Table H-11.

The estimate of net value added of 346 million yuan in 1952 prices is derived by multiplying the estimate of 212 million 1933 yuan by the deflator for the wage of government employees estimated at 163 per cent for 1952 with 1933 as 100.

The number of workers employed in finance is estimated at 0.14 million by dividing total net value added of 212 million yuan by the net value added per worker of 1,490 yuan estimated on the basis of data given in Ou (National Income, Vol. I, pp. 114-115).

1952-57

Net value added in 1952 is derived on the assumption that net value added per worker for 1952 in real terms remained at the 1933 level. As shown in Table 63, the number of workers in financial institutions in 1952 is estimated at 0.54 million. Net value added per worker being 1,490 yuan, net value added for 1952 in 1933 prices amounts to 805 million yuan. The estimate in 1952 prices is obtained at 1,312 million yuan by multiplying the figure in 1933 prices by the price index of 163 per cent for 1952 with 1933 as 100.

For 1953-57, estimates of net value added in both 1933 and 1952 prices are derived by extrapolating from the figures for 1952 on an index of changes in the sum of net value added in the principal sectors of the

Table H-11

NET VALUE ADDED, FINANCIAL INSTITUTIONS, 1933
(million yuan)

Chinese-owned banks[a]	66
Foreign-owned banks[b]	38
Traditional money shops[c]	30
Trust companies, insurance, and savings institutions[d]	31
Pawn shops[e]	28
Others[f]	19
Total	212

Notes:

[a]Gross value added by the Chinese-owned modern banks has been estimat by T. C. Liu at 71 million yuan (Income, p. 53). China Yearbook, 1936-37 (p. 790) lists depreciation as about 10 per cent of total general expenses. Total general expenses being 48.4 million yuan, depreciation is 4.8 millio and net value added, 66 million yuan.

[b]Data on the financial accounts of the foreign banks in China are totally lacking. This rough estimate of net value added is made on the basis of 134 million yuan total paid-up capital (Wu Cheng-hsi, Chung-kuo ti yin-hang (China's Banks), Shanghai, 1934, p. 103 and Appendix) and the rati of net value added to total capital in the Chinese-owned banks calculated a 28 per cent (based on Ou, National Income, Vol. I, p. 114).

[c]Estimated on the basis of total capital for lack of other relevant data. Total capital of these money shops in 1934 has been estimated by the Bank of China at 100 million yuan (F. T. Tamagna, Banking and Finance in China, New York, Institute of Pacific Relations, 1942, p. 62). It is assumed that the ratio of value added to capital would be slightly higher for the money shops than for the modern banks because of higher interest rates charged by the money shops and relatively higher labor-capital ratio for the traditional money shops. The ratio for the money shops is assumed to be 30 per cent as compared with a figure of 28 per cent for the modern Chinese banks. Net value added is derived by applying this ratio to total capital.

Notes (continued):

[d]The estimates of net value added by trust companies, savings institutions and insurance companies are those made by Ou, National Income, Vol. I, pp. 112-113.

[e]Ou estimates 64 million yuan total capital for the pawn shops. Ibid., Vol. I, p. 113. However, as Ou himself admits, this figure is too low. Lacking any information, we raise the estimate by 10 per cent to 70 million yuan to allow for that portion not enumerated by Ou. The ratio of net value added to capital is assumed to be the average of the ratio for pawn shops in Lanchow, given at 50 per cent, and the ratio for traditional money shops estimated at 30 per cent, that is, 40 per cent. (Pan Yi-min, Lanchow tzu kung-shen-yeh yu chin-yung (Industry, Trade and Finance in Lanchow), quoted in Ou. Ibid.) Net value added by pawn shops is thus derived at 28 million yuan.

[f]To allow for net value added by personal lending and by certain financing institutions in Manchuria, we add 10 per cent of the net value added in the financial institutions already accounted for above, or 19 million yuan.

economy to which financial institutions provide their services -- agriculture, manufacturing, mining, trade and construction. The results are shown in Table H-12.

As with trade and government, depreciation in finance can only be estimated. On the basis of very fragmentary data from financial reports, Ou has computed depreciation in modern financial institutions in 1933 at about 3 per cent of net value added (Ou, National Income, Vol. I, p. 114). For finance, government, and trade as a whole, the percentage is likely to be much lower because of the relatively low figure of fixed assets in the traditional sectors of these industries. Depreciation is arbitrarily assumed to be 1 per cent of net value added. Therefore rough estimates of depreciation for 1933 and 1952-57 are calculated at 0.10, 0.14, 0.15, 0.16, 0.16, 0.18, and 0.18 billion 1952 yuan, and 0.04, 0.05, 0.06, 0.06, 0.06, 0.07, and 0.07 billion 1933 yuan.[50]

PERSONAL SERVICES

Included in this sector are the services of medical doctors, teachers, lawyers, accountants, domestic servants, and others in the service industry Net value added in this sector for 1933 is derived at 343 million yuan by multiplying the number of workers in each profession by the respective average earnings per person as shown in Table H-13.

The estimate for 1933 in 1952 prices is derived by multiplying the estimate in 1933 prices by the price deflator for the wage payments to government employees, that is, 163 per cent for 1952 with 1933 as 100 as discussed earlier.

The estimates for 1952-57 in both 1933 and 1952 prices are obtained by extrapolating from the 1952 estimates, which are assumed to be the

TABLE H-12

NET VALUE ADDED IN FINANCE, 1952-57

(in 1933 and 1952 prices)

	1952	1953	1954	1955	1956	1957
Net value added in agriculture, manufacturing, mining, trade, and construction						
Total (**billion** 1952 **yuan**)	53.60	56.81	59.85	61.94	69.98	72.29
Index (per cent)	100	106	112	116	130	135
Net value added in finance						
Billion 1933 **yuan**	0.80	0.85	9.90	0.93	1.04	1.08
Billion 1952 **yuan**	1.31	1.39	1.47	1.52	1.70	1.77

<u>**Sources**</u>: **Tables** 36, 37, 47, 49.

Table H-13

NET VALUE ADDED IN PERSONAL SERVICES, 1933

(in 1933 yuan)

Occupation	Number of persons (million)	Average annual income (yuan)	Total income (million yuan)
Teachers			
Old-fashioned tutors	0.33[a]	70	23
Private school teachers	0.16	240	38
Physicians and others in medical service	0.30[b]	240	72
Lawyers and accountants	0.01	1000	10
Domestic servants	2.30[c]	65[d]	150
Other nonagricultural workers	0.53[e]	95[f]	50
Total	3.63		343

Notes:

[a]There were 0.65 traditional tutors per 1,000 persons in prewar China. Multiplying this figure by the total population of 500 million in 1933 estimated in Chapter IV, we obtain 0.33 million traditional tutors.

[b]The number of persons in the medical service is estimated at 0.6 per thousand. Total number in this profession is derived by multiplying this figure by the total population.

[c]The number of domestic servants is derived separately for cities and small towns. The percentages of population employed as domestic servants in Shanghai, Wuhan, and Nanking are estimated at 3.30, 4.09, and 6.89 per cent. The median, 4.09, is used in our calculation. Population in cities of 100,000 persons or over is estimated at 5 per cent of total population, that is, 500 x 0.05 = 30 million (Djang Gee-hung, "An Estimate of the Working Population of China," She-hui ko-hsueh tsa-chih (Quarterly Review of Social Sciences), Shanghai, Vol. IX, No. 2, December 1947, p. 86). The number of domestic servants in large cities is therefore 30 x 0.041 = 1.23 million. Total nonagricultural population in 1933 has been estimated at 135 million in Table 55. Hence, nonagricultural population residing in small towns is 135 - 30 = 105 million. The number of domestic servants in this 105 million is unavailable. Since the per capita number of domestic servants in small towns would probably be much lower than in large cities, we assume a figure of 1 per cent, which, together with the total population

Notes (continued):

of 105 million, gives a rough estimate of 1.05 million domestic servants. Total number of domestic servants thus comes to 1.23 + 1.05 = 2.28 million. This figure is rounded to 2.30 million to allow for servants in the households of rich landlords and local officials in rural areas.

[d]The per-worker earnings of domestic servants are assumed to be one-half of the per-worker earnings of handicraftsmen, that is, 65 yuan per person. (Value added per worker in handicrafts is discussed in Chapter IV.)

[e]Total number of other workers is derived at 8.89 million. (That is the sum of 7.91 million workers in nonagricultural occupations, given in Table 55, plus 0.98 million man-labor units to account for the part of the agricultural population engaged in other nonagricultural occupations, as given in Table 54.) Deducting the sum of persons in the service industry, government, and finance (3.10, 5.12, and 0.14 million) from 8.89 million, we obtain a residual of 0.53 million.

[f]In the absence of any information, the figure is assumed to be the average of the earnings of other persons in this sector, 293/3.10 = 95 yuan.

Sources:

Ou, National Income, Vol. I, pp. 122, 125, 126, 129. Djang Gee-hung, "An Estimate of the Working Population of China," She-hui ko-hsueh tsa-chih (Quarterly Review of Social Sciences), Shanghai, Vol. IX, No. 2, December 1947, pp. 86-87.

same as for 1933, on an index of employment in this sector for 1952-57 computed from data given in Table 63. The results, in billions of yuan, are as follows:

	1952	1953	1954	1955	1956	1957
Net value added in services						
In 1933 prices	0.34	0.34	0.34	0.33	0.31	0.31
In 1952 prices	0.55	0.55	0.54	0.54	0.51	0.51

Depreciation of fixed assets in this industry is presumably very small. Hence, no depreciation allowance is made.

RESIDENTIAL RENT

Gross expenditure of rent per person during the 1930s has been estimated at 3.52 yuan in Shanghai and 5.47 in Peiping in two budget studies.[51] The unweighted average of these two figures, 4.50 yuan, is multiplied by the 135 million total nonagricultural population to obtain the gross rent of the nonagricultural population at 608 million yuan. For the farm population, gross rent per person is estimated at 2.10 yuan on the basis of data from J. L. Buck's two field studies.[52] Agricultural population being 365 million, gross rent amounts to 766 million yuan. Total gross rent for the entire population, therefore, comes to 1,374 million yuan. Allowing 15 per cent of this total for repairs and miscellaneous expenses and 10 per cent for depreciation, we obtain net residential rent at 1,030.5 million yuan and depreciation at 137 million yuan.

A price index for rent is derived from data for Tientsin as follows: The price index of residential rent in Tientsin in 1936-37 with 1933 as 100 is given at 97 per cent, and the cost-of-living index in 1952 with 1936-37 as 100 at 207 per cent.[53] On the assumption that the price index of rent increased from 1936 to 1952 in proportion to the cost-of-living index over the same period, we link the two indexes together and derive a price index of rent at 194 per cent in 1952 with 1933 as 100. By multiplying the estimates of gross and net rent and depreciation for 1933 in 1933 prices by this price index, the estimates in 1952 prices are obtained at 2,665, 1,998, and 267 million 1952 yuan.

For 1952-57, it is assumed that per capita expenditure on rent remained at the same level as in 1933. The per capita rent in 1933 and the total population in 1952-57 being known (see Chapter IV), the estimates of gross and net rent and depreciation for residential buildings in 1952-57 are derived and shown in Table H-14.

WORK BRIGADES

Value added by work brigades is estimated at 80 per cent of the value of earth work done in connection with construction projects.[54]

Railroad Construction

The 1952 Communique reported 480 kilometers of newly built railroad and 753 kilometers of restored and repaired track in 1952. To build one kilometer of new railroad, an average of roughly 63,000 cubic meters of earth work was involved,[55] and to restore or repair one kilometer of old railroad requires about 50,000 cubic meters of earth work, according to Chinese railroad veterans. Therefore, the total earth work done in railroad construction during 1952 can be estimated at (480 x 63,000) + (753 x 50,000) = 67.9 million cubic meters, and the amount done by forced labor, 67.9 x 0.8 = 54.3 million cubic meters.

Mileage of railroads built and repaired from 1953-57 are taken from Great Ten Years. The earth work done per kilometer in these years is assumed to be the same as given for 1952. The annual amounts of earth work are estimated in Table H-15.

Table H-14

GROSS AND NET RENT AND DEPRECIATION, RESIDENTIAL BUILDINGS, 1952-57

(billions of yuan)

	1952	1953	1954	1955	1956	1957
In 1933 prices						
Gross rent	1.56	1.59	1.62	1.67	1.70	1.75
Net rent	1.17	1.19	1.22	1.25	1.28	1.31
Depreciation	0.16	0.16	0.16	0.17	0.17	0.18
In 1952 prices						
Gross rent	3.04	3.10	3.16	3.25	3.31	3.40
Net rent	2.28	2.32	2.37	2.44	2.48	2.55
Depreciation	0.30	0.31	0.32	0.32	0.33	0.34

Table H-15

EARTH WORK IN RAILROAD CONSTRUCTION, 1953-57

Newly built railroads		Reconstructed railroads		Total earth work done	Earth work done by work brigades
Mileage (kilometers) (1)	Earth work (million cubic meters) (2)	Mileage (kilometers) (3)	Earth work (million cubic meters) (4)	(million cubic meters) (5)	(million cubic meters) (6)
587	37.0	119	6.0	43.0	34.4
831	52.4	301	15.1	67.5	54.0
1222	77.0	184	9.2	86.2	69.0
1747	110.1	495	24.8	134.9	107.9
474	29.9	692	34.6	64.5	51.6

s:

Columns (1) and (3): Great Ten Years, p. 60.

Column (2) = Column (1) times 63,000.

Column (4) = Column (3) times 50,000.

Column (5) = Column (2) plus column (4).

Column (6) = Column (5) times 0.8.

Highway Construction

Data on the mileage of highways constructed and restored in 1952-55 are also taken from Great Ten Years, p. 63. For 1956 and 1957, mileages given are not usable because they include many simple and substandard roads. Mileage data given in the 1956 Communique and FFYP Communique provided the basis for our estimate for those two years.

The total amount of earth work done in connection with the highway program in 1952 is given at 24 million cubic meters, and the total mileage of highway constructed and restored at 11,168 kilometers.[56] The earth work per kilometer is computed at 2,150 cubic meters. On the assumption that such earth work per kilometer did not change significantly in subsequent years, the earth work accomplished in highway projects is obtained by multiplying the mileage in 1953-57 by 2,150 cubic meters. As in the case of railroad construction, 80 per cent of the earth work is assumed to have been done by work brigades. The results are given in Table H-16.

Water Conservation Projects

Dredging rivers, repairing and reconstructing dikes and dams, and many other flood-prevention and water-conservation projects require tremendous manual labor. The achievements in this field are usually expressed directly in terms of earth work completed. The annual volume of earth work done for 1952-57 and our estimated portion done by work brigades are presented in Table H-17.

The earth work in construction projects was done mainly by manual labor with very little mechanical help. The productivity of this kind of manual labor was very low. A Communist high official indicated that in the early 1950s the digging and moving of one cubic meter of earth (including stone

Table H-16

EARTH WORK IN HIGHWAY CONSTRUCTION, 1952-57

Year	Mileage added (kilometers) (1)	Total earth work (million cubic meters) (2)	Earth work done by work brigades (million cubic meters) (3)
1952	11,168	24.0	19.2
1953	9,654	20.8	16.6
1954	7,164	15.4	12.3
1955	8,138	17.5	14.0
1956	17,499	37.6	30.1
1957	22,814	49.1	39.3

Notes:

Column (1). 1952-55 figures are from Great Ten Years, p. 63. Mileage is taken from 1956 Communique. Mileage in 1957 is obtained by deducting the 1956 year-end mileage from the 1957 year-end mileage given in 1956 Communique and First Five Year Plan. (Figures for 1956 and later years are not usable because of their inclusion of simple country roads.)

Column (2). Column (1) times 2,150, except 1952. For that year the total volume of earth work is given by Economic Yearbook, 1953, Hong Kong, Ching-chi tao-pao-she, 1953, p. 24. One kilometer of highway constructed requires 2,150 cubic meters of earth work.

Column (3). Column (2) times 0.8, the ratio of earth work done by work brigades.

Table H-17

EARTH WORK IN WATER CONSERVATION, 1952-57

(million cubic meters)

Year	Total earth work accomplished (1)	Earth work done by forced labor (2)
1952	1,110.0	888.0
1953	541.0	432.8
1954	659.0	527.2
1955	1,415.0	1,132.0
1956	1,500.0	1,200.0
1957	1,650.0	1,320.0

Notes:

Column (1). Figures for 1952, 1954, and 1955 are taken from the respective annual Communiques. The figure for 1953 was derived as follows: according to Fu Tso-yi, Communist Minister of Water Conservancy, the water conservation projects completed during 1949-54 amounted to 2,900 million cubic meters and from 1949 to 1952 to 1,700 million cubic meters. (See Jen-min shou-ts'e (People's Handbook), Tientsin, Ta-kung-pao-she, 1955, p. 514.) The earth work accomplished during 1953-54 was 2,900 - 1,700 = 1,200 million cubic meters. Since the earth work accomplished in 1954 is 659 million cubic meters (1954 Communique), that in 1953 should be 1,200 - 659 = 541 million cubic meters. Figures for 1956 and 1957 are not readily available; however, the total amount of earth work done in the first five year plan period, 1953-57, was reported to be about 6,300 million cubic meters. (See Jen-min shou-ts'e (People's Handbook), Peiping, Ta-kung-pao-she, 1958, p. 533.) Deducting the amount completed during 1953-55, 2,600 cubic meters, from the five-year total, the aggregate work done for 1956 and 1957 should be about 3,700 million cubic meters. This figure is much higher than that reported for the first three years. Since there is no specific explanation for this sudden increase, the earth work reported for 1956-57 could probably include a part of the work done in the small irrigation projects and not included in previous reports on water conservation. This is evidenced by the large expansion of irrigated acreage in the last two years of the first plan period. According to the Communist reports, the total increase of irrigated acreage during the first period was 210 million mow (ibid.), and this increase in the first three years, 1953-55, was only 20 million mow (HHPYK, No. 17, 1956, p. 42). Therefore, the increase of irrigated acreage in 1956 and 1957 should have been 190 million mow, which is nearly ten times the increase that occurred in the first

Notes (continued):

three years. To eliminate this probable duplication of accounting, 15 per cent of the total earth work done in 1956 and 1957 is discounted for portions of farm irrigation projects to arrive at a net water conservation accomplishment of 3,150 million cubic meters for these two years. Based on the scattered progress reports of water conservation jobs, more work was done in 1957 than in 1956; hence, the total amount of work of 3,150 million cubic meters is arbitrarily split into 1,500 for 1956 and 1,650 cubic meters for 1957.

Column (2). Column (1) times 0.8.

and cement) required one whole day's work of manual labor.[57] In other words the value of one cubic meter of earth work is equivalent to the value produce by one day's work of an unskilled worker. Value added per unskilled worker, estimated at 0.5 yuan, is roughly the average value added per day by the agricultural workers, handicraftsmen, and old-fashioned transportation workers.[58] Total value of earth work done by the work brigades in each category is then obtained by multiplying the amount of work by the unit value of 0.5 yuan. The net values so computed are given in Table 50.

In addition to the temporary workers drafted from various occupational groups to work on the public construction projects, civilians under the Communist regime are also compelled to serve for a certain period each year as militiamen. The function of this group appears to be similar to that of the national guards. However, the draftees do perform many productive jobs beyond the call of their normal duties. These include the protection of forests, maintenance of public roads, cooking and laundering for the cadres, and numerous odd jobs.[59]

The total number of militia is said to have been about 12 million men and women in 1952.[60] The draftees are not known to have received any regula pay, but those who served in remote places might have been given food, sleeping accommodations, and sometimes uniforms.

There is no information on the amount of productive work done by the militiamen in each year. Beside their military duties, we assume that each one contributed 2 days per month, or 24 days a year, of his free service to the state for those productive works of which the value added has not been included in other sectors, and the net value added by his service is also 0.5 yuan per day. The annual value produced per each militiaman would, therefore, be 12 yuan and the total value produced by the whole militia force in 1952 is computed at 12 million times 12 = 144 million yuan.

The size and the function of the militia in 1953-57 are not known to have changed from 1952. Hence, the net value produced by them in each of these years is assumed to be the same as in 1952, that is, 144 million yuan at 1952 prices.

FOOTNOTES TO APPENDIX H

1. The derivation of estimates for 1933 in 1952 prices and for 1952-5 in 1933 prices was explained in Chapter IV.

2. The amount of depreciation and the price of coal and iron ore per ton are given in Ou, National Income, Vol. II, pp. 13-14; and Vol. I, Table 3, p. 53.

3. See Table 40.

4. The modern sector refers to those portions of mineral output that are presumably included in the Communist gross value of industrial producti

5. See Table 57.

6. The number of miners is estimated in Ou, National Income, Vol. II, pp. 19-28, and the ratio is obtained on the basis of data in Vol. I, pp. 5

7. SSB, Industry Study, p. 97.

8. The figure for China proper is the sum of electricity generated by the utilities and by the industrial power plants for their own use, given in Electric Utility Regulation Board, National Construction Commission, "Electric Power Development in China," Transactions of the Third World Powe Conference, Vol. II, Washington, D.C., 1938, p. 112; and Statistical Abstra 1945, p. 85. The estimate for Manchuria is given in Manchuria Electric Company, Manshû niokeru denki jigyô gaisetsu (A Survey of the Electric Powe Industry in Manchuria), Hsinking, 1938, p. 12.

9. Great Ten Years, p. 69.

10. The first estimate is obtained by dividing the gross output by the physical quantity of output for 1933 given in Liu, Income, Table 15, p. 44. The second and third estimates are derived in a similar manner on the basis

of data on gross output and electricity production given in Ou, National Income, Vol. II, Tables 3 and 4, pp. 68-69.

11. TCKT, No. 4, 1957, p. 7.

12. The prices are 0.19 yuan per ton in NFJP, Canton, August 3, 1952, p. 3, and 0.60 yuan per ton in Nankai Economic Research Institute, Nankai chih-shu tzu-liao chun-pien (Source Materials on Nankai Indices), Peiping, T'ung-chi chu-pan-she, 1958, p. 320.

13. Computed from data on prices of coal in Table H-1.

14. Output of hydroelectric power in 1952 totalled 1.26 billion kwh. (SSB, Industry Study, p. 64.) Deducting this figure from the total output of 7.26 billion kwh, we obtain the output generated by thermoelectric plants.

15. SSB, "Technological Level of Industrial Production in China," TCKT, No. 8, April 1957, p. 31.

16. The ten cities are Shanghai, Nanking, Tientsin, Tsinan, Canton, Sian, Chungking, Shanyang, Hankow, and Taiyuan. For sources, see KSHW, Canton, December 3, 1952; SSJP, Taiyuan, August 31, 1952; CCJP, Hankow, July 6, 1952; and CCCP, Shanghai, Vol. 13, No. 25, December 20, 1951, p. 498.

17. The amount of electricity supplied to consumers in 1952 totalled 6.23 billion kwh. (SSB, Industry Study, p. 48.) The amount of power plant consumption and loss is thus equal to total output minus electricity supplied to consumers (7.26 - 6.23 billion kwh).

18. This price is the rate charged for industrial use of electricity. It is derived as follows. The national average price in 1952 is given at 0.06 yuan per kwh. Available data on electricity rates indicate that the price structure consists of two differential rates, household and industrial. The latter is generally one-half of the former. (People's Daily, March 2,

1950; HHJP, Chungking, April 19, 1952; NFJP, Canton, July 2, 1952; HSCJP, Soochow, July 9, 1952.) Household use of electricity can be calculated at 11 billion kwh, that is, 15 per cent of total output from data on total electricity supplied to all consumers and output supplied to industrial users given in SSB, Industry Study, p. 48. On the basis of this informatic the price charged for industrial use of electricity, 0.052 yuan per kwh, ca be calculated from the following relation: 0.15 times 2x plus 0.85x = 0.06 where x represents the price for industrial use.

19. Computed on the basis of prices in 1933 and 1952 given in Table H

20. Computed from data on the price of coal in 1933 and 1952 given in Table H-1. This price index comes close to the price index of fuels (254 per cent in 1952 with 1933 as 100) computed from data given in Nankai Economic Research Institute, pp. 15, 17.

21. See Appendix F, Table F-15.

22. Obtained by multiplying 10 per cent by the ratio of the price index of fuels to that of water supply, that is, 10 times 250/267 = 9.

23. The price index of water supply is assumed to be the same as that of raw materials in our calculation of the amount of raw materials for 1952 in 1952 prices.

24. Table H-4.

25. SSB, Industry Study, p. 67; however, these figures are considerab lower than the estimates for 1953, 1955, and 1957 obtained from other sourc at 133,000, 185,000, and 290,000. The figure for 1953 is given in Jen-min shou ts'e, 1955 (People's Handbook), Shanghai, Ta-kung-pao-she, 1955, p. 38 The union members in the electric power industry in 1955 are reported at 151,691, or 82 per cent of the total number of workers. (Ibid., 1957, p. 2

The total number of workers is calculated at 151,691/0.82 = 185,000. The figure for 1957 is given in KJJP, Peiping, December 8, 1957, p. 7.

26. For data used in this computation, see output data for 1933 and 1952 in Table H-4 and the numbers of workers in these two industries in 1933.

27. The prices of cement in 1933 and 1952 are given in Appendix F, Table F-6, and limestone prices in Table H-1. The price of lumber in 1933 is computed at 18 yuan per cubic meter on the basis of gross value and amount of lumber used by factories in Shanghai given in Lieu, Industry Survey, Vol. II, Table 14, p. 30. The quantity of lumber is given in square feet which is expressed in cubic meters on the assumption that boards commonly used for construction are 1/2-inch thick. The price of lumber in 1952 is given under Forestry Products in Appendix D.

28. The output of cement, limestone, and lumber at users' prices are 35, 20, and 517 million yuan. The proportions are 6, 4, and 90 per cent.

29. The net value added per worker in handicrafts is equal to 130 yuan per worker. (See the discussion under Other Agricultural Sectors in Chapter IV.) Net value added in mining is calculated at 270 yuan per worker from data on total net value added and number of workers given in Tables H-1 and H-3. The estimate of 220 yuan for construction is the weighted average of these two figures, the weights being two-thirds for mining and one-third for handicrafts.

30. Yang Po, "On the Distribution of National Income in China," CCYC, No. 6, December 1957, p. 5.

31. SSB, "A Preliminary Study of the Production and Distribution of China's National Income," TCYC, No. 1, January 1958, p. 11.

32. Basic construction in current prices for 1953-57 is given at 8.00, 9.07, 9.30, 14.80, and 13.83 billion yuan in Great Ten Years, p. 46. The

figures are then deflated by the price index of basic construction for 1952-57 with 1952 as 100 given in Table 74 to obtain basic construction in 1953-57 in 1952 prices.

33. The Nankai Economic Research Institute gives the list of fuels on p. 5 and the wholesale price index on pp. 15 and 17.

34. Djang Gee-hung, "An Estimate of the Working Population of China," She-hui ko-hsueh tsa-chih (Quarterly Review of Social Sciences), Shanghai, Vol. IX, No. 2, December 1947, p. 78.

35. Net value added per worker in agriculture is derived at 92 yuan by dividing net value added in agriculture given at 18.76 billion yuan in Table 36, by the total number of agricultural workers given at 204.9 million in Table 11. Net value added per worker in the handicraft industry is estimated at 130 yuan by Ou (National Income, Vol. I, pp. 73-74).

36. The derivation of the price index of handicraft products is given in the discussion of Table I-2 in Appendix I.

37. For net value added in these three industries in 1952-57, see Table 8. Net value added by modern transportation and communications in 1952-57 is given in Table H-9, and net value added by old-fashioned transportation in 1957 is given in Table H-10.

38. If the adjusted estimate of net value added by agriculture, manufacturing, and mining in 1952-57 given in Table 68, is used to compute the index, the following adjusted estimates of net value added by old-fashioned transportation are obtained for the years 1952 through 1957: 2.69, 2.31, 2.08, 2.22, 2.26, and 2.43 billion 1952 yuan.

39. The corresponding adjusted estimates of depreciation based on the adjusted estimates of net value added for 1952-57 given above are 0.03, 0.03 0.02, 0.02, 0.02, and 0.03 billion 1952 yuan.

40. Ou, National Income, Vol. I, pp. 100-105, and Vol. II, pp. 247-268.

41. Liu, Income, p. 55, and Ou, National Income, Vol. I, pp. 137, 140.

42. Liu, Income, p. 60.

43. The total money wage paid to 15.02 million workers and employees in 1952 is given at 6.7 billion yuan. (SSB, "Statistical Materials Concerning Improvements in the Workers' Living Conditions," TCKT, No. 14, July 1957, p. 13.) Fringe benefit payments in 1952 totalled 0.66 billion yuan. (People's Daily, October 7, 1957, p. 3.) The average annual wage rate is equal to (6.7 + 0.66)/15.02 = 490 yuan per worker.

44. See Table 62.

45. The average wage rates for 1952-57 are given at 446, 496, 519, 534, 610, and 637 yuan in Great Ten Years, p. 191. The wage rates for 1952 used in our calculation are the Communist figures raised by 9 per cent to allow for fringe benefits.

46. The cost-of-living index is given at 100, 105.6, 106.9, 107.3, 107.1, and 109.2 per cent for 1953-57 with 1952 as 100 in SSB, "Changes in the Market Prices in 1957 and Its Effects on People's Living Conditions," TCYC, No. 4, April 1958, p. 25; and HHPYK, No. 8, 1959, p. 51.

47. A Japanese research institute estimated the 1953 number at 2.9 to 3.4 million, see Tsu kuo (China Weekly), Hong Kong, No. 13, March 30, 1953, p. 10; R. B. Rigg gives a figure of 2.7 million in "Red Army in Retreat," Current History, Vol. 32, No. 185, January 1957, p. 4; David Chipp reported a figure of 2.5 million in the Washington Post and Times Herald, July 28, 1957, p. A-7; and an estimate of 2.5 million, presumably by the Communist general, Lin Piao, is given in the New York Times, February 16, 1960, p. 6.

48. Ti Chao-pai, "Fiscal and Economic Conditions in 1950," quoted in Ho Yu-wen, Chung-kung ts'ai-cheng chieh-foh (An Analysis of Communist China's Public Finance), Hong Kong, The Asia Press, 1953, pp. 91-92.

49. People's Daily, April 2, 1952.

50. Net value added by finance, government, and trade in 1933 and 1952-57 is shown in Table 8. If the adjusted estimate of net value added by these three industries given in Table 68 is used, the corresponding adjusted estimate of depreciation for the years 1933 and 1952-57 amounts to 0.10, 0.14, 0.16, 0.17, 0.18, 0.20, and 0.21 billion 1952 yuan, and 0.04, 0.05, 0.06, 0.06, 0.07, 0.08, and 0.08 billion 1933 yuan.

51. Yang Hsi-mung, A Study of the Living Standards of Workers in Shanghai, quoted in Ou, National Income, Vol. I, p. 119; and S. P. Gamble, How Chinese Families Live in Peiping, 1933, Table 2, p. 315, Table 12, p. 321, quoted in Liu, Income, p. 33.

52. Farm Economy, p. 400, and Land Utilization, Vol. I, p. 369.

53. Nankai Economic Research Institute, pp. 49, 69. The figure for 1952 is the average for January to April only.

54. The term "earth work" used in this study includes stone and cement work.

55. The Communists reported that a total of 30 million cubic meters of earth work was involved in building up the 505 kilometers of Chengtu-Chungking railway. Earth work per kilometer was 59,400 cubic meters (Economic Weekly, Hong Kong, combined issue 290-291, September 30, 1952, p. 16). In building up the 347 kilometer Tienshui-Lanchow railway, the total earth work was reported to be 23 million cubic meters, or 66,300 cubic meters per kilometer (Huai Fu, "New China's Great Achievements in the Reconstruction of Transportation during the Past Year," Ching-chi nien-p 1953 (Economic Yearbook, 1953), Hong Kong, Ching-chi tao-pao-she, 1953, pp. 23-27). The average of these two, about 63,000 cubic meters of earth work per kilometer, is used here.

56. Ibid., p. 24.

57. Fu Tso-yi, Communist Minister of Water Conservancy, "Our Country's Great Achievements of Water Conservancy in the Past Three Years," San-nien-lai hsin-chung-kuo ching-chi ti cheng-chiu (New China's Economic Achievements during the Past Three Years), Peiping, Jen-min chu-pan-she, 1953, p. 142.

58. Total net value added by agriculture, handicrafts, and old-fashioned transportation has been estimated at 34.19 + 4.72 + 2.65 = 41.56 billion yuan in 1952 (Table 8). Total number of workers in these three sectors in 1952 has been estimated at 199.89 + 13.50 + 10.90 = 224.29 million (Table 11). The net value added per worker per day in these industries is therefore estimated at 41.56/224.29/365 = 0.5 yuan.

59. CCJP, Hankow, July 29, 1952; and HHJP, Chungking, May 20, 1953.

60. According to Chou En-lai, Communist premier, the number of militiamen in 1951 was about 12 million (KMJP, Peiping, November 3, 1951). The figure for 1952 was said to be from 2 to 10 per cent of local population in various localities (CCJP, Hankow, June 7, 1952). Assuming that the number constantly kept in service was close to the lower percentage, the number of militiamen in 1952 can be estimated by applying the 2 per cent to the total population of 569 million, or about 12 million.

61. CCJP, Hankow, December 26, 1951.

Appendix I

PRICE DEFLATORS FOR DOMESTIC PRODUCT AND EXPENDITURE

This appendix presents the price indexes that have either previously been used in this study or that can be readily derived from the estimates already obtained, and explains the derivation of those indexes that have not been given elsewhere. In the first two sections, the price indexes for the individual industries and the major types of expenditures for 1952, with 1933 as 100, are given. The third section explains the price indexes for 1957, with 1952 as 100, that are used to derive product and expenditure estimates in constant 1957 prices.

PRICE INDEXES FOR GROSS VALUE AND VALUE ADDED BY INDUSTRIES, 1952

Table I-1 summarizes the price indexes for value added by industries for 1952, with 1933 as 100. The sources and methods used in deriving these figures are as follows:

1. Agriculture. The Laspeyre index, 180 per cent for 1952 with 1933 as 100, is the deflator derived by dividing the estimate of net value added for 1933 in 1952 prices by the corresponding figure in 1933 prices given in Table 36. The Paasche index is similarly derived at 186 per cent on the basis of the estimates of net value added for 1952 in constant 1933 and 1952 prices given in Table 36. The ideal index is the geometric mean of the two indexes.

2. Manufacturing. The Laspeyre indexes are obtained by dividing the gross output and gross value added for 1933 in 1952 prices by those in 1933 prices given in Appendix F, Table F-6. The Paasche indexes are derived by the same procedure. (See Appendix F, Table F-13.) The ideal index is the geometric mean of the two price indexes.

Table I-1

PRICE INDEXES FOR VALUE ADDED BY INDUSTRIES, 1952[a]

(1933 = 100)

	Laspeyre (1933 quantity as weights)	Ideal	Paasche (1952 quantity as weights)
1. Agriculture	181	183	186
2. Manufacturing			
Producers' goods			
Gross value	482	488	495
Gross value added	520	582	652
Consumers' goods			
Gross value	329	332	335
Gross value added	497	490	483
3. Handicrafts	216	218	220
4. Mining	242	238	234
5. Utilities	109	104	99
6. Construction	304	304	304
7. Transportation and communications			
Modern	254	254	254
Old-fashioned	216	218	220
8. Trade			
Stores and restaurants	350	350	350
Peddlers	216	218	220
9. Government			
Civil service	163	163	163
Military service	216	218	220
10. Finance	163	163	163
11. Services	163	163	163
12. Residential rent	194	194	194
13. Work brigades	216	218	220
14. Net domestic product	206	213	220

Note:

[a]Price indexes for the output of producers' goods and consumers' goods are also given in this table.

3. Handicrafts. The derivation of the price indexes for handicraft products is explained with reference to Table I-2. The price index with 1933 output as weights is computed at 216 per cent for 1952, with 1933 as 100, by dividing the gross value of output of nine products for 1933 in 1952 prices by that in 1933 prices. The price index with 1952 output as weights is derived at 220 per cent by a similar procedure on the basis of gross value of output of these nine products for 1952 in constant 1933 and 1952 prices. The ideal index, 218 per cent, is the geometric mean of the two price indexes.

4. Mining. The computation of the price indexes for mineral products is explained with reference to Table I-3. The price index for 1952, with 1933 output as weights, is obtained at 242 per cent by dividing the gross value of these six products for 1933 in 1952 prices by that in 1952 prices. The price index with 1952 output as weights is obtained at 234 per cent by a similar procedure. The geometric mean of these two indexes is equal to 238 per cent.

5. Utilities. Computed from data given in Appendix H, Table H-4.

6. Construction. See the discussion in Appendix H, especially Table H-6.

7. Modern transportation and communications. See Appendix H.

Old-fashioned transportation. The price indexes are assumed to be the same as for handicrafts.

8. Trade -- stores and restaurants. See the section on trade in Chapter IV.

Trade -- peddlers. The price indexes are assumed to be the same as for handicrafts.

OUTPUT, PRICES, AND GROSS VALUE OF NINE HANDICRAFT PRODUCTS,

1933 AND 1952

	Output		Price		Gross Value			
					1933		1952	
	1933	1952	1933	1952	In 1933 prices	In 1952 prices	In 1933 prices	In 1952 prices
	(million piculs)		(yuan/picul)		(million yuan)			
Wheat flour	282.80	177.90	7.6	13.0	2,149.3	3,676.4	1,336.8	2,286.7
Tea	3.00	0.99	59.0	160.0	177.0	480.0	58.4	158.4
Sugar	5.96	4.04	7.9	17.0	47.1	101.3	31.9	68.7
Soybean Sauce	15.00	16.00	9.0	16.0	135.0	240.0	144.0	256.0
Wine and liquor	12.50	5.32	13.0	30.0	162.5	375.0	69.2	159.6
Edible Vegetable oils	28.29	12.78	18.3	36.7	517.7	1,038.2	233.9	469.0
Paper	7.18	4.63	7.8	23.5	56.0	168.7	36.1	108.8
Cotton Yarn	3.04	3.09	41.4	163.9	125.8	498.2	127.9	506.4
Cotton Cloth[a]	74.00	52.03	7.0	24.6	518.0	1,820.4	364.2	1,279.9
Total					3,888.4	8,398.2	2,402.4	5,293.5

(Notes to this table are on the following page.)

Note:

[a]Output in millions of bolts; price in yuan per bolt.

Sources:

1933. Data on output and prices of the nine handicraft products are given in Appendix G. Specific computations made for edible vegetable oils, paper, and sugar are as follows:

Edible vegetable oils. Total output in 1933 is given at 33.5 million piculs in Table G-4. Gross handicraft output of these oils accounted for 719.9/875.4 = 82 per cent of the total. Applying this percentage to 33.5 million piculs, we derive the output of 28.29 million piculs shown in the table above. The price of edible vegetable oils is obtained at 18.3 yuan per picul by dividing the gross output, 613.5 million yuan, by the quantity of output, 33.5 million piculs.

Paper. On the basis of data on output and gross output of native paper in nine provinces and one city (compiled by Ou, National Income, Vol. II, pp. 152-153), an average price of paper at 7.82 yuan per picul is derived. Total gross output of paper for 1933 has been estimated at 56.2 million yuan. Output of paper is calculated at 56.2/7.82 = 7.18 million piculs.

Sugar. Appendix G gives the gross value of sugar output at 47.2 million yuan. The price of sugar is computed at 7.4 yuan per picul on the basis of 6,734 million piculs (Ou, National Income, Vol. II, pp. 138-139

1952. See the discussion in Appendix G under 1952-57.

Table I-3

OUTPUT, PRICES, AND GROSS VALUE OF SIX MINERAL PRODUCTS, 1933 and 1952

	Output		Price		Gross value			
					1933		1952	
	1933	1952	1933	1952	In 1933 prices	In 1952 prices	In 1933 prices	In 1952 prices
	(thousand tons)		(yuan per ton)		(million yuan)			
Coal	28,379.0	63,528.0	5	12.5	141.9	354.7	317.6	784.1
Copper	0.5	2.2	585	2,530	0.3	1.3	1.3	5.6
Zinc	0.2	6.7	210	3,685	(*)	0.7	1.4	24.7
Tin	8.0	8.0	2,327	3,200	18.6	25.6	18.6	25.6
Antimony regulus	11.0	8.0	201	2,530	2.2	27.8	1.6	20.2
Crude oil	91.0	436.0	140	160	12.7	14.6	61.0	69.8
Total					175.8	424.7	401.6	1,940.0

Note:

(*) Less than 0.06 million yuan.

Source:

Compiled from data given in Appendix H, Table H-1.

9. Government -- civil service. This price index is derived by dividing the total wage payments to government employees for 1933 in 1952 prices by the corresponding estimate in 1933 prices given in Appendix H under 1952-57.

Government -- military service. The price indexes are assumed to be the same as for handicrafts.

10-11. Finance, services. The price indexes are assumed to be the same as for civilian government services.

12. Residential rent. See the discussion in Appendix H under the same title.

13. Work brigades. The price index is assumed to be the same as for handicrafts.

14. Net domestic product. Computed from data on net domestic product for 1933 and 1952 in constant 1933 and 1952 prices given in Tables 8 and 9.

PRICE INDEXES FOR DOMESTIC EXPENDITURE, 1952

Table I-4 presents a summary of the price indexes for the major categories of domestic expenditure. The sources and methods used in deriving these estimates are as follows:

1. Personal consumption. The price index for 1952, with 1933 quantities as weights and with 1933 as 100, is derived by dividing total personal consumption in 1933, in 1952 prices, by that in 1933 prices, that is 56.53/28.02 = 202 per cent. The corresponding figure with 1952 quantities as weights is derived similarly on the basis of total personal consumption in 1952 in constant 1933 and 1952 prices, that is, 54.60/27.56 = 198 per cent.[1] The geometric mean of these index numbers is equal to 200 per cent.

Table I-4

PRICE INDEXES FOR DOMESTIC EXPENDITURES, 1952

(1933 = 100)

	Laspeyre (1933 quantity as weights)	Ideal	Paasche (1952 quantity as weights)
1. Personal consumption	202	200	198
a. Food	183	187	191
b. Clothing	348	340	332
c. Residential rent	194	194	194
d. Fuels and light	208	208	208
e. Miscellaneous	206	170	141
2. Communal services	228	235	242
3. Government consumption			
a. Goods	329	332	335
b. Services	163	163	163
4. Net domestic investment	500	500	500
5. Net domestic expenditure	208	215	222

1.a. Food. The price index numbers are the implicit deflators derived by dividing food consumption in 1952 prices by 1933 prices. With 1933 quantities as weights, the price index for 1952, with 1933 as 100, is 33.19/18.13 = 183 per cent. With 1952 quantities as weights, the price index is 33.08/17.28 = 191 per cent.[2] The geometric mean of these two figures is 187 per cent.

1.b. Clothing. The price index with 1933 quantities as weights is derived by dividing clothing consumption in 1933, in 1952 prices, by 1933 prices, that is, 7.56/2.17 = 348 per cent for 1952, with 1933 as 100. With 1952 quantities as weights, the price index is equal to 7.89/2.38 = 332 per cent.[3] The geometric mean of these two figures is 340 per cent.

1.c. Residential rent. See Appendix H under the same heading.

1.d. Fuels and light. In China, materials used for fuels consist mainly of stalks and straw, wood, and coal briquettes, and for the majority of the population, light is provided by burning vegetable oils. According to the field survey by Buck, kaoliang stalks are one of the most important sources of fuel among the stalks and straws of various crops.[4] The price index of other stalks and straw is assumed to vary with that of kaoliang stalks which, in turn, is assumed to be the same as that for kaoliang over the same period.

To determine the price index of fuels and light the following procedure is used. The price index of kaoliang (and hence stalks) is computed at 178 per cent for 1952, with 1933 as 100.[5] The price index for fuel wood is roughly estimated at 162 per cent for 1952, with 1933 as 100.[6] The price index for coal briquettes is assumed to vary with that of coal which is computed at 250 per cent for 1952, with 1933 as 100.[7] The price index of vegetable oils is assumed to be the same as for edible vegetable oils estimated at 245 per cent for 1952, with 1933 as 100.[8] The unweighted average of these four index numbers, that is, 208 per cent, is taken to be the price index for fuels and light.

1.e. Miscellaneous personal consumption. For 1933, the price index for miscellaneous personal consumption is assumed to be the same as for domestic product as a whole, that is, 206 per cent for 1952, with 1933 as 100.[9] For 1952, the price index is derived by dividing the estimates of miscellaneous consumption for 1952, in 1952 prices, by that in 1933 prices.[10]

2. Communal services. Computed from data given in Table 78.

3.a. Government consumption: goods. The price indexes are assumed to be the same as for manufactured consumers' goods given in Table I-1.

3.b. Government consumption: services. See Table I-1.

4. Net domestic investment. The price index for investment for 1933 is computed by dividing the estimate of investment for 1933 in 1952 prices by that in 1933 prices. Investment in 1933, in 1952 prices, is derived as follows: Net domestic expenditure for 1933, in 1952 prices, is first derived at 61.76 billion yuan by summing up net domestic production in 1952 prices already obtained, and import balance of trade given at 2.27 billion yuan.[11] Deducting personal consumption, communal services, and government consumption for 1933, in 1952 prices, estimated at 56.53, 0.32, and 2.36 billion 1952 yuan,[12] from net domestic expenditure of 61.76 billion yuan, we obtain the estimate of net domestic investment for 1933, in 1952 prices, at 2.55 billion yuan. Net domestic investment in 1933 prices has already been estimated at 0.51 billion yuan.[13] The price deflator for investment is thus calculated at 500 per cent for 1952 with 1933 as 100. Available

statistical data are insufficient for us to compute a price index for investment in 1952 separately. We assume that the price index obtained above is applicable to the estimate for 1952-57 in 1952 prices. Furthermore, for lack of a better alternative, the same price index is assumed to be applicable to depreciation charges.

PRICE INDEXES FOR DOMESTIC PRODUCTION AND DOMESTIC EXPENDITURE, 1957 (1952 =

The procedure for deriving the product and expenditure estimates in constant 1957 prices involves multiplying the estimates in constant 1952 prices by appropriate price indexes for 1957 with 1952 as 100. In all cases the price indexes are drawn from Communist sources, and, as previously observed, Communist price indexes (particularly those for personal consumption) generally tend to understate the extent of price increases.[14] Unfortunately, the magnitude of the error cannot be estimated, for it would require just the detailed statistical information we lack.

The price index used to deflate personal consumption is the Communist workers' cost-of-living index for 12 cities, given at 109.2 per cent for 1957 with 1952 as 100.[15] The same index is used for deflating government purchases of services and income payments to those in communal services. The price index for government consumption of goods and for the expenditure of goods for communal services is the Communist retail price index for 1957 given at 108.6 per cent with 1952 = 100.[16] That for investment was estimated in Chapter V in the text following Table 74. The same price index is used for gross and net investment. Estimates of domestic expenditure by end use for 1933 and 1952-57, in 1957 prices, are derived by applying these price indexes to the corresponding estimates of personal consumption, government consumption of goods and services, and investment in 1952 prices. The results were presented in Table 10.

The deflation of domestic product and its components is carried out separately for the following items: domestic product; agriculture, factories, mining, and utilities; and an "others" category. On the assumption that the price index for domestic product for 1957, with 1952 as 100, is the same as for domestic expenditure over the same period, estimates of domestic product in 1957 prices are derived by multiplying the estimates in 1952 prices by a factor equal to the ratio of domestic expenditure in 1957 prices to the corresponding estimates in 1952 prices.[17]

Net value added by agriculture for 1933 and 1952-57, in 1957 prices, is derived by applying to the estimates in 1952 prices a price index of 106.3 per cent in 1957, with 1952 as 100, derived on the basis of rough estimates of net value added by agriculture in 1957 in constant 1952 and 1957 prices. Gross output in 1957, including preliminary processing of farm products, handicraft products for farm home consumption, and processing of farm products for consumers, is given at 60.35 billion 1952 yuan.[18] Deducting the gross output of the three subsidiary items estimated at 2.35, 6.94, and 0.36 billion 1952 yuan[19] from 60.35 billion, we obtain the gross output of agricultural products in 1952 prices at 50.70 billion yuan. The comparable estimate in 1957 prices is given at 53.70 billion.[20] The price index for gross output is, therefore, equal to 53.70/50.70 = 105.9 per cent in 1957 with 1952 as 100.

Deductible costs incurred in agricultural production in 1952 prices is estimated at 22 per cent of gross output, that is, 13.28 billion yuan. Of this total, purchases from the nonagricultural sector amount to 10.02 billion, the residual being purchases from the agricultural sector itself. Net value added in 1952 prices is thus derived at 37.42 billion yuan by deducting total purchases (13.28) from gross output (50.70).

On the assumption that the price index of retail products sold to farmers, given at 101.6 per cent in 1957 with 1952 as 100,[21] is applicable to purchases of nonagricultural input by the farmers, and that the price index of gross agricultural product estimated at 105.9 per cent in 1957, with 1952 as 100, is applicable to intrasector purchases of input, we derive the estimate of purchases from the nonagricultural sector in 1957 prices at 3.31 billion yuan, and intrasector purchases at 10.61 billion, totalling 13.92 billion yuan. Net value added in 1957 prices thus amounts to 53.70 minus 13.92 billion, that is, 39.78 billion yuan. Dividing this figure by net value added in 1952 prices (37.42 billion), we obtain the price index of 106.3 per cent in 1957 with 1952 as 100.

The price index for net value added by factories, handicrafts, mining, and utilities is assumed to be the same as the price index for the gross industrial output derived at 89.8 per cent in 1957, with 1952 as 100, by dividing the Communist estimates of gross industrial output for 1957, in 1957 prices, by that in 1952 prices.[22] This price index is then applied to the estimates of net value added by these four sectors in 1952 prices to arrive at the net value added in 1957 prices.

Net value added in industries other than agriculture, manufacturing, handicrafts, mining, and utilities in 1957 prices is derived as a residual by deducting the estimates for these industries from domestic product in 1957 prices. The results are summarized in Table 9.

FOOTNOTES TO APPENDIX I

1. For estimates of personal consumption for 1933 and 1952 in constant 1933 and 1952 prices, see Table 10.

2. For estimates of food consumption for 1933 and 1952 in constant 1933 and 1952 prices, see Table 79.

3. For estimates of clothing consumption for 1933 and 1952 in constant 1933 and 1952 prices, see Table 88.

4. Land Utilization, Vol. I, Table 24, p. 238, and discussion, p. 239.

5. The price of kaoliang is estimated at 2.8 yuan per picul in 1933 and 5.0 yuan per picul in 1952. See Appendixes B and D.

6. An arithmetic mean of nine quotations for the price of fuel wood in 1933 is calculated at 1.30 yuan per picul on the basis of data given in Survey. The average of five price quotations for 1952 is computed at 2.10 yuan per picul. (Sources of these five quotations are TKP, Shanghai, March 20, 1952, p. 3; CCJP, Hankow, August 31, 1952, p. 4; NPJP, Ningpo, August 31, 1952, p. 3; KSJP, Nanchang, September 2, 1952, p. 4; SNJP, Wuhsi, September 4, 1952, p. 4.)

7. The price of coal is estimated at 5 yuan per ton in 1933 and 12.5 yuan per ton in 1952. See Table I-3.

8. See Appendix F, Table F-6.

9. See Table I-1.

10. For miscellaneous personal consumption for 1952, in 1933 and 1952 prices, see Table 10.

11. For net domestic product in 1933 in 1952 prices, see Table 8, and for import balance, see Table 87.

12. See Table 10.

13. See Table 71.

14. See the discussion on the expenditure gaps and inflationary pressure in Chapter III, including Figure 10.

15. FFYP Communique, No. 8, 1959, p. 51.

16. Great Ten Years, p. 153.

17. For a summary of these estimates, see Tables 8 and 10.

18. Great Ten Years.

19. See Appendix J, Table J-1.

20. Great Ten Years.

21. Ibid.

22. Gross industrial output (including handicrafts) in 1957 is given at 78.39 billion and 70.40 billion yuan in constant 1952 and 1957 prices. Ibid., p. 76.

Appendix J

RECONSTRUCTED COMMUNIST ESTIMATE OF DOMESTIC PRODUCT AND ITS RECONCILIATION WITH THE ADJUSTED ESTIMATE, 1952-57

This appendix explains the reconstruction of the Communist estimate of domestic product and its reconciliation with the adjusted estimate for 1952-57 presented in Table 70. The four sections below will describe the data, sources, and methods used in deriving the following four major items given in the table: the reconstructed Communist estimate; adjustments of the reconstructed Communist estimate because of differences in concept, coverage, and classification; the unexplained balance; and the adjusted estimate.

RECONSTRUCTION OF COMMUNIST ESTIMATE, 1952-57

Agricultural and Farm Subsidiary Production

Since 1956, the Communists have published estimates of the gross value of agricultural and farm subsidiary production for 1952 and subsequent years. Figures of the gross value produced by some of the component groups and the percentage shares of some others in the total value are also available for 1952-55. We have pieced these data together and made up the missing percentages for 1956-57 in Table J-1.

Data on deductible costs of production have not been published by the Communists for the country as a whole. A survey of income and expenses of 856,131 farms made in 1955 indicates that the production expenses accounted for about 25 per cent of the gross value of agricultural and subsidiary production, of which about 22 per cent was for agricultural production and 3 per cent for farm subsidiary production.[1] By deducting these expenses

Table J-1

COMMUNIST DATA ON GROSS VALUE OF AGRICULTURAL AND FARM SUBSIDIARY PRODUCTION, 1952-57
(in 1952 yuan)

	1952		1953		1954		1955		1956		1957	
	Billion	Per cent	Billion	Per cent	Billion	Per cent	Billion	Per cent	Billion	Per cent	Billion	Per cent
1. Gross value of agricultural and farm subsidiary production	48.39	100.0	49.91	100.0	51.57	100.0	55.54	100.0	58.29	100.0	60.35	100.0
2. Agricultural production	38.47	79.5	39.24	78.6	40.64	78.8	43.71	78.7	45.87	78.7	47.50	78.7
Plant products	33.10	68.4	33.75	67.6	34.96	67.8	37.60	67.7	39.46	67.7	40.86	67.7
Animal products	5.37	11.1	5.49	11.0	5.68	11.0	6.11	11.0	6.41	11.0	6.64	11.0
3. Subsidiary production	9.92	20.5	10.68	21.4	10.93	21.2	11.83	21.3	12.42	21.3	12.85	21.3
Hunting and collecting	2.08	4.3	2.14	4.3	2.27	4.4	2.95	5.3	3.10	5.3	3.20	5.3
Preliminary processing for farm household consumption	1.89	3.9	2.05	4.1	2.11	4.1	2.17	3.9	2.27	3.9	2.35	3.9
Handicraft work for farm household consumption	5.71	11.8	6.24	12.5	6.29	12.2	6.38	11.5	6.70	11.5	6.94	11.5
Processing of farm products for consumers	0.24	0.5	0.25	0.5	0.26	0.5	0.33	0.6	0.35	0.6	0.36	0.6

Sources:

Line 1. *Great Ten Years*, p. 104.

Lines 2 and 3. Figures for 1952-55 are based on the gross values given in line 1 and the percentage breakdowns of the gross value into various component groups given in Chao Ching-hsin, "Seasonal Variations of the Market after Agricultural Cooperation," *CCYC*, No. 5, 1956, p. 25, and Wang Keng-chin, "My Opinions on the Methods of Computing Gross Value of Agricultural Production," *TCKT*, No. 4, 1957, p. 3. Those for 1956-57 are based on the gross value given in line 1 and the 1955 percentage breakdowns of the various component groups in the total.

from their respective gross value figures, we obtained the net value of agricultural and subsidiary production for 1952-57 given in Table J-2. Our reconstructed net value added by agriculture, and subsidiary production in 1954-55 and 1957 and the Communist estimates for 1952-53 and 1956 given at 36.19, 36.95, and 42.88 billion yuan[2] are used in the reconciliation of the Communist estimate with the adjusted estimate in Table 68.

Because of the inclusion of products such as night soil and animal and green manures in both output and costs, the Communist figures of gross value of agricultural production and of the percentage shares of deductible costs in the gross value are higher than our estimates for the corresponding items.[3] However, the differences between the reconstructed Communist net value figures and our estimates of net agricultural products are much smaller.[4] The fact that the deductible costs of subsidiary production accounted for only 3 per cent of the gross value of agricultural and subsidiary production is easily explained, as the values of raw material costs do not exist (as in the case of hunting and fishing) or are not included in the gross value.[5] The deductible costs presumably consist only of such small expenses as the repair and maintenance of processing equipment and tools.

Nonagricultural Sectors

The reconstructed Communist estimates of net value added in the nonagricultural sectors are summarized in Table J-3. The sources and methods used in the calculation of these figures are as follows:

1. Industry. Estimates of net value added for 1952 and 1956 are derived by multiplying the Communist estimates of national income by the proportions of national income originating in industry as given by the

Table J-2

RECONSTRUCTED COMMUNIST DATA ON NET VALUE OF AGRICULTURAL AND FARM SUBSIDIARY PRODUCTION, 1952-57

(billions of 1952 yuan)

	1952	1953	1954	1955	1956	1957
1. Gross value of agricultural and subsidiary production	48.39	49.92	51.57	55.54	58.29	60.35
2. Gross value of agricultural production	38.47	39.24	40.64	43.71	45.87	47.50
3. Deductible production expenses	10.65	10.98	11.35	12.22	12.82	13.28
4. Net value of agricultural production	27.82	28.26	29.29	31.49	33.05	34.22
5. Gross value of subsidiary production	9.92	10.68	10.93	11.83	12.42	12.85
6. Deductible production expenses	1.45	1.50	1.55	1.67	1.75	1.81
7. Net value of subsidiary production	8.47	9.18	9.38	10.16	10.67	11.04
8. Net value of agricultural and subsidiary production	36.29	37.44	38.67	41.65	43.72	45.26

Notes:

Lines 1, 2 and 5. Taken from Table J-1.

Line 3. 22 per cent of line 1.

Line 4. Line 2 minus line 3.

Line 6. 3 per cent of line 1.

Line 7. Line 5 minus line 6.

Line 8. Line 4 plus line 7.

Table J-3

RECONSTRUCTED COMMUNIST ESTIMATES OF NET VALUE ADDED

IN NONAGRICULTURAL SECTORS, 1952-57
(billions of 1952 yuan)

	1952	1953	1954	1955	1956	1957
1. Industry	11.00	14.75	17.15	18.44	23.43	25.87
Factories	6.45	8.64	10.15	10.93	15.69	17.26
Utilities	0.31	0.37	0.43	0.48	0.59	0.71
Mining	1.47	1.46	1.82	2.32	2.38	3.07
Lumbering and fishing	0.53	0.68	0.87	1.03	1.05	1.37
Handicrafts	2.24	3.60	3.88	3.68	3.72	3.46
2. Construction	1.83	2.28	2.68	2.93	4.97	4.62
3. Transportation and communications	2.45	3.04	3.20	3.43	3.90	4.33
4. Trade	9.66	12.53	12.18	12.35	13.76	13.45
5. Total	24.94	32.60	35.21	37.15	46.06	48.27

State Statistical Bureau.[6] The estimate for 1955 is also given by the Communists.[7] On the basis of these three estimates of net value added and the Communist figures of gross output of industry for 1952 and 1955-56,[8] the ratios of net value added to gross output are calculated at 32.0, 33.6, and 33.3 per cent. We assume that for 1953-54 and 1957, the ratios are equal to the average of those for 1952, 1955, and 1956, that is, 33 per cent. The gross output for 1953-54 and 1957 being known,[9] net value added for these years can be calculated.

The estimates of net value added by factories, utilities, and mining have been derived elsewhere.[10] The derivation of net value added by lumbering and part of fishing is explained below. The figures for handicrafts are residuals obtained by deducting those for factories, utilities, mining, lumbering, and fishing from total net value added by industry.

2. Construction. See the discussion under 1952-57 in Appendix H.

3. Transportation and communications. The Communist estimates of national income for 1952 and 1956 are given at 61.13 billion and 88.75 billion yuan, and the proportions of income originating in transportation and communications, at 4.0 and 4.4 per cent.[11] By multiplying the national income figures by the corresponding percentages, we obtain the estimates of net value added for 1952 and 1956. Net value added for 1953-55 and 1957 are derived on the basis of the 1956 figure and the index of net value added by agriculture, factories, handicrafts, and mining given in Table 68.

4. Trade. The estimates for 1952 and 1956 are derived on the basis of Communist national income figures for 1952 and 1956 and the proportion of national income originating in trade for the same years.[12] For 1953-55

and 1957, estimates of net value added in trade are derived by deducting the estimates already obtained for all the agricultural and nonagricultural sectors except trade from the Communist estimates of national income for these years.[13]

ADJUSTMENT OF DIFFERENCES BETWEEN RECONSTRUCTED COMMUNIST FIGURES AND THE ADJUSTED ESTIMATE

Agricultural and Farm Subsidiary Production

Agriculture proper. Items classified by the Communists as income from other sectors but included in the adjusted estimate as agricultural income are (a) cotton ginning (classified by the Communists as income from farm subsidiary production); (b) lumbering and fishing (income derived from modern lumber products and natural fishery products are classified by the Communists as a part of the value of industrial production); and (c) hunting and collecting (classified by the Communists as a part of farm subsidiary production).

(a) Cotton ginning (footnote b. to Table 70). Data on the costs of ginning in 1952-57 are not available. It is known, however, that during the pre-Communist period the costs of ginning were about 4 per cent of the farm price of lint cotton.[14] By assuming that this ratio still prevailed in 1952, the cost of ginning in 1952 can be derived by multiplying this ratio by our estimate of the farm price of lint cotton in 1952.[15] The resultant figure, 3.4 yuan per picul, is then multiplied by the output of lint cotton in each year, 1952-57,[16] to obtain the value added by cotton ginning in 1952 prices.

(b) Lumbering and fishing (footnote c. to Table 70). The net value added by modern lumber products is obtained by deducting costs or production and depreciation from their gross value of output. The gross value added by modern lumber products is derived from the gross value of all lumber products and percentages of the modern sector in the total. The data and computation are given in Table J-4.

Although the entire fishery production is included in our agricultural sector, it is divided by the Communists into cultured and natural fishery. The former is considered by the Communists as a part of agricultural production; the latter, a part of industrial production. The gross and net values of all fishery products for 1952-57 have been estimated in Appendix E in Table E-3. The value of the natural fisheries is derived from the total values and the percentage of the natural fisheries in the total given by the Communists. The data and computation are presented in Table J-5.

Total net value added by modern lumbering and natural fishery products in each year is the sum of figures given in the last lines of Tables J-4 and J-5.

(c) Hunting and collecting (footnote d. to Table 70). The net value added by wild animals caught, wild plants and herbs collected, etc., is derived from the gross value of the output of the group[17] on the assumption that the ratio between the net and gross values in each year during 1952-57 was the same as for all farm subsidiary production.[18]

Subsidiary. This item does not appear in our estimates. The components of this item are either included in the adjusted estimate as a part of income from other sectors or are not included at all. Those in the former category are: (a) hunting and collecting (footnote d. to Table 70), (b) cotton ginning (footnote b. to Table 70), and (c) other handicraft works.

Table J-4

NET VALUE ADDED BY MODERN LUMBER, 1952-57

(in 1952 prices)

	1952	1953	1954	1955	1956	1957
1. Gross value of all lumber products (billions of yuan)	0.48	0.80	1.01	1.15	0.99	1.34
2. Percentage in modern sector (per cent)	17	22	27	32	37	42
3. Gross value of modern lumber products (billions of yuan)	0.08	0.18	0.27	0.37	0.37	0.56
4. Net value of modern lumber products (billions of yuan)	0.07	0.16	0.24	0.33	0.33	0.51

Notes:

Line 1. See the discussion following Table E-4 in Appendix E.

Line 2. Percentages for 1952 and 1957 are given in TKP, Peiping, October 1, 1957. Those for other years are interpolations from the 1952 and 1957 figures on the assumption that annual increment was even over the 1952-57 period.

Line 3. Line 1 times line 2.

Line 4. Net values are obtained by deducting 10 per cent from the gross values for costs of production and depreciation. This deduction doubles the 5 per cent deduction (including 3 per cent for costs of production and 2 per cent for depreciation) for all lumber products discussed in Appendix E because of more expensive equipment and facilities being used in modern lumbering.

Table J-5

NET VALUE ADDED BY NATURAL FISHERIES, 1952-57

(billions of 1952 yuan)

	1952	1953	1954	1955	1956	1957
1. **Gross value of all fishery products**	0.63	0.72	0.87	0.96	1.01	1.18
2. **Gross value of cultured fishery products**	0.14	0.16	0.19	0.21	0.23	0.26
3. **Gross value of natural fishery products**	0.49	0.56	0.68	0.75	0.78	0.92
4. **Net value of all fishery products**	0.59	0.67	0.81	0.89	0.93	1.10
5. **Net value of natural fishery products**	0.46	0.52	0.63	0.70	0.72	0.86

Notes:

Line 1. Obtained by multiplying the output of fishery products, given in Table 33, by the 1952 price of fishery products of 19 yuan per picul, as given in Appendix D. These gross values are also shown in Table 36.

Line 2. Gross value in 1957 is estimated on the basis of a statement that 22 per cent of all fishery products was pond-reared in that year. See Chang Yu-tien, "Fishermen's Record Hauls," Peking Review, No. 11, 1959, p. 13. Percentages for the other years are assumed to be the same as for 1957.

Line 3. Line 1 minus line 2.

Lines 4 and 5. Obtained by deducting 7 per cent (5 per cent for costs of production and 2 per cent for depreciation; see Fishery Production in Appendix E) from the corresponding gross values given in lines 1 and 3.

The first two have been discussed above; the last one will be discussed here together with the portion of subsidiary production that is not included in our estimate.

The components of farm subsidiary production and their gross values for 1952-57 in constant 1952 prices have been given in Table J-1. Aside from hunting and collecting, which has been discussed above, the gross values of the other subgroups are used to derive the net values of the respective subgroups on the assumption that the ratio of net value to gross value for each subgroup is equal to the ratio (given earlier in this Appendix) for farm subsidiary production as a whole. The net values of the respective subgroups thus derived are shown in Table J-6.

A large part of the net values of production in these subgroups is not considered as income in the adjusted estimate. For instance, in "preliminary processing for farm household consumption," work such as salting vegetables, making bean curd, farm slaughtering of animals, etc.; and in "handicraft work for farm household consumption," work such as making clothes, shoes, stockings, etc., are all not included in the adjusted estimate.[19] Detailed data on the values of the components of these subgroups are not available. We have assumed that the portions not included in the adjusted estimate constituted about 80 per cent of each of the two subgroups. The resultant figures (footnote e. to Table 70) are shown in Table J-7.

The remaining 20 per cent of net value added by these two subgroups, and net value added by "processing of farm products for consumers" (excluding the net value added by cotton ginning which is included in our "agriculture proper") are all included in the adjusted estimate as part of the net value added by handicrafts. They are shown in Table J-8.

Table J-6

NET VALUE ADDED: SELECTED SUBGROUPS, FARM

SUBSIDIARY PRODUCTION, 1952-57

(billions of 1952 yuan)

Year	Preliminary processing for farm household consumption	Handicraft work for farm household consumption	Processing of farm products for consumers
1952	1.61	4.88	0.21
1953	1.76	5.36	0.22
1954	1.81	5.40	0.22
1955	1.87	5.48	0.28
1956	1.95	5.76	0.30
1957	2.02	5.96	0.31

Table J-7

COMMUNIST NET VALUE: FARM SUBSIDIARY PRODUCTION

NOT INCLUDED IN HANDICRAFT ESTIMATES, 1952-57

(billions of 1952 yuan)

Year	Preliminary processing	Handicrafts	Total
1952	1.29	3.90	5.19
1953	1.41	4.29	5.70
1954	1.45	4.32	5.77
1955	1.50	4.38	5.88
1956	1.56	4.61	6.17
1957	1.62	4.77	6.39

Table J-8

COMMUNIST NET VALUE OF CERTAIN FARM SUBSIDIARY PRODUCTION

INCLUDED IN OUR HANDICRAFTS ESTIMATES, 1952-57

(billions of 1952 yuan)

Year	Preliminary processing	Handicrafts	Processing for consumers	Cotton ginning	Total (excluding cotton ginning)
1952	0.32	0.98	0.21	0.09	1.42
1953	0.35	1.07	0.22	0.08	1.56
1954	0.36	1.08	0.22	0.07	1.59
1955	0.37	1.10	0.28	0.10	1.65
1956	0.39	1.15	0.30	0.10	1.74
1957	0.40	1.19	0.31	0.11	1.79

Manufacturing

Factories. There is no difference between the Communist and the adjusted estimates.

Handicrafts. The value of certain handicraft works considered by the Communists as a part of farm subsidiary production is included in the adjusted estimate of the value of handicrafts. See discussion on subsidiary, above.

Utilities. No difference.

Mining. No difference.

Lumbering and fishing. Classified by the Communists as a part of the value of industrial output, but included in the adjusted estimate of agricultural income. See discussion on agriculture proper, above.

Construction. No difference.

Transportation and communications. Net value added by passenger transportation is not included in the Communist estimate, but is included in our estimates. The figure for this item is obtained by taking the difference between the adjusted estimate and the reconstructed Communist estimate for transportation and communications as given in Table 68 and Table J-3.

Trade. No difference.

Government, finance, services, residential rent, and work brigades. Net value added is not included in the Communist estimate, but is included in the adjusted estimate. The figure for this item is taken from Table 68.

UNEXPLAINED BALANCE

These figures represent the difference between the adjusted estimates of domestic product and the sum of reconstructed Communist estimates, and the adjustments because of differences in concept, coverage, and classification.

ADJUSTED ESTIMATE

These estimates are taken from Table 68.

FOOTNOTES TO APPENDIX J

1. TCKTTH, No. 17, 1956, p. 8.

2. See Appendix E, Table E-11. These figures are the only ones available for 1952-57.

3. Compare Table J-2, lines 2 and 3, with corresponding figures given in Table 36.

4. Compare line 4 of Table J-2 with the last line of Table 36.

5. For instance, in the case of preliminary processing of plant products for farm household consumption or for consumers, the value of raw materials used is believed to be excluded from the gross value of subsidiary production but is included in the gross value of agricultural production. SSB, "Several Important Problems of Calculating Total Value of Agricultural Production," TCKTTH, No. 22, 1956, pp. 1-2.

6. SSB, "A Preliminary Study of the Production and Distribution of China's National Income," TCYC, No. 1, January 1958, p. 11.

7. Li Hui-hung, Chung Chi-ren, and Wang Hua-hsin, "The Problem of Classifying Light and Heavy Industries," TCKT, No. 18, September 1957, p. 15.

8. 1956 Statistical Abstract, p. 23.

9. See Appendix F, Table F-16.

10. See Table 68.

11. SSB, "A Preliminary Study of the Production and Distribution of China's National Income," TCYC, No. 1, January 1958, p. 11.

12. Ibid.

13. For Communist estimates of national income in 1952-57, see Table 69.

14. Shanghai Bank of Commerce and Savings, Mien (Cotton), Shanghai, 1931, p. 54; Honan Cotton Improvement Bureau, Honan mien-yeh (Cotton Industry of Honan), Shanghai, 1936, pp. 35-47; and Chi Chun-mien, Chih-mie shou-tse (Handbook of Cotton Planting), Shanghai, 1951, p. 91.

15. For the farm price of lint cotton in 1952, see Appendix D, Table D-4.

16. For output of lint cotton in 1952-57, see Table 33.

17. As given in Table J-1.

18. The calculation of the ratio of net value to gross value of subsidiary production in each year is based on data given in Table J-2.

19. For description of the components in these subgroups, see TCKT, No. 4, 1957, p. 3; and Editorial Committee of the Statistical Press, Handbook of Agricultural Statistical Work, Peiping, Tung-chi chu-pan-she, 1956 (English translation), pp. 31-32.

Appendix K

COMPUTATIONS FOR THE 1958-59 ESTIMATE OF DOMESTIC PRODUCT

This appendix presents the detailed computations for "A Conjectural Estimate of Domestic Product, 1958-1959," in Chapter III, summarized in Table 8.

Table K-1 summarizes in detail our estimate of domestic product for 1958-59 and the adjusted estimate based primarily on Communist data. The derivation of the estimates in this table is explained below.

AGRICULTURE

Estimates of gross output and value added in the agricultural sector in 1958-59 are given in Table K-2.

Gross Value of Output

Gross value of output is primarily obtained by multiplying the physical quantities of output of agricultural products in 1958-59 by their respective prices in 1952 given in Appendix D. The adjusted and authors' estimates of output are presented in Table K-3. The reader may wish to compare these estimates with the figures in Table 33. The estimates are derived as shown below.

Adjusted estimate: plant products. Except for sesame, cottonseed, hemp crops, tobacco, and vegetables, the output of all plant products in 1958 is taken from Great Ten Years, pp. 105, 109, 110, and 112. The output of sesame in 1958 is given in NCNA, Peiping, January 7, 1959. Output of cottonseed is assumed in Appendix A to be twice the output of ginned cotton. The output of hemp crops in 1958 is derived by multiplying the corresponding figure for 1957 (9.9 million piculs given in Appendix C under Hemp Crops)

Table K-1

DOMESTIC PRODUCT BY INDUSTRIAL ORIGIN, 1958-59

(billions of 1952 yuan)

	Authors' estimate		Adjusted estimate	
	1958	1959	1958	1959
Value added				
Agriculture	40.09	42.13	51.08	56.00
Factories	18.93	25.06	30.35	43.56
Handicrafts	6.00	6.48	7.76	8.69
Mining	4.19	5.34	5.55	7.16
Utilities	0.97	1.32	0.97	1.32
Construction	6.24	7.77	6.24	7.77
Modern transportation and communications	4.13	5.17	6.66	9.07
Old-fashioned transportation	2.87	2.83	3.72	3.56
Trade	12.38	13.56	19.31	23.47
Government administration	4.87	6.11	4.87	6.11
Finance	2.00	2.29	2.91	3.58
Personal services	0.51	0.51	0.51	0.51
Residential rent	2.60	2.67	2.60	2.67
Work brigades	2.50	3.27	2.50	3.27
Net domestic product	108.28	124.52	144.97	176.75
Depreciation	6.45	7.91	8.97	11.73
Gross domestic product	114.73	132.43	153.94	188.48

Table K-2

GROSS VALUE OF OUTPUT AND NET VALUE ADDED BY AGRICULTURE, 1958-59

(billions of 1952 yuan)

	Authors' estimate		Adjusted estimate	
	1958	1959	1958	1959
Gross value of output	46.42	48.74	59.04	64.64
Plant products	33.87	35.30	42.85	46.57
Animal products	6.02	6.11	8.98	9.87
Forest products	2.44	2.75	2.44	2.75
Fishery products	1.54	1.91	1.54	1.91
Miscellaneous	2.54	2.67	3.24	3.54
Gross value added	41.02	43.10	52.27	57.29
Plant products	30.11	31.38	38.09	41.40
Animal products	4.81	4.87	7.46	8.26
Forest products	2.37	2.67	2.37	2.67
Fishery products	1.47	1.81	1.47	1.81
Miscellaneous	2.26	2.38	2.88	3.15
Depreciation	0.93	0.98	1.18	1.29
Net value added	40.09	42.13	51.08	56.00

Table K-3

OUTPUT OF AGRICULTURAL PRODUCTS, 1958-59

	Authors' estimate		Adjusted estimate	
	1958	1959	1958	1959
Plant products				
Food crops (million piculs)	5830.00	5960.00	7724.00	8333.00
Paddy rice	1720.00	1760.00	2274.00	2458.00
Wheat	440.00	450.00	579.00	626.00
Miscellaneous food crops	940.00	960.00	1239.00	1339.00
Potatoes (in natural weight)	2740.00	2800.00	3632.00	3910.00
Soybeans (million piculs)	190.00[a]	200.00[a]	210.00	230.00
Oil-bearing crops (million piculs)				
Peanuts	81.00[b] (Peanuts, Rapeseed, Sesame combined)	81.70[b] (Peanuts, Rapeseed, Sesame combined)	56.00	61.20
Rapeseed			22.00	22.00
Sesame			11.00	11.00
Cottonseed	69.40	80.30	84.00	96.40
Plant fibers (million piculs)				
Cotton	34.70	40.20	42.00	48.20
Hemp crops	10.70	10.70	10.70	10.70
Other industrial crops (million piculs)				
Sugar cane	270.50	283.30	270.50	283.30
Sugar beets	58.00	73.70	58.00	73.70
Tobacco	19.60	21.50	19.60	21.50
Tea	2.80	3.20	2.80	3.20
Vegetables (billion 1952 yuan)	1.52	1.59	1.89	2.06
Fruits (million piculs)	78.00	85.00	78.00	85.00
Animal products				
Increase in number of livestock (billion 1952 yuan)				
Large livestock	0.09	0.03	0.09	0.03
Sheep and goats	0.08	0.03	0.08	0.03
Hogs	0.09	0.11	0.65	0.92
Poultry	0.03	0.04	0.03	0.04

(continued)

Table K-3 (continued)

	Authors' estimate		Adjusted estimate	
	1958	1959	1958	1959
Livestock and poultry utilized (million head)				
Large livestock	0.58	0.58	0.58	0.58
Sheep and goats	0.33	0.35	0.33	0.35
Hogs	3.23	3.31	5.63	6.26
Poultry	0.55	0.59	0.55	0.59
Other animal products				
Eggs (billion 1952 yuan)	0.57	0.65	0.57	0.65
Wool (million piculs)	1.62	1.68	1.02	1.68
Silk cocoons (million piculs)				
Domesticated	1.69	1.69	1.69	1.69
Wild	1.14	1.14	1.14	1.14
Forest products				
Tung nuts (million piculs)	15.7	15.7	15.7	15.7
Timber (million cubic meters)	35.00	41.20	35.00	41.20
Other forest products (billion 1952 yuan)	0.64	0.65	0.64	0.65
Fishery products (million piculs)	81.20	100.36	81.20	100.36

Notes:

[a]Gross output given in Table K-5 divided by 7 yuan per picul given in Appendix D.

[b]Gross output given in Table K-5 divided by the average price of the three oilseeds of 10.9 yuan per picul. This price is derived from data on output and the gross value of output in 1957 given in Appendixes C and E.

by an index computed at 108 per cent in 1958 with 1957 as 100 on the basis of the output of flax in 1957-58 given in Appendix C and People's Daily, August 27, 1959. Similarly, the output of tobacco is derived by using the 1957 output figure (13.2 million piculs given in Appendix C). The output index of tobacco is assumed to be the same as that for cured tobacco computed from data given in Great Ten Years, p. 109. The output of vegetables in 1958 is derived by the same procedure as for 1952-57, that is, by assuming that gross output of vegetables amounts to 4.8 per cent of the output of all other plant products except fruits.[1]

The total output of food crops in 1959 is given in People's Daily, January 23, 1960. Production of food crops by the four major categories is derived on the assumption that the percentage composition of total food crops output in 1959 was the same as in 1958. The figures for soybeans and cotton in 1959 are also given in the same source. Output of peanuts is derived on the basis of the 1958 output given at 56 million piculs and the output index given at 109.2 per cent in 1959 with 1958 as 100 in Peking Home Service (a Communist radio broadcast), January 24, 1960. The output of rapeseed, sesame, and hemp crops in 1959 is assumed to be the same as the corresponding output in 1958. The 1959 output of cottonseed is assumed to be twice the output of ginned cotton. The output of sugar cane, sugar beets, cured tobacco, and tea in 1959 are 3, 27, 11, and 8 per cent higher than those for 1958 (ibid.). The 1959 figures are computed on the basis of these indexes and the 1958 output. The 1959 output of vegetables is derived by the same procedure as used for 1958. For lack of a better alternative, the output of fruits in 1959 is assumed to have increased from 1958 in proportion to that of all plant products (except vegetables) over the same period.

Animal products. The gross value of the increase in the number of large livestock is derived at 91 and 26 million 1952 yuan for 1958 and 1959, on the basis of the gross value of year-end total number of large livestock in 1957, computed at 6,509 million yuan from data given in Appendix C, Table C-2, the discussion on livestock in Appendix D, and the annual percentage increase in number in 1958-59 reported at 1.4 and 0.4 per cent in Great Ten Years, p. 117; and People's Daily, January 23, 1960. Increases in the number of sheep and goats in 1958-59 are derived at 10.4 and 3.6 million head from the respective total numbers in 1957-59 given in the same sources. Multiplying the increases by the respective 1952 prices of 8 yuan per head given in Appendix D, we obtain the gross value of increase at 83 and 29 million yuan in 1958 and 1959. From the total number of hogs in 1957-59, 145.9, 160.0, and 180.0 million head, the increase in the number of hogs in 1958-59 can be calculated at 14.1 and 20.0 million head. The 1952 prices of hogs, 46 yuan per head, given in Appendix D, and the gross value of increase in hogs in 1958-59 amounts to 649 and 920 million yuan. The increase in poultry in 1958-59 is assumed to be in proportion to the increase in number of livestock over the same period (given in Appendix E, Table E-6) and is based on the 483 million yuan given in Table K-4.

Gross value of large livestock, sheep and goats, and hogs utilized are derived by multiplying the corresponding estimates for 1957 by the indexes of the respective midyear total numbers in 1958-59 with 1957 as 100. The 1957 figures are taken from Appendix E, Table E-7. The midyear totals for 1958-59 are computed by averaging the totals at the beginning and end of the year for 1957-59 given in Appendix C, Table C-2; Great Ten Years, p. 117; and People's Daily, January 23, 1960. It is

Table K-4

TOTAL NUMBER AND GROSS VALUE OF LIVESTOCK AND POULTRY
1957-59

	1957	1958	1959
Total number (million head)			
Year-end total			
Large livestock	83.9	85.1	85.4
Sheep and goats	98.5	108.9	112.5
Hogs	145.9	160.0	180.0
Midyear total			
Large livestock	84.3	84.5	85.2
Sheep and goats	97.7	103.7	110.7
Hogs	114.0	153.0	170.0
Gross value of livestock and poultry at midyear (million yuan)			
Large livestock	6,532	6,548	6,602
Sheep and goats	782	830	886
Hogs	5,244	7,038	7,820
Poultry	483	555	589
Total	13,041	14,971	15,897
Gross value of livestock and poultry utilized (million yuan)			
Large livestock	574	575	580
Sheep and goats	313	332	354
Hogs	4,195	5,630	6,256
Poultry	483	555	589
Total	6,565	7,092	7,779

assumed that the total gross value of poultry increased from 1957 to 1959 in proportion to gross value of all livestock over the same period and that the entire midyear stock in a given year is utilized.[2]

Table K-4 summarizes the data on the number of livestock and, for later computation of feed expenses, the data on gross value of livestock and poultry at midyear, derived by multiplying the midyear total by the prices given in the discussion on livestock and poultry in Appendix D.

The gross value of poultry eggs in 1958-59 is derived on the basis of the estimate for 1952 (0.47 billion 1952 yuan, given in Appendix E, Table E-2) and the index of the total gross value of poultry in 1958-59 with 1952 as 100 (computed from above data and from the discussion under Poultry, 1952-57, in Appendix E). The gross value of wool in 1958-59 is estimated from the gross value of wool output in 1957, given in Appendix C, Table C-5, and the index of the total number of sheep and goats given above. The output of domesticated and wild cocoons in 1958 is taken from Great Ten Years, p. 110, assuming the same figure for 1959.

Forest products. Output of tung nuts in 1958 is estimated at 15.7 million piculs by dividing the output of tung oil in 1958 given at 4.4 million piculs in People's Daily, December 14, 1958, by the quantity of tung oil produced from one picul of tung nuts given at 0.28 picul in Appendix A. For lack of information, we assume that the output in 1959 is the same as in 1958. The output of timber in 1958-59 is given in Great Ten Years, p. 85, and People's Daily, January 23, 1960. The gross value of other forest products in 1958-59 is assumed to have increased from 1957 in proportion to total population. The 1957 estimate of other forest products is given under Timber and Other Forest Products in Appendix E.

Fishery products. Output in 1958 is given at 81.20 million piculs in People's Daily, March 13, 1959. The 1959 output is reported at 23.6 per cent above the 1958 level. Ibid., January 23, 1960. The output in 1959 is calculated at 100.36 million piculs.

Miscellaneous agricultural products. Gross value of miscellaneous agricultural products in 1958-59 is derived on the assumption that the ratio of the four major categories of agricultural products to miscellaneous agricultural products in 1958-59 remained the same as in 1957.[3]

The authors' estimate. Except for food crops, soybeans, oil bearing crops, cotton, hogs, vegetables, and miscellaneous agricultural products, the adjusted estimates of output and the authors' estimates are the same. The gross value of vegetables and miscellaneous agricultural products is derived on the same assumption as the adjusted estimate, but the basic data are now different. The other figures are obtained as follows.

Food crops. Total consumption of food crops is estimated at 3,159 and 3,232 million piculs for 1958-59 by multiplying total population in 1958-59 (650 and 665 million) by the per capita consumption of food crops in 1957 given at 486 piculs in Table 32. For total population in 1958, see Ts'ai-cheng (Public Finance), Peiping, No. 18, 1959, p. 23. The 1959 population is estimated on the basis of the 1958 figure and the average annual rate of increase in total population in 1953-56, that is, 2.22 per cent per annum, derived from data given in TCKT, No. 11, 1957, p. 25. Total output of food crops is derived by dividing total consumption by 83.7 per cent, the percentage of total food crops output used for food in 1957, also given in Table 32. Total output in 1958-59 is then divided into four major categories (rice, wheat, miscellaneous food crops, and potatoes) on the assumption that the proportion of each category in total production is the same as that derived from the adjusted figures for 1958.

Soybeans and oil bearing crops. Exports of soybeans and oil seeds in 1957-59 are first roughly estimated. The exports in 1957 are then deducted from total gross output given in Appendix E, Table E-1, to arrive at total domestic consumption in 1957. Estimates of total consumption in 1958-59 are obtained on the assumption that per capita consumption of soybeans and oil seeds in these years remained the same as in 1957. Total population in 1957-59 being given above, total consumption in 1958-59 can be calculated. Total consumption and exports sum up to total gross output. Of this total output of soybeans and oil seeds, gross output of cottonseed in 1957-59 can be derived by multiplying the output of cottonseed obtained at twice the output of ginned cotton in 1957-59, given in Great Ten Years, p. 105 and this appendix below, by the price of cottonseed given at 3.6 yuan per picul in the discussion on Cottonseed in Appendix D. The ratio of cottonseed to ginned cotton is discussed under Cottonseed in Appendix A. The breakdown of the residual into figures for soybeans and other oil bearing crops is made on the assumption that the percentage share of each group in the residual is the same as that derived from the adjusted estimate of output of soybeans, peanuts, rapeseed, and sesame already obtained above. The details are presented in Table K-5.

Cotton. Output of cotton in 1958-59 is derived on the basis of the 1957 output (32.8 million piculs given in Great Ten Years, p. 105) and an index of the authors' estimates of gross output of cotton yarn,

Table K-5

GROSS VALUE OF OUTPUT, SOYBEANS AND OIL SEEDS,

1957-59, THE AUTHORS' ESTIMATE

(millions of 1952 yuan)

	1957	1958	1959
Exports[a]	296	241	309
Oil seeds	98	63	-
Soybeans	198	178	-
Domestic consumption[b]	2,171	2,215	2,266
Gross output[c]	2,467	2,456	2,575
Soybeans	1,407	1,324	1,394
Cottonseed	236	250	289
Peanuts, rapeseed, and sesame	824	883	891

Notes:

- Not available.

[a] The 1957-58 figures are the sums of exports to the USSR and Western countries as given in Economic Planning Administration, Ministry of Foreign Trade, USSR, Foreign Trade of the USSR, 1958 (Statistical Survey), Moscow, 1959 (English translation), p. 190, and U.S. Department of State, Summary of East-West Trade in 1958, U.S. Government Printing Office, Washington, D.C., 1960, p. 46. The 1959 figure is derived on the assumption that total exports increased from 1958 at the same rate as exports of oil seeds to Soviet Russia over the same period given in China Trade and Economic Newsletter, October 1960.

[b] The figure for 1957 is derived by deducting exports from gross value of output given in Table E-1, Appendix E. The 1958-59 figures are derived on the assumption that domestic consumption increased from 1957 to 1959 at the same rate as total population (given earlier) over the same period.

[c] Total gross output is the sum of exports and domestic consumption. Output of cottonseed is calculated at twice the output of cotton given in the text. Outputs of soybeans and other oil seeds are derived on the assumption that their share in the total gross output (minus cottonseed) is the same as that derived from the corresponding adjusted estimate.

cotton cloth, and clothing and knitted goods in 1957-59, given in Table 39, and Table K-7 below.

Hogs. The total number of hogs at the end of the year for 1958-59 is assumed to have increased from 1957 at the same rate as total population over the same period. The year-end total for 1957 being 101.6 million head (Appendix C, Table C-2), the total for 1958-59 is calculated at 103.6 and 106.0 million head. Increases in the number of hogs in 1958-59 are, therefore, 2.0 and 2.4 million head. Multiplying the latter figures by the 1952 price of 46 yuan per head (included in the discussion on Chickens, Ducks, and Geese in Appendix D), we derive the gross value of the increase in the number of hogs in 1958-59 at 92.0 and 110.4 million yuan. By a similar procedure, the total number of hogs at the middle of the year for 1958-59 is derived at 87.9 and 89.9 million head on the basis of the 1957 estimate of 86.2 million head given in Appendix C, Table C-2, and the percentage increase in total population in 1957-59. Assuming the slaughter rate to be 80 per cent of the midyear total, the number of hogs utilized in 1958-59 is derived at 70.3 and 71.9 million head, and the gross value at 3.23 and 3.31 billion yuan.

GROSS VALUE ADDED, DEPRECIATION, AND NET VALUE ADDED

The percentages of deductible costs in total gross output for the five categories are assumed to be the same as for 1952-57 given in Appendix E. Gross value added is derived by deducting the costs of production from the gross value of output. Allowing 2 per cent of gross value of output for depreciation, we obtain the estimates of net value added.

Factories

The derivation of net value added by factories in 1958-59 given in Table K-1 is explained in Table K-6. For expository convenience, the adjusted estimate is first explained below.

The adjusted estimate. Essentially, the derivation of value added for 1958-59 follows the same procedure adopted in estimating value added for 1952-57: (1) estimating the gross output and gross value added by the products for which data on output and prices are available; (2) estimating total gross output of factories as a whole; (3) deducting the gross output obtained in step (1) from total gross output to derive the gross output of those products not yet covered in (1); (4) estimating the gross value added of those products not covered in (1); and (5) allowing 5 per cent of gross output for depreciation.

Statistical data on the output of 9 producers' goods and 14 consumers goods in 1958, and 7 producers' goods and 12 consumers' goods in 1959 are available, or can be roughly estimated. Gross value of output of these identified products is then derived by multiplying the output figures by the price of these products in 1952. Applying the ratio of gross value added to gross output for each of these products in 1952 to the corresponding gross output in 1958-59, we obtain the gross value added by these identified products. The results are presented in Table K-7.

The total gross value of output of producers' goods from factories as a whole in 1958-59 is estimated at 58.71 and 85.90 billion 1952 yuan, and that of the consumers' goods at 30.58 and 41.68 billion 1952 yuan, again by the same methods used in obtaining the estimates for 1952-57. The calculations are shown in Table K-8.

Table K-6

GROSS VALUE OF OUTPUT AND VALUE ADDED BY FACTORIES, 1958-59

(billions of 1952 yuan)

	Authors' estimate		Adjusted estimate	
	1958	1959	1958	1959
Gross value of output	54.14	71.67	89.29	127.58
Producers' goods	35.18	50.27	58.71	85.90
Identified	22.82	21.34	25.75	29.58
Unidentified	12.36	28.93	32.96	56.32
Consumers' goods	18.96	21.40	30.58	41.68
Identified	14.07	14.96	15.74	18.56
Unidentified	4.88	6.44	14.84	23.12
Gross value added	21.64	28.64	34.81	49.94
Producers' goods	15.40	21.55	24.99	36.55
Identified	10.46	9.69	11.81	13.46
Unidentified	4.95	11.86	13.18	23.09
Consumers' goods	6.24	7.09	9.82	13.39
Identified	4.78	5.16	5.37	6.45
Unidentified	1.46	1.93	4.45	6.94
Depreciation	2.71	3.58	4.46	6.38
Producers' goods	1.76	2.51	2.93	4.30
Consumers' goods	0.95	1.07	1.53	2.08
Net value added	18.93	25.06	30.35	43.56
Producers' goods	13.64	19.04	22.06	32.25
Consumers' goods	5.29	6.02	8.29	11.31

Source:

Table K-9 and text of this appendix.

Table K-7

OUTPUT, GROSS VALUE OF OUTPUT, AND GROSS VALUE ADDED BY MANUFACTURED PRODUCTS, 1958-59, THE ADJUSTED ESTIMATE

(billions of 1952 yuan)

Product and unit of measurement	Output[a]		Gross value of output[b]		Gross value added[c]	
	1958	1959	1958	1959	1958	1959
Producers' goods			25.75	29.58	11.81	13.46
Pig iron (million tons)	9.53	20.50	1.91	4.10	0.76	1.64
Steel (million tons)	8.00	13.35	4.80	8.01	2.88	4.81
Rolled steel (million tons)	6.37	10.64	6.37	10.63	2.36	3.94
Machinery (million tons)	-	-	7.71	-	3.55	-
Cement (million tons)	9.30	12.27	0.79	1.04	0.29	0.38
Coke (million tons)	16.30	27.20	0.72	1.20	0.37	0.62
Chemicals (million tons)			1.05	1.49	0.39	0.55
Ammonium sulfate	0.65	1.06	0.26	0.43	0.10	0.16
Caustic soda	0.27	0.36	0.34	0.45	0.12	0.17
Pure soda	0.64	0.80	0.22	0.28	0.08	0.10
Sulfuric acid	0.74	1.05	0.23	0.33	0.09	0.12
Paper (million tons)	1.22	1.70	2.23	3.11	1.09	1.52
Gunny sacks (million pieces)	86.19	-	0.17	-	0.12	-
Consumers' goods			15.74	18.56	5.37	6.45
Cotton yarn (million bales)	6.10	8.25	4.39	5.94	2.24	3.03
Cotton cloth (million bolts)	147.58	199.59	3.98	5.39	0.76	1.02
Silk (thousand tons)	7.55	7.55	0.37	0.37	0.11	0.11

Table K-7 (continued)

Product and unit of measurement	Output[a]		Gross value of output[b]		Gross value added[c]	
	1958	1959	1958	1959	1958	1959
Silk piece goods (million meters)	79.44	79.44	0.24	0.24	0.06	0.06
Woolen textiles (million tons)	-	-	0.57	0.63	0.27	0.30
Grass cloth (million tons)	-	-	(*)	(*)	(*)	(*)
Clothing and knitted goods (million tons)	-	-	0.24	0.32	0.11	0.15
Sugar (million tons)	0.58	0.73	0.64	0.80	0.31	0.39
Milled rice (million tons)	2.16	2.26	0.43	0.45	0.03	0.03
Wheat flour (million tons)	3.95	3.84	1.22	1.19	0.13	0.13
Edible vegetable oils (million tons)	-	-	0.46	0.53	0.08	0.10
Cigarettes (million cases)	4.75	5.49	2.33	2.69	0.98	1.13
Matches (million cases)	10.60	-	0.13	-	0.05	-
Rubber footwear (million pairs)	182.36	-	0.73	-	0.24	-

(Notes to this table are on the following pages.)

Notes:

- Not available.

(*) Less than 0.01 billion yuan.

[a] Output. For the output of pig iron, steel, cement, cotton yarn, cigarettes, and rubber footwear in 1958-59, see Great Ten Years, pp. 84-89, and People's Daily, January 23, 1960, p. 1. The output of rolled steel and coke in 1957-59 is assumed to have increased in proportion to that of steel over the same period. The output of steel in 1957 is given in Appendix F, Table F-8. The output figures for caustic soda, pure soda, and sulfuric acid in 1958 are given in Great Ten Years, p. 85. The corresponding estimates for 1959 are derived on the basis of the 1958 figures and percentage increases in 1959 over 1958 reported at 25, 35, and 42 per cent in NCNA, Peiping, February 1, 1960. The output of ammonium sulfate in 1958-59 is derived on the assumption that it increased from 1957-59 in proportion to that of chemical fertilizers over the same period. For the output of ammonium sulfate in 1957, also see Table F-8, and for the output of chemical fertilizers in 1957-59, see Great Ten Years, p. 86; and People's Daily, January 23, 1960, p. 1. The output of machine-made paper in 1958-59 is given in People's Daily, October 10, 1959, p. 7, and January 23, 1960, p. 1. The output of gunny sacks in 1958 is the planned figure for 1958 given at 110.3 per cent of the 1957 output in TKP, Peiping, February 7, 1958, p. 1. Table F-8 gives the 1957 figure. The output of cotton cloth in 1958-59 is derived on the basis of this 1957 figure and the assumption that it increased from 1957 to 1959 in proportion to that of machine-spun yarn over the same period. The output of silk and silk piece goods are similarly derived from the corresponding figures for 1957 and an index for 1957-59 computed from data on the output of silk cocoons in 1957-59 given in Great Ten Years, p. 110, and Table K-3 above. The outputs of sugar, milled rice, and wheat flour in 1958-59 are also derived by a similar procedure. The outputs of these products in 1957 are shown in Table F-8. The indexes of output of these products are assumed to have changed in proportion to total sugar output given in Great Ten Years, p. 89; and People's Daily, January 23, 1960, p. 1; urban population in 1958-59; and the output of wheat in 1956-58 given in Appendix C, Table C-1, and Table K-3 above. The urban population in 1959 is given at 100 million in People's Daily, October 25, 1959; the figure for 1958, 95 million, is the average of the figures given in Table 68 for 1959 and 1957. The output of matches in 1958 is the planned figure for that year given at 103.4 per cent of the 1957 figure in TKP, Peiping, February 7, 1958, p. 1. The 1957 output is given in Table F-8.

[b] Gross value of output. The gross value of output of all the products except machinery, woolen textiles, grass cloth, clothing and knitted goods, and edible vegetable oils, is obtained by multiplying the output figures of these products by their respective prices in 1952, given in Appendix F, Table F-10. The gross value of machinery output in 1958 is given at 41 times that of 1949 in Chao Er-lu, "The Machinery

Notes (continued):

Industry in the Past Ten Years," People's Daily, September 24, 1959, p. 9. The output in 1949 is 188 million yuan as given in 1955 Statistical Abstract, p. 40; thus the 1958 figure is calculated at 7,708 million yuan. The gross outputs of woolen textiles, grass cloth, clothing and knitted goods, and edible vegetable oils in 1958-59 are assumed to have increased from 1957 to 1959 in proportion to the output of wool and hemp crops in 1956-58 given in Appendix C, Table C-5, the text under Hemp Crops, and Table K-3 above; the output of cotton yarn in 1957-59 given above; and the total output of edible vegetable oils in 1957-59 given in Great Ten Years, p. 89; and People's Daily, January 23, 1960, p. 1.

[c] Gross value added. These figures are derived by applying the ratio of gross value added to gross output for each of the products given in Appendix F, Table F-11, to the gross value of output in 1958-59 already obtained.

Table K-8

GROSS VALUE OF OUTPUT OF FACTORIES, 1958-59

(billions of 1952 yuan)

	1958	1959
Gross output of producers' goods[a]	65.06	93.23
Deduct:		
Mineral products[b]	5.82	7.91
Electric power[b]	1.65	2.49
Lumber[c]	0.79	1.03
Add: Pig iron	1.91	4.10
Equals: Factory output of producers' goods	58.71	85.90
Gross output of consumers' goods[a]	31.90	42.75
Deduct:		
Output of salt[b]	1.41	1.50
Water and gas supply[b]	0.57	0.60
Part of fishery products[d]	1.20	1.49
Add: Part of cotton yarn	1.86	2.52
Equals: Consumers' goods output of factories	30.58	41.68
Total gross value of output of factories	89.29	127.58

Notes:

[a] Industrial output: gross output of producers' goods and consumers' goods. Total output of producers' goods and consumers' goods in 1958 is derived at 77.03 and 54.08 billion 1952 yuan by deflating the corresponding estimates in 1957 prices (67.0 and 50.0 billion 1957 yuan) by price indexes for 1957 with 1952 as 100 (87.0 and 92.4 per cent), computed from gross output of producers' and consumers' goods in 1957 in constant 1952 and 1957 prices. For data used in this calculation, see Great Ten Years, p. 76. The gross output for 1959 is derived at 110.38 and 72.47 billion 1952 yuan by multiplying the 1958 figures by the indexes for 1959 with 1958 as 100, given at 143.3 and 134.0 per cent for the producers'

Notes (continued):

and consumers' goods in People's Daily, January 23, 1960, p. 1. On the assumption that the output of factories increased in 1957-59 at the same rate as total output over the same period, we derive the gross output of producers' goods in 1958-59 at 65.06 and 93.23 billion 1952 yuan, and gross output of consumers' goods at 31.90 and 42.75 billion 1952 yuan. The gross output of factory producers' goods and consumers' goods is given in Appendix F, Table F-16.

[b] Gross value of mineral products, electric power, salt, water and gas supply. Table K-10 and K-11.

[c] Gross value of lumber. Total gross output of lumber has been estimated at 1.68 and 1.98 billion yuan for 1958-59 earlier in this appendix. The proportion of output produced by the modern sector is roughly estimated at 47 and 52 per cent of the total gross output for 1958-59 by linear extrapolation from the figures for 1952-57. These figures are given in Appendix F under Gross Value Output of All Factories. The 1952 price of timber, 48 yuan per cubic meter, is given in Appendix D.

[d] Gross value of part of fishery products. This item represents the gross output of natural marine products, estimated at 78 per cent of total marine products given in Table K-3 and under Fishery Products in Appendix D. For the derivation of the percentage of natural fishery products in total marine products, see Appendix F, in the section on Gross Value of Output of All Factories.

Gross outputs of those producers' goods in 1958-59 not covered in Table K-7 are 32.96 and 56.32 billion yuan, obtained by deducting the gross output of the identified products given in Table K-7 from the corresponding totals given in Table K-8. Similarly derived, the gross output of consumers' goods not covered in Table K-7 are 14.84 and 23.12 billion 1952 yuan for 1958 and 1959.

For lack of a better alternative, we assume that the percentages of gross value added by the unidentified producers' and consumers' goods in the gross value of output of these goods in 1958 are the same as for comparable products in 1957. The latter figures are computed at 40 per cent for producers' goods and 30 per cent for consumers' goods.[4] Applying these percentages to the gross output of unidentified producers' and consumers' goods in 1958, we obtain the gross value added by them at 14.84 and 4.45 billion yuan. By a similar procedure, gross value added by unidentified producers' goods in 1959 is derived at 23.09 billion yuan, and consumers' goods at 6.94 billion yuan.[5]

Total gross value added by producers' and consumers' goods thus amounts to 24.99 and 13.18 billion yuan in 1958, and 36.55 and 23.09 billion yuan in 1959. Allowing an arbitrary 5 per cent of gross output for depreciation, we obtain net value added by producers' and consumers' goods in 1958 at 22.06 and 8.29 billion yuan, totalling 30.35 billion yuan, and the corresponding estimates for 1959 at 32.25 and 11.31 billion yuan, totalling 43.56 billion yuan.

The authors' estimates. The methods used in deriving the authors' estimate of net value added by factories in 1958-59 are essentially the same as those used in deriving the adjusted estimates. First, the gross output and gross value added by identified products are estimated separately for producers' goods and consumers' goods, as shown in Table K-9. Except for four producers' goods (pig iron, steel, rolled steel, and coke) and three consumers' goods (cotton yarn, cotton cloth, and clothing and knitted goods) for which adjustments have been made, gross output and gross value added by identified products are taken from Table K-7. The gross output of producers' goods and consumers' goods are explained in turn.

According to the Communist claims, output of modern steel in 1958 reached 8 million tons.[6] However, a considerable portion of this total must have been produced by the small converters during the period of the Great Leap Forward in 1958-59, and is excluded from our estimate for modern factories by the following procedure.[7] On the basis of the gross output of machinery and steel in 1952-57, given in Table 39, a linear regression of machinery output on steel output is obtained. With a gross output of machinery in 1958 equal to 7.71 billion yuan in 1958 and on the assumption that this linear regression relationship holds also for 1958, a rough estimate of the gross output of steel can be obtained at 3.80 billion yuan for 1958.[8]

The Communist figure of steel output for 1959 must also be adjusted to exclude the output of the small converters. Unfortunately, data on machinery for 1959 are not available and an even more arbitrary method of revision must be adopted. This revision is made on the assumption that the ratio of the authors' estimate to the adjusted estimate of the increase in steel output from 1958 to 1959 is the same as for 1957 to 1958, that is, 37 per cent.[9] Since the adjusted gross outputs of steel in both 1958 and 1959 are known, the authors' estimate of gross output

Table K-9

GROSS VALUE OF OUTPUT AND GROSS VALUE ADDED BY IDENTIFIED MANUFACTURED PRODUCTS, 1958-59

(billions of 1952 yuan)

	Authors' estimates			
	Gross value of output		Gross value added	
	1958	1959	1958	1959
Producers' goods	22.82	21.34	10.46	9.69
Pig iron	1.45	2.43	0.58	0.97
Steel	3.80	5.36	2.28	3.21
Rolled steel	5.04	7.11	1.87	2.63
Machinery	7.71	-	3.54	-
Cement	0.79	1.04	0.29	0.38
Coke	0.57	0.80	0.30	0.42
Chemicals	1.05	1.48	0.39	0.55
Paper	2.23	3.11	1.09	1.52
Gunny sacks	0.17	-	0.12	-
Consumers' goods	14.08	14.96	4.78	5.16
Cotton yarn	3.55	4.11	1.81	2.10
Cotton cloth	3.20	3.70	0.61	0.70
Silk	0.37	0.37	0.11	0.11
Silk piece goods	0.24	0.24	0.06	0.06
Woolen textiles	0.57	0.63	0.27	0.30
Grass cloth	(*)	(*)	(*)	(*)
Clothing and knitted goods	0.21	0.24	0.10	0.11
Sugar	0.64	0.80	0.31	0.39
Milled rice	0.43	0.45	0.03	0.03
Wheat flour	1.22	1.19	0.13	0.13
Edible vegetable oils	0.46	0.53	0.08	0.10
Cigarettes	2.33	2.69	0.98	1.13
Matches	0.13	-	0.05	-
Rubber footwear	0.73	-	0.24	-

Notes:

- Not available.

(*) Less than 0.005 billion yuan.

of steel in 1959 can be estimated at 5.36 billion yuan.[10] The gross output of pig iron, rolled steel, and coke produced by modern factories in 1958-59 are then obtained on the assumption that their outputs increased from 1957 in proportion to that of steel.[11]

The authors' estimate of gross output of cotton yarn, cotton cloth, and clothing and knitted goods in 1958-59 are obtained by summing net exports and domestic consumption of these products.[12] Exports in 1957-59 are roughly estimated at 0.72, 0.96, and 1.93 billion yuan on the basis of fragmentary data on clothing exports to Soviet Russia and Western countries.[13] By deducting exports of 0.72 billion yuan from total output of 6.57 billion yuan given in Table 39, domestic consumption in 1957 is equal to 5.85 billion yuan. For 1958-59, domestic consumption is derived at 5.99 and 6.13 billion yuan on the assumption that domestic consumption in 1958-59 increased from 1957 at the same rate as total population over the same period as discussed earlier in this appendix. The sum of exports and domestic consumption in 1958-59 is equal to total gross output, imports (if any) being negligible. We assume that the percentage composition of the three products in the total is the same as that derived from the adjusted estimate given in Table K-7. The gross output of each of these three products in 1958-59 can then be easily calculated.

To derive gross value added by the seven products (pig iron, steel, rolled steel, coke, cotton yarn, cotton cloth, and clothing and knitted products) given in Table K-9, the percentages of gross value added in gross output given for 1952 in Appendix F, Table F-11, are used.

The gross output of unidentified producers' goods in 1958-59 is assumed to have increased from 1957 in proportion to identified products over the same period. The results are 12.36 and 28.93 billion yuan for 1958-59.[14] By a similar procedure, the gross output of unidentified consumers' goods is derived at 4.88 and 6.44 billion yuan for 1958 and 1959.[15] By applying the percentages of gross value added in gross output of unidentified producers' and consumers' goods used for the correspondir adjusted estimates given earlier, gross value added by the unidentified producers' goods in 1958-59 are computed at 4.95 and 11.86 billion yuan, and those of unidentified consumers' goods, 1.46 and 1.93 billion yuan.

Total gross output of producers' goods in 1958 and 1959 thus amounts to 35.18 and 50.27 billion yuan, and that of consumers' goods, 18.96 and 21.40 billion yuan. The gross values added for these two years are 15.40 and 21.55 billion yuan for producers' goods, and 6.24 and 7.09 billion yuan for consumers' goods. Again, allowing 5 per cent of gross output for depreciation, we obtain estimates of net value added by producers' goods in 1958-59 at 13.64 and 19.04 billion yuan, and by consumers' goods at 5.29 and 6.02 billion yuan.

HANDICRAFTS

Net value added by handicrafts in 1958-59 is derived on the assumption that it increased from 1957 in proportion to the gross output of agriculture and mining over the same period, the two latter industries being suppliers of raw materials to handicrafts. On the same assumption, but using the adjusted estimates of gross output of agriculture and minin we also derive the adjusted estimate of net value added by handicrafts at 7.76 and 8.69 billion yuan for 1958 and 1959. For the authors' estimates of gross output of agriculture and mining in 1957, see Tables 36 and 47, and Tables K-2 and K-10 in this appendix. For the adjusted estimates, see Appendix E, Table E-4, Appendix H, Table H-2, and this appendix, Tables K-2 and K-10.

MINING

Table K-10 summarizes the estimates of gross output and net value added by mining in 1958-59. For expository convenience, the adjusted estimates are first explained. Gross output of all the products, except miscellaneous products, is derived by multiplying output of each of these products by their 1952 prices given in Appendix H, Table H-1. The total output of coal in 1958-59 is given at 270 and 347 million tons; that of crude oil, 2.264 and 3.700 million tons; and that of salt, 10.40 and 11.04 million tons in Great Ten Years, pp. 84-89; and People's Daily, January 23, 1960, p. 1. The proportions of native and other output in total coal and salt output in 1957 given in Table H-2 are used to split total outputs of coal and salt in 1958-59 into these two categories. The outputs of iron ore and manganese ore in 1958-59 are assumed to have increased at the same rate as the output of pig iron over the same period; and the output of limestone in 1958-59, at the same rate as that of cement over the same period. For the output of pig iron and cement in 1957-59, see Appendix F, Table F-8, and Table K-7 of this appendix. Gross output of the miscellaneous products, in turn, is assumed to have increased in 1957-59 in proportion to the total gross output of all the other mineral products, except salt, over the same period. The reason for excluding the gross output of salt in this calculation is that the output of miscellaneous products is not likely to fluctuate as erratically as the output of salt, which depends heavily on weather conditions.

Net value added by these seven product groups is derived by applying the percentage of net value added in gross output of each of these product

Table K-10

GROSS VALUE OF OUTPUT AND NET VALUE ADDED

BY MINING, 1958-59

(billions of 1952 yuan)

	Adjusted estimate		Authors' estimate	
	1958	1959	1958	1959
Gross value of output	9.40	12.10	6.76	8.55
Coal	4.96	6.38	2.73	3.44
Native	1.76	2.26	0.97	1.22
Other	3.20	4.12	1.76	2.22
Crude oil	0.36	0.59	0.36	0.59
Iron ore	0.89	1.34	0.89	1.34
Manganese ore	0.08	0.12	0.08	0.12
Limestone	0.30	0.40	0.30	0.40
Salt	1.81	1.93	1.81	1.93
Native	0.41	0.43	0.41	0.43
Other	1.41	1.50	1.41	1.50
Miscellaneous	0.99	1.34	0.58	0.73
Net value added	5.55	7.16	4.19	5.34
Coal	2.37	3.05	1.30	1.65
Native	0.69	0.79	-	-
Other	1.68	1.26	-	-
Crude oil	0.32	0.48	0.32	0.48
Iron ore	0.69	1.04	0.69	1.04
Manganese ore	0.07	1.10	0.07	0.10
Limestone	0.27	0.36	0.27	0.36
Salt	1.13	1.19	1.13	1.19
Native	0.25	0.26	0.25	0.26
Other	0.88	0.93	0.88	0.93
Miscellaneous	0.70	0.94	0.41	0.52

Note:

Not available.

groups for 1957 to the gross output in 1958-59. Allowances for depreciation in 1958-59 are assumed to account for the same proportion of total gross output as in 1952-57, that is, 5 per cent.

With the exception of coal and miscellaneous mineral products, the authors' estimates of gross output of all other products are the same as the adjusted figures. For coal, net value added in 1958 is first estimated at 1.30 and for 1959 at 1.65 billion yuan on the basis of the total of the net value added by the three most important coal consuming industries (factories, utilities, and modern transportation) in 1958-59, given in this appendix, and a linear regression of net value added by these three industries on the net value added by coal mining in 1952-57, obtained from data given in Tables 37, 47, and 48. The gross output of coal and miscellaneous mineral products and the net value added by the latter are then derived by multiplying the corresponding adjusted estimates for 1958-59 by a factor equal to the ratio of the adjusted net value added by coal mining to the corresponding adjusted estimate for 1958-59.

UTILITIES

Estimates of gross output and value added by electric power, water supply, and gas supply are derived separately. Estimates for electric power in 1958 and 1959 are obtained by extrapolation from the estimates for 1957 given in Appendix H, Table H-5, on the basis of an index of electric power output in 1957-59 given in Great Ten Years, p. 84; and People's Daily, January 23, 1960, p. 1. The estimates for water supply are derived similarly. The output index of water supply for 1957-58 is computed from output data given in Great Ten Years, p. 69, and the index for 1958-59 is assumed to be the same as for urban population in 1958-59, given in notes to Table K-7. For gas supply, it is assumed that the figures are the same as in 1957. The results are shown in Table K-11.

CONSTRUCTION

Net value added by construction in 1958 is derived by extrapolating from the estimate for 1957 given at 4.62 billion in Table 47, on the basis of an index of the number of workers in construction in 1957-58. The number of workers in 1957 has already been estimated at 2.40 million in Table 59. The figure for 1958 is estimated at 3.25 million by summing the number of regular workers in August 1958 given at 3 million in "The Big Leap Forward in Basic Construction Work," TCYC, No. 9, 1958, p. 10, and the number of temporary workers which is assumed to be the same as in 1955, given in Table 59.

Net value added by construction in 1959 is derived on the assumption that it increased from 1958 in proportion to the volume of basic construction work included in the state investment plan. Basic construction work increased from 21.44 billion yuan in 1958 to 26.70 billion yuan in 1959, as reported in Great Ten Years, p. 47; and People's Daily, January 23, 1960, p. 1.

MODERN TRANSPORTATION AND COMMUNICATIONS

For convenience, the adjusted estimate of value added by this industr in 1958-59 is first derived as follows. Gross receipts and value added in 1958-59 are derived by extrapolating from the estimates for 1957 on the basis of appropriate indexes for 1958-59 with 1957 as 100. Separate indexes of the 1958 volume of freight by railroads, trucks, and ships, the volume of passenger traffic, and gross receipts from communications and postal service in 1952 prices, with 1957 as 100, can be derived from data given in Great Ten Years, pp. 138-139. The index for railroad freigh

Table K-11

GROSS VALUE OF OUTPUT AND NET VALUE ADDED

BY UTILITIES, 1958-59

(billions of 1952 yuan)

	1958[a]	1959[a]
Gross value of output	2.22	3.09
Electric power	1.65	2.49
Water supply	0.50	0.53
Gas supply	0.07	0.07
Gross value added	1.30	1.75
Electric power	0.86	1.29
Water supply	0.40	0.42
Gas supply	0.04	0.04
Depreciation	0.32	0.44
Electric power	0.22	0.33
Water supply	0.10	0.11
Gas supply	0.01	0.01
Net value added	0.97	1.32
Electric power	0.64	0.97
Water supply	0.30	0.32
Gas supply	0.03	0.03

Note:

[a] No adjustment has been made in these figures. Hence, they represent both the adjusted and the authors' figures.

in 1959 with 1958 as 100 is derived from data on the tonnage of freight carried by the railroads in 1958-59. *Ibid.*, p. 129; and *People's Daily*, January 23, 1960, p. 1. The index for the total volume of freight carried by trucks and ships and that for the total volume of passenger traffic in 1959 with 1958 as 100 are assumed to be the same as the corresponding indexes for 1958, with 1957 as 100. For communications and postal service it is assumed that gross receipts in 1958-59 increased at the same rate as the average rate for 1952-57 derived from data given in *Great Ten Years*, p. 138. The results are shown in Table K-12.

As noted in Chapter III, the output data for modern factories are probably exaggerated. Since the workers and managers in the modern transportation and communications industry are working under the same incentive system and under the same tremendous pressure of the Great Leap Forward to fulfill and overfulfill the output quota as those in modern factories, it is likely that the statistics of the modern transportation and communications industry are also exaggerated. To allow for this exaggeration, we assume that the degree of exaggeration is the same in the statistics for transportation and factories. The authors' estimates of net value added in modern transportation and communications in 1958-59 are thus derived at 4.13 and 5.17 billion yuan by multiplying the corresponding adjusted estimates by the ratios of the authors' estimates to the adjusted estimates of net value added by factories in 1958-59 given in Table K-6.

OLD-FASHIONED TRANSPORTATION

The derivation of net value added by old-fashioned transportation follows the same procedure as that used to derive the estimate for 1952-57. The underlying assumption is that the total volume of transportation of

Table K-12

GROSS RECEIPTS AND NET VALUE ADDED, MODERN TRANSPORTATION, COMMUNICATIONS AND POSTAL SERVICE, 1958-59

(billions of 1952 yuan)

	1958	1959
Gross receipts	12.36	16.83
Freight[a]	10.47	14.66
Passenger[a]	1.31	1.51
Communications and postal service	0.58	0.66
Gross value added	7.19	9.78
Freight	6.08	8.51
Passenger	0.67	0.77
Communications and postal service	0.44	0.50
Depreciation	0.52	0.70
Net value added	6.66	9.07

Note:

[a] Modern transportation includes truck, rail, and ship; excludes air.

both the modern and traditional sectors varies proportionately with the output of agriculture, factories, handicrafts, and mining, the major industries to which the transportation industry provides its services.[16] Net value added by these four industries in 1957-59 and total net value added by the entire transportation industry in 1957 being known (see Table 8 and Table K-1), total net value added by the entire transportation industry in 1958-59 can be calculated at 7.00 and 8.00 billion yuan. Deducting the net value added by the modern sector, 4.13 and 5.17 billion yuan, given above, we obtain net value added by the traditional sector in 1958-59 at 2.87 and 2.83 billion yuan. By a similar procedure and using the adjusted estimate of net value added by the four industries given in this appendix and in Table 68, the adjusted estimates of net value added by old-fashioned transportation in 1958-59 are derived at 3.72 and 3.56 billion yuan.

TRADE

The derivation of net value added by trade in 1958 and 1959 (12.38 and 13.56 billion yuan) is based on the linear regression of the sum total of net value added by agriculture, factories, handicrafts, and mining on the net value added by trade for 1952-57 given in Table 49, and the net value added by the four industries in 1958-59, given earlier in this appendix. The adjusted estimates of net value added by trade in 1958-59 are derived similarly at 19.31 and 23.47 billion yuan.

GOVERNMENT ADMINISTRATION

Net income originating in government administration in 1958-59, including social, educational, and health services supported by the government but excluding military subsistence, is 3.85 and 5.09 billion yuan. These figures are estimated by extrapolating from the corresponding estimate for 1957 given at 4.01 billion yuan in Appendix H (under Government, 1952-57) on an index of total state expenditures on administration and cultural and social services for 1958-59 with 1957 as 100 (computed from data given in Great Ten Years, p. 21, and Li Hsien-nien, "Report on the Implementation of the State Budget for 1959 and the Draft State Budget for 1960," People's Daily, April 1, 1960, p. 2). Military subsistence in 1958-59 is assumed to be the same as in 1957 given at 1.02 billion yuan in Appendix H. Total net income originating in the government sector, therefore, amounts to 4.87 and 6.11 billion yuan for 1958 and 1959.

FINANCE

Net value added by finance in 1957-59 is assumed to have increased in proportion to net value added by agriculture, factories, mining, trade, and construction as a whole over the same period. Net value added by finance in 1957 and net value added by these five industries in 1957-59 being known (Table 8, and earlier sections of this appendix), net value added by finance in 1958 and 1959 can be derived at 2.00 and 2.29 billion yuan. The corresponding adjusted estimates of net value added by finance in 1958-59 are similarly derived at 2.91 and 3.58 billion yuan.

PERSONAL SERVICES

Income originating in personal services in 1958-59 is assumed to be the same as in 1957 given at 0.51 billion yuan in the discussion of personal services in Appendix H.

RESIDENTIAL RENT

Residential rent in 1958-59 is assumed to have increased from 1957 in proportion to total population over the same period. For data on total population in 1957-59, see Table 32 and the first section of this appendix.

WORK BRIGADES

Net value added by work brigades in 1958 and 1959 is derived at 2.50 and 3.27 billion yuan by summing up the estimates for their value added in railroad construction, highway construction, water conservation, and militia services.

The mileage of newly constructed railroads in 1958 is reported at 1,332 kilometers and that of reconstructed railroads, 1,044 kilometers in Great Ten Years, p. 60. Multiplying these figures by the amount of earth work done per kilometer of construction, given at 63 and 50 thousand cubic meters in Appendix H, Table H-15, and summing, we obtain the total volume of earth work done in railroad construction at 136 million cubic meters. Assuming that 80 per cent of this was done by work brigades and that the value added per cubic meter of work done amounts to 0.50 yuan, we derive the total value added by work brigades in railroad construction in 1958 at 54 million yuan.[17] Net value added in 1959 is derived at 70 million yuan on the assumption that it increased from 1958 in proportion to the mileage of railroad track laid over the same period, reported at 29 per cent above the 1958 figure in NCNA, Peiping, January 29, 1960.

Total mileage of highway construction in 1958 is reported at 150,000 kilometers in People's Daily, April 14, 1959. As mentioned in Appendix H, earth work done per kilometer was 2,150 cubic meters. Assuming that 80 per cent of the total earth work was done by work brigades, and that the value added per cubic meter was 0.50 yuan, we derive total value added by the work brigades in highway construction in 1958 at 129 million yuan.

The estimate for 1959 is derived at 166 million yuan by assuming that it increased in proportion to railroad construction over the same period.

According to People's Daily, April 15, 1959, the volume of work done in water conservation in the period October 1957 to September 1958 totalled 5.8 billion cubic meters. The volume of work done in the first three quarters of 1958 is estimated at three-fourths of the total, that is, 4.35 billion cubic meters. The estimate for the last quarter is assumed to be one-half of the amount done in other quarters since the entire nation was preoccupied with backyard blast furnaces which must have drawn away considerable amounts of labor from water conservation. Total earth work done is thus calculated at 5.08 billion cubic meters, of which 80 per cent, or 4.06 billion cubic meters, is assumed to have been done by work brigades. At 0.50 yuan per cubic meter, total net value added is derived at 2.030 million 1952 yuan.

The total earth and stone work done in water conservation and irrigation in 1959 is assumed to be the same as for the period October 1958 to September 1959, reported at 13 billion cubic meters. Ibid., January 23, 1960. The volume of work done in water conservation alone is arbitrarily assumed to be one-half of the total, that is, 6.5 billion cubic meters. Assuming, further, that 80 per cent of this total was done by work brigades and that net value added per cubic meter was 0.50 yuan per cubic meter (see Appendix H, the notes to Table H-17), we derive the net value added by work brigades in water conservation projects in 1959 at 2,600 million 1952 yuan.

Since the establishment of the communes in 1958, militia services presumably increased substantially. For lack of information, we arbitrarily assume that the imputed value of militia services in 1958 and 1959 is two and three times that of the 1957 figure of 144 million 1952 yuan.[18]

DEPRECIATION

Depreciation in agriculture and factories have already been estimated in Tables K-2 and K-6. Depreciation in other sectors is roughly estimated by the same methods as those used in deriving depreciation in 1952-57.[19]

FOOTNOTES TO APPENDIX K

1. The derivation of the 1952-57 figure is described in Appendix E.

2. The assumption of 100 per cent utilization does not mean that there is no increase in stock.

3. For the computation of this ratio, see Miscellaneous Products in Appendix E. For the gross value of the four major categories of agricultural products in 1958-59, see Table K-2.

4. Data used in calculating the percentages for 1957 are given in Tables 37 and 39.

5. The percentages of gross value added in gross output are computed at 41 and 30 per cent for the unidentified producers' and consumers' goods. For data used in this calculation, see Tables K-7 and K-8.

6. HHPYK, No. 17, 1959, p. 22.

7. By 1956, the rate of utilization of modern steel producing equipment was already close to 90 per cent of capacity. (See CHCC, Peiping, July 1957, p. 6.) This means that any further expansion in the output of the modern mills must come primarily from increase in capacity. However, productive capacity increased only by 0.53 million tons in 1957 over 1956, and the only important plants completed in 1958 were the No. 4 and No. 5 converters in Anshan, which could hardly account for the increase of 2.65 million tons of modern steel in 1958 over 1957. The increase of capacity in 1957 is derived by deducting the increase in 1953-56 (2.29 million tons given in SSB, Industry Study, p. 16) from the total increase in 1953-57 (2.82 million tons given in FFYP Communique, p. 49). For the list of major construction projects completed or partially completed, see 1958 Communique, p. 53. In another reference, the total productive capacity at the end of

1957 is given at 6.48 million tons, and the 1958 output at 8.0 million tons. (SSB, "Rapid Development in China's Industrial Construction," TCYC, No. 9, September 1958, pp. 4-5). For the two figures to be consistent, there must be an increase in capacity of more than 1.5 million tons in 1958 and for the above reasons this does not seem plausible.

8. For a discussion of the reasons why the output of steel in 1958 is derived indirectly, see Chapter III under A Conjectural Estimate of Domestic Product, 1958-59.

9. The gross value of output in 1957 has been estimated at 3.21 billion yuan and the 1958 authors' estimate and adjusted estimate of gross value of output, 3.80 and 4.80 billion yuan. (See Tables 39, K-7 and K-9. The authors' estimate of the increase in gross value of output from 1957 to 1958 is therefore equal to 3.80 - 3.21 = 0.59, and the estimated adjusted increase, 4.80 - 3.21 = 1.59 billion yuan. The ratio of the authors' estimated increase to the adjusted increase is thus calculated at 0.59/1.59 = 37 per cent.

10. The adjusted increase from 1958 to 1959 is equal to 8.01 - 3.80 = 4.21 billion yuan (Table K-7). Multiplying 4.21 by 37 per cent, we obtain our estimated increase at 1.56 billion yuan. This amount is then added to our 1958 estimated total output of 3.80 billion yuan to obtain gross output of 5.36 billion yuan for 1959.

11. For the gross output of pig iron, rolled steel, and coke in 1957, see Table 39, and for the adjusted gross output in 1958-59, see Table K-7.

12. See the section, A Conjectural Estimate of Domestic Product, 1958-59, in Chapter III.

13. 1957 exports -- the sum of exports of cotton cloth, knitted goods, semifinished and finished textile products, and one-half of the export of miscellaneous clothing products given in Table 91.

1958 exports -- based on the 1957 figure and an index of cotton cloth exports of 134 per cent in 1958 with 1957 as 100, computed from exports to Soviet Russia given in Economic Planning Administration, Ministry of Foreign Trade, USSR, Foreign Trade of the USSR, 1958 (Statistical Survey), Moscow, 1959 (English translation), p. 192, and exports to Western countries in 1958-59 reported in Department of State, Summary of East-West Trade in 1958 (Thirteenth Report to Congress), U.S. Government Printing Office, Washington, D.C., 1960, p. 47.

1959 exports -- the index of exports of cotton cloth and related products to Soviet Russia in 1958-59, given in China Trade and Economic Newsletter, October 1960, p. 7. The original data on exports are given in rubles and U.S. dollars; in our computation, they have been converted to yuan at the official exchange rates given in CHCC, No. 12, 1957, p. 29.

14. Data used in this calculation are in Tables 37, 39, and K-9.

15. Data used in this calculation are in Tables 39, 43, and K-9.

16. This assumption presupposes that transportation capacity itself is not a limiting factor. Although there might well be temporary and regional bottlenecks, such as those that occurred in the latter part of 1958, over longer periods this assumption appears reasonable. In the modern sector, the most important carrier is the railroad. Considerable increase in the rolling stock and improvements in management have been reported (see, for example, People's Daily, January 25, 1960, p. 1; and

Wang Shou-tao, "The Transportation and Communications Industry in the Continuous Big Leap Forward," People's Daily, February 19, 1960, p. 7). Railroad construction since 1949 apparently has been determined more by strategic than by economic considerations. Consequently, overloading of the newly constructed railroads, particularly in the northwestern part, does not appear likely. In the traditional sector, human labor is primarily the means of transport, and the supply of unskilled labor used in transport is generally rather elastic.

17. Derivation of the value added per cubic meter of earth work done is explained under Water Conservation Projects in Appendix H.

18. See the discussion on value of militia services under Water Conservation Projects in Appendix H.

19. Depreciation is also discussed under most of the sections in Appendix H and immediately preceding the discussion on mining in Chapter IV.

Appendix L

AN ALTERNATIVE VIEW OF BASIC CONSTRUCTION AND INVESTMENT IN WORKING CAPITAL[1]

INTRODUCTION

Some Communist investment series can be given a different interpretation from that adopted in Chapter V. One possible reinterpretation involves the definition of investment in basic construction. This term as defined in the text includes ancillary expenses and new fixed assets. A possible redefinition includes these two elements plus changes in unfinished construction.

A second reinterpretation involves a new estimate of investment in working capital. The estimate in the text is derived from Communist estimates of accumulation and basic construction. Somewhat different results can be obtained by use of the percentage of accumulation accounted for by working capital investment, as given in Communist sources.

These two interpretations and their effects on the estimates of total investment and investment in working and fixed capital are discussed in this appendix. The original interpretation and the underlying assumptions are explained first, and then the alternative estimate is derived and compared with the original estimate given in the text.

NET DOMESTIC INVESTMENT

The Original Estimate

Net domestic investment is defined in the text as accumulation less ancillary expenses, plus items omitted from the Communist data.

In calculating net domestic investment, we made the following assumptions:

(1) Ancillary expenses (defined below) are included in accumulation. Survey and design expenses for a project, probably a major item in ancillary expenses, are presumably included, for they are included in total value of the fixed asset when the latter becomes an entry in the capital account, and accumulation is estimated from the capital accounts.[2] It is not clear from the sources whether ancillary expenses other than survey and design costs are also included in accumulation. Here it is assumed that they are.

(2) Part of the value added by work brigades, passenger transportation, and finance is not included in Communist national income estimates, and therefore is not included in accumulation.

Accumulation is derived from Communist data on national expenditures and the percentage of these expenditures accounted for by accumulation. Items presumably omitted from the accumulation figures are estimated elsewhere in the study. Ancillary expenses are obtained by deducting new fixed assets from investment in basic construction on the following definitions and assumptions.

Investment in basic construction -- called "basic construction" for short -- is defined as "funds used to increase fixed assets in the national economy," which includes (a) expenditures on construction; (b) purchases of equipment, tools, and instruments; (c) installation expenses, and (d) expenses of prospecting, design, and scientific experiments and research directly related to the construction project, expenditures of training cadres to operate the new project when completed, expenses necessary to compensate former residents of the construction site for moving them out, and so on.[3] Item (d) in this definition is designated as "ancillary expenses."

The value of a "new fixed asset" is the sum of (a) through (c) above plus "certain expenses connected with increasing fixed assets."[4] Exactly what is included in "certain expenses connected with increasing fixed assets" is not clear; nor is there any reasonable way of estimating it. The item is assumed to be negligible. If this assumption does not hold, then ancillary expenses will be overestimated and total net investment underestimated.

Other assumptions underlying the calculation of ancillary expenses are (3) that both basic construction and new fixed assets are gross of depreciation; (4) that the scope for both concepts is the same -- both include certain basic construction or new fixed assets outside the state plan but exclude others, such as basic construction by cooperative farms; and (5) that no ancillary expenses are involved in basic construction in the individual or cooperative sector.

<u>An Alternative Estimate</u>

An alternative definition of basic construction can be given as follows: At any given point of time, three categories of investment work can be distinguished according to their stages of construction and installation: (1) uninspected work in progress, which includes all construction work in progress before it reaches a certain stage of partial completion and before it is inspected; (2) unfinished construction, which includes the partially completed work that has been inspected, the total value of equipment being installed, the value of equipment and tools that do not require installation but have been shipped to the construction site, and completed plants that are ready to operate but have not yet been inspected; and (3) new fixed assets, which include completed plants (not necessarily a completed project) that are ready to operate and have been inspected.

If a project consists simply of laying a foundation, putting up walls, and covering the structure with a roof, the value of the unfinished foundation at any given point of time is uninspected work in progress. After the foundation is completed and inspected, its value becomes unfinished construction. After the whole building is completed and inspected, it becomes a new fixed asset.

Basic construction is defined as the sum of new fixed assets, changes in unfinished construction, and ancillary expenses.[5] If this definition is used, then ancillary expenses cannot be derived as the difference between basic construction and new fixed assets, for this difference includes not only ancillary expenses but also changes in unfinished construction.

For lack of information, the amount of ancillary expenses can be roughly estimated only by making some more or less arbitrary assumptions. In the Soviet case, ancillary expenses constitute 6 to 9 per cent of basic construction.[6] It is probably higher in the Chinese case because most of the surveying, designing, and training was done by Soviet experts, presumably with high salaries. We assume it to be 10 per cent. The results, as compared with the original estimates, in billions of 1952 yuan, are as follows:

Year	Original	Alternative	Difference
1952	1.25	0.44	0.81
1953	1.35	0.75	0.60
1954	1.67	0.89	0.78
1955	1.32	0.96	0.36
1956	4.03	1.64	2.39
1957	1.01	1.53	-0.52

Because the estimates of ancillary expenses are different, total net and gross domestic investment would also be different. The new estimates for the two items, both in billions of 1952 yuan, are as follows:

	Net Domestic Investment		Gross Domestic Investment	
Year	Original	Alternative	Original	Alternative
1952	11.26	12.07	14.52	15.33
1953	15.45	16.05	19.11	19.71
1954	16.74	17.52	20.77	21.55
1955	18.04	18.40	22.31	22.67
1956	20.39	22.78	25.59	27.98
1957	20.62	20.10	26.10	25.58

These changes will also affect the estimates of total and miscellaneous personal consumption, the percentage distribution of gross domestic expenditure, per capita expenditure and consumption, the comparison of the adjusted with the authors' estimate of domestic expenditure, and the reconciliation of the adjusted estimate and the Communist estimate of net domestic expenditure.

It should be noted that both the original and the alternative estimate of net and gross domestic investment are likely to be high because the Communists tend to understate depreciation, therefore overestimating accumulation.[7]

INVESTMENT IN WORKING CAPITAL AND FIXED CAPITAL

The Original Estimate

Accumulation is first defined as the sum of (a) increase in fixed assets (net of depreciation) and (b) increases in working capital and inventory reserves. Working capital and inventory reserves include such items as raw materials, supplementary raw materials, fuels, low-priced perishable goods, industrial semifinished products and goods in process, "unfinished projects," and inventory reserves of marketing or supply organizations and state organizations.[8]

Increase in fixed assets is defined as the sum of new fixed assets, miscellaneous new fixed assets, ancillary expenses, and major repairs, less depreciation.[9]

Total new fixed assets are separated into new fixed assets (that is, those in the state sector) and miscellaneous new fixed assets (that is, those in the private and cooperative sector) because there is reason to believe that the Communist statistics given for "new fixed assets" refer to those in the state sector only. Basic construction, apparently comparable in scope to new fixed assets, does not include the basic construction of agricultural cooperatives.

There is no satisfactory way of estimating miscellaneous new fixed assets, major repairs, and the Communist figure for depreciation.

In general, depreciation should exceed major repairs because depreciation allows for funding of both major repairs and replacement. On the other hand, there are likely to be some miscellaneous new fixed assets, that is, new fixed assets in the private and cooperative sector. This item will tend to offset the excess of depreciation over major repairs, so that it may not be far wrong to assume that the algebraic sum of these three items is rather small.

Increase in fixed assets is therefore equal to new fixed assets plus ancillary expenses, which in turn is equal to basic construction. Investment in working capital is equal to accumulation minus the increase in fixed assets, that is, accumulation minus basic construction. And net fixed investment is equal to total domestic investment minus investment in working capital. Underlying this calculation is the assumption that the service items omitted in accumulation are now allocated to fixed investment alone. Whatever error there may be in this allocation would be relatively small, for the total amount of services added back to accumulation for any given year is about 0.5 billion yuan, that is, about 3 to 4 per cent of total domestic investment.

A more serious difficulty arises in connection with the estimate of net fixed investment in each sector. As in the case of increase in fixed assets, it is assumed that the algebraic sum of miscellaneous new fixed assets, major repairs, and depreciation is negligible. Net fixed investment in each sector is then derived by summing new fixed assets and the omitted items in each sector. However, depreciation is likely to exceed major repairs by a considerable amount. If, as is probable toward the end of the First Plan Period, this amount is not fully compensated for by miscellaneous new fixed assets, net fixed investment should be lower than the figures given in Table 76. In other words, the original estimate is high. Consequently the capital stock figures for pre-1956 years are underestimated and those for post-1955 years are overestimated, since the capital stock estimates are obtained by adding (algebraically) the net fixed investment to the Communist estimate of net capital stock at the end of 1955. The rather rapid rate of growth of capital stock for the trade sector may be partly explained in this way, although to some extent it may be due to the construction of storage facilities for grain since 1953 when the planned purchase and sale system was first put into effect.

An Alternative Estimate

An alternative estimate of working capital investment can be derived by multiplying accumulation by the percentage of accumulation accounted for by increase in working capital investment. This calculation by-passes the assumptions underlying the original estimate, but it involves two others: (1) it is not clear whether the percentages are computed from absolute figures in constant 1952 prices or not, but we assume that they are; (2) it is not clear whether working capital investment includes changes in unfinished construction, but we assume that it does not. In the calculation of ancillary expenses above, the amount of change in unfinished construction is implicit. The sum of the estimate for unfinished construction plus the estimate of working capital obtained directly from Communist figures is the alternative estimate of working capital investment.

Net fixed investment is then obtained by deducting working capital investment from total net domestic investment. The results, in billions of 1952 yuan, are as follows:

Year	Working Capital Investment		Net Fixed Investment	
	Original	Alternative	Original	Alternative
1952	7.08	7.72	4.18	4.35
1953	7.86	7.83	7.59	8.22
1954	7.91	8.48	8.83	9.04
1955	8.24	7.16	9.80	11.24
1956	6.32	4.48	14.07	18.30
1957	6.53	5.47	16.13	16.67

The new estimate of total net fixed investment will not affect the allocation of fixed investment by sectors shown in Table 76, except for the "others" sector, which, being the residual, becomes larger.

It seems desirable to separate fixed investment in the state sector (which includes investment in the state plan and other investment such as investment by state enterprises financed with union funds) and fixed investment outside the state sector. The total for the state sector is the sum of new fixed assets (deflated) and the omitted items (work brigades, passenger transportation, and finance, which have been allocated entirely to the state sector). Fixed investment in the non-state sector is derived as the residual after deducting fixed investment in the state sector from total fixed investment. The results, in billions of 1952 yuan, are as follows:[10]

	1952	1953	1954	1955	1956	1957
Other investments by the state						
(1) Culture, education, and research	0.21	0.48	0.58	0.55	0.86	1.00
(2) Public health and welfare	0.04	0.11	0.13	0.10	0.09	0.14
(3) Geological prospecting	0.05	0.15	0.24	0.23	0.34	0.32
(4) Government administration	0.01	0.22	0.18	0.13	0.13	0.20
(5) Omitted service items	0.11	0.16	0.16	0.11	0.11	0.10
(6) Miscellaneous	0.39	0.91	0.86	0.58	0.70	0.66
(7) TOTAL	0.81	2.03	2.15	1.70	2.23	2.42
Other investments in the non-state sector						
(8) Original	0	0.55	0.65	0.23	0.32	0.35
(9) Alternative	0.17	1.18	0.86	1.67	4.55	0.89
Total other investments, state and non-state sectors						
(10) Original [row (7) + row (8)]	0.81	2.58	2.80	1.93	2.55	2.77
(11) Alternative [row (7) + row (9)]	0.98	3.21	3.01	3.37	6.78	3.31

There is yet another way of using the Communist figures for new fixed assets by sectors without involving the many assumptions mentioned earlier. One may simply regard the sum of new fixed assets and the omitted items as fixed investment by the state, gross of depreciation and net of major repairs, and use them in the discussions of the pattern of investment by the state and the trends in capital-output relationships. But since the margin of error in the Communist figures and hence in our investment estimates is probably large, further refinements along these lines are not likely to produce significant improvements, and have therefore not been attempted.

FOOTNOTES TO APPENDIX L

1. We are greatly indebted to RAND colleague Richard H. Moorsteen for many stimulating comments and constructive suggestions.

2. Hsu Chien, *et al.*, p. 131; Yueh Wei, "The Method of Computing National Income," *CCYC*, No. 3, June 1956, p. 63.

3. *First Five Year Plan*, p. 23.

4. Hsu Chien, *et al.*, p. 131.

5. *Ibid.*, pp. 129-131; Yang Pin-chuan, "Unfinished Construction," *TCKTTH*, No. 1, 1956, pp. 29-30.

6. Central Statistical Board of the U.S.S.R.; Council of Ministers, *U.S.S.R. in Figures for 1959*, Moscow, Foreign Language Publishing House, p. 167.

7. Hsu Yi, "A Discussion of Some Aspects of Economic Accounting," *CCYC*, No. 4, April 1958, p. 66.

8. Yueh Wei, "The Method of Computing National Income," *CCYC*, No. 3, June 1956, p. 63.

9. This definition is based on a discussion of increases and reductions of fixed assets in an enterprise given in Hsu Chien, *et al.*, p. 48. The original discussion includes two items not given in the definition here: purchase or sale of fixed assets by the enterprise, and withdrawal of depreciated assets and losses. The first item does not appear in our definition because for the economy as a whole inter-firm purchases and sales cancel out. The second item is presumably negligible.

10. Total investment in the "others" sector is obtained by deducting fixed investment in factories, mining, and utilities;

construction; trade; modern transportation and communications; and agriculture from total fixed investment. The estimates of other investments by the state are primarily based on the Communist figures for new fixed assets and basic construction. For sources, see the notes to Table 76. Other investments in the non-state sector are residuals.

INTRODUCTION TO REFERENCE MATERIALS

The arrangement of materials adopted here is designed to serve three groups of readers: (1) those who do not read Chinese; (2) those who are particularly interested in either the pre-1949 or post-1948 periods; (3) those who are interested in Communist Chinese official statistics or statements on economic policy. The references are therefore arranged by language, period, and nature of the source.

Section I(B)(3), "State Statistical Bureau," is for the convenience of those who are particularly interested in the nature and reliability of Communist statistics. Section I(B)(4), "Official reports and statements," lists articles by officials of the Communist regime who are of cabinet rank or higher. In this way we have attempted to distinguish statements made by major policy makers.

The following Table of Organization shows the arrangement of references.

TABLE OF ORGANIZATION

LIST OF SHORT TITLES

Agricultural Estimates	National Agricultural Research Bureau, National Government, *Agricultural Estimates,* Shanghai, 1947.
AMJP, Amoy	*Amoy jih-pao* (Amoy Daily), Amoy.
CCCP, Shanghai	*Ching-chi chou-pao* (Economic Weekly), Shanghai.
CCJP, Hankow	*Chang-chiang jih-pao* (Chang-chiang Daily), Hankow.
CCJP, Sian	*Chun-chung jih-pao* (The Mass Daily), Sian.
CCTP	*Ching-chi tao-pao* (Economic Bulletin), Hong Kong.
CCYC	*Ching-chi yen-chiu* (Economic Research), Peiping.
CFJP, Shanghai	*Chieh-fang jih-pao* (Emancipation Daily), Shanghai.
Chang, *Crop Estimates*	Chang, C. C., *An Estimate of China's Farms and Crops,* Nanking, 1932.
CHCC	*Chi-hua ching-chi* (Planned Economy), Peiping.
CKJP, Chungking	*Chungking jih-pao* (Chungking Daily), Chungking.
CKJP, Hangchow	*Chekiang jih-pao* (Chekiang Daily), Hangchow.
CPJP, Tientsin	*Chin-pu jih-pao* (Progress Daily), Tientsin.
Crop Reports	National Agricultural Research Bureau, *Nung-ch'ing pao-kao* (Crop Reports), Nanking. Monthly.
Economic Yearbook, 1934	Ministry of Industry, National Government, *Chung-kuo ching-chi nien-chien* (China Economic Yearbook), Nanking, 1934.
FAO	Food and Agricultural Organization of the United Nations.
Farm Economy	Buck, John Lossing, *Chinese Farm Economy,* Chicago, University of Chicago Press, 1930.

FCJP, Foochow	*Foochow jih-pao* (Foochow Daily), Foochow.
FFYP Communique	SSB, "Communique on the Fulfillment of the First Five Year Plan," *Hsin-hua pan-yueh-k'an* (New China Semimonthly), Peiping, 8, April 1959, pp. 48–54.
First Five Year Plan	*Chung-hua-jen-min-kung-ho-kuo fa-chan kuo-min ching-chi ti-y wu-nien-chi-hua* (The First Five Year Plan for National Economic Development of the People's Republic of China), Peiping, Jen-min chu-pan-she, 1955.
FKJP, Foochow	*Fukien jih-pao* (Fukien Daily), Foochow.
Food Balance Sheets	Food and Agriculture Organization of the United Nations, *Food Balance Sheets,* Washington, D.C., 1949.
Food Crops	Liu, Ta-chung, Chong Twanmo, and Kung-chia Yeh, *Production of Food Crops on the Chinese Mainland: Prewar and Postwar,* Santa Monica, Calif., The RAND Corporation, January 1964.
Great Ten Years	*Wei-ta ti shi-nien* (The Great Ten Years), Peiping, Jen-min chu-pan-she, 1959.
HHJP, Chungking	*Hsin-hua jih-pao* (New China Daily), Chungking.
HHJP, Nanking	*Hsin-hua jih-pao* (New China Daily), Nanking.
HHPYK	*Hsin-hua pan-yueh-k'an* (New China Semimonthly), Peiping.
HHYP	*Hsin-hua yueh-pao* (New China Monthly), Peiping.
HNJP, Kaifeng	*Honan jih-pao* (Honan Daily), Kaifeng.
HPJP, Hankow	*Hupeh jih-pao* (Hupeh Daily), Hankow.
HPJP, Paoting	*Hopei jih-pao* (Hopei Daily), Paoting.
HSCJP, Soochow	*Hsin Soochow jih-pao* (New Soochow Daily), Soochow.

HWJP, Shanghai	*Hsin-wen jih-pao* (News Daily), Shanghai.
Industrial Handbook: Chekiang	Bureau of Foreign Trade, National Government, *Chung-kuo shih-yeh-tze: Chekiang-sheng* (Industrial Handbook of China: Chekiang), Shanghai, 1933.
Industrial Handbook: Hunan	Bureau of Foreign Trade, National Government, *Chung-kuo shih-yeh-tze: Hunan-sheng* (Industrial Handbook of China: Hunan), Shanghai, 1935.
Industrial Handbook: Kiangsu	Bureau of Foreign Trade, National Government, *Chung-kuo shih-yeh-tze: Kiangsu-sheng* (Industrial Handbook of China: Kiangsu), Shanghai, 1933.
Industrial Handbook: Shansi	Bureau of Foreign Trade, National Government, *Chung-kuo shih-yeh-tze: Shansi-sheng* (Industrial Handbook of China: Shansi), Shanghai, 1936.
Industrial Handbook: Shantung	Bureau of Foreign Trade, National Government, *Chung-kuo shih-yeh-tze: Shantung-sheng* (Industrial Handbook of China: Shantung), Shanghai, 1934.
KJJP	*Kung-jen jih-pao* (Workers' Daily), Peiping.
KMJP, Peiping	*Kuang-ming jih-pao* (Kuang-ming Daily), Peiping.
KSHW, Canton	*Kung-sheng hsin-wen chou-k'an* (Industrial and Commercial News Weekly), Canton.
KSJP, Hong Kong	*Kung-sheng jih-pao* (Industrial and Commercial Daily), Hong Kong.
KSJP, Lanchow	*Kansu jih-pao* (Kansu Daily), Lanchow.
KSJP, Nanchang	*Kiangsi jih-pao* (Kiangsi Daily), Nanchang.
Kwangsi Yearbook	Kwangsi Provincial Government, *Kwang-si nien-chien* (Kwangsi Yearbook), 1934.

Land Utilization	Buck, John Lossing, *Land Utilization in China,* 3 vols., Chicago, University of Chicago Press, 1937.
Lieu, *Industry Survey*	Lieu, D. K., *Chung-kuo kung-yeh tiao-tsa pao-kao* (Report on a Survey of China's Industry), Nanking, 1937.
Liu, *Income*	Liu Ta-chung, *China's National Income, 1931–36: An Exploratory Study,* Washington, D.C., The Brookings Institution, 1946.
Manchurian Factories, 1933	South Manchurian Railway, *Manshū kojō tōkei, A, 1933* (Statistics of Manchurian Factories, A, 1933), 1935.
Manchurian Factories, 1934	South Manchurian Railway and the Manchurian Government, *Manshū kojō tōkei, B, 1934* (Statistics of Manchurian Factories, B, 1934), Hsinking, 1936.
NCNA	New China News Agency.
NFJP, Canton	*Nan-fang jih-pao* (Southern Daily), Canton.
NMKJP, Huhehot	*Nei-meng-ku jih-pao* (Nei-meng-ku Daily), Huhehot.
Northeast Economic Handbook	Northeast Natural Resources Control Committee, National Government, *Tung-pei ching-chi hsiao-ts'ung-shu* (Economic Handbook of Northeast China), Shenyang, 1947.
NPJP, Ning-po	*Ning-po jih-pao* (Ning-po Daily), Ning-po.
Ou, *National Income*	Ou Pao-san, *1933 Chung-kuo kuo-min so-te* (China's National Income, 1933), 2 vols., Shanghai, Chung-hua Book Co., 1947.
People's Daily	*Jen-min jih-pao* (People's Daily), Peiping.
Po, *1956–57 Plan*	Po I-po, "Report on the Fulfillment of the 1956 National Economic Plan and the Draft Plan for 1957," *Hsin-hua pan-yueh-k'an* (New China Semi-monthly), Peiping, 14, July 1957, pp. 28–39.
Po, *1958 Plan*	Po I-po, "Report on the Draft 1958 Na-

tional Economic Plan," *Hsin-hua pan-yueh-k'an* (New China Semimonthly), Peiping, 5, March 1958, pp. 12–23.

SCCJP, Shihchiachuan — *Shihchiachuan jih-pao* (Shihchiachuan Daily), Shihchiachuan.

Shen, *Agricultural Resources* — Shen Tsung-han, *Agricultural Resources of China*, Ithaca, N.Y., Cornell University Press, 1951.

Shen Pao Yearbook, 1933 — *Shen Pao nien-chien, 1933* (Shen Pao Yearbook, 1933), Shanghai, Shen-pao nien-chien-she, 1933.

Shen Pao Yearbook, 1935 — *Shen Pao nien-chien, 1935* (Shen Pao Yearbook, 1935), Shanghai, Shen-pao nien-chien-she, 1935.

SKJP, Tihua — *Sinkiang jih-pao* (Sinkiang Daily), Tihua.

SNJP, Wuhsi — *Su-nan jih-pao* (Southern Kiangsu Daily), Wuhsi.

SPJP, Yangchow — *Su-pei jih-pao* (Northern Kiangsu Daily), Yangchow.

SSB — *State Statistical Bureau.*

SSB, *Commercial Network* — SSB, "The Development of China's Commercial Network and Basic Conditions in 1955," *Hsin-hua pan-yueh-k'an* (New China Semimonthly), Peiping, 24, December 1956, pp. 80–83.

SSB, *Industry Study* — SSB, *Wo-kuo kang-tieh, tien-li, mei-t'an, chi-hsieh, fang-chih, tsao-chih kung-yeh ti chin-hsi* (Past and Present of China's Iron and Steel, Electric Power, Coal, Machinery, Textile, and Paper Industries), Peiping, T'ung-chi chu-pan-she, 1958.

SSB, *1955 Employment* — SSB, "Size, Structure and Distribution of Total Employment in 1955," *Hsin-hua pan-yueh-k'an* (New China Semimonthly), Peiping, 2, January 1957, pp. 87-889.

SSB, *Population Statistics* — SSB, "Population Statistics, 1949–56," *T'ung-chi kung-tso* (Statistical Work), Peiping, 11, June 1957, pp. 24–25.

SSB, *Socialist Industrialization* — SSB, "A General Survey of China's Socialist Industrialization," *Hsin-hua*

	pan-yueh-k'an (New China Semi-monthly), Peiping, 2, January 1957, pp. 54–62.
SSB, *Technological Level*	SSB, "The Technological Level of Industrial Production in China," *T'ung-chi kung-tso* (Statistical Work), Peiping, 8, April 1957, pp. 30–33.
SSJP, Taiyuan	*Shansi jih-pao* (Shansi Daily), Taiyuan.
Statistical Abstract, 1935	Directorate of Statistics, National Government, *Chung-hua min-kuo t'ung-chi ti-yao, 1935* (Statistical Abstract of the Republic of China, 1935), Nanking, 1936.
Statistical Abstract, 1940	Directorate of Statistics, National Government, *Chung-hua min-kuo t'ung-chi ti-yao, 1940* (Statistical Abstract of the Republic of China, 1940), Chungking, 1940.
Survey	Ministry of Communications, Post Office Administration, National Government, *Chung-kuo t'ung-yu ti-fang wu-chan-chih* (A Survey of Products along China's Mail Routes), Shanghai, 1937.
SYJP, Kuai-sui	*Sui-yuan jih-pao* (Sui-yuan Daily), Kuai-sui.
TCJP, Tsinan	*Ta-chung jih-pao* (The Public Daily), Tsinan.
TCKT	*T'ung-chi kung-tso* (Statistical Work), Peiping, succeeding *T'ung-chi kung-tso-t'ung-hsin* since January 1957, beginning January 1959 succeeded by *Chi-hua yu t'ung-chi*.
TCKTTH	*T'ung-chi kung-tso t'ung-hsin* (Statistical Work Bulletin), Peiping.
TCYC	*T'ung-chi yen-chiu* (Statistical Research), Peiping.
TKP, Peiping	*Ta kung pao* (Impartial Daily), Peiping.
TKP, Shanghai	*Ta kung pao* (Impartial Daily), Shanghai.
TKP, Tientsin	*Ta kung pao* (Impartial Daily), Tientsin.

TPJP, Shenyang — *Tung-pei jih-pao* (Northeast Daily), Shenyang.

The Trade of China — Inspectorate General of Customs, National Government, *The Trade of China, 1933,* Shanghai, 1934.

TTJP, Tientsin — *Tientsin jih-pao* (Tientsin Daily), Tientsin.

TTJP, Tsingtao — *Tsingtao jih-pao* (Tsingtao Daily), Tsingtao.

WHP, Hong Kong — *Wen-hui pao* (Wen-hui Daily), Hong Kong.

WPJP, Hofei — *Wan-pei jih-pao* (North Anhwei Daily), Hofei.

YNJP, Kunming — *Yunnan jih-pao* (Yunnan Daily), Kunming.

1952 Communique — SSB, "Communique on National Economic Cultural and Educational Rehabilitation and Development in 1952," *Jen-min jih-pao* (People's Daily), Peiping, September 28, 1954, p. 1.

1953 Communique — SSB, "Communique on National Economic Development and Fulfillment of the State Plan in 1953," *Jen-min jih-pao* (People's Daily), Peiping, September 28, 1954, p. 1.

1954 Communique — SSB, "Communique on National Economic Development and Fulfillment of the State Plan in 1954," *Jen-min jih-pao* (People's Daily), Peiping, September 23, 1955, p. 1.

1955 Communique — SSB, "Communique on Fulfillment of the National Economic Plan in 1955," *Hsin-hua pan-yueh-k'an* (New China Semimonthly), Peiping, 13, July 1956, pp. 39–42.

1956 Communique — SSB, "Communique on Fulfillment of the National Plan in 1956," *Hsin-hua pan-yueh-k'an* (New China Semimonthly), Peiping, 17, September 1957, pp. 201–205.

1958 Communique — SSB, "Communique on the Development of the National Economy in

1958," *Hsin-hua pan-yueh-k'an* (New China Semimonthly) Peiping, 8, April 1959, pp. 51–54.

1959 Communique — "Press Communique on Economic Development in 1959," *Jen-min jih-pao* (People's Daily), Peiping, January 23, 1960, p. 1.

1954 Statistical Abstract — SSB, "Statistical Abstract of the National Economic, Cultural and Educational Achievements in 1949–54," *Hsin-hu yueh-pao* (New China Monthly), Peiping, 11, November 1955, pp. 181–189.

1955 Statistical Abstract — SSB, "Economic Statistical Abstract," *Hsin-hua pan-yueh-k'an* (New China Semimonthly), Peiping, 17, September 1956, pp. 39–50.

1956 Statistical Abstract — SSB, "Economic Statistical Abstract," *Kuo-chia t'ung-chi-chu kwan-yu 1956 nien-tu kuo-min ching-chi chi-hua chi-hsing che-kuo ti kung-pao* (State Statistical Bureau Communique on the Fulfillment of the National Economic Plan for 1956), Peiping, T'ung-chi chu-pan-she, 1957.

LIST OF PERIODICALS AND NEWSPAPERS CONSULTED

I. *Chinese Language, Pre-1949*

Academica Sinica, *She-sui ko-hsueh tsa-chih* (Quarterly Review of Social Scientists), Shanghai. Quarterly.

Chung-nung ching-chi t'ung-chi (Economic Statistics of the Farmers' Bank of China), Chungking. Monthly.

Geological Survey of China, *General Statement on the Mining Industry*. Irregular.

Nankai Institute of Economics, *Quarterly Journal of Economics and Statistics,* Tientsin. Quarterly.

National Agricultural Research Bureau, *Nung-ch'ing pao-kao* (Crop Reports), Nanking. Monthly.

T'ung-chi yueh-pao (Statistical Monthly), Nanking and Chungking. Monthly.

Tung-fang tsa-chih (Eastern Miscellany), Shanghai. Monthly.

II. *Chinese Language, Post-1948*

A. Newspapers

Amoy jih-pao (Amoy Daily), Amoy.

Chang-chiang jih-pao (Chang-chiang Daily), Hankow.

Chekiang jih-pao (Chekiang Daily), Hangchow.

Chieh-fang jih-pao (Emancipation Daily), Shanghai.

Chin-pu jih-pao (Progress Daily), Tientsin.

Chun-chung jih-pao (The Mass Daily), Sian.

Chung-king jih-pao (Chungking Daily), Chungking.

Foochow jih-pao (Foochow Daily), Foochow.

Fukien jih-pao (Fukien Daily), Foochow.

Honan jih-pao (Honan Daily), Kaifeng.

Hopei jih-pao (Hopei Daily), Paoting.

Hsin-hua jih-pao (New China Daily), Chungking.

Hsin-hua jih-pao (New China Daily), Nanking.

Hsin Soochow jih-pao (New Soochow Daily), Soochow.

Hsin-wen jih-pao (News Daily), Shanghai.

Hupeh jih-pao (Hupeh Daily), Hankow.

Jen-min jih-pao (People's Daily), Peiping.

Kansu jih-pao (Kansu Daily), Lanchow.

Kiangsi jih-pao (Kiangsi Daily), Nanchang.

Kuang-ming jih-pao (Kuang-ming Daily), Peiping.

Kung-jen jih-pao (Workers' Daily), Peiping.

Kung-sheng jih-pao (Industrial and Commercial Daily), Hong Kong.

Nan-fang jih-pao (Southern Daily), Canton.
Nei-meng-ku jih-pao (Nei-meng-ku Daily), Huhehot.
Ning-po jih-pao (Ning-po Daily), Ning-po.
Shansi jih-pao (Shansi Daily), Taiyuan.
Shihchiachuan jih-pao (Shihchiachuan Daily), Shihchiachuan.
Sinkiang jih-pao (Sinkiang Daily), Tihua.
Su-nan jih-pao (Southern Kiangsu Daily), Wuhsi.
Su-pei jih-pao (Northern Kiangsu Daily), Yangchow.
Sui-yuan jih-pao (Sui-yuan Daily), Kuai-sui.
Ta-chung jih-pao (The Public Daily), Tsinan.
Ta kung pao (Impartial Daily), Peiping.
Ta kung pao (Impartial Daily), Shanghai.
Ta kung pao (Impartial Daily), Tientsin.
Tientsin jih-pao (Tientsin Daily), Tientsin.
Tsingtao jih-pao (Tsingtao Daily), Tsingtao.
Tung-pei jih-pao (Northeast Daily), Shenyang.
Wan-pei jih-pao (North Anhwei Daily), Hofei.
Wen-hui pao (Wen-hui Daily), Hong Kong.
Yunnan jih-pao (Yunnan Daily), Kunming.

B. Periodicals

Chi-hua ching-chi (Planned Economy), Peiping. Monthly.
Chien-she yueh-k'an (Reconstruction Monthly), Peiping. Monthly.
Ching-chi chou-pao (Economic Weekly), Shanghai. Weekly.
Ching-chi tao-pao (Economic Bulletin), Hong Kong. Bimonthly.
Ching-chi yen-chiu (Economic Research), Peiping. Bimonthly.
Chung-kuo chin-yung (China's Finance), Peiping. Semimonthly.
Chung-kuo ch'ing-kung-yeh (China's Light Industry), Peiping. Semimonthly.
Chung-kuo fang-chih (China's Textile Industry), Peiping. Semimonthly.
Chung-kuo kung-jen (Chinese Worker), Peiping. Semimonthly.
Chung-kuo lin-yeh (China's Forestry), Peiping. Monthly.
Chung-kuo shiu-li (China's Water Conservancy), Peiping. Semimonthly.
Chung-kuo shiu-li (China's Water Conservancy), Peiping. Monthly.
Hsin-chien-she (New Construction), Peiping. Monthly.
Hsin-hua pan-yueh-k'an (New China Semimonthly), Peiping (beginning January 1956, succeeding *Hsin-hua yueh-pao*). Semimonthly.
Hsin-hua yueh-pao (New China Monthly), Peiping. Monthly.
Hsueh-hsi (Study), Peiping. Monthly until December 1956. Semimonthly since then.

Hung-chi (Red Flag), Peiping. Semimonthly.

Jen-min shou ts'e (People's Handbook), Shanghai, Tientsin, and Peiping. Published annually by Ta-kang-pao-she since 1950, except 1954.

Kung-sheng hsin-wen chou-k'an (Industrial and Commercial News Weekly), Canton. Weekly.

Liang-shih (Food Grain), Peiping. Monthly.

Min-tsu ping-lun (Democratic Review), Hong Kong. Semimonthly.

Shih-shih shao-ts'e (Current Events Handbook), Peiping. Semimonthly.

Shih-yu kung-yeh t'ung-hsin (Petroleum Industry Bulletin), Peiping. Semimonthly.

Ti-li chih-shih (Geographic Knowledge), Peiping. Monthly.

Ts'ai-cheng (Public Finance), Peiping. Monthly.

Ts'ai-ching yen-chiu (Financial and Economic Research), Shanghai. Quarterly.

Tsu-kuo (China Weekly), Hong Kong. Weekly.

T'ung-chi kung tso (Statistical Work), Peiping, succeeding *T'ung-chi kung-tso t'ung-hsin* since January 1957. Beginning January 1959 succeeded by *Chi-hua yu t'ung-chi.* Semimonthly.

T'ung-chi kung-tso t'ung-hsin (Statistical Work Bulletin), Peiping. Semimonthly.

T'ung-chi yen-chiu (Statistical Research), Peiping. Monthly.

Yeh-chin pao (Metallurgy News), Peiping. Weekly.

III. *English Language*

China News Analysis, Hong Kong. Weekly.

China Reconstructs, Peiping. Bimonthly.

China Trade and Economic Newsletter, London. Monthly.

China Travel Service Gazette, Hong Kong.

China Weekly, Hong Kong. Weekly.

Chinese Economic Journal, Peiping. Monthly.

Contemporary China, Hong Kong. Irregular.

Far Eastern Economic Review, Hong Kong. Weekly.

Foreign Broadcast Information Service. *Daily Report—Far East.* Daily.

Peking Review, Peiping, succeeding *People's China* beginning with January 1958. Weekly.

People's China, Peiping. Semimonthly.

The Economist Intelligence Unit, Ltd. *Three-Monthly Economic Review of China, Hong Kong and North Korea,* London. Quarterly, with annual supplement.

Union Research Service, Hong Kong. Irregular.

BIBLIOGRAPHY

I. *Chinese Language Materials*

A. Pre-1949 Publications

1. OFFICIAL

Bureau of Foreign Trade, National Government, *Chung-hua min-kuo t'ung-chi nien-chien, 1948* (Statistical Yearbook of The Republic of China), Nanking, 1948.

——— *Chung-kuo jen-kou wen-ti chih t'ung-chi fen-hsi* (A Statistical Analysis of China's Population Problems), Chungking, 1944.

——— *Chung-kuo shih-yeh-tze: Chekiang-sheng* (Industrial Handbook of China: Chekiang), Shanghai, 1933.

——— *Chung-kuo shih-yeh-tze: Hunan sheng* (Industrial Handbook of China: Hunan), Shanghai, 1935.

——— *Chung-kuo shih-yeh-tze: Kiang-su sheng* (Industrial Handbook of China: Kiangsu), Shanghai, 1933.

——— *Chung-kuo shih-yeh-tze: Shansi sheng* (Industrial Handbook of China: Shansi), Shanghai, 1936.

——— *Chung-kuo shih-yeh-tze: Shantung sheng* (Industrial Handbook of China: Shantung), Shanghai, 1934.

——— *Mien-tze-yu* (Cotton Seed Oil), Changsha, 1940.

Bureau of Statistics, National Government, *Chung-hua min-kuo t'ung-chi nien-chien, 1948* (Statistical Yearbook of the Republic of China), Nanking, 1948.

——— *Chung-kuo jen-kou wen-ti chih t'ung-chi fen-hsi* (a Statistical Yearbook of the Republic of China), Nanking, 1948.

——— *Chung-kuo tu-ti wen-ti chih t'ung-chi fen-hsi* (Statistical Analysis of China's Land Problems), Chungking, 1941.

Central Planning Board, National Government, *Wu-tse chien-she wu-nien chi-hua tsao-an ti-yao* (Draft Five Year Plan for Economic Reconstruction), Chungking, 1945.

Directorate of Statistics, National Government, *Chung-hua min-kuo t'ung-chi ti-yao, 1935* (Statistical Abstract of The Republic of China, 1935), Nanking, 1936.

——— *Chung-hua-min-kuo t'ung-chi ti-yao, 1940* (Statistical Abstract of The Republic of China, 1940), Chungking, 1940.

Inspectorate General of Customs, National Government, *The Trade of China, 1933*, Shanghai, 1934.

Kwangsi Provincial Government, *Kwang-si nien-chien* (Kwangsi Yearbook), 1934.

Ministry of Agriculture and Forestry, National Government, *Nung-lin t'ung-chi shou-t'se* (Handbook of Agricultural and Forestry Statistics), Nanking, 1948.

Ministry of Communications, Post Office Administration, National Government, *Chung-kuo tung-yu ti-fang wu-chan-chih* (A Survey of Products Along China's Mail Routes), Shanghai, 1937.

Ministry of Education, National Government, *Ti-erh-tsi chung-kuo chiao-yu nien-chien* (The Second Chinese Education Yearbook), Shanghai, Commercial Press, 1948.

Ministry of Industry, National Government, *Chung-kuo ching-chi nien-chien* (China Economic Yearbook), Nanking, 1934.

——— *Shih-yeh t'ung-chi tzu-liao* (Industrial Statistical Data), Nanking, 1934.

Ministry of Interior, National Government, *Min-kuo shi-chi-nien ko sheng-shih hu-kuo tiao-cha t'ung-chi* (Population Statistics by Province, 1928), Nanking, 1933.

National Agricultural Research Bureau, National Government, *Agricultural Estimates,* Shanghai, 1947.

——— *Nung-ch'ing pao-kao* (Crop Reports), Nanking.

National Economic Commission, National Government, *Shih-tang kung-yeh pao-kao-shu* (Report on the Sugar Manufacturing Industry), Shanghai, 1936.

Northeast Natural Resources Control Committee, National Government, *Tung-pei ching-chi hsiao ts'ung-shu* (Economic Handbook of Northeast China), Shenyang, 1947.

2. OTHER

Chang, C. C., *An Estimate of China's Farms and Crops,* Nanking, 1932.

——— "Statistical Estimation of Agriculture by Hsien," *T'ung-chi yueh-pao* (Statistical Monthly), Nanking, Vol. II, No. 7, July 1930.

Chang Hsiao-mei, *Sze-chwan ching-chi tsan-kao tzu-liao* (Reference Materials on Szechwan Economy), Shanghai, 1939.

Chang Hsiao-mei and Chao Chun-po, *Sze-chwan shang chi tung-yu* (Tung Oil of Szechwan Province), Shanghai, Commerical Press, 1938.

Chen Chang-heng, "A Preliminary Comparison of China's Land and Population and Discussion on Policies Concerning the National Economic Reconstruction," *Ti-li hsueh-pao* (Journal of the Geographical Society of China), Nanking, Vol. II, No. 4, December 1935, pp. 1–44.

Chen Chung-wei, *Si-kang wen-ti* (Problems of Sikang), Shanghai, 1930.

Chiao Chi-ming and Chiang Chieh, *Chung-kuo jen-k'ou yu shih-liang wen-ti* (China's Population and Food Problems), Shanghai, Chung-hua Book Co., 1939.

Ching-chi-pu fang-chi kung-yeh shan-charn hui-yi chi-lu (Proceedings of the Conference on Textile Production Held by the Department of Economic Affairs), Shanghai, 1947.

Chu Lien-tsing, "Suggestion on the Utilization and Amelioration of the Soils in Ningsia," *Tu-jang chi-k'an* (Soil Quarterly), Chungking, Vol. V, No. 2, April 1946, pp. 63–74.

Chung-hua nien-chien (Chinese Yearbook), Chung-hua nien-chien-she, Nanking, 1948.

Djang Gee-hung, "An Estimate of the Working Population of China," *She-hui ko-hsueh tsa-chih* (Quarterly Review of Social Sciences), Shanghai, Vol. IX, No. 2, December 1947, pp. 71–91.

——— *Tiao-tsa pao-kao* (Report on an Agricultural Survey of Szechwan Province), Chungking, 1941. 5 vols.

Farmers' Bank of China, *Chung-nung ching-chi t'ung-chi* (Economic Statistics of the Farmers' Bank of China), Chungking, Vol. II, No. 7, July 31, 1942.

Honan Cotton Improvement Bureau, *Honan mien-yeh* (Cotton Industry of Honan), Shanghai, 1936.

Hsu Fang-kan, Wang Mou-shui, and Kung Chun, "Survey of Farmers' Living Conditions in Ihsin and Wuching," *Tung-fang tsa-chih* (Eastern Miscellany), Shanghai, Vol. 24, No. 16, August 1927, pp. 85–89, 105–109.

Hsu Ming, *Yu-tung chi tsai-pai yu kai-liang* (Planting and Improvement of Tung Trees), Chungking, 1943.

Koh Tso-fan, *Chung-kuo kung-yeh-hua tung-lun* (A General Discussion of China's Industrialization), Shanghai, Commercial Press, 1947.

Kwan Chi-yu, *Tien-fu cheng-shih chih li-lun yu shih-wu* (Theory and Practice of Land Taxation in Kind), Chungking, 1944.

Lee Ching-han, *Peiping chiao-wai chih hsiang-t'sun chia-ting* (Rural Families in Suburban Peiping), Peiping, Social Science Research Department, China Foundation, 1929.

Lieu, D. K., *Chung-kuo kung-yeh tiao-tsa pao-kao* (Report on a Survey of China's Industry), Nanking, 1937.

Lu Ping-teng, *Sze-chwan nung-t'sun ching-chi* (Rural Economy of Szechwan), Shanghai, 1936.

Ma Li-yuan, "Another Estimate of China's Farm Area," *Ching-chi chien-she chi-k'an* (Economic Reconstruction Quarterly), Chungking, Vol. III, No. 2, October 1944, pp. 157–164.

Ou Pao-san, *1933 Chung-kuo kuo-min so-te* (China's National Income, 1933), 2 vols., Shanghai, Chung-hua Book Co., 1947

Pan Kung-chao, *Jin-jih chih Mung-ku* (Mongolia Today), Shanghai, 1947.

Pei Yu-lin, "National Income, Consumption and Investment of China," *Shi-yeh jin-yung* (Journal of Finance and Industry), Shanghai, Vol. I, No. 1, May 1948, pp. 65–77.

Shanghai Bank of Commerce and Savings, *Mien* (Cotton), Shanghai, 1931.

Shanghai Civic Association, *Shanghai-shih ti-fang t'ung-chi* (Statistics of Shanghai), Shanghai, 1933.

Shen Pao nien-chien, 1933 (Shen Pao Yearbook, 1933), Shanghai, Shen-pao nien-chien-she, 1933.

Shen Pao nien-chien, 1935 (Shen Pao Yearbook, 1935), Shanghai, Shen-pao nien-chien-she, 1935.

Shen Pao nien-chien, 1936 (Shen Pao Yearbook, 1936), Shanghai, Shen-pao nien-chien-she, 1936.

Szechwan Agricultural Improvement Bureau, *Sze-chwan nung-t'sun wu-chia chih-shu* (Farm Price Index of Szechwan), Chengtu, 1942.

Tsou Hsu-pu, *Chung-kuo yu-tung yu tung-yu* (China's Tung Plant and Tung Oil), Shanghai, Chung-hua Book Co., 1944.

Tsou Hsu-pu and Chang Hsiao-mei, *Chung-kuo chan-hou nung-yeh chien-she chi-hua kang-yao* (Outline of Postwar Agricultural Reconstruction Plan in China), Chengtu, 1944.

Tu Tsun-tung, "Production and Consumption of Food Crops in Fukien," *Fu-kien hsien-cheng pan-yueh-k'an* (Fukien Local Administration Semimonthly), Foochow, Vol. II, No. 1, March 1937, pp. 6–17.

Wang Fu-shun, "The Proportion of Industrial Production by Foreign-owned Factories in Total Industrial Production in Prewar China," *Chung-yang yin-hang yueh-pao* (Central Bank Monthly), Shanghai, Vol. II, No. 3, March 1947, pp. 1–19.

Wang Shih-ta, "A New Estimate of Recent Chinese Population," *She-hui ko-hsueh tsa-chih* (Quarterly Review of Social Sciences), Shanghai, Vol. VI, No. 2, June 1935, pp. 191–266.

Wu Cheng-hsi, *Chung-kuo ti yin-hang* (China's Banks), Shanghai, 1934.

Yen Kwang-kuo, *Tung-yu* (Tung Oil), Shanghai, Cheng-chung Book Co., 1947.

B. Communist Regime Publications

1. COMMUNIST PARTY

"Communique on the Sixth Conference of the Eighth Central Committee," *Hsin-hua pan-yueh-k'an* (New China Semimonthly), Peiping, 24, December 1958, pp. 1–3.

"Communique on the Eighth Conference of the Eighth Central Committee," *Hsin-hua pan-yueh-k'an* (New China Semimonthly), Peiping, 17, September 1959, pp. 1–2.

"Communique on the Ninth Conference of the Eighth Central Committee," *Hung-chi* (Red Flag), Peiping, 3–4, February 1961, pp. 1–3.

"Draft Program for the Development of Agriculture, 1956–67," *Hsin-hua pan-yueh-k'an* (New China Semimonthly), Peiping, 4, February 1956, pp. 2–5.

"Program for the Development of Agriculture, 1956–67 (Revised)," *Jen-min jih-pao* (People's Daily), Peiping, April 12, 1960, pp. 2–3.

"Proposal of the Second Five Year Plan," *Hsin-hua pan-yueh-k'an* (New China Semimonthly), Peiping, 20, October 1956, pp. 164-170.

"Resolution on the Problem of Agricultural Cooperativization," *Hsin-hua yueh-pao* (New China Monthly), Peiping, 11, November 1955, pp. 9–13.

"Resolutions on Certain Problems in People's Communes," *Hsin-hua pan-yueh-k'an* (New China Semimonthly), Peiping, 24, December 1958, pp. 3–11.

2. STATE COUNCIL

Chung-hua-jen-min-kung-ho-kuo fa-chan kuo-min-ching-chi ti-yi wu-nien-chi-hua (The First Five Year Plan for National Economic Development of the People's Republic of China), Peiping, Jen-min chu-pan-she, 1955.

"Decisions on the Development of Hog Production," *Hsin-hua pan-yueh-k'an* (New China Semimonthly), Peiping, 7, April 1957, pp. 75–77.

"Directive on Banning the Outflow of Farm Population," *Ta kung pao* (Impartial Daily), Peiping, December 19, 1957, p. 1.

"Directive on Curbing the Inflow of Peasants into Cities," *Jen-min jih-pao* (People's Daily), Peiping, April 17, 1953, p. 1.

Financial and Economic Commission, State Council, *Chung-yang ts'ai-ching cheng-tse fa-ling hui-pien* (Collection of Laws, Regulations and Statements Concerning the Fiscal and Economic Policies of the Central Government), Peiping, Hsin-hua Book Co., Vol. 1, August 1950; Vol. 2, June 1951.

"On the Classification of Rural and Urban Areas," *Hsin-hua pan-yueh-k'an* (New China Semimonthly), Peiping, 3, February 1956, p. 7.

"On Planned Purchase and Supply of Cotton Cloth," *Jen-min jih-pao* (People's Daily), Peiping, September 15, 1954, p. 1.

"On Planned Purchase and Supply of Food Grain," *Jen-min jih-pao* (People's Daily), Peiping, November 24, 1953, p. 1.

"On Planned Purchase of Cotton Yarn," *Hsin-hua yueh-pao* (New China Monthly), Peiping, Vol. III, No. 3, January 1951, p. 622.

"On Planned Purchase of Raw Cotton," *Jen-min jih-pao* (People's Daily), Peiping, September 15, 1954, p. 1.

"Provisional Measures for Planned Purchase and Planned Supply of Food Grains in Rural Areas," *Hsin-hua yueh-pao* (New China Monthly), Peiping, 9, September 1955, pp. 160–162.

"Provisional Measures for Rationing of Food Grains in Urban Areas," *Hsin-hua yueh-pao* (New China Monthly), Peiping, 9, September 1955, pp. 163–164.

"Regulations on the Reorganization of the System of Control for Industry, Trade and Public Finance," *Jen-min jih-pao* (People's Daily), Peiping, November 18, 1957, p. 3.

3. STATE STATISTICAL BUREAU

"A General Survey of China's Socialist Industrialization," *Hsin-hua pan-yueh-k'an* (New China Semimonthly), Peiping, 2, January 1957, pp. 54–62.

"A General Survey of National Industrial Capital," *T'ung-chi kung-tso* (Statistical Work), Peiping, 1, January 1957, pp. 31–33.

"A General Survey of Supply of Goods in the Domestic Market in 1957," *T'ung-chi yen-chiu* (Statistical Research), Peiping, 4, April 1958, pp. 24–25.

"A General Survey of the Distribution of the Centrally Allocated Commodities in the Past Years," *T'ung-chi kung-tso* (Statistical Work), Peiping, 13, July 1957, pp. 29–31.

"A Preliminary Analysis of the Production and Distribution of China's National Income," *T'ung-chi yen-chiu* (Statistical Research), Peiping, 1, January 1958, pp. 11–15.

"A Study of Gross and Net Value of Output," *T'ung-chi yen-chiu* (Statistical Research), Peiping, 2, February 1958, pp. 27–30.
"A Survey of Domestic Market Prices in 1956," *T'ung-chi kung-tso* (Statistical Work), Peiping, 7, April 1957, pp. 31–32.
"A Survey of Market Prices in the First Quarter of 1957," *T'ung-chi kung-tso* (Statistical Work), Peiping, 11, June 1957, pp. 26–27.
"Agricultural Production in the Past Seven Years," *T'ung-chi kung-tso* (Statistical Work), Peiping, 14, July 1957, pp. 9–13.
"Basic Conditions in China's Coal Industry," *T'ung-chi yen-chiu* (Statistical Research), Peiping, 4, April 1958, pp. 18–23.
"Basic Conditions in China's Construction Industry," *T'ung-chi kung-tso t'ung-hsin* (Statistical Work Bulletin), Peiping, 24, December 1956, pp. 31–33.
"Basic Conditions in China's Mineral Survey and Prospecting Work," *T'ung-chi kung-tso* (Statistical Work), Peiping, 5, March 1957, pp. 31–32.
"Basic Conditions in the Construction Enterprises in the Past Four Years," *T'ung-chi kung-tso* (Statistical Work), Peiping, 18, September 1957, pp. 31–32.
"Changes in the Market Prices in 1957 and Their Effects on People's Living Conditions," *T'ung-chi yen-chiu* (Statistical Research), Peiping, 4, April 1958, pp. 25–26.
"Changes in the Price Ratios of China's Industrial and Agricultural Products Since Liberation," *T'ung-chi kung-tso* (Statistical Work), Peiping, 17, September 1957, pp. 4–7.
"Changes in the Standard of Living of Workers in Shanghai in the Past 27 Years," *T'ung-chi kung-tso* (Statistical Work), Peiping, 13, July 1957, pp. 6–7.
"Communique on Adjustment of the Agricultural Statistics for 1958," *Hsin-hua pan-yueh-k'an* (New China Semimonthly), Peiping, 17, September 1959, p. 69.
"Communique on the Development of the National Economy in 1958," *Hsin-hua pan-yueh-k'an* (New China Semimonthly), Peiping, 8, April 1959, pp. 51–54.
"Communique on the Fulfillment of the First Five Year Plan," *Hsin-hua pan-yueh-k'an* (New China Semimonthly), Peiping, 8, April 1959, pp. 48–54.
"Communique on Fulfillment of the National Economic Plan in 1955," *Hsin-hua pan-yueh-k'an* (New China Semimonthly), Peiping, 13, July 1956, pp. 39–42.

"Communique on Fulfillment of the National Economic Plan in 1956," *Hsin-hua pan-yueh-k'an* (New China Semimonthly), Peiping, 17, September 1957, pp. 201–205.

"Communique on National Economic, Cultural and Educational Rehabilitation and Development in 1952," *Jen-min jih-pao* (People's Daily), Peiping, September 28, 1954, p. 1.

"Communique on National Economic Development and Fulfillment of the State Plan in 1953," *Jen-min jih-pao* (People's Daily), Peiping, September 28, 1954, p. 1.

"Communique on National Economic Development and Fulfillment of the State Plan in 1954," *Jen-min jih-pao* (People's Daily), Peiping, September 23, 1955, p. 1.

"Data on Farm Income and Expenditure in 1954," *T'ung-chi kung-tso* (Statistical Work), Peiping, 10, May 1957, pp. 31–33.

"Data on Labor and Production Costs on High Yield Land," *T'ung-chi kung-tso* (Statistical Work), Peiping, 22, November 1958, pp. 23–24.

"Data on the 1955 Survey of Income and Expenditure of Agricultural Cooperatives," *Hsin-hua pan-yueh-k'an* (New China Semimonthly), Peiping, 24, December 1956, pp. 63–65.

"Data on the 1957 Representative Survey of the Distribution of Income in 228 Agricultural Cooperatives," *T'ung-chi yen-chiu* (Statistical Research), Peiping, 8, August 1958, pp. 8–12.

"Development of China's Tea Production," *T'ung-chi kung-tso* (Statistical Work), Peiping, 3, February 1957, pp. 5, 33.

"Development of New China's Education," *T'ung-chi kung-tso* (Statistical Work), Peiping, 22, November 1957, pp. 30–33.

"Development of State Capitalism in China's Industry," *Hsin-hua pan-yueh-k'an* (New China Semimonthly), Peiping, 2, January 1957, pp. 66–70.

"Economic Statistical Abstract," *Hsin-hua pan-yueh-k'an* (New China Semimonthly), Peiping, 17, September 1956, pp. 39–50.

"Economic Statistical Abstract," *Kuo-chia t'ung-chi-chu kwan-yu 1956 nien-tu kuo-min ching-chi chi-hua chi-hsing che-kuo ti kung-pao* (State Statistical Bureau Communique on the Fulfillment of the National Economic Plan for 1956), Peiping, T'ung-chi chu-pan-she, 1957.

"From the Four-part Partition Policy to the Re-purchase Policy of Fixed Interest Payment," *T'ung-chi kung-tso* (Statistical Work), Peiping, 6, March 1957, pp. 30–32.

"Great Achievements in China's Basic Construction in the Past

Seven Years," *T'ung-chi kung-tso* (Statistical Work), Peiping, 17, September 1957, pp. 1–3.

"Great Achievements in China's Economic Construction in the Past Nine Years," *T'ung-chi yen-chiu* (Statistical Research), Peiping, 9, September 1958, pp. 1–3.

"Input-Output Coefficients of Major Products, 1953–56," *T'ung-chi kung-tso* (Statistical Work), Peiping, 18, September 1957, pp. 18, 33.

"Output of China's Light Industry under the Increase-Production Practice-Economy Drive," *T'ung-chi yen-chiu* (Statistical Research), Peiping, 2, February 1958, pp. 12–15.

"Population Statistics, 1949–56," *T'ung-chi kung-tso* (Statistical Work), Peiping, 11, June 1957, pp. 24–25.

"Press Communiqué on Economic Development in 1959," *Jen-min jih-pao* (People's Daily), Peiping, January 23, 1960, p. 1.

"Rapid Development in China's Industrial Construction," *T'ung-chi yen-chiu* (Statistical Research), Peiping, 9, September 1958, pp. 4–5.

"Several Important Problems of Calculating Total Value of Agricultural Production," *T'ung-chi kung-tso t'ung-hsin* (Statistical Work Bulletin), Peiping, 22, November 1956, pp. 1–2.

"Several Problems in the Compilation of Constant 1957 Industrial Prices," *T'ung-chi kung-tso* (Statistical Work), Peiping, 19, October 1957, pp. 11–13.

"Size, Structure and Distribution of Total Employment in 1955," *Hsin-hua pan-yueh-k'an* (New China Semimonthly), Peiping, 2, January 1957, pp. 87–89.

"Some Preliminary Experience in Statistical Analysis of China's Industry," *T'ung-chi yen-chiu* (Statistical Research), Peiping, 1, January 1958, pp. 22–28.

"Statistical Abstract of the National Economic, Cultural and Educational Achievements in 1949–54," *Hsin-hua yueh-pao* (New China Monthly), Peiping, 11, November 1955, pp. 181–189.

"Statistical Materials Concerning Improvements in the Workers' Living Conditions," *T'ung-chi kung-tso* (Statistical Work), Peiping, 14, July 1957, pp. 13–14.

"The Basic Situation of Planned Purchase and Planned Supply of Food Grains in China," *T'ung-chi kung-tso* (Statistical Work), Peiping, 19, October 1957, pp. 28, 31–32.

"The Big Leap Forward in Basic Construction Work," *T'ung-chi yen-chiu* (Statistical Research), Peiping, 9, September 1958, pp. 10–12.

"The Development of China's Commercial Network and Basic Conditions in 1955," *Hsin-hua pan-yueh-k'an* (New China Semimonthly), Peiping, 24, December 1956, pp. 80–83.

"The Development of China's Education in the Past Few Years," *Hsin-hua pan-yueh-k'an* (New China Semimonthly), Peiping, 24, December 1956, pp. 93–94.

"The Problem of Classifying Producers' and Consumers' Goods," *T'ung-chi kung-tso* (Statistical Work), Peiping, 3, February 1957, pp. 1–4.

"The Problem of the Living Standards of the Workers and Peasants," *T'ung-chi kung-tso* (Statistical Work), Peiping, 13, July 1957, pp 4–5, 24.

"The Scale and Speed of Development in China's Basic Construction Investment," *T'ung-chi kung-tso t'ung-hsin* (Statistical Work Bulletin), Peiping, 18, September 1956, pp. 4–6.

"The Technological Level of Industrial Production in China," *T'ung-chi kung-tso* (Statistical Work), Peiping, 8, April 1957, pp. 30–33.

Wei-ta ti shih-nien (Great Ten Years), Peiping, Jen-min chu-pan-she, 1959.

Wo-kuo kang-tieh, tien-li, mei-t'an, chi-hsieh, fang-chih, tsao-chi kung-yeh ti chin-hsi (Past and Present of China's Iron and Steel, Electric Power, Coal, Machinery, Textile and Paper Industries), Peiping, T'ung-chi chu-pan-she, 1958.

4. OFFICIAL REPORTS AND STATEMENTS

Central Bureau of Administrative Control of Industry and Trade, *Sze-ying kung-shan-yeh ti-she-hui-chu-i kai-tsao cheng-tse fa-ling hsuan-pien* (A Collection of Directives and Decrees Relating to the Socialist Transformation of Private Industry and Trade, 1949–1952), Vol. I, Peiping, Ts'ai-ching chu-pan-she, 1957.

Chao Er-lu, "Produce More and Better Machines To Ensure a High Rate of Development in Socialist Reconstruction," *Jen-min jih-pao* (People's Daily), Peiping, May 31, 1958, p. 3.

Chen Yun, "Concerning the Problem of Socialist Transformation of Private Industry and Trade," *Hsin-hua pan-yueh-k'an* (New China Semimonthly), Peiping, 14, July 1956, pp. 51–54.

——— "Internal Trade and the Problem of Its Relation to Industry," *Hsin-hua pan-yueh-k'an* (New China Semimonthly), Peiping, 15, August 1956, pp. 141–143.

——— "Major Problems in Current Basic Construction Work,"

Jen-min jih-pao (People's Daily), Peiping, March 1, 1959, pp. 1–2.

——— "New Problems Following the High Tide of Transformation of Capitalistic Industry and Trade," *Hsin-hua pan-yueh-k'an* (New China Semimonthly), Peiping, 21, November 1956, pp. 64–67.

——— "Statement Before the National Congress of People's Representatives," *Jen-min jih-pao* (People's Daily), Peiping, September 24, 1954, p. 3.

——— "The Problem of Increasing Production and Economizing," *Hsin-hua pan-yueh-k'an* (New China Semimonthly), Peiping, 7, April 1957, pp. 15–18.

——— "The Problem of Planned Purchase and Sale of Food Grain," *Hsin-hua yueh-pao* (New China Monthly), Peiping, 8, August 1955, pp. 50–54.

Chia Chi-yun, "Communes Shining Brilliantly," *Jen-min jih-pao* (People's Daily), Peiping, September 25, 1959, p. 4.

——— "Statistical Work in 1954 and Suggestions for 1955," *Hsin-hua yueh-pao* (New China Monthly), Peiping, 4, April 1955, pp. 149–154.

Chia To-fu, "Problems in the Development of the Light Industry," *Hsin-hua pan-yueh-k'an* (New China Semimonthly), Peiping, 21, November 1956, pp. 100–102.

——— "Report on Drafting of the 1957 Economic Plan," *Chi-hua ching-chi* (Planned Economy), Peiping, 4, April 1957, pp. 1–9.

——— "Speech before the People's Congress," *Hsin-hua yueh-pao* (New China Monthly), Peiping, 8, August 1955, pp. 90–93.

Chou En-lai, "Political Report," *Hsin-hua pan-yueh-k'an* (New China Semimonthly), Peiping, 5, March 1956, pp. 11–20.

——— "Report on Adjustment of Major Targets in the 1959 National Economic Plan and the Launching of the Campaign To Increase Production and To Economize," *Hsin-hua pan-yueh-k'an* (New China Semimonthly), Peiping, 17, September 1959, pp. 19–24.

——— "Report on Draft Second Five Year Plan," *Hsin-hua pan-yueh-k'an* (New China Semimonthly), Peiping, 20, October 1956, pp. 35–49.

——— "Report on Government Work," *Hsin-hua pan-yueh-k'an* (New China Semimonthly), Peiping, 14, July 1957, pp. 1–16.

——— "Report on Government Work," *Hsin-hua pan-yueh-k'an*

(New China Semimonthly), Peiping, 9, May 1959, pp. 2–15.
——— "Report on the Problem of the Intellectuals," *Hsin-hua pan-yueh-k'an* (New China Semimonthly), Peiping, 5, March 1956, pp. 1–10.
——— "Struggle for the Consolidation and Development of People's Victory," *Hsin-hua yueh-pao* (New China Monthly), Peiping, Vol. II, No. 6, October 1950, pp. 1213–1222.
——— "The Great Ten Years," *Hung-chi* (Red Flag), Peiping, 20, October 1959, pp. 1–15.
Fu Tso-yi, "Our Country's Great Achievements of Water Conservancy in the Past Three Years," in China Council for the Promotion of International Trade, *San-nien lai hsin-chung-kuo ching-chi ti cheng-chiu* (New China's Economic Achievements during the Past Three Years), Peiping, Jin-min chu-pan-she, 1953.
"Government Receipts and Expenditures in the First Five Year Plan Period," *Ts'ai-cheng* (Public Finance), Peiping, 8, August 1957, pp. 32–33.
Hsieh Mu-ch'iao, "Our Experience in Statistical Work During the First Five Year Plan Period and Our Future Tasks," *T'ung-chi kung-tso* (Statistical Work), Peiping, 21, November 1957, pp. 1–21.
——— "Socialist Transformation of China's National Economy," *Jen-min jih-pao* (People's Daily), Peiping, September 17, 1959, p. 3.
——— "Summary Report to the Fourth National Statistical Work Conference," *Hsin-hua yueh-pao* (New China Monthly), Peiping, 6, June 1955, pp. 147–151.
——— "We Must Strive To Improve Agricultural Statistical Work," *T'ung-chi kung-tso* (Statistical Work), Peiping, 22, November 1957, pp. 7–11.
Jung Tzu-ho, "A Summary and Review of Public Finance Work in 1950 and the Policy and Task for 1951," *Hsin-hua yueh-pao* (New China Monthly), Peiping, Vol. III, No. 6, April 1951, pp. 1354–1356, 1363.
——— "China's Public Finance in the Past Ten Years," *Ts'ai-cheng* (Public Finance), Peiping, 18, September 1959, pp. 14–22.
Kao Kang, "Strengthen National Defense; Develop the Economy," *Hsin-hua yueh-pao* (New China Monthly), Peiping, Vol. III, No. 5, March 1951, pp. 1061–1063.
Lai Chi-fa, "Production Problems of the Construction Material

Industry in 1957," *Chien-she* (Reconstruction), Peiping, 1, January 1957, pp. 3–5.

Li Fu-chun, "Achievements of the First Five Year Plan in Its First Three Years and the Tasks for the Coming Two Years," *Ta kung pao* (Impartial Daily), Peiping, September 29, 1955, p. 2.

——— "Raise High the Red Flag of the General Line and Continue To Advance," *Jen-min jih-pao* (People's Daily), Peiping, August 17, 1960, pp. 2–3.

——— "Report on the Achievements of the First Five Year Plan and the Tasks and Direction in Future Socialist Construction," *Ta kung pao* (Impartial Daily), Peiping, December 8, 1957, p. 3.

——— "Report on the Draft 1959 Economic Plan," *Hsin-hua pan-yueh-k'an* (New China Semimonthly), Peiping, 9, May 1959, pp. 15–20.

——— "Report on the Draft 1960 Economic Plan," *Jen-min jih-pao* (People's Daily), Peiping, March 31, 1960, pp. 2–3.

——— "Report on the First Five Year Plan," *Hsin-hua yueh-pao* (New China Monthly), Peiping, 8, August 1955, pp. 1–22.

——— "Strengthen the Planning Work for Socialist Construction," *Hsin-hua pan-yueh-k'an* (New China Semimonthly), Peiping, 21, November 1956, pp. 104–107.

——— "The Achievements of China's First Five Year Plan and the Future Tasks of Socialist Reconstruction," *Hsin-hua pan-yueh-k'an* (New China Semimonthly), Peiping, 1, January 1958, pp. 13–18.

——— "The Implementation of China's First Five Year Plan," *Hsin-hua pan-yueh-k'an* (New China Semimonthly), Peiping, 14, July 1956, pp. 46–51.

——— "Welcome the New Leap Forward in 1960," *Hung-chi* (Red Flag), Peiping, 1, January 1960, pp. 1–8.

Li Hsien-nien, "Problems in Public Finance and Financial Work," *Hung-chi* (Red Flag), Peiping, 1, January 1960, pp. 9–13.

——— "Report on the Final Accounting of the 1954 State Budget for 1955," *Hsin-hua yueh-pao* (New China Monthly), Peiping, 8, August 1955, pp. 23–32.

——— "Report on the 1955 State Budget and the Draft Budget for 1956," *Hsin-hua pan-yueh-k'an* (New China Semimonthly), Peiping, 14, July 1956, pp. 1–9.

——— "Report on the Final Accounting of the 1956 State Budget and the Draft Budget for 1957," *Hsin-hua pan-yueh-k'an* (New China Semimonthly), Peiping, 14, July 1957, pp. 16–28.

——— "Report on the Final Accounting of the 1957 State Budget and the Draft Budget for 1958," *Hsin-hua pan-yueh-k'an* (New China Semimonthly), Peiping, 5, March 1958, pp. 3–12.

——— "Report on the Final Accounting of the 1958 State Budget and the Draft Budget for 1959," *Hsin-hua pan-yueh-k'an* (New China Semimonthly), Peiping, 9, May 1959, pp. 20–23.

——— "Report on the Final Accounting of the 1959 State Budget and the Draft Budget for 1960," *Jen-min jih-pao* (People's Daily), Peiping, April 1, 1960, p. 2.

——— "The Use of Our Pricing Policy To Stimulate Production," *Hsin-hua pan-yueh-k'an* (New China Semimonthly), Peiping, 21, November 1956, pp. 84–87.

Li Shu-cheng, "National Agricultural Production in 1950," *Hsin-hua yueh-pao* (New China Monthly), Peiping, Vol. III, No. 5, March 1951, pp. 1070–1072.

Liao Lu-yen, "Explanation of the Plan for Agricultural Development, 1956–1967," *Hsin-hua pan-yueh-k'an* (New China Semimonthly), Peiping, 4, February 1956, pp. 6–9.

——— "Strive Hard for a Bumper Harvest," *Hung-chi* (Red Flag), Peiping, 3–4, February 1961, pp. 26–32.

——— "Summary Report on Agricultural Production in 1956 and the Task for 1957," *Hsin-hua pan-yueh-k'an* (New China Semimonthly), Peiping, 8, April 1957, pp. 81–88.

Liu Shao-chi, "Political Report," *Hsin-hua pan-yueh-k'an* (New China Semimonthly), Peiping, 20, October 1956, pp. 2–23.

Ma Wen-ray, "A Decade of Struggle To Develop Productivity Rapidly and To Improve the Living Conditions of the Workers," *Jen-min jih-pao* (People's Daily), Peiping, September 25, 1959, p. 10.

Mao Tse-tung, "On the Correct Handling of People's Internal Contradictions," *Hsin-hua pan-yueh-k'an* (New China Semimonthly), Peiping, 13, July 1957, pp. 1–14.

——— "On the Problem of Agricultural Cooperativization," *Hsin-hua yueh-pao* (New China Monthly), Peiping, 11, November 1955, pp. 1–8.

——— "Strive for the Upturn of the National Financial and Economic Conditions," *Jen-min shou-t'se 1951* (People's Handbook, 1951), Shanghai, Ta-kung-pao-she, 1951, Vol. II, H 1–4.

Ministry of Agriculture, "China's Food Crop Production During the First Five Year Plan Period," *Hsin-hua pan-yueh-k'an* (New China Semimonthly), Peiping, 9, May 1958, pp. 80–83.

Ministry of Commerce, "Report on the Problem of Cotton Cloth Supply for Consumers' Use in the Fourth Year of Planned Supply," *Jen-min jih-pao* (People's Daily), Peiping, August 20, 1957, p. 1.

——— "Report on the Problem of Cotton Cloth Supply in 1957," *Jen-min jih-pao* (People's Daily), Peiping, April 20, 1957, p. 3.

Ministry of Water Conservancy, "Summary Report on Water Conservancy Work in 1950 and Policy and Tasks for 1951," *Hsin-hua yueh-pao* (New China Monthly), Peiping, Vol. III, No. 5, March 1951, pp. 1079–1082.

Ministry of Water Conservancy and Electric Power, "Outline of Technological Revolution in Water Conservancy and Electric Power," *Shui-li shui-tien chien-she* (Water Conservancy and Hydro-electric Power Construction), Peiping, 6, June 1959, pp. 6–13.

National Economic Commission, "Explanation of Major Changes in the Tabulation Forms for the 1958 National Economic Plan," *Chi-hua ching-chi* (Planned Economy), Peiping, 8, August 1957, pp. 24–27.

Pai Ju-ping, "Report Before the First National Congress of China's Handicraft Cooperatives," *Ta kung pao* (Impartial Daily), Peiping, December 17, 1957, p. 3.

People's Congress, "Model Regulation for Higher-stage Agricultural Producers' Cooperatives," *Hsin-hua pan-yueh-k'an* (New China Semimonthly), Peiping, 14, July 1956, pp. 19–25.

Po I-po, *Kuan-yu 1953-nien kuo-chia yu-hsuan ti pao-kao* (Report on the Draft State Budget for 1953), Peiping, Jen-min chu-pan-she, 1953.

——— "On the Correct Handling of the Problem of the Relationship Between Accumulation and Consumption," *Hsin-hua pan-yueh-k'an* (New China Semimonthly), Peiping, 20, October 1956, pp. 72–76.

——— "Problems of Correcting the Style of Work in Economic Departments," *Hsin-hua pan-yueh-k'an* (New China Semimonthly), Peiping, 7, April 1958, pp. 103–111.

——— "Report Before the National Conference of Model Agricultural Workers," *Hsin-hua pan-yueh-k'an* (New China Semimonthly), Peiping, 6, March 1957, pp. 57–59.

——— "Report on the Draft 1958 National Economic Plan," *Hsin-hua pan-yueh-k'an* (New China Semimonthly), Peiping, 5, March 1958, pp. 12–23.

——— "Report on the Fulfillment of the 1956 National Economic Plan and the Draft Plan for 1957," *Hsin-hua pan-yueh-k'an* (New China Semimonthly), Peiping, 14, July 1957, pp. 28–39.

——— "Strive for a New Victory in China's Industrial Production and Construction," *Hung-chi* (Red Flag), Peiping, 3–4, February 1, 1961, pp. 19–25.

——— "The Task and Role of Statistical Work in China's Socialist Reconstruction," *T'ung-chi yen-chiu* (Statistical Research), Peiping, 1, January 1958, pp. 4–10.

Sa Chien-li, "The Glorious Achievements in Food Management," *Ta kung pao* (Impartial Daily), Peiping, October 25, 1959, p. 3.

State Planning Commission, "Labor and Wages in 1956," *Chi-hua ching-chi* (Planned Economy), Peiping, 3, March 1957, pp. 14–15.

——— *Ti-yi-ke wu-nien-chi-hua-ti ming-tsi chieh-hsi* (Explanation of Terms Used in the First Five Year Plan), Peiping, Jen-min chu-pan-she, 1955.

Tan Chun-lin, "A Preliminary Study of Income and Standard of Living of the Peasants," *Hsin-hua pan-yueh-k'an* (New China Semimonthly), Peiping, 11, June 1957, pp. 105–111.

——— "Problems of China's Farm Mechanization," *Hung-chi* (Red Flag), Peiping, 6, March 1960, pp. 1–8.

Teng Tzu-lui, "Report Before the Conference on Animal Husbandry," *Ta kung pao* (Impartial Daily), Peiping, December 20, 1957, p. 3.

——— "Report Before the National Conference of Model Agricultural Workers," *Hsin-hua pan-yueh-k'an* (New China Semimonthly), Peiping, 6, March 1957, pp. 49–56.

——— "Report on the Coordinated Plan To Prevent Floods Permanently and To Develop Water Resources of the Yellow River," *Hsin-hua yueh-pao* (New China Monthly), Peiping, 8, August 1955, pp. 33–39.

——— "Social Transformation of China's Agriculture," *Jen-min jih-pao* (People's Daily), Peiping, October 18, 1959, p. 6.

Tsao Chu-ju, "The Financial Industry in the Past Ten Years," *Ta kung pao* (Impartial Daily), Peiping, October 12, 1959, p. 3.

Tseng Shan, "Report Before the Conference on the Census of

Private Trade and Restaurants," *T'ung-chi kung-tso t'ung-hsin* (Statistical Work Bulletin), Peiping, 8, April 1955, pp. 12–15.

Wang Shou, "Conditions and Current Problems of Food Crop Production in Our Country," *Ko-hsueh t'ung-pao* (Science Bulletin), Peiping, 5, 1954, pp. 17–20.

——— "The Transportation and Communications Industry in the Continuous Big Leap Forward," *Jen-min jih-pao* (People's Daily), Peiping, February 19, 1960, p. 7.

Wang Shou-tao, "Carry Out the Transportation Work Well and Support the Agricultural Cooperative Movement," *Hsin-hua yueh-pao* (New China Monthly), Peiping, 2, December 1955, pp. 219–221.

Wu Po, "Explanation of the Regulations on Agricultural Tax," *Hsin-hua pan-yueh-k'an* (New China Semimonthly), Peiping, 12, June 1958, pp. 84–87.

Yeh Chi-chuang, "Great Cooperation and Selfless Aid," *Jen-min jih-pao* (People's Daily), Peiping, November 3, 1957, p. 5.

——— "Report Before the Fourth Session of the People's Congress," *Hsin-hua pan-yueh-k'an* (New China Semimonthly), Peiping, 16, August 1957, pp. 90–94.

——— "Report Before the Second Session of the First People's Congress," *Hsin-hua yueh-pao* (New China Monthly), Peiping, 8, August 1955, pp. 168–170.

——— "The Development of Sino-Soviet Trade in 1958," *Ta kung pao* (Impartial Daily), Peiping, November 6, 1958, p. 4.

5. Books and Articles

"Anti-conservative and Anti-extravagant in Drafting and Implementation of the Second Five Year Plan," *Chi-hua ching-chi* (Planned Economy), Peiping, 3, March 1958, pp. 1–4.

"Certain Problems in Basic Construction Planning," *Chi-hua ching-chi* (Planned Economy), Peiping, 6, June 1957, pp. 8–9, 33.

Chan Cheng-jen, "On the Ownership and Distribution System of Communes," *Jen-min jih-pao* (People's Daily), Peiping, October 18, 1959, p. 7.

Chan Tieh-chang, "Tabulation Forms for Transportation Planning," *Chi-hua ching-chi* (Planned Economy), Peiping, 3, March 1957, pp. 29–33.

Chang Chung-wan and Hwang Wei-yi, *Tsu-kuo ti hsu-mo yu hsu-chan tzu-yuan* (Animal Husbandry and Animal Products of Our Fatherland), Shanghai, Yung-hsiang Book Co., 1953.

Chang Sun and Wang En-juen, "A Brief Discussion of the

Fixed Assets of Industrial Enterprises and Their Depreciation," *Ching-chi yen-chiu* (Economic Research), Peiping, 5, October 1956, pp. 69–78.

Chang Yi-fay, "The Problem of the Price Ratios Between Industrial and Agricultural Products," *Hsin-chien-she* (New Construction), Peiping, 11, November 1958, pp. 22–25.

Chao Ching-hsin, "Seasonal Variations of the Market After Agricultural Cooperation," *Ching-chi yen-chiu* (Economic Research), Peiping, 5, October 1956, pp. 19–38.

Chao Yi-wen, *Hsin-chung-kuo ti kung-yeh* (New China's Industry), Peiping, T'ung-chi chu-pan-she, 1957.

——— "The Process of Socialist Transformation of China's Capitalist Industry," *Hsin-hua pan-yueh-k'an* (New China Semimonthly), Peiping, 2, January 1957, pp. 62–66.

Chen Hsin-wen, "Reconstruction of the Electric Power Industry in the Past Four Years," *Chien-she yueh-k'an* (Reconstruction Monthly), Peiping, 7, July 1957, pp. 35–36.

Chen Ju-lung, "The State Budget and the Problem of Bank Credit Balance," *Ta kung pao* (Impartial Daily), Peiping, April 17, 1957, p. 3.

Cheng Chu-yuan, "Trends in Mainland China's National Income," *Tsu-kuo* (China Weekly), Hong Kong, 189, August 13, 1956, pp. 17–23.

Cheng-fu kung-tso pao-kao hui-pien (Collection of Reports on Government Work), Peiping, Jen-min chu-pan-she, 1951.

Chi Chun-mien, *Chih-mien shou-t'se* (Handbook of Cotton Planting), Shanghai, 1951.

Chi Chung-wei, "China's Industry Should Support and Spur the Development of Agriculture," *Ching-chi yen-chiu* (Economic Research), Peiping, 2, February 1958, pp. 1–11.

——— "How To Achieve a More Balanced Development in China's Industry," *Chi-hua ching-chi* (Planned Economy), Peiping, 7, July 1957, pp. 4–8.

Chia Hung-yu and Chen Yung-ping, "Economic Survey of the Advanced Agricultural Producers' Cooperatives in Kingshan, Haining Hsien, Chekiang Province," *Ts'ai-ching yen-chiu* (Financial and Economic Research), Shanghai, 1, March 1957, pp. 49–57; 2, June 1957, pp. 51–60.

Chiao Yue, "Develop the Uncultivated Land and Increase the Cultivated Area," *Chi-hua ching-chi* (Planned Economy), Peiping, 2, February 1958, pp. 21–24.

Chien Hung, "Facts Prove That China Has Enough Food

Grain," *Jen-min jih-pao* (People's Daily), Peiping, November 3, 1955, p. 2.

Chien-kuo shih-nien (Ten Years of National Reconstruction), Hong Kong, Chi-wen chu-pan-she, 1959, Vols. I and II.

Chien Tzu-kuang, "Develop the Textile Industry Rapidly," *Hung-chi* (Red Flag), Peiping, 8, April 1959, pp. 1–11.

China Council for the Promotion of International Trade, *San-nien-lai hsin-chung-kuo ching-chi ti cheng-chiu* (New China's Economic Achievements During the Last Three Years), Peiping, Jen-min chu-pan-she, 1953.

Ching Chih, "Planned Purchase Is the Socialist System of Purchasing Agricultural Products," *Hsin-hua yueh-pao* (New China Monthly), Peiping, 11, November 1955, pp. 172–177.

Ching Hua, Liang Sze-ta, *et al.*, *Chi-nien-lai wor-kuo sze-ying kung-shang-yeh ti pien-hua* (Changes in China's Private Industry and Trade in the Past Seven Years), Peiping, Ts'ai-ching chu-pan-she, 1957.

Ching Lin, "The Proportionate Relation Between the Steel Industry and the Machinery Manufacturing Industry," *Jen-min jih-pao* (People's Daily), Peiping, September 22, 1957, p. 5.

——— *Ti-yi-ke wu-nien-chi-hua chung ti chi-che chi-tso-yeh* (The Machinery Manufacturing Industry in the First Five Year Plan Period), Peiping, Chung-huo chuan-kuo k'o-hsueh pu-chi hse-hui, 1955.

Chu Cheng-ping, "Production and Consumption Under the First and Second Five Year Plans," *Hsin-chien-she* (New Construction), Peiping, 2, February 1957, pp. 1–6.

——— "Some Questions Concerning National Income," *Ching-chi yen-chiu* (Economic Research), Peiping, 3, June 1957, pp. 129–140.

Chu Chi, "The Analytical Work in Drafting Plans for Factory Prices of Producers' Goods," *Chi-hua ching-chi* (Planned Economy), Peiping, 3, March 1957, pp. 18–21.

Chu Ching and Chu Chung-chien, "Variations in Our Rural Market Commodity Turnover," *Ching-chi yen-chiu* (Economic Research), 3, June 1957, pp. 100–126.

Chu Han, "The Basic Condition of China's Food Grain Supply in the Current Year," *Ta kung pao* (Impartial Daily), Peiping, October 8, 1956, p. 2.

Chung Chi, "People's Living Conditions as Viewed from Several Angles," *Ching-chi tao-pao* (Economic Bulletin), Hong Kong, 649, December 14, 1959, p. 11.

Chung-hua jen-min kung-ho-kuo fen-sheng ching-tu (Detailed Provincial Maps of the People's Republic of China), Shanghai, Ti-tu chu-pan-she, 1953.

"Comparative Diagrams Showing China's Foreign Trade in 1950," *Hsin-hua yueh-pao* (New China Monthly), Peiping, Vol. III, No. 6, April 1951, pp. 1343–1345.

"Develop Agriculture and Industry Simultaneously Is a Major Law in China's Socialist Economy," *Hung-chi* (Red Flag), Peiping, 22, November 1960, pp. 1–6.

"Develop More, Faster, Better and Economically the Local Industry," *Jen-min jih-pao* (People's Daily), Peiping, May 12, 1958, p. 1.

Electric Utility Regulation Board, National Construction Commission, "Electric Power Development in China," *Transactions of the Third World Power Conference,* Vol. II, Washington, D.C., 1938.

Fan Jo-i, "Further Remarks on Price Policy of the Heavy Industrial Products," *Ching-chi yen-chiu* (Economic Research), Peiping, 3, June 1957, pp. 54–67.

——— "Price Policy and the Law of Value," *Ching-chi yen-chiu* (Economic Research), Peiping, 5, May 1958, pp. 45–49.

Fang Fa, "Tabulation Forms for Industrial Production Planning," *Chi-hua ching-chi* (Planned Economy), Peiping, 1, January 1957, pp. 26–31.

"Fraternal Economic Cooperation," *Jen-min jih-pao* (People's Daily), Peiping, October 2, 1956, p. 3.

"Fulfill and Over-fulfill the Industrial Production Plan for 1958 in a More, Faster, Better and Economical Manner," *Chi-hua ching-chi* (Planned Economy), Peiping, 2, February 1958, pp. 1–5.

Fung Chi-hsi, "Growth of China's Economy as Viewed from the State Budget," *T'ung-chi kung-tso* (Statistical Work), 12, June 1957, pp. 28–33.

Han I-chun, "Try for a Big Leap Forward in Animal Product Production," *Chi-hua ching-chi* (Planned Economy), Peiping, 8, August 1958, pp. 36–37.

Han Po, "Economize Current Expenditures on Agriculture," *Chi-hua ching-chi* (Planned Economy), Peiping, 2, February 1958, pp. 17–21.

Ho Cheng, "The Past and Prospects of Light Industry," *Ta kung pao* (Impartial Daily), Peiping, February 27, 1958, p. 3; March 13, 1958, p. 3.

Ho Pai-sha, "Follow Closely the Policy of Developing Both the

Large and Small Scale Enterprise in Coal Mining Construction," *Jen-min jih-pao* (People's Daily), Peiping, March 3, 1958, p. 3.

Ho Wei, "The Meaning and Method of Comparing Prewar and Current Agricultural Prices," *Hsueh-hsi* (Study), Peiping, 7, April 1957, pp. 15–17, 21.

Ho Yu-wen, *Chung-kung ts'ai-cheng chieh-foh* (An Analysis of Communist China's Public Finance), Hong Kong, The Asia Press, 1953.

Hsing Ke-an, "Several Problems in Agricultural Statistical Work as Reflected in the Quality of Some Statistics," *T'ung-chi kung-tso* (Statistical Work), Peiping, 10, May 1957, pp. 22–23.

Hsu Cheng-ying, *Chung-kuo chih hsu-mo* (Animal Husbandry in China), Shanghai, Yung-hsiang Book Co., 1950, p. 41.

Hsu Chien, Tai Shih-kuang, and Yu Tao, *Ching-chi-t'ung-chi-she chian-hua* (Lectures on Economic Statistics), Peiping, T'ung-chi chu-pan-she, 1957.

——— "On the Problem of Comparing the Standard of Living of the Workers and the Peasants," *T'ung-chi kung-tso* (Statistical Work), Peiping, 16, August 1957, pp. 31–33.

Hsu Kang, "Have the Living Conditions of the Workers and Peasants Improved Since Liberation?" *Ta Kung Pao* (Impartial Daily), Peiping, August 9, 1957, p. 2.

Hsu Ti-hsin, *Chung-kuo kuo-tu she-chi kuo-min ching-chi ti fen-hsi* (An Analysis of the National Economy During China's Transition Period), Peiping, Ko-hsueh chu-pan-she, 1959.

Hsu Yi, "A Discussion of Some Aspects of Economic Accounting," *Ching-chi yen-chiu* (Economic Research), 4, April 1958, pp. 62–74.

Hu Ming, "Key Problems in Food Industry," *Ta kung pao* (Impartial Daily), Peiping, January 17, 1958, p. 3.

Huai Fu, "New China's Great Achievements in the Reconstruction of Transportation During the Past Year," *Ching-chi nien-pao, 1953* (Economic Yearbook, 1953), Hong Kong, Ching-chi tao-pao-she, 1953, pp. 23–27.

Huang Ching, "The Problem of Farm Mechanization in China," *Jen-min jih-pao* (People's Daily), Peiping, October 24–25, 1957, p. 4.

Huang Ching-hsiu, "A Method of Studying Farm Income, Expenditure and Consumption Level on the Basis of Farm Budget Survey Data," *T'ung-chi kung-tso* (Statistical Work), Peiping, 10, May 1957, pp. 9–15.

Huang Hsiao-chuan, "Actively Raise the Local Highway Transportation Capacity," *Chi-hua ching-chi* (Planned Economy), Peiping, 3, March 1957, pp. 11–13.

Kao Chang-chu, *Hsi-tsang kai-kwang* (General Conditions in Tibet), Taipeh, Taiwan, 1953.

Ko Chih-ta, *Kuo-tu shi-chi ti chung-kuo Yu-shuan* (China's Budget in the Transition Period), Peiping, Ts'ai-cheng chu-pan-she, 1957.

——— "The Nature of China's National Budget and Its Role in the Transition Period," *Ching-chi yen-chiu* (Economic Research), Peiping, 3, June 1956, pp. 67–80.

Ko Hu, "Tabulation Forms for Prospecting Design," *Chi-hua ching-chi* (Planned Economy), Peiping, 8, August 1957, pp. 31–33.

Kuan Mei-chu, "Reconstruction of China's Communications During the First Five Year Plan," *Chien-she yueh-k'an* (Reconstruction Monthly), Peiping, 10, October 1957, pp. 35–36.

Kung Chi-chih, *Nung-yeh shih-yung shou-t'se* (Practical Agricultural Handbook), Shanghai, Chung-kuo wen-hua shih-yeh-she, 1951.

Kung Chung-hua and Li Yuan, "A Balance Sheet for the Timber Industry," *T'ung-chi kung-tso* (Statistical Work), Peiping, 14, July 1957, pp. 29–30.

Kung Yin-ping, "The Rehabilitation and Adjustment of the Light Industry," *Hsin-hua yueh-pao* (New China Monthly), Peiping, Vol. III, No. 2, December 1950, pp. 361–363.

Kung Yin-ping and Wang Hsin-yuen, "The Light Industry in the Past Year," *Hsin-hua yueh-pao* (New China Monthly), Peiping, Vol. III, No. 4, February 1951, pp. 859–862.

Kuo-min shou-ju lun-wen-chi (A Collection of Essays on National Income), Peiping, T'ung-chi chu-pan-she, 1956.

Lau Tzu-wei, "Several Problems in Handicraft Production," *Jen-min jih-pao* (People's Daily), Peiping, March 18, 1957, p. 4.

Lau Wen and Shan-Kuan Chang-chun, "The Problem of Developing Farm Irrigation," *Chi-hua ching-chi* (Planned Economy), Peiping, 10, October 1957, pp. 15–17.

Li Chang, "Technical Assistance from Soviet Russia and East European Countries in the Past Ten Years," *Jen-min jih-pao* (People's Daily), Peiping, September 28, 1959, p. 11.

Li Chien, "Arrange the Basic Construction Plan for 1957 Properly on the Basis of the Nation's Financial and Resource

Capability," *Chi-hua ching-chi* (Planned Economy), Peiping, 3, March 1957, pp. 4–5, 13.
Li Hui-hung, Shung Chi-ren, and Wang Hua-hsin, "The Problem of Classifying Light and Heavy Industries," *T'ung-chi kung-tso* (Statistical Work), Peiping, 18, September 1957, pp. 13–15.
Li Liang, "Technical and Economic Norms in the Cotton Textile Industry," *Chi-hua ching-chi* (Planned Economy), Peiping, 5, May 1956, pp. 27–28.
Li Lin-ku, "The Structure of Socialism and the Population Problems," *Hsin-chien-she* (New Construction), Peiping, 4, February 1960, pp. 49–55.
Li Pei-fang, "Actively Strengthen the Organization of Sources of Supply for Exports," *Chi-hua ching-chi* (Planned Economy), Peiping, 2, February 1958, pp. 28–31.
Li Shu-teh, "Peasants' Burden in 1956: Conditions and Problems," *Ts'ai-cheng* (Public Finance), Peiping, 8, August 1957, pp. 3–5.
Li Si-heng, "The Problem of Food Grain Exports," *Kung-jen jih-pao* (Workers' Daily), Peiping, November 19, 1957, p. 3.
Li Wei, "Proportional Relationship Between Accumulation and Consumption in National Income," *Ta kung pao* (Impartial Daily), Peiping, December 2, 1956, p. 1.
Liao Chi-li, "Only If We Accelerate Agricultural Development Can We Speed Up Industrial Development," *Chi-hua ching-chi* (Planned Economy), Peiping, 8, August 1957, pp. 4–6.
Liao Hsien-hao, "Tabulation Forms for Agricultural Production Planning," *Chi-hua ching-chi* (Planned Economy), Peiping, 4, April 1957, pp. 30–33.
Liao Kai-lung, "Certain Tasks of Reforming Capitalist Trade in the First Five Year Plan," in Yang Ying-chieh, *et al.*, *Hsueh-hsi ti-yi-ke wu-nien-chi-hua tsarn-kow wen-chi* (A Collection of Reference Materials for Studying the First Five Year Plan), Vol. I, Peiping, T'ung-hsu tu-wu chu-pan-she, 1955.
Lu Hsi-kang and Huang Yun-ting, "The Role of Import Trade in the First Five Year Plan Period," *Ta kung pao* (Impartial Daily), Peiping, December 15, 1957, p. 3.
Lung Hua-yung, Chi Hsi-yung, and Chen Ming-hsi, "Several Problems Concerning the Computation of Value Added by the Construction Industry," *T'ung-chi kung-tso* (Statistical Work), Peiping, 8, April 1957, pp. 14–16.

Ma Ming-fang, "Workers at the Financial and Commercial Front Advancing Vigorously," *Jen-min jih-pao* (People's Daily), Peiping, June 23, 1958, p. 3.

Ma Yin-chu, "New Population Theory," *Hsin-hua pan-yueh-k'an* (New China Semimonthly), Peiping, 15, August 1957, pp. 34–41.

——— *Wo-ti ching-chi-li-lun tse-hsueh si-hsian ho cheng-chi li-chang* (My Economic Theory, Philosophy and Political Stand), Peiping, Ts'ai-cheng chu-pan-she, 1958.

Mao Yue, "China's Population," *Ta kung pao* (Impartial Daily), Peiping, March 22, 1957, p. 3.

Mung Chun-hu and Liu Fu-yuan, "On Certain Problems in the Supply of Edible Vegetable Oils," *Liang-shih kung-tso* (Grain Work), Peiping, 12, June 1956, pp. 9–12.

Nankai Economic Research Institute, *Nankai chih-shu tzu-liao chun-pien* (Source Materials on Nankai Indices), Peiping, T'ung-chi chu-pan-she, 1958.

Niu Chung-huang, *Chung-kuo she-hui chu-i kung-yeh-hua wen-ti* (The Problem of China's Socialist Industrialization), Peiping, Chung-kuo ching-nien chu-pan-she, 1956.

——— "The Problem of Technological Improvement in China's Agriculture," *Jen-min jih-pao* (People's Daily), Peiping, August 26, 1960, p. 1.

——— *Wo-kuo kuo-min-shou-ju ti chi-lai ho hsiao-fei* (Accumulation and Consumption in China's National Income), Peiping, Chung-kuo ching-nien chu-pan-she, 1957.

Pao Kuo-pao, "The Problem of Developing the Electric Power Industry," *Jen-min jih-pao* (People's Daily), Peiping, March 19, 1957, p. 3.

"Problems To Be Borne in Mind When Implementing the Basic Construction Plan for 1958," *Chi-hua ching-chi* (Planned Economy), Peiping, 2, February 1958, pp. 4–8

"Purchase and Sale of Food Grain in the Past Ten Years," *Ta kung pao* (Impartial Daily), Peiping, October 6, 1959, p. 5.

"Reorganization, Consolidation and Improvement," *Jen-min jih-pao* (People's Daily), Peiping, November 25, 1958, p. 3.

Shanghai College of Social Sciences, "Survey of the Costs of Producing Major Agricultural Products (Rice, Cotton, and Vegetables)," *Ts'ai-ching yen-chiu* (Financial and Economic Research), Shanghai, 7, October 1958, pp. 28–31.

Sheng Ping, "China's Industrial and Commercial Tax in the Past Ten Years," *Ts'ai-cheng* (Public Finance), Peiping, 18, September 1959, pp. 27–31.

Statistical Bureau of the Liaoning Province, "Why Is the Cost of Coal Production in Liaoning Rising?" *T'ung-chi kung-tso* (Statistical Work), Peiping, 5, March 1958, pp. 21–23.

Sun Tze-fang, "Tabulation Forms for Commercial Planning," *Chi-hua ching-chi* (Planned Economy), Peiping, 2, February 1957, pp. 27–31.

Sun Wei-tsu, "Principles for Drafting the Plan for Food Grain Supply," *Chi-hua ching-chi* (Planned Economy), Peiping, 2, February 1958, pp. 24–27.

Sung Chao-wen, "Light Industry Must Maintain the Standard of Quality and Economize the Use of Raw Materials," *Hsin-hua yueh-pao* (New China Monthly), Peiping, 11, November 1955, pp. 150–151.

Sung Tzu-yung, "Develop the Production of Sugar To Ensure Market Supply," *Ta kung pao* (Impartial Daily), Peiping, January 1, 1958, p. 3.

Tang Fay, "The Present Conditions in the Transformation of Rural Private Traders and Comments on Future Work," *Hsin-hua pan-yueh-k'an* (New China Semimonthly), Peiping, 17, September 1956, pp. 65-68.

Tien Chi, "Several Problems in the Revision of Constant 1952 Industrial Prices," *T'ung-chi kung-tso* (Statistical Work), Peiping, 1, January 1957, pp. 15–17.

Tseng Wen-ching, *Chung-kuo ti she-hui chu-yi kung-yeh-hua* (China's Socialist Industrialization), Peiping, Jen-min chu-pan-she, 1958.

Wang Chien-chun, "People's Living Conditions as Reflected in the Price Statistics," *Ta kung pao* (Impartial Daily), Peiping, September 24, 1957, p. 3.

Wang Hsing-fu and Lan chien-chiao, "Develop Vigorously the Chemical Fertilizer Industry," *Chi-hua ching-chi* (Planned Economy), Peiping, 10, October 1957, pp. 11–15.

Wang Keng-chin, "My Opinions on the Methods of Computing Gross Value of Agricultural Production," *T'ung-chi kung-tso* (Statistical Work), Peiping, 4, February 1957, pp. 3–4.

Wang Kuang-wei, "On the Allocation of Agricultural Labor," *Chi-hua ching-chi* (Planned Economy), Peiping, 8, August 1957, pp. 6–9.

Wang Si-hua, "The Role of Statistics in Our Economic Construction and Questions Pertaining to Some Statistical Indicators," *Ching-chi yen-chiu* (Economic Research), Peiping, 5, May 1958, pp. 26–32.

Wang Tzu-ying, "Lessons from the Drafting and Implementation of the 1956 State Budget," *Hsin-hua pan-yueh-k'an* (New China Semimonthly), Peiping, 5, March 1957, pp. 91–93.

Wei Yi, "The Problem of Developing Rapidly the Light Industry," *Hsin-hua pan-yueh-k'an* (New China Semimonthly), Peiping, 19, October 1956, pp. 50–53.

Wen Liang, "General Conditions in Railroad Transport on the Mainland," *Tsu-kuo* (China Weekly), Hong Kong, 11, March 16, 1953, pp. 6–8, 11.

Wu Chiang, *Chung-kuo tzu-pan chu-i ching-chi kai-tso wen-ti* (The Problem of Transformation of China's Capitalist Economy), Peiping, Jen-min chu-pan-she, 1958.

——— "The Transition from a Capitalist Economy to a National Capitalist Economy," *Ching-chi yen-chiu* (Economic Research), Peiping, 2, April 1956, pp. 54–99.

Wu Ching-chao, "A New Discussion of China's Population Problem," *Hsin-chien-she* (New Construction), Peiping, 3, March 1957, pp. 1–9.

——— "China's Rate of Industrial Growth in the First Five Year Plan Period," *Hsin-chien-she* (New Construction), Peiping, 9, September 1955, pp. 7–12.

——— "Several Important Ratios in the First Five Year Plan," *Kuang-ming jih-pao* (Kuang-ming Daily), Peiping, August 30, 1955, p. 3.

Wu Hua-pao, *Fu-yao ti chung-kuo nung-yeh tzu-yuan* (The Abundant Agricultural Resources of China), Shanghai, 1951.

Wu Shih, "An Analysis of China's Food Problem During the Transition Period," *Hsin-hua pan-yueh-k'an* (New China Semimonthly), Peiping, 10, May 1957, pp. 104–109.

Yang Chien-pai, "A Comparative Analysis of China's and Soviet Russia's First Five Year Plan," *Hsin-hua yueh-pao* (New China Monthly), Peiping, 9, September 1955, pp. 193–197.

——— *Chung-hua jen-min kung-ho-kuo hui-fu ho fa-tsan kuo-min ching-chi ti cheng-chao* (The Achievements of the People's Republic of China in Rehabilitation and Development of the National Economy), Peiping, T'ung-chi chu-pan-she, 1956.

Yang Fang-hsun, "The Great Nine Years of China's Agricultural Production," *T'ung-chi yeh-chiu* (Statistical Research), Peiping, 9, September 1958, pp. 6–9.

Yang Pei-hsin, "The Ways of Financing Agricultural Development," *Ching-chi yen-chiu* (Economic Research), Peiping, 1, January 1958, pp. 22–37.

Yang Pin-chuan, "Unfinished Construction," *T'ung-chi kung-tso t'ung-hsin* (Statistical Work Bulletin), Peiping, 1, January 1956, pp. 29–30.

Yang Po, "Has the Peasants' Standard of Living Been Raised or Lowered?" *Kung-jen jih-pao* (Workers' Daily), Peiping, September 12, 1957, p. 3.

——— "On the Distribution of National Income in China," *Ching-chi yen-chiu* (Economic Research), Peiping, 6, December 1957, pp. 1–11.

Yang Pong-chieh, "A Proposal To Use Constant Prices in Drawing Up the Basic Construction Plan and Budget," *Chi-hua ching-chi* (Planned Economy), Peiping, 2, February 1958, pp. 30–31.

Yao Hui-pin, "Production of Hogs and the Law of Value," *Hsueh-hsi* (Study), Peiping, 4, April 1957, pp. 25–26.

Yen Chung-ping, *Chung-kuo chin-tai ching-chi-she t'ung-chi tzu-liao shuan-chi* (Selected Statistical Materials on the Contemporary Economic History of China), Peiping, San-lien shu-tien, 1955.

Yen I-sheng, "On the Production of Producers' Goods and Consumers' Goods in Relation to Government Revenue and Expenditures," *Ching-chi yen-chiu* (Economic Research), Peiping, 7, July 1959, pp. 7–11.

Yi Lin, "Several Problems in Developing Fully the Effectiveness of Investment in Industrial Construction," *Chi-hua ching-chi* (Planned Economy), Peiping, 6, June 1957, pp. 5–7.

Yin Hsin, "Emphasizing the Economy of Labor Is an Effective Means of Increasing Accumulation of the Enterprise," *Lao-tung* (Labor), Peiping, 6, 1955, pp. 9-10.

Yu Chien-ting, "The Problem of the Proportional Relationship Between the Iron and Steel Industry and the Machinery Industry," *Ching-chi yen-chiu* (Economic Research), Peiping, 6, December 1957, pp. 20–26.

Yu Shu-fang, "Changes in the Form of Wage Payment in the Past Six Years," *Lao-tung* (Labor), Peiping, 5, May 1956, pp. 46–47.

Yu Tien, "On the Proportion of Consumption and Accumulation in China's National Income," *Ta kung pao* (Impartial Daily), Peiping, March 24, 1957, pp. 1, 3.

Yueh Wei, "Problems of Computing National Income," *T'ung-chi kung-tso t'ung-hsin* (Statistical Work Bulletin), Peiping, 1, January 1956, pp. 15–17.

——— "The Method of Computing National Income," *Ching-*

chi yen-chiu (Economic Research), Peiping, 3, June 1956, pp. 48–66.

II. *Materials in Other Languages*

Abraham, William I., "Investment Estimates of Underdeveloped Countries: An Appraisal," *Journal of the American Statistical Association,* Vol. 53, No. 283, September 1958, pp. 669–679.

American Consulate General, Hong Kong, (1) *Survey of China Mainland Press;* (2) *Selections from China Mainland Magazines* (succeeding *Extracts from China Mainland Magazines*); (3) *Current Background.*

Barnett, A. Doak, *Communist Economic Strategy: The Rise of Mainland China,* Washington, D.C., National Planning Association, 1959.

Bergson, A., *Soviet National Income and Product, 1937,* New York, Columbia University Press, 1953.

Brown, Phelps E. H., "The Meaning of the Fitted Cobb-Douglas Function," *Quarterly Journal of Economics,* Vol. LXXI, No. 4, November 1957, pp. 546–560.

Buck, John Lossing, *Chinese Farm Economy,* Chicago, University of Chicago Press, 1930.

——— *Land Utilization in China,* 3 vols., Chicago, University of Chicago Press, 1937.

Central Statistical Board of the U.S.S.R., Council of Ministers, *U.S.S.R. in Figures for 1959,* Moscow, Foreign Language Publishing House, 1960.

Chang, C. C., *An Estimate of China's Farms and Crops,* Nanking, 1932.

Chang Yu-tien, "Fishermen's Record Hauls," *Peking Review,* Peiping, 11, March 17, 1959, pp. 12–13.

Chen Ta, *New China's Population Census of 1953 and Its Relations to National Reconstruction and Demographic Research,* Stockholm, International Statistical Institute, 1957.

Cheng Chu-yuan, *The People's Communes,* Hong Kong, Union Press, 1959.

China Handbook Editorial Board, *China Handbook, 1951,* Taipeh, Taiwan, China Publishing Co., 1951.

China-U.S. Joint Commission on Rural Reconstruction, *A Decade of Rural Progress,* Washington, D.C., U.S. Government Printing Office, 1958.

"China's Foreign Trade Organizations," *Peking Review,* Peiping, 28, September 9, 1958, pp. 13–15.

The Chinese Yearbook, 1935–1936, Shanghai, Commercial Press, 1935.

Chou En-lai, "Report on China's 1959 Economic Plan," Supplement to *China Reconstructs,* Peiping, October 1959, pp. 1–15.
——— "Report on the Work of the Government," *People's China,* Peiping, 20, October 16, 1954, pp. 3–31.
Chu Chi-lin, "China's Skyrocketing Oil Output," *Peking Review,* Peiping, 23, August 5, 1958, pp. 9–11.
Coal and Iron Ore Resources of Asia and the Far East, New York, United Nations, 1952.
Department of Economic Affairs, *A System of National Accounts and Supporting Tables,* New York, United Nations, 1953.
East Asia Research Institute, *Nihon no taishi toshi* (Japanese Investments in China), 1942.
——— *Shogaikoku no taishi toshi* (Foreign Investments in China), 1943.
Economic Commission for Asia and the Far East, *Economic Bulletin for Asia and the Far East,* United Nations. Quarterly.
——— *Economic Survey of Asia and the Far East,* United Nations. Annually since 1948.
Economic Planning Administration, Ministry of Foreign Trade, USSR, *Vneshniaia torgovlia* (Foreign Trade), Supplement, Moscow, Foreign Trade Publishing House, 1959.
Editorial Committee of the Statistical Press, *Handbook of Agricultural Statistical Work,* Peiping, T'ung-chi chu-pan-she, 1956.
Far East Yearbook, 1941, Tokyo, Far East Yearbook Co., 1941.
Faure, Edgar, *The Serpent and the Tortoise,* London, Macmillan, 1958.
Food and Agricultural Organization of the United Nations, *Food Balance Sheets,* Washington, D.C., 1949.
——— *Report of the Second Session of the International Rice Commission,* Bangkok, Thailand, 1950.
"Future Growth of Chinese Population During Industrialization," May 1946 (unpublished).
Gamble, S. D., *How Chinese Families Live in Peiping,* New York, Funk and Wagnalls, 1933.
——— *Ting Hsien: A North China Rural Community,* New York, Institute of Pacific Relations, 1954.
Gel'bras, V., "Achievements of the People's Republic of China in the Fields of Labor and Wages During the Past Ten Years," *Sotsialisticheskii trud* (Socialist Labor), Moscow, 9, September 1959, pp. 27–38.
Guillain, Robert, *The Blue Ants,* London, Secker and Warburg, 1957.
Handbook on People's China, Peking, Foreign Language Press, 1957.

Hollister, William W., *China's Gross National Product and Social Accounts, 1950–1957,* Glencoe, Ill., The Free Press, 1958.

Hou Chi-ming, "Foreign Capital in China's Economic Development, 1895–1937," Ph.D. Thesis, Columbia University, New York, 1952.

India, Government of, Ministry of Food and Agriculture, *Report of the Indian Delegation to China on Agricultural Planning and Techniques,* New Delhi, 1956.

International Tin Study Group, *Statistical Yearbook, 1956,* The Hague, International Tin Study Group, 1956.

Ishikawa, Shigeru, "An Analysis of Economic Growth in China," *Asian Affairs,* Tokyo, Vol. II, No. 1, March 1957, pp. 21–46.

Ivanov, N., *et al., Razvitie ekonomiki stran narodnoi demokratii* (Development of the Economies of the People's Democratic Countries), Moscow, 1958.

Japan Kwantung Bureau, *A Thirty-Year Collection of Statistics by the Kwantung Bureau,* 1937.

Japan-Manchoukuo Agricultural Policy Research Society, *Manshū-Nogyo Yoran* (Brief Views on Manchurian Agriculture), 1940.

Japan-Manchoukuo Yearbook Company, *Japan-Manchoukuo Yearbook, 1936,* Tokyo, 1936.

——— *Japan-Manchoukuo Yearbook, 1941,* Tokyo, 1941.

Japanese Embassy, Peiping, *Kahoku kojo tokei* (Statistics of Factories in North China), Peiping, 1943.

Kinmond, William, *No Dogs in China,* New York, Thomas Nelson & Sons, 1957.

Koh, Tso-fang, *Capital Stock in China,* China Council Paper No. 2, Part 2, Eighth Conference of the Institute of Pacific Relations, December 1942.

Krader, L. and John S. Aird, "Sources of Demographic Data on Mainland China," *American Sociological Review,* Vol. XXIV, No. 5, October 1959, pp. 623–630.

Kuznets, Simon "National Income and Industrial Structure," in Simon Kuznets, *Economic Change: Selected Essays in Business Cycles, National Income and Economic Growth,* New York, W. W. Norton, 1953.

——— *National Income and Its Composition, 1919–38,* New York, National Bureau of Economic Research, 1941.

——— *Quantitative Aspects of the Economic Growth of Nations,* Supplement to *Economic Development and Cultural Change,* Vol. V, No. 4, July 1957.

Li Choh-ming, *Economic Development of Communist China,* Berkeley and Los Angeles, Calif., University of California Press, 1959.

Lieu, D. K., *Industrial Development in Communist China,* New York, Sino-American Amity, 1955.
Lieu, D. K., and C. M. Chen, "Statistics of Farm Land in China," *Chinese Economic Journal,* Peiping, Vol. II, No. 3, March 1928, pp. 181–213.
Liu, Ta-chung, *China's National Income, 1931–36: An Exploratory Study,* Washington, D.C., The Brookings Institution, 1946.
Liu, Ta-chung, Chong Twanmo, and Kung-chia Yeh, *Production of Food Crops on the Chinese Mainland: Prewar and Postwar,* Santa Monica, Calif., The RAND Corporation, January 1964.
Lu Kuang, "China's National Income," *Peking Review,* Peiping, 6, April 8, 1958, pp. 7–9.
Manchoukuo Yearbook Co., *Manchoukuo Yearbook, 1934,* Hsinking, 1934.
——— *Manchoukuo Yearbook, 1941,* Hsinking, 1941.
——— *Manchoukuo Yearbook, 1942,* Hsinking, 1942.
Manchurian Electric Power Company, *Chūka minkoku denki jigyo, 1933* (The Electric Power Industry of the Republic of China, 1933), Hsinking, 1935.
——— *Manshū ni okeru denki jigyo gaisetsu* (A Survey of the Electric Power Industry in Manchuria), Hsinking, 1938.
Meng, C. Y. W., "Our Silk, Tung Oil, and Tea," *China Trade Monthly,* Shanghai, March 1947, pp. 161–162.
Metal Statistics, 1956, New York, American Metal Market, 1956.
Ministry of Economic Affairs, Manchurian Government, *Manshū kojō tōkei, A, 1940* (Statistics of Manchurian Factories, A, 1940), Hsinking, 1941.
——— *Manshū kojō tōkei, 1939* (Statistics of Manchurian Factories, 1939), Hsinking, 1940.
National Agricultural Research Bureau, National Government, *Agricultural Estimates,* Shanghai, 1947.
Phillips, Ralph W., *Livestock Improvement in China,* Chungking, 1944.
Phillips, R. W., R. G. Johnson, and R. T. Moyer, *The Livestock of China,* Washington, D.C., U.S. Government Printing Office, 1945.
Po I-po, "How Much To Invest and How Much To Consume," *People's China,* Peiping, 21, November 1956, pp. 16–22.
Remer, C. F., *Coal Production in Communist China,* Ann Arbor, Mich., University of Michigan, 1956.
Rigg, R. B., "Red Army in Retreat," *Current History,* Philadelphia, Vol. 32, No. 185, January 1957, pp. 1–6.
Shen Tsung-han, *Agricultural Resources of China,* Ithaca, N.Y., Cornell University Press, 1951.

South Manchurian Railway, *Manshū keizai tōkei nempo, 1933* (Manchurian Statistical Yearbook, 1933), Dairen, 1934.

——— *Manshū kojō tōkei, A, 1933* (Statistics of Manchurian Factories, A, 1933), 1935.

——— *Manshū koku keizai teigō* (Statistical Abstract of the Manchurian Economy), 1938.

South Manchurian Railway and the Manchurian Government, *Manshū kojō tōkei, B, 1934* (Statistics of Manchurian Factories, B, 1934), Hsinking, 1936.

Stevenson, William, *The Yellow Wind,* Boston, Mass., Houghton Mifflin, 1959.

Su Chung, "Facts about China's Population," *Peking Review,* Peiping, 18, July 1, 1958, pp. 9–10.

Swen, W. Y., "A Study of the Consumption of Staple Food Products in China," *Crop Reports,* Vol. II, No. 8, August 1, 1934, pp. 63–65.

Tai Shih-kuang, *1953 Population Census of China,* Calcutta, Indian Statistical Institute, 1956.

Tamagna, F. T., *Banking and Finance in China,* New York, Institute of Pacific Relations, 1942.

T'ao Lu-kung, *Livelihood in Peking; An Analysis of the Budgets of Sixty Families,* Peiping, Social Research Department, China Foundation, 1928.

——— *The Standard of Living Among Chinese Workers,* Shanghai, China Institute of Pacific Relations, 1931.

United Nations, Statistical Office, *International Standard Industrial Classification of All Economic Activities,* Statistical Papers, Series M, No. 4, Lake Success, N.Y., 1949.

U.S. Bureau of Mines, "Mineral Resources of China," *Foreign Minerals Survey,* Washington, D.C., Vol. II, No. 7, January 1948.

U.S. Department of Agriculture, *Report of the China-U.S. Agricultural Mission,* Washington, D.C., Government Printing Office, 1947.

U.S. Department of Commerce, *Business Statistics,* Washington, D.C., Government Printing Office, 1957.

U.S. Department of State, *Soviet Bloc Economic Activities in the Free World,* Washington, D.C., Government Printing Office, 1955.

——— *Summary of East-West Trade in 1958,* Washington, D.C., Government Printing Office, 1960.

——— *The Strategic Trade Control System, 1948–1956,* Washington, D.C., Government Printing Office, 1957.

——— *The 1958 Revision of East-West Trade Controls,* Washington, D.C., Government Printing Office, 1959.

Wang Tzu-ying, "Financing the First Five Year Plan," *People's China,* Peiping, 20, October 16, 1957, pp. 13–19.

Willcox, Walter F., "The Population of China and Its Modern Increase," *Studies in American Demography,* Ithaca, N.Y., Cornell University Press, 1940.

Wu Cheng-ming, *Manufacturing Industries in China: A Preliminary Report,* New York, 1946 (mimeographed).

——— "Socialist Transformation of Private Trade," *People's China,* Peiping, 10, May 1956, 11–15.

Wu Yuan-li, *An Economic Survey of Communist China,* New York, Bookman Associates, 1956.

——— "Communist China's Economic Challenge," *Current History,* Philadelphia, Vol. 32, No. 185, January 1957, pp. 19–25.

Yeh, K. C., *Electric Power Development in Mainland China: Prewar and Postwar,* Santa Monica, Calif., The RAND Corporation, 1956 (mimeographed).

Yin, Helen, and Yin Yi-chang, *Economic Statistics of Mainland China (1949–1957),* Cambridge, Mass., Harvard University Press, 1960.

INDEX

The letter t preceding a page reference indicates tabular material; the letter n following a page reference indicates a footnote.

SELECTED RAND BOOKS

Arrow, Kenneth J., and Marvin Hoffenberg. *A Time Series Analysis of Interindustry Demands.* Amsterdam: North-Holland Publishing Company, 1959.

Baum, Warren C. *The French Economy and the State.* Princeton, N.J.: Princeton University Press, 1958.

Bellman, Richard. *Adaptive Control Processes: A Guided Tour.* Princeton, N.J.: Princeton University Press, 1961.

Bellman, Richard. *Dynamic Programming.* Princeton, N.J.: Princeton University Press, 1957.

Bellman, Richard, and Stuart E. Dreyfus. *Applied Dynamic Programming.* Princeton, N.J.: Princeton University Press, 1962.

Bergson, Abram. *The Real National Income of Soviet Russia Since 1928.* Cambridge, Mass.: Harvard University Press, 1961.

Bergson, Abram, and Hans Heymann, Jr. *Soviet National Income and Product, 1940–48.* New York: Columbia University Press, 1954.

Brodie, Bernard. *Strategy in the Missile Age.* Princeton, N.J.: Princeton University Press, 1959.

Chapman, Janet G. *Real Wages in Soviet Russia Since 1928.* Cambridge, Mass.: Harvard University Press, 1963.

Dantzig, G. B. *Linear Programming and Extensions.* Princeton, N.J.: Princeton University Press, 1963.

Davison, W. Phillips. *The Berlin Blockade: A Study in Cold War Politics.* Princeton, N.J.: Princeton University Press, 1958.

Dole, Stephen H. *Habitable Planets for Man.* New York: Blaisdell Publishing Company, Inc., 1964.

Dorfman, Robert, Paul A. Samuelson, and Robert M. Solow. *Linear Programming and Economic Analysis.* New York: McGraw-Hill Book Company, Inc., 1958.

Galenson, Walter. *Labor Productivity in Soviet and American Industry.* New York: Columbia University Press, 1955.

Halpern, Manfred. *The Politics of Social Change in the Middle East and North Africa.* Princeton, N.J.: Princeton University Press, 1963.

Hirshleifer, Jack, James C. DeHaven, and Jerome W. Milliman. *Water Supply: Economics, Technology, and Policy.* Chicago: The University of Chicago Press, 1960.

Hitch, Charles J., and Roland McKean. *The Economics of Defense in the Nuclear Age.* Cambridge, Mass.: Harvard University Press, 1960.

Hoeffding, Oleg. *Soviet National Income and Product in 1928.* New York: Columbia University Press, 1954.

Hsieh, Alice L. *Communist China's Strategy in the Nuclear Era.* Englewood Cliffs, N.J.: Prentice-Hall, Inc., 1962.

Kershaw, Joseph A., and Roland N. McKean. *Teacher Shortages and Salary Schedules.* New York: McGraw-Hill Book Company, Inc., 1962.

Kramish, Arnold. *Atomic Energy in the Soviet Union.* Stanford, Calif.: Stanford University Press, 1959.

Lubell, Harold. *Middle East Oil Crises and Western Europe's Energy Supplies.* Baltimore, Md.: The Johns Hopkins Press, 1963.

McKean, Roland N. *Efficiency in Government through Systems Analysis.* New York: John Wiley & Sons, Inc., 1958.

Moorsteen, Richard. *Prices and Production of Machinery in the Soviet Union, 1928–1958.* Cambridge, Mass.: Harvard University Press, 1962.

Whiting, Allen S. *China Crosses the Yalu: The Decision To Enter the Korean War.* New York: The Macmillan Company, 1960.

Wolf, Charles, Jr. *Foreign Aid: Theory and Practice in Southern Asia.* Princeton, N.J.: Princeton University Press, 1960.